1 MONTH OF
FREE
READING

at
www.ForgottenBooks.com

By purchasing this book you are eligible for one month membership to ForgottenBooks.com, giving you unlimited access to our entire collection of over 700,000 titles via our web site and mobile apps.

To claim your free month visit:
www.forgottenbooks.com/free756564

ISBN 978-0-483-56947-8
PIBN 10756564

This book is a reproduction of an important historical work. Forgotten Books uses
state-of-the-art technology to digitally reconstruct the work, preserving the original format
whilst repairing imperfections present in the aged copy. In rare cases, an imperfection in
the original, such as a blemish or missing page, may be replicated in our edition. We do,
however, repair the vast majority of imperfections successfully; any imperfections that
remain are intentionally left to preserve the state of such historical works.

For support please visit www.forgottenbooks.com

The Southern Workman

VOLUME XLIII

JANUARY THROUGH DECEMBER, 1914

The Press of
The Hampton Normal and Agricultural Institute
Hampton, Virginia
1915

INDEX TO VOLUME XLIII

January through December, 1914

JANUARY 1914

THE SOUTHERN WORKMAN

The Basis of Indian Ownership of Land and Game

FRANK G. SPECK

Negro Progress in Virginia

BOOKER T. WASHINGTON

Robert C. Ogden's Labors in the South

SAMUEL CHILES MITCHELL

The Hampton Institute Trade School

Press of
The Hampton Normal and Agricultural Institute
Hampton, Virginia

e Hampton Normal and Agricultural Institute

HAMPTON VIRGINIA

H. B. FRISSELL., Principal

G. P. PHENIX, Vice Principal

H. B. TURNER, Chaplain

F. K. ROGERS, Treasurer

W. H. SCOVILLE, Secretary

It is   An undenominational industrial school founded in 1868 by Samuel Chapman Armstrong for Negro youth. Indians admitted in 1878.

To train teachers and industrial leaders

Land, 1060 acres; buildings, 140

Academic, trade, agriculture, business, home economics

Negroes, 1215; Indians, 37; total, 1252

Graduates, 1709; ex-students, over 6000
Outgrowths: Tuskegee, Calhoun, Mt. Meigs, and many smaller schools for Negroes

$125,000 annually above regular income
$4,000,000 Endowment Fund
Scholarships

A full scholarship for both academic and industrial instruction - - -	$ 100
Academic scholarship - - -	70
Industrial scholarship - - -	30
Endowed full scholarship - - -	2500

Any contribution, however small, will be gratefully received and may be sent to H. B. FRISSELL, Principal, or to F. K. ROGERS, Treasurer, Hampton, Virginia.

FORM OF BEQUEST

*I give and devise to the trustees of The Hampton Normal and Agri-
    Institute, Hampton, Virginia, the sum of   dollars,*

Is

The Southern Workman

Published monthly by

The Hampton Normal and Agricultural Institute

Contents for January 1914

THE SOUTHERN WORKMAN was founded by Samuel Chapman Armstrong in 1872, and is a monthly magazine devoted to the interests of undeveloped races.

It contains reports from Negro and Indian populations, with pictures of reservation and plantation life, as well as information concerning Hampton graduates and ex-students who since 1868 have taught more than 250,000 children in the South and West. It also provides a forum for the discussion of ethnological, sociological, and educational problems in all parts of the world.

CONTRIBUTIONS: The editors do not hold themselves responsible for the opinions expressed in contributed articles. Their aim is simply to place before their readers articles by men and women of ability without regard to the opinions held.

EDITORIAL STAFF

H. B. FRISSELL   W. L. BROWN
HELEN W. LUDLOW   W. A. AERY, Business Manager
J. E. DAVIS   W. T. B. WILLIAMS

TERMS: One dollar a year in advance; ten cents a copy
CHANGE OF ADDRESS: Persons making a change of address should send the *old* as well as the *new* address to

THE SOUTHERN WORKMAN, Hampton, Virginia

Entered as second-class matter August 13, 1908, in the Post Office at Hampton, Virginia, under the Act of July 16, 1894

THE HAMPTON LEAFLETS

Any twelve of the following numbers of the "The Hampton Leaflets" may obtained free of charge by any Southern teacher or superintendent. *A charge of fi cents per dozen is made to other applicants.* Cloth-bound volumes for 1905, '06, ' and '08 will be furnished at seventy-five cents each, postpaid.

Address: Publication Office, The Hampton Normal and Agricultur Institute, Hampton, Virginia

The
Southern Workman

VOL. XLIII   JANUARY 1914   NO. 1

Editorials

The Southern Race Commission at Hampton — Hampton welcomes many groups of interesting people to its grounds. Missionaries from Africa and Asia come to study its methods. Chinamen, Japanese, East Indians, governors of distant colonies come to Hampton to find out what it is doing toward the solution of race problems. Representative educators desiring to know how to meet the demand for vocational training have found the Hampton School an object of interest.

The superintendents of schools in the Southern states visited the school in a body. So did the county superintendents of the State of Virginia. For a number of years parties of Northern friends, each numbering over a hundred, have come to Hampton at Anniversary time. Many teachers from different cities in New England have made pilgrimages to the Institute. The Chamber of Commerce of the city of Newport News, and more recently the Merchants' Association of Hampton and Phoebus have been guests of the school. But it is doubtful if Hampton has ever had a more interesting or a more intelligently interested group than the Commission of Southern Universities on the Race Question, which came to Hampton in December.

To Dr. James H. Dillard, formery dean of Tulane University and now president of the Jeanes Board and director of the Slater Fund, is due much credit for the bringing together of this group of earnest young professors, who are devoting much time and thought to the condition of the Negroes in the South. The meeting of the Southern Sociological Congress last spring in Atlanta, Georgia, and especially the gathering of the group which had to do with race problems, was an important event in the history of the South. The strong feeling there manifested that the Southern white man must interest himself in his brother in black is most hopeful. The sympathy for the Negro expressed by the various speakers argues well for the future of race adjustment.

Professor DeLoach, of the University of Georgia, who visited Hampton as a member of this Commission, urged at the Atlanta Conference the education of the Negro farmer. Speaking of the result of certain Negro farmers' conferences he had attended, he said, "In almost every individual instance there has been great improvement in the farms represented at the meetings. * * It is interesting to learn that in the counties generally, though not always, where the majority of landowners are Negroes, the farm-crop yields per acre are greater than in the counties where the majority of landowners are whites. Where the Negroes are mostly tenants, the crop yields are not so high as where they own their own land."

Professor Josiah Morse, of the University of South Carolina, another member of Hampton's visiting group, in speaking of the social and hygienic condition of the Negro, made these significant remarks at Atlanta. "Our people," he said, "have been persuaded by a generation of short-sighted, uneducated, and unscrupulous demagogues that the development and elevation of the Negro are somehow incompatible with the best interests of the white men ; that prosperity for the black man spells ruin for the white man ; that what is good for the one is bad for the other; that what is true for one is false for the other. And so this strange state of affairs has come to pass : that those traits and things we admire when possessed by ourselves we dislike when they appear in the Negro. Thus we recognize that education is a good thing, and those who strive for it are deserving of approbation and even praise. Likewise, manliness and self-respect are commendable ; and ambition and thrift and the pursuit of happiness are not to be condemned. And yet there are too many who prefer the ignorant, lazy, diseased, immoral Negro—even the vicious and criminal one—to the self-respecting, progressive, property-owning, educated one."

Speaking of the hopeless view that is often taken of the Negro's future, Professor Morse referred to Frederick Hoffman's

"Traits and Tendencies of the American Negro," where Mr. Hoffman states that "of all races for which statistics are obtainable the Negro shows the least power of resistance in the struggle for life." Commenting on this statement, Professor Morse says, "Mr. Hoffman's prepossessions have led him to commit the fallacy of 'false cause.' For it is also a fact that there is more poverty among the Negroes, more illiteracy and ignorance of the laws of health, of modern sanitation and personal and public hygiene; that their living quarters are inferior, their physical environments less sanitary, and that a much larger percentage of their mothers are bread-winners, which means neglect of the children, malnutrition, etc. And inasmuch as these are causes of disease among all peoples the world over, why may they not account for the excessive death rate among the Negroes? Mr. Hoffman would hardly maintain that the larger disease and death rate of the Russian-peasants, for example, half of whose children die before one year of age, or of our own factory and mill workers, indicate that they possess the least power of resistance in the struggle for life."

What it means to the Negro race to have a company of Southern white professors in state universities holding and proclaiming such sane and hopeful views in regard to their colored neighbors it is not easy to state. No wonder that they were welcomed with enthusiasm at Hampton Institute.

Our Wards in the Philippines Bishop Charles H. Brent, who was in this country in the fall, attending the Episcopal Convention in New York, has gone back to the Philippine Islands to continue with new plans and new encouragement the work of helping the Moro tribes to found real homes and maintain civilized communities until their savagery is fully outgrown. His friends in this country have organized the National Committee for Upbuilding the Wards of the Nation, which will work under the auspices of the Harmony Club of America and will have for its aim the raising annually of a fund sufficient to carry on the non-sectarian work which has been planned for the Moro tribes.

Bishop Brent's plans include social, industrial, educational, and evangelical work among the million or more queer little brown people who subsist on camotes and corn, wear no garments, and make their homes in treetops. He hopes to cure them of their chronic ills, such as malaria, hookworm, black fever, and the like, and teach them to live so as to avoid the tropical diseases, most of which are due, not to climate, but to unhygienic habits.

The industrial work is one of the chief features. Dr. Brent's aim is to make the Moros self-supporting and masters of several trades and occupations. He will teach them how to reclaim thousands of acres of productive land; how to build and care for sanitary dwellings; and, in short, through the trade school, bring them out of their present bondage of poverty and degradation. In the academic work the boys and girls will be taught the duties of citizenship, and will be given such ethical and moral guidance as will prevent the cruelty and immorality so prevalent among their elders.

Any readers who may be especially interested in Bishop Brent's work may learn further details by addressing the Secretary of the National Committee, 30 Church Street, New York

Colored
Y. M. C. A.
Work

The recent Y. M. C. A. building fund campaign in New York, which attracted nation-wide publicity, brought about a unity of effort never before known among the colored people of New York. It called up latent energies which were heretofore undreamed of. It established self-confidence among the colored people, who worked earnestly to do their share in securing funds for the big Y. M. C. A. building campaign, and it resulted in the collection of over $40,000 in a fortnight from those who had little to give.

This co-operation indicates what may be brought about when men and women realize that they have important interests in common and that they win for themselves a new place in the estimation and respect of their white friends when they become active workers instead of willing beneficiaries. The daily reports from the colored people raising money in the campaign evoked prolonged applause. Analytical minds were active in giving, by comparison, true value to the gifts of colored men and women—gifts from a race with few avenues open for earning even a bare living in a great cosmopolitan city.

Dr. J. E. Moorland, national secretary of the colored men's department of the Y. M. C. A., and his able assistants deserve a great deal of praise for their untiring work in raising money for the large fund from which the colored people will receive back enough money for two well-equipped buildings to meet the needs of a deserving people. More important than the added material equipment of the colored Y. M. C. A. work will be the improved social re-action among the colored people, who will have more opportunity to develop along the lines of physical conservation, wholesome amusements, and a rational form of religion.

The fact that colored men will have in New York an Association building costing $150,000 and colored women one costing $100,000, will put more pressure on men and women in other cities so that they will follow the far-sighted wisdom of such a man as Julius Rosenwald, of Chicago, and help the colored people, financially and otherwise, to have, in cities and towns where there are a large number of Negroes, first-class organizations and buildings for the Young Men's and Young Women's Christian Associations.

▨

Demonstration in Industrial Training A school especially designed for children of mill operatives is a feature of the industrial education system of Columbus, Georgia. The school was established with the idea of encouraging attendance among the large class of mill children in Columbus, many of whom were not going to school at all.

A handsome colonial residence in the mill district was purchased by the board of education for the new school. Special pains were taken to adapt the course of study and the hours in the school to the conditions of mill work. School hours are from eight to eleven, and from one to three-thirty. The long intermission is to enable the children to take lunches to parents, brothers, sisters, and others who may be employed in the mills. This is a regular daily task with most of the children, some of them earning several dollars a week as "dinner-toters." The school itself is frequently termed by the children "the dinner-toters' school."

Although the aim of the school is industrial, the "three R's" are insisted upon even more severely than in the regular schools, because of the limited time the children have for schooling. "Although the prescribed course contemplates seven years," says Roland B. Daniell in a bulletin which has been recently issued by the United States Bureau of Education, "few of the pupils continue after the fifth or sixth year, so strong is the call of the mills. Not more than one per cent finish this school and pursue their studies further."

The three morning hours and the first hour of the afternoon are devoted to academic studies, while the last hour and a half of the day is given to practical work. All the boys are required to take the elementary course in woodwork and gardening. The girls take basketry, sewing, cooking, poultry raising, and gardening. The school is in session all the year round, and pupils are promoted quarterly. The teachers live at the school and keep "open house" to the people of the community at all times.

This school is only one part of a carefully developed system of industrial training in Columbus that is intended to reach the needs of all parts of the population. Mr. Daniel says, concerning the industrial work for Negroes:

"In the Negro schools the industrial, as well as the academic work of the primary department, which includes the first, second, third, and fourth grades, is directed by the grade teacher. The industrial work in grades five, six, seven, eight, and nine is conducted by special teachers for the various subjects taught. One

hour per day is given in each of these grades to industrial work.
"The boys divide their time equally between the work in the
carpentry department and the blacksmith shop. The section of the
grade that gives one hour to carpentry today will spend one hour
in the blacksmith shop tomorrow. The girls give equal time to
cooking, sewing, and laundering. When a class leaves the academic department it is divided, one part taking cooking, another
sewing, and the other laundering ; and the next day, of course,
they change.

"The child is therefore given industrial work five hours a
week for five years. This is thought to be sufficient to give his
education a practical turn and in a measure help him to begin the
work of life on a higher level than he could possibly do otherwise.
Then, too, such training enables the boy or girl to advance more
rapidly.

"The value of the equipment for the blacksmith shop does
not exceed $150, not counting the cost of the special building.
The wood shop is equipped only with benches and hand tools, not
exceeding $200 in value. The sewing department is equipped
with tables, chairs, and a half dozen sewing-machines, etc., costing in all $200. The kitchen has one coal-burner range, one gas
range, and individual equipment for classes. The value of this is
about $150. The equipment for the department of laundering is
very simple, consisting of tubs, ironing boards, ordinary flatirons,
electric irons, etc., worth $75.

"The main purpose in the work for the Negroes is to prepare them for the lines of industrial work open to them. No
attempt is made to give them training in the use of high-grade
machinery. The school has developed a number of good blacksmiths, carpenters, cooks, seamstresses, and laundresses. Pupils
who remain in the schools long enough to complete the course
receive upon leaving school in compensation for their labor about
twice what they would receive for unskilled labor such as they
would be able to render without such training. It is often the
case that one of these boys is able to earn $2 a day at the age of
17, when his father, without such preparation, receives $1.25 for
unskilled labor. "

The Society of American Indians, at its third
Opening the annual Conference in Denver last October, inserted
Court of Claims
to the Indians in its adopted platform a plank urging that the
United States Court of Claims be opened to all
the tribes and bands of Indians in the nation, for bringing suit
against the Government to settle claims for money which many
of the tribes believe is due them and has been owing them for
many years.

For this a special Act of Congress is necessary, because
only by approval of Congress may the Indians sue the Government. To promote its campaign and to create a public
sentiment which will impress upon Congress the need of such
action, the Society has issued from its headquarters in Washington

a little pamphlet, under the caption, "An Appeal to the Nation," in which are set forth the arguments in favor of this movement as a matter of simple justice.

Everybody familiar with the situation has long felt that some method should be found for settling or eliminating all the claims of the tribespeople against the United States. Yet it happens that year after year and even decade after decade goes by and the tribes still wait for some relief. While action is delayed the Indian suffers, not more by privation perhaps than by a sense of injustice which rankles in his breast. Hope deferred makes him sick at heart and paralyzes all effort for progress. Until this matter is settled the Indian will wait, and will stand still. Surely some remedy should be found, and that soon, for such a situation, and the one urged by the Society of American Indians seems to be a good one. Some safeguard against the ravages of the grafter will be necessary in any plan for settling these claims and this should be carefully looked after.

The proposal to open the Court of Claims to the Indians is not new. It has been discussed before. The Commissioner of Indian Affairs, in his report of June 30, 1912, said: "As a further preliminary [to the segregation of trust funds] all Indian tribes that have claims against the United States should receive legislative authority, under a general statute, to have their claims adjudicated by the Court of Claims. In this way claims of Indians can once for all be adjudicated, those which are just ascertained and prepared for consideration of Congress, and an element of discontent among Indians and of expectation which may often be unfounded will be permanently removed."

It will be noted that the Commissioner cites this action as an essential preliminary to the segregation of the tribal funds into individual holdings. It will be remembered that the Mohonk Conference has declared in favor of such segregation of the trust funds and that the Indian Rights Association has stoutly favored it. Moreover, the Indians have themselves petitioned for it, beginning as far back as 1898. It is evident that some legal aid for the Indians towards the settlement of their claims is a pressing necessity.

A means to this end is found in a bill introduced by Honorable Mr. Stephens of Texas in the House of Representatives on February 3, 1912. The Legal Aid Committee of the Society of American Indians has found that this bill meets the ideal requirements to a remarkable degree. Only two or three slight changes are recommended by way of safeguarding the interests of all parties involved. And it is for this amended bill that the Society solicits the support of all good citizens interested in the progress and welfare of the Indians.

Tuskegee
Meetings

A special meeting in the interest of the Tuskegee Institute will be held in Trinity Church, Boston, on Sunday evening, January 18, 1914. Among the speakers will be Bishop William Lawrence, Dr. Alexander T. Mann, and Principal Booker T. Washington of the Tuskegee Normal and Industrial Institute.

The Tuskegee fall and winter campaign work is usually inaugurated each year in New England through a large and important meeting in some one of the Boston churches. The Trinity Church meeting offers àn opportunity for friends of Negro advancement to be present and hear some of the results of Negro education in the South, for which they have given so much in the way of money and encouragement.

For the past three or four years a party of friends from the North has accompanied the trustees to Tuskegee Institute, where the semi-annual trustees' meeting is hèld. It is the plan to repeat this visit during the present winter.

The trustees, together with any friends who may choose to accompany them, will probably leave New York in a compartment car on the morning of February 19, reaching Tuskegee on the night of the twentieth and returning to New York on or before the morning of the twenty-fifth.   It will be noted that this plan gives friends the opportunity of celebrating Washington's Birthday at Tuskegee.   Details of the trip will be furnished to those who are interested, by Honorable Seth Low, Chairman of the Tuskegee Institute Board of Trustees, 30 East Sixty-fourth Street, New York City.

The Francis
Memorial

Surely there is great reason for men to be hopeful when the Secretary of State for a great nation pays his simple and public tribute to the memory of a colored physician whose life was devoted to the service of his fellow-men.   There was held in Washington, D. C., on November 24, 1913, a rather unique meeting of some fifteen hundred people, most of them Negroes, who paid their respect and tribute to Dr. John R. Francis—a man who devoted himself to the advancement of the work of the Colored Settlement of Washington.

The speakers included Honorable William Jennings Bryan, Dr. William M. Davidson, then superintendent of public schools in Washington, Professor George W. Cook, of Howard University, Dr. Thomas Jesse Jones, of the U. S. Bureau of Education, and Major R. R. Moton, of Hampton Institute.   The presiding officer was Roscoe Conkling Bruce, assistant superintendent of Washington schools and the present president of the Colored Social Settlement of Washington.

Mr. Bryan spoke of the importance of the service which Dr.

Francis rendered to his fellow-men. He did not introduce any-thing concerning the race question. He simply showed the impor-tance of measuring men's greatness by the service that they ren-der continuously and unselfishly. He said that the memory of Dr. Francis could be best honored by continuing the social settle-ment movement, of which he was such a vital part.

Major Moton emphasized the fact that Dr. Francis, like other Negroes of education and means, might have gone to a commu-nity where race feeling was less intense and there won for him-self a certain degree of success. He showed clearly, however, that Dr. Francis made the better choice when he devoted his life to the service of his own people.

The Francis memorial meeting calls attention to the fact that men are thinking more and more in terms of service and less in terms of class or race distinction.

The Virginia Educational Conference
The eighth annual Virginia Educational Conference was held in Lynchburg Thanksgiving week. This Conference is a three days' meeting of all the edu-cational forces in the state—the Teachers' Asso-ciation, State Department of Public Instruction, State Superin-tendents, State Board of Education, the Co-operative Education Association, School Trustees' Association, and affiliated organiza-tions, such as the Peace League, Folklore Society, Library Asso-ciation, and the School Athletic Association of Virginia.

There was a note of joyous adventure about this gathering which is usually lacking in such meetings. One of the leaders explained the situation when he said, "It is strange to see pioneer life in an old state." True, it is strange, and exhil-arating too. Everyone in Virginia, from the Governor in the Executive Mansion to the teacher in the one-room schoolhouse, is busy creating a public school system that shall fit the needs of the state. Such work of all, high and low, united for one object which is a source of satisfaction and pleasure to all classes of society, is true democracy.

Many teachers' conferences are dry because they are devoted to polishing and repolishing an inherited system, but this was alive because it was full of creative enthusiasm. This fresh enthusiasm was explained when one of the leading educators of the state said, referring to past school conditions, "I never was in school a day in my life until I went to the university," and a teacher hardly out of her teens gaily quoted the proverb, "Free school flea school." The present Virginian is forming a public school system untrammeled by the past. He is fitting the school to serve the state, he is firing the teachers and pupils with the new civic consciousness of the twentieth century.

In what way can these boys and girls serve the state? Virginia has six million acres of untilled land. This is an opportunity ready for the teacher, and every teacher is preaching from the text: "Better homes, better schools, better farms." Every child and parent is being taught how to raise more food, how to market it, and how to cook it. Crusades for better roads or buildings, for consolidated schools or better sanitary accommodations, are gaily carried on in every community, and the service of the state adds dignity to the simplest daily life. This was the general impression made upon the visiting stranger.

This does not mean that the State of Virginia is leading the world in achievement. In buildings and in quality of teaching she hardly competes with many old states, and an automobile trip convinces one of the great need of good roads; but perhaps in no state in the Union does school work occupy the attention of so many different classes of people, and only in new states does the school so reflect the people.

The Co-operative Education Association
On Friday, the twenty-eighth, the rally of the Co-operative Education Association summed up the forces at work in the new school life of Virginia. At the morning meeting, presided over by Mrs. B. B. Munford, president of the Association, a full and interesting report of the year's work was given by Mrs. Dashiell, director of the Citizens' Leagues. Miss Ella G. Agnew told of a league meeting in the interest of better farming. A student of the Luray High School told of the work done by a junior league. Rev. Mr. Carter, of Hampton, Virginia, spoke of the value of extension leagues ; Mr. Binford, of the school as a neighborhood center.

No one could read over the program or listen for even five minutes without feeling how vital the work of the leagues is. Such a report as that made by Superintendent Dickinson of Cumberland County on building a consolidated school and two miles of good road shows how they take hold of a community. The county secured $2500 for a building, then got a loan on the building for $2500 more, and sold three one-room schools, making a total of $6000 for the schoolhouse; but when finished it was two miles from a good road, cut off by as bad a piece of red clay road as the state affords. So they waited until January when things could be no worse, and then invited everyone to a patrons' meeting. By the time they reached the building everyone was convinced of the need of a new road! The parents raised $2000 then and there, then went to the County Road Superintendent and said, "Now match that money," then to the state for an engineer to build it, and, finally, the citizens kept an eye on it and refused three times to accept it. So, when at last it was accepted as perfectly satisfactory, it was an object lesson to the county.

Such work is a moral stimulus to the people of a community. It is their work and they are responsible, not that vague somebody, "the government." Superintendent Dickinson asked a patron who gave $200 at the meeting why he did so and received this shrewd bit of arithmetic. "I have ten children. If I send my oldest girl away to school this winter, it will cost me $200 down, and if I keep her there three years it will cost me $600. That would mean at least $6000 to educate all my children. It's cheap to me to get off with $200." The feeling that it is an economy for a family to pay for a good school and good food and good fun, so that their children will love and support the home life, is being taught in a hundred ways by the co-operative work.

Miss Webb, who was presented by Mrs. Munford as a woman road-builder, told of the variety of work in rural communities. She described the keeping of patrons' day, health day, good-roads day, better-farm day, athletic meets, and other social meetings, and told of exhibits of corn and canning clubs. The discussion closed with a lively "experience meeting" where school by school or county by county told what it had done to make better schools and better homes.

The School Fairs In a large hall in Lynchburg, during the educational conference, the exhibits from the school fairs of Virginia were displayed. Each county had held its fair during the early weeks of school, gathering the children and parents together for a children's day when the work of the summer vacation was exhibited. A hundred thousand people— parents, neighbors, and friends of the children—had visited these fairs. They had offered the prizes; they knew the children; and the ears of corn and the fruit in the cans had been grown in their counties, on their land, and by their children. That was a great economic lesson.

But it was not all utilitarian. Such an exhibit as Gloucester County made was of the very essence of patriotism, for the children had each prepared and sent in pictures of their daily life. There was a little fish-pond, with its tiny net, set on a blue-painted board, just as every boy sees it in the blue water of York River. There was a log cabin, made by a boy, of little logs collected from all the varieties of trees in Gloucester County. There was a collection of fifteen varieties of nuts, and there was a rabbit trap made from a hollow sweet-gum log. Collections of weeds and their seed pods, of flowers, grasses, and leaves, seed corn and beans, cans of fruits and vegetables—in every way the life of the woods and water and farm and garden, a child's natural kingdom, were represented. Besides this, there was hand work—drawing, carving, sewing, cooking—all forms of activity had their place.

President J. D. Eggleston of the Virginia Polytechnic Institute took for his text on Friday morning, "The School Exhibit" and told the story of these school fairs.

To many a teacher who has toiled over exhibitions of children's work it was a vision of freedom to hear Dr. Eggleston declare that the value of the school fair is that it shows, at the end of vacation, what the child has done for himself instead of showing, at the end of school, what the teacher has done for the child.   He showed the moral value of all this work.   He urged that the child should be encouraged to compete with himself, saying that a prize should be given when the boy had reached a certain standard, when he had conquered himself—his own awkwardness or laziness—and that the teacher should not exhibit the last and finished product but the steps by which the child had come, so that the boy could see what growth he had made. Prizes and exhibitions to be moral must prove to the growing child "the value of labor and the shallowness of luck."   He admitted that this was difficult, but "its difficulty is the measure of the duty."   The object of this work should be to train the child as a citizen, to teach him to conquer and direct his own energies, and to serve the state.   "This," he declared, "is essential democracy; this is essential Christianity; he who would be first among you, let him serve."

***

News from China
Hampton is pleased to have news from Miss Margaret Jones, a valued former worker who resigned last year in order to take up missionary work among Chinese girls.   She is a teacher at the True Light Seminary in Canton, a mission of the American Presbyterian Board. Miss Jones writes:

"It is just three weeks since the *Mongolia* landed us in Hongkong, after an almost perfect voyage, with very interesting stops at Honolulu, Manila, and three Japanese ports.   Fair as were the countries we touched at, I am glad that my work is to be in China and in Canton.   The millions of faces that one passes here in the streets are, almost without exception, patient, clean, honest, rugged faces.

"In spite of reports to the contrary, political affairs are unusually quiet in Canton just now, although many predict that it is simply the lull before the storm.   There is everywhere a decided reaction against the more progressive republican ideas.   It is the old story of the headstrong eagerness of young leaders.

Most of those elected to office here in the South immediately after the Revolution were returned students, whose ideas were too much in advance of those possessed by the Government officials in Peking, and who, from their long absence, were personally out of touch with their own people. The changes they demanded would, no doubt, have benefited China if they had been willing to wait for the Government to grow accustomed to their ideas. As it is, last summer's revolt has set things back for years. ·

"Mr. Chung Meng Kwong, the governor, and Dr. Chung, the commissioner of education, who was doing splendid work, have fled to America for their lives. The chief of police and several minor officials have been beheaded. Last week three coolie women were shot out here on the land back of our school. Bombs had been discovered hidden in their baskets. The present governor, Lung Tsai Kuong, was formerly a bandit chief. He is a rough, cruel man, wholly out of sympathy with progressive ideas. It is galling to these ambitious young progressives to have a man of that type placed over them. Even the argument that a poor government is better than none may not be sufficient to restrain them long. Indeed, the report is abroad this morning that the governor has been secretly speared. This, if true, is probably the direct result of Yuan Shi Ki's last edict, that no one shall become a member of his assembly who has not held an office in China for ten years.

"There are the usual accompaniments of an unstable government. The pirates and robbers, so the older missionaries say, are more bold than they have ever known them. A boat was robbed by the pirates last week only five hours' journey from Hongkong. It is only in such indirect ways that foreigners are liable to suffer from present conditions. No foreigners have ever been injured in the actual skirmishes between the two parties.

"The life of Mr. Wong, the man whose sermons I listen to each Sunday (and do not understand), is very representative of the ups and downs that come to the Chinaman who is in advance of his age. Mr. Wong was educated in one of the mission schools in this city. Through his influence Christian teachers first made an entrance into Tien Chow, his native city. The Chinese in authority did not like this and, for punishment, Mr. Wong was beaten three hundred times with a bamboo rod. It was a miracle that his back was not broken. He fled at once to Honolulu where he worked among his own people until the Revolution broke out. He then returned and was appointed governor of the province where he was beaten. Since the reaction has again set in he has resigned from the governorship and become pastor of the Second Presbyterian Church here. His church is always packed and the majority in the audience are young men.

"At present the Republic may seem a disappointment here in the South, but God sometimes has to teach his people by hard lessons, and all who love China have faith that from this last struggle stronger and more tactful leaders will come forth. Living and working behind the ivy-covered walls of this old school with these sweet-mannered Chinese girls, war and the rumors of war seem strange and out of place. But the Revolution did leave bullet holes in our front gate!

"My chief duty in life at present is to devote myself to language study some six hours a day, so that as soon as possible I may take a more active part in the work. I find the study interesting simply because the language is so tantalizingly difficult. I can now write some seventy characters, and read the first twelve verses of Mark in character. By the way, I have a new name—Miss Chung. That is the nearest the Chinese language comes to Jones."

Jane Augusta Stevens A former Hampton worker, Mrs. Jane Augusta Stevens, who served the school most untiringly from 1896 to 1910, died recently at the age of 69. Mrs. Stevens was born in Westmoreland, N. H., on December 14, 1844, and was educated in the public schools of Concord, N. H.

More than a year ago Mrs. Stevens was obliged to give up active work on account of failing health. She leaves a sister, a nephew, and a niece (Mrs. George D. Young), all of Springfield, Mass. The funeral was held at the home of Mr. and Mrs. Young, who, for a number of years, were also valued workers at Hampton.

One of the important contributions of Mrs. Stevens's life to Hampton Institute was her constant insistence on high standards of work among the students. She was never satisfied with anything that was done in a slipshod manner. She was always most painstaking herself, and she never failed to bring the Hampton students up to a faithful and efficient performance of their everyday tasks.

THE HAMPTON INSTITUTE TRADE SCHOOL

II BLACKSMITHING AND WHEELWRIGHTING

" Self-support must go along with Christian living. It is hard to be honest if you are starving. A man who can support himself is more likely to lead a Christian life. " SAMUEL CHAPMAN ARMSTRONG

" IF you don't believe that it takes some real, worth-while education to shoe a horse properly, then try to shoe the next horse you see. " William Hodges Mann, of Virginia, frequently uses words to this effect to give added force to his public appeal for practical, common-sense training of all classes for special service to the community. Hampton understands fully the importance of applying Governor Mann's idea to the making of blacksmiths and wheelwrights, as well as other tradesmen, teachers, and farmers.

Why is it that blacksmiths and wheelwrights who are trained at Hampton meet unusual emergencies when they are thrown out in the world to make their own way as journeymen, as teachers of blacksmithing and wheelwrighting, or as independent owners of their shops ? What is there in Hampton's system which promotes initiative, application, and general efficiency ?

From the minute a Negro or Indian boy enters the blacksmith shop at Hampton he is put to work at his trade. He is shown how to move about his forge in a comfortable, natural manner. He is shown how to build a fire properly and then he is assigned the task of building a fire which will stand the test of inspection. At every turn, the boy is shown, not only how to do the work that the blacksmith must know how to do, but he is given the why and wherefore of the processes which enter into the blacksmithing trade and must be mastered.

The beginner is not merely a shop helper or handy man who mechanically does the striking for another man or simply waits on some superior. From the start, the blacksmith-in-the-making comes in touch with a system of instruction which abounds in common sense and practicality. He learns to do his work accurately and neatly. He learns his first lessons partly through imitation, for shop demonstrations are frequent and to the point. The student is encouraged to ask questions and to work out, with the help of his instructor, satisfactory answers. If the task, for, example, is that of building properly a forge fire, then the properties of coal, the heating of iron, and the control of the blast are some of the questions which receive careful attention.

Hampton takes boys who are "green from the woods" and, by careful training, through tasks of graduated difficulty, develops tradesmen who learn to do the so-called common tasks of life with skill and understanding. The school itself, which is an industrial village, furnishes a variety of work, which makes it possible to give Negro and Indian students the tasks which they need to develop their latent powers. Whenever a wagon is built in the wheelwright shop, it is passed to the blacksmiths to have the necessary iron work properly fitted. The axles are welded; the wheels are fitted with the tires; and the springs are fastened or clipped to the wagon gear. The iron which is used on the wagon is carefully measured, worked into shape, and properly fitted on the body and gear built by the wheelwrights. If work has to be done on a school boat, then the blacksmiths and wheelwrights, along with other tradesmen, are on hand to do the necessary repair or construction job.

When fire escapes and fire ladders were needed for the dormitories, the blacksmiths were assigned to the work. When ornamental iron work was called for in the construction of the new Y. M. C. A. building, Clarke Hall, and the remodeling of the Principal's house, the blacksmiths were again assigned some difficult and important work. Then, again, the necessary repair work on farm implements and farm wagons, which are in daily use on the home farm and at Shellbanks, the large school farm some six miles away from the main Hampton buildings, is done satisfactorily by the Trade School blacksmiths and wheelwrights.

Hampton tradesmen not only do the repair and construction work for the school, but they also do a considerable amount of commercial work. This includes, for the blacksmiths and wheelwrights, the making of railroad and wharf trucks in some twenty-five styles, and the building and repairing of wagons, as well as a variety of carts and wheelbarrows. Attractive andirons, sets of fire tools, fire screens, well-made forging tools—these are some of the interesting products of the blacksmith shop.

The boys at Hampton who take the regular course in agriculture, spend half a day a week for two months in the blacksmith shop, and there they learn to make the simple iron articles which are commonly used on the farm, including staples, links for chains, lap links for traces, and hame hooks. These agriculture boys receive drill in the principles of blacksmithing and are given enough practice so that at the end of their brief course they are able to do the ordinary blacksmithing work required on the farm.

WHERE GOOD BLACKSMITHS ARE MADE

They also find out that they can buy a small and suitable black-smithing outfit at a small cost.

To understand how the Trade School is able to do such a

BLACKSMITHS IRONING WAGONS AND CARRIAGES

variety of blacksmithing work with boys who are crude at the beginning, one must follow, step by step, the training that is offered
in the Trade School. After a boy has learned to make his forge
fire, he is given a piece of iron about half an inch in diameter and
thirty inches long and is first required to make a square point on
one end. This apparently simple operation requires patient practice. Hampton insists that no work shall be accepted until it is
well done. After a boy has mastered the making of a square
point, he passes to the making of a round one, and then a flat one.
Meanwhile, he learns how to handle the blacksmith's hammer ;
how to get the proper wrist and elbow motion ; and how to handle
his muscles to the greatest advantage. Then, too, he learns more
and more about the handling of his forge fire. Such knowledge
as the proper use of green coal, and of heat itself, becomes his
own through the mastery of carefully supervised and graduated
tasks. When the thirty-inch piece of iron gets so short that a
boy cannot hold it without burning his hands, he receives a new
piece of iron and is taught how to make a weld. Step by step, he
turns out, according to specifications and blueprint drawings,
some seventy-odd technical exercises during his first year of
Trade School work. Drawing out iron, making staples, bending
rings, making a hook and eye, developing a gate hook, fashioning
bolts and nuts of various sizes and shapes, welding rings, constructing braces, chain links, square bands, making chisels, drills,
springs, lathe tools, horseshoes, carriage steps, scrapers—these
are some of the technical exercises in iron and steel which the
Hampton blacksmith learns to do.

The students in the blacksmith shop take regular turns in
shoeing the horses and mules that belong to the school. Nobody
is ever allowed to abuse a horse or a mule. Every boy is taught
to do his horseshoeing work with due regard to the animal's
needs.

Along with the practical work over the forge and anvil, the
tradesman studies from a simple text the facts concerning iron
and iron working, iron forging and welding, fuels, steel and steel
working. He also studies the use of the tools that the blacksmith
needs in his everyday shop practice. The text, which is carefully
studied, contains, in question and answer form, the facts which
the blacksmith needs to know.

During the Saturday morning lectures and demonstrations,
students take up in greater detail the technical side of their work
and learn the ins and outs of their trade by coming in contact
with definite problems and by reasoning out together with their
instructors the *how, when,* and *why* of processes with which they
have to deal every day.

The story of a typical Hampton tradesman follows: "A student

FULL-SIZE DRAWINGS ARE USED IN MAKING GEARS

who now has a blacksmith shop in Richmond, Virginia, by his
attention to business, settling his accounts promptly, and general
good character and habits, so impressed a salesman for a

TO MAKE GOOD WHEELS REQUIRES PATIENCE AND SKILL

Baltimore firm with the value of the training Hampton students receive that he has been recommending them for positions in Virginia and North Carolina for several years. He has also called attention, from time to time, to good openings for shops and has helped some of the Hampton students to get started in business for themselves. He recently said that not one of the students he had recommended had failed to please or to make good, and that by their good work they are inspiring confidence in their race. "

Although blacksmithing and wheelwrighting are taught at Hampton as two distinct trades, every effort is made to show students the close relation of one to the other. The blacksmith, during his course, receives some training in wheelwrighting, and the wheelwright, in turn, receives some practice in blacksmithing. In a number of cases, a blacksmith will take, after finishing his own trade, a year of special work in the wheelwright shop, while the boy who has received his wheelwrighting certificate will often take a year of special work in the blacksmith shop. The fact is recognized that the wheelwright and the blacksmith must work over many problems in common. For this reason, all that has been said concerning blacksmithing can be applied, with appropriate changes, to the work of wheelwrighting.

Technical work is given the wheelwrighting students to teach them how to use their tools effectively and how to make the common and special joints required in their work ; how to select and dress timber and work it to given sizes. To do the essential operations, a boy has to use a number of different tools and woodworking machines, cross-cut, rip, and bandsaws, planer, jointer, shaper, mortiser, turning lathe, and boring machine. Then there are working drawings of a variety of joints which are made so as to give training for wagon work in which some joints must not show. When a boy builds a wheelbarrow he must know at every turn why he does this or that. As a part of his work he must lay out full-size drawings in the shop.

Later in the course, the wheelwright applies his technical knowledge to commercial work—the making of railroad and wharf trucks, the building of carts and wagons, the repairing of carriage and wagon bodies, the putting on of rubber tires, making new rims, respoking wheels, and doing general repair work. On the repair jobs boys labor together and thereby learn to develop initiative and the ability to work well with their fellows.

The wheelwrights have good tools to use, and also good general equipment for all their trade work. They are required to take the very best care of the material and tools that Hampton has placed at their disposal.

The shop talks cover such matters as the care and dressing of tools, the proper methods of laying out work, cutting and fitting

WHEELWRIGHTS BUILD CARTS, WAGONS, VANS, AND CARRIAGES

timber for regular wheelwright problems, discussions dealing with suitable materials for the various parts of wagons and carriage construction, cost of material and labor, seasoning and handling of timber. Students keep written notes and sketches

HAMPTON'S HORSES AND MULES ARE CAREFULLY SHOD

of the shop talks, which are regularly given every Saturday morning, and, indeed, whenever some important question comes up during the working out of a regular wheelwrighting problem.

Wheelwrights and blacksmiths, when they leave the Hampton Trade School, can readily find work as journeymen in the South. The Negro or Indian boy who is prepared to do his trade work well does not lack the opportunity of securing profitable employment. The demand for skilled workmen is growing.

The students are encouraged to return to their home communities and there put in action the ideas which they have gained at Hampton. Service and efficiency are emphasized at every turn during the courses which are given in the Hampton Institute Trade School.

THE RED CROSS IN JAPAN

BY SAINT NIHAL SINGH

THAT the Red Cross, whose foundation rests entirely upon Christianity, should be adopted bodily by a heathen nation and grow into a healthy and sturdy organization, is a matter to be greatly wondered at. That is precisely what has happened in Japan ; though, curiously, while the military and naval exploits of the Japanese are noised about the world, little is known of the success which has attended the efforts made by this non-Christian nation to minimize the unhappy results of warfare, and also to help alleviate, through the agency of the Red Cross, the suffering caused by disasters of various kinds.

The first attempt to induce the Japanese Government to adopt this institution was made soon after the War Department had been organized in 1871. The officials connected with its medical bureau had heard rumors of a humanitarian agency which nursed and healed sick and wounded soldiers irrespective of whether they were friends or foes, and whose doctors, nurses, and attendants were not molested by the fighters on either side ; and they asked the " Council of State " to grant permission to establish a similar institution in connection with the native army.

But this request was made before the time was ripe for the innovation. The Mikado's advisers could not reconcile themselves to the idea of adopting the cross for their symbol, and they disdainfully rejected the suggestion as one proceeding from the " abject followers of Western medicine. " However, soon afterwards, the promoters of the movement induced the War Department to allow the medical bureau to adopt as its badge a horizontal red line on a white ground. These sagacious men believed that in the course of time they would be permitted to add the perpendicular line that would make it a red cross—the universal emblem of humanitarianism.

In the meantime the civil war of 1877 broke out, and Mr. (afterwards Count) Tsumétami Sano, who, during his sojourn in Europe, had studied the work and methods of the Red Cross League, secured the co-operation of a few other philanthropists and started a small organization patterned after the Western institution, naming it the *Hakuaisha*—"The Society of Universal

THE MANCHURIAN RED CROSS HOSPITAL AT PORT ARTHUR

Love. " A red line with a dot over it was adopted as the badge of the association, a small medical corps was hastily organized, and, with the permission of the Imperial commander-in-chief, the work of affording relief to both the Government and rebel soldiers commenced in a leased house located in the heart of the fighting operations.

After the expiration of the civil war, which lasted only eight months but was extremely sanguinary, the organizers of the *Hakuaisha* constantly used all the influence they could command to induce the Government to accord the Society the position which it is given in Christendom. In 1886 the War Department was completely won over, Japan entered the Geneva Convention, and

the unofficial association was converted into a semi-state organization.   The red cross became the symbol of the Japanese military
medical agency.   Special steps were taken to imbue the soldiers
with the spirit of the institution, and to teach them, while waiting
for scientific aid, how to bandage their own and their comrades'
wounds with antiseptic bandages which were sewn inside their
tunics.

But the difficulties did not end here.   When Japan sought, in
1887, to join the International Red Cross Society, some reaction-
ary delegates attending the Fourth International Conference held
at Karlsruhe, Germany, made a motion to the effect that the
assistance and protection which the Red Cross League rendered
in time of war should not be extended to countries outside the
boundaries of Europe, even when those countries happened to be
members of the League. '' The Japanese delegates, under the
leadership of Surgeon-General Baron Tadanori Ishiguro, at once
resisted this proposal, which was actuated purely by racial prejudice.   The better sense of the assembly prevailed, and finally the
motion was dropped, Japan becoming a full-fledged member of
the International League, bearing its equal share of the responsibilities and enjoying equal privileges.

Ever since the admission of the Japanese Red Cross Society
into the Geneva Convention, its officials have displayed great
activity in establishing hospitals, training doctors and nurses, and
inducing men and women to join as members and subscribe to its
funds.   In these endeavors they were materially assisted by their
Imperial Majesties, the late Emperor and the Empress Haruku,
and other members of the Royal Family, the court nobles, and
high officials.

As a result of this, when the war broke out with China in
1894, the organization had acquired great strength and was able
to do considerable work.   Relief corps numbering 1587 were sent
to the front.   Besides those who were attended to in and about
the scenes of battle, 1484 (mostly Chinese prisoners) were transported to Japan to be treated at the reserve hospitals, where, for
the first time in the history of this country, Japanese gentlewo-
men trained by the Red Cross Society acted as nurses, and by
creditably discharging their duties, put an end to the prejudice
entertained by the Japanese against middle- and upper-class
women engaging in nursing.

During the Boxer troubles in China in 1900 the Red Cross
Society of Japan sent 491 helpers to the front, and transported
125 white soldiers (and most of them French), caring for them
at the base hospitals.   The Red Cross also rendered invaluable
aid in the Russo-Japanese War.   No less than 4700 nurses were
mobilized, and 11 hospital ships engaged to transport the wounded.

OFFICERS OF THE PATRIOTIC WOMEN'S ASSOCIATION OF JAPAN

The work was so well done by the relief corps of the Society, in conjunction with the regular military sanitary authorities, that a new record of saving the wounded was established, showing that Japan had so mastered the Western system as to be able to teach the Occidentals how to improve on their own methods.

The record of the Japanese Red Cross in alleviating distress during times of catastrophe has been equally splendid. During the famine of 1906 ; in the event of holocausts like the big fires at Hakodaté in Hokkaido in 1907 and at Osaka in 1909 ; of terrible mine disasters such as the explosion, in 1907, at the Toyokuni mine, Fukuoka ; on the occasion of the Shiga earthquake in 1909; of the sanguinary riots during the strikes at the Ashiwo mine; of the sickness attendant upon the pilgrimage, in 1907, of great masses of people to Hongwanji, one of the greatest Buddhist sanctuaries in the Empire; and in many accidents such as an explosion in a railway train, and another in a gunpowder factory, the Society saved thousands of lives and held out hope to hundreds of thousands, who, but for the assistance thus given, would have been helpless and hopeless.   An ambulance station has been established at

TOKYO HEADQUARTERS OF THE JAPANESE RED CROSS SOCIETY

Tokyo to care for those injured in street and factory accidents.

In addition to the relief given at home, much has been done by the Japanese Red Cross to help the necessitous in its over-seas dominions in Formosa and Korea.   On several occasions members have been sent to nurse the military men injured in conflicts, in the remote districts of Formosa, with the cannibals who constantly harrass them.   They were even anxious to attend to the wounded savages ; but these proved so vicious that this was found to be impracticable and the idea had to be given up.

Not content with relieving suffering within the Empire, like true Red Cross crusaders they collected and forwarded $146,000 to aid the California earthquake sufferers, and also sent a large donation to Italy at the time of the earthquake which devastated Messina and Reggio in 1908.

STRETCHER PRACTICE OF THE JAPANESE RED CROSS NURSES

The Japanese Red Cross Society has now (in 1913) grown into a sturdy institution. It has a membership of about 1,750,000 (that is, one person out of every 36 in Japan). Its funds exceed $1,500,000 and its buildings, ships, and equipment are worth more than $8,150,000. It has a large hospital in a suburb of Tokyo which serves as the central institution. In addition, it maintains eleven other hospitals in various parts of the Empire, including Manchuria and Formosa.

The Red Cross nurse's hospital uniform consists of a long, white, over-all apron and a large, high, square, snowy cap with a

RED CROSS DOCTORS AND NURSES IN THE RUSSO-JAPANESE WAR

red cross on its front.   The traveling, or out-door habit, is a neat,
plain dress of dark material, not unlike that worn by American
nurses.   In order to join the Society as a nurse, the candidate
must be over seventeen and under thirty, and be willing to serve
a probationary term of three years in the hospital as a student.
After graduation all the nurses but those required to staff the
Red Cross Hospitals, used during times of peace as ordinary medical institutions, are placed on the reserve list.   They vow to be
ready at any moment, for a period of fifteen years, to answer the
call from headquarters and go wherever they may be sent,
whether it be to the battlefield, to the scene of political disturbances or of devastation due to an act of nature, or to engage in
manœuvres.

Young men are educated in medical science free upon their
vowing to serve as reserve physicians after their graduation for a
period of five years.   Some of the most promising ones are even
sent abroad to finish their training.

In addition to the salary they receive, the Red Cross workers
are paid their traveling expenses at any time they may be mobilized for any purpose whatsoever.   If they are injured or become
ill during their active service, or on account of it, they are
granted pensions, which are continued to their families if they
die.

The real reason why the Japanese have scored such great
success in assimilating Red Cross methods is the fact that they
are a kind-hearted nation.   Another cause which has contributed
to the same end is the shrewdness displayed by the organizers of
the institution in opening a channel in which the mother-love of
the Japanese gentlewoman can flow, which, but for that avenue,
would remain pent up and of no direct use to the nation.

NEGRO NURSES IN FRONT OF PROVIDENT HOSPITAL

NEGRO WOMEN AS TRAINED NURSES

BY ROBERT McMURDY

TO most people the "Negro problem" means the problem of the Negro man. They do not realize how much graver is the problem of the Negro woman. But a moment's reflection will bring to mind the tragedy of her condition.

Not the least cruel of the incidents of slavery was her loss of home and family life and consequently of a normal point of view. Even now, in these days of so-called freedom, normal existence is difficult for the colored woman to attain; for fate still decrees that she make what progress she can in spite of odds for which her race is not to blame. She must strive against a tradition of immorality (a tradition assumed to be conclusive), against a prejudice which closes to her the door of nearly every employment that could ensure her progress and self-development, against wretched environment, and against a poverty almost hopeless in such circumstances. Rarely as yet are the learned professions open to colored women. Only here and there is there opportunity

* Reprinted, with permission, from the *Survey*

for them in industrial positions, or in dressmaking, millinery, and other lines of business.

In the fine arts, transcendent genius has won recognition; but the artistic instinct, undeniably present in the race, is as yet undeveloped. The one door only too widely open before her is the door of vice. Reports show that Negro women are employed in large numbers as maids or housekeepers in places of ill-fame, and are sooner or later dragged downward. And in many cities the segregated vice district is located in the Negro section.

Certainly students of the Negro question have difficulties in finding any path through the woods which promises a way out. Yet gradually they are discovering a few lines of broken branches

DR. GEORGE C. HALL,
SURGEON AT PROVIDENT HOSPITAL

which seem to indicate the trails, and now and then a clear vista shows the way. One such vista is the vocation of the trained nurse. For this work nature has endowed the Negro woman, and race experience laid sound foundations. Add to natural qualifications the discipline of scientific training, and there results for the colored woman a means of skilled employment. Such an aim possesses both a human and a patriotic aspect; and its accomplishment is a fact of interest and significance.

For instance, visit the Hope Day Nursery, in New York. Here in kindergarten hours you will see some of the most appealing pickaninnies to be found outside a frame. Here are Italian children too, who have not yet imagined such a thing as race prejudice—Italian-Americans accepting benevolence from Negroes! The nursery, maintained by Negroes to fill a need among their own people, was started by an enthusiastic, unassuming colored woman who gave up a lucrative position as private nurse to lend help in the upward struggle of her people, and who has recently taken up a yet larger work in the San Juan Hill region. She will tell you concerning her preparation, "I was educated as a trained nurse at Provident Hospital in the 'black belt' of Chicago."

In one of your Georgia trips you might meet a colored woman who is nursing in Atlanta. Her story is one of ambition and struggle: "My mother was a washerwoman. I left the iron-ing-table and went to the industrial university in which Dr. DuBois was a leading influence. I learned to be a printer. At this trade I earned enough to take the course in dressmaking, to complete the academic work, and later to graduate as a nurse. I heard of Provident Hospital in Chicago, gained admission, was graduated, and returned to work among my own people."

In an institution for white people located in a large city of Iowa is a colored physician and teacher. From others rather than from himself you can best learn of his achievement. Coming north from Texas he took his medical course at Northwestern. At an examination for the position of interne, he passed first, leaving in the rear twenty-five white men, and was appointed to the only hospital in the Northwest which admits colored men to its staff. He himself will tell you gladly of the hospital and its work, and of its fund from which he drew enough to start in surgical practice, repaying the loan from his first case. He owes his start to Provident Hospital.

The hospital is really and distinctively a Negro enterprise. Founded twenty years ago with the purpose of affording colored women the nurse's training, it was then the only institution of its kind in this country, except the Government hospital, Freedmen's, at Washington. Through its earlier years it was managed by colored people, and even to this time members of both races are on its staff and board of trustees. It is supported largely by colored people. Its endowment started from the pathetic bequest of an old colored woman who, dying, had just fifty dollars to leave after providing for her burial. Her direction was, "Give it to two charities established for my people, one-half going to Provident Hospital." To this "widow's mite" have been added generous gifts from friends of all races sympathizing with the aim of Provident and enthusiastic over its splendid record of achievement. It has graduated over 118 nurses and now has in training 25 colored women.

These nurses are from twenty-four states—Canada, the West

Indies, and Poland. From the Provident Training School many have gone into institutional work, especially in the South. One graduate established the training school at Tuskegee which others have carried on. Another was in sole charge of Provident and managed it with distinguished success. Still another has been for two years the head of the Freedmen's Hospital Training School. Two have become physicians; three are in the Visiting Nurses' Association, with a record of having cared for more than 5200 people in the three years of their connection. The hospital has cared for a total of more than 14,000 patients in the wards; 88,000 in the dispensary. These patients have not been Negroes only, but of all races. Connected with the dispensary is a laboratory conducted by nurses and devoted to the problem of skilfully feeding infants. A children's clinic is held by the staff doctors; and during the summer, a fresh-air tent is erected on the hospital roof where scores of babies find in hot weather their only chance for life.

But do these colored women really make efficient nurses? An answer may be found in the words of Sophie P. Palmer, after a month's visit at Provident: "From the standpoints of order, dignity, and technical skill the nursing force of this hospital seems to compare more than favorably with hospitals of the same size and class in other cities where the nursing service is composed of white women."

Opportunities exist for comparing the work of these colored nurses with that of nurses in other schools. When the Provident students took their training in dietetics at Northwestern University their record was in no way inferior to that of the white students; in similar classes of the School of Domestic Arts and Sciences, they took the lead. Recently a graduate took a civil service examination in Chicago. Failing at the first test, she passed later at the head of a class of fifty-four. And these nurses not only maintain their average but show in crises the skill, endurance, and devotion which is rightfully expected from the nurse, regardless of her color.

Lately a white boy was hurried to the hospital gravely ill with pneumonia. The telegraph summoned his parents from the East. His mother, a Southern-bred woman, rebelled at his surroundings, but the boy was too ill to be moved. Between life and death he wavered for days. The doctors gave him up. But the Negro nurse refused to yield. For thirty-six hours she fought for his life with every known means, hardly leaving his bedside, and taking not an instant's rest. Finally the nurse's devotion and skill won a two-fold victory—disease was conquered in the child and a life-long prejudice was conquered in the mother's heart.

What is, after all, the deepest significance of Provident Hospital—the actual work within its wards, the skilled employment which its scientific training places within the reach of colored women, or the influence it radiates, through the association of races in its work, upon one of the very grave problems of this country?

THE BASIS OF INDIAN OWNER-SHIP OF LAND AND GAME

BY F. G. SPECK

"TO recognize Indian ownership of the limitless prairies and forests of this continent (that is, to consider the dozen squalid savages who hunted at long intervals over a territory of a thousand square miles, as owning it outright) necessarily implies a similar recognition of the claims of every white hunter, squatter, horse thief, or wandering cattleman. In fact, the mere statement of the case is enough to show the absurdity of asserting that the land really belonged to the Indians. The different tribes have always been utterly unable to define their own boundaries. "

— T. Roosevelt in " *The Winning of the West.*"

In making the above statement Mr. Roosevelt is quite in error as regards most, if not all, of the hunting tribes of the northern part of this continent. Not only is his erroneous deduction promulgated among his own readers, who may have · no opportunity to correct it, but the statement, taken for reliable authority, is copied, quoted, and used as the basis for an adverse decision against the rights of the Indians in general, by the compiler and author of a fairly well-known historical series. [1] To disseminate misconceptions resulting disadvantageously to a weaker race seems an injustice, though perhaps excusable through ignorance, which one feels challenged to correct. The attack upon the fundamental claims to their domains is a matter of considerable importance to the Indians, both in the United States and Canada. Accordingly, I take occasion to present a brief outline of some facts, part of my own studies of the past few years among the hunting tribes of the northern forests, and in particular

1 The Historian's History of the World. Henry Smith Williams, LL. D., volume XXII—The British Colonies and the United States, 1904

the statement of a Canadian Ojibway chief concerning the actual family claims to territory. I will present this testimony first, the following being a translation of the matter, which very appropriately at this time was left in my charge this summer, while visiting the tribes of northern Ontario to make public to the white people encroachments upon Indian rights to the land.

TESTIMONY OF ALECK PAUL (OSHESHEWAKWASINOWININI,[1])
SECOND CHIEF OF THE TEMAGAMI BAND OF OJIBWAYS,
BEAR ISLAND, TEMAGAMI,[2] ONTARIO

'' In the early times the Indians owned this land where they lived bounded by the lakes, and rivers, and hills, or determined by a certain number of days' journeys in this direction or that. These tracts formed the hunting grounds owned and used by the different families. Wherever they went the Indians took care of the game animals, especially the beaver, just as the Government takes care of the land today. So these families of hunters would never think of damaging the abundance or the source of supply of the game, because this had come to them from their father and grandfather and those behind them. It is, on the other hand, the white man who needs to be watched. He makes the forest fires, he goes through the woods and kills everything he can find, whether he needs its flesh or not, and then, when all the animals in one section are killed, he takes the train and goes to another where he can do the same.

'' The Indian families used to hunt in a certain section for beaver. They would only kill the small beaver and leave the old ones to keep on breeding. Then when they got too old they too would be killed, just as a farmer kills his pigs, preserving the stock for his supply of young. The beaver is the Indian's pork, the moose his beef, the partridge his chicken. And there was the caribou or red deer, that was his sheep. All these formed the stock on his family hunting ground, which would be parceled out among the sons when the owner died. He says to his sons, 'You take this part. Take care of this tract. See that it always produces enough.' That was what my grandfather told us. His land was divided among two sons, my father and Pisha'bo (Tea Water), my uncle. We were to own this land so no other Indians could hunt on it. Other Indians could travel through it and go there, but could not go there to kill the beaver. Each family had its own district where they belonged and owned the game. That was each one's stock, for food and clothes. If another Indian hunted on our territory we, the owners, could

---

1 This means " Noise-of-sighing-wind-in-the-trees man."

2 It would be desirable for those who are interested in these matters to communicate with Chief Paul.

shoot him. This division of the land started in the beginning of time, and always remained unchanged. I remember about twenty years ago some Nipissing Indians came north to hunt on my father's land. He told them not to hunt beaver, 'This is our land,' he told them; 'you can fish but must not touch the fur, as that is all we have to live on.' Sometimes an owner would give permission for strangers to hunt for a certain time or on a certain tract. This was often done for friends or when neighbors had had a poor season. Later the favor might be returned.

"When the white people came they commenced killing all the game. They left nothing on purpose to breed and keep up the supply, because the white man don't care about the animals. They are after the money. After the white man kills all the game in one place he can take the train and go three hundred miles or more to another and do the same there. But the Indian cannot do that. He must stay on his own section all the time and support his family on what it produces. So he has to preserve his game stock and live on what is bred, on the increase. If the Indian did like the white man and should go to the old country, England, what would the white man do? He would send soldiers to shoot him or send him back where he came from.

"You can write this down for me. If an Indian went to the old country and sold hunting licenses to the old country people for them to hunt on their own land, the white people would not stand for that. The Government sells our big game, our moose, for $50.00 license and we don't get any of it. The Government sells our fish and our islands or gets the money, but we don't get any share.

"What we Indians want is for the Government to stop the white people killing our game, as they do it only for sport and not for support. We Indians do not need to be watched about protecting the game; we must protect the game or starve. We can take care of the game just as well as the game warden and better, because we are going to live here all the time. We don't like to be watched, when the Government don't watch the people he should watch. When the treaty was made, about sixty years ago, the Government said, 'You Indians own the game.' There are a great many Indians in this country. People do not see them much at the towns because they stay in the bush. These Indians need to have their rights in the land and the game recognized and protected as much as the new settlers."

A few brief results of my own investigation of social life may be pertinent here, especially as they show how widespread the above conditions were among the northern tribes. Fundamentally these conditions formed the primary social institution from the Atlantic Coast across the continent. The whole territory claimed by each tribe was subdivided into tracts, owned from time immemorial by the same families and handed down from generation to generation. The almost exact bounds of these districts were known and recognized, and trespass, which, indeed, was of rare occurrence, was summarily punishable. These family groups form the social units of most of the tribes and bands, having not only kinship ties but a community of land and interests. In some tribes these bands had developed into clans, with prescribed rules of marriage, some social taboos, and totemic emblems. The territorial bounds, indeed, are so well established and definite that it has been possible to show on maps the exact tract of country claimed by each family group. The districts among the Algonquins seem to average between two and four hundred square miles to each family. I have already prepared such maps of the Penobscot territory in Maine, where the tribal domains were divided into twenty-two families; of the Temiskaming, of eight families; of the Nipissing, Lake Demonie, Temagami, Matachewan, and Mattawa bands of Algonquin and Ojibway in Ontario and Quebec. From other authorities we learn of the same social foundation among the Narragansetts of Rhode Island (authority of Roger Williams), the Indians of New Brunswick, Labrador, and the western plains north of the Missouri; while it is very probable that inquiry will disclose something similar among the Central Plains tribes.

In conclusion, briefly, we encounter in this instance another illustration of one of the popular fallacies entertained by historical writers when dealing with the complicated inside life of the American Indians.

NEGRO PROGRESS IN VIRGINIA*

BY BOOKER T. WASHINGTON

Principal of Tuskegee Institute, Alabama

THE members of the colored race who live outside of Virginia are beginning to grow somewhat jealous of the progress which our race is making in this commonwealth. The Negro race in Virginia is going forward, in my opinion, in all the fundamental and substantial things of life, faster than the Negro himself realizes and faster than his white neighbor realizes. I say this notwithstanding there are many existing weaknesses and much still to be accomplished. This progress which Virginia Negroes are now experiencing is owing to two causes.

First, they have been fortunate for a number of years in having governors with foresight, vision, liberality, and courage; and in having superintendents of education and other state officials who have considered the interests, prosperity, and progress of all the people, regardless of race or color. Though I have done so at a distance, I have watched with the greatest interest and satisfaction the interest which Governor Mann has shown in the education and uplift of all the people in this state. Governor Mann is in the highest degree a model executive. It is because of the leadership and guidance of such state officials that the Negro in Virginia has gone forward as fast as he has. I have always noticed that the character of the colored race in any community or state is patterned very largely after the character of the white people in that community or state.

The second reason why the Negroes of Virginia have made, and are making, such great strides, grows out of the fact that they are blessed with the leadership and guidance of such level-headed, conservative, safe, unselfish, and able colored men as Major R. R. Moton, the leader in the Negro Organization Society, and dozens of others I could mention.

The Negro Organization Society has for its object the unifying and focusing of all the organizations among our people in Virginia on certain fundamentals of life, such as education, health, and cleanliness. It is not the purpose of this Society to seek to interfere with the special work and purpose of any of the individual organizations represented, but to co-operate with them

* Address delivered before the Negro Organization Society, Richmond City Auditorium, November 7, 1913

so as to promote education in its broadest sense, without which there can be no permanent prosperity. The work which it is doing under the general direction of Major Moton, Prof. J. M. Gandy, of Petersburg, the Rev. A. A. Graham, of Phoebus, and others equally interested, is worthy of all praise and encouragement.

The work of this Society is fundamental. It touches the life and the interests of every white citizen in Virginia. I have watched its growth with a great deal of interest and I believe that it is one of the most potent factors for our uplift. Here is a great example of co-operation. It is sometimes said that black people cannot get together and work for the general improvement of a community, but we have here, in a great state, an example of Negro organizations, of every sort, with diverse interests, being able to get together and co-operate for better schools, better farms, better homes, better morals, and better health.

I find that for educational improvement in Virginia during the past year this Society assisted in raising money for the building of schools to the value of $10,000, that in one county it aided in raising $900 for school improvement and extension of school terms; also that a large number of schools were inspired to make adequate provision for ventilation, as well as to have individual drinking cups, sanitary outhouses, and improved surroundings.

I am especially interested in the efforts which are being made for better morals among our people. Special emphasis is being placed upon the idea that parents should devote more time and thought to the rearing of their children, and that they should inculcate in their offspring correct habits of morality.

One of the greatest things that the Negro Organization Society is doing is that of improving the health of the masses of the black people throughout Virginia. At the last meeting of the National Negro Business League, I was particularly interested in the report that Professor Gandy gave concerning the work of this Society. Among other things, he told about the "Clean-up Day" that the Negroes of Virginia had last April, when 100,000 Negroes were influenced to observe the day. I am especially pleased to know of the hearty response and sympathetic co-operation that were shown by the white people, and by the white papers in reporting this state-wide "Clean-up Day." I was particularly pleased to note the editorials in the *Times-Dispatch* and other leading white papers of the state, commending the effort and calling upon the white citizens to use their influence with the colored people in their employ to get them to observe the day. I was equally gratified to observe the great interest that the colored people themselves manifested and the large amount of work they did in cleaning up Virginia.

The Bible tells us that cleanliness is next to godliness. When the colored people in a great state like Virginia all get together and co-operate for a general housecleaning—whitewashing their houses, fences, and outbuildings, cleaning out their wells and springs, and seeing that their schoolhouses and homes are properly ventilated—this people is making progress, not only along health lines, but also along educational and religious lines. Through the Organization Society the Negroes of Virginia are contributing, not only towards their own improvement, but also towards the improvement of the state as a whole.

Virginia is setting a great example for the remainder of the South in the matter of showing how the white and colored people may co-operate for general improvement. I find that not only have the efforts of the Negro Organization Society received the hearty support of the white people of the state, but that other special lines of endeavor have likewise received their most cordial support. This is particularly true in the matter of education. Virginia was the first state to have a state supervisor of rural colored schools, and by so doing set an example for the remainder of the South. The work of Mr. Jackson Davis in improving the Negro schools of Virginia is an indication of how the best white people of the South are ready to give their time and talent for the betterment of conditions among Negroes.

It has been my pleasure, under the auspices of Hampton Institute, to make several trips recently, with Major Moton and others, through the tidewater counties of Virginia, and in each one of those counties I was most gratified at the evidences of progress on the part of our race in getting land, building better houses, establishing schools and churches, and in contributing their part toward law and order and a higher and better civilization. In Gloucester County, for example, we found that there was not a single individual of either race in the county jail. That is a record which can be mentioned by few counties, North or South, or indeed anywhere in the United States.

In Virginia there are about 675,000 black people, and I find that they are making considerable progress along religious lines. They are building up-to-date churches which cost from $10,000 to $40,000. In connection with the material progress of Negro churches, there is also improvement intellectually and morally. You have here some of the most capable and intellectual ministers among colored people. There are in Virginia about 2000 colored church organizations with a membership of over 300,000. Another evidence of the progress that is being made is the growth in Sunday-school work. There are in the state over 2000 Sunday schools with 13,000 teachers and officers and 115,000 pupils. The value of the church property owned by colored people in Virginia is over $4,000,000.

Perhaps in no other section of the country is there a body of Negroes who, on the whole, are more progressive than the Negroes of Virginia. Here the first Negro bank was established, and now there are more banks operated by Negroes in Virginia than in any other state. I understand that there are altogether twelve such banks. Richmond has the distinction of having the first Negro bank in the country that is run by a woman.

Along other lines of business Virginia Negroes have made great progress in the past few years. There are today more Negroes in the state than ever before who are operating grocery stores, undertaking establishments, real estate, and other business enterprises. In practically every city in Virginia where there is any large number of Negroes, there are business blocks owned by them.

The most notable progress of the race in Virginia has been along agricultural lines. Thirty-four per cent of all persons engaged in farming in the state are Negroes. Almost one-half of all the Negroes in the state are engaged in farming. There are 48,000 who are operating farms; and they are operating 26 per cent of all the farms in the state. Although Virginia gained only 10,000 in its Negro population, or a little more than one per cent from 1900 to 1910, in the same period the number of Negroes owning farms increased 20 per cent. Something like 2,250,000 acres of land are under the control of Negroes; that is, owned or rented by them. The Negro farmers in Virginia control over $55,000,000 worth of farm property. This is 123 per cent more than they controlled ten years ago.

These Negro farmers, along with Negro farmers in other parts of the South, are using more and more machinery in their farming operations. Ten years ago they owned $1,000,000 worth of farm machinery. Now they own $2,000,000 worth. There are 32,000 Negroes in Virginia who own land. No other state has so many. Mississippi is next with 25,000 farm owners among her Negro population. Virginia Negroes own over 1,600,000 acres of land, which is over 300,000 acres more than they owned ten years ago. The remarkable thing about these Negro farmers is that they own over half the land they cultivate. Except in Kentucky, this is true in no other Southern state. I find that, according to the census, in the ten years from 1900 to 1910, the value of land and buildings owned by the Negroes of Virginia increased from $10,000,000 to $28,000,000, or 180 per cent.

In the matter of education Virginia Negroes are making progress also, but, as in most of our Southern states, much remains to be accomplished. It is true that a large percentage of the colored population of Virginia cannot read or write. We must not, however, be deceived by the mere fact that a person can read or write. Unless he has received that broader training which enables him to know the object of education, the uses of education, unless he receives that broader training which will make him realize that book education is useless without character, without industry, without the saving habit, without the willingness to contribute his part toward law and order and the highest and best in the community, his mere book education will in many cases mean little or nothing. It is the object of the Negro Organization Society to help the colored people of Virginia to digest their education, to utilize it in the common, ordinary affairs of life for the benefit of white people and black people.

In the foregoing remarks I have merely hinted at some of the instances of progress in Virginia. I have done so to show what can be done, but one must not get the idea that all the work is done or that the Negro race is on its feet. In Virginia, as in other Southern states, we are just beginning to teach the Negro how to make progress and the two races how to co-operate with each other. Under the leadership of such men as Major Moton and such institutions as Hampton and others, we shall soon leave behind all doubt and uncertainty as to the future relations of the two races in the South.

THE question with the Negroes is not one of special proficiency, of success in one direction—the pursuit of knowledge—but of success all around. It is one of morals, industry, self-restraint; of power to organize society, to draw social lines between the decent and indecent, to form public sentiment that shall support pure morals, and to show common sense in the relations of life.

—*From " Education for Life "*

ARMSTRONG

BY EMMA L. DILLINGHAM

A royal heritage was thine,
  A soul imbued with love divine,
A heart that throbbed with sympathy,
A life for service through eternity.

A royal thought forever crowned
With words and deeds that knew no bound
Of pity, patience, tenderness,
And grace to uplift and to bless.

A royal courage, thine, to face
Dark problems, untried ways to trace
Through many a maze of prejudice,
That men their manhood should not miss.

A royal battle decades long
With poverty, mistrust, and wrong,
Till right and light dispelled the gloom
And for a ransomed race made room.

A royal rest for thee remains,
Where faithful service honor gains,
Where heart of man unfolds anew
In heart of God forever true.

From the "*Pacific Commercial Advertiser*"

THE WHITE MAN'S DEBT TO
THE NEGRO *

BY L. H. HAMMOND

WE hear the phrase with increasing frequency—"the white man's debt to the Negro," but there is no debt white people owe to the Negroes on the ground of race. As a descendant of slave-owners, a long-time friend of the Negro, and a lover of my own people, Southern problems are for me both an inheritance and an environment; and I believe both the North and the South have obscured and magnified the task of Negro uplift by continually talking and thinking about it in terms of race. If we would see life sanely, we must see it whole. No race can be understood when regarded as a detached, and consequently anomalous, fragment, cut off from its wide human relations. Races are human first and racial afterwards. Differences go deep, and abide; but likenesses go deeper yet; the most radical evolutionist and the most ultra-orthodox Christian must agree on that point.

There are just two things in the so-called Negro problem which are really questions of race. One of them is the desire of the better classes of both races to keep whites and blacks racially, and therefore socially, distinct. This is expensive, especially in the matter of separate public schools; but no wise man, in either race, objects to that. In such a case, however, both justice and statesmanship require that school provision be made, not according to a man's ability to support the schools, but according to the children's needs. This standard is far from being attained in the South, or in many other sections; yet our best men see its wisdom, and we do move toward it, though slowly and haltingly.

The other purely racial ingredient of the "Negro" problem is prejudice; and it is not confined to either race. Yet, after all, though racial and local in its manifestations, as race prejudice must always be, it is as wide as humanity and as old as time. It cannot be charged upon the South alone, nor are its manifestations in the South, in any respect, peculiar to Southern whites or Southern blacks; they are peculiar to that stage of intellectual and moral growth which those manifesting the prejudice have attained. And, knowing this, one may regard it, not without

* This article by Mrs. L. H. Hammond of Paine College, Augusta, is reprinted from the special number of *The Annals*, entitled "The Negro's Progress in Fifty Years."

sorrow, but without bitterness, and with hope.   It is a stage of
life, and it will pass.

With these two exceptions, all that we white Amercicans
North and South, have so long known as the Negro problem is
not Negro or racial, but human ; and the sooner we all recognize
this fact the sooner our racial and sectional prejudices and animos-
ities will give place to mutual sympathy and co-operation.   There
can be, in the nature of things, no successful sectional appeal
between North and South, nor successful racial appeal from black
to white, or *vice versa* ; a successful appeal must be made from a
common standing-ground, and that we find, not in our differences, but in our common humanity.

Our Negro problem is, with the exceptions noted, our fragment of the world-problem of the privileged and the unprivileged,
of the strong and the weak, dwelling side by side.   It is human
and economic.   We say, here in the South, that the mass of the
Negroes are shiftless and unreliable ; that their homes are a menace to the health of the community ; and that they largely furnish
our supply of criminals and paupers.   And most of us believe that
all this is the natural result, not of the Negro's economic status,
but of the Negro's being Negro.

There is truth in the indictment ; yet it is by no means so
largely true as many of us believe.   Take a single instance :   The
census of 1910 shows the value of Negro-owned farm lands in the
South to be $272,922,238, a gain of over 150 per cent for the
decade.   The same decade shows a decrease in Negro illiteracy
from 48.1 per cent in 1900 to 33.4 per cent in 1910.   These
figures prove that the race is advancing' rapidly, no matter how
much ignorance, incompetence, and criminality remain for future
elimination.   They also prove, lynching and other barbarities to
the contrary notwithstanding, that Southern whites, as a whole,
are not as bad neighbors for Southern blacks as some of our
Northern brethren fear.

A main reason for disregarding, in our estimates of Negro
life, the extraordinary progress of a large and growing section of
the race, and for our fixing our attention almost entirely upon its
less desirable members, is that the latter are the Negroes most
prominent in our own lives.   As the Negro gains in culture, in
efficiency, in his struggle for a competence, he withdraws into a
world of his own, a world which lies all about us white folk, yet
whose existence we rarely suspect.   The inefficients of the race,
the handicapped, the unambitious, the physically and morally degenerate—all these remain in that economic morass which we
regard as purely racial ; and from them we draw the bulk of our
supply of unskilled laborers and servants.   From this class, too,
we fill our jails ; and to many of us it is all the class there is.   As
fast as a man rises out of it he disappears from our field of vision.

I have been impressed increasingly by these facts since my husband and I have laid aside other things and come to live at a school for the higher education of Negroes. In our many previous years of effort to aid the race we had become aware of this withdrawn world, of course ; but it remained remote, intangible, save for brief, bewildering glimpses. It is not yet an open world ; but since we have taken this public and decisive stand of sympathy we pass the threshold, and come upon that deeper life which aspires in the breasts of those who carry in their own hearts the sorrows and burdens of a race. One must be struck with a sense of the sacrificial instinct of this class. It is with Negroes as with other races : under pressure of misfortune or of calamity a race or a nation, like an individual, sinks down to the sources of life, and rises to wider vision ; brotherhood becomes real to them. The Negro who has risen to higher intellectual and industrial levels and who does not realize his debt of service to the less fortunate of his race is rather the exception than the rule.

But the mass of the Negroes are still in the economic morass ; and we of the South do not yet realize that conditions such as it furnishes produce exactly the same results in men of all races the world around. In a population racially heterogeneous, like that of New York or Chicago, or in one racially homogeneous like that of London or Rome, or in a bi-racial population like our own, the people who live on the edge of want, or over it, furnish nearly the whole of the world's criminal supply. Insufficient food, housing conditions incompatible with health or decency, a childhood spent unprotected in the streets—these things produce, not in this race or that, but in humanity, certain definite results : ill-nourished bodies, vacant and vicious minds, a craving for stimulants, lack of energy, weak wills, unreliability in every relation of life. French slums breed French folks like that; Chinese slums breed such Chinamen; English slums, Englishmen of the same kind; and Negro slums, such Negroes.

When we see this, approaching our "Negro" problem by world-paths, grasping it in its world-relations, we will begin to do what the privileged classes are learning to do elsewhere—to widen the bounds of justice, to open the door of opportunity for all, to give our slum-dwellers a living, human chance.

It is not for a moment claimed that when they have a human chance slum dwellers of many races and of diverse inheritances will be all of one pattern. It is only in the depths of undevelopment that differences disappear. In the lowest forms of life even animal and vegetable seem one ; but as life develops it differentiates. Slum-dwellers, when the way of growth is opened for them, come true to type, and will render each his own racial service to the human brotherhood.

Here in the South, as elsewhere, the stability of civilization is to be measured by the condition of the masses of our working people. Men of all nations have been prone to think that enduring national strength can be built up on rottenness ; that national and industrial life can be broad-based and firm though it rests on injustice to the poor and the despised, on ignorance, immorality, inefficiency, disease ; that the great huddled mass of workers can be safely exploited and then ignored ; that a people may defy the fundamental law of human life and prosper. So, from the beginning, have nations fallen, until, at last, men began to learn. In the old world and in the new we are moving slowly, along much lauded paths of science, to that ignored simplicity of Jesus Christ, whose word of human brotherhood we have forgotten.

Here in the South we are moving too. Some of our best are turning to serve our neediest. In Louisville, Ky., is a man, the son of an Alabama banker, a man of substance and family, who is conducting settlement work for Negroes, serving them in the same ways that other college-bred men and women serve folk of other races in the same economic class elsewhere. One of the International Y. M. C. A. secretaries, a Southern man, has enrolled six thousand young men in our Southern colleges to study the white man's debt to the Negro ; and another Southern secretary is following up the work by organizing these young men for social service among Negroes. The Southern University Commission on the Negro, an outgrowth of the first Southern Sociological Congress, held a year ago, is composed of men both young and old from every Southern state university, who are agreed as to the duty of the favored race to secure justice and opportunity for the backward one. The Woman's Missionary Council of the Southern Methodist Church, an organization representing over two hundred thousand of our white women, recently adopted a plan for co-operation between their own local societies, some four thousand in number, and the better class of Negroes, for the uplift of the poorer classes, locally, throughout the South. Through their secretary for Negro work, efforts in this direction are already being made at several points. The Southern Baptists have still more recently decided to open a theological seminary for Negro preachers. It is to be in connection with their seminary for white preachers, and the same man, one of their most honored leaders, is to be the head of both institutions. The Southern Presbyterians have long had a theological seminary for Negroes, where Southern white college men have taught their darker brothers. In South Carolina white members of the Episcopal church, both men and women, are giving their personal service to the Negroes. The Southern Methodists have for thirty years maintained a school for the higher education of the race

where college-bred Southern white men and women have taught
from the beginning.   The work of a man like the Virginia state
superintendent of Negro rural schools is something for both races
to be thankful for.   Southern club women, too, in more than one
state, are showing both by word and deed a spirit of sympathy
with the Negro life in their midst.   Among the many encouraging and inspiring utterances by both whites and blacks at the
recent meeting of the Southern Sociological Congress in Atlanta
no single speech summed up the race situation as did that of a
young Negro on the closing night.

"I have always known," he said, "that the old Southern
white man understood and trusted the old Negro, and that the old
Negro understood and trusted the old Southern white man ; but
before this Congress I never dreamed that the young Southern
white man and the young Negro could ever understand or trust
one another ; and now I know they can, and that, shoulder to
shoulder, each in his own place, they can work out together
the good of their common country."   In all the Congress, no
speech won from the white people heartier applause than this.
But the white men who spoke—college professors, lawyers, business men, preachers—had their audience with them also, as they
called for justice and brotherhood and service in the spirit of
Christ.

The millennium is probably far to seek ; but vision is coming
to our leaders—a vision of human onenesss under all racial separ-
ateness, of human service fitted to human need.   And as the
leaders are, the people will be.   When even one man sees truth
its ultimate triumph is always assured.   Whatever may happen
in between, the final issue is inevitable.

The educational needs of the Negroes are great.   The mass of
them, like the mass of every race, must always work with their
hands, doing what we call the drudgery of life.   They need to
learn, as we all do, that drudgery is not in work, but in the worker's habit of mind.   We need, not merely in the South, but in
America, to approach the German standard in regard to industrial
training for the rich and the poor of all races.   As we grow more
rational ourselves the Negroes will catch the infection, as they
have caught from white folks, North and South, an irrational
scorn of "common" work.   Our public and private schools,
especially our normal schools, for both races, need large development in industrial training.   We are awakening to this fact, particularly in regard to our white schools ; and as they progress
along broader lines progress in schools for Negroes will be easier.

The only absolutely untouched need of the Negro, and it is a
need most fundamental, most disastrous in its long neglect, is.
the need for decent, healthful houses for the poorer classes.   We

are just developing a social consciousness in the South, and it is
naturally first aroused by the needs of the poor whites.   We know
little, as yet, of slum populations elsewhere, and we think of the
Negro slum-dweller as a separate fragment of life, unrelated, a
law unto himself, creating his slum as a spider spins his web,
from within.   We build him shacks and charge heavy rents, as
landlords of this economic class do the world around.   Cheap as
the shelter furnished is, it deteriorates so rapidly, through neglect and misuse, that the owners of such property, the world over,
declare that the high rentals are necessary to save them from
actual loss.

We need an experiment station in Negro housing in the South.
Fifty thousand dollars would buy a city block of six acres, and
put on four of the meighty well-lighted, three-roomed houses,
with water and a toilet in each, and with a tiny garden-spot.
Two acres would furnish a playground for the children, otherwise
doomed to ruin in the city streets; and there would be money
enough left to put up a settlement house providing for a kindergarten, free baths, boys' clubs, industrial classes, a place of recreation for young people whose only present refuge is a low dance
hall or a saloon.   At two dollars per room per month, the price
paid in my own town by people of this class for houses which are
a menace to the whole community, the income from such an
investment would pay the salary of a social worker who would
collect the rent on the Octavia Hill plan, and would yet yield 10
per cent gross on the investment, in dollars and cents.   In character-building, in the cutting off of our pauper and criminal supply, in convincing our white people that the slum breeds the
Negro we find in the slum, the return on the investment would
be incalculable.

An experiment like this, worked out to success and advertised
through the South, would awaken the interest and win the
approval of very many Southern business men who deplore the
Negro slum but see no hope of abolishing it.   Money would be
invested in decent homes for this class as soon as white men saw
it could be done without financial loss.   Such an experiment station would do more than any other one thing I know of to help
the Negroes who most need help; but the money for this initial
enterprise will have to come from beyond the South, where these
methods have already been successfully tried.   That it will come
I firmly believe.   When things ought to be done they get done,
somehow; and this fundamental need is to be met.

ROBERT C. OGDEN'S LABORS IN THE SOUTH *

BY SAMUEL CHILES MITCHELL

President of the Medical College of Virginia

THE projectile power of personality was happily set forth in the results of the labors for the South of Robert C. Ogden. It is instructive to study his plans for the improvement of public schools, for the betterment of farming, for the enrichment of rural life, for racial adjustment and social progress. It is pleasing to tabulate the statistics that show the increase in school revenues, in the attendance of children, in the efficiency of teaching, and in the moral support given to public education during the past decade in the South. But unless we regard all of these achievements as simply bodying forth the dynamic force of personality, we shall not interpret aright this educational renaissance, so far as our leader affected the results.

Mr. Ogden's personality was contagious. He became a center in organizing constructive friendships. When he began his labors in the South for universal education, there were isolated workers in the several states unacquainted with one another, without any large view of the general task, and without an interchange of common experience. His presence instantly caused all of these workers to leap together, just as atoms form a new combination in the laboratory induced by the presence of a single new element. He had a rare faculty for the discovery of men and of their aptitude for social leadership. Surpassing even his joy in the discovery of talent was his delight in opening up a career for a man of this sort to deploy his power. His eye seemed to rest upon every worker, and all of us shared in the inspiration and strength that his sympathetic interest daily imparted.

The great thing, however, about Mr. Ogden was not merely his sagacity as to the way in which to do the things that were really worth while in the national life, unerring as his sagacity was in the choice of men and measures. It was not even his passionate love for people, and especially people dis-

* An address at the Ogden Memorial Service in New York, October 26, 1913

advantaged and in need. But the great thing in him was his faith in the capacity of men to grow, his faith in the essential goodness of the human heart, his faith in the subtle potency of reason when trained and rightly directed—in a word, his faith in man under the influence of truth and love. It was this structural faith that sustained him in his great labors, that enabled him to overcome all barriers, and that swept him forward with a purpose that moved majestically, like a force in nature.

I can never forget the first time that I saw him, when he stood upon the platform at Hampton Institute giving a fatherly message to the graduating class of Indian and colored youth that stood before him. He seemed to breathe into the characters of those people his own large spirit of faith, encouragement, aspiration, and spirit of social service. My thought of divinity became clearer and more concrete as I listened to his words of wisdom and of love.

His philanthropy took naturally the form of a structural purpose; namely, to achieve for the South through the training of children and through the process of social growth, results which all other means, including war and politics, had been unable to produce. The chief evil of slavery was not economic nor political, but mental and moral. Slavery tended to gag the South. Its sole imperative was: Thou shalt not think. Hence this movement sought to revive discussion, to interpret in terms of education all the factors in the life of the South. "Democracy is government by discussion," says Woodrow Wilson, and the principle implied in this remark was invoked in the South. Future-heartedness marked the movement from the beginning. It was forward-looking. It cherished the past, to be sure, in order to draw thence strength for the tasks of today. The word education does not begin to cover the complex bundle of activities surging in this movement. It developed in the South a party of progress, a platform for frank discussion of present-day facts. It called forth a body of literature surcharged with social and moral energies of transforming power. These structural purposes bespeak the statesman rather than the schoolman. Mr. Ogden was a statesman, a state-builder after the order of Horace Mann, Cavour, and Gladstone, all of whom put their trust in truth and relied upon the subtle force of growth to achieve great national ends. They knew full well that "in the long run the forces go with the virtues." Mr. Ogden was the greatest benefactor that the South has known since Appomattox.

Sir Horace Plunkett, while sitting in the British Parliament for eight years, discerned that England, in applying for centuries political remedies to Ireland's economic wrongs, had failed.

It occurred to him one day that it might be well to apply economic remedies to Ireland's economic wrongs. He left his seat in Parliament, went to Ireland and began to improve the farms, to sweeten the homes, to establish co-operative dairies and to enrich the life of the people through efficient schools, libraries, and social gatherings. A humble program, to be sure, but it is remaking Ireland—something that eight centuries of "blood and iron" had been unable to do.

So in the South the strong wind, the earthquake, and the devastating fire swept by. God was in none of these, but in the still small voice that whispered an electric message to the heart of the child and strung his arm with energy for the achievement of great social and national ends. I believe that it was given to a business man to hit upon a sounder principle for economic progress, racial adjustment, and national integration than has been vouchsafed to any politician or general in the annals of America. The conquests of education alone are enduring. "One former is worth a dozen reformers." What a lurid glare is shed upon the follies and wastes of War and Reconstruction in view of the beneficent changes wrought by these silent forces of light and love. Never was more finely revealed the regenerative impulse in the heart of man than the signal results of. this educational movement through the power of public opinion. In the case of millions of children Mr. Ogden "thinks in their brain, throbs in their heart, speaks in their conscience, and makes their will leap like a resolute muscle to its task in fulfilling the will of God."

While Mr. Ogden was a statesman in his grasp of the complex situation in the South, he was also a teacher, but a teacher through inspiring companionships, after the order of Socrates and Jesus. He trained a group of social workers who even at this early time are displaying power in foreign embassies, in the Cabinet at Washington, in the Federal Bureau of Education, and in the international task of public health and sanitation. These men all account it among the highest privileges in their lives to have felt the throb of his loving heart.

He was by instinct a leader, a big brother of mankind, yet he delighted to follow. In many instances he took up other men's tasks and pushed them to a completion hardly dreamed of by the men who first conceived the enterprises. At Hampton he took up the task of Armstrong. In 1900 he took up the task of public education in the South begun by J. L. M. Curry and the elect band of men who had met three years before at Capon Springs to concert plans for bettering the common schools. Mr. Ogden was daring in conception, but he was no less great in his appropriating power. Like a master builder, he made a wise use of all materials at hand. He entered into the vision that had come to such men as George Foster Peabody, Edwin A. Alderman, Hollis B. Frissell, Wallace Buttrick, P. P. Claxton, Walter H. Page, Charles W. Dabney, and F. T. Gates. Mr. Ogden's sympathies grasped the situation in the South, emerging slowly from the waste of war and sorrow of defeat. He discerned at a glance what an aroused public opinion could do for progress through the common schools. His strategy consisted, not in money, not in the creation of new agencies, not in the attempt to impose ideas and institutions upon a people, but in his belief in the ability of the people of the South to do for themselves the things necessary for their own well-being. He coveted the privilege of sympathizing with the South in accomplishing these great social ends and in sharing and strengthening the impulses of the men who were bent on their accomplishment.

He had no ambition to be the founder of an institution. His name is identified with a movement, and not with an institution. He preferred to vitalize the nascent common school system. He integrated all his efforts with what the towns, counties, and states had already undertaken. The wisdom of this plan has been abundantly justified. He multiplied himself a million times by inciting the whole citizenship to get underneath the task and to energize the schools as a means of social progress. The principle upon which he thus acted is of wide and present application. Only the state, through the power of public taxation, is equal to the task of training all the children for the duties of citizenship in democracy. The main thing is to stimulate the people of a community to do well by their own schools. The principle of local taxation, the necessity of community control, and the power of public opinion were the three prime factors in his plan of educational campaign for the South. The fruitfulness of his labors sprang naturally out of the force inherent in these three principles. He built, therefore, not for a day, but for the ages. Instead of being able to point to a single school that bore his name, he could point to state systems of schools into which he had breathed the energy of his own great personality.

Once, as I sat in his office in New York City talking with him about educational plans for the South, I started to go, feeling that I had detained him far too long from his business. I can never forget the tone of his voice as he said, in a firm and manly way, beckoning me to remain seated, "*This* comes first." The impulse of civic duty then borne in upon me was worth more than all the formal lessons that any college can give. He put life above livelihood. He revealed in his own career a fresh discovery of the divine order, "Seek ye first the kingdom of heaven and all these things shall be added unto you." So unstintedly did he give himself in service to humanity that it seems irrelevant to dwell upon the fact that he was generous in giving of his own substance to the various causes that found a home in his great heart. Money, even his own money, means so little in all this as compared with the consecration of his life and personality to the good of others. He was a wise worker, but all of his plans displayed the dynamics of love, the motive force of faith.

The progress of the South in education during the past decade is unprecedented. The figures are like a fairy tale. And yet the fine enthusiasm of the people surpasses by far the import of any numerical statement. Take, for instance, Georgia. In 1902 the state was spending upon its public schools $1,125,000. Last year it spent about $5,125,000. In 1902 the value of school property was $4,000,000 and within the decade it climbed to more than $11,000,000, an actual increase of about $7,000,000. Within the same period the number of school days rose from 113 to 140. During the same decade the increase in enrollment was 115,000 children. The actual increase in the per capita expenditure according to enrollment was $6.18. Illiteracy among the whites was reduced from 12 to 7 per cent and among the Negroes from 52 to 36 per cent. This bare recital of the advance of schools in the single state of Georgia is an index of the beneficent changes wrought throughout the entire South by the co-operation of all the agencies at work for social betterment. About $20,000,000 was added annually to the revenues of public schools within a period of ten years. Since 1906 about 1000 high schools have been established and developed. The significance of these figures is beyond the power of words to express.

In 1779 Thomas Jefferson drew out a liberal scheme for public education in the South, beginning with elementary schools for all the people and rising through the high school to the state university. In accordance with the social structure of the South at that day, the only part of his scheme which was carried out was the apex ; namely, the University of Virginia. It fell to a later day to build beneath that apex the solid body of the pyramid, consisting of the common schools as the base and the high schools resting upon them, all capped by the state university. This solid structure of public education is now rising in every Southern state.

Aiming in the beginning at the betterment of the common schools through an awakened public sentiment, Mr. Ogden's purposes gradually widened until they embraced all the activities

makjng for progress in the South.   He became in turn connected
with the country life movement, with vast plans in the interest
of public health and endowment of colleges; with the effort to
make the state university the moral fortress of a democratic
commonwealth; with the causes of social unrest throughout the
nation; with the housing problem and the diverse evils growing
out of industrial conditions in this country. The sweep of his
activity in all these fields of human need is suggested by his
membership in the General Education Board, the Russell Sage
Foundation, the Southern Education Board, the Jeanes Board,
and other agencies dedicated to the common good.

When George Adams Smith was asked how he accounted
for the marvelous intellectual output of Scotland during recent
decades, he said that he attributed it in no small degree to the
fact that in the seventies Mr. Moody put every man and woman
in Scotland to reading the Bible with fresh interest. The intellectual energies thus aroused had taken, to be sure, a direction
in literature, science, and religion undreamed of by Mr. Moody,
who in this way imparted the initial impulse to the Scottish
mind.

We have been witnessing in recent months a similar renaissance in the South's constructive energies in the realm of statesmanship that is intoning a new day in the national life—a passion
for fair play in politics, a searchlight of publicity thrown upon all
stages of legislation, a conviction that the whole is greater than
the parts, as shown by an embargo on all forms of class rule, the
public conscience quickened to the point where it is sensitive
to the appeals of right and responsive to the demands of progress, a desire to set our own house in order because of a clearer
vision of the moral mission of America in bringing in an era of
good will among mankind.

I am inclined to think that many of these fine results
are due to the stirring of the mind of the South during the
last decade to serious thought and high endeavor as regards
the rights of childhood, racial adjustment, social service, and
the spirit of nationality. The South during this time has passed
through an educative process of rare power. It has taken stock
of untoward factors in its life, such as ignorance, poverty,
inefficiency, sanitation, public health, and the twin forces of
sectionalism and sectarianism. It has reviewed the past in con-
templative mood. It has revived the memories of the constructive part that Southern men took in the formative period
of the republic as well as recounted the facts in the later period
of slavery, war, and reconstruction. It has studied the State's
duty to educate the children for citizenship, to insure social order,
and to safeguard public health. These vital matters have been

discussed frankly, not only in the great Conferences for Education in the South, but likewise in rural communities throughout the entire region. The discussion has divided families, furnished new views to editors, and has proved the pivot upon which many a political campaign has turned.

It was impossible for the minds of millions of people to be thus stirred to the depths by elemental forces without the generation of large civic impulses and new ideals. This educational movement modernized the Southern mind, related it anew to the larger facts in the world today, and gave the people of the South a new sense of their latent power and the possibilities of co-operation for nobler ends. The decade marked a return to fundamentals, such as the fertility of the soil, upon which the home, school, and church depend; such as the duty of the State to the child in a democracy like ours; such as the relation of health to social progress and intellectual power; such as the necessity of co-operation for the growth of community life; such as the benefits to be derived from international experience in working out local problems touching the farm, school, sanitation, and racial adjustment.

Mr. Ogden's career was as a golden clasp binding together the North and South in sympathy and co-operation for the integrity of national life. He enlisted throughout the North men and women of initiative as co-workers in the tasks of the South. With him this noble band of friends would make an annual pilgrimage to the Conference for Education, study the facts in the Southern situation for themselves, and strike friendships there of enduring and fruitful character. It is not too much to say that Mr. Ogden in this way changed radically the viewpoint of the North with reference to the South, rendering editors, publicists, and educators in the North sympathetic with the struggle of the South and eager to aid on all occasions the forces there making for practical righteousness. These kindly, interlacing influences of the North and South have perhaps done more toward reuniting the sections in a common purpose and like-mindedness than any other single agency in the history of our country since the Civil War.

Thus in these two ways Mr. Ogden's efforts in behalf of public education have had a distinctly national bearing: First, by stirring to the very depths the mind of the South through the discussion of the vital facts involved in democratic education ; and, secondly, by knitting the sympathies of the leaders in the North and in the South, revealing their oneness in the fellowship of social service and in a common purpose embracing the good of the whole country. Never more happily was illustrated the meaning of that Scripture : ''A little child shall lead them,'' for it was the efforts to open for the child the door to a larger life that brought about these signal results in social progress and national unification.

Mr. Ogden gave a new interpretation to the meaning of American citizenship. He had a scent for human need. He socialized his life and energies. Friendship was the essence of his working program. His hospitality was kingly and the list of his friends would make up the honor roll of America. There can be no pessimism in the presence of such an example. All problems dissolve as retreating clouds before the outreach of such a personality. So long as exalted citizenship in the private walks of life reveals the sanity and sacrifice that characterized Robert C. Ogden, there can be no doubt as to America's fulfilling the moral expectancy of mankind. "The character of the citizen is the strength of the State."

Book Reviews

The Vanishing Race: a record in picture and story of the last great Indian Council * * * and the Indians' story of the Custer fight, written · and illustrated by Dr. Joseph K. Dixon --the concept of Rodman Wanamaker. Doubleday, Page & Co., New York. Price, $3.50.

THE attention which is now given to the "vanishing race" in books and pictures reminds one of the familiar saying that "blessings brighten as they take their flight." The Indian has for many years been seriously studied from all points of view, and both the scientific and the popular interest in him appear to be steadily increasing. His sociological and industrial status, his political significance, his native art, his inherited religion, his racial characteristics, and his past life—all are the objects of careful study. The result is a considerable accumulation of valuable material which will some day, perhaps, form the basis of a great epic of the Indian.

Dr. Dixon's book is a valuable addition to the accumulation because it contains some narrations by the Indians not hitherto published. For example, there is the story of the Custer fight on the Little Big Horn in June 1876, about which the voice of the Indian has hitherto been largely silent, so far as publication is concerned, and which is now claimed to be told for the first time by Custer's four Indian scouts and by leaders of the Sioux and Cheyenne tribes. The story of these surviving scouts shows how much the services of Indian scouts contributed to the success of the United States troops in their warfare on the Western frontier, and reminds us how much the bravery, sagacity, and endurance of these loyal allies call for our patriotic gratitude.

There is valuable biography, too, in the life stories of the chiefs who attended the last great Council, and the full-page portraits of these chiefs, each in costume and war bonnet, make a striking series of character studies.

The last great Council referred to was held in the valley of the Little Big Horn River, in Montana, in September 1909, and was attended by chiefs from most of the great tribes. When all had assembled, Plenty Coups rose and made a speech of welcome in the sign language which is reported in the book. The others all responded and then these chiefs, all of them warriors and former enemies one of another, smoked the peace-pipe together and departed. "To realize," as the author says, "that, as their footfalls leave this council lodge, they have turned their backs upon each other forever, and that, as they mount their horses and ride away to their distant lodges, they are riding into the sunset to be finally lost in the purple mists of evening, is to make the coldest page of history burn with an altar fire that shall never go out."

As its full title suggests, the book is not a consecutive narrative but a collection of more or less unrelated chapters. Its special value, therefore, is as a book of reference. The illustrations are unusually fine and of rare artistic merit. The human interest, however, is particularly intense in the final chapter, for in this account of the last great Council, recent though it was, we have vividly presented to us for one brief moment the real Indian of the past, the vanishing element of the race.

W. L. B.

Hazel: By Mary White Ovington. Published by the Crisis Publishing Company, New York. Price, $1.00 *net*.

"HAZEL" is a well-educated, attractive little colored girl who leaves her home in Boston to spend the winter with her father's mother in Alabama. Miss Ovington, who is on the *Crisis* staff, says in her preface: "I have thought for some time that the colored children of the United States might also like to have their intimate books telling of happenings that were like their own." The book resembles the best stories for white children in its unpretentious, wholesome plot and simple language. The "color prejudices," as the little girl meets them, are neither exaggerated nor ignored, but wisely and sanely treated. Some of the illustrations by Harry Roseland are very characteristic, but unfortunately the frontispiece drawing of Hazel does not portray a typical Negro child. The chief importance of the book lies in the fact that it is a literary pioneer.

M. I. H.

At Home and Afield

HAMPTON INCIDENTS

THE CHRISTMAS HOLIDAYS

THE first real event of the Christmas Holidays, the Christmas concert, occurred on the evening of December 18, the day before the vacation began, so that all the students might, as usual, hear and take part in one of the most enjoyable entertainments of the year. The numbers on the program were fairly difficult for student performers, but every number was strongly and surely sung with true harmony of the parts. Two choruses which the audience received with special enthusiasm were Gounod's "Nazareth," sung by the Night School boys, and Adams's "Child divine," sung by the Junior Day School girls. "My heart at thy dear voice," from "Samson and Delilah," the solo part of which was sung by Carolyn Murie, an Indian girl, to a very difficult accompaniment, received much applause. The most interesting item on the program was an original composition for a barytone horn, composed without assistance, by J. A. Watkins, a Negro student, and beautifully played by him to a piano accompaniment written and played by Mr. R. N. Dett, director of music. This composition, as Mr. Dett explained, was unconsciously based on the Negro scale, which characteristically omits the tones fa and ti and ends with the tones $la, do.$ "Go tell it on the mountain," which embodies, for Hampton audiences at least, all

the romance of Christmas, was beautifully sung by the four quartets that are soon to go North for the winter campaign. The concert closed with the new Hampton song, "Hampton, my home by the sea," composed by Mr. Dett and enthusiastically sung by the entire student body. The program was not intended so much as a Christmas celebration as a demonstration of the music work of the term in the various classrooms.

TWO evenings of Christmas week, Monday and Friday, were devoted to "movies," quaint pictures presenting the story of David Copperfield being shown on the first occasion. Two student socials were held on Saturday evening, December 20, and on Christmas evening. On Monday, December 29, Coleridge-Taylor's cantata, "Hiawatha," was given in Cleveland Hall chapel by the Norfolk and Portsmouth Choral Society.

ENTERTAINMENTS

THANKS to the intervention of American friends, "The Revenge of Shari-hot-su" was not so horrible as two shy Japanese lovers feared, and the audience at Huntington Hall auditorium on Saturday evening, November 29, witnessed a "happy ending," with two engagements. The play was given for the benefit of the Armstrong League, and the actors were Hampton workers who played their parts with spirit and dramatic effect. The Japanese costumes and make-ups were most successful and the beauty of the setting in the second scene, a Japanese garden, elicited whispers of admiration from the interested audience of Hampton teacher and workers.

THE dramatic ability of the students finds occasional expression both in classic drama and in more modern plays. Two of the latter were presented by the Shakespeare Literary Society in Huntington Hall on the evening of December 14 to a "capacity house " of students and teachers. The first play, "Fooling Father," with only three characters, was exceptionally well acted, and the cool shrewdness of Father, who successfully turned the tables on a mischievous son and an ardent suitor for his daughter's hand, was very enjoyable. The second farce, "The Bachelor's Club Baby," with little William Miller in the title role, was a much shorter and less ambitious production. The impudent bellboy and the good-natured butler who ministered to the needs of club members furnished considerable merriment, and the smiling baby did not need any "lines " to arouse the interest and sympathy which always greet children on any stage.

THREE ILLUSTRATED LECTURES

ON the evening of November 18, Mr. Charles K. Graham, director of Hampton's Agricultural Department, gave an informal illustrated talk on rural Ireland to Farmers' Conference guests in Clarke Hall, showing excellent pictures of beautiful Irish country and describing conditions and life among the Irish peasants as he observed them last summer. The pictures showed the methods of farming, the quality of land and of crops, the rough character of the carts, the straw-thatched, one-story, stone houses, the fairs or market days in small town squares, the cattle and hogs, and the wonderful mountains and lakes which beautify Ireland. Mr. Graham answered many questions about agricultural methods asked by the Negro farmers in the audience.

At a special teachers' meeting on December 10, Dr. Alexander Johnson, an extension lecturer of the Training School for the Feeble-Minded in Vineland, New Jersey, gave an interesting stereopticon lecture on the different types of feeble-mindedness, emphasizing the part which heredity plays in the disease, and the need of institutions which shall segregate irresponsible members of society in all states. He showed pictures of children in the Vineland school at work and at play and told of the ways in which nearly every child manages to be happy and useful.

Pictures of the wonderful monuments of the ancient cliff dwellers and Pueblos in the southwestern states, Mexico, and Central America, were shown and described most interestingly by Dr. Edgar L. Hewett, Director of the American School of Archæology at Santa Fé, New Mexico, in Cleveland Hall Chapel on Monday evening, December 15. Dr. Hewett is a world authority on the cliff dwellers. He has had charge of the excavations in the Mesa Verde Park, which has been reserved by the Government that the American people may see the ruins of a remarkable civilization which precedes their own in this country. The ruins are strangely like those in Egypt.

RELIGIOUS WORK

DURING the second week in December Dr. Frank K. Sanders, President of Washburn College, Topeka, Kansas, delivered before the entire school six helpful lectures on the four gospels interpreted as literature and history. On Sunday morning, December 14, he preached in Memorial Church on "reasonable religion."

THE first *Y. M. C. A. Triangle*, "a circular to be issued from time to time during the year" appeared the last of November. It contained news of the work of committees, notices of special programs, plans for the future, and other items of interest. Its object is to acquaint the students, graduates, teachers, and honorary members with the work of the Association and thus arouse their interest.

An illustrated lecture on the Passion Play was given by Miss Alta Reed before the Y. M. C. A. on November 30. The pictures, interesting in themselves, were accompanied by a description of the location and scenes of the play, which seemed to carry the listeners right to the spot. Miss Reed went back of the scenes, moreover, and showed how the characters of the men who took the various parts fitted them for what was required.

On December 14, Mr. W A. Hunton, International Y. M. C. A. Secretary for the Colored Men's Department, gave an inspiring summary of the achievements of the Y. M. C. A. among colored men in schools and cities of the South. The same evening Mr. Hunton spoke to the Shellbanks branch of the Y. M. C. A. on "Stickability."

THE first meeting of the boys' club at the Whittier School was held on Monday, December 8. About twenty-five boys gathered for a jolly evening of entertainment. A few games were played, and a few slides were shown in the stereopticon, accompanied by humorous recitatioñs by S. D. Spady. Mr. J. E. Scott and Mr. McGill, who are to have the work of this club in hand, gave a summary of the plans of the organization. The organization has been tentatively named "The Armstrong Guards," and the plans of organization are similar to those of the Boy Scouts, many of the principles and ideals being incorporated. Mr. Jinks is having the pupils in his manual training classes make some games which can be played by the boys, and Mr. McGill is also planning to instruct the boys in the making of game tables similar to those in use in Clarke Hall. Permission has been obtained to use the main room of the Whittier two nights a week. Several Hampton men are also working with the boys in the afternoons after school, coaching them in outdoor sports. Both Mr. McGill and Mr. Scott are well qualified for the work, Mr. McGill from his experience in dealing with the young boys of his own town, and Mr. Scott from his experience with the boys of Mrs. Barrett's night school.

THE KING'S DAUGHTERS FAIR

BY five o'clock on December 1, when the teachers were admitted to the King's Daughters rooms with the privilege of purchasing, most of the pretty gifts which they had been invited to inspect only at one o'clock had been bought by the girls. The articles for sale, all of which were contributed by students and teachers, were classified according to price, an arrangement which was an excellent advertising scheme and at the same time avoided confusion and loss of time. Prices ranged from five cents to fifty cents; more elaborate fancy work and embroidery lent by the teachers and girls was also on exhibit, but not for sale. The Indian girls had charge of a very popular candy table. Victrola music added to the festivity. The proceeds of the fair will be used for a rug for the King's Daughters parlor. The Society, having fallen heir to a home, is anxious to furnish it comfortably and attractively.

ATHLETICS

THE Union University team, playing its bravest at Richmond on November 22, succeeded in preventing Hampton from scoring more than 30 points. Shaw at Hampton on Thanksgiving Day in the last game of the season was defeated by a score of 70-0. The championship of the Colored Interscholastic Athletic Association (with a membership of five institutions—Hampton, Howard, Lincoln, Shaw, and Virginia Union) therefore goes to Hampton. Six of the All-Star Colored Eleven, picked by Edwin B. Henderson of Washington, are Hampton men—Gayle, Stoney, Aiken, Wildy, Jamison, and Oliver.

The first basket-ball game of the season, played in the school gymnasium with a fast, light-weight team from Armstrong Manual Training School of Washington, D. C., resulted in a score of 28-16, Hampton's victory. The Armstrong School team has held the championship of the Interscholastic Athletic Association for several seasons. Hampton's schedule includes games with the Hiawatha Club of Washington, Howard University, and Lincoln University.

HAMPTON WORKERS

A memorial meeting for Dr. John R. Francis, a colored physician whose loss is keenly felt by members of his race and also by many white people in the District of Columbia, was held in Washington at the Metropolitan A. M. E. Church on November 25. The leading speakers were Secretary Bryan, Dr. William M. Davidson, Superintendent of Schools in Washington, and Major R. R. Moton, Commandant of Hampton Institute.

Three of a series of patrons' meetings in the eight colored schools of Elizabeth City County have recently been held in the vicinity under the supervision of Mrs. John H. Evans, the industrial supervising teacher. At the Salter's Creek school on November 24, after a fine entertainment by the children, Miss Sarah Walter and Mr. W. A. Aery spoke to the assembled crowd of patrons on the subject of co-operation between parents and teachers.

"Do You Like To Be Poor?" was the first line of a poster which brought a large audience of the colored people of Bates District to the schoolhouse on December 4 to hear Mr. William S. Dodd and Major R. R. Moton tell why the colored man should own property. Miss Anne Scoville, Miss Henrietta Graves, Miss Marie Fuller, and Mrs. Evans were among the other speakers. Music was furnished by a quartet of Hampton students.

At the afternoon tea and patrons' league meeting at the Union Street school on December 15 Miss Sarah Walter spoke again on the co-operation of parent and teacher. Miss Caroline Pratt talked to the girls about tasteful, economical, neat dress. Miss Elizabeth Hyde discussed the question of safeguarding girls, and Dr. George P. Phenix congratulated the patrons on the success of the meeting. Refreshments were prepared and served by girls wearing caps and aprons which they had themselves made in sewing classes.

A new academic teacher, Miss Hattie M. Lombard, who is a graduate of the Farmington Normal School, Farmington, Maine, was engaged the last of November to fill a vacancy.

THE MERCHANTS' ASSOCIATION

ON December 3, Hampton Institute had the honor of entertaining forty-six of the fifty-three members of the Hampton-Phoebus Retail Merchants' Association, together with the white clergymen of the town and various town and county officials.

The guests arrived on the school grounds about ten o'clock; they were met by the Faculty and conducted to the Mansion House where they were received by Dr. and Mrs. Frissell. They were then taken to inspect the laundry, the trade school, the domestic science department and other parts of the school's work. At noon the visitors watched the battalion drill and march to dinner and at one o'clock the student body met in Cleveland Hall Chapel to sing plantation songs to the guests and to hear brief, interesting speeches from President Hunter R. Booker, Honorable Harry R. Houston, and Rev. Charles Friend. After lunching at the Mansion House, the company met for a short conference in the Museum, and later visited the barn and learned something of the agricultural course at Hampton.

The school is pleased to have the best people in the community inspect the work it is doing and especially pleased to hear such visitors express their approval of this work, as the merchants did in their speeches in Cleveland Hall Chapel.

WHITTIER SCHOOL

NOT the least of the numerous fairs and sales held on the school grounds during December was that given by the Whittier children, which included a supper and a sale of candy, cakes, doughnuts, and fancy work. All of the food and materials for food were contributed by the children and their parents and friends, and practically everything eatable that was sold was prepared by the Whittier girls in their cooking classes. There was no child in the school who did not bring something for the fair, even if it were only an egg, which is not so small a contribution in these days. Many proud fathers and mothers came in to enjoy the supper of chicken salad, fried oysters, potato salad, baked beans, and other good things cooked and daintily served by their daughters. From the fair the children cleared thirty-five dollars to add to the piano fund and could probably have sold as much again if they had had more contributions of food materials.

On the last day of school before Thanksgiving vacation the Whittier pupils made their usual visits to the Weaver Orphans' Home and to the aged poor in Phoebus, carrying vegetables, preserves, and provisions. The chariot took as many children as could be accommodated and some of the new teachers to the Weaver Home, where the little orphans welcomed them with delight and gave them a charming entertainment.

In spite of the fact that November 21 was a Farmers' Conference day, there were forty present at the meeting of the Parents' Association to discuss "The outside life of the child." Among the speakers was the president of a Parents' Association in Baltimore who told something of her work.

The Whittier School closed for the Holidays on December 19, with the usual Christmas exercises and tree.

HAMPTON VISITORS

THE success of the Farmers' Conference was greatly increased by the presence of Governor William Hodges Mann, who addressed the farmers on Wednesday afternoon, November 19, expressing his good will to ward the Negro farmers of Virginia. A number of other distinguished guests were present.

Mr. P. S. Khankhoje, a native of India, who hopes to establish industrial schools in his country and has been studying trades and agriculture in the United States with that object in view, was at Hampton for two days recently, studying the school's methods of instruction. He spoke to the students at evening chapel, telling something of the work he hopes to do. He has lately been traveling through this country lecturing on India, conditions there, and manners and customs, hoping to arouse interest in the needs of his native land.

Miss Alice P. Tapley, treasurer of the Boston Hampton Committee, and her friend, Miss Elizabeth Thornell, of Princeton, N. J., spent some time at Hampton in December. Miss Anne Beecher Scoville, who is arranging for an educational campaign trip for Hampton among girls' schools in the North, has been at Hampton for the past month. Mrs. S. C. Armstrong was a welcome visitor at the school Thanksgiving week. The Misses Richards, who have for many years been interested in Hampton's Indian work, have arrived at Holly Tree Inn for their usual winter visit. Mr. Elbridge Adams, chairman of the executive committee of the New York Armstrong Association, with friends, Mr. and Mrs. William Curtis Demarest, spent several days at the school in December. Mrs. Alexander Purves, Miss Ruth Purves, and Mr. Ogden Purves, with several guests, spent Christmas Holidays at "The Moorings." A number of the young people who are away during the year at school or at work, spent Christmas week at their homes on the school grounds.

FEBRUARY 1914

THE SOUTHERN WORKMAN

Press of
The Hampton Normal and Agricultural Institute
Hampton, Virginia

e Hampton Normal and Agricultural Institute

HAMPTON VIRGINIA

H. B. FRISSELL, Principal   P. K. ROGERS, Treasurer
G. P. PHENIX, Vice Principal   W. H. SCOVILLE, Secretary
H. B. TURNER, Chaplain

t it is   An undenominational industrial school founded in 1868 by Samuel Chapman Armstrong for Negro youth. Indians admitted in 1878.

To train teachers and industrial leaders

Land, 1060 acres; buildings, 140

Academic, trade, agriculture, business, home economics

Negroes, 1215; Indians, 37; total, 1252

Graduates, 1709; ex-students, over 6000
Outgrowths: Tuskegee, Calhoun, Mt. Meigs, and many smaller schools for Negroes

$125,000 annually above regular income
$4,000,000 Endowment Fund
Scholarships

A full scholarship for both academic and industrial instruction - - -	$ 100
Academic scholarship - - -	70
Industrial scholarship - - -	30
Endowed full scholarship - - -	2500

Any contribution, however small, will be gratefully received and may be sent to H. B. FRISSELL, Principal, or to F. K. ROGERS, Treasurer, Hampton, Virginia.

FORM OF BEQUEST

I give and devise to the trustees of The Hampton Normal and Agri-Institute, Hampton, Virginia, the sum of   *dollars,*

le

The Southern Workman

Published monthly by

The Hampton Normal and Agricultural Institute

Contents for February 1914

THE SOUTHERN WORKMAN was founded by Samuel Chapman Armstrong in 1872, and is a monthly magazine devoted to the interests of undeveloped races.

It contains reports from Negro and Indian populations, with pictures of reservation and plantation life, as well as information concerning Hampton graduates and ex-students who since 1868 have taught more than 250,000 children in the South and West. It also provides a forum for the discussion of ethnological, sociological, and educational problems in all parts of the world.

CONTRIBUTIONS: The editors do not hold themselves responsible for the opinions expressed in contributed articles. Their aim is simply to place before their readers articles by men and women of ability without regard to the opinions held.

EDITORIAL STAFF

H. B. FRISSELL   W. L. BROWN
HELEN W. LUDLOW   W. A. AERY, Business Manager
J. E. DAVIS   W. T. B. WILLIAMS

TERMS: One dollar a year in advance; ten cents a copy
CHANGE OF ADDRESS: Persons making a change of address should send the *old* as well as the *new* address to

THE SOUTHERN WORKMAN, Hampton, Virginia

Entered as second-class matter August 13, 1908, in the Post Office at Hampton, Virginia, under the Act of July 16, 1894

THE HAMPTON LEAFLETS

Any twelve of the following numbers of the "The Hampton Leaflets"
obtained free of charge by any Southern teacher or superintendent. *A charge
cents per dozen is made to other applicants.* Cloth-bound volumes for 1905, '
and '08 will be furnished at seventy-five cents each, postpaid.

VOL. I

1　Experiments in Physics (Heat)
2　Sheep : Breeds, Care, Management
3　Transplanting
4　Birds Useful to Southern Farmers
5　Selection and Care of Dairy Cattle
6　Care and Management of Horses
7　How to Know the Trees by Their Bark
8　Milk and Butter
9　Commercial Fertilizers
10　Swine: Breeds, Care, Management
11　Fruits of Trees
12　December Suggestions

VOL. II

1　Suggestions to Teachers Preparing Students for Hampton Institute
2　Experiments in Physics (Water)
3　Spring Blossoms : Shrubs and Trees
4　School Gardening
5　Drainage
6　Mosquitoes
7　Roots
8　Seed Planting
9　Housekeeping Rules
10　Prevention of Tuberculosis
11　Thanksgiving Suggestions
12　Some Injurious Insects

VOL. III

1　Proper Use of Certain Words
2　Winter Buds
3　Domestic Arts at Hampton Institute
4　Beautifying Schoolhouses and Yards
5　Responsibility of Teachers for the Health of Their Children
6　Manual Training in Rural Schools
7　Rotation of Crops
8　Life History of a Butterfly
9　How Seeds Travel
10　Nature Study for Primary Grades
11　Arbor Day
12　Evergreen Trees

VOL. IV

1　Plants
2　How to Attract the Birds
3　The Story of Corn
4　The Story of Cotton
5　The Meaning of the Flower
6　A Child's Garden
7　The Winged Pollen-Carriers
8　Soils
9　Care of Poultry
10　Plowing and Harrowing
11　Transplanting of Shrubs and Vin
12　Transplanting and Pruning of T

VOL. V

1　Teaching Reading to Children
2　Culture and Marketing of Peanu
3　The House Fly a Carrier of Di
4　Culture and Marketing of Tobac
5　Virginia's Fishing Industry
6　Farm Manures
7　Soil Moisture and After-cultivati
8　Patent Medicines
9　Hookworm Disease
10　Reading in the Grammar School
11　Oystering in Hampton Roads
12　Common Sense in Negro Public

VOL. VI

1　Sewing Lessons for Rural Schoo
2　Housekeeping and Sanitation in Rural Schools
3　Canning Fruits and Vegetables
4　Manual Training, Part II
5　Patrons' Meetings
6　Correlation of Industrial and Ac Subjects in Rural Schools
7　Southern Workman Special Inde
8　Community Clubs for Women an
9　Housekeeping and Cooking Less, Rural Communities
10　Fifty Years of Negro Progress
11　Approved Methods for Home La
12　Number Steps for Beginners

Address: Publication Office, The Hampton Normal and Agric
Institute, Hampton, Virginia

The

Southern Workman

VOL. XLIII   FEBRUARY 1914   NO. 2

Editorials

The Tuskegee Conference and Negro Farming
For the twenty-third time the Tuskegee Negro Conference says to the Negroes of the South: "Stay on the soil, buy land, improve your farms, have more gardens, raise your foodstuffs, build better churches and schoolhouses, lengthen your school terms, and have better equipped preachers and teachers. The report made that 225,000 Negro farm owners have acquired 20,000,000 acres of land, an area greater than the State of South Carolina, and the many instances of improvement in methods of farming, in building better farm homes, and in improving rural churches and schools, indicate that the advice of the Conference is being heeded.

"There is, however, much room for improvement along all lines. Almost 80 per cent of the Negro farmers in the South still rent the soil that they till. A large majority of the farm homes are yet without gardens. Too many colored people are still living out of the stores. Too often there is the tendency for a farmer to buy too much land. The Conference strongly advises the people when buying land not to buy more than they can profitably farm and successfully pay for. The Conference further advises that more attention be given to the business side of farming and that careful accounts be kept of all receipts and expenditures so that each farmer may know whether he is making or losing money.

"The boll weevil is here. In order to meet its ravages the Conference says to the Negro farmers of Alabama and other states : "Follow the directions of the agricultural experts ; diversify your crops ; grow more oats, corn, and sweet potatoes ; raise more live stock ; do not depend entirely on cotton.

"Every intelligent Negro farmer helps to advance the farming progress of the South ; every ignorant Negro farmer retards this progress. The Conference requests that through individual planters, state aid, and otherwise, more be done to improve Negro rural schools, provide more prizes for Negro farmers, and furnish more agricultural demonstration agents to teach the farmers on the soil. All of these things will help to increase the efficiency of the Negro farmer.

"Appreciation is expressed for what has already been done; for the growing spirit of helpfulness and co-operation that is manifested by the white people of the South ; and for the increasing number of planters who are taking a deeper interest in their tenants, providing for them better school facilities, better homes, and in every way encouraging them to improve and help keep up the property on which they live. Attention is called to the pitiable condition of a majority of Negro rural schools, too many of which are still unprovided with school buildings, have teachers receiving from $15 to $18 per month, and have terms that are only two or three months in length. To help teach the one million Negro farmers better methods of farming, and thus make them more efficient, there are throughout the South less than fifty Negro agricultural demonstration agents."

A report of this Conference may be expected in the next issue of the SOUTHERN WORKMAN.

Report of the Board of Indian Commissioners

The increased activity and possibility for usefulness of the Board of Indian Commissioners is evidenced in its forty-fourth annual report recently made public. The most important fact in connection with the work of this Board during the past year, the report states, was the recognition, by the Secretary of the Interior, of the growing importance of the Board's co-operation in the administration of Indian affairs, as indicated in his recommendation to Congress of an increase of from $4,000 to $10,000 in the appropriation for the expenses of the Board for the fiscal year 1914. To the lay mind there seems no reason to doubt that this Board, independent as it is of political parties or Government bureaus, and composed as it is of men of sterling integrity and high ability earnestly giving their efforts to the cause, might well render a service of peculiar value by making wholly independent investigations and by giving to Congress as well as to the President and the Interior Department, the results of its labors. The field of activity is broad enough, for undoubtedly there are more problems today vitally affecting the property rights and the future physical, social, and moral welfare of the Indians which require the earnest, careful exercise of this Board's legal functions than at any time heretofore.

Some of these problems are reviewed in the report. Among others is the pressing need of relief for the Pimas in the matter of water for irrigation. It is generally agreed that the Government should restore to these Indians the water rights which they have lost, and vigorous steps to this end are strongly urged. The distressing conditions at White Earth, too, are discussed with recommendation for legislation to protect the property rights and improve the living conditions of these Indians. The need of more adequate educational facilities for the Navahos is cited, as is also that for proper protection of all the "restricted" Indians and proper supervision of probate matters affecting the estates of minor Indians among the Five Civilized Tribes.

In view of the abnormal death rate among Indians from tuberculosis and the spread of that disease and of trachoma among them, for the relief of which Congress has increased the appropriation from $90,000 for 1913 to $200,000 for 1914, it is recommended that hospitals should be provided for the treatment of cases among adult Indians in order to supplement the hospitals already established in connection with many of the best Indian schools.

The report, though brief, is comprehensive and indicates the wide scope of activities that come within the purview of the Board. Announcement is made of the resignation of Mr. H. C. Phillips as Secretary and the succession of Mr. F. H. Abbott to that office. Mr. Abbott's long connection with the Indian Office culminating in his service as Acting Commissioner of Indian Affairs gives him an intimate knowledge of the whole Indian situation which must needs be of considerable value to the Board in the increased activities to which it is addressing itself.

Conference of Secondary Schools The Conference of Principals and Teachers of Secondary Colored Schools of Virginia, which met in its eighth annual session at Virginia Union University in Richmond the day after Christmas, had an interesting and significant program. Seventeen schools were represented. The members of this body come mainly from the smaller colored schools of the state. Hitherto they have concerned themselves primarily with subjects bearing upon the development of their institutions. As a result, considerable good has been done. Isolated schools have been brought into touch and sympathy with each other. Through contact with the stronger institutions they have gained broader and clearer notions of education. Better courses of study in keeping with their needs have been worked out, and more efficient methods of administration have been presented. Interest in the public schools near these institutions has been increased, and better relations with the public school authorities have been established. At the last session the discussions turned from the schools themselves to a consideration of what it is possible for these schools to contribute directly to the welfare of their communities.

Many of the primary needs of the country districts were impressively set forth in reports on such subjects as the homes, health, and moral conditions in rural districts, religious and public school conditions, farming and business methods and principles among the country people. Each report was followed by a paper outlining such practical work as the schools might do to improve the conditions presented. Attention was also called to the help the communities might receive from outside sources, such as the larger educational institutions through their extension work, publications, and conferences, the Negro Organization Society, and the state through its departments of health, education, and agriculture.

The reports and the general discussions which followed were frank and incisive. It is clear that wretched conditions obtain in many localities, while in a number of others notable improvement is evident. The worse sections, however, are usually the neglected localities where no good schools have been at work and into which no farm-demonstration agents, industrial supervisors for rural schools, or good preachers have been sent. Over against these bad conditions, such a section as Charlotte County stands in striking contrast. Here, it is reported, Negro country homes have improved fifty per cent in twenty years. Only a few one-room cabins are said to remain. And tenant houses also show marked improvement in recent years. Homes that are clean, warm, well lighted, and amply supplied with simple furniture are not uncommon. The colored church also is strong and effective in this section. For a long time it has maintained a good local school. And the very efficient industrial teacher for this county has for years been a potent civilizing influence in this part of the state. The Conference was fortunate in the direct, helpful instruction given the schools.

THE NEGRO'S PROGRESS IN FIFTY YEARS OF FREEDOM *

BY JAMES HARRISON WILSON

Retired Brigadier-General, United States Army

TWENTY-THREE papers, covering the population, business activities and labor conditions, social conditions and problems, educational progress and needs of the American Negro are included in "The Negro's Progress in Fifty Years."

As these papers are contributed by public officials, university presidents, professors of economics and sociology, resident physicians, supervisors of colored schools, and agents of educational funds of the highest standing from nearly all portions of the country and especially from the Southern states, they constitute an invaluable survey of all the topics touched upon and as such are entitled to the careful and respectful consideration, not only of those especially interested in such subjects, but of all statesmen and publicists throughout the country. So far as we know they are the first of the kind ever collected and need but to be read and considered to be acknowledged as setting forth the fundamental facts relating to a large and important group of American laborers.

The first paper, prepared by Dr. Thomas Jesse Jones, specialist in the United States Bureau of Education, shows that our entire Negro population as shown by the census in 1910 was 9,827,763; in 1860 it was 4,441,830; increase in 50 years, 5,385,933, or 11.2 per cent, which is about equal to the average national increase of the European people.

Many interesting figures are given proving that the Negro race is slowly decreasing in its rate of increase in the Southern states and increasing somewhat more rapidly in the Northern states. Careful calculations show that 89.7 per cent of our entire Negro population are found in the Southern states, 10.3 per cent in the Northern states. They also show that only about 10 per cent of the colored population of the country are of mixed blood or mulattoes. It will surprise many to learn that there is but little if any increase of this class either in the North or the South and

* Review of "The Negro's Progress in Fifty Years," *Annals* of the American Academy of Political and Social Science, September 1913, pp. v, 244. Published by the Academy, 2419 York Road Baltimore, Md.

that the movement of Negroes from one state to another is almost negligible.

There is a slight tendency of Negroes from the South towards the Northern and Western states, but the proportion of Negroes living in the cities and towns of the South is "practically the same as the proportion of white population." There is nowhere any evidence that there is any preceptible relative decrease of the native Negroes as compared with the native whites.

In other words, the Negroes, whatever be their deficiencies or aptitudes, are here to stay. They are far too numerous;to deport to other countries, and far too prolific at present to justify the thought that they may die out from natural causes. The real question therefore is, What is to be done to increase the usefulness or economic value of the Negro as he increases in population ?

Manifestly, in the South at least, where he is treated as a race apart, he has been called upon to play his part in the skilled and professional occupations and the extent and success with which he has done this has been well set forth by Dr. Kelly Miller, dean of Howard University.

He tells us the world's workers are divided into (1) those who are concerned in the production of wealth and (2) those who regulate physical, intellectual, moral, spiritual, and social life. The bulk of the toiling masses is found under the first head, while the small number of the so-called learned professions is found under the second. In the United States they stand approximately as twenty to one. In days not altogether past, it was generally believed that the Negro could not rise above the lowest level of menial service, and should not aspire to the least of the learned professions. It is believed by many even yet, that the time, money, and effort spent upon the Negro in this direction have been worse than wasted, and that industrial education or the training of the hand is the only means through which the Negro can properly fill his appointed place in our country.

In 1900, there were 47,210 Negroes, engaged in professional service, by far the larger number of whom were clergymen, doctors, and teachers. But, withal, the tables show only one Negro in every 84 is engaged in professional pursuits of the various kinds, whereas one white in every 20 is found in this class. If this is the true standard, then the Negro has less than one-fourth of his professional quota.

The Negro ministry was the first to take the lead in directing the moral and spiritual life of their people, setting up separate places of worship, till today the Methodist and Baptist denominations practically control the entire race. They have more than 30,000 church organizations, 3,560,000 communicants, and 56,000,000 dollars' worth of church property.

It should be remembered that the Negro church is not merely a religious institution. It deals with all the features of Negro life—political, educational, social, and religious. It has been well said that it is, so far, "the only field in which the Negro has displayed initiative and executive energy on a large scale."

The rise of the colored teacher was due to the abolition of slavery, but in neither the white race nor the colored, has the teacher yet risen to the highest place as a member of the learned professions.

The Negro doctor is a later comer, but as he had farther to travel in his education, his progress has been slower. The Negro lawyer labors under a still heavier handicap, but both are slowly making their way, and as the prosperity of their race continues they will find increasing spheres of influence and usefulness.

From the fact that the race is forced to live apart, it has found itself called upon to furnish its own quota of merchants, bankers, contractors, engineers, electricians, authors, artists, and even editors, and in most cases these have performed their various functions with increasing credit to themselves and to their race. While the most of them are of mixed blood, it must not be forgotten that they are subjected everywhere to the retarding influences of race prejudice.

The paper on "The Negro in Unskilled Labor" was written by Dr. R. R. Wright, Jr., the editor of the *Christian Record* of Philadelphia. It covers that class which requires the least training of mind and the least training of hand—the farmers, agricultural workers, domestic servants, and general helpers. Many figures are given showing the number and percentage of the five main classes into which the Negroes are subdivided. They show that during the past fifty years significant changes have taken place :

(1) The Negro race, which freedom found almost entirely unskilled, has developed more than a million of semi-skilled workers, business and professional men and women ; (2) the standard of the unskilled worker has been raised everywhere ; (3) he has adapted himself to a system of wages as against the slavery system ; (4) his average intelligence has been greatly increased ; (5) he has become more reliable ; (6) he has survived the competition of the immigrant ; (7) he has migrated largely to the cities; (8) he has become to a large extent the foundation on which the Negro business, the Negro church, and the Negro secret societies have grown up.

The remarkable development in Tidewater Virginia has been frequently alluded to in these pages, but the paper of Thomas C. Walker of Gloucester Court House, gives a mass of interesting details. At the close of the war, the Negroes of twenty-four

Virginia counties owned less than 5000 acres, with improvements valued at less than $70,000. They now hold 421,465 acres, valued, with improvements, at $4,282,947, with not a single man, white or black, in the county jail!

According to the Auditor of Virginia for 1912, the Negroes of the entire state held 1,692,626 acres, valued, with improvements, at $14,156,757 and these lands are increasing in value year by year owing to the increasing knowledge and better farming of the Negroes, which, it is but fair to say, is in turn due to the influence of the Hampton Institute and the demonstration work of the United States Department of Agriculture. And one of the most encouraging factors of the marked improvement which is still going on is due to the encouragement and friendly feeling of the better element of the white people of Virginia.

"The Negro and the Immigrant in the Two Americas," "The Tenant System and its Changes since Emancipation" are too long and far too interesting for summarization.

One of the most interesting and valuable additions to the series comes from the University of Arkansas where "the problem of the economic, social, hygienic, educational, moral, and civic uplift of the Negro race is at present challenging the best thought of Southern scholars and philanthropists."

The Southern universities have appointed a commission to study the race question, and under the leadership of Dr. Dillard, formerly of New Orleans, president of the Jeanes Fund, aided by distinguished scholars to the number of ten or more, representing all the old Southern states and universities, are making a complete study of the Negro problem in all its phases. They seem to realize the importance of a correct understanding of the problem and are devoting much thought and reading to the subject. Many individual students are hunting books which will bring them in contact with the leading thinkers in this new field of sociological endeavor. A library of over 400 volumes has been collected and additions are being constantly made and catalogued for use.

Professor Charles H. Brough's admirable paper shows conclusively that the Negroes of the South have made remarkable progress. In 1880, 70 per cent were illiterate. By 1890 this was reduced to 57.1 per cent, and by 1900 it had declined to 44.5 per cent. By 1910 the percentage was only 30.4.

Arkansas and Texas have caught on to the movement and are doing their part of the work nobly. While those states, as well as most of the others, have shamefully neglected the rural schools, under the counsel of Dr. Dillard and his co-laborers they are waking up to the necessity of further exertion and further progress.

The four principal retarding forces to further development

are said to be the tenant system, the one-crop system, the abuse of the credit system, and the depressing effect of isolation. But all these are receiving careful consideration, and "the splendid efforts" of Booker T. Washington, Major R. R. Moton, and Joseph Price; of Charles Banks and Isaiah Montgomery of Mississippi; and of Joseph A. Booker and E. T. Venegar of Arkansas, in behalf of the industrial education and uplift of their race, are receiving the unstinted praise of leading white men in all the states.

Niels Christensen, editor and proprietor of the *Beaufort Gazette* which is published in Beaufort, S. C., discusses the character of the Sea Island Negroes, where the proportion of whites to blacks is as 13.1 to 86.9 and where the mulattoes are only 4.6 per cent, as against 16 per cent for the state at large. He considers their morality, criminal records, church connections, industry, literacy, and economic progress from such records as are attainable, and shows conclusively that even in the Sea Islands "there is progress" through farming and truck-raising and especially in land-owning, all of which are on the increase.

Mrs. L. H. Hammond, of Paine College, Augusta, Georgia, wisely and sympathetically discusses "The White Man's Debt to the Negro." A descendent of slave owners, she declares that Southern problems are both an inheritance and environment to her. She contends that "both the North and the South have obscured and magnified the task of Negro uplift by continually thinking and talking about it in terms of race" instead of in terms of sociology and economics. She acknowledges that the Negro as a mass is generally regarded as "thriftless and unreliable," merely because "the Negro is a Negro" rather than because of his economic status. While she admits that "there is truth in the indictment," she boldly claims that "it is by no means so largely true as many of us believe."

She cites a single instance: "The census of 1910 shows the value of Negro farmlands in the South" to be $272,922,238, a gain of over 150 per cent for the decade; in Negro illiteracy (in the South) "a decrease from 48 per cent in 1900 to 33.3 per cent in 1910." She truthfully adds: "These figures prove that the race is advancing rapidly, no matter how much ignorance, incompetence, and criminality remain for future elimination."

The whole of this article with its wise reflections and humane suggestions, coming as they do from a Southern white woman, is most encouraging to those face to face with the Negro problem as well as to the country at large.

The discussion of "Negro Criminality in the South" by Monroe N. Work, of Tuskegee Institute, shows, contrary to the belief of many, that, so far as prison population is an index, Negro criminality in recent years has not only not increased, but in

1894-5 began decreasing.   He also shows that lynching for murder and sexual crimes is on the decrease, but admits that in both
North and South, the crime rate for Negroes is much higher than
it is for whites.   He points out, however, that the Negro has a
relatively lower crime rate than several of the immigrant races
now coming to this country, and that much is being done with
encouraging results for the decrease of crime in both Northern
and Southern communities, especially in the cities of both sections.

There are interesting papers on "Negro Churches and Religious Conditions," and on "Negro Organizations " and their history both before and since the Civil War.   Alluding briefly to the
uprising of the slaves in New York in 1812, the first of ten similar outbreaks, the latter article gives an account of the Negro
conventions in Philadelphia, 1830–1831, and 1832 ; at Syracuse in
1864 ; the Equal Rights Congress at Harrisburg in 1865 ; the
Washington Convention of 1869 ; the organization of the independent Negro churches ; the Negro secret and benevolent orders ;
the colored women's National Christian Temperance Union ; the
Afro-American Protective League ; the American Association of
Educators of Colored Youth ; the Colored Press Convention at
Washington 1889 ; the Tuskegee Conference in 1890 ; the National
Association of Physicians, Dentists, and Pharmacists in 1895 ; the
National Federation of Colored Men for the social, economic, and
political uplift of the colored people," 1895 ; the National Association of Colored Women and its branches, in 1896, for the estab-
lishment of kindergartens, mothers' meetings, sewing classes,
sanatoriums, and welfare work.

The mere enumeration of the foregoing associations shows
beyond a doubt that the Negro race aspires to higher civilization,
and is making substantial progress in that direction.

The race has founded the American Negro Historical Society;
the National Business League, which has 11 chartered affiliated
leagues, 221 local leagues, and 450 allied leagues, covering 32
states of the Union, Jamaica, and the British West Indies.   It
represents four national associations, the first of which is the
National Negro Bankers, representing 64 Negro banks, capitalized
at $1,600,000 with an annual business of $20,000,000.

Besides, the National Funeral Directors, the Negroes have a
National Press Association organized in 1909, which stands for
249 newspapers and 149 periodicals, published by Negroes.   And,
finally, the Negroes have national organizations of Oddfellows,
Knights of Pythias, Elks, and Mosaic Templars, as well as
mutual, provident, and beneficial insurance companies, law and
order leagues, literary societies, educational congresses, professional and business clubs, and labor unions.

In matters of Negro public health, Dr. S. B. Jones of the

Agricultural and Mechanical College at Greensboro, N. C., takes a wide survey of the race tendencies towards "an increasing death rate, a decreasing birth rate, the influence of alcoholic and sexual intemperance, and particularly to the alleged racial predisposition to tuberculosis." While the investigation is hampered by the absence of statistics prior to 1860, he points out that for the war period the rejection of white recruits exceeded in all forms of disease that of colored, as 264 against 170 per thousand. He shows that since slavery was abolished infant mortality has increased, but looks to the force of education and the improvement of "Negro homes and standards of living" for the improvement of sanitary conditions both in the cities and the country at large.

Dr. Robert E. Park, of Wollaston, Massachusetts, in an article of 16 pages, makes a wide survey of "Negro Home Life and Standards of Living, " giving many interesting details and examples of Negro progress in all parts of the South. His paper is too long, as well as too important, for condensation, but no one can read it without agreeing with the author that "the Negro has made great progress in many directions during the past half century, but nowhere more than in his home, and nowhere," he adds, "do the fruits of education show to better advantage than in the home of the educated Negro."

"Race Relationship in the South" is ably and impartially discussed by Dr. Weatherford of Nashville, Tennessee, who is a Southern man trained in a Southern university and widely acquainted by his travels for the last twelve years with the actual conditions in the old slave states. Passing rapidly over the period from 1619, when Negroes were first introduced, to the invention of the cotton gin and the establishment of the big plantation, which he calls "a period of good feeling on both sides, " he comes to forced labor and the dark days of the Civil War when "the Negroes were intrusted with the lives, property, and honor of the Southern white homes and no Negro was found faithless in this sacred trust. "

The period of reconstruction, following peace and manumission, lasted to the early nineties, "during which all men seemed to be blind. " There were "only two redeeming rays of light"—one was that "the Negro was never denied the right to work," and the other, that he "must be trained and made efficient." The South settled this question once for all, in the early seventies; and since then "has put multiplied millions of dollars into the enterprise, which, however discouraging in the past, is now beginning to show signs of rich fruitage."

It was not until far into the nineties that the true race relationship between whites and blacks began to show itself. Under the guidance of such men as Chancellor Barrow of the University of Georgia, Bishop Galloway of Mississippi, and Edgar Gardner Murphy of Alabama, the "new epoch was slowly ushered in." But it was not till the first half of the first decade of the present century that the larger hope "began blossoming into a rose of beauty," and "the idea of brotherhood between the races" began to take a practical and definite shape.

Eight events and tendencies illustrate the present feeling between the races : (1) Since 1870 the Southern states have spent "more than $200,000,000 on Negro public schools," and now that the Negro owns $700,000,000 worth of property, he is rapidly coming to bear his share of the taxes for education. But it must be remembered that the Negro who produced much of the wealth has always paid, indirectly at least, a considerable part of the cost of education.

(2) The Southern white man has a growing sense of friendliness to the Negro—"a new appreciation of the value of naked humanity—which is coming not only in the South but also slowly all over the world." The determination is growing in the hearts of thousands of the best Southern whites that "the lynching of Negroes must stop."

(3) There is also a decided movement on the part of the lawyers, business men, and others to see that more justice is done to the Negroes. * * *

(4) Never before has there been so much talk of improving the sanitary conditions in which Negroes live. The Southern Sociological Congress at Atlanta last April discussed health, housing, sanitation, education, religious life, and economic progress— all "in the spirit of constructive co-operation between the races."

(5) Another indication of better relations between the races is found in the eager attention given by the Southern white colleges to this whole topic. Six thousand students have been enrolled to study the books bearing on the progress of the Negro race. Many of the churches are doing the same, and under Dr. James H. Dillard of the Jeanes and Slater Funds a commission of state university professors is making "first-hand investigation of the whole subject of Negro uplift."

(6) The outcome of this study is that many of the choicest young men and women of the South "are giving much first-hand social investigation and more social service."

(7) Under this impulse "a goodly company of our choicest white college men and women are offering their lives to the uplift of the Negro race. An entirely new attitude toward the whole race problem is showing itself throughout the South."

(8) An increased interest on the part of Southern white men in Negro progress, is stimulated "by the growth of race pride

and race consciousness on the part of the Negro. When the Negro has become economically efficient, intellectually more advanced, and racially self-conscious, there will be far less friction, for the Negro will then feel as the white man feels that racial integrity and social separation are best for both races." The fear of amalgamation will disappear and the two races will dwell side by side in a spirit of increasing brotherhood, and each will find the place for which he is best fitted in the economic and political world.

The work of the Jeanes and Slater Funds is discussed at length by B. C. Caldwell of New York. Negro illiteracy is treated by Professor Lichtenberger, of the University of Pennsylvania, in a broad and philosophic manner. Starting at 95 per cent fifty years ago, it has been reduced to 30.4 per cent and this is justly regarded as "a phenomenal race achievement."

An instructive paper is furnished by Howard W. Odum, of the University of Georgia, on the Negro children of the public schools of Philadelphia, and another on "The Higher Education of Negroes in the United States" by President Edward T. Ware of the Atlanta University.

Finally, Dr. Booker T. Washington, principal of Tuskegee Institute, contributes a careful and judicious article on "Industrial Education and the Public Schools," which, in connection with his paper in the January number of this magazine on "Negro Progress in Virginia," shows beyond controversy that Negro education and Negro progress have been distinct, praiseworthy, and encouraging from the first.

He also shows that industrial education, as provided at Hampton and Tuskegee Institutes and their many offshoots, has finally come to be acknowledged in both the North and the South as a distinct step upward in the science as well as in the actual furnishing of education, not only for Negroes, but as an example for the imitation of all other people throughout the world.

My personal conviction is that the ten million of Negroes now in the United States, with their twenty-two Negro universities, hundreds of "institutes" and thousands of students, are not only making satisfactory progress in all directions open to them, but also will ultimately find an honorable place in the economic, educational, and political world which will be peacefully conceded, if not guaranteed to them by every section and by all the people of our common country. The road is open and although it may be obscured at times, no one who reads "The Negro's Progress in Fifty Years," written by men of the highest calling and character, can doubt that Negro progress, as there recorded, will continue to the end and add to the common glory of both races.

THE NATIVE AFRICAN TRIBES
OF THE UGANDA HILLS

BY ALEXANDER G. FRASER

President of Trinity College, Kandy, Ceylon

TEN years ago, when I went to Uganda, the railway was only half way to the lake and we had to walk a great part of the way in the old fashion, with our luggage carried on the heads of porters who went in single file through the long grass. Our porters belonged to many tribes and were of many varieties. The Wa Kikuyu were a small and peaceful race, once in terror of their lives from the Masai, and they carried bundles on the small of their backs with a leather thong attached to the sides of the box and going round the forehead, thus keeping the box in position. The Masai themselves, once the great warriors and the scourge of the Great Rift Valley, never carry or do any labor that they can help. Once a very powerful nation, they have now gone all to pieces through immorality, and have lost their population as well as their strength. The strongest carriers we had, the Wa Kamba, came from the South of the Victoria Nyanza. I remember a man carrying one day a double load, or 120 pounds, on his head for twenty-two miles, walking hard the whole way, and when he came into camp among the first of the porters, dancing round the camp twice before laying down his box.

As we went up-country, we saw men and women dressed sometimes in cloth, sometimes in a few beads, sometimes in red clay, and sometimes in nothing. But when we came to Uganda, it was a very different type of civilization that we met. Here there was a historical tradition going back some 400 years, and a well-developed form of government. In many ways the latter resembled the old feudal system in England, being in some respects well up to the standard of the government introduced by Henry II. Each village had its council ; each group of villages, a chief over them ; and each shire or province its ruling chief and his lieutenant. The ruling chiefs formed a sort of senate house, and under the king ruled the country, each of them being responsible for the full administration of his own district as well as being a councillor in the national senate. When absent in council, his lieutenant carried on his administration work for him.

KING'S HILL

"A great chief may have a space as large as four acres around his house"

The country, of course, was organized largely with a view to war, and service was expected of every man in charge. Bribery was practically unknown ; a man's chance of rising to the position of chieftain depended upon his reputation for administering justice truly and well. A man could rise from the rank of peasant to the highest chieftainships, first by the election of a village to its headship, and later by attracting the notice of the greater chiefs above him. The people struck me as being an exceedingly able race. Twenty-five years before, they had not the slightest knowledge of reading and writing, and yet their language was splendidly developed, the verb being almost as fully developed as that of the Greeks, though their other parts of speech were not of course developed to the same extent. But their vocabulary contains in all probably at least 15,000 words. The fact that their vocabulary and grammar has been developed without the aid of writing says an immense amount for the quality and flexibility of the intelligence of the people. They had already produced, ten years ago, a literature of their own in the short time in which they had had the teaching of missionaries, having a book of travel, a history of their people, a church history, two or three commentaries on the books of the New Testament, a book of local proverbs and another of folklore. As a rule, they were keen students of the Bible, which formed for most of them their only literature. Their constitution did not develop as the feudal system in England because there was no public opinion or community power to limit the abuse of the royal autocracy. The king used to sacrifice large numbers to his fears of the next world. Once, I believe, Mtesa killed three thousand human beings in one great sacrifice. Frequently the king, to raise money for the carrying on of the government, would carry war into a neighboring country, but when he was not strong enough to do that, one of his own provinces was devoted to murder and destruction in order that the goods of the people in it should be taken for the treasury.

In 1822 or thereabouts, when the last of the great kings died, immorality was punished by instant death. But there succeeded him a monarch of the temperament of Charles II. Uganda, which had been a terror to the neighboring peoples and seemingly above the buffets of fortune in the days of her Puritan kings, fell as England did under Charles II. into an orgy of lust and became weak, and her borders were at the mercy of neighboring peoples. In 1877, when the first missionaries arrived in the country, the population of Uganda had dwindled immensely, and was probably not much more than 30 per cent of what it had been in 1822. Sir Harry Johnson says that if it had not been for the Christian missionaries, the population of Uganda would by now have been wiped out, just as the population of the Masai is perishing from the face of the earth and for the same reason today.

Uganda is a country of hills, and almost all of them are small. As you look over the undulating country, you see hill after hill rising like waves of the sea and varying from one hundred to two hundred feet in height. Around the bases of most of these are small rivers or swamps covered with thick vegetation. The sides of the hills are covered with grass six or seven feet long except where the plantain gardens have displaced it. On the top of most are situated the little villages. Here and there on the biggest hills and on their broadest tops are the mansions of the greater chiefs surrounded by the village houses. The remarkable cleanliness of every house is a thing that must strike even the most casual observer. Each chief has a large, clean-swept square around his house; the greater his position, the larger the square. An African loves illimitable spaces; he likes the things which are vast and soul-swelling. So a great chief may have a space as large as four acres, or even more, around his house, all of it clean swept, unbroken by any growth, and surrounded by a large fence.

When one goes into the capital of Uganda, Mengo, one finds a city set on, the people say, twenty hills, such little round hills as are described above. It is said that some 80,000 people live in the city, but as the traveler goes along its broad roads, all he sees is the golden reed fences bordering the public roads, most of the houses being hidden in the trees of their gardens. Inside these gold reed fences are the trees which provide the bark cloth, a cloth which forms the dress of the great majority of women and of all the peasantry. Among the bark cloth trees and large plantain gardens are hidden the houses.

It is a land of great thunderstorms and of lightning, and is supposed to be more the victim of these than any other land on earth. The average number of thunderstorms in the year is calculated at over two hundred, and so there is a rule that when lightning strikes a house and sets it on fire and the warning

"IN EVERY TOWN THERE IS A MARKET-PLACE"

is given, everyone who hears the warning must immediately rush to the rescue, and if anyone at such a time tries to seize the property of a rescuer or a victim, the punishment is extremely severe. The alarm is given by a peculiar cry made by calling and at the same time beating the mouth with the fingers of the hand. To do this is called to *kuba indulo*. I remember once being on the top of one of the hills in the capital in a great thunderstorm. Every now and again the whole country flashed out of its darkness, and every dwelling and fence stood out in dazzling light. Suddenly the *kuba indulo* rose from near the King's Hill, and then immediately the little narrow roads between the long grass and the broader roads between the fences were lit up in the darkness by a tracery of torches moving like lines of living fire, as men hastily lit them and dashed off to the rescue. Soon the alarm was sounded from another quarter, and fresh paths of flame lit the country as rescuers went in the new direction.

From the capital we can just see the Murchison Gulf and the blue waters of the Victoria Nyanza. The land is a beautiful land. In the early morning, the great snowy mists fill the valley below like a great white sea, and all the hill tops rise like islands above it. Then, as the mists rise, away, as far as the eye can reach, stretch the undulating uplands of Central Africa, here and there the glorious forests showing and far off the blue waters of the Victoria.

In every town there is a market-place, generally under a large tree. The currency in my time was the cowry shell, though the Indian rupee was also coming in, and just as I left, they were bringing in the Indian pice. The cowry shells generally went about a thousand to a rupee, or a thousand to a third of a dollar. Prices were extraordinary. We used to get about seven eggs for a cent, a hen for two cents, a goat for a third of a dollar, and twenty plantains for a cent. On the other hand we would have to pay seven dollars for two gallons of kerosene oil when it was at its highest, and always, even at its cheapest, two and one-half dollars. European flour or biscuits

THE NATIVES BRINGING GRASS TO THATCH THE CATHEDRAL ROOF

THE INTERIOR OF A UGANDA CATHEDRAL

were also extraordinarily exorbitant, and we were never able to eat bread except on very great occasions, but lived as the people did, chiefly on plantains or bananas. The wages of a chief, if paid in shells, would have weighed some three tons, but the government found it expensive paying them in the common currency and so paid them in rupees. Of all things the people loved salt. Their own salt was brownish in color and very coarse, but little children would buy it as a sweetmeat, and if they could get the white, refined salt of Europe, they were more than delighted and would give largely for it.

The cruelty of heathen times was very great, and often one saw men and women who had lost an ear or an eye or had a nose slit, or in some other way had been mutilated, either by the revenge of a chief or in punishment for some crime. I once found an old women abandoned by the side of a swamp ·who had been there for over three days. Her children had brought her in from a distant part of the country, found her ill with fever and not able to walk further, and so had abandoned her. For at least three days she had lain within sight of the road. Many had passed and no one had given her either to eat or to drink. I tried to get some one to help me to carry her into the capital about ten miles distant. At first I could get no one, and finally I had to add to money and to persuasion, force. They objected to carrying her in as they felt it was a work derogatory to their self-respect; it was such a useless bit of labor. She died in hospital a week or so later, having been too far gone and too emaciated to recover.

Under Christianity, the people have advanced tremendously. I have just spoken of the heartless way in which an old woman was left in a swamp. On the other hand, I knew an old Christian woman who found a small boy covered with small-pox abandoned in a swamp, and who, at the risk of her own life, took him into her own cottage, nursed him through and brought him up as her own son.

Again the chiefs of Uganda met in their Council and abolished slavery. They abolished it without indemnity although they themselves were the greatest of slave owners, and they did it on the stated ground that it was against the law of Jesus Christ. I remember, too, how when sleeping sickness, the most dreaded scourge and the one which most hits the imaginations of the African, came to Busoga, a foreign country, our Uganda men working there as missionaries were attacked by it and came back stricken to the capital. Others were asked at the risk of their lives to go out and fill their places, and more than three times the number required for the posts volunteered to go out, knowing the cost and that it meant not the risk only but the probability of the most terrible form of death.

It would be unfair to leave the country without saying something of its beauty—the glorious birds, the splendid animals, the magnificent trees, and gorgeous flowers. No one who has lived in Central Africa, be it even for a short time, can fail to feel homesickness when he thinks of it. No land, I should think, casts such a spell over the man who has seen it—its splendid, virile people, brave, alert, keen; their splendid glossy skins and graceful movements; the swift spear, the ready laughter, the geniality and brightness of everything. It is a great land, and the people there have a great future before them. They are stronger in physique than probably almost any other race. Their power of reproduction is immense. Hitherto sin has laid a blight upon their growth and upon their mental development. That sin and its effects are being taken away by Christ, and to Africa the words have come, " Arise and shine for thy light is come and the Glory of the Lord has risen upon thee."

One can hardly leave the story of Uganda without touching on that of some of its great men. No nation can rise as quickly as Uganda has risen, without great leaders. The leading man in the country is no doubt Sir Apolo Kagwa, prime minister, or, as he is called, *Katikiro*. He was Uganda's leading representative at the coronation of King Edward VII. About the middle of the day, at a fixed time, a white handkerchief is hung up at the door of his office, and at that time no one may disturb him, however great the power and reputation of the visitor, for he is at that hour in prayer. He is a man keenly interested in the social

welfare of his country. He has done much to put down the
immorality which existed to so extraordinary an extent ; he has
made segregation of the insane and due care of them compulsory ; he has introduced the telephone and the typewriter and
is doing much towards bringing in a reasonable system of drainage and an improvement in agriculture ; a man upright, powerful
in body, keen in mind, with a capable pen, and in council strong
and sagacious.

FOLLOWING A FOREST TRAIL IN UGANDA

H. W. D. Kitakule is the senior clergyman of the church. He
was one of the first Christians who passed through the fiery
persecutions and was offered at one time the premiership, but
believed he could do more for his country as a minister. He
is the champion athlete of the country, though now of course
too old, but along with his interest in church services he carries
quite as deep an interest in wrestling contests.

THE REVEREND SAMWELI GUKASA AND HIS FAMILY

Then there is Samweli, who in my time was *Kangao*, or fourth in rank of the great administrating nobles, a position he still holds. Samweli as a boy was a page in Mwanga's court. Mwanga, the King, sent him to gather the taxes in Kyagwe, one of the great provinces. He gave his oath to bring back the taxes and deliver them to the King in ·person. On his way back to the capital, a friend met him and warned him that a fiery persecution had broken out against the Christians and that his name was on the list of those who were to be executed. Samweli entered the capital by a round-about road and hid in a swamp. He consulted Ashe, a missionary, as to his duty—should he fulfil his oath and go in person with the taxes or should he escape for his life? Ashe recommended escape as the King had forfeited all right to his allegiance. But with the usual independence of the people of Uganda, Samweli, having received the advice, went back to consider it. He left the swamp in the early morning, having determined on his course. The moment the doors of the palace were opened, he rushed in through all the maze and network of courtyards till he came to the King's chamber house in the very center. He rushed in there, delivered up his taxes, and fled pursued by the King's guard, but made good his escape. He became ordained later but afterwards accepted a chieftainship in the belief that then the country needed a Christian ruler more than it needed a Christian pastor. He does not give a tithe of his income merely to the spread of the Gospel, but a very great deal more.   Once when a church was in debt, a messenger at night, under cover of darkness, brought a pair of handsome ivory tusks and a large sum of money and laid it at the door of the church with the inscription, "From one who has received more than he can ever pay." It was found out accidentally that the messenger had come from this chief.

Of course there are other types of Christians in Uganda, but the country that has produced these great types and has such leaders is safe for a very great future. It has been thought that the missionary must dominate in Central Africa. Nothing is further from the truth. The missionary is a very small person beside the great chief, and his influence in the country, great and good though it is, is not that of the inspirer of the chief. The chief and many of his people stand in their Christian manhood, not below, but at least alongside the missionary who has brought the message of light to them. When the history of Uganda is written, in the front rank will stand names like those of Mackay and of Pilkington and of Bishop Tucker, but in the very same rank and with no whit less luster will stand the names of Samweli, the *Kangao*, Sir Apolo Kagwa, and others.

It was, however, the rank and file of the Christians, not the apologists, or apostles, who won the Roman Empire. So today in Uganda the moral, social, and intellectual resurrection which is taking place is due not to one here and there, but to the 4000 Christian teachers and evangelists, who at salaries less than an unskilled laborer's are working for the elevation of their people, and for the coming of the Kingdom of God.

THE BURIAL OF MWANGA, THE KING, IN A ROYAL TOMB

THE LOVE OF THE NORTH

BY EDITH A. TALBOT

BACK to the pines that lower in the snow,
The murky skies, frost-filled and hanging low,
  Back to the brooks ice-bound,
  Gray-looming rocks snow-crowned ;
My heart, why move the passing hours so slow !

There where the sun reluctant rising makes,
As from the mist his copper luster breaks,
  There reigns the night supreme,
  Lit by the white moon's stream.
The cold alone my ardent longing slakes.

How in the darkness, silence lies in wait,
Seizes unwary travellers voyaging late,
  And with the first cock-crow
  Slinks to the woods and snow——
I would my restless soul with silence sate.

As in the North strange lights will gleam and glow, —
Flower of the Arctic, winter-blooming—so
  Thought flashes clear and high
  Under a frosty sky,
And in the cold strong souls take root and grow.

THE PLAINS OJIBWAY

BY ALANSON SKINNER

Assistant Curator in the American Museum of Natural History

THE Ojibway Indians, as we generally think of them, are a true forest people, dwelling mainly about Lakes Superior, Michigan, and Huron, and in northern Minnesota. They are one of the most populous of our Indian nations, numbering nearly thirty thousand in Canada and the United States, and have almost always been on friendly terms with the whites since the day of the first settlements.

There is, however, one little group of these people which separated from the main body and wandered out into the Western plains in pursuit of the buffalo, and which, in the course of years, became differentiated from the parent stock to a considerable extent, taking over the life of the prairie Indians.

The younger Henry, John Tanner, and other traders and frontiersmen, writing of the Northern plains during the early part of the nineteenth century, tell us considerable about this wandering fragment of the Ojibway, but in later years they have been rather forgotten. At the present time most of these people are scattered on small reserves throughout Manitoba and Saskatchewan; a few have gone farther, for Dr. P. E. Goddard, of the American Museum of Natural History, met only this past summer a wandering party of "Saulteaux" (as they are called from the tradition that the home of their ancestors was at Sault Ste. Marie) far up the Athabaska River.

The Plains Ojibway have so long been separated from the main body of their nation that they no longer recognize the fact that they once formed a component part of the tribe. On the contrary they firmly assert their independence, and call themselves "Bungi," but their language and our historical records dispose of their contention in short order.

WINDIGOKAN, OR CANNIBAL DANCERS, IN CHARACTERISTIC COSTUMES

The "cultural" position which these Indians hold is midway between their true forest dwelling relatives and the buffalo hunting tribes of the plains. They have discarded their ancestral bark and mat wigwams for tepees of buffalo hide, they have adopted the *travois* for dogs and horses, and have retained the dugout canoe. Their art shows at once the flower designs common to the people of the woodlands and the angular figures of the plains. They still practice the Medicine Dance, or *Midéwiwin*, of the

A DANCING LODGE AT LONG PLAINS, MANITOBA
The hoop is used in dancing, the performers squirming through it as they dance

THREE OJIBWAY GENERATIONS
The old woman on the right saved her husband, wounded by the Sioux, and is therefore
entitled to wear an eagle feather and to dance with the warriors in the soldiers' tent

forest tribes, and they have acquired the Sun Dance of the
plains.

Naturally, to the student of ethnology such an intermediate
group is of great interest, so that it was with no doubtful pleasure that I betook myself last summer to one of the Saulteaux

HOUSE OVER AN OJIBWAY GRAVE TO SHELTER THE "JABAI" OR GHOST
Note the door for the passage of the spirit and the offering of food for its sustenance

reserves in Manitoba, situated near Portage La Prairie, and not far from Turtle Mountain, North Dakota.

This particular band of Indians originally roamed over the country between Fort Garry and Turtle Mountain, making their headquarters at or near Portage La Prairie. They were warriors and buffalo hunters, a proud and independent people ; rich, in that they had all that they desired in food, raiment, and shelter, until the buffalo suddenly vanished in a couple of years, whereupon they were reduced to starvation and absolute poverty, from which they are only now beginning to emerge by turning their attention to the raising of wheat.

In olden times the "Bungi," like many of our Eastern tribes, were divided into a large number of gentes, each member of which was supposed to be descended from a common animal ancestor, or totem. Consequently, a man belonging to the bear totem was putatively the brother of any woman belonging to the

OGIMANWININI OR "CHIEF OF MEN," AN OLD TIME WARRIOR

In his hand he bears his staff or badge of office as a war leader. The two eagle feathers
he wears denote blows struck against the Sioux

A WARRIOR AND HIS SON

same group, even though she hailed from a different tribe, and therefore he was obliged to marry out of his gens, taking a woman from some one of the other families. In addition, the "Bungi" were further split up into local bands, each having its own chief, a man chosen because of his unusual valor, wisdom, and generosity. These bands had their own hunting grounds, and when the tribe camped together, they pitched their tents in a large circle on the prairie, each band occupying its own segment of the ring.

In the great camp circle order was maintained and quarrels were prevented by the "Okitcita," or "strong-hearted men," who acted as police. These "strong-hearted men" were warriors who had accomplished one or more of a series of recognized brave deeds, such as killing or scalping a foe, striking a foe with the hand or a hand weapon, rescuing a wounded comrade from the clutches of the enemy, or stealing an ememy's horse. Anyone who had achieved one of these brave deeds was accounted "Okitcita," and was entitled to wear an eagle feather in his hair marked to show the nature of his exploit.

AN OJIBWAY LOG CANOE ON THE ASSINIBOINE RIVER
The Plains Ojibway employ both the canoe and *travois*

The Okitcita had a huge tent of their own at one side of the encampment, which was emblazoned with paintings of their warlike exploits. They had their own servant, who fed them and filled their pipes, and they were personages of great import- ance and honor. It was their duty, if trouble broke out in the camp, to suppress all quarrels, and if two men came to blows, the Okitcita would come out and hold a pipe between them, whereupon the wranglers were obliged to cease and submit their difficulty to arbitration. If any one resisted or threatened an Okitcita, the Okitcita might kill him, for they were exempt from blood vengeance. The "strong-hearted men" also guarded the horses at night, and when there was danger of an attack they would announce through the village that the young men were forbidden to go courting in the evening, lest they should be shot by mistake, for when danger was at hand the Okitcita were not obliged to challenge a suspicious character.

One of the most important duties of the Okitcita was to regulate the buffalo hunt. In olden times it was important that, when a herd was sighted, the men should surround the herd and attack it all at once, so that enough animals might be killed to feed the entire camp. If one man stole a march on the others, he might easily stampede the buffalo, and so place all the people in danger of starvation. To hunt alone, therefore, was strictly forbidden, and it was the business of the Okitcita to see that no one violated this rule. If a man did so, no notice was taken of it at the time, but that evening the whole band of Okitcita would appear before his tepee and call him out. They would then flog him severely, cut his garments and his tent to pieces, or kill his horses and dogs; in short, destroy all his property. If the man objected, he might be expelled from the band or even killed, but if, on the other hand, he said nothing and offered no resistance, at the end of four days the Okitcita would go about the camp and confiscate from others enough property to restore his estate once more, for it was thought that the social disgrace he had suffered was punishment enough.

The buffalo were taken by several methods, chief of which was by impounding. In the winter a large enclosure was made of stumps and stones, with an opening at one side, which connected with two huge fan-like wings, forming a great funnel-shaped approach. In the center of the enclosure a pole was erected, and on it were hung various sacred medicines. When all was in readiness, a man was sent out to toll the buffalo in. Riding to the herd, he would stop nearby, remove his blanket or buffalo robe, and sway it slowly backwards and forwards in front of him, crying, *Wu! Wu! Wu!* to attract the attention of the grazing buffalo. When they looked up he would begin to ride slowly away, zigzagging as he went. The buffalo, full of curiosity, would follow him, and he would gradually entice them into the entrance of the wings. Once they were inside, men who had previously concealed themselves behind snow banks arranged at intervals along the wings would spring up, whooping and waving their robes, until the herd was stampeded. At the entrance of the circular enclosure the horseman would urge his pony through a secret door and escape, while the herd would pile in, sometimes overflowing the high walls, running on top of each other. The Indians on the stockade now tried to get the herd to mill, and once they had succeeded in this, they could shoot the buffalo at their leisure.

Sometimes they drove the buffalo on the ice, where the great beasts were unable to stand, or bogged them in the marshes. In summer, however, they preferred to surround the herd and charge it in a body, as has been described. Occasionally, men would disguise themselves as wolves, and thus stalk an animal or two. The old men tell me that often they were not the only hunters, and I have heard them describe most graphically how they have seen titantic combats between grizzly bears and buffalo ; how the bear would endeavor to get the buffalo by the horns and twist its neck, and how, sometimes, a young bull would succeed in killing his antagonist.

The two great religious ceremonies of the Plains Ojibway were the Sun Dance, which they acquired from their Western neighbors, and the *Midéwiwin*, or Medicine Dance, which they brought with them from their forest homes. These ceremonies are now sternly put under by the Canadian authorities, and so it is very hard to gather data upon them. The Sun Dance was a

great festival which had nothing whatever to do with the sun,
despite its popular name which has been given by the settlers.
It was given in early summer, each year, by some man who had
had a vision of the Thunderbirds. He would cause a large
structure to be built, containing a central pole, at the top of
which was placed a bunch of leaves representing the nest of the
Thunderers. A great company of his tribespeople now gathered
and held a ceremony lasting four days, during which time all the
participants refrained from food or drink.

They entered the lodge prepared for them, and danced almost
continuously, gazing at the "Thunderers' nest" at the top of the
pole, and blowing incessantly upon little bone whistles which
they held in their mouths. During a certain phase of the dance,
youths who wished to achieve social distinction for their valor, or
in fulfillment of a vow made during sickness, would come
forward, half naked, and present themselves to a medicine man
who would make cuts in the flesh of their breasts, through which
skewers of wood were thrust. These skewers were attached to
thongs made fast to the central pole, and as soon as they were
ready the youths would throw themselves back, straining and
tugging in an endeavor to tear loose. If successful they had
achieved a great honor, but if one of them fainted or cried out,
he was disgraced. Often the muscles refused to yield, and the
young men would pull for a long time, dancing and whistling,
before they could break away. Others circled the camp dragging
buffalo skulls skewered into their backs in the same way, and
still others led spirited horses, attached to the flesh of their
backs, around the village. It was largely because of these
terrible torture features that the Sun Dance has been frowned
upon by the Canadian Government.

The Medicine Dance, on the other hand, had no features of
self-mutilation. It was the public performance of a society
founded upon the teachings of Nänibozhu, the culture hero, allied
to the Memomini Mänäbus, and had for its object the cure of the
sick and the instruction of people in "the true path of life,"
that they might successfully reach the hereafter and dwell in peace
in the happy land situated beyond the sunset.

The public performance consisted of the recitation of the
ritual myths and songs, and the initiation of a new member by
instruction in the lore of the society, with the passing of the
power contained in the animal skin medicine bags of the older
members into his body. At a certain part in the ceremony the
performers danced up to the novice and presented their medicine
bags, pointing them at him. It was supposed that the essence of
the contents of the bags flew out and penetrated his body,
knocking him unconscious. After a time he was revived and was

thought to be possessed of the power that had entered him and able to impart it to others in the same way.

The Plains Ojibway have an enormous pantheon of various gods, which are, for the most part, natural forces personified. They believe as well in a host of genii, hobgoblins, and ogres, which haunt the forests and prairies, hills and streams, and which have to be constantly placated with offerings of tobacco, which they are most scrupulous to give.

Among other monsters, a large panther is supposed to dwell beneath the water, and from time to time a dog is killed and thrown with tobacco into the Assiniboine River for the delectation of the mythical beast. Another belief of theirs is in a huge horned snake who seeks to destroy mankind, issuing from dismal places in search of his prey only when the day is cloudless, for he in turn is preyed upon by the Thunderbirds, who champion the people. The Thunderbirds are gigantic, supernatural eagles, whose flashing eyes cause the lightning, and whose cries are the thunder which we hear. None of these concepts are unique among the Plains Ojibway; on the contrary, they are shared with many another tribe.

In the old days the Plains Ojibway were mighty warriors, waging fierce battles with the Sioux, whom they hated with an implacable enmity. The old men can still tell many exciting tales of their exploits.

One of the most interesting of Plains Ojibway institutions is that of the Cannibal Dancers, or "Windigokan," as they are called. Certain men had the right to make for themselves ridiculous costumes of rags and masks of the same material. When the band was gathered in the great camp circle, one of these persons would dress and search for comrades. Armed with a staff he would go from tent to tent until he found some one whom he wished to associate with himself. At this time he would point his stick, whereupon it was the duty of the chosen party to make himself a costume and accompany his captor, willy nilly. If, however, he saw the "Windigokan" approaching and escaped before the fateful wand was leveled at him, it was well.

When a sufficient number of recruits had been gathered, a tent was erected to house them, and there they dwelt, issuing forth from time to time to capture food, or to exorcise the demons of disease from some sick person. Their method of procuring food was extremely amusing. The entire party, headed by the leader, would make the rounds of the camp, singing and frolicking. When they came upon buffalo meat hung out to dry, they would immediately proceed to stalk it most elaborately, until finally, one of the party, who was armed with a bow and arrow, would shoot at it. If he missed his aim, the party proceeded,

never even picking up the arrow. If the meat was struck, they
would flee in pantomime of terror, falling over backwards and
performing many ludicrous antics, returning, however, to carry
off the food in triumph. When they reached the door of their
tepee they never thought of carrying the meat in ; instead they
would attempt to throw it in through the smoke hole. If, however, the meat missed the hole and fell outside, the "Windigokan"
would never touch it, and it became the prey of the bystanders,
who thronged to see the fun.

Another peculiarity of the cannibals was that they used
"inverted speech." That is to say, they expressed themselves
by opposites. If one wished to drink, he would announce that he
was not thirsty, and if a bystander wanted him to dance, he
commanded the clown not to do so.

With the loss of the buffalo herds, the Plains Ojibway sank
from absolute wealth and prosperity to abject misery and
starvation. The buffalo supplied everything. His flesh was food;
his hide made garments, robes, bedding, lodges ; his hair, ropes;
his bones, tools ; his hoofs, glue ; his horns, spoons. All of these
commodities were lost at once, and the Plains Ojibway and their
neighbors starved and died by hundreds. The duck tents of the
white man were not so good as the buffalo skin lodges ; the
blanket was far inferior to the robe. Our food was unpalatable
to the Indians, nor did they understand how to prepare it.

But of late years a change has set in. Settlers have crowded
out on the Manitoba plains. Cities and towns have grown up about
the reservation ; the well-tilled wheat fields of the whites furnish
a daily object lesson to the Indians ; efficient missionaries are
coming in. The Plains Ojibway has learned to build log houses.
He can farm, if he will, and already members of his nation have
turned to the plow. At Long Plains, the most backward reserve,
the Indians are beginning to send their children to school in order
that they may be able to compete with their neighbors.

Slowly, but surely, the past is sinking into oblivion. The
mice gnaw the medicine man's rattle, but he will soon be too
busy keeping them from his granaries to notice it. In a few
years more, the great grandchildren of the buffalo hunters will
be nearly equipped to take their places among the citizens of
Canada, but, in justice to the Indian, let us not expect too much
of him at once; give him time ; and what I say applies not only
to the Plains Ojibway, but to all Indians. They have the poten-
tiality, if properly developed, of becoming worthy citizens of any
land.

JOHN CHAVIS

ANTEBELLUM NEGRO PREACHER AND TEACHER

BY STEPHEN B. WEEKS

WHEN an individual who is born in the lower ranks of life, by energy, ambition, and industry wins recognition and respect from his superiors, he is worthy of becoming a model and guide for others to follow. When therefore a black man, born in the midst of an aristocratic slaveholding oligarchy, develops such intellectual power and force of character as to command, despite race and social position, not a grudging, but a cheerful recognition from the exclusive aristocracy among whom he lives, he can well be pointed to as a source of inspiration and help to all future generations of his people ; for his career should convince them that personal excellence will win its way even though faced by the heaviest odds.

Such was the career of John Chavis, a full-blooded North Carolina Negro of the last century, who served the white race, as well as his own, as a minister and teacher for many years. Of his early life we really know nothing. In 1832 he said of himself, "If I am black, I am a free-born American and a Revolutionary soldier." With this exception we have no authentic information until we turn to the Acts and Proceedings of the General Assembly of the Presbyterian Church in the United States, where, under the year 1801, we find the following resolution : "That . . Mr. John Chavis, a black man of prudence and piety, who has been educated and licensed to preach by the Presbytery of Lexington in Virginia, be employed as a missionary among people of his color, until the meeting of the next General Assembly ; and that for his better direction in the discharge of duties which are attended with many circumstances of delicacy and difficulty, some prudential instructions be issued to him by the Assembly, governing himself by which, the knowledge of religion among that people may be made more and more to strengthen the order of society."

The next year it is stated in the Acts and Proceedings "That the journal of Mr. John Chavis, a black man licensed by the Presbytery of Lexington, in Virginia, was read in the Assembly. He appears to have executed his mission with great diligence, fidelity, and prudence. He served as a missionary nine months. " It was again resolved "That Mr. John Chavis be appointed a missionary for as much of his time as may be convenient. " In 1803 (not before) Chavis is officially reported as a licentiate of the Presbytery of Lexington, Virginia, and it was again resolved that he be employed as a missionary "for the times and on the routes specified in the report. " The missionaries so employed were to be "left at discretion as to the time of the year in which to perform their services, provided their terms be completed so as to enable them to report agreeably to the instructions of the committee of missions. "

In May 1804, the General Assembly again employed him as a missionary for three months and he was to travel in the southern part of Virginia and in North Carolina. The next year the Synod of Virginia reported "That Mr. Chavis, a missionary to the blacks, itinerated in several counties in the south part of the state ; but owing to some peculiar circumstances, stated in his journal, his mission to them was not attended with any considerable success. " Notwithstanding this seeming lack of success he was again employed (for 1805) for six months, "to pursue nearly the same route as last year, and employ himself chiefly among the blacks and people of color. " In 1806 he was employed for two months and directed to spend his time "among the blacks and people of color in Maryland if practicable ; otherwise at his discretion, " and in 1807 it was ordered that he be employed three months among the blacks in North Carolina and Virginia and that his route be left to his discretion.

After 1807, Chavis disappears from the Acts and Proceedings of the General Assembly. It is said that he returned to North Carolina about 1805 and the records of the Hanover Presbytery show that he was dismissed by it in 1805 to join the Orange Presbytery in North Carolina. In 1809 he was received by the latter as a licentiate and for the next twenty years seems to have preached pretty regularly in Granville, Wake, and Orange Counties. It is perhaps impossible at this late date to say whether he held regular pastorates of white churches. It is certain that he continued more or less regularly the work which he had already been doing for the General Assembly, performing missionary service among the Negroes and preaching from time to time to white congregations.

As a result of the Nat Turner insurrection in Southampton County, Virginia, in August 1831, the North Carolina legislature in 1832 passed an act silencing all colored preachers. With reference to this act, as applied to Chavis, we find an entry in the Proceedings of the Orange Presbytery, under date of April 21, 1832, as follows :

"A letter was received from Mr. John Chavis, a free man of

color, and a licentiate under the care of the Presbytery, stating his difficulties and embarrassments in consequence of an act passed at the last session of the legislature of this state, forbidding free people of color to preach: whereupon, *Resolved*, That the Presbytery, in view of all the circumstances of the case, recommend to their licentiate to acquiesce in the decision of the legislature referred to until God in His providence shall open to him the path of duty in regard to the exercise of his ministry. "

It does not appear that Chavis preached after this date. Of his abilities as a minister we have the testimony of the late George Wortham, a lawyer of Granville County, who wrote in 1883: ''I have heard him read and explain the scriptures to my father's family and slaves repeatedly. His English was remarkably pure, contained no *negroisms*; his manner was impressive, his explanations clear and concise, and his views, as I then thought and still think, entirely orthodox. He was said to have been an acceptable preacher, his sermons abounding in strong, common-sense views and happy illustrations without any effort at oratory or any sensational appeal to the passions of his hearers. He had certainly read God's Word much and meditated deeply upon it. He had a small but select library of theological works, in which were to be found the works of Flavel, Buxton, Boston, and others. I have now two volumes of Dwight's Theology which were formerly in his possession. He was said by his old pupils to have been a good Latin and a fair Greek scholar. He was a man of intelligence on general subjects and conversed well. I do not know that he ever had charge of a church, but I learned from my father that he preached frequently many years ago at Shiloh, Nutbush, and Island Creek churches to the whites. "

He even aspired to religious authorship and published in 1837 a pamphlet entitled '' Chavis' letter upon the Doctrine of the Atonement of Christ, '' in which, although a Presbyterian, he argues strongly against the popular conception of Calvinism and insists that the atonement ''was commensurate to the spiritual wants of the whole human family. '' This pamphlet is said to have been widely circulated but no copy has come under the eye of the present writer.

It was not, however, as a minister but as a teacher of white boys (and apparently of white girls also) that this free-born, full-blooded Negro was of most service to the State of North Carolina. For the greater part of the time after he was silenced as a preacher in 1832, and most probably for a large part of the time from his return to North Carolina until his death in 1838, he conducted a private school in Wake County and perhaps in Chatham, Orange, and Granville Counties. The school was a peripatetic one and changed its location from time to time according to the encouragement offered. He numbered among his pupils some who became distinguished in the next generation. Among those who are known to have attended his school were Priestly H. Mangum, brother of Senator Mangum and himself a lawyer of distinction ; Charles Manly, Governor of North Carolina ; Abram Rencher, minister to Portugal and Governor of New Mexico ; Mr. James H. Horner, founder of the Horner School ; as well as others of less distinction. His school served as a high school and academy for the section in which it was located. One of the extracts already quoted gives us some idea of his scholarship and it seems that he prepared some of his pupils for the University of North Carolina.

His abilities as preacher and teacher and his high character brought him an acquaintance with the leading citizens of that section of the state, by whom he was treated with every mark of respect. We have a very pleasing account of this from Mr. Paul C. Cameron, who wrote in 1883 :

"In my boyhood life at my father's [Judge Cameron's] home I often saw John Chavis, a venerable old Negro man, recognized as a free man and as a preacher or clergyman of the Presbyterian Church, As such he was received by my father and treated with kindness and consideration, and respected as a man of education, good sense, and most estimable character. He seemed familiar with the proprieties of social life, yet modest and unassuming, and sober in his language and opinions. He was polite, yes, courtly, but it was from his heart and not affectation. I remember him as a man without guile. His conversation indicated that he lived free from all evil or suspicion, seeking the good opinion of the public by the simplicity of his life and the integrity of his conduct. If he had any vanity, he most successfully concealed it. He conversed with ease on the topics that interested him, seeking to make no sort of display, simple and natural, free from what is so common to his race in coloring and diction. . . . I write of him as I remember him and as he was appreciated by my superiors, whose respect he enjoyed. "

His relations with Judge Mangum were very intimate. I might say they were affectionate, even fatherly. He was an occasional visitor at the house of the Judge and was treated with all deference and courtesy, so much so that it caused astonishment and questioning on the part of the younger children, which was met in turn by, "Hush, child, he is your father's friend. " The letters of Chavis to Judge Mangum which have come down to us indicate no social inequality. They are written in the frank friendship which has bridged all social distinctions, and when read between the lines give us glimpses of the power of intellect and character to overcome the mere conventionalities of society. They give us also an insight into the political views of the writer. We learn something of the history of private schools in the state, something of his ideas of pedagogy, and above all they serve as an inspiring example to others. They extend from 1823 to 1836 and cover all sorts of subjects, but in particular politics and teaching. I have room for only a few extracts.

In his first letter he says: "I am very anxious respecting the presidency. I am very fearful that Mr. Crawford will not be elected. . . . There is much rumor abroad that you will not be elected again because you support the election of Mr. Crawford." In May 1826: "I am teaching school where I did last year and should you be traveling this road I shall thank you to call on me." He was opposed to agitating the question of Federal amendments, "because once a beginning is made to amend the Constitution away goes the best of human compacts." He did not hesitate to oppose the wishes of Judge Mangum. In 1827 he writes: "You know that I have ever opposed every stage of your political life, preferring your continuance at the bar until you have acquired a competent fortune."

In March 1828, he writes: "I am much more helpless than when you saw me. You cannot conceive what it costs me to attend to my school. My number at present is 16 and it may probably amount to 20." In September 1831: "I must plainly and honestly tell you that I have ever been grieved that you were the professed political friend of G[eneral] Jackson. Please to give my best respects to Mrs. Mangum and tell her that I am the same old two and sixpence towards her and her children, and that she need not think it strange that I should say that her children will never be taught the Theory of the English Language unless I teach them. I say so still. I learnt my Theory from Lindley Murray's Spelling book which no other Teacher in this part of the country Teaches but myself and I think it preferable to the English Grammar."

In March 1832, he returns to the same subject: "It is four weeks today since I left your house at which time Mrs. Mangum and myself wrote to you respecting my teaching school for you. . . . So anxious am I to Teach your children the Theory of the English Language that I am truly sorry that I had not told Mrs. Mangum to write to you . . . that if nothing else could be done that I would come and teach Sally [Judge Mangum's oldest child, then eight years old] for the same you would have to give for her board in Hillsborough, provided you would board me and let me have a horse occasionally to go and see my family." Then he falls into politics: "Oh, my son, what will you do with the overwhelming eloquence and masterly disquisitions of Mr. Clay?"

In July 1832, he writes that if Mrs. Mangum "will condescend to board out Sally and send her to a man of my stamp I can have her boarded at an excellent house. . . I desire to teach her the Theory of the English Language which she never will be taught unless I teach her, because no other person in this part of the country teaches it but myself, and my manner I deem far preferable to the English Grammar. I wish you to make this statement to Colonel Horner and tell him that I want his daughter Juliana for the same purpose. ''

I have space for but one more quotation on politics and for his définition of character : ''You appear to think that I have become unsound in politics. If to be a genuine Federalist is to be unsound in politics I am guilty. But pray how has it been with yourself? How often have [you] changed your Federal coat for a Democratic or Republican one? . . . I have ever been opposed to the election of G. J. [General Jackson] from the beginning to this day. . . . For honesty, integrity, and dignity is my motto for character.''

THE ELECTION OF AN INDIAN
GOVERNOR IN NEW MEXICO

BY ALBERT B. REAGAN

AT about three o'clock in the morning of December 29, 1900, Victoriana Gachupine, the Indian who chored for me, woke me and said : ''They have built the fires of the gods. '' I went to the house roof and sure enough a huge fire was burning just without the pueblo in each of the cardinal directions, one to each of their deities. The one to the south represented the Sun, the one to the north the Moon, the one to the east the Morning Star, and the one to the west the Evening Star.

''Today is election day, '' broke in Mr. Gachupine as he joined me on the house top. ''Last night, '' he continued, ''the *cacique* and chief religious men and medicine men met and cast corn (cast lots) to see who would be a suitable man for governor (this is the Jemez mode of nominating a candidate.) Today we will vote for the governor and other officers. ''

At that instant the heavy, guttural command of the governor and his aids, who just then entered the plaza on their commanding tour, broke the stillness of the early morning : '' *O-wah bah kwal-la-shoo ka whee pang-a-oonghung* (Go to the south *estufa* to vote for the governor today).'' This they repeated time after time as they made the circuit of the entire village.

After this commanding tour was completed nothing further of interest happened until about ten o'clock in the forenoon, except that guards were put out on every side of the village to prevent any of the male Indians above twenty years of age from leaving the place. At ten o'clock the governor and his aids again appeared in the public square, and as they walked around and around the streets of the village, they gave the command : *"Bah-ka-whee pang-oo* (Go to the election)." This order was not obeyed. The Jemez never care to attend an election. If there, they stand a chance of being elected to some office ; and, if elected, they must serve, whether they want to or not.

At noon, the governor and his aids again appeared and in gruff, coarse, emphatic voices gave the following and last command of the day : " *Sho yosch-shee tang-aka-whee pang-oo* (We command you in the name of all the gods of our fathers, go to the election). " This order likewise was not obeyed. So the Indian constables were compelled to force attendance ; some of the Indians were dragged from their dark rooms and carried, struggling, to the *estufa.*

When all were within the secret religious hall, the *cacique*, standing with his back against the post which separates the north wall of that edifice into two rainbow sections—the section of the Rainbow in the West and that of the Rainbow in the East, lifted his hands to heaven and out toward the symbolic paintings of the house as he prayed long and earnestly to his deities. After his prayer was completed, the retiring governor, Augustine Pecos, gave his farewell address in the form of a prayer as follows :

"O God of the Day, O God of the Night, O God of the Morning, O God of the Evening, O Montezuma, O all the Gods of our fathers, we indeed and in truth thank you for all things. We thank you for the infants, we thank you for the young women, we thank you for the young men, we thank you for the middle-aged and old women, we thank you for the old men, we thank you for the horses, we thank you for the mules, we thank you for the cattle, we thank you for the corn, we thank you for the wheat, . . . we thank you for our kind neighbors (*kya-ba*), we indeed and in truth thank you for all things. "

Then turning to his associates in office he said : "In the name of the God of Day, of the God of Night, of the God of the Morning, of the God of the Evening, of the Great Water Snake, of the Flower-producing Flash Lightning, of Montezuma, . . . and of all the gods of our fathers, I thank you all for your faithful work. I thank you, *cacique.* I thank you, first assistant *cacique.* I thank you, second assistant *cacique* I thank you, my first lieutenant governor. I thank you, my second assistant lieutenant governor. I thank you, war captain. I thank you,

assistant war captain. I thank you, our east-side ditch commissioner. . . . I indeed and in truth thank you all for your
faithful work. ''

Then as he turned his face heavenward he continued, ''In
the year to come as in the past, O God of the Rain, give us
water. As in this year, O God of Bloom, give us flowers in
abundance. O, may the gods of our fathers give us a bountiful
harvest . . . and O God of Day, O God of Night, . . .
gods of all our fathers, give us for the year to come a good
governor.

Then with one of his official canes raised toward the heavens,
the other suspended over his visible hearers, he said : '' I indeed
and in truth thank you all, both those present and those above.
Amen. ''

After the farewell address was finished, nominations were in
order; the result of the casting lots the night before was supposed
to be secret and not known to the populace. Mr. José Reyes Gal-
lena was the candidate for governor. As soon as his nomination
was announced, the vote was taken by acclamation, all rising and
saying ''nop. '' It was unanimous. Had it not been unanimous,
a new candidate must have been proposed ; everything must be
by unanimous consent with the Jemez.

As soon as declared elected, the governor elect went to the
cacique and got down on his knees before him. Then that august
person, the cacique, as he bent over the man at his feet, first
prayed to his deities ; second, he gave the new governor instructions as to the duties of his office ; and, third, he gave him the two
gold-headed canes of authority, which go with the office of governor. The now inaugurated governor rose from his humble
position and seated himself at the right side of the cacique beneath
the section of the Rainbow in the West.

The election of the other officers immediately followed. The
election of each remaining officer was somewhat similar to that of
governor, except in the case of the minor officer. Each of these
was nominated by the retiring officer ; and, as soon as elected, the
retiring officer turned his rod of authority over to him without
any ceremony. In all, thirty-one officers were elected.

When all the officers had been elected, the cacique again
prayed long and earnestly to his gods and to their symbolic paintings on the estufa walls. With his prayer the election closed.

CIVIC REFORMS IN THE TREAT-
MENT OF THE NEGRO *

BY W. O. SCROGGS

· Professor of Economics and Sociology in the Louisiana State University

IT is a noteworthy fact that in 1912, for the first time since the
Civil War, the Republican national platform contained no
reference to the problem of the Negro. It is equally significant
that the platform of the new-born Progressive party was also
silent on this subject. These omissions have been bewailed by
certain types of Negro leaders and also by some of their Northern sympathizers, but it seems to me a cause for rejoicing that
Northern politicians have ceased to find it profitable at regular
four-year intervals to deplore the wrongs of the black man. The
race problem as a national political issue will now probably be
relegated to that limbo whither Anti-Masonry, Know-Nothingism,
and the "bloody shirt" have already wended their way. If the
politicians of the South would only follow the example of their
Northern brethren and leave the race question severely alone,
the country would profit still further, though a few individuals
now holding high office might have to retire to private life.

The removal of the race question from politics must precede
any far-reaching reform in the treatment of the Negro, and the
sooner this is accomplished the sooner shall we be able to carry
out one part of the program of this Southern Sociological Congress— "the solving of the race question in a spirit of helpfulness to the Negro and of equal justice to both races." If we
as members of this Congress are to co-operate in promoting this
spirit of equal justice, we must necessarily familiarize ourselves
with the present civic status of the Negro. None of us, I am
sure, will have the hardihood to affirm that the Negro's treatment as a member of our citizen-body is quite what it should be.
In saying this I do not have in mind any criticism of that basic
fact in the relations of whites and blacks, social segregation. This
is a phenomenon found in all ages and in all countries where members of diverse races have been brought together in anything
like equal numbers. It is based on human instinct and confirmed by reason and experience ; and it is in vain that Northern

* An address at the Southern Sociological Congress, Atlanta, April 1913, reprinted, with
permission, from "The Human Way"

enthusiasts may rail at it as "senseless prejudice" and "unreasoning antipathy." In doing so they run counter to the opinion of the vast majority of their fellow citizens and thus virtually repudiate that very democracy which they advocate so effusively.

The Southern people have accorded the Negro a large measure of civil rights. He enjoys protection of life, limb, and property; he has in the South, perhaps, a greater measure of industrial freedom than elsewhere in this country; and he can obtain at least an elementary education for the asking. But comparative well-being is not necessarily absolute well-being. The most optimistic leaders of the race are unable to overlook the dark side of the Negro's civic condition, and at times they give evidence of discouragement. Some of these disheartening aspects of the problem I shall now indicate.

1 The Negro does not get equal accommodations with the whites on railway passenger trains, although he pays the same fare. The laws of the Southern States prescribe separate accommodations on trains for whites and blacks, and this principle, inasmuch as it reduces friction between the races, is for the best interests of both. Railways, however, while providing separate accommodations, have not undertaken to make these equal for both races. A short time ago I made a journey which involved travel on local trains over six different railway lines, and on only one of these did I find equal conveniences for white and black. On two trains the whites were furnished with modern vestibuled coaches, while the Negro coaches were of the antiquated open-platform pattern, very dingy and much less comfortable than the cars for whites. The rear half of one of these inferior coaches served as a smoking compartment for white men, while in the forward half Negro men and women, smokers and non-smokers, were herded together, with a single toilet for all. Another train carried its white passengers in a steel coach and its Negro patrons in a coach of wood. When I commented upon this to a gentleman from the West, he remarked: "Well, I guess it costs the road more to kill a white man than a nigger, and so it takes extra precautions for us." On through trains with interstate passengers the accommodations for the two races are more nearly equal, though they are rarely identical.

This unfair treatment of the Negro by common carriers is inexcusable. No honest Southerner would countenance a white merchant's selling his Negro customers inferior goods at the same price at which he supplied his white patrons with a better article. Yet we allow our railways to do practically the same thing with impunity. Such a policy can only engender bitterness in the Negro, and if persisted in it may put in jeopardy the whole principle of racial segregation in interstate travel. The Interstate Commerce Commission has already been appealed to, but without any appreciable result. The most serious discrimination is found on local trains and on branch roads, where Negro patronage is generally greatest. The remedy lies with the several states, and it should be applied as a measure of simple justice.

2 North and South the urban Negro population is forced to live in poorly built, unsanitary dwellings, on filthy and neglected streets, and frequently in an atmosphere permeated with vice. Abominable as his housing facilities are, the Negro is compelled to pay an exorbitant rent. Southern real estate dealers will tell you that Negro shacks and cabins are among the best investments, often yielding from 15 to 20 per cent on their cash value. This, of course, is only true when the landlord exercises due diligence in collecting his rent. The Negro accepts such conditions because he wants nothing better. There can be no effective remedy save through the gradual raising of his standard of living.

3 It is a matter of common knowledge that in the division of the school fund the Negro is not fairly treated. Politicians have won many votes by advocating that the moneys be divided in proportion to the direct contributions to the treasury by the respective races. They are either ignorant, or else they deliberately blind themselves to a fact that every student of elemetary economics fully understands—namely, that the taxpayer is not always the tax-bearer. The white man pays many taxes whose burdens rest upon the black man's shoulders either wholly or in part. Whether the man who hands the money to the tax collector is white or black is a matter of minor importance. That our taxes as at present administered fall most heavily on those least able to pay is everywhere recognized, and from this it must follow that the Negro, in proportion to his ability, bears a greater burden from taxation than does the white man. Professor Charles L. Coon, of North Carolina, has demonstrated that the education of the Negro is no burden on the white race, at least in the states where statistics are available for determining this question. Forty per cent of the children of school age in eleven states are Negroes, and yet they receive only fifteen per cent of the school fund. Only fifty-three per cent of the Negro children of school age in the South ever enter a schoolhouse. There is evidence that in some communities the Negro is actually being taxed to support white schools. A mere policy of enlightened selfishness would cause us to give the black man a better educational opportunity. What will it profit us to spend millions in the uplift of one race if the other be left close by its side in ignorance and vice ? Separate schools, like separate

coaches, are a necessity ; but the fair-minded citizenship of the
South should exert itself to see that separation does not produce
injustice.

4 Inequalities like those in the administration of the school
fund are even more noticeable in the case of such municipal improvements as parks, driveways, and public libraries. A few
cities, like Jacksonville, Florida, and Louisville, Kentucky, provide library facilities for their Negro citizens, but generally for
these and other civic improvements like those just mentioned
the black man must contribute his quota and expect little or
nothing in return. North and South, nearly all the special activities for social uplift, such as settlement work, day nurseries,
and fresh air funds, seem to overlook the Negro, though there
are many notable exceptions.

5 Intelligent and highly respectable Negroes are sometimes
disfranchised for no other reason than that of color. The unfitness of the race for the exercise of the suffrage at the time
it was bestowed is now generally admitted. Today the Negro
is disfranchised by legal restrictions based on illiteracy, ownership of property, payment of poll tax, good character, good
understanding of the constitution, military service, and a voting
grandfather. The exclusion of the ignorant and propertyless
from the ballot is not to be condemned if impartially enforced ;
but the good character and good understanding clauses vest too
much arbitrary power in the hands of the registration officers,
and the "grandfather clause" is a piece of class legislation
utterly opposed to American ideals. The only saving feature of
this last measure was its temporary nature, but I regret to say
that in my own state at the election in November, 1912, the
"grandfather clause" was revived by constitutional amendment
until September, 1913, and a premium was thus placed on white
illiteracy.

There are those who would disfranchise every Negro regardless of his fitness for the ballot, and their name is legion.
Supported by such sentiment in their communities, registration
officers have even gone to the extreme of rejecting Negro
college graduates while registering the most degraded of white
men. The suffrage should be held before the Negro as a reward
of character. If our present electoral laws are properly enforced,
every worthy colored man can have the ballot.

6 The Negro is accorded legal, but nevertheless unequal,
treatment in our courts of law. It is not that the Negro is dealt
with unlawfully, but that the punishment of the Negro rests on
a different basis from that of the white man. It is not that
the Negro gets more than his legal deserts, but that the white
man gets less. This is due partly to racial animosity and partly

to the fact that the Negro has little money and very few influential friends. The poor and obscure 'white man in all parts of the country too often suffers in the same way. It is further claimed that a Negro lawyer does not have a fair chance before a white jury when the opposing attorney is a white man, and that a Negro litigant is discriminated against when his opponent and the jury are both white. Juries are sometimes loath to convict white men on the testimony of Negroes, and grand juries likewise have failed to find true bills on such evidence. That the proportion of convictions is greater and the terms of sentence longer for Negroes than for whites has been urged by Southern governors in justification of their extensive use of the pardoning power. Time and again we read in the papers of the execution of "the first white man ever hanged in this county." These facts seem to indicate that the Negro experiences the full rigor of the law, while in the case of the white man justice is likely to be over-tempered with mercy.

As a remedy for this condition it has been proposed that Negroes should serve on juries to try members of their own race, but those who urge that the law should take no account of color must find it hard to defend such a proposition with consistency. The average Southerner demurs to this proposal because he has come to believe that there exists a kind of freemasonry among Negroes that causes them to shield one another from the consequences of their acts ; but in spite of this widespread belief it has been observed that the Negro himself sometimes prefers to place his fate in the hands of a white jury.

7 Finally, the Negro is too frequently the victim of mob violence. With sorrow must we confess that lynching is the evil *par infamie* of the Southland. In 1912 seventeen states were disgraced by lynching atrocities, and the evil was not confined entirely to our section. Montana, North Dakota, Oklahoma, Oregon, and Wyoming each furnished an example. It is no consolation, however, to know that in this respect the Southern states have some company. The most deplorable fact in connection with lynching is the wide hearing given to its defenders. The opponents of such lawlessness, who constitute practically all the enlightened people of the South, have shown a strange timidity in voicing their sentiments, while leather-lunged demagogues, posing as champions of Southern womanhood, have condoned and advocated it from one end of the continent to the other. The only ground upon which they defend lynching is that it furnishes protection to Southern women, but our statistics show that 75 per cent of our lynchings are for crimes other than the one they are supposed to avenge. Happily, the number of lynchings is slowly but surely decreasing. As compared with the black

year, 1892, when there were 225, the number in 1912 was only sixty-five. Of these, only ten were for what is wrongly called "the usual crime," and two were for attempts to commit that crime. In the first three months of 1913 there were thirteen known lynchings, and not one of these was for a crime against women.

The crime of lynching is undoubtedly the source of more irritation, distrust, and despair on the part of the Negro than the sum total of all the other ills to which black flesh is heir. But its degrading effect is even worse upon the white man who sanctions it and upon him who joins the mob. The former is an anarchist and the latter a murderer. In the face of such prevalence of the mob spirit among the ignorant masses, why have bench and bar, preacher and teacher so long remained silent? When will Southern manhood muster sufficient courage to challenge effectively the sovereignty of the mob?

In considering remedies for these untoward conditions it is easy to say what should be done, but difficult to indicate the way to do it. Our hope lies in further education for white and black, in co-operation between the best elements of both races, in greater publicity for those whose views are rational, and last, but not least, in the development of an infinite amount of patience. Civic progress for the Negro is to be secured by educational and economic improvement rather than by political methods. His condition as a citizen will improve with his economic progress; his economic progress is dependent upon an increase of his wants; and an increase of his wants will come with better education. Where the white man is guilty of injustice no merely external reforms will suffice. Such injustice is an outward sign of a lack of inward grace. There must be a reform of men's souls. Better education, higher moral ideals, a general awakening of mind and spirit, the substitution of reason for prejudice and tradition, the socialization of religion—these are the fundamental needs of the hour. Above all, we must realize that as a race we cannot live wholly unto ourselves; that if the black man is sinking we are not rising; that if he is going backward we are not going forward; and finally, that no social regime can long endure that is not founded on justice.

Book Reviews

Our Southern Highlanders: By Horace Kephart. Published by the Outing Publishing Company, New York, 1913. Price, $2.50 *net*.

THOSE to whom the "mountain white" is nothing more than a moonshiner and a feudist, a man without regard for law or life, picturesque, but of small account as an American citizen, should read Mr. Kephart's book, if they would know what makes the "Southern Highlander" the kind of man he is.

The book is an interesting and valuable study of the mountaineer by one who has lived with him and seen him in his daily life. Mr. Kephart does not seek to hide his faults, but he does give a reasonable explanation of them, and he shows that the mountain people have many virtues also.

In a detailed description of the physical geography of Appalachia, the region inhabited by these people, taking in the western part of the states of Georgia, the Carolinas, Tennessee, Kentucky, Virginia, and West Virginia, he shows how environment has been the chief factor in forming the characters of the mountaineers. They have been shut away from the rest of the world from the time they entered this region, and, consequently, "the mountain folk still live in the eighteenth century. In order to be fair and just with these, our backward kinsmen, we must *decivilize* ourselves to the extent of going back, and getting an eighteenth century point of view." In the light of this reasoning, suspicion of strangers, disregard of law, carelessness of human life, are naturally explained. Mr. Kephart makes this the basis of his explanation of those characteristics of the people who are so different from other Americans, and draws many interesting comparisons between the Southern highlander of today and the Scotch highlander of two centuries ago. He feels that the mountaineer's problem is fundamentally an economic one, and that "the future of Appalachia lies mostly in the hands of those resolute native boys and girls who win the education fitting them for leadership," and this education Mr. Kephart believes they will find in vocational schools.   M. L. S.

Soils and Crops: By Hunt and Burkett. Published by the Orange Judd Company, New York. Price, $1.50 *net*.

THIS is a book admirably adapted for use in agricultural high schools. It shows that crop production is the result of two factors. The first factor is environment. This includes the soil properties, such as texture, moisture, heat, air, and plant food. It also includes the atmospheric conditions surrounding the plant, their insect enemies, and plant diseases. The second factor is inheritance. This the farmer makes use of in seed selection and in propagation by cuttings and graftings.

In connection with environment, the book teaches that clay soil is compact because the particles are fine and fit closely together. In order to make a clay soil more productive, the particles must be grouped together, thus making the soil less compact and more congenial to root growth. It also teaches that drainage is a factor in soil improvement in all humid regions, for it influences the air and temperature properties of the soil.

The authors solve the fertilizer problem by first considering the materials that make up a plant; then, the plant foods needed to make these materials; and next, the sources of these plant foods, which are air and soil. The plant food furnished by the air amounts to ninety per cent of all the food. The remaining ten per cent is furnished by the soil. The soil has some of its plant foods in abundance, others have to be supplied by commercial fertilizers.

In trying commercial fertilizers the author maintains it is necessary to apply business methods. For instance, the yield of a crop must be sufficiently increased to pay for the fertilizers, and that grade of fertilizer should be chosen which will produce the greatest increase in yield at the least cost.

The management of farm manure is shown to be an important problem to the farmer. Theoretically, it is best to apply it to the field daily. In practice, this is not usually possible, and good results can be obtained by having the manure in an open shed with a tight floor and walls. On those farms in which the amount of manure is insufficient to keep up the soil fertility, the farmer must rely upon green manuring crops, of which the legumes are the best.

Tillage, the author claims, is possibly the most expensive part of the crop production. The classes of tools used, and the standards of results to be obtained by each, help the farmer to check up his work and estimate its money value.

The farmer's work is not over with preparing for the crop and planting the seed. He must also know how to control insect enemies and plant diseases.

Rotation of crops, to enrich the soil and deprive insect and plant enemies of their food supply, is practiced by all successful farmers; for diversified farming is still the most profitable for the average farmer.

Lastly, the work includes a study of soil requirements, culture methods, and the harvesting and marketing of the leading crops in the various sections of the country. The aim is to give the pupil a chance to compare the yield and value of a crop in his locality with that in other sections of the country. This knowledge will stimulate better crop production and it will lead the pupil to consider whether changes of crops could not wisely be made in his locality.   E. B. G.

The Boy with the U. S. Indians: By Francis Rolt-Wheeler. Published by Lothrop, Lee and Shepard Company. Boston, 1913. Price, $1.50.

THIS is the story of Lost Wolf, a young Arapahoe who was picked up from beside his dead mother after the Wounded Knee Massacre, and his white chum, Virgil Keen. Brought up and educated as a white boy, Lost Wolf's longing for Indian life overcomes his training, and, with no other clue to his identity than his pair of baby moccasins and a few bits of picture writing, he starts West with his friend; to find out who he is and where he belongs. The story of their wanderings forms a slender thread on which hang adventures in many tribes, from the Crows in Montana to the Pueblos and Navahos in the Southwest. From their travels one learns much of Indian life and custom. There are thrilling bits of history, interspersed with descriptions of such ceremonies as attend the Cherokee ball dance or the Hopi snake dance. There is a great deal of information concerning Indian etiquette, the naming of children, why and when warriors are allowed to wear feathers, the division of labor between men and women, and many other things that are told in so interesting a way that one learns without realizing that one is being instructed.

To the boy or girl who longs to read about Indians this book will be a boon. It is exciting enough to hold the attention, and adds to that the virtue of unusual accuracy. It is the fifth volume in the United States Service series, the manuscripts of which are censored by the heads of the Departments with which they deal. This book, therefore, goes forth bearing the approval of both the Bureau of Ethnology and the Indian Office.

The illustrations deserve especial mention. They are obtained from authentic sources, mainly from the Bureau of Ethnology, the American Museum of Natural History, and Mr. E. W. Deming, the well-known illustrator of Indian life. They add greatly to the interest of the book, and all are accompanied by clear and concise descriptions.   C. W. A.

Hampton! My Home by the Sea

R. Nathaniel Dett   R. Nathaniel Dett

1. When the glo-rious day has paled a-way, Great moons in splen-dor shine,
2. As a dove in flight, so flies the night, The stars fade o'er the brim,

At.. Hamp - - ton; Hark! how sweet-ly on the air,
At.. Hamp - - ton; How the soul is stirred with-in,

At Hamp - ton

Then the bells of eve - ning chime! At.. Hamp - - ton!
As we sing each old, old, hymn! At.. Hamp - - ton!

At Hamp - ton

Now the night o'er-flown with glad-ness, Pours its joy from shore to shore;
Say, what is the spell of mag-ic That doth ev-'ry-where a-bound?

Hampton! My Home by the Sea

The dream-ing wa - ters spar - kle, And old caves of o - cean roar!
What tones di - vine - ly trag - ic, Ring with high ce - les - tial sound!

All the world is filled with mus - ic Ech - o an - swers o'er and o'er,
'Tis the blood of all "The Mar-tyr'd Faith - ful" cry - ing from the ground,

"Hamp - - - ton!" Shout, shout the cho - rus, o'er

moun-tain, vale, and plain, The no - ble deeds, the hearts that would be free!
· moun-tain

Then, in a sweet-er, yet more ten-der strain, Sing Hampton, my home by the sea!

At Home and Afield

HAMPTON INCIDENTS

THE HAMPTON CHRISTMAS TREE

"PATTERNIN' after Paris," remarked Hampton's veteran night guard, as he viewed critically the shining glory of hundreds of colored lights in the fir branches of the Hampton community Christmas tree. The brilliancy of the scene might readily suggest the gay streets of the French capital, as they are commonly described, but the comparison could hardly proceed.

The big, growing fir-tree, with the glowing star of light at its tip forty feet above the ground, which shone out "Peace on earth, good will to men" was significant not only of the first Christmas, but also of the present-day spirit of bringing cheerfulness and light to others—that spirit of Christianity and brotherhood which prompted the illumination of the tree in Times Square—and this significance was strongly felt both by the Hampton students and by the hundreds of community visitors who gathered around the tree on the night before Christmas to sing carols and to listen to Christmas music by the band.

The tree was first lighted on the cold, clear Christmas Eve at eight o'clock, the big star blazing out first, growing brighter and brighter, followed by row after row of little, many-colored lights distributed among the branches from the top to the bottom. Every evening during the holiday week it expressed its silent message of cheer from eight o'clock until midnight, ending with New Year's night, when a large number of visitors again joined the students in the singing of carols.

Perhaps no one more enjoyed the tree than groups of little children (and the grown people who watched warily from a distance) who came and danced around it with shouts of glee early in the evening, spiritually unencumbered by any restraining elder presence.

Toward the kind Northern friend who conceived the plan of a community Christmas tree at Hampton and who made possible the realization of the plan after the decision of Hampton's authorities that the school could not this year afford such a luxury, much gratitude is felt by all who enjoyed the beautiful scene.

NEW YEAR'S DAY

JANUARY first has a double celebration at Hampton and its significance to the colored people as Emancipation Day is probably greater than its importance as the first day of the year.

In the morning occurred the New Year prayer meeting and the annual exercises of the Senior Class, whose custom it is to unveil their class motto on this date. At nine o'clock the Class of 1914, girls in white and boys in uniform, marched into chapel and took their seats on the platform. Brief devotional exercises were followed by a speech from the president of the class, Solomon D. Spady, who had for his text the motto itself, "To co-operate and uplift." As he pronounced the words two members of the class came forward and lifted the covering from their chosen escutcheon, which will, during the coming year, according to custom, inspire Hampton students from the wall of the main dining-room.

In the afternoon, Emancipation exercises were held in the Gymnasium. A large number of the colored population of Hampton formed ranks and marched to the Institute grounds, headed by the school band under the leadership of a mounted chief marshal, Mr. C. H. Jarvis. Rev. A. A. Graham, the presiding officer, introduced several prominent Negro citizens who made excellent ten-minute speeches. The Emancipation Proclamation was read, and received with ·enthusiasm, and addresses of welcome were given by a Hampton Negro student and a Hampton Indian student.

In the evening, students and teachers with a few outside friends met in Huntington Memorial Library for an informal observance of the library's tenth anniversary, January 1, 1904, being the date that the building was first opened for the circulation of literature. The dedication hymn, written by Miss Helen Ludlow to Haydn's music, which appears in most hymn-books with Addison's words on "The Creation," and first heard on April 28, 1903, the date of the dedication of the library in Anniversary week of that year, was sung by all present. Dr. Frissell then spoke of the great value which the library, under the charge of competent and interested workers, has been to the school. A printed notice showing statistics for the past ten years gave the following figures : January 1904 to January 1914—Attendance, 578,742; volumes added, 23,943; books circulated,133,899; pictures circulated, 26,780 ; magazines circulated, 8,496.

When the building was opened ten years ago the library had 13,000 volumes ; it has now approximately 35,000 volumes.

ENTERTAINMENTS

" RUBBER BOOTS " was the title of an amusing, one-act farce presented by the King's Daughters in Cleveland Hall Chapel, Saturday evening, January 17, to an appreciative audience. Three sisters, left alone in the house and very much afraid of tramps, tried to show their bravery in a crisis, and a series of funny events ensued, in which the sisters succeeded in thoroughly scaring each other, and a harmless tramp reaped all the benefit. A pair of rubber boots figured largely in the plot and occasioned most of the mistakes in identity which furnished the fun. The parts were all well taken and won much applause, the tramp being especially good.

The farce was followed by very interesting moving pictures, including scenes from "The Merchant of Venice " and two comic reels which were cordially received by the student audience.

On Sunday evening after chapel exercises a large audience in Cleveland Hall Chapel, including many visitors from the Fort and from Hampton, saw the moving pictures representing "John Henry's" four years at Hampton, which will be a feature of the Northern campaign meetings this winter. The majority of those present had never seen the pictures, as they have been shown at Hampton only once before, last July, when there were but few teachers and students on the grounds. Nothing is more vitally interesting than "to see ourselves as others see us" and laughter and applause testified to the intimate appreciation of scenes showing the trials and triumphs of a Hampton student.

RELIGIOUS WORK

THE Rev. Dr. John R. Gow, pastor of the Calvary Baptist Church, Minneapolis, Minnesota, was the only visiting minister heard by Hampton audiences during the past month. He preached in Memorial Church on Sunday, January 11, from a text in the eleventh chapter of John : "Lazarus, come forth." At chapel exercises in the evening, he spoke forcefully on the subject of "Self-mastery." Other religious exercises have been conducted by Dr. Eldridge Mix, Dr. Turner, and school officers.

The first week in January, observed at the school as] a week of prayer, proved a great inspiration to all. The central theme for the discussions of the week was Christ. The leaders of the boys' meetings were Dr. Frissell, Dr. Mix, Dr. Turner, Major Moton, and Mr. Gates. As the meetings progressed and enthusiasm livened, an invitation was extended to all those who were not professing Christians to openly signify their intention to live a Christian life. Thirteen of the sixty-four who are not church members rose. The girls' meetings were led by Miss Johnston, Miss Holmes, Miss Walter, Miss Flora Low, and Mrs. W. T. B. Williams. Thirteen of the twenty-two girls who are not now church members expressed a desire to join the communicants' class to be conducted by Miss Johnston and Miss Holmes. The week of prayer was observed by the Shellbanks Farm Y. M. C. A. during the second week in January, the meetings being in charge of Dr. Mix, Mr. Aery, Rev. J. W. Patterson, Major Moton, and student leaders from the main branch. All but one of the non-professing boys professed Christ before the week was over.

Mr. Charles B. Randall, a Hampton graduate of 1899, now engaged as Y. M. C. A. county secretary in Brunswick County, Virginia, addressed the Y. M. C. A. on January 18, in a most inspiring talk. He presented conditions throughout the district where he works as typical of most of the rural communities in the South. He spoke of the crying need of the country for educated colored men to go back to their own communities and just live according to their education as examples for the people to follow. If the country boy, after receiving an education, should return to his own people and help build up the community, the problem in the South would be largely solved. There is a dead-level of existence throughout the country, a lack of inspiration and high ideals to work for. Preparation for

such service is best attained at Hampton by doing something in the community work carried on by the school.

During the vacation holidays, a social was held for the boys in Clarke Hall, at which "fairy bowling" was again played and thoroughly enjoyed. "Blow football" tested the lung capacity of another group, besides furnishing much laughter for the onlookers.

ATHLETICS

HAVING defeated the Armstrong Manual Training School, of Washington, D. C., interscholastic champions of last season, by the score 28-16, and the Hiawatha Club, of Washington, by a score of 40-16, the Hampton basket-ball team went up to New York on January 16 with hope in their hearts that this year might mark a double triumph over Howard. The result, however, proved that Hampton must be content with her football glory, for Howard, in a very close game, won by a score of 27-24.

During the holidays, interclass football games and basket ball between the Indians and the soldiers at the Fort were the source of much interest and enthusiasm. Two of the three games played by the Indian team and the soldiers resulted in victories for the Hampton boys.

HAMPTON WORKERS

AT a patrons' meeting held recently at the Buckroe School, one of the series of meetings being held this winter in the Negro schools of Elizabeth City County, words of encouragement were given to the assembled parents and friends by Miss Ida A. Tourtellot, Miss Sarah J. Walter, Major R. R. Moton, Mr. Frank K. Rogers, and Mr. W. A. Aery, all Hampton workers : and by Mrs. Ellen A. Weaver, General Armstrong's sister, who is spending the winter at the school. Mrs. Smith, the president of the Patrons' League, told of the improvements that have already been made and urged further co-operation with the teacher, Miss

Mamie Bassette, to increase the attractiveness of the school.

At the eighth annual conference of principals and teachers of the secondary colored schools of Virginia, held in Richmond on December 26 and 27, two Hampton workers, Capt. G. W. Blount, and Mr. W. T. B. Williams, were among the speakers. Captain Blount's paper was on "Practical Instruction in Business Methods and Principles" and Mr. Williams discussed "The Association of Industrial and Secondary Schools."

A bulletin of the National League on Urban Conditions among Negroes, issued in December 1913, stating the purposes, plan of organization, achievements, and further plans of the association, has on its list of officers Major R. R. Moton as vice chairman.

A meeting in the interest of neighborhood work in Phoebus was held in Zion Church in January, at which Mrs. Bowles, who is connected with the New York Y. W. C. A. and is assisting Mrs. Hunton in the organization of branch associations, helped to make plans for future work. It is hoped to revive the work which was carried on under the leadership of Mrs. Morton, who has recently moved to Norfolk. Miss Elizabeth Hyde and Miss Carrie Erskine, of Hampton Institute, were present, and Miss Hyde spoke to those assembled on the subject of "Safeguarding Girls."

Several new workers have come to Hampton to take the places of those who have left during the past term. Miss Rowena Jackson, a graduate of Mechanics' Institute, Rochester, N. Y., is teacher of domestic science at the Holly Tree Inn, a position left vacant by Miss Anna Barnum. Miss Jackson has been connected with the Colored Orphan Asylum at Riverdale-on-Hudson, New York. Miss Virginia Diestel, of Hampton, is filling Miss Rebecca Barnum's place in the post office. Miss Katherine L. MacMahan, of Philadelphia, Pa., has been engaged as teacher of physical culture to succeed Miss Isabel Dowell. Mr. Charles

E. Brett, who has studied at the Massachusetts Agricultural College and at Rhode Island Agricultural College, is teaching agricultural subjects, there being a vacancy in that department, through the resignation of Miss Ethel B. Gowans.

Announcements of the marriage, in New York City on January 10, of Mr. Jerome Faber Kidder, a Hampton worker, and Miss Lavinia Barker Frissell, niece of Hampton's principal, were received at Hampton the first of the month. Mr. and Mrs. Kidder arrived at the school on January 19.

WHITTIER SCHOOL

THE membership of the Armstrong Guards, under the direction of Mr. Harrison M. Magill, Hampton, '08, manual training teacher at the Whittier, has increased to thirty. Meetings are held three evenings a week from seven to nine o'clock. On Monday, business is transacted and some such instruction as the Boy Scouts receive is given to the members by the leader; on Wednesday, the meeting is held in the Gymnasium and is devoted principally to basket ball; and on Friday, the members play indoor games, some of which have been made by the boys in the Whittier manual training classes. Only the boys of the upper grades are eligible for membership in the Guards, and the smaller children, who are not encouraged to go out on the streets in the evening, enjoy games in the Gymnasium one afternoon a week. All of this work, which contributes much to the activity and usefulness of the Whittier School, is under the personal supervision of Mr. Magill.

VISITORS

HAMPTON is glad to welcome Miss Mary T. Galpin, a former worker, for a winter visit among friends on the grounds. Other ex-Hampton workers who have been recent visitors are Miss Mary Gray Clark, of Westfield, N. J., niece of Miss Emma Johnston, and Miss Mary Alma Coe, of Boston. Miss

Louise Dodd, Mrs. Frissell's sister, is spending several weeks at the school.

Holiday guests at Hampton were Dr. and Mrs. George W. Crary at "The Moorings;" Miss Mix, a teacher at the Farmville Normal School, who came to spend a few days with her father, Dr. Eldridge Mix; Dr. and Mrs. Henry W. Nelson and Miss Margaret Nelson, of Marshfield Hills, Massachusetts; and Sir Horace Plunkett, of Ireland, who spent Christmas Day at Hampton and spoke to the students in chapel on the evening of Dec. 24.

Other distinguished visitors during the past month have been Professor Frank Day of the Carnegie Institute of Technology, Pittsburgh, and Mrs. Day; Miss Elizabeth Gilman, daughter of the late president of Johns Hopkins University; Miss Grace Miller, of New York, a cousin of Mrs. Frissell; Professor Bruce Wyman, formerly of the Harvard Law School, and Mrs. Wyman; Mr. and Mrs. Finley J. Shepard, of Lyndhurst, Irvington-on-Hudson, and Mr. Finley's sister, Mrs. Wright; Mr. George Morris, of Villa Nova, Pa., whose wife was formerly Miss Fanny Hillard, a teacher at Hampton; Dr. J. N. Roy, of Montreal, Canada; and Dr. P. H. Thompson, president of Koskiusko Industrial College, Mississippi.

GRADUATES AND EX-STUDENTS

THE position as sales manager, at St. Paul's School, Lawrenceville, Va., left vacant by Royal A. B. Crump '09, who is now studying at Virginia Union University, Richmond, has been filled by Solomon Phillips, '03.

James D. Washington, '10, who has for two years been principal of the graded school in Denton, Md., is now teaching at his own home in Essex Co., Va.

Georgia W. Walker, '08, is teaching at Woods Cross Roads, Va.

Eustace A. Selby, '10, formerly teacher of printing at the Chistiansburg Institute, Cambria, Va., is now manager of the Eastern Clarion Printing Company at Lynchburg, Va.

Alma M. Stanton, '10, has recently been appointed industrial teacher in the Brownsville School at Hamilton, Loudoun Co., Va.

James F. McCoy, '06, has resigned the position of farm manager at the Christiansburg Institute, Cambria, Va., which he has held for six years, to become principal of the Gainsboro Graded School in Roanoke, Va.

A school near Williamsburg, Va., is under the management of two Hampton graduates—Mrs. Josephine Taylor Harris, post graduate, '03, and Bessie B. Reed, '11, who has this year been appointed her assistant.

Russell C. Atkins, '10, is teacher of agriculture at the Slater Normal and Industrial School, Winston-Salem, S. C., where his father, Dr. S. G. Atkins, is principal.

Alice G. Bryant, post graduate '12, is teacher of cooking and dining-room matron at Clafflin University, Orangeburg, S. C.

Gertrude N. Norman, '10, is teaching at her home in Dunbrook, Essex Co., Va.

Vivian R. Trigg, '09, who has since her graduation been a teacher at the Whittier School, is now assistant in the public graded school at her home in Lynchburg, Va.

THE position of industrial supervisor of rural schools in York and Warwick Counties, Va., is being filled by Lucy Lee Jones, '98.

Major M. Hubert, post graduate, '12, is teacher of agriculture at the Prentiss Normal and Industrial Institute, Prentiss, Miss.

Henry S. Ewell, '04, is teaching printing at the Manassas Industrial School, Manassas, Va.

Lorenzo E. Hall, '03, who has been for the past three years assistant farm manager at the Penn School, Frogmore, S. C., is now a farm-demonstration agent at Whiteville, Columbus Co., N. C.

Clarence M. Grey, '12, is now a contractor and builder at Roanoke, Va.

MARRIAGES

THE marriage of Nancy R. Walker, '08, and Edward G. Bryant, Trade School, '03, occurred at the bride's home at Mt. Meigs, Alabama, on November 19. Mr. and Mrs. Bryant will live in Savannah, Georgia.

Antoinette Norvell, '02, was married to Simeon R. Cohen on November 26 in Charleston, S. C. They will make their home at Summerville, S. C.

Announcement has been received of the marriage on December 21, of Maggie J. Ross, '95, to Charles A. Evans, in New York City.

A letter from Ella L. Hawes, '05, tells of her marriage to William H. Holloway, professor of sociology and in charge of extension work at Talladega College, Ala.

The marriage of K. Josephine Minter, '09, and Junius W. Boyd took place at Roanoke, Va., on November 1.

The wedding of Ethel Geneva, '11, to Walter G. Young, Agriculture '10, occurred in December, at the Carmel Presbyterian Church in Chester, South Carolina.

Announcement of the marriage of Grace D. George, '11, to Solomon G. Slade, at the bride's home in Runnymede, Virginia, has been received.

The marriage of Hattie C. Daggs, '08, to John Lattimore, of Hampton, Va., occurred on November 20.

DEATHS

THE death of Mrs. Ellen White Reid at her home near Suffolk, Va., occurred on November 26, 1913.

Robert H. Evans, '99, died in Los Angeles December 8, 1913. He had been following his trade as carpenter for several years in that city.

George L. Pryor, '72, died in New York City in November, 1913.

David D. Weaver, '72, died at his home in Newport News, Va., on December 14, 1913.

News has been received of the sudden death of Dr. Malcolm J. Winn, '94, in Columbus, Ohio, on December 18, 1913.

INDIAN NOTES

SEVERAL former Hampton students are now employed] in the Government Boarding School at Oneida, Wisconsin. Lena Ludwick,| Normal Course, '10, is teaching, Minnie Skenandore is assistant seamstress, Lydia Webster House is baker, Jesse Cornelius holds the position of carpenter, as he has for a number of years, and Reuben Baird, '04, has recently been appointed farmer.

Robert Blodgett writes that he is working on a fruit ranch in Wineville, California.

Ralph White, who finished the business course in 1910, is employed in the Reclamation Service, and has been working for some time on the Fort Peck Project in Montana.

Martin Sampson is general mechanic at the Indian School on the Fort Peck Reservation.

Gilbert Lowe is this year attending school at Heidelberg University, Tiffin, Ohio.

Word has recently reached Hampton of the death of Mrs. Louisa Quinney Dextater, who graduated from the Normal Course in 1901. She was a teacher for a number of years after leaving school, and since her marriage in 1908 has been occupied with the duties of her home. She leaves a husband and children.

Stella O'Donnell, '10, who since leaving Hampton has completed the Business Course at the Haskell Institute, has recently been appointed stenographer at the Pawnee Agency in Oklahoma.

Word has reached Hampton of the marriage of Ruth McIntosh, '07· She is now Mrs. George Rebo,and is living in Dooley, Montana.

THE following letter is from a former student, who came to Hampton as a care-free little girl more than thirty years ago. That time has not dimmed her recollections or her affection is very evident, and it is in such results as this shows that Hampton feels most pride and pleasure. She writes:

"It is many years since I was at Hampton, but everything is as fresh in my memory as though it was yesterday. There never is a Christmas that passes but somehow I feel lonesome for Hampton, for it was there that I learned what Christmas meant. I look back and think what a careless, thoughtless girl I was. I never could settle myself down to be sober and thoughtful. I only thought of fun all the time, and now I am a grandmother. I have nine living children and I have certainly had some rough places to travel over, but I have tried to stick to my principles. When those that I knew failed to do right, and fell, I never went back on them, but gave them my right hand and helped them to right their wrongs, sometimes at my own cost. If there is any evil plot going on that I know about I generally put a stop to it. Of course I have never distinguished myself, but in my own quiet, unknown way I have tried to lead those that I have had anything to do with to the right. It isn't much. I wish I could have done great things, when I remember my teachers that tried so hard to educate me, but I have never had time. I have been busy with my children, and now it's my grandchildren. I shall try and send some worthy boys to Hampton. I hope Hampton lives on and grows in grace and strength as the years come and go."

NOTES AND EXCHANGES

INDIANS AS FARMERS

THE most remarkable fair ever held in the state of Nevada was in progress during last September. Practically all of the exhibits of this fair were the individual contributions of the Indians on the Pyramid Lake Reservation. The exhibition comprised cattle, horses, poultry, vegetables, farm products of all descriptions, bead and basket work, leather work, and domestic science exhibits, including pies, cakes, doughnuts, jellies, and canned fruits. The most notable feature of the fair was an exhibit by an Indian of fifty-three different varieties of grain and vegetables, which he had raised on a farm of fifteen acres. Stalks of corn eleven feet high, pumpkins weighing from fifty to ninety pounds, squashes, beets, tomatoes, and potatoes of excellent quality and size were shown. Wheat and oats had large full heads and some stalks were seven feet high. The fruit display was splendid, the apples, peaches, and plums being the equal of any on the Eastern market.

The Indian's Friend

George Kapayou, of the Iowa Sac and Fox Agency, took first prize on his yellow dent seed-corn at the Tama County Fair. There were five white men who had entered against him, and this is the first time that an Indian ever showed in competition with white men at this fair.

Indian School Journal

C. W. Crawford, federal agricultural agent for the full-blood Indians, reports that the Indians of Carter County, Okla., took ten of the fourteen prizes offered at the new state fair at Muskogee. The full-blood exhibit was taken to the Dry Farming Congress at Tulsa.   *The Oklahoman*

NEGRO WOMEN

IN the *Individualist* of September-October, an English paper published in London, Dr. Frances Hoggan, an Englishwoman who has traveled and observed widely and who is particularly interested in the development of the Negro race, has an article on "American Negro Women During Their First Fifty Years of Freedom." She says:

"Working with determination and energy when once they realized the dignity of labour, numbers of Negro women obtained education and training. Having cast away from them the feeling that work was lowering, they set themselves to become practically efficient. I could tell much of the special aptitude shown by so many Negro women for the work of education, including the power of imparting to the children that courtesy which is one of their own most marked characteristics, both in Africa and America. Fifty years ago Negro women were uneducated, poor, downtrodden; they are now rapidly emerging into a state of civilized and cultured prosperity."

LEARNING TO PLAY

THE author of "Education by Plays and Games," George E. Johnson, has been made head of the newly created Department of Play and Recreation in the New York School of Philanthropy. This is the first department of the kind in any educational institution in this country. Professor Johnson will develop and train superintendents and secretaries of playground and recreation associations.

NEGRO TAXABLE WEALTH

THE following is from a 20-page booklet containing "Facts of Interest to the People of Laurens County [Georgia]":

"In 1910 the Negroes in Laurens County owned 33,194 acres of land, an increase of 76 per cent in ten years; household goods and utensils, $101,885, an increase of 377 per cent; farm animals, $163,309, an increase of 361 per cent. Total aggregate wealth $589,597, an increase of 322 per cent. The total aggregate wealth on the tax digest for both races in the county was a little more than doubled in 10 years, but taxable wealth of the Negroes was more than quadrupled during this period. This enormous gain in property ownership by Negroes in the county is most largely due to the fact that standing-rent tendency is the rule. They increase in wealth less rapidly where share-renting is the rule. The standing-rent tenants in Laurens outnumber the share tenants about two to one."

A comment by the county superintendent in the preface says: "I think it is as essential that the people know these facts as it is to know any other secular facts in the world. I would be glad if every teacher would require every pupil above the fourth grade to master the facts herein contained as thoroughly as they require the mastery of any lesson."

U. S. HELPING STATE SCHOOLS

THREE hundred thousand dollars of Government money are about to be distributed to the rural schools in 40 counties of eastern Oklahoma that were formerly in Indian Territory. This is money appropriated by Congress to assist the schools in lieu of making the land of the Indians non-taxable and thereby cutting off the income for schools by taxation. The idea of the Government is to furnish sufficient funds to keep the rural schools running eight months, and to put enough Government money in to make up what the school district lacks in money raised by taxation. There are 2000 rural schools that will share in the money in one way or another.

Indian School Journal

A COURSE FOR SOCIAL WORKERS

THE American Interchurch College of Nashville, Tenn., is offering a six years' course for religious and social workers from January 7 to February 17. The schedule includes six courses: The home and public health; child welfare and eugenics; crime and mental hygiene; the care and treatment of a city's dependents; the church and social service; race relationships and co-operation for civic betterment. Mornings will be devoted to research and visits to Nashville institutions, afternoons to classroom lectures and conferences with specialists, and evenings to Bible study and public lectures delivered in the churches by some of the most prominent ministers, educators, and social workers in the country.

"The value of this school work is enhanced one hundred per cent by repeating the same courses for colored people at the Nashville Institute, which is the Negro Department of the Interchurch College."–*Taken from preliminary announcement*

Song of the Armstrong League.

H. W. LUDLOW.

Air :—Hawaiian Hymn.

1. Not where our he - ro lies, Seek ye with weep - ing eyes,
Far front his ban - ner flies, Rings his com - mand.

REFRAIN.

Strong arm to cleave the way, Strong will to win the day,
Strong soul to live for aye, For God and land.

2 March on to duty then,
  Quit you like valiant men;
  Pledge now and once again
    Head, heart and hand.—*Ref.*

3 On, where the colors lead,
  On, for the people's need,
  On, truth and right to speed,
    Do all, and stand.—*Ref.*

4 E'er see that banner wave,
  Give as he freely gave,
  Live as he lived to save,
    Brave Hampton band.—*Ref.*

MARCH 1914

THE
SOUTHERN
WORKMAN

Press of
The Hampton Normal and Agricultural Institute
Hampton, Virginia

The Hampton Normal and Agricultural Institute

HAMPTON VIRGINIA

What it is   An undenominational industrial school founded in 1868 by Samuel Chapman Armstrong for Negro youth. Indians admitted in 1878.

Object   To train teachers and industrial leaders

Equipment   Land, 1060 acres; buildings, 140

Courses   Academic, trade, agriculture, business, home economics

Enrollment   Negroes, 1215; Indians, 37; total, 1252

Results   Graduates, 1709; ex-students, over 6000
Outgrowths: Tuskegee, Calhoun, Mt. Meigs, and many smaller schools for Negroes

Needs $125,000 annually above regular income
$4,000,000 Endowment Fund
Scholarships

A full scholarship for both academic and industrial instruction	$ 100
Academic scholarship	70
Industrial scholarship	30
Endowed full scholarship	2500

Any contribution, however small, will be gratefully received and may be sent to H. B. FRISSELL, Principal, or to F. K. ROGERS, Treasurer, Hampton, Virginia.

FORM OF BEQUEST

I give and devise to the trustees of The Hampton Normal and Agricultural Institute, Hampton, Virginia, the sum of   dollars, payable

The Southern Workman

Published monthly by

The Hampton Normal and Agricultural Institute

Contents for March 1914

THE SOUTHERN WORKMAN was founded by Samuel Chapman Armstrong in 1872, and is a monthly magazine devoted to the interests of undeveloped races.

It contains reports from Negro and Indian populations, with pictures of reservation and plantation life, as well as information concerning Hampton graduates and ex-students who since 1868 have taught more than 250,000 children in the South and West. It also provides a forum for the discussion of ethnological, sociological, and educational problems in all parts of the world.

CONTRIBUTIONS: The editors do not hold themselves responsible for the opinions expressed in contributed articles. Their aim is simply to place before their readers articles by men and women of ability without regard to the opinions held.

EDITORIAL STAFF

H. B. FRISSELL
HELEN W. LUDLOW
J. E. DAVIS

W. L. BROWN
W. A. AERY, Business Manager
W. T. B. WILLIAMS

TERMS: One dollar a year in advance: ten cents a copy

CHANGE OF ADDRESS: Persons making a change of address should send the *old* as well as the *new* address to

THE SOUTHERN WORKMAN, Hampton, Virginia

Entered as second-class matter August 13, 1908, in the Post Office at Hampton, Virginia, under the Act of July 16, 1894

THE HAMPTON LEAFLETS

Any twelve of the following numbers of the "The Hampton Leaflets" obtained free of charge by any Southern teacher or superintendent. *A charge cents per dozen is made to other applicants.* Cloth-bound volumes for 1905, ' and '08 will be furnished at seventy-five cents each, postpaid.

VOL. I

1 Experiments in Physics (Heat)
2 Sheep: Breeds, Care, Management
3 Transplanting
4 Birds Useful to Southern Farmers
5 Selection and Care of Dairy Cattle
6 Care and Management of Horses
7 How to Know the Trees by Their Bark
8 Milk and Butter
9 Commercial Fertilizers
10 Swine: Breeds, Care, Management
11 Fruits of Trees
12 December Suggestions

VOL. II

1 Suggestions to Teachers Preparing Students for Hampton Institute
2 Experiments in Physics (Water)
3 Spring Blossoms: Shrubs and Trees
4 School Gardening
5 Drainage
6 Mosquitoes
7 Roots
8 Seed Planting
9 Housekeeping Rules
10 Prevention of Tuberculosis
11 Thanksgiving Suggestions
12 Some Injurious Insects

VOL. III

1 Proper Use of Certain Words
2 Winter Buds
3 Domestic Arts at Hampton Institute
4 Beautifying Schoolhouses and Yards
5 Responsibility of Teachers for the Health of Their Children
6 Manual Training in Rural Schools
7 Rotation of Crops
8 Life History of a Butterfly
9 How Seeds Travel
10 Nature Study for Primary Grades
11 Arbor Day
12 Evergreen Trees

VOL. IV

1 Plants
2 How to Attract the Birds
3 The Story of Corn
4 The Story of Cotton
5 The Meaning of the Flower
6 A Child's Garden
7 The Winged Pollen-Carriers
8 Soils
9 Care of Poultry
10 Plowing and Harrowing
11 Transplanting of Shrubs and Vin
12 Transplanting and Pruning of T

VOL. V

1 Teaching Reading to Children
2 Culture and Marketing of Peanu
3 The House Fly a Carrier of Dis
4 Culture and Marketing of Tobac
5 Virginia's Fishing Industry
6 Farm Manures
7 Soil Moisture and After-cultivati
8 Patent Medicines
9 Hookworm Disease
10 Reading in the Grammar Schools
11 Oystering in Hampton Roads
12 Common Sense in Negro Public

VOL. VI

1 Sewing Lessons for Rural Schoo
2 Housekeeping and Sanitation in Rural Schools
3 Canning Fruits and Vegetables
4 Manual Training, Part II
5 Patrons' Meetings
6 Correlation of Industrial and Ac Subjects in Rural Schools
7 Southern Workman Special Inde
8 Community Clubs for Women an
9 Housekeeping and Cooking Less Rural Communities
10 Fifty Years of Negro Progress
11 Approved Methods for Home Lau
12 Number Steps for Beginners

Address: Publication Office, The Hampton Normal and Agric Institute, Hampton, Virginia

The
Southern Workman

VOL. XLIII   MARCH 1914   NO. 3

Editorials

An Indian Get-together Meeting

A new phase in the work of the Society of American Indians was inaugurated on February 14 by a meeting and banquet in Philadelphia. Inasmuch as the annual Conference is held in the West the officers of the Society feel that many deeply interested persons are unable to attend, and that a series of "get-together-and-get-acquainted meetings" should be held at points convenient to the Indians and their friends.

The initial meeting was a most pleasant and successful one, and seems to justify the extension of the idea. At the afternoon session, held in the Academy of Natural Sciences, speeches were made by Hon. Gabe Parker, Register of the Treasury, Herbert Welsh, of the Indian Rights Association, General Pratt, P. J. Hurley, attorney for the Choctaw Nation, H. B. Peairs, Supervisor of Indian Schools, and others. The banquet in the evening was followed by more addresses, the guest of honor being Hon. Cato Sells, Commissioner of Indian Affairs. Commissioner Sells' speech showed his genuine interest and the very real earnestness with which he regards the work of directing the affairs of a race, and, to quote from his own words, his "desire to understand the viewpoint of the Indian." That his attitude is appreciated was shown by one of the speakers of the afternoon who referred to the Commissioner as a man who "regarded his work, not as a job, but as an opportunity."

Possibly the most valuable and significant feature of the meeting was the coming together of so many individuals and r epresentatives of societies who, with such widely varying methods and ideas, are all working toward the same end. Good results can hardly fail to be brought about by the cordial relations and mutual understanding fostered by such a gathering. That the Indian's voice is welcomed, perhaps for the first time, in advising and consulting in matters which so vitally concern him is in itself a great step, and one which augurs well for the future of the race and for the Society whose members are so unselfishly and earnestly trying to bring about better days for their people.

A School for the Unprivileged In the depths of a beautiful forest of oak and pine in the highlands of northwestern Georgia may be found a unique institution, or rather, two institutions—one twelve years old for boys, one four years old, for girls. These three hundred girls and boys are of homogeneous stock—pure Anglo-Saxon. To gain a place in this school they must belong to the "unprivileged" class. Miss Martha Berry, daughter of an aristocratic Southern family, is the principal of both schools, and has devoted the two thousand acres of land which was her inheritance, and also her time and strength and love since the beginning of the boys' school in a log cabin in 1902, to "giving a chance" to the neglected children of the mountain whites. Miss Berry has rigidly adhered from the beginning to her desire to help only the unprivileged, refusing flattering offers of money for the tuition of those able to pay but also able to obtain an education elsewhere.

These mountain boys and girls are asked to pay only fifty dollars a year for the privilege of developing hearts, heads, and hands under the direction of devoted, capable, cultured men and women. The boys in their school and the girls in theirs (a village of log cabins) do all the work of washing, ironing, mending, cooking, gardening, and dairying, besides receiving instruction in college preparatory studies and in all kinds of hand work. No outside labor of any kind, except that of instructors, is employed. Some of the pupils are backward and awkward, but a spirit of helpfulness seems to pervade the institution, and a sixteen-year-old may be in the beginners' class without provoking a smile. Life is too earnest and everybody is too intent on making the most of the "chance" Miss Berry has given them.

All these young people are poor and, as a rule, go back to work hard on poor mountain farms or at their trades in small mountain hamlets. Yet, at the tenth anniversary of the boys' school, the one thousand former students showed their devotion to the school by presenting their beloved founder with one thousand dollars to help her in the expansion of her work. Such loyalty and devotion promise well for the future of the Berry School.

Significance of the Lincoln Memorial In the course of a sermon preached by Dr. Eldridge Mix in Memorial Church, Hampton Institute, on the Sunday morning following the birthday of Abraham Lincoln, on the text, "And the Lord was with Joseph, and he was a prosperous man, and he was in the house of the Egyptian," the following reference was made to Lincoln:

"Is there not a striking parallel between Joseph and Abraham Lincoln, whose birth a grateful nation commemorated the other day? They each had to struggle against almost hopeless outward conditions in their youthful days; the one with bondage and all its degradation in an alien land, alone and unprotected by human hand; the other in bondage to abject poverty, not of his own making, with all its seeming helplessness. Both, with help vouchsafed from Heaven, won the respect and confidence of their fellow-men, and of those superior to them in position, by their indomitable will in rightdoing, their sterling worth of character, their uprightness and trustworthiness, their unselfish service in behalf of others. They conquered adverse outward conditions by self-mastery, made formidable hindrances stepping stones in upward climbing, surmounted seemingly insuperable difficulties by transforming them into helps upward. At length they were each exalted to the highest seats of power and supremacy by the will and choice of those whom they had so unselfishly served. They in turn honored their high office by delivering the people they governed in time of greatest peril from impending destruction. Their names will alike be held in everlasting remembrance on earth and in heaven.

"Only fifty years have elapsed since Lincoln fell by the hands of an assassin, leaving the country terribly torn and impoverished by the ravages of war, and still rent with the enmity and bitterness by which the war was engendered, though peace had been declared and the contending armies disbanded. The birthday of the savior of the Republic was celebrated the other day in its capital city by breaking ground for the erection of a worthy national monument to his memory, for which Congress, whose members are largely from the South, has appropriated

$2,000,000. It was truly a fitting thing, and withal singularly significant, that a former Confederate army officer, with uncovered head, should open the proceedings on that occasion; that an ex-senator from Kentucky, also with head uncovered, should be the first to put the spade into the ground and in so doing speak in high praise of the President against whom he fought a half-century ago; that one of the senators of the present Congress, representing the same Southern state, should be heard to say, 'This monument will show to the world who it is that is regarded as the greatest of Americans, and that he is so held by the South as well as by the North.' It was a member of the Senate from North Carolina who made the motion, of his own accord and without pre-arrangement, that the Senate adjourn out of respect to the memory of Lincoln. That motion was preceded by the reading of Lincoln's Gettysburg address by another senator from the South. One cannot but exclaim in view of these facts, What hath God wrought by this man of His choosing!''

The Indians' Opportunity for Service In Indian affairs it seems evident that as fast as general policies are settled unforeseen questions constantly arise. On another page of this issue will be found an article by Mr. John M. Oskison on Arizona and her Indian problems. This article reflects the conflict of interests between the Indian and the white man, inevitable whenever the increasing population of the West brings the two people together. That these problems are difficult and perplexing is evident to even the casual reader. To the parties interested they may well become so acute, as this article says, that "every man who touches upon them becomes excited and suspicious towards every other man. '' How they will be solved remains to be seen, but it is probably safe to say that, however justly they are settled, some interests must suffer, and in such cases we have usually seen the Indian suffer most. In Arizona there is, for the most part, a friendly feeling towards the Indians and it is to be hoped that here the more powerful race will deal fairly with the natives and will recognize their rights.

But, even so, the Indians cannot expect to have it all their own way. At best, there will have to be concessions on both sides. In the matter of grazing lands, for example, one side is as badly off as the other ; for all the grazing lands are said to be full already, and the organizations of white stockmen are reported to be taking steps for limiting the size of their flocks and herds. How, then, may the Indian expect to be given extensive additional grazing lands ? What is the just and all-around fair thing to be done ? These are interesting questions—the more interesting in proportion as they are the more dispassionately studied. And they must be studied dispassionately in order to arrive at, or help others to reach, fair conclusions.

Here, then, is an opportunity for the educated young Indians to be of real service to their people and perhaps also to the Government. They might very well study this Arizona situation, for instance, and become familiar with the problem here in all its bearings. With their better education and broader knowledge they could understand many things which would not be understood by the older Indians. It seems evident that if, with this advantage, some of them would take up these questions, get at the actual facts, and make a thorough investigation in a calm and temperate spirit, they might not only help their people to see clearly and act wisely, but also be of real service to the Government in finding a way out which would be as fair to both sides as the circumstances permit.

Hampton in the North Twenty cities have recently heard Hampton. Twenty thousand people, old and young, in six states have applauded the songs and have watched the faces of the Hampton singers. Thousands have clapped hands as they saw a country Negro boy pass from his cabin home through Hampton's daily round and lead his company of trained men, "marching in the light," ready for service. Thousands have caught the meaning of Hampton as never before from the motion pictures of a black boy's struggles interpreted by plantation melodies in a manner that no words convey.

A dozen men whose names loom large in the affairs of education, politics, religion, and philanthropy, have pled for Hampton in various cities of the East. Such leaders as Hon. George McAneny, Congressman Samuel Walker McCall, Judge Job Hedges, President John Finley, President Rush Rhees, ex-Governor Mann, Bishop Perry, Dr. Welch, and Dr. John Brashear, were willing to bear witness to the value of Hampton's work.

Among Hampton's own trustees who spoke for the school were George Foster Peabody, Dr. Wm. Jay Schieffelin, and Dr. Francis Peabody ; and Hampton's greatest graduate came far and gave freely of his strength and time to win new friends for the school through his great gift of speech. More than five hundred patronesses, representing the best life of a dozen great cities, welcomed the little company from Hampton as they traveled from Philadelphia to Boston, from Albany to Buffalo, from Pittsburgh to Wilkes-Barre, and back South through Baltimore.

Can one ask if such a campaign is worth while ? If only for the new aid of a few thousand dollars which come instantly to Hampton, the effort is worth while. For the new lives made possible at Hampton, for the income starting and continuing from new sources, the effort has paid. Most of all for the new friends of Hampton and the Negro, this winter's long campaign has proved worth while.

Hampton stands for the best in Negro and Indian life as perhaps no other institution in America. Hampton can plead for the Indian and Negro races as no other institution today. If the larger campaign which Hampton has inaugurated of late can accomplish this broader mission of winning respect and sympathy for those peoples for whom the school stands sponsor, the generous response which follows may be regarded as but an exponent of a far greater good than the increase of donations upon the books of the Treasurer.

A notable result of the campaign just closed was the formation of new associations in the interest of Hampton in schools, colleges, and cities.

At Phillips Academy, Andover, at the Groton School, at Williams College, Armstrong Leagues were formed for the sympathetic study of the Negro and Indian, and for aid to Hampton. There was not a Hampton club, from Philadelphia to Boston, which failed to make the coming of "the singers" a successful rally.

The growth and devotion of the Hampton associations of Philadelphia, New York, Brooklyn, Springfield, Boston, and Taunton this winter, have made the journeys of the large company from Hampton more than ever effective and far-reaching.

Another important phase of the winter campaign was the renewal of interest in territory which the singers have not visited in many years, territory in which many loyal friends of Hampton have kept up their interest and support. Albany, Rochester, Syracuse, and Buffalo, saw large and enthusiastic meetings which bid fair to greatly strengthen Hampton's constituency in that territory.

The enthusiasm and instant response from the crowded meetings of Pittsburgh and Baltimore were the encouraging result of a journey into a territory long untried.

In this year of financial depression, when the need of friends for the Negro is as urgent as the need of funds for the school, the generous response to Hampton's call for help in the North has been inspiring.

Ellen Dickson
Wilson

Mrs. Ellen Dickson Wilson passed away on Monday, January 26, at the home of her son, Hugh I. Wilson, in Rosemont, Pa., where she had made her home for a number of years. For the last five years she had suffered from an illness which baffled the skill of eminent physicians. But she was strong enough to attend the Hampton meeting in Philadelphia on the Saturday evening preceding her death, and when the principal of the Hampton School visited her the next day, she seemed bright and cheerful and expressed the hope that she might be able to attend the Hampton Anniversary in April.

Mrs. Wilson was the daughter of Hugh Dickson, a Presbyterian clergyman born in County Down, Ireland, who emigrated to this country at the age of twelve and settled in Pennsylvania. She was the widow of Colonel William Potter Wilson, whom she accompanied soon after her wedding to Fort Union, New Mexico, near Las Vegas, riding three hundred ninety miles by overland stage. After her husband's death she took up her residence in Philadelphia and became a member of Holy Trinity Church. Largely owing to the influence of its then rector, Dr. McVickar, she became deeply interested in the Hampton School. Although she had never known General Armstrong, the story of his soldierly life attracted her strongly and she became the devoted friend of his children. She was the guest of Mr. Ogden on a number of his Southern trips, when her Irish wit and wonderful story-telling power added greatly to the pleasure of her fellow-travelers. As long as her health allowed it, she was an annual visitor at Hampton where she was a universal favorite. Her "Aunt Hannah Stories," which have since been published in the *Southern Workman*, she was accustomed to tell at Hampton to the great entertainment of both teachers and students.

Mrs. Wilson had a genius for loving. She loved men and women and children of all sorts and conditions. She seldom took a journey without finding and bringing cheer and comfort to some boy or girl who was friendless and homesick. Often she helped a young mother to care for her children. She seldom went North from Hampton without carrying with her to a Northern hospital, some lame or deformed Negro boy or girl who needed care. She not only gave her help to these afflicted children, but to a wonderful degree she gave herself. The stories she told of their devotion and friendship would make a most interesting volume.

When she became too ill to take much part in the social life around her, her thoughts dwelt largely on Hampton. Like Bishop McVickar, she was continually endeavoring to persuade people to go and see Hampton. It was largely through her influence that Mrs. Grover Cleveland and other friends visited the school. In her death Hampton Institute has lost a devoted friend.

The Virginia Negro Teachers Association   One of the most encouraging and hopeful signs of genuine Negro progress is the way in which Negro leaders have been able to secure the co-operation of their fellow-men in school and welfare work. Those who question the wisdom of assisting Negroes to get an education and fit themselves for leadership would do well to study closely the facts dealing with the steady development of Negro school improvement leagues, health organizations, and social settlements.

A few years ago there was formed, for example, the Negro Teachers' Association and School Improvement League of Virginia, whose object was to aid in advancing the social, civic, and school interests of Negro communities. The beneficial results that have already come to light indicate that in one year the school improvement leagues have raised some $25,000. Of this amount, about $20,000 was used for school improvements and $5000 for the extension of school terms. Some 400 leagues have been organized in connection with 600 schools.

The figures for a few Virginia counties will suggest the value of the work of the school improvement leagues : Henrico County raised in one year $2155 ; Brunswick, in which St. Paul's School is located, $1831 ; and Gloucester, in which there is, according to Dr. Washington, less race prejudice than in Boston or New York, $1724.

The Negro Teachers' Association has encouraged the development of a professional spirit among Negro teachers and has induced a friendly rivalry among the counties in the work of raising money for local school improvements. It has helped to awaken the colored people to the material needs of their own schools and the importance of having well-trained teachers. It has won the interest and moral support of some of the very best white people of Virginia, including those who are actively engaged in the work of the Co-operative Education Association. It has served to call attention to the short terms and meagre equipment of the Negro schools of Virginia. It has attempted to show the Negroes the importance of supporting and improving the public school and has not favored the old rivalry that existed between the private or denominational school and the free public school. It has advocated the establishment of county high schools for Negroes so that teachers may be prepared for the regular, elementary school work.

An interesting teacher's creed has been adopted by this association. Even a cursory study of a portion of the creed, which follows, will show how much stress the Negroes of Virginia, and this is true of other Negroes as well, are placing on education :

'' I believe in universal education as a cure for all the ills to which society is subject, and I consecrate my life to the service of teaching, because in so doing I believe I am hastening the coming of the time when the nation shall be exalted in righteousness.

"I believe in the public school as the greatest heritage of the common people, and I pray that the dawn of that fair day is not far distant when the public schools shall do the work for which they were designed.

"I believe it is the business of the school authorities to furnish adequate facilites for the carrying on of the work of the school; but, if things are not what they should be, I believe it is my duty to try to make them so by every legitimate means at my command.

"I believe in work with the hands as a supplement to work with the brains, and that it is a part of my duty to teach both to those who come to me.

"I believe in adequate compensation for the teachers, but I also believe that what I do and how I do it is more important than what I get for doing it."

English Ballads in Virginia One of the most interesting events at the Virginia Educational Conference in Lynchburg last December was the meeting of the Virginia Folklore Society. Professor C. Alphonso Smith of the University of Virginia, president of the Society, presided and told of the work accomplished in the six months since it was organized.

Its first work has been to collect old English ballads in Virginia. In a way we all know that "Barbara Allen" and other old songs of England have lived on in the Virginia mountains, but it certainly came as a surprise to find that already the Society has found there twenty English or Scotch ballads and thirty variants. Among these are "The Douglas Tragedy, "Lady Isobel," "Twa Sisters o' Binorie," "Lord Randolph," "Young Bichen," three variants of "Robin Hood," and "Sir Hugh of Lincoln."

These ballads were sung by old people or others in rural districts, and Dr. Smith gave many interesting pictures of the people who were accustomed to sing them—sometimes a grandmother whose mother had sung her to sleep with the old songs, sometimes a shoemaker or woodman in the country, who had always known them. "Sir Hugh of Lincoln" came from an old Negro mammy in Alabama! One group was contributed by an elderly gentlewoman who said that when she was young the girls sang them while spinning. In collecting, it was found that Tidewater Virginia has these ballads as well as the mountains. Not only were the talks on these ballads most entertaining, but three of them were sung to quaint old tunes in a most delightful manner by Randolph-Macon students.

Perhaps nothing shows more conclusively what a homogeneous people the Virginians are than this discovery that the songs sung by our English ancestors two hundred years ago have lived from lip to lip to this very day.

A "STATESMAN–EDUCATOR"

*An address delivered in Memorial Church, Hampton Institute,
by Stephen S. Wise, Rabbi of the Free Synagogue of New York
City, on Sunday, February 1, 1914, in celebration of Founder's
Day*

THOUGH deeply appreciative of the generous words of Dr.
Scheiffelin,[1] I yet feel that the invitation to deliver the
Founder's Day address was extended to me by your Principal,
Dr. Frissell, because he felt that there might be a certain fitness
in asking a representative of one of the oldest of the civilized
peoples of earth to bring the message of the hour to you, who
are the sons and daughters of one of the youngest of earth's
races.   Much that I shall say to you in this hour will be an
offering from out the rich and full storehouse of my people's
experiences, gathered in the course of a history of forty centuries of moral and spiritual culture.   And this message I am to
bring to you, who are of the latest of the races of the world to
step out of the darkness of the past and to enter upon the better,
brighter, joyfuller way that lies before you.

I have been thinking of the man we are met to commemorate,
not only during the past few days, but ever since that hour,
nearly fourteen years past, in which I first was privileged to
enter within the walls of this Institute.   No man in modern
times, or even in earlier days, could be more fitly likened to
Moses, the great leader of my people, than Samuel Chapman
Armstrong.   Moses was first the liberator, the emancipator, of
his people, resting his eternal faith upon the word of God—
"Let my people go that they may serve Me."   Having freed
Israel from the bonds and fetters of Egypt, Moses rendered the
Children of Israel the second and the greater service of leading
them to the foot of Sinai, from the summit of which God's moral
law was proclaimed unto Israel and through Israel for all time to
the peoples of earth.   Moses was not content merely to be the
emancipator of bondmen.   Having freed Israel physically and
politically, he then became the moral leader, the compelling legis-
lator.   He freed Israel from itself, from its baser, unworthier
self, and, at Sinai, he set Israel upon that broad highway of
freedom that the soul of Israel was to pursue through centuries
then unborn.

---

[1] Dr. Wise was introduced by Dr. Schieffelin.   For his words see "Hampton Incidents."

In the same way, General Armstrong fought, with lion-hearted courage, throughout the Civil War in order to emancipate your race. But he, as little as Moses, was content to bring a race out of bondage. He knew that even after the issuance of the Emancipation Proclamation your souls awaited and demanded another deliverance; he knew that you were still in bondage to yourselves. He divined the truth of the words of the German poet, "Nur das Gesetz kann uns die Freiheit geben"—"The moral law alone can make man free." He, who was destined to become the most wise of friends and the most helpful of teachers, somehow foreknew that, while you must be freed from bondage to your long-time owners, the supreme thing was to free and to save the Negro from himself. For you he wished for both kinds of freedom—freedom from without and, above all, what Thomas Hughes called "freedom to do as you ought." What other man fought for both throughout his life as did Armstrong, through the bitter days of war and the wearying years of peace ? Even, I repeat, as Israel was freed, not in Egypt but at Sinai, so General Armstrong was among the first to understand that, though your race was forever freed from without on the first day of January, 1863, the emancipation would not really be until crowned by the acceptance of the higher law of moral and spiritual freedom.

I name General Armstrong today statesman-educator of democracy. He was far-sighted and fore-sighted enough to understand the importance of obeying the command of the New England poet of the humanities, who bade men substitute

" For slavery's lash the freedman's will,
    For blind routine, wise-handed skill."

No words of mine could encompass the measure of the service of Armstrong as did Whittier in these prophetic lines, which might well have been chosen for the motto of Hampton. It was as though Armstrong had remembered, too, the earlier words of the Elizabethan dramatist :

" O what a world of profit and delight,
    Of power, of honor, of omnipotence,
    Is promised to the studious artisan."

It was left to the genius of this statesman-educator of the highest order to translate the dreams of poets separated by centuries into an abiding reality for the good of a newly awakened race.

I name Armstrong not only statesman-educator but statesman-philanthropist as well, for Armstrong was that if ever man was. He loved not only his own neighbor but all men as his neighbors. He loved not only his own race but he loved and served the races of the earth. He could not love the stranger as himself, for stranger was an alien term in the vocabulary of his soul. Statesman-patriot of the brotherhood of democracy he may well be called, who was among the first to understand the possibilities of the slogan inscribed upon the Robert Gould Shaw Memorial in the city of Boston—"The white officers—the black men—together"—that in the togetherness of service lay the solution of the problem which involved the destinies of two races, that the white and the Negro races must together work out their common salvation.

Again I name General Armstrong a statesman-philanthropist of democracy, who, to cite the words of his official report of 1866, clearly saw that the "education of the freed men is the great work of the day. It is their only hope, the only power that can lift them up as a people." He seemed to understand, perhaps better than any man of his day understood, that which a noble pagan had declared centuries and centuries before—"No man can permanently be kept erect by others." All that men can do for man is to help him to rise to the largest possibilities of his moral and spiritual stature. This was the self-chosen task of the statesman-philanthropist-educator of democracy who conferred upon you, and upon a whole generation that went before you, the highest of all boons, all that a man can do for men—the boon of helping you to stand erect.

I would, however, not dwell upon Armstrong's achievements, but rather, as far as I may, seek to learn the secret of his life, or, better yet, the motive-power that lay back of that life, simply great and greatly simple, that life of finest, rarest human worth. Armstrong was a visionary, an idealist. Unconsciously, even in the earliest days of army service, he seemed ever to vision the future, though he concerned himself solely and alone with tasks of the immediate present. "And so I do not bother myself much about possibilities, but strive rather to obey the calls of the present and trust in God." In speaking to young men, I have sometimes ventured to say that the only truly practical man in the world is the visionary, for he alone is the man who foresees and foreknows today that which will come to pass on the morrow. The man who was placed in charge of the construction of the earlier buildings at Hampton says : "I sat on a log and looked at him. I thought he was a visionary. It all came to pass." Sometimes the idealist is imagined to be an impatient man. Even Lord John Morley expressed something of impatience with the so-called impatient idealist. But, in truth, the idealist is the most patient being on earth, for he takes the long look, the far look ahead, and patiently and laboriously strives for that which may be centuries in the future. Such a finely patient, withal never-wearied, idealist was

Armstrong who, in the words of his daughter, said, when a promising pupil went to the bad, "If we were not working for two hundred years hence, this might be discouraging."

As I have read and re-read the story of Armstrong's life, it has seemed to me that one of the most significant things in that life, and perhaps the most potent formative influence throughout his days, was the home influence which happily fell to his lot. That home, on the borders between the far West and the farther East, tells at every point in his great career. The life to which he was born was the life of missionaries, of God-fearing, God-dedicated souls, giving themselves to the high task of humanizing and moralizing and religionizing the souls of a people that dwelt in darkness. What a background of high enterprise and noble endeavor the memories of that home furnished throughout his days!

Dr. Frissell finely said in his last annual report that the founder of Hampton Institute, when confronted with the problems of men and women but lately freed from slavery, a race without the tradition of self-respecting family life, unconsciously adopted the home as the model for his school and chose that type of home where each member contributes his share of service to the common need. I trust that my words may command the assent of Dr. Frissell, who knew his predecessor so well and follows so truly in his footsteps, when I say that I believe that Armstrong not only wished to make of Hampton a home, but that he must surely have forefelt that he could render you no finer service nor better lead you in the direction of self-reverence than by making you understand and love the values of home life. Surely it must have come to his wise and far-seeing soul that no race could become truly self-respecting until it had built itself up, as it were, upon the basis of the family unit, and the home foundation. Into Hampton, General Armstrong carried the home spirit, the home influence, the home atmosphere. He could make no finer contribution to Hampton Institute as a home than to show forth, as he did from day to day, what the inspirations and the values of the home had become in his own life. He never rendered you, nor those men and women who have gone before you, greater service than when he made you love Hampton as a home and then go out from Hampton and magnify your own homes. No finer service can be rendered to any man or woman at Hampton than to send him or her forth a lover and cherisher of home values. The surest test of a people's culture lies in the value which it attaches to the home. Until you become a people of homes, a home-loving and home-prizing people, you are still at one of the earliest stages of human progress and culture. The higher a race rises, the more deeply it values and cherishes the home.

One of the perils in the life of our own time lies in the breaking down of home standards and the lowering of home values. If the family and its self-sufficing integrity are to go, then this American democracy of ours will not be worth while. May not I, as a teacher of moral and spiritual values, warn you, young men and women of the race that is yet in the making or re-making, against the peril of thinking lightly of the home? If you would build wisely and lastingly, you must build upon the foundation of the home, magnifying the home, glorifying the family life. It is something to gain houses and land and implements and so-called position and even power, but I say to you, young men and women, that all these things are as nothing beside the home which alone can give, these things a soul. Cherish the home ties and the home joys, magnify the home duties and the home simplicities, revere the home sanctities and the home tendernesses, so that these shall mean more to you than aught else in the world; and these in turn will serve to enrich and to ennoble your own lives.

I speak with deep feeling here, because I am come from a people which has ever magnified the home. The world shut out Israel and so Israel had to shut itself up as it were within the home. Israel enriched the home and the home in turn exalted Israel. Israel magnified home values and held home ties priceless. Although the world without battered against the walls of Jewish life and integrity, Jewish self-respect was maintained and a fine Jewish dignity was perpetuated from generation to generation, because the light was never suffered to die out of the Jewish home. The Jew fought at one and the same time for the altar and the hearth. He brought his altar to his hearth and he made of his hearth a veritable altar before God, with father and mother as its ministering priest and priestess, a veritable shrine, such as you must dream of making your home, sun and shield of your own race. If ever Israel's home passes, Israel will and ought to perish, for all that is finest and noblest will have passed out of the life of Israel.

The moral genius of the man we this day remember is nowhere more clearly shown than in his lifelong conquering of difficulties and, what was even finer, his life-long seeking out of life's hardest places. "There is a certain spirit of conquest in this work that I like. We have lots of strong places to take and we have the force to do it. . . Not very easy, but it can be done." Above all things, General Armstrong was a pioneer, choosing life's outposts in his own day as his father had chosen them before him. "I am glad I am on the outposts doing frontier and pioneer work, for the South is just now a heathen land and Hampton is on the borders thereof. I see my whole nature calls me to the work that is done there—to lay foundations strong, and not do frescoes and fancy-work." Throughout his days, he welcomed and even sought out difficulties in order that he might triumph- antly overcome them.

What finer service could any man render the nation than to show, as Armstrong did, that America means the doing of what cannot be done, the doing of the impossible in the strength of God, translating the impossible to the possible, the unattainable into the achieved. "Doing what cannot be done is the glory of living." This principle was the chiefest compulsion of his life, and made him a resistless conqueror. "I feel happy when all my powers of resistance are taxed; I must win. God has not dark- ened the way. His hand points to a steep and craggy height. It must be climbed; I will climb it." Thus he served three races in America by constantly teaching and living by the maxim that life's so-called impossibilities are not to be accepted as insupera- ble obstacles and hindrances but to be hailed as spurs and stim- uli to the soul. If I were to indulge in a moment of self-revela- tion, I should lay bare as one of the secrets of my own life that nothing has helped me more than the mandate of General Arm- strong, which his lips proclaimed and his life illustrated—the impossible vanishes as the morning mist before the soul of a man who trusts in God and dares all things with the might of his own soul.

If it fell to me to analyze the life and spirit of General Arm- strong in a very few words, I should venture to say that the secret of his days is to be found in the truth that he never con- cerned himself about the best that the Republic could offer him but ever about the best which he could offer to the Republic. He never thought of sacrifice upon the altar of the Republic as grim and austere, for, as he sacrificed, sacrifice was rich and glad- some, pouring itself forth as the inevitable expression of his soul. The man who makes the highest and the finest sacrifices in life is usually so enamoured of his task that he knows not that he is making sacrifices. The beauty and the bloom of sacrifice were vanished if a man were ever thinking of sacrifice. If Gen- eral Armstrong rose to the supreme height of unwearied and unending, withal unconscious, sacrifice throughout his days, it was because he sounded the keynote of his life when, in 1864, at the age of twenty-five, he wrote to his mother: "It is no sacri- fice for me to be here. It is rather a glorious opportunity and I would be nowhere else than here if I could and nothing else than an officer of colored troops if I could. This content, this almost supreme satisfaction, sheds a rich glow upon my life." Not of sacrifice he thought but of glorious opportunity, though that glo- rious opportunity lay on the field of carnage and death. All his life he was thinking, not of what he was giving up, but of the content and the supreme satisfaction which, as he put it, shed a rich glow upon his life. I am merely giving you his own thought, for you will remember the words found among his memoranda: "What is commonly called sacrifice is the best use of one's self and one's resources, the best investment of time, strength, and means. He who makes no such sacrifice is most to be pitied."

General Armstrong was never conscious of self-sacrifice, because he never thought of himself at all. If he thought of self at all it was ever last. A biography of five or ten thousand pages would not tell as much about the man as a word which he wrote on New Year's Eve in 1890: "It pays to follow one's best light, to put God and country first, and ourselves afterward." Contrast him for a moment with the men who live for themselves, who live for their stomachs and their appetites and their passions, who live in order to gain money and nothing else, who live in order to achieve fame and nothing more. Samuel Chapman Armstrong never thought of himself, and because he never thought of himself the world will never cease to think of him. The man who ever thinks of himself the world soon forgets. The man who never thinks of himself the world will never suffer to pass out of its remembrance. The man who thinks most about himself is the man who is soonest forgotten, if remembered at all. Daringly, selflessly, gloriously, Armstrong spent himself, first in war and then in peace, while the prudent and conventional thought him rashly daring and wondered why he did not dedicate his gifts to some gainful callings—to callings which would help him occupy a great seat among the places of men. Today, this man who spent himself in peace and in war in utter self-forgetfulness lives and will live in the hearts of your race and in the memory of the white race—a precious and kindly heritage to us all.

If the spirit of Armstrong could be summoned to this scene in this hour, would he not say: Do not think of me but remember only the men and the women whom I sought to serve. So be it! Shall I not then express the conviction of all of us when I say that there never lived a man of finer self-respect and deeper self-reverence than was Armstrong. And yet that self-respect was not rooted in insistence upon self. He never insisted upon himself; upon you he ever insisted. His was that highest imaginable self-reverence, which takes little or no thought of self and which is reached through pursuing the pathway of self-surrender, self-forgetfulness.

There are times when men must insist upon themselves, when men's insistence upon themselves must be manful, earnest, uncompromising, when nothing worse could happen to a race than to assent, in the words of Kelly Miller, to "self-obliter-ation." But before any race can insist upon the reverence of the world, it must find its way to self-reverence through self-surrender, through that forgetfulness of self which is wrought out of the exalting ideal of service and dedication.

I should be the last man in the world to urge upon you, men and women of the Negro race, that you waive your rights or submit to wrongs. If I were speaking to white men, I would insist solely upon the rights of the Negro. Speaking as I am, however, to young men and women of the Negro race in this hour and under the inspiration of this truly august day which gave Armstrong to American history, I say to you that the surest way to secure rights is to meet duties gladly, greatly, conqueringly. I do not maintain that no wrongs will be done you, nor would I ask that you should even for a moment refrain from protest against wrong. But do not forget that while there are times when insistence upon rights by men is absolutely inevitable if they would continue to have the regard of their fellow-men, the doing of the right will, in God's providence, prove for you the surest way of safe-guarding your rights as men and as Ameri-cans. There are times when you must insist upon your rights, but it is ever your business to insist upon duty, and *duty*, and DUTY yet again.

If I failed to urge you to protest against wrong when wrong is done you, I should not have the right to ask you to accept me as your friend. For well do I know that there are times when protest against wrong must be sounded, and this knowledge is born out of the experience of a people who have been deeply wronged through the ages. Within a few weeks, my people, which gave to the world the idea of a God regnant in righteous-ness, my people, which gave to the world the Bible old and new, my people, from whose loins sprang generations of patriarchs, and judges and kings and prophets—*my people*—have had to face the tribunal of the world's judgment on the charge of ritual-murder. I say my people, for if that Russian Jew was guilty of ritual-murder, then is every Jew guilty of ritual-murder, living or dead, then were the founders of Christianity sharers of the guilt of Russia's hapless victim. Can you imagine what it means to my people, nineteen hundred years after the birth of Him you name Master, him we call the latest in the great order of Hebrew prophets, that we in this twentieth century should be arraigned before a Russian court of justice on the charge of ritual-murder. And yet, in the despite of this unutterable calumny against a proud and honorable people, do you think that we are to give our days to protest against this hideous charge? "Assailed by slander and the tongue of strife, the only answer is a blameless life."

Lest I be misunderstood, I repeat that there may be times in your life when wrong will be done, when you will be so assailed that it will be the part of your manhood and your womanhood to protest. But by my people's experience of centuries and centuries of injury and wrong, I adjure you, men and women, never to forget that the only answer to assailing slander is a blameless life, that in truth there is something infinitely finer and greater than defending one's self against charges of wrongdoing, and that is to offend not in the sight of God or man. To some of you my counsel will commend itself little if at all, but I say to you again that which I have said to my people again and again and shall continue to say whilst I live—the surest way of meriting, even though one gain it not, the reverence of the world without, is through that self-reverence which rests forever on the doing of the right. The world may choose to withhold its reverence, but it cannot lessen the worth of my life if worthy I be. The world may impinge upon that outer fate of which I am not wholly master ; but it cannot mar my inmost soul, of which I am forever captain.

In stressing duties rather than rights, for rights come from without and obedience to duty comes out of the inmost soul, I am but echoing a word of another friend of the Negro race, General Howard, who, speaking many years ago, of certain conditions that bore very hard upon you, said that on the whole it was better for you, for it put you at the bottom of the ladder. What you have the right to demand is that the ladder stand and remain open and accessible to you all. You may not demand that you have the first nor the second place, but that, no matter where you begin, the top shall not be barred nor shut nor denied to you. A fair field and no favor, withal no disfavor, is all that a man may ask—and with God be the rest !

I revert for the last time to the possibility of times coming in your life when wrong will be done, when iniquity shall darken the ways of men in their dealings with you. What, I ask for the last time, shall be your attitude toward occasional injustice, toward the wrong when wrong is inflicted upon you ? Two attitudes there are, alike wrongful—the one is the attitude of uncomplaining and cowardly acquiescence, and the other is the no less intolerable attitude of ceaseless whining. Men never whine ; men complain, protest, rise up. Men speak out and speak up and speak on, but they do not whine, for they are men. It is your business to be men, first, last, ever—firm in protest against wrong, protesting as men, nor leaving it wholly to others to protest for you—but never whining.

One other word of counsel I venture to offer you, phrasing it in the word of one of the noblest friends of your race, Wendell

Phillips, who, in 1868, said "Let us give to the Negro a chance to show that Toussaint L'Ouverture was not a splendid monster, but a fair representative of the capacity of his race." Upon a deep truth I would here lay emphasis. Far better that you produce not a few exceptional and extraordinary persons, though that, too, were fine, but a multitude of fair representatives of the capacity of your race. Your constant aim must be to produce the highest possible average and not a few extraordinary and unaccountable beings. The world is going to judge you by what you are in the aggregate and not because of what a few of your outstanding and exceptional men may be or do. When the world without assails you, the blameless or even the matchless life of a single representative, or a handful of representatives, of your race will not and ought not to avail. The Negro race is not going to be saved by its Washingtons and its Dunbars, its DuBoises and its Tanners and its Millers, but it will be saved, as it must be served, by the men and the women within my hearing. Neither will office-holding by a chosen few save your race. Some of you vainly imagine that a millennium will be at hand for your race, if only a few of the representatives of the Negro race achieve political position. It is far more important for you that the average Negro, in the despite of every obstacle cruelly placed in his pathway, shall earnestly strive to be a good citizen. Barter not away the soul of your race for a few political jobs.

Above all, I would say to the members of the Negro race here assembled that which you never have the right to ignore—no one man at his best can save you, but one man at his worst can terribly disserve and almost damn your whole race. "He who commits a crime helps the enemy." He who among you commits a wrong does that which wrongs your whole race. Every Negro bears upon his own shoulders for weal or woe the burden of his people. If you are men and women you will accept this burden as a challenge, as a glorious opportunity to be met in the spirit of finest manhood and noblest womanhood. No man liveth unto himself alone—is peculiarly true of the Negro if he fail or fall. Who among you will ever be ready to do wrong, knowing as you must know that it is not alone the doer of the wrong who will suffer but the whole of your race ?

I have wondered as I have stood before you whether you feel that the recital of the life of Armstrong cannot help you, for he was a man who dwelt apart. Apart he seems, it is true, for, as Renan says, the man whom God has touched is always a being apart. In that sense, Armstrong was a being apart. And yet those of you who, like Dr. Frissell, knew Armstrong well, will, I think, hold as I have felt who knew him not at all in the flesh, that though he stood apart, and walked with God, he was yet completely, splendidly, radiantly human. Far from being discouraged by the contemplation in this hour of the nobleness of the man, let us never forget that any man may dare to rise unto the heights which he gained who, like Armstrong, walks with God and serves his fellow-men.

A few months ago I stood at the grave of the great Doge in honor of whom one of the two matchless columns in the Piazza of Venice was erected, the Doge Michael. On that tomb is written : "Here lies the terror of the Greeks. Whosoever thou art who comest to behold this tomb of his, bow thyself down before God because of him." Men and women, you and I are met this day to commemorate the life and the service of a great man. We think not chiefly, if at all, of the terror that he brought to the heart of his enemies, though he dared during war's bitterest hours all that did become a man. War's days are forever past and they that once were foes are now bound together in the bonds of indissoluble friendship.

May I not say, however, that all of us together of the North and the Southland, white man and Negro, Jew and Christian, as we come to behold the grave wherein his dust lies buried, bow ourselves down before God because of him and, having bowed ourselves, rise up again in spirit to a nobler stature such as was his because of

>" . . . . all that human and divine
>I' the weary, happy face of him—half god,
>Half man, which made the god part god the more."

We bow ourselves down because of him and reverently, gratefully, even lovingly, we ask God to make us worthy of the memory of Samuel Chapman Armstrong.

"TO GIVE A CHILD A CHANCE"

BY L. HOLLINGSWORTH WOOD

ABOUT forty miles out on Long Island, and not far from its center, the Howard Orphanage and Industrial School, thanks to the energy and far-sightedness of Rev. James H. Gordon and his wife, has found a big, roomy farm, and with faith in its future has built seven new cottages, remodeled some older buildings, and started real life in the country, where children belong.

This is a philanthropic farm where two hundred and fifty children live, and play, and work, and learn how to do all three—an enterprise started and supported and developed by Negroes.

Its story is unlike Cinderella's in one thing. There was no fairy godmother. Perhaps some of the children had step-sisters—who can tell?—but at any rate it was no wave of a wand

which produced the buildings at Kings Park and transplanted the two hundred and fifty children to their country home.

There was a fairy spirit somewhere, for one of the children—they are all under sixteen—wrote this little moving song to celebrate the change from the old brick building in the City of Brooklyn to the broad fields of Long Island.

A MOVING SONG

Moving Day ' way down in Howard Home,
All the children carrying brush and comb,
Mrs. Gordon standing clapping her hand;
She means order and we understand.
Mr. Gordon strutting down the street,
A band of children tripping at his feet.
Run, ye women; children, run, run, run,
We are going to our country home.

But there was no fairy wand, unless the lives of men and women who have given time and money and love and, in the end, their very lives, to bring true their dream of something really good for the little waifs of the large and growing Negro population of the Northern cities, make up a fairy wand.

The story of those lives sounds very familiar. Sheep without a shepherd, and lambs straying about, have always interested somebody, and in the spring of 1866 Mrs. S. A. Tillman saw so many of the children of her own race in New York and Brooklyn who could not be cared for in the institutions existing, that she took them into her own home at 104 East Thirteenth Street, New York.

She could care for only twenty, and there were so many more that, with the help of some ministers and Negro churches, the "Home for Freed Children and Others" was organized in August 1866, with the rooms of the Colonization Society, corner of Dean Street and Troy Avenue, in Brooklyn, as its home.

General O. O. Howard saw the chance to aid and, as witness to his work and helpful advice and influence, his name was used in the corporate title, when in September 1868 the Legislature of New York granted the Society a charter, and the corporate existence of the Brooklyn Howard Colored Orphan Asylum began.

To visit churches where Christ's name is used and beg for any worthy object, and especially for children, ought to be easy. In those days it was cold and snowed in the winter, and rained and was hot and uncomfortable sometimes in summer, and some people were busy with other things and had no time to stop and think about the hungry little children in the Asylum. But there were also some who did think and feel for them, and when the old rooms had to be given up, a new house was provided, and the little family of children and their caretakers grew and moved into the new brick building which was built for them. Perhaps it was easier for William F. Johnson, a colored minister, to give up his life to raising the money to pay for this building because he was blind, but perhaps it took a still higher courage, than if he could see, to grope his way about to visit churches and kind people in faith that they would do what should be done to help the children of his race.

While this growth of the institution was going on, Brooklyn was taking rank with the great cities and becoming a part of New York, and the managers longed to have their charges on a farm where they could have room and better air, and a chance to work out of doors.

MAKING USE OF THE FARM BY-PRODUCTS

In 1910 the Brooklyn Rapid Transit Company offered to buy the property in the city, and the Jewish Agricultural and Industrial Aid Society was willing to sell its farm of 572 acres at Kings Park, and so, with the help of the moving spirit of Superintendent Gordon, and the managers, and our little girl who is a poet, the Orphanage came to its own in the country. Arbutus in your own woods is a good exchange for asphalt or even a chance in a city park; and pigs and chickens, and cows and horses, and lots of room for baseball, and a chance to climb a cherry tree—what do they not mean for boys, and why not for girls! There is a pond, too, with frogs, and an ice house and

AT WORK ON THE FARM

an apple orchard and two hundred and fifty happy children.

Seven new cottages were built; things are a little bare yet, but the trees will grow. There is abundance of light and the ventilation is good, and there is water in plenty. The school-house is an old cottage remodeled and it is pretty crowded, but the children learn, though the exercises at graduation, or on holidays, or when some great man comes for a visit, have to be held out of doors. There are 145 boys and 105 girls, so it requires a large building to bring them all together comfortably.

The cost of all this opportunity to live makes a budget which it is a business problem to meet. Last year the expenditures were $44,839.35, and the money came, first, from the City of New York and the near-by counties; second, from donations by churches, individuals, and entertainments; and third, from the sale of produce from the farm.

For the coming year the budget will be larger, for the school needs an expert in agriculture to aid Mr. Gordon, and the new schoolhouse, assembly hall, and hospital are all to be built, while the two hundred and fifty children are to be fed, and clothed, and taught, and helped to ability and happiness.

The classes in cooking, needlework, and laundering are turning out useful workers for the things which have to be done, and when the girls have found places, their letters to Mother Gordon, which she shows with proper pride, give good accounts of their appreciation of the training at "The Home." The Howard

Orphanage hopes to send representatives to many a home to show the kind of training which Mr. and Mrs. Gordon are giving.

The cobbling class always has work ready at hand, and the carpenters turn out very creditable tables, racks, and stools. The boys made a new dormitory out of an unused attic, finishing it with yellow pine, and it is now very presentable. They also made over an outbuilding for a domestic science classroom.

The care of the cows, and pigs, and chickens, planting and hoeing corn and potatoes, cabbage and turnips, and "making garden," keep the children busy in this country school of life.

The market for the produce of the farm and dairy is convenient. The city folk come to the edges of Long Island to live in the summer, and they stay later and later each year. The baskets of fresh eggs, and butter, and garden vegetables from the school can come to the railway station in the morning in time to be delivered to the conveyance which brings the business man to his train.

Spirits of Mrs. Tillman, General Howard, Mr. Johnson, and all the other good, hardworking fairies of the Howard Orphanage's history, happy in its progress, sad in its failures, stand at the shoulders of those who yearn today for growth in the trees you planted. In humility the present workers listen to your voices, in courage they follow in your footsteps, helping to make an institution for the self-help of Negroes, for Negroes, by Negroes.

THE CARE OF THE COWS HELPS TO KEEP THE CHILDREN BUSY

ARIZONA AND
FORTY THOUSAND INDIANS

BY JOHN M. OSKISON

IT came upon me gradually, as I made my first pilgrimage last fall among the Western Navahos, the Pimas and Maricopas, and the Apaches of Arizona, that this Western state has the greatest variety of live Indian problems on its hands that confront any of our organized communities.

Only in one other state (Oklahoma) is there a greater Indian population; and in Oklahoma the Five Civilized Tribes, which make up 101,000 of the state's 117,000 Indians, are no longer thought of as Indians requiring special guardianship. Arizona holds 40,000, and the state is deeply concerned about all of them. For these 40,000 are real Indians, not "mixed-bloods"; they are reservation Indians, among whom the allotment idea is new ; they are just beginning to feel the pressure and the irritations which follow from a first sharp clash with the white man.

"They've been dancing more this summer than I've ever known before," said the traders among the Western Navahos, as I talked with them in September. "I don't know why—they just seem to be restless. No, we don't expect any trouble; we're long past the time, of course, of 'uprisings'."

Then, two and a half months later, came the widely advertised break of a few renegade Navahos to the Beautiful Mountains, and the expedition of General Scott, the famous Indian tamer. You couldn't blame the citizens of Arizona for getting nervous about the Navahos ! Not unless you knew all the facts— and the average citizen of Arizona certainly couldn't be expected to know them.

For a number of years, the Navahos have been spreading outside the boundaries of their twelve-million-acre reservation. Between 5000 and 9000 of them are on public land; the growth of their herds and flocks has forced them to seek pasture outside the limits of their mountain and desert reservation. For perhaps half of those who live off the reservation, allotments have been scheduled (though not yet confirmed); but there is a hitch in the proceedings, and no one knows when the rest of them will be assured of their right to Government land.

Why the hitch ? Grazing land is precious in Arizona, and the white stockmen are unanimous in the belief that they can make use of it all. White men are voters and pay taxes; the three men who represent Arizona in Congress have been sent there by the whites. They prefer to see the wealth-creating resources of the state in the hands of white voters and taxpayers. The matter is simple !

Simple as it is at bottom, the problem of the Arizona Navahos is perplexing and highly interesting on the surface. It is going to offer a pretty study in tactics ; and the white men of Arizona have beaten the Indian Office to the first move.

Their nearest neighbors like and trust the Navaho stockmen. I rode for half a morning with a blue-eyed, drawling cattleman, whose range, north of Flagstaff, lies at the edge of the public-land ranges used by the Navahos. His friends say that this man has held cattle on this same range for nearly forty years. They call him "Rimmy Jim," because he rides the rim of the canyon through which the Little Colorado River twists.

"Shucks ! these Indians are the finest people in the world to get along with," said "Rimmy Jim" when I asked him if he had ever been troubled. "They'll look after my stock, when any of it gets over on their range, just like it was their own; of course, they know I'll do the same for them. I ain't never had a bit of trouble—don't ever expect to have any ! "

But "Rimmy Jim" plays his hand alone—the big cattle companies are vastly more concerned over the question of making profit than this blue-eyed neighbor of the Navahos. They have no sentiment, and they want the Navahos kept on their reservation. If the reservation is not adequate to support the Navaho herds and flocks, the Arizona cattlemen and sheepmen don't feel that they are responsible.

So (I am going to quote the President of the Indian Rights Association), "the national policy of allowing the Indians to locate on the public land was held up in Arizona and New Mexico by the indirect method of introducing an amendment into an appropriation bill, whereby the Indian Office was forbidden to use any of the money appropriated for the current year to effectuate such allotments. This amendment was championed by certain senators from New Mexico and Arizona because they claimed that the reservations, which Senator Fall describes as ' immensely rich reserves, ' are the proper place for the Indians, and that the states of Arizona and New Mexico are entitled to have these public lands settled by white people, who will be voters and taxpayers.''

Naturally, it would help to get the Navahos back on the reservation if the public were convinced that they were trouble-makers and not fit to be trusted to live alongside the whites.

With Dr. Montezuma of Chicago, I started, early in October, on a round of visits to the Pimas and Maricopas and the Apaches. So far as the Pimas and Maricopas are concerned, it was only a start. We attended one meeting at the small settlement of Lehi, near Mesa, but when we drove, next day, to listen to the talk of some hundreds of Pimas and Maricopas who live under the Sacaton Agency, we were met by the Superintendent's Indian police and asked to come to the Agency to explain the purpose of our visit. Dr. Montezuma was charged with being a trouble-maker and a contract-seeker, and we were ordered not to hold any meetings with the Indians.

Now, the Superintendent who chased us with his police from Santan to Blackwater and back again, zealous in carrying out his purpose to prevent a meeting, was merely reflecting a state of acute strain. There exists, among these Indians of Lehi, of Santan, of Sacaton, of Blackwater, and of Gila Bend, problems so acute that every man who touches them becomes excited and suspicious of every other man. There are factions among the Indians which have split on matters of water and the question of allotment, on the sale of surplus land, on the building of the storage reservoir at San Carlos; and we who went to listen and learn (and add, if we might, our influence toward harmony) were bundled off the reservation as meddlers !

At the Lehi meeting, I heard talk so specific and so convinc-ing as to the injustices suffered at the hands of white water users that I do not wonder the Superintendent doesn't want the Indians to talk to outsiders. That Superintendent believes the Indian Office will be able to settle the matter satisfactorily ; and he has his faction among the Lehi Indians who counsel patience, who favor allotment on terms which do not please the older people, and who are optimistic in the face of dry irrigating ditches and withering crops. These Pimas and Maricopas are truly at close grip with the problems which follow the whites into any Indian country.

The impression was forced upon me that the Indian Office was arranging compromises on behalf of the Salt River and Gila River Indians which will prove too costly. For instance, I was told by Indians who supported his policy that the Superintendent at Sacaton is going to have restored to the Pimas their ancient rights in the natural flow of the Gila River. Meanwhile, he urges the Indians to use the well water (which most of them don't like), and to refuse to push their claim for a proper share of the water which will be impounded by the San Carlos dam.

I don't know, of course, that it is beyond the power of the Superintendent and of the Indian Office to have restored to the Gila River Indians their old rights, but for thirty years the fight has been going on without result. I don't believe it will ever be done. If it can't, the Indian Office is wrong to encourage its representative to make such a promise in order to avoid facing a troublesome alternative—that of securing from an organized asso-

CHIEF YUMA FRANK OF THE FORT MCDOWELL APACHES

ciation of white water users the Indians' fair share of the water which is expected to make fertile the Gila Valley when the San Carlos dam is built. For not only will the whites who have usurped the natural flow of the Gila keep what they have been using for a long time, but those newcomers who are already building their ditches in anticipation of the completion of the San Carlos project will demand that the Indians pay their proportionate share of the cost of the project before they take water from the dam.

So far as these newcomers are concerned, that is a perfectly fair attitude. Now, the question comes, Who is to pay—the Indians or the Government ? The Indians don't feel that they ought to be compelled to sell any part of their land (they say they have no more than they need) in order to raise the money to pay for water from the San Carlos dam. They feel that they can stand pat on the plea that the Government owes them restoration of the water they lost.

On the other side, the Government (represented by the Indian Office) finds it hard to get money from Congress to meet the bill. As a result, there is dissention within the reservations. One faction believes that the Superintendent's promise will be made good ; another does not. One faction is for immediate allotment, in 5- or 10-acre tracts, of the land, and the sale of what is left over ; another says that this is a Government scheme to saddle upon the Indians the cost of securing for them an adequate water supply.

Few of the Arizona Apaches have yet come to close quarters in the conflict between their interests and those of the whites. But the little band of two hundred seventy at Fort McDowell constitute an exception. I accompanied Dr. Montezuma on his flight from the Gila to the little reservation of the McDowell Apaches on the Verde River ; and there I heard the story of the attempt which is being made to transfer this band from their lovely old home on the Verde to a flat stretch of desert under the main ditch which comes from the Roosevelt dam.

Here it is a question of another compromise between the Government and the hungry white water users. If the McDowell Indians will give up their little 24,000-acre reservation and relinquish their rights to the flow of the Verde River, they will be given allotments on a bare desert under the Salt River ditch and a right in the water of the Roosevelt dam. And if the Indians will get busy, build houses, plant trees, clear off the sage brush and greasewood, and open up fields, this Salt River water will enable them to make homes just as attractive as those they now occupy—in time.

All this will result—if the Roosevelt reservoir doesn't go dry! And throughout the Salt River Valley last fall, I heard many prophecies that this is exactly what will happen if the winter of 1913-14 stores as little snow in the mountains as did the winter of 1912-13, or if there is any further great extension of ditches in the valley.

But the Government's advocates of this compromise say that if the McDowell Indians move under the Salt River ditch, they will take along their priority of right in the water. That is what the Pimas and Maricopas who live in the Lehi settlement near Mesa thought when they abandoned their old ditches and took a share of the water from the Roosevelt dam through the ditches

of the white users in the valley; and now they must see their
crops wither because they are classed, through some manipula-
tion of the contract which they do not understand, with those
users who are supplied after the rest are satisfied. They are in
class "C"—and they can't get water until the users in classes
"A" and "B" are supplied.

The McDowell Indians know this, and they prefer to stick to
the reservation on the Verde. They want to stay there, and they

AN APACHE PAPOOSE

want a permanent irrigation system installed there. But that
would cost about $90,000 ; and how is the Indian Office to get the
money ?

And vital to the whites who are crowding the Salt River Valley to suffocation, is the question : Won't the McDowell Indians
block the plan to build a great storage reservoir on the Verde to
supplement the Roosevelt supply if they are allowed to remain on
their present reservation ? As a guardian, the Government is
certainly having its troubles with the Indians of Arizona.

If the Fort McDowell Apaches are like children just emerging into a faint understanding of what is meant by bucking white

APACHE BASKET-MAKERS

civilization, the 5000 Apaches of the White Mountain Reservation, under the San Carlos and Fort Apache Agencies, are still real infants.

Their nursery is a great body of mountain country, with strictly limited areas of land capable of cultivation when water is led on it. At San Carlos, on the upper reaches of the Gila, and, on the San Carlos River, a good many of the Indians do support themselves by farming. Many of them own some cattle and horses, but the greatest part of the excellent mountain pasture belonging to these Apaches is leased to white cattlemen ; and so long as the Government can't, or won't, induce the Indians them- selves to make use of the range, there is no reason why the white cattlemen should not be permitted to lease it. But it is hard to see why the Government permits the use of money received by the Indians from the cattlemen in a way to benefit only the whites ! For example :

There is a public highway from Globe to Southern Arizona which runs across the White Mountain Reservation, crossing the Gila and the San Carlos Rivers. Bridges over these two streams are needed, and Arizona's representative in Congress set out to get those bridges built with money collected by the Apaches for grazing fees. His argument was that the bridges would be on Indian land and would be of beneficial use to the Indians, there- fore the Indians ought to pay for them. But the fact is that the bridges would not be of the slightest use to the Indians. The nearest of the Fort Apache Indians lives at least fifty miles away, and to use the bridges to cross the two rivers, the San Carlos Indians would have to make a twelve-mile detour! Yet that authorization of the use of Apache money was successfully included in a bill which went through Congress.

San Carlos faces a situation a good deal more serious than the misuse of grazing fees, however. If that storage reservoir is built at San Carlos (and the site is an ideal one), practically every one of the San Carlos Indian farmers will be flooded out. While I was at San Carlos, surveyors and reclamation engineers pushed their work, and a Government man was there to assist the Superintendent in appraising the value of the property which will be covered by water when the dam is built. It certainly looks as if the project, which has been delayed a very long time, is going through.

What provision has been made to take care of the San Carlos Indians who will lose their land? I asked the Superintendent that question, and he replied:

"No provision has been made; I have no idea what will be done."

It certainly would not be fair to ask the thousands of settlers on the Gila below the dam site to forego indefinitely the chance to put water on fertile land because a handful of Indians

INDIAN HUNTERS IN THE HILLS EAST OF THE VERDE

would be flooded out. They would resent being held up by a handful of white men in the same way.

What is the Indian Office going to do with those San Carlos Apaches? Both the Indians and the people of Arizona are anxious to get an answer to that question.

What is going to become of the 6000 Papago Indians down in the southern part of Arizona? These industrious and always peaceable people have been shifting for themselves, living on public land, getting crops from the desert by an ingenious system of conserving the scanty rainfall, and grazing their stock over immense areas of poor range. Now, are they going to give way before the demands of the white stockmen for all the public range, and be crowded into a reservation to become dependents and drawers of rations? If they are not, it devolves upon the Indian Office to find a way to insure them in the possession of their water holes and their widely scattered fields.

In Arizona, I did not find any general sentiment hostile to the Indians. What was evident was a strong determination among the whites to push the state along the road to prosperity as fast as possible. It is regarded as a very great handicap that so large a part of the state's resources are either in the Indian reservations or in the national forests. The people of the new state who have to support its government feel unjustly burdened by taxes, and they see little relief ahead as long as conditions remain as they are.

No one can blame the citizens of Arizona for thinking of their own welfare. But this very determination to save for taxpaying whites every resource of the state it is possible to save is making the Indian problem of Arizona one of the most acute and one of the most interesting we face today.

TUSKEGEE INSTITUTE AND ITS CONFERENCES*

BY J. E. DAVIS

A visitor who has not seen Tuskegee Institute for ten years marvels at its wonderful growth.   Here are fine, large dormitories and dining hall, new agricultural and academic buildings, a beautiful campus, a thousand-acre farm under excellent cultivation, another thousand acres in pasture, lawn, and woodland, a modern, fully equipped hospital with training school attached, well-organized academic and industrial departments, sixteen hundred students, and, over all, that untiring, practical "worker of miracles" who learned thirty years ago from his great teacher, Samuel Chapman Armstrong, that "doing what 'can't be done' is the glory of living."

Everything is on a vast scale—enormous buildings, large rooms, high ceilings, long roads, big crops, endless corridors, battalion line like a battle array, agricultural parade a mile and a half long but occupying only two stretches of the miles of road on the estate.   One hears much of the progress of the Negro in fifty years.   Surely the progress of Negro Tuskegee in less than thirty years is like a fairy tale.

And that not all of this improvement is on the outside is evident to anyone who remains long enough at the school to see some of its inner life.   While there is doubtless in Dr. Washington's opinion much in the school which still falls short of his high ideal, it is evident that vast improvement has been made in the quality and thoroughness of the academic work ; in the standards set in shop, kitchen, dining-room, and farm ; in the cleanliness and order in the dormitories ; and in the ideals of life placed before the students.

There is a healthy dissatisfaction with what is not yet ideal, an insistence on practical, sensible work in shop and classroom, a thoroughness of inspection and supervision, and a strong desire to go on working out original methods of finally reaching the best in all lines, all of which speak well for the future of the institution.   From faithful "Old Brandon," dressing vegetables in the kitchen and chatting of the time when "Me and Booker started

* Illustrated with photographs of the parade by Dr. R. R. Clark of Hampton Institute

this school,'' up to "Booker" himself, the head of the Institute,
who mounts his waiting grey each morning, no matter what the
weather, for his daily inspection of the various departments, there
is a fine devotion to the institution and an earnest wish to see it
forge ahead on right lines.

THE FARMERS' CONFERENCE

January twenty-first was the date set this year for the annual
Farmers' Conference first organized by Dr. Washington twenty-
three years ago. Even ten years ago an "acre of mules" was

THE TYPE OF FARMER THAT "USED TO COME " TO THE
TUSKEGEE CONFERENCE

a picturesque accompaniment of this Conference. The few vehicles were all of them more or less of the ramshackle order and the
dress and speech of the poor tenant farmers, held down by the
crop-lien system, was of a style to correspond. Without doubt the
Conference has lost in picturesqueness as it has gained in intelligence. This year there was no "acre of mules" but, rather,
a mile of buggies ; the audience was made up chiefly of landowners, as well dressed and intelligent as one could wish to see, and the
improvement in the aims, interests, and personal habits of the visiting farmers was remarked upon even by the student guides in
their excellent classroom resumé of the Conference next day.

An interesting feature, new this year, was an agricultural
parade, headed by an army of farmers and agricultural students

THE RUTABAGO ARMY AT THE HEAD OF THE AGRICULTURAL PARADE

carrying as ammunition rutabagoes fastened to sticks. These were followed by "the Negro farmer of fifty years ago," a bent old man with his cob pipe, his dog, his mule, and his wooden plow. Other old-time farmers followed, the last being a man with two mules and a two-horse turning plow.

The second section of the parade was made up of the up-to-date machinery used on the Institute farm and driven by students—a four-horse gang plow, a disc harrow, a roller, a seed drill, a mower, a binder, a thresher, a corn harvester, a cotton-

THE NEGRO FARMER OF FIFTY YEARS AGO
The roads were torn up for a new steam-heating system.

THE BIBLE TRAINING SCHOOL IN THE PARADE
"A good church is clean"—" A good church is well ventilated "

stalk chopper and transplanter. This section was enthusiastically cheered by the visiting farmers. It was followed by floats representing the orchard, the canning factory, the poultry yard with boys plucking chickens, the creamery with girls making butter, the veterinary division, an old-time bush-arbor school, and a modern school with a county supervisor present. The live-stock was well represented, as were also the agricultural products of the Institute.

Several county organizations took part in the parade, which ended with a long procession of Negro farmers and their wives and families in their own conveyances. It was remarked later

THE VEGETABLE FLOAT OF THE GARDENING DIVISION

that one could see more in an hour's time in the parade than one could learn in school in a month.

In the chapel, where the large audience, perhaps 2500 people, gathered after the parade, Dr. Washington, showing in every sentence, as he talked informally to the farmers, a marvelous, intimate knowledge of their home conditions, finally settled into the address which opened the Conference.

DR. WASHINGTON'S ADDRESS

Time and money spent every year by farmers coming here in large numbers will be thrown away unless each one is determined to get something out of this Farmers' Conference that he can take home and put into practice himself. If each one will do that, these meetings from year to year will be worth while.

Many of us here in the South fail to realize as farmers the value of time. We are continually talking about the saving of money, but time is just as valuable as money. In not a few sections of the South people are throwing away the days in December, January, and February, but they are just as valuable as the days in March and April. In every one of these months something can be done on the farm. Ditches can be put in order, fences repaired, stables and outhouses improved, the land turned over by deep plowing, root and grain crops cultivated, seed corn selected, tools repaired, and the dwelling house improved.

To be perfectly plain, too large a proportion of our race spend the winter months waiting until the first of March, when they expect some white man to begin making "advances" to them. We have now been free fifty years and I know that throughout the South the white man—and the colored man too—is getting tired of carrying so many Negro farmers on his back year by year through the system of "advances." The white man thinks it is time to *wean* the colored people. Let us get weaned. We ought to be able to help ourselves more, to "carry" ourselves, to provide enough grain, meat, vegetables, and other food to carry us from year to year without having to go in debt to buy what the farm ought to produce.

A county or community can only grow wealthy as it has a large number of individual producers. If a man has only what he can buy at a store he does not increase the wealth of the community. Now, after fifty years, let us be free. If the colored farmers will make up their minds to work every month in the year, and teach their wives and children to be continually producing something in the way of vegetables, poultry, milk, and butter while the husband is doing his part in raising something to sustain the family, it will not be necessary for them to get "advances" from anybody. Give your wives and children a chance *in the house*. At present you make them help you in the fields, so that they have no chance to plan meals, to raise vegetables, or to can fruit. Give them a chance and they will make and save as much as you do.

White people throughout the South are beginning to see that the kind of farmer who brings prosperity to the county is the one who produces more than he consumes, owns a little piece of land, and has some money in the bank. This kind of man becomes an asset instead of a liability to the county in which he lives. When this kind of man drives into town on Saturday, the merchant, the banker, and everybody else welcome him, because he brings into town more than he takes out.

Our people in many parts of the South are trying to buy more land than they can pay for, or take proper care of. Some who are buying large tracts are letting their children grow up in ignorance. I heard a farmer say about his boy, "I wu'ked him and wu'ked him and wu'ked him 'twell he had to leave home." Another said that he did better than that. "I got nine chillun," said he, "I jes' wu'ks 'em all, I jes' wu'ks 'em and wu'ks 'em an' I don' has to do nothin' myself." I don't care how many acres you own, you are not prosperous if you don't have a comfortable house with conveniences in it for your wives and children. I went to see a colored man the other day who owns hundreds of acres, and I had to go out of doors to wash my hands! Among these people who own too much land, the school and the church are often poor, for the farmers are not doing anything for the community.

Don't try to buy so much land—not over one hundred acres. Cultivate a little land well, and see that your house is fit to live in, and that your wives and children have a chance to work in the house instead of in the field. Instead of investing a little extra money in more land, put it into your house, build a bathroom, and make the home in every way attractive to your children.

There is no set of black people anywhere in the world who are permitted to occupy such a rich, genial, and beautiful section of the country as we are. Let us make up our minds that we are each going to do our part to develop the farms, the gardens, the orchards, the stock, the poultry, the fruit, the vegetables, and have the best of everything, including houses. In proportion as we do this, there will be less effort to replace us by another class of farmers. No matter what anybody says to the contrary, the average Southern white man likes the Negro, likes to have him near him. In the great big fundamental things of life, he is ready to encourage him and help him, and protect him. Any people who can change from the types that used to come here at the beginning of these conferences to the good-looking, intelligent men and women who are here today is a great people.

THE DISCUSSION

While the audience sang with enthusiasm, "Give me dat ole-time religion," there was no disposition to shout for the old-time ways of farming. The slogan of the Conference was "better farms, better homes, better schools, better health," like that of the Negro Organization Society of Virginia, whose work was very ably described the evening before by Rev. A. A. Graham of Phoebus, Virginia, chairman of its executive committee.

As one farmer after another rose to tell how he had begun with nothing, or less than nothing (one having had to borrow his wedding clothes, and another to ask his wife to buy the license!) and by hard work had earned money and bought acre after acre of land, Dr. Washington, by a rapid fire of questions, kept them to the point and insisted on knowing about the homes, the schools, and the churches. He finally forced one old man, who boasted that he owned one hundred and twenty-four acres of land and said that if he had had anything mortgaged "since Jonah swallowed the whale" he would give ten dollars, to admit that he would sell his house for twenty-five dollars!

In contrast to this was the man who began on less than a dollar and celebrated his wedding by hauling wood all day for fifty cents. He then made up his mind that he would save fifty cents a day for "me and Frances" as long as they lived together, and he has done it for thirty years. He not only owns a farm of three hundred and ninety acres and holds mortgages on other farms, but has exchanged his patched-up log cabin for a seven-room house *with a bathroom* and hot and cold running water. Another is so prosperous that he owns a *painted*, six-room house in which he lives and four brick stores on the main street in town, which he rents to people of both races, and is so forehanded that he has his coffin "all bought and paid for" as well as a "monument thirteen feet high"! This man reported a good, eight-months' school in his town, with four teachers.

Favorable reports were made in regard to the supplementing of school terms by patrons in several localities; of 45 colored schools in one county, one-third were said to have good houses, the term being 110 days. Representatives of the Tallapoosa County Fair presented the Conference with $6.00, this being the gift, partly of the boys' corn club, 15 boys having made 733 bushels of corn on 13 acres, and partly of the Rural District School Association of that county, 10 school farms having made $442 to supplement the school fund.

The most unfavorable report was in regard to the "no-count teachers and no-count preachers" who are said to be actually selling whisky themselves to the people under their charge, and to be encouraging all the other "blind tigers" in their communities. Dr. Washington called upon the farmers present to do all in their power to change this condition, which is the cause of the immorality, crime, and lack of progress in certain sections.

Hon. R. L. Smith of Texas, when called upon to speak as a representative of the Negro Farmers' Association of Texas, which has 10,000 active members and includes 400 organizations, told how the Tuskegee Conference had inspired him to start an agricultural school at Waco, which now owns 95 acres of land and 5 buildings worth $20,000 and is crowded with students. Inspired by a meeting of the Negro Business League he went home and established a farmers' bank, whose shares of stock are sold at $10 and $15. Three-quarters of a million dollars have passed through the hands of its directors and its resources have increased from $7000 to $93,000.

All about the chapel hung large charts showing the progress of the Negro farmer in the United States in the past fifty years. These charts were carefully prepared from authorized sources by Professor Monroe N. Work, of the research department of the Institute. The most important of the facts presented are given in the following table.

AGRICULTURAL PROGRESS OF NEGRO FARMERS IN FIFTY YEARS

	1863	1913
Negro farmers	. . . 15,000 . . .	. . . 937,000 . . .
Acres operated	. . . 600,000 . . .	. . . 42,000,000 . . .
Farm owners	. . . 4,000 . . .	. . . 225,000 . . .
Acres owned	. . . 300,000 . . .	. . . 20,000,000 . . .
Value domestic animals . . .	. . . $150,000 . . .	. . . $180,000,000 . . .
Value farm machinery	. . . $100,000 . . .	. . . $37,000,000 . . .
Value lands and buildings . .	. . . $700,000 . . .	. . . $275,000,000 . . .
Value all property of Negro farmers	. . . $1,000,000	. . $500,000,000 . . .

One of the tables which follow shows that ten of the Southern states have each ten thousand or more Negroes who own large farms. The other shows the crops raised by Negro farmers, indicating the economic value of the race to the South.

STATES HAVING 10,000 OR MORE NEGROES OWNING FARMS

STATES	NUMBER OF FARMERS	NUMBER OF ACRES OWNED	VALUE OF LAND AND BUILDINGS
Virginia	. . . 32,228 . . .	. . 1,381,223 . . .	. $28,059,534
Mississippi	. . . 25,026 . . .	. . 2,227,194 . . .	. 34,317,764
North Carolina . . .	. . . 21,443 . . .	. . 1,197,496 . . .	. 22,810,089
Texas	. . . 21,232 . . .	. . 1,866,742 . . .	. 30,687,272
South Carolina . . .	. . . 20,372 . . .	. . 1,089,044 . . .	. 22,112,291
Alabama	. 17,082 . .	. . 1,466,719 . . .	. 17,285,502
Georgia	. . . 15,698 . . .	. . 1,349,503 . . .	. 20,540,910
Arkansas	. . . 14,662 . . .	. . 1,202,114 . . .	. 20,694,215
Louisiana	. . . 10,725 . . .	. . 834,695 . . .	. 12,779,570
Tennessee	. . . 10,700 . . .	. . 590,676 . . .	. 12,179,780

The Declarations of the Farmers' Conference were published in the last issue of the *Southern Workman*.

CROPS RAISED BY NEGRO FARMERS

CROP	QUANTITY PRODUCED		PER CENT TOTAL CROP RAISED IN UNITED STATES
	UNIT OF MEASURE	TOTAL	
Cotton	. . Bale . . .	. . 4,000,000 . . .	. . . 39.0 . . .
Corn	. . Bushel . . .	. . 100,000,000 . . .	. . . 3.5 . . .
Oats	. . Bushel . . .	. . 4,500,000 . . .	. . . 0.4 . . .
Wheat	. . Bushel . . .	. . 4,000,000 . . .	. . . 0.5 . .
Rice	. . Pound . . .	. . 20,000,000 . . .	. . . 9 0 . . .
Potatoes { white	. . Bushel . .	. . 4,000,000 . . .	. . . 1.0 . . .
sweet	. . Bushel . . .	. . 12,000,000 . . .	. . 21.0 . . .
Tobacco	. Pound . . .	. . 90,000,000 . . .	. . . 10.0 . . .
Hay and forage . .	. . Ton . . .	. . 500,000 . . .	. . . 0.5 . . .

THE WORKERS' CONFERENCE

The Farmers' Conference took a look backward over fifty years, but the Workers' Conference, on the contrary, took a look forward over fifty years, with a view to estimating what may be saved to the South in that time by the conservation of the health of the Negro people. If the load of ignorance of sanitary precautions and the methods of disease prevention now oppressing the masses of Negroes can be removed, it is estimated that in fifty years the death rate of the race and the annual economic loss to the South resulting from the sickness and death of Negroes may be decreased one-half. The amount that might thus be saved, it is calculated, would be sufficient to provide good schoolhouses and six months' schooling for every child in the South. The charts giving these estimates, like those shown at the Farmers' Conference, were made by Professor Work, and the figures used in making them were pronounced by an educational expert present to be as accurate as it is possible to get them.

The second day's conference, therefore, resolved itself into a committee of the whole to consider the best methods of removing the ignorance which causes this economic loss and to present some concrete illustrations of these methods. The audience was a more representative one than has ever before gathered at Tuskegee for this conference, nearly every important colored school in the South sending delegates, as well as state and national boards of health, and the National Child Welfare Committee. There were a number of Negro physicians present, but it was felt that many more should have taken this opportunity of learning how to make a concerted effort to teach their people preventive measures.

The text of the health sermons was ''pure air, pure water, pure food.'' Dr. Oscar Dowling, president of the Louisiana State Board of Health, who had come to Tuskegee in person with the two state health cars, had spoken to the farmers the previous day on the importance of sleeping with windows open, and of using plenty of water, giving them a plan for building an inexpensive and rather crude but perfectly practical bathroom in a lean-to which can be attached to the smallest cabin. He also urged the building, in connection with every home, of the Stiles sanitary closet. On the second day Dr. Dowling read a paper covering the various aspects of the health question and announcing the purpose of his Board to make a state-wide campaign this spring among the colored people of Louisiana, to teach them how to prevent tuberculosis, typhoid, and other common diseases. He also said that he has planned comfortable, sanitary homes for colored people on a tract of six hundred and forty acres and hopes to carry the details into execution within a short time.

Dr. A. M. Brown of Birmingham, president of the National Medical Association, divided the causes of disease into two classes—those which the people can control and those which they cannot. The first class includes all diseases resulting from neglect of health, sanitation, and preventive measures and from indulgence in vice; the second includes those caused by improper or unenforced state and city legislation. He spoke particularly of the duties devolving on the Negro physician. "It is the Negro doctor," he said, "who should teach the Negro how to sleep, how to dress, and how to feed his children." Dr. Sanders, president of the Alabama State Board of Health, was most concerned in regard to the intemperance of the colored people in eating and drinking and in the use of tobacco and snuff. In fact, it became clear at both conferences that, next to ignorance, the greatest obstacle in the Negro's path of progress is the use of intoxicating liquor.

Dr. Washington, in his opening address, called attention to the facts set forth on the charts hanging about the room and spoke particularly of the importance of co-operation by white people in the effort to conserve Negro health. "The life of the humblest black person in the South," he said, "touches the life of the most exalted white person in the South. It is impossible for the Negro to have a weak and diseased body without affecting the life of the whole community. For this reason and also on the higher ground of justice, honor, and humanity, I plead for the interest and help of our white friends."

One of the most important questions discussed was how to get before the masses of the people the information given at the Conference, and here again ignorance, even the ignorance of many preachers, was admitted to be the obstacle in the way. "Our people do not read," said a speaker. "We can talk and discuss here, but the majority of our ministers and leaders are not here. The masses of our people must be taught to read." Dr. Washington announced that the material on the charts and other information given at the Conference would be printed and distributed, and the Declarations requested that "every minister, teacher, and physician constitute himself a committee of one to teach health and sanitation to the people." The Conference also recommended that an organization for the conservation of Negro health be formed in the South, that it include the various organizations for this purpose which already exist, aud that it meet biennially in connection with the Tuskegee Workers' Conference.

THE HEALTH EXHIBITS

Adding enormously to the value of the discussions were the various health exhibits. In the rooms on the right and left of the hall leading to the assembly room in which the Conference was held, and in the hall itself, was the exhibit of the National Child Welfare Committee under the care of Miss Emily Coye of New York City. Even more interesting than the graphic charts and the objects sent from place to place by this Committee was the result of "linking-up" this exhibit with local conditions at Tuskegee and among the people whom the school is trying to reach. Under Miss Coye's direction the various departments prepared supplementary exhibits showing in a most practical manner how sanitary laws may be obeyed even by the poorest and most ignorant person. From the dainty cradles made from baskets and crates to the meals for a working man set on small tables; from the proper care of milk to the proper care of a tuberculosis patient, there was nothing omitted that could carry a suggestion for better living.

The Louisiana Health Car was visited by the thousands present and was a veritable storehouse of information and warning in matters of ventilation, drainage, food, and disinfection. Similar truths were pressed home by the moving pictures on health and sanitation given by Dr. Dowling on the lawn in front of the new girls' dormitory on Wednesday evening. In fact, nothing was left undone that might help in any degree to impress the necessity of conserving the health of the Negro or to teach the people how to accomplish this object.

THE PROBLEM OF HEALTH ON INDIAN RESERVATIONS

BY ELSIE E. NEWTON

PUBLIC attention has been widely called to health conditions among Indians by a report of an investigation made last year by the Public Health and Marine Hospital Service at the request of Congress.[1] Those familiar with reservations were not surprised at the prevalence of trachoma and tuberculosis disclosed, but doubtless a good many people were set to wondering why such prevalence is possible and what the Government is doing to check it.

Particular conditions have arisen through specific causes, but in general they are the usual symptoms of that change from the modes of life and thought of the uncivilized to the civilized, accentuated by the rapidity of the change. The diseases of civilized life necessitate a protective and preventive method of living; in his former free and wide existence, where the unfit lost out and disease was frequently left behind, the Indian had little need of such a method, which he must now, however, understand and acquire.

On the part of the public, there has been a tardy recognition of the true offices of the physician as a teacher and a sanitarian as well as a doctor of disease, and the Government has shared in the general sentiment in this regard. A school for Indians, with its white employees, required that a physician be employed to care for illness when it occurred, but that his efforts should be directed towards a regulation of health conditions on the reservations was, until recently, not to be thought of. Nor is there any blame to be attached to such an attitude, since public opinion even five years ago was not as educated along health lines as it is now. Moreover, in Indian administration, there were other things concerned besides health, and many a complication might have arisen from giving too much authority to physicians who were not dealing with whites but with an ignorant race.

The early experiences of the white practitioner among Indians make a chapter of encounters with aboriginal prejudice not wholly finished. Even his own life was not safe if the doctor ventured too near the borderland of prejudice, and if a death occurred at the beginning of his practice, he was likely to be avoided for the rest of his sojourn. This in itself was discouraging.

1 Senate Document, 1088; 62nd Congress: *Contagious and Infectious Diseases among Indians*

If added to it there was the inability to follow up a case or to prescribe proper remedies because they were unsafe except under supervision, it can easily be seen that a practitioner's life was not one round of joy.   Many an Indian came for a first dose and was never seen or heard of afterwards—whether death or distaste was the result of his visit the doctor might never know. Or an entire bottle of cough syrup would be consumed at once, on the theory that if a teaspoonful was good, a bottleful would be better !   I recall the case of an Indian with heart trouble for whom the physician prescribed digitalis.   Two doses were prepared with minute directions for each, the Indian appearing to be more intelligent and trustworthy than the average.   As a precaution, the man was to camp in the front yard under the doctor's eye.   But all this elaboration was vain, since the man took the two doses at once.   Consider what could have been done with such a case at a distance of twenty-five miles !

An Indian Service physician had to await the coming of his patients ; he could not go out into the highways and byways and compel them to come in, even though he was paid to serve them and his help was badly needed.   Although he might be sure of his ability to relieve, he had to stand by and see the most desperate case suffer and maybe die, because he could not afford to run the risk of an unfortunate ending to any case treated under compulsion.

Some people are ready to criticise the Government for not using compulsion in instances where life might be saved, but they are those who do not understand the extent to which the Indian is superstitious and ignorant.   Let us imagine a young and enthusiastic physician, late an interne in an up-to-date Eastern city, coming to a reservation where the Indians are rather backward.   Finding that there are few facilities to work with, he asks for a hospital.   A hospital is forthwith built and a nurse established.   Many Indians come and go at the dispensary but none stay to be treated,   The doctor, becoming impatient to use his hospital, asks that a certain case of pneumonia, for instance, be brought in because there are no facilities at home for the proper care of the patient.   The patient refuses to leave his tepee ; his friends refuse to bring him.   Force is required ; he is brought in, but although the best of care is given him, he dies.   What, then, is the plight of the young enthusiast ?   He is avoided entirely by the rest of the Indians, and because they believe in the return of the spirit after death, they will not for a generation inhabit his hospital because it is now haunted.   Moreover, excited by the medicine man who dislikes his white rival, they threaten to mutiny or otherwise make trouble for the agent.   Such an instance would not have been hypothetical in former days, and there are some reservations at the present time to which it might be equally applicable.

Not long since, on a reservation where the Office had forbidden the sun dance, one of the most prominent and most influential Indians was stricken with spotted fever and died. His friends said that the misfortune was the result of the omission of the dance. This will serve to illustrate the deep-rooted superstitions of Indians even as they are today; how much more in the past their prejudices have hampered the cause of health, may easily be inferred.

Reservation physicians have immense distances to cover. Until recently, adequate means for getting over the country were not provided. It was not an uncommon occurrence for a physician to be two weeks on the road in visiting only a few cases. To be gone several days was usual. Imagine one doctor to the entire state of Connecticut and obliged to go by team from one end to the other, and it will be realized what it meant to be a reservation doctor. Occasionally he had to provide his own team, and more often than not had to care for it at all times. Unless he became familiar with the language, or by grace was furnished with an interpreter, his intercourse was very limited and unsatisfactory. Certainly, under such conditions, a thorough sanitary reformation of the Indian country would have been a miracle, especially where there were neither nurses nor field matrons to assist.

The era of improvement may be said to have begun with the International Congress on Tuberculosis held in Washington in 1908. There was a great awakening of the general public at that time, in which the Indian Service' shared, and from which it reaped immediate reward. There had never been a medical supervisor previously; one was authorized, and sanitary reforms begun. The schools were made the first object of effort. Double beds were eliminated, the individual drinking cup tabooed, and regular and thorough physical examination of pupils required. Children found to have even incipient tuberculosis were returned to their homes. Other measures have been undertaken, such as the introduction of the Pullman system of towels, the taking out of obsolete types of closets and installing the newest and most sanitary kind above ground instead of in the basements. Playgrounds have become common, and more than one school has an expensive gymnasium. But all reforms require money with which to make them. For instance, when the order went out to substitute single beds for double ones , it was found that it would cost twenty thousand dollars, and without a special appropriation, two years, to accomplish it. When the amount of air space required was increased from 400 cubic feet to 500 cubic feet, the capacity of each school was reduced and enlarged quarters made necessary to accommodate the rightful enrollment. The building of sleeping porches has been carried on as rapidly as funds allow, but for each child who sleeps out of doors in a cold climate, there must be extra clothing and bedding which the current allowance of a school may not have taken into account. The enlargement of the school rations, now allowing such substitutive articles and quantities as will give a more nourishing and varied diet, would have been impossible under the old law that penalized a superintendent who did not keep current expenses down to $167 per capita a year. The limit has had to be removed in the interest of good administration.

An element in school life for Indians that used not to be taken into account, is the effect of restraint and routine on children who have hitherto been used to no restraint. It has a physical depression which, coupled with the nostalgia to which an Indian child is liable, may tend to lower the resistance of the pupil. For this reason, even more pains should be taken to suit the environment to his needs than is taken with the white child, who, even away at school, is not among aliens in language, thought, and habits.

With all the handicaps, important strides have been taken in the improvement of health conditions and more are being made each year, so that in time the schools will have become the radiating points of standards of good living. That they have done much to dispel the prejudice against the white physician on the reservations must not be overlooked. The children have become used to his ministrations at school and have taken home a very different idea of him from the one they brought.

Compared with that of the school, the task of improving health conditions on the reservation is serious. Over pupils, there is control and authority with the ability to enforce regulations, but there are many perplexities to discourage the sanitarian in Indian homes, and until we can strike at the root of the matter and improve the Indian home, we can have little hope for the betterment of the race.

Records will show that as regards the full-bloods, the Indian population is not increasing. The mortality among full-bloods is greater; in some places the death rate is greater than the birth rate, in others about even, or slightly below, in others a little above, while only a few tribes are growing numerically stronger, one of these being the Navahos.

The reasons may be classified as (1) lack of resistance to disease, due to poor or irregular food supply, lack of regular employment, liquor, and inbreeding ; and (2) the prevalence of disease due to insanitary habits of living.

Tuberculosis causes the greatest number of deaths, the diges-

tive disorders of early childhood the next greatest, while incur-
sions of such epidemics as whooping cough and measles come
third on the list of fatal causes. The incidence of tuberculosis is
everywhere acknowledged to be greater than among whites.
The reasons for an Indian's susceptibility have been widely discussed. It is not within the scope of this article to discuss them
except to point out some of the very obvious weak spots in the
Indian economy. First of all, with a few exceptions, the food
supply is not satisfactory. It is a fact that tuberculosis is less
frequent among the Pueblos of the Southwest than among other
tribes. These Indians have lived in houses for generations, and
they have a fine climate. But other Indians in the same climatic
conditions are more afflicted with tuberculosis, living either in
camps or houses ; it is reasonable to suppose, therefore, that the
greatest factor in the resistance of the Pueblo is his food supply
and the habits of industry necessary to procure it. They own
irrigable lands which they cultivate industriously. They raise corn
in plenty, melons, peaches, apricots, squash, peppers, also a few
sheep.   The corn is hand-ground, very fine, and made into paper-
like bread. It is also boiled on the cob and then dried for winter
use. Melons and squash last into the winter. Seldom is it that a
Peublo family knows what it is to stint food, unless perchance there
may have been some agricultural catastrophe. The supply is
such, and their providence so general, that there is no danger of
the feast-or-famine custom which prevails among the tribes where
the supply is more haphazard.

Contrast with such circumstances those of some of the tribes
of the North who were formerly hunters and warriors, living
almost entirely upon meat. When they were limited to their reservations, the Government provided beef as a substitute for the
buffalo they formerly hunted. Much of their country is not fit for
the amateur farmer, such as they would probably be if farmers at
all, and as stock-raisers they had more interest in the food a herd
would supply, than in the income from its increase. Meat is
still their favorite diet, but meat is getting scarce. On one of
these reservations the physician told me that it was his opinion
that all of the Indians in his district were living on one-fourth
rations—that is, one-fourth were receiving rations and the entire
population of the community were living off the one-fourth.
Certainly their appearance bore out the statement. At this place
I went to call upon an ex-schoolgirl who was dying with tuberculosis. There were two or three grown men in the family, but
very few signs of prosperity about the place. I asked the girl
what she had to eat ; she answered, "Crackers and meat."
I asked her husband if he did not have a cow. Yes, he said,
he had two, but they were somewhere on the range, he did

not know where. He had owned a fresh cow, he said, but had sold it for fifty dollars. There were no chickens to furnish eggs for the sick woman, and the only resource of the family was a hundred and fifty dollars to her credit at the Agency ; this was being doled out to her, but it would have needed a daily guard to see that the whole of it was not appropriated or its value consumed by the relatives. Yet it was the husband, ineffectual as a provider, who was taking almost tender care of the woman and who kept in decent order the little sickroom.

This is one of the many painful instances of a house-to-house inspection on a reservation, and it serves to illustrate one of the problems we have to meet. In the premises, how would it have been possible to set these grown men to work to supply needed food to the sick woman ? What assurance is there that the whole family, a part of which is already infected, will not succumb to the disease through a lowered vitality due to lack of food?

The constant hospitality practiced by Indians, and the custom of sharing the last crumb, is another phase of the food question, difficult to be appreciated by whites. As long as an Indian has any subsistence, his neighbors and friends come a-visiting, to remain as long as the food holds out. To be inhospitable or ''stingy like the white man '' is an opprobrium which only the hardiest Indian can socially survive. This Indian virtue bars the way to an equalization of any distribution of food, and I may remark incidentally that it is the cause of many of those cases of '' Indians Starving, '' which the newspapers make much of. Of the rations issued to the old and infirm, the younger and abler bodied have no code that forbids them to be self-invited sharers, and thus the benovolent purposes of the Government are thwarted.

To learn what is the food taste of the reservation, one needs only to glance at the stock of goods carried by the local trader. Thus, among the Sioux, I found the best brands of canned vegetables and fruits. ''The Indians will have no others,''say the traders. The most of the supplies are good—coffee, tea, condensed milk, canned goods of all sorts, sugar, flour, baking powder, and crackers. One trader I met makes weekly shipments of bread and cookies. I have seldom seen an Indian woman making light-bread at home. In a Shoshone tepee, not long ago, I saw a young girl soaking a cake of yeast. I asked her what she was going to do. ''Make bread, '' she answered. ''And where did you learn to make bread?'' I asked. ''At the Mission School, '' she told me. Some of the white settlers' wives make light-bread regularly for the Indians, but they seem to prefer crackers where native bread has fallen out of use.

The Pueblos keep chickens, the Navahos occasionally milk

their goats, and among some of the other tribes the custom of keeping cows and chickens is gradually creeping in, but very slowly. It is still rare to find milch cows even among those who own stock, so that milk is never found except where the Indians are unusually well advanced. Among the Sioux, dog meat is still used, while a few of the Indians in Oklahoma have not ceased to use carrion. In general, however, the Indian's taste is steadily approximating that of the white man, because he is, after all, quite as dependent upon the same sources of supply.

So closely is the lack of occupation connected with the economic state as a cause of predisposition to disease, that it needs but a brief notice. There is nothing healthier for mind and body than a compelling industry, not too hard. With idleness comes the mischief to morals, and mental and physical flabbiness, all conducive to disease. Unfortunately, physical labor has been looked upon by the Indian as the woman's work; indeed, in one of the Indian languages the word for chores means "woman's work."

That the close intermarriage of many of the tribes is a reason for their gradual disappearance cannot be disregarded in any discussion touching their physical condition. The former constant movement of the Plains Indians, their sorties and warfare, resulted in many mixed unions which kept the blood fresh. Since their segregation and their limitations, the tendency has been otherwise. One tribe is said to have decreased from about 2800 to 1700 in 20 years. These Indians have intermarried very little with whites, and as they have not been a moral tribe, the chances are that inbreeding has been entirely too frequent. The Pueblos have already become extinct in one or two villages; the marriages outside of the tribe had been few, and it was inevitable that they should have become inbred.

Of the causes for the spread of disease, that of insanitation is the greatest, and although it is a contested point, I believe that a too sudden change to the permanent home has been a factor. The old Indian custom of burning or abandoning a dwelling where a death had occurred was not a bad measure except from an economic point of view. But when an Indian had expended considerable money in a house, as of late the Government has induced him to do, it was quite necessary to teach him that such a dwelling could not be burned when death had visited it. Fumigation would solve the problem, if it were possible to fumigate in every instance, but without it the house has meant the annihilation of those infected families who did not know how to make it sanitary. The camp had the advantage of being easily moved and of being less occupied during the day. Also, for some reason I do not understand, the Indian keeps a house much hotter than he does a tepee or a tent. When the tepee was used, there was some ventilation assured. With the house, there is none. Many of the houses are of logs with few windows, and such windows as there are are firmly fastened in the wall. It is a matter of remark that Indians wish to lock themselves in after dark because of some superstitious fear of the night. Frankly, the Indian is afraid of the night, probably because of the spirit stories told in his youth. Thus, at bedtime, you are likely to find nearly every window and door in the Indian country not only shut but sealed, and until this prejudice is outgrown, ventilation will remain the serious problem that it is.

It is noticeable, however, that the number and size of windows has perceptibly increased. Even the log houses have more light, while all the houses of the newer type are abundantly provided with doors and windows. One young Navaho, who was assistant carpenter at one of the schools, employed his vacation at home in building more windows in his father's house.

The Navaho hogan affords plenty of ventilation, for the opening at the top takes almost the entire roof of the truncated cone which a hogan represents. The arbor is almost universal. It is built of brush and trees situated near the house, and to it the family escapes as soon as the weather allows. One sees it among the Papagoes in Arizona and the Sioux of the North. On the Kiowa Reservation this very excellent feature has been preserved by the superintendent; when he built new houses for his Indians, he put a shingled pavilion near by. Some have cement floors, and a few are screened. This makes an ideal resort for the family during the day and I have no doubt has added much to their health.

With the traveling dentists, the traveling trachoma specialists, the field nurses, the field matrons, and the increased number of local physicians at better salaries, we are acquiring a fair amount of machinery to attack the problem of health. Last year Congress generously made a special appropriation of $200,000 with which to build hospitals, carry on special work in trachoma, enlarge the campaign against tuberculosis already begun, and strengthen the sanitarium work. The trachoma campaign is already showing results. Where formerly the number of sore eyes or bad eyes, from whatever cause, was noticeable, there are now but few. On one of the Sioux reservations, as an example, a prevalence of twenty per cent was reported two years ago, ten per cent a year ago, and this year, at the opening of school, there could not have been more than three per cent. This is due to the persistent and continuous treatment given by the employees at the day schools, following the visit of an eye specialist who operated on many of the eyes and prescribed for others.

Of the two diseases, tuberculosis presents the greater problem. The loss or impairment of vision is bad enough, but tuberculosis threatens life itself, not only of a single person, but of a wide circle of people. It is still the greatest single menace to the red race. Its treatment is long, expensive, and presents more complexities than that of trachoma. An Indian may submit himself to eye treatment for a few weeks, months, or even a year, but to put himself under restraint with possible separation from friends for the years required, in a sanitarium for tuberculosis, is a proposition not likely to appeal to him. Being a fatalist, he submits himself to the disease rather than to the treatment.

There are three successful sanitariums for school children already in operation, and a fourth is now being opened. These are situated at Fort Lapwai, Idaho; Phoenix, Arizona; Laguna, New Mexico; and Toledo, Iowa. The combined capacity is probably three hundred and fifty. All merely curative institutions have an educational value and much is to be expected from their establishment in the effect upon those both directly and indirectly concerned.

But, after all, the best results will be obtained when we all, employees and Indians, have learned to think in terms of prevention and resistance, in our everyday lives. This can come only from continuous agitation, education, and persistent effort from the center to the circumference ; and the great element of success is individual effort rather than elaborate machinery.

SUBSTITUTES FOR THE CONVICT LEASE SYSTEM

BY E. STAGG WHITIN

Chairman of the Executive Board of the National Committee on Prison Labor

PRISONERS are public property. The public is aroused to the need of sane reform in the use of these state chattels. Negro slavery derived its better side from the good master's responsibility for his slave. Good people throughout this country and high-minded state officials are alike realizing this responsibility and seeking substitutes for the prevailing evil system of penal discipline, together with a broad, constructive program for administrative development.

The convict lease system is no Southern problem, but a nation's problem. When Rhode Island, Connecticut, Delaware, Indiana, Iowa, or Wisconsin say they contract for the labor of their convicts, they are only admitting the existence of the lease system itself, adapted to meet the climate and the demands of the industrial interests which held the lessee. What the lessee wants is the labor of the convicts under his control. In the Southland he has had to provide for the convict's maintenance to get his labor ; in the Northland he gets his labor without the embarrassment of his maintenance. Be not deceived, the exploitation of the convict by business interests is national in its scope, respects neither color nor previous condition of servitude, nor the limitations of the Mason and Dixon line.

When our forefathers wanted cheap labor, in all the original colonies, except Georgia, they bought the convicts at the ship-landing, from the captain who brought them from the jails of England ; when they wanted the mines of Connecticut worked by cheap labor it was the shackled convict who was forced into their depths; when machinery developed the first knitting and shoe factories, it was the children in the reformatories of New York and the men and women in the prisons of Wisconsin who were bought for a song. The building of great institutions in the name of reform has in large part supplied salaried positions for the idle voter and graft for the political henchman—all in the name of scientific penology, with a laugh and a wink to the dominant business interests which controlled the political destinies of many a

state. Be not deceived, this movement for the abolition of penal
servitude, for which the labor organizations and the sincere prison
reformer have worked for years, found its expression in many
a Northern state, along with the movement against Negro slavery ; but it is interesting to note that, despite the anguish of the
great conflict, the close of the war left upon the constitution of
the United States an amendment which, abolishing slavery and
involuntary servitude, definitely by prescription perpetuated the
system of penal servitude. The South, the seat of the war, had
none but military prisons ; the North, with its victorious army,
had its prisons packed with offenders that the lawlessness of war
had produced. To prohibit the exploitation by penal servitude of
the Northern white prisoner was forgotton, and his lot was overlooked by the press and the public, while the attempts of the
South to control the wayward, shiftless class of vagrants left by
the fortunes of war and emancipation, were derided and suppressed by martial law on the basis of race oppression.

I do not pretend to justify the black code, to analyze the
motives of reconstruction, or to moralize on the results of the last
fifty years. It is sufficient to remember that the same penal servitude which turned over in large numbers the colored man of the
South, together with a few white Southerners, to the exploitation
and tyranny of the slave-driving convict lessee, also turned over
large numbers of Northern white convicts, together with a few
Negroes, to be exploited for the benefit of similar business interests. Would that some Southerner had risen in Congress, in reply
to Blaine, and told this uncomfortable truth. As a Northerner, I
ask for the abolition of this human exploitation in the North, in
the South, in the East, and in the West.

The shifting hand of political fate has placed today in the
hands of the South a large share of the responsibility for the government of this nation. While the party of the South may still
be a minority, it is dominant in the nation. Before a Congress
dominated by this party, led by Southern men, will come the
question of the perpetuation of the lease and contract system.
For many years, bills before Congress have failed of passage ;
what if from the Southland the new stimulus for social righteousness should sweep on and cause the passage of these bills which
will forever abolish this last form of slavery in the Northland—
what irony of fate !

What substitute have we for this exploitation of the convicts by
lessees ? For some score of years, the struggle has waged for the
control by the state of its own convicts. New York, in 1894, put
a provision to this effect into its constitution ; Ohio made it part
of the constitution last year ; the principle has been put into the
statutes of New Jersey by Woodrow Wilson, of Ohio by Harmon,

of Missouri by Hadley, of Wyoming by Carey, and of California by Johnson. Hatfield in West Virginia has begun the work of reconstruction ; Goldsborough in Maryland has made it his slogan for the next campaign. State control means state responsibility ; state responsibility means efficient management for the use of adequate business methods in the state's government ; it means stopping the renting of North Carolina convicts to fake railroad concerns ; it means taking the convicts of South Carolina out of the knitting mills ; it means the abolition of the contracts at Frankfort ; it means the end of coal-mining by convicts in Alabama ; it means the establishment of farm and road work, properly supervised under competent officers, with all the means for uplift which the genius of management can produce ; this is no small task, but it is one definitely possible of accomplishment.

I present a definite recommendation for road and farm work based upon a gathering together of suggestions of those things in management which have proved best in the experience of practical men. The adaptation to local conditions must be left and only the broad lines sketched.

County convict gangs are usually composed of misdemeanant prisoners, black and white, from sixteen years up. Where state or felony convicts are included, little difficulty is found in treating them in the same way as the misdemeanants, provided this treatment is humane.

Convicts should be divided into gangs which should follow the sex and color line, and upon these divisions should be based the housing regulations ; the supervising officers should be of the same sex as those supervised. Within broad lines, the organization, type of food, type of guarding, and recreation should be based upon the industrial needs, viewed from an educational standpoint. Work on a county farm is preferable to road work because the farm produce may be consumed by the charitable institutions of the county, thus making direct return to the county treasurer ; while in the case of road work, the product of the labor has no direct market value and while it adds to the general wealth of the county or state and to taxing power, it often happens that individual landowners secure the largest profit therefrom. In the case of either roads or farms, the work should be organized along lines which will produce efficiency, and at the same time minimize the hardships of the prison. Certain accepted principles have been found to operate in securing efficiency among workmen, upon road gangs as within factories, and in some instances have been applied to convicts with remarkable success. Applying these principles, we will get the following organization:

The gang should be divided into three grades, each grade or squad or subdivision of squad, being worked separately, so that the same speed of work may prevail throughout the grade. Men should be promoted from one squad to another because of efficiency attained in the work.

The incentive for efficiency should be in the shape of money, which should be paid to the convicts according to a fixed scale to be determined by the following method : In the case of roads, the exact cost of building all the roads constructed by convict labor for the last three years should be ascertained ; from this could be reckoned the average cost of building the average mile of road and the value of the work of the average convict in its construction. Each convict gang should consider this amount as its stint per man, and it should be understood that work done over this amount will be credited to the gang. The value of this credit should be figured out in dollars and cents. It will be apparent that the credit given the gang will in no way increase the cost of building the road per mile, for, as the mile is completed in a shorter time than formerly, there is a direct saving per mile in the cost of maintenance of prisoners and guards, the cost of housing, and the wages of guards, owing to the time saved by the efficiency system. These items being known, the saving per mile is easily determined and can be distributed to the prisoners without loss to the county.

The distribution of gang savings should be upon the basis of the grades or squads. Each grade which does the amount of task set it under the above system should be given either a plug of tobacco per man or an extra dish in diet, amounting to one-eighth of the savings of the gang. Failure to make the stint should result in the loss of this reward. The second grade, which, on account of the selective process, will on the average make something more than the stint in each day, should be given the extra food ration of one-eighth of the saving, and another eighth should be deposited to the credit of the men, each man recording his share in a wage-book, which he himself should keep, preferably with penny provident stamps. The third grade, which has been selected for the greatest efficiency of its men, should receive the extra food ration plus two-eighths of the savings in money, which should be distributed as suggested above. The above would total three-fourths of the savings of the gang, the balance being used as an incentive to the guards.

The guards should receive one-fourth of the savings over and above all wages which shall be paid them, and, should any guard be able to have his men under such discipline that he can supervise the work at the same time that he guards, and thus make unnecessary the hiring of a supervising guard, he should receive the same bonus of three-eighths as the highest grade of convicts.

Under a co-operative sharing system like the one above outlined, the danger of escape would decrease in the same proportion as the interest in the work induced by the record increased. The desire of the guard to produce efficiency could be trusted to gradually eliminate the leg-iron from all but the exceptional prisoner, and he, on account of his inability to be efficient, would fall to the lowest group. The increase in nourishing food would increase the vigor of the prisoner and would tend to eliminate laziness and inefficiency. A thorough medical examination should be given those prisoners who fail to make good in the lowest grade, and those found sick or defective should be removed from the gangs. Little or no discipline of the corporal type should be necessary, in that the lazy man who is strong enough to work will feel the ostracism of the rest of the gang, which is probably the strongest compelling force known to society. The educational value of such training is so obvious that it need not be pointed out. Hard work, under the right type of incentive, is the education needed by most convicts of this type.

The application of efficiency to road work has been outlined. On the farm, whether the workers be women or men, a similar scheme for the distribution of earnings can be adopted, but the method of ascertaining just wages must be different. The farm, having been purchased by the county, should return to the county treasurer sufficient money to pay for the bonds issued for its purchase. To this amount should be added a just amount to cover the interest on buildings, insurance, and annual repairs, together with the cost of maintenance, supervision, and guarding; these costs should be deducted from the value of the farm products, estimated on their market value. The supervisor of the farms should collect from the county institutions taking the farm supplies the amount due the farm for these products, and on failure to pay should discontinue the sale to such institutions. The surplus after these payments have been made should be divided among the convicts and guards as suggested above.

The funds belonging to the convicts should be cared for by a duly authorized agency, which, when not the Penny Provident Association or other duly incorporated society, should give bond. The earnings should be distributed to those legally entitled to them, as, for instance, the family of the prisoner or officers of the county to whom costs must be paid.

The change herein advocated will establish a new concept of what incarceration for crime really means. With the change will come a changed attitude in the courts; juries will not hesitate to convict guilty men, or the judge to give the full extent of the penalty; this will mean much for justice, and aid in making firm law and order in your state. But it will do more. The day has passed when the community will tolerate in any state the seizure of men for trivial offences, and their incarceration for a long series of years to satisfy the avarice of business interests. The gathering in of the convicts when there is work to be done must cease with exploitation, and political jobbery in connection with the courts and the penal administration. It is in this connection that public spirit and pride must play their part. We are at the beginning of a period of social education. We must combine in committees and associations to spread the gospel and to establish the new spirit. In this field, the National Committee on Prison Labor has its place, dealing with the nation's problem, contrasting state with state, governor with governor, calling on local pride, and developing local support. Its local committees, inspired by broad knowledge and striving ever to educate the convicts of their community through that opportunity and that spirit of hope which Oglethorpe implanted in his little colony, must hold up the hand of the administrators who sincerely desire to accomplish results amid the embarrassment of antiquated laws, ancient forms, and the evil influences which permeate political organisms and tend to drive out ideals. We ask men and women to join us in our endeavor ; there is work for all to do ; there is an opportunity for service. Who could ask a greater cause or better issue ?

Book Reviews

Better Rural Schools: By George Herbert Betts and Otis Earle Hall. Published by the Bobbs-Merrill Company, Indianapolis. Price, $1.25

AN inspiring and suggestive book, supplemented by clear and convincing photographs and charts, with a short but well-chosen bibliography, and an excellent table of contents outlining the whole volume by the use of the topical side-headings, is here offered. The authors, Mr. George Herbert Betts, a psychologist who has published several other books on educational subjects, and Mr. Otis Earle Hall, superintendent of schools in Montgomery County, Indiana, have contributed to the volume a knowledge of the theory and practice of rural education and have presented it in a spirit of practical idealism which compels the attention and, one might almost say, the active co-operation of the reader.

Besides the introductory and concluding chapters which discuss respectively the present demand and the future outlook for better rural schools, there are four main sections of the book: The Curriculum of the Rural School; The Teacher and the Rural School; Consolidation and Rural School Efficiency; and Rural School Administration. So enthusiastic and patriotic a spirit pervades the two middle sections that the glory of being a successful teacher of rural life in a rural community, or a successful promoter of rural school consolidation in a district which has failed to realize its potentialities, seems very alluring.

The book has, to recommend it, not only eloquence in the propagation of a movement which has proved itself valuable, but also suggestions of methods already successfully used in the United States for improving the curriculum, for encouraging and carrying out consolidation, and for managing both the consolidated rural school and the one-room district school, which latter is at least a temporary necessity.

If the authors seem too sanguine in their representation of the average farmer as a well-to-do citizen who can easily afford to pay adequate taxes for up-to-date schools, they answer any objection to this premise in their demonstration that the increased tax, per capita, demanded for the efficient rural school economically managed, by no means equals the increased value of the school to the community.   M. I. H.

A **Woman Rice Planter**: By Patience Pennington, with an introduction by Owen Wister and illustrations by Alice R. H. Smith.   The Macmillan Company, New York.   Price, $2.00

AS Mr. Wister says in his introduction to Mrs. Pennington's book, "This is a Southern picture unsurpassed. . . . a native document of permanent historic value." It is an almost daily record of the duties, pleasures, successes, and disappointments of the owner of a rice plantation in South Carolina.   That the owner happens to be a woman—a very gentle and sympathetic but withal a plucky and courageous woman—adds tremendously to the interest of the book. Mrs. Pennington's attitude towards her Negro servants is one typical of the old-time plantation mistress—almost maternal in its solicitude for their comfort, appreciative and generous when they render faithful service, and over considerate and indulgent to them in their weaknesses and flagrant abuses of her confidence.   One would like to know what "the still, small voice," to which she was so obedient, said to her about continuing her lonely struggle to eke out an existence on the fields where rice-planting has become a thing of the past. Such courage and endurance as Mrs. Pennington's amid the thousand distractions and discouragements and deceptions which fell to her lot deserve a generous reward.

The pictures which the author gives of Southern life are charming—the days out of doors enjoying the beauty of the woods and fields and sky, the long drives with funny little "Dab" sitting up behind, the perilous crossing of the flatboat ferry with the spirited horses, the long rows across the river to visit a neighbor, the days of planting and harvesting in the fields directing the picturesque workers—all are vivid and interesting.   The illustrations have, for the most part, the real charm of the South, and are Millet-like in their characterization of peasant life.   J. E. D.

At Home and Afield

HAMPTON INCIDENTS

FOUNDER'S DAY

THE stories and reminiscences of General Armstrong recalled at each anniversary of his birth make it very clear that, although Hampton has lost the man, his personality is still one of the school's most powerful assets. The testimony of many of the older and more influential graduates who knew him—"I am trying to do what General Armstrong would like to have me do"— together with the genuine affection which characterizes every mention of him by his former students and co-workers, declare that he is still a moving influence in their lives.

On the Saturday evening before Founder's Day, celebrated this year on February 1, the Armstrong League of Hampton Workers held a meeting in the Museum, and five graduates talked informally of their memories of General Armstrong. The speakers were Mr. George J. Davis, '74, now manager of Whipple Farm; Mr. Fred D. Wheelock, '88, of Hampton, Va.; Mrs. Laura Titus, '76, president of the Colored Y. W. C. A. in Norfolk, Va.; Capt. Allen Washington, '91, now assistant disciplinarian at Hampton; and Mrs. Harris Barrett, '84, of Hampton, Va. Mr. Louis Armell, ex-student, '97, an Indian farmer of Winnebago, Nebraska, who came to Hampton after General Armstrong's death, told of the interesting circumstances of his coming, of his disappointment at being too late to see "the great man," and of the work which Hampton's returned Indians are doing in the West.

Each graduate had instances to relate of the General's sense of fairness in dealing with culprits and in looking after the comfort and pleasure of his students and helpers. One speaker summarized his speech happily by saying, "He taught us all lessons of self-reliance, self-help, and self-confidence." Mrs. Titus, who, as one of the original Hampton singers, helped to "sing up" Virginia Hall, described amusing incidents of their Northern trip, how the boys were "mighty fastidious" when they walked on Fifth Avenue, and suffered from the cold rather than cover their elegant "Prince Alberts" with the old blue army coats which General Armstrong offered them, until the General himself unexpectedly appeared on the city's most fashionable thoroughfare in one of the despised garments; how the General saw a croquet set on a lawn and told the boys and girls to go and play with it, how the owners came out and discovering that their surprise party was made up of Hampton singers, said, "Help yourselves; have a good time." She told also of early days at Hampton, how the girls and the "roach-bugs" shared the old Barracks, and the girls were sure the "roach-bugs" were the ghosts of dead soldiers; and how there used to be an orchard beyond the barn that Mr. Howe watched at night! Mrs. Titus sang very sweetly three of the songs that had been General Armstrong's favorites: "Nobody knows de touble I see;" "Swing low, sweet chariot;" and "I hope my mother will be there."

I was a pleasure to Hamptonians to have present at this meeting Mr. and Mrs. Benjamin F. Dillingham, of Honolulu, and to hear a few words from each of them. Mrs. Dillingham, who was introduced by Mrs. Ellen Weaver, knew General Armstrong during his youthful days in the Hawaiian Islands, and after telling of some of his activities there and of the esteem in which he is still held in his birthplace, she read the poem "Armstrong" which she wrote for the dedication exercises of the Armstrong Memorial at Punahou held on January 30, 1913. The poem was published in the January 1914 issue of the *Southern Workman.*

AT the Sunday morning service Rabbi Stephen S. Wise, of the Free Synagogue, New York City, delivered the Founder's Day Address. Dr. Wise was introduced by Dr. Wm. Jay Schieffelin, of New York, a Hampton trustee, who told of the Rabbi's twenty-one years' service in the fight against corrupt government in Portland, Oregon, and in New York City. Dr. Schieffelin said : " It is most appropriate that the speaker on Hampton's Founder's Day should be a man who has been fighting so manfully to get people out of slavery. He can fully appreciate the great and unselfish life which he commemorates."

The eloquence and earnestness of Dr. Wise's words, and his sympathetic understanding of the spirit in which General Armstrong approached his work, although he himself never met the founder of Hampton, deeply impressed his hearers, most of whom had known and loved General Armstrong. His message to the students, as a member of one disfavored race to members of other disfavored races showed appreciation of their discouragements and difficulties which doubled the value of his words. The address will be published in full in this magazine.

HAMPTON'S TRUSTEES

HAMPTON workers are always glad of a chance to meet the school's

trustees, and the trustees' meeting which brought five of them to Hampton at this season gave that opportunity. Rev. Francis G. Peabody, D. D., of Cambridge, Mass.; Dr. Wm. Jay Schieffelin, Rev. James W. Cooper, D. D., and Mr. Clarence H. Kelsey, all of New York City; Dr. Samuel C. Mitchell, of Richmond, Va.; Mr. Frank W. Darling, of Hampton, Va.; and Dr. Frissell were present at meetings held in connection with Founder's Day.

Dr. Peabody, who spent several days at the school the last of January, spoke to the students in chapel of the recently increased interest throughout Massachusetts in the work of Hampton, resulting in the organization of a state association to promote the school's work. This association will include the large and active Boston Committee and Springfield Club as well as a number of new Hampton leagues in various cities. Dr. Peabody spoke also of the recent loss of two good friends of the school—Mr. Robert C. Ogden, for many years president of the board of trustees, and Mrs. William Potter Wilson, whose great interest in Hampton and its work has been shown in many ways. He told of a brief visit to General Armstrong's home in Hawaii and of his pleasure at finding him loyally honored there as one of the island's great men. On January 30 the Hampton workers had the pleasure of hearing Dr. Peabody's impressions of Japan and the Japanese, received during his recent stay of several months in that country as exchange professor at the University of Tokyo.

At chapel exercises on the Saturday evening before Founder's · Day, Dr. Schieffelin made one of his always entertaining speeches, and was followed by Dr. Mitchell, who took for his text "the Big Four—the public school, the public road, the public library, and public health."

INDIAN CITIZENSHIP DAY

THE thirty-six Indian students at Hampton held their twenty-seventh annual celebration of Indian Citizenship Day on February 8. The day falling on Sunday, the exercises were substituted for the usual evening chapel service in Cleveland Hall. The speaker of the day was Mr. Arthur C. Parker, a Seneca Indian, who is an archæologist connected with the State Education Department, Albany, N. Y., and is also the secretary-treasurer of the Society of American Indians. His subject was "The Relation of 'Surplus' to Indian Progress." Two brief, manly addresses on the duties of the younger Indians to their race and to the country were delivered by Arthur Harris, a Mohave-Apache and Fred Bender, a Chippewa Indian student. A representative of the Negro students offered their greetings and congratulations in an impressive, sincere speech. Four Indian songs delighted the large audience, many of whom were from Fort Monroe and Hampton. The meeting closed with the customary singing of "America," the first verse by a trio representing the three races, the second by the Indian students, the third by the colored students, and the last by the whole audience.

HAMPTON WORKERS

A vacancy in the Domestic Science Department is being filled by Miss Mary R. Kennedy, of Pittsfield, Mass. Miss Kennedy is a graduate of Pratt Institute and has been active in social work in Pittsfield, where she taught cooking to a working girls' club.

Miss M. Louise Sugden of Hampton Institute, a graduate of Vassar College, is employed in the Publication Office, there being a vacancy through the reorganization of the work of that department and the resignation of Miss Marion Swan.

The engagement of Mr. Alfred G. Gilbert, manager of Shellbanks Farm, and Miss Amelia A. Cooke, in charge of the Domestic Science Department, was announced early in the winter.

ATHLETICS

DURING the past month Hampton has gained two basket-ball victories, the first in Baltimore where the team defeated Lincoln University by a score of 27-24, and the second at Hampton on February 14 when Howard University, in a hard fight, was able to score only 23 points to Hampton's 25. The latter game was one of the most exciting that has been played in the Gymnasium. Howard is recognized as Hampton's greatest athletic rival and had, less than a month before, defeated the Hampton team in New York by a score of 27-24. Football supremacy had given Hampton a tantalizing taste of victory. During the entire game on February 14 there was at no time a difference of more than a few points between the scores of the two teams, and the interest was intense. Unless a third game can be arranged, Hampton and Howard will be obliged to share the basket-ball honors for this season.

Two baseball games have been scheduled for this spring, both with Union University. Hampton will also send athletes to an outdoor track meet in Washington, D. C., to compete against representatives from the most prominent colored colleges in this section of the country.

THE WHITTIER SCHOOL

A piano, for which the Whittier has been working for some time, has finally been secured and the school is very proud of it. Part of the money was raised by the children, and it was not found necessary to draw upon Hampton Institute for any of the amount.

At the last meeting of the Parents' Association, white friends in Hampton, who have been active in the school leagues of Virginia, were invited to speak. The meeting was opened with prayer by Rev. Mr. Carter of St. John's Church. Mrs. Henry Lane

Schmelz, president of the Elizabeth City County leagues, told of the work done in the county and spoke of the good that might be done by a strong organization in the Whittier School. Mrs. Frank W. Darling, who was influential in forming a league at the West End School in Hampton, told of the work taken up in the various parts of the state. Mrs. Haw, of Hampton, chairman of the Character-Building Committee in the West End School, said that work similar to that of her committee should be introduced into every school throughout the county. Mr. Carter spoke of the work of the Junior leagues. After the speeches, there was some discussion about forming a Whittier School League then and there, but it was suggested that a strong county association, including all of the colored schools, might be more helpful, and the president called for a meeting of the executive committee the following week to consider the matter.

General Armstrong's birthday, January 30, was celebrated at the Whittier School as usual with appropriate exercises. Mr. Frank Banks, a Hampton graduate and head bookkeeper in the Treasurer's Office, talked to the children most interestingly about his reminiscences of General Armstrong. He told them what freedom ought to mean to them, comparing their lot with the life of little colored children before the war, and said that they were indebted to General Armstrong for the Whittier School, which they so much enjoy. Mr. Banks introduced the General's sister, Miss M. J. Armstrong, his daughter, Mrs. William Scoville, and his grandson, Armstrong Scoville, who sat on the platform, that the children might feel the reality of General Armstrong's life. One of General Armstrong's letters to his mother was read, Hawaiian songs and the General's favorite hymns were sung, and "The Grand Army of Workers," written by Miss Helen Ludlow for Armstrong Day exercises, was acted by little boys and girls.

ENTERTAINMENTS

SIX barrels of steamed oysters turned out hot on long tables and made hotter with horse-radish and tabasco; crackers, pickles, coffee, and sugary doughnuts, cheered the members of the Armstrong League who attended the oyster "roast" in Huntington Hall Auditorium on January 24. The lively entertainment which followed brought before the audience some unexpected talent. Among the numbers were a spirited performance on jawbones to accompany a clog dance, a topical song given with much spirit by a "quartet" of six, and several comedy acts.

"The Japanese Girl," a very pretty operetta, was presented in Cleveland Hall Chapel by the Treble Clef Club for the benefit of the Dixie League on Saturday evening, February 7. The plot of the operetta was light, with little action, but the Japanese scenery was charming and there were a number of delightful solos and choruses.

TRADE SCHOOL NOTES

THE Technical Carpentry Shop has recently completed several hatracks, umbrella racks, and magazine stands; also a set of mission furniture in children's size, consisting of an arm chair, a rocking-chair, and a settee. These articles, all made by firstyear students and often from very simple sketches, show many examples of superior workmanship. The agricultural students, in their short session in this shop, have made, among other things of a practical nature, some wooden molds for concrete troughs, and are now constructing a full-sized poultry house.

The Wheelwright Shop is building a medium-weight farm wagon for use at the school, a covered delivery wagon for a Washington firm, and a new body for a large, open-platform wagon belonging to another Washington firm. It is also constructing, after Mr. S. J. Scott's design, a light farm wagon and a "utility cart." The latter is a light, two-wheeled, driving rig which may be used for carrying light loads. It is hoped to build these in some numbers and so greatly extend, for the blacksmith boys, the valuable practice in "ironing off" wagons, carts, and other vehicles.

THE Machine Shop has recently furnished a six-inch, vertical, steam separator for a New York firm, and is now preparing the patterns for a four-inch separator of the same style for another firm in the same city. It has also added desirable variety to the experience of the machinists by overhauling a large Packard truck belonging to a near-by branch of a Chicago firm. Another large job, now well started, is the rebuilding of a two-cylinder, compound, steam engine for a York River tow-boat. The engine is to be completely overhauled and a new supporting frame and air pump are to be supplied. The work on the new parts is nearly done and the arrival of the tow-boat is expected shortly.

The Bricklaying Shop is building, as a practice exercise, a full-sized brick baking-oven. This is an interesting exercise, as it is the first time in some years that the students have had a chance to build such an oven. It has a long, arched space for the baker's "peels" in what is usually waste space underneath. It is made from a special design by Mr. Wm. A. Webster, the instructor.

VISITORS

RECENT visitors to Hampton were Dr. Karl Rathgen, of the Colonial Institute, Hamburg, with his wife and daughter. Dr. Rathgen was apppointed, upon the nomination of the Prussian Ministry of Education, Kaiser Wilhelm Professor in Columbia University for the year 1913-14, and has been giving a course on the economic problems of modern Germany. He served for eight years in the Imperial University at Japan and has traveled extensively in the East. Professor Rathgen spoke before the Y. M. C. A., one Sunday evening on "The Problems of Slavery in Tropical Africa," mentioning the excellent work done by Tuskegee students in the teaching of agriculture in West Africa.

Dr. John R. Mott, chairman of the Continuation Committee of the World Conference, Associate General Secretary of the International Committee of the Y. M. C. A., and a world authority on missions, visited Hampton with friends on February 8.

Rev. Mr. Ross, a missionary in Surat, India, and Rev. C. S. Ikenberry, of Daleville College, Virginia, visited the school in February to inspect the methods of teaching agriculture and the trades. Mr. William L. Ricks, who is making plans for the founding of a colored industrial school in Cincinnati, Ohio, half a million dollars having been given for that purpose, has been spending several days at the school with his wife, studying the way in which Hampton conducts industrial courses. It is Mr. Ricks's intention to use the vacant lots in Cincinnati for agricultural instruction.

Mr. Henry Pitt Warren, Jr., whose father delivered the Founder's Day address on February 2, 1913, is planning to form a Junior Hampton League in Albany, and has been visiting the school in order to become familiar with its work and needs. Mr. W. H. J. Beckett, director of physical education in the colored branch of the Y. M. C. A. in Washington, D. C., was a recent visitor.

GRADUATES AND EX-STUDENTS

many schools taught by Hampton graduates and ex-students, January 30 is celebrated as Armstrong Day, and chapters of the Armstrong League, whose membership includes former Hampton students, are loyal in their observance of the anniversary. Three accounts of Armstrong Day exercises, which have been sent to the *Southern Workman*, follow :

Exercises were held in celebration of General Armstrong's birthday in the Tuskegee Institute Chapel, Friday night, January 3. Night school was suspended. Charles W. Greene, Class of '75, gave a very instructive talk on General Armstrong as he knew him at Hampton. Harrison Finch, a member of the Senior Class, spoke on the General's student life. Fifteen "Hampton grandchildren" sang "The Song of the Armstrong League." The annual address was delivered by the chaplain, Rev. J. W. Whittaker.

ON Sunday, February 1, services celebrating the seventy-fifth anniversary of the birth of General S. C. Armstrong were held by the Richmond chapter of the Armstrong League at the Ebenezer Baptist Church in Richmond, Virginia, one of the finest colored churches in the South. It seats one thousand people, but hundreds were turned away on this occasion. Devotional exercises were conducted by Professor J. W. Barco of Virginia Union University, a Hampton ex-student in 1894; an address of welcome in behalf of the church was given by Rev. W. H. Stokes, and the response in behalf of the League by Mr. W. B. Davenport, ex-student, '78, who knew the General personally and gave many illustrations of the greatness of the head and heart of Hampton's founder. The address of Rev. R. O. Johnson, ex-student, '87, on the life of General Armstrong was most interesting. Mr. Johnson lived with General Armstrong

for a long time, and was probably better acquainted with him than any other student present.

Over fifty graduates and ex-students of Hampton were present and sang the songs which the General loved so much. The scene was like a real day at Hampton. The students from Hartshorn College and Virginia Union University were out in a body with many of their teachers, and seemed to enjoy the program immensely. Though the meeting lasted two hours and a half, no one seemed tired, for many lingered to shake hands with the Hampton students, many of whom were at Hampton as far back as 1872-75. The League meets each month, to enroll new members, to get better acquainted,.to help each other, and for social enjoyment.

A graduate of the Class of '90, Mary E. Fisher Foster, sends the following account of the celebration at her school and of her own work :

"Armstrong Day was celebrated by School No. 3, Pocomoke City, Md., on January 30 in memory of our beloved friend, the late General Samuel Chapman Armstrong. The children of the school gave the Armstrong Day exercises written by Miss Helen Ludlow. There were other poems read and speeches made, and of course we sang the songs that he loved: 'They look like men of war,' 'The Battle Hymn of the Republic,' 'O Freedom,' 'He is King of kings,' and others. We had an audience that enjoyed it, for some were heard to say it was the best they had ever attended. We had manual training work and sewing on exhibition at the time, which was viewed with pride by the parents.

"When my school closes, I shall have taught fifteen years since leaving Hampton, and I am now teaching the same school for the fourth year. I am a Sunday-school worker, and have a mothers' and a young girls' club. It does not seem that much has been accomplished in these fifteen years, but I hope some good seed has been sown."

DOMESTIC SCIENCE in the public school at Bowling Green, Ky., is under the charge of Eugenia A. Mundy, ' 99. The similar position which she resigned in Winchester, Ky., has been filled by Mattie E. Cheeks, '07, who was for three years teacher in the Southern Industrial Classes in Norfolk and vicinity.

Homer Thomas, '01, who was graduated from Oberlin College in 1911 and received an M. A. degree from Yale in 1912, has accepted the position of instructor in mathematics and physics at the Agricultural and Mechanical College, Tallahassee, Florida.

THE Teachers' Association of Northern West Virginia, an active and progressive league of colored teachers, met in Morgantown, W. Va., in November for its eighth annual session in answer to the call of its president, Mattie S. Pronty, '02, who two years after her graduation from Hampton went to Morgantown as a teacher in the public school. In 1910 she became principal of the school, a position which she still holds.

Nettie E. Dolly, '04, is this year teacher of one of the grades in the Calhoun Colored School.

Marcia B. Stillwell, post graduate '05, was graduated last June from the Montclair State Normal School, and has been appointed kindergarten teacher at Camden, N. J.

Dr. Samuel A. Thomas, '06, who was graduated in dentistry at Meharry Dental College in 1913, has opened an office in Newport News, Va.

THE industrial department of the Mayesville Institute, Mayesville, S. C., is under the supervision of Robert L. Page, '07, who is also instructor in bricklaying and mechanical drawing. His wife, Delmo E. Lucas, ex-student '07, is principal of the primary department in the same institution.

Geneva O. Mackey, '10, is teaching in one of the public schools of Norfolk, Virginia.

Joseph E. Herriford, '11, has this year accepted the position of manual training teacher in one of the public schools in Kansas City. Three other Hampton men hold similar positions there—Wm. G. Moore, '12, Harvey L. Watkins, '03, and Wm. T. White, '03. The principal of one of the schools is Richard T. Coles, '78.

Wm. T. Coleman, '12, has been made superintendent of the Wissahickon Boys' Club in Germantown, Pa., where with six assistants he has charge of two hundred and sixty-five boys.

Ethel G. Dabney, '12, is teaching at Ivanhoe, Wythe Co., Va.

Pattie F. Miller, post graduate '12, formerly a teacher at the Penn School, Frogmore, S. C., is this year an assistant in the Gregory Public School, Roanoke, Va.

Ruth B. Oates, post graduate '13, is filling the position of matron at Selma University, Selma, Ala.

George R. Thomas, Trade Class '06, having completed a course at the Leonard Medical School of Shaw University, is now a pharmacist at Kimball, W. Va.

Hugh C. Smith, '13, is working at his trade of bricklaying at his home in King William, Va.

Roscoe C. Lewis, Night School Senior '01, left before the completion of his course to become teacher of wheelwrighting at the Manassas Industrial School at his home, Manassas, Va. In 1903 he opened a wheelwrighting and blacksmithing business in the town, in which he is still employed. During the past summer he was made one of the trustees of the Manassas Industrial School.

Theodore A. Fountain, who finished the course in cabinet-making in 1911, is now teacher of manual training at the Bartlett Agricultural and Industrial School in Dalton, Missouri.

The position of assistant matron in the Nursery House in Kansas City, Missouri, is held by Sarah Grady, Senior Middler, '12.

Estella Busbee, Senior Middler '08, is matron and teacher of sewing at the Garnett School in Pollocksville, N. C.

MARRIAGES

THE marriage has been announced of Dr. Bennette M. Starks, '00, a physician in Baltimore, Md., to Ellen C. McGuinn, daughter of Mrs Nannie Servant McGuinn, '89. Dr. Starks is also a graduate of the Medical College of Howard University.

Eleanora M. Brandon, ex-student '12, and Lee L. Wise, ex-student '11, who is following the carpenter's trade in Portsmouth, Va., were married in Portsmouth on Sept. 21, 1913. Mrs. Wise is the daughter of George W. Brandon, '82, and Clara Bowser Brandon, '85.

Word has been received of the marriage in Hampton, on October 16, 1913, of Pearl L. Miles, '05, to Richard T. Ward, ex-student, '10, of Baltimore, Md.

DEATHS

NEWS has been received of the death of North T. Reid, Trade Class '11, on April 22, 1913.

Fannie E. Smallwood, post graduate '06, died at the home of her sister in Buffalo on January 13, 1914. Immediately after finishing her course at Hampton, she went to Wilmington, Delaware, to become teacher of domestic science in the graded public school, a position which she held until last spring, when she was obliged to stop teaching on account of her health.

Mrs. Sudie Smith, of Cape Charles, Va. writes of the death of her husband, Wm. R. Smith, ex-student, '87, on August 8, 1913. He was for twenty-five years car inspector for the N. Y. P. & N. Co. at Cape Charles.

ON December 30, 1913, Roscoe C. Anderson, ex-student '97, a much respected citizen of Utica, N. Y., died at his home there. He was a member of Hope Chapel Union Church and of several lodges, in some of which he held offices.

The death of Rev. R. Grant Riley, ex-student '90, occurred in November, 1913. After leaving Hampton he graduated from the Theological Department of Morgan College, Baltimore, and joined the Delaware Conference of the M. E. Church.

INDIAN NOTES

A friend from the San Carlos Agency in Arizona writes of the death of Dewey Martine nearly a year ago. The letter says, "He was a fine worker, and a good, all-round man." Martine was a student here during the year of '05-'06.

The *Brulé Rustler* mentions Leon de Shuquette, who was a Hampton student from '85 until '86, as being one of the most successful stockraisers and cattle dealers on the Lower Brulé Reservation.

Emma E. Jackson of the Klamath Agency, Oregon, who was a student from '04 until '07, is now Mrs. Wilson. She writes that she has a good home and is trying to live up to the standard set at school.

Louis Armell, ex-student '97, a farmer in Winnebago, Neb., visited Hampton the last of January with his wife and little daughter. Rachel Sheridan Walthill, Senior Middler '09, of Macy, Neb., was also a recent visitor.

John E. Curran, Trade Class '07, has been for some time employed on one of the irrigation projects in Arizona. The *Native American* says that during the absence of the electrical engineer for the project Mr. Curran has had entire charge of the pumping plant.

Mrs. Kate Henderson Calvert, '91, is living in Seattle, Washington. One of her daughters is with her and is attending the State University.

APRIL 1914

THE
SOUTHERN
WORKMAN

Press of
The Hampton Normal and Agricultural Institute
Hampton, Virginia

The Hampton Normal and Agricultural Institute

HAMPTON VIRGINIA

What it is An undenominational industrial school founded in 1868 by Samuel Chapman Armstrong for Negro youth. Indians admitted in 1878.

Object To train teachers and industrial leaders

Equipment Land, 1060 acres ; buildings, 140

Courses Academic, trade, agriculture, business, home economics

Enrollment Negroes, 1215 ; Indians, 37 ; total, 1252

Results Graduates, 1709 ; ex-students, over 6000
Outgrowths ; Tuskegee, Calhoun, Mt. Meigs, and many smaller schools for Negroes

Needs $125,000 annually above regular income
$4,000,000 Endowment Fund
Scholarships
  A full scholarship for both academic and
    industrial instruction - - - $ 100
  Academic scholarship - - - - 70
  Industrial scholarship - - - - - 30
  Endowed full scholarship - - - - 2500
  Any contribution, however small, will be gratefully received and may be sent to H. B. FRISSELL, Principal, or to F. K. ROGERS, Treasurer, Hampton, Virginia.

FORM OF BEQUEST

I give and devise to the trustees of The Hampton Normal and Agricultural Institute, Hampton, Virginia, the sum of   *dollars, payable*

The Southern Workman

Published monthly by

The Hampton Normal and Agricultural Institute

Contents for April 1914

THE SOUTHERN WORKMAN was founded by Samuel Chapman Armstrong in 1872, and is a monthly magazine devoted to the interests of undeveloped races.

It contains reports from Negro and Indian populations, with pictures of reservation and plantation life, as well as information concerning Hampton graduates and ex-students who since 1868 have taught more than 250,000 children in the South and West. It also provides a forum for the discussion of ethnological, sociological, and educational problems in all parts of the world.

CONTRIBUTIONS: The editors do not hold themselves responsible for the opinions expressed in contributed articles. Their aim is simply to place before their readers articles by men and women of ability without regard to the opinions held.".

EDITORIAL STAFF

H. B. FRISSELL   W. L. BROWN
HELEN W. LUDLOW   W. A. AERY, Business Manager
J. E. DAVIS   W. T. B. WILLIAMS

TERMS: One dollar a year in advance; ten cents a copy

CHANGE OF ADDRESS: Persons making a change of address should send the old as well as the new address to

THE SOUTHERN WORKMAN, Hampton, Virginia

Entered as second-class matter August 13, 1903, in the Post Office at Hampton, Virginia, under the Act of July 16, 1894

THE HAMPTON LEAFLETS

Any twelve of the following numbers of the "The Hampton Leaflets" may obtained free of charge by any Southern teacher or superintendent. *A charge of cents per dozen is made to other applicants.* Cloth-bound volumes for 1905, '06, ' and '08 will be furnished at seventy-five cents each, postpaid.

Address: Publication Office, The Hampton Normal and Agricultu Institute, Hampton, Virginia

The
Southern Workman

VOL. XLIII   APRIL 1914   NO. 4

𝔈𝔡𝔦𝔱𝔬𝔯𝔦𝔞𝔩𝔰

"The Negro Farmer"   The *Negro Farmer*, which is now being issued every other week at Tuskegee Institute "in the interest of the home, farm, and garden," and which is "especially devoted to the interest of Negro land own-ers, tenant farmers, and those who employ Negro labor," com-mands attention and wins respect because it shows what can be done by colored men and women through independent thinking and acting.

Who can begin to realize the economic and social possibili-ties of two million black farmers? What may we not expect in the coming decade from the continued development of the farming industry among Negroes, who now cultivate over one hundred million acres of Southern land and own about seventy dol-lars out of every one hundred dollars possessed by the Negro race? What are some of the best agencies for reaching and helping this vast army of Negro farmers who form such a vital part of the life of the South and the life of the nation? The *Negro Farmer* is throwing light on these questions and is arousing public interest in the problem of the man on the land.

To present clearly, simply, and attractively to the colored

children in the school, to the working people on the land, and to
the older people active in the home and church, the essential
facts of rural-life improvement is a difficult and, therefore, a
most attractive problem.   The United States Government, with
all the money that it is spending on agricultural work and various kinds of extension projects, finds it almost impossible to present in the simplest terms the elemental facts concerning common farm operations.   The United States Government, and other
agencies as well, find that the men and women who can make
research studies often have great difficulty in adjusting their
writings to the capacities of readers at large.   Those who can
do things successfully with their hands are frequently unable
to write out, simply and forcefully, the ideas they have been
skilful enough to put into execution.   Frequently those who can
write interestingly are neither exact in their thinking nor
reliable in their judgment.   In the *Negro Farmer* the student
of Negro life in the South will find the present-day economic
and social problems discussed in the simplest and most direct
language and with telling force.   The facts tell the story of
human progress through adjustment.

That this paper has received the hearty endorsement of
Southern governors and officials who are connected with the federal and state departments of agriculture means much for the
success of the adventure in constructive, economic journalism.
This endorsement is another instance of the Southern white man
and the Southern black man joining forces for the systematic
development of farming as an industry and as a factor in civic
and social development.

A careful study of the topics discussed in the published
numbers of the *Negro Farmer* suggests its common-sense inter-
pretations and hopeful outlook on life for the colored farmer in
the prospering Southland.   The periodical deserves the loyal
support of white men and black men who wish to see the Negro
win prosperity for himself and for the nation.

**Encouraging
Indian Art**   About ten years ago, when first public attention
was generally directed to Indian music and Indian
art, there were printed in these pages a few songs,
transcribed by Miss Curtis, as sung by Indian students at Hampton.   The gain in public recognition for this kind of music and
for all kinds of native art has been great within ten years.   Among
other signs of it we have the imitations of Indian art work and
near-Indian manufactures flooding our department stores ; and we
have at least three so-called Indian operas written by white men,
besides innumerable adaptations of Indian themes for piano and

violin compositions. Thus, while the Indian is bringing genuine gifts of his own to the civilization that absorbs him, his ingenious imitators are trading upon the popularity of his handiwork.

In a recent number of the *Outlook* Miss Natalie Curtis has contributed an article on "The Perpetuating of Indian Art." On the subject of music, which is the particular art to which she refers, Miss Curtis speaks with authority, for her sympathetic and intelligent study of it during all these years has led her deep into its mystery and meaning. Her particular plea is for the teaching of the native music to Indian youth by the older Indians. She finds that, in spite of our systematic efforts in the past to destroy the song impulse in the Indian, the native music is still a live force in native life. For the schools, therefore, to encourage in the younger generation the creative instinct in music would earn for them the thanks of all who are interested in art, in ethnology, and in the true progress of the Indian. But this is a native art, and obviously it can be taught only by the natives. The suggestion that the songs, collected from the older Indians, might be "harmonized," and that these inevitably distorted versions should then be taught to the young Indians by white school-teachers seems to her palpably absurd. Manifestly there could be nothing of true value to the Indian in the white man's arrangement of his songs. Her argument is that if anyone is to teach Indian songs 'in the 'schools it would seem that the older Indians should do it.

Certainly the co-operation of the old Indians, so far as it is practically possible, must prove the most effectual way of perpetuating music or any other art inherent in Indian life. Only an Indian could do in music what Mrs. Angel DeCora Dietz, for instance has done in drawing at Carlisle. This young and gifted Winnebago woman has developed their native arts among the Carlisle students by creating a school of applied design and decoration in which only Indian themes and Indian art traditions are used. And the argument that somehow and somewhere the younger Indians should learn the native music from their elders is reasonable and sound. Whether or not it should be in the schools is perhaps largely a question of expediency.

And there will probably be few to dissent from Miss Curtis's further argument that there should be some opportunity for art education for the few gifted individuals. Not all men can make songs, as she herself once said somewhere. And our educational efforts must necessarily just now be focused on getting the Indian upon his feet industrially. Yet there are always the gifted few in every race to whom an art education may be accorded with reasonable assurance of good results, and if the creative instinct in music, as in drawing, is to be kept alive, a few selected Indian youths might well be provided with an opportunity tor a thorough education in music.

🏵

"Tau₃ht by an ex-slave"   The following story, written by Richard Hamilton Byrd for the *Springfield Republican*, is here reprinted in the belief that it contains a lesson for many readers of the Southern Workman.

"It has been left to an unlettered ex-slave on a tiny farm in Alabama to unwittingly put into practice the scientific principles which the mighty power of the Department of Agriculture with its millions of appropriations is exerting itself to demonstrate to the farmers of the country. Sam McCall, the poor Negro, knows no science or the why or wherefore of scientific agriculture, but through the exercise of native sense and keen observation he has every year raised crops on two acres of soil, which at first would hardly sprout beans, that are not only the envy of his neighbors, but likewise the wonder of Government experts, who have many times visited his humble home.

"The average cotton yield of the Southern states is about one-third of a bale to the acre, and two bales to the acre is a splendid crop; yet McCall has raised over seven bales on his two acres. Fifty bushels of shelled corn to the acre is a good crop, and 100 bushels is a magnificent yield; McCall has raised on these two acres two corn crops in the same year, with a total of 320 bushels. During the past four or five years he has, on much of his land, raised three crops each year—corn, oats, and cotton. In 1908 he raised 125 bushels of oats, 50 bushels of corn, and four bales of cotton—all from two acres. Could such yields be won by all the farmers of America, or even half such yields, the total result would be fabulous. Either the farmers would all be millionaires or else the cost of living would be cut in half. Verily it may be said, when land which could not produce one quarter of a bale of cotton to the acre can be made to yield by natural improvement nearly four bales, then there are no waste acres in the country.

"How does the ex-slave, who cannot even read or write, secure such bountiful returns? Through irrigation or the application of great quantities of commercial fertilizers? Neither. He cultivates his soil in the usual manner, except that he cultivates it with great care and frequency, and he has not used a pound of commercial fertilizer. He has simply plowed under every vestige of green stuff which he has grown, instead of burning off the stalks and litter, as is common practice among his neighbors; and he has also added to this all the leaves and other trash he could gather and has applied to his soil all the manure furnished by his horse and cow. Each year he has plowed a little deeper until, instead of the soil only three inches deep that he started with, he now has a rich loam eleven or twelve inches deep. His farming is truly intensive and not an ounce of straw or cotton or cornstalk is wasted. All organic material is returned to the soil and forms food for the next crop.

"The soil and farm experts of the Department of Agriculture recognize in McCall's practices the most exact and complete carrying into effect of the principles which they are endeavoring to get the average farmer of the country to adopt."

The Indian Rights Association has recently issued **The Indian Y. M. C. A.** a circular letter from Rev. Henry Roe Cloud in regard to the present situation in Indian Y. M. C. A. work. Because of a deficit the International Committee feels obliged to drop its Indian department, at a time when the work is tremendously valuable. For several years Rev. Robert D. Hall and his assistants have worked faithfully to establish associations in the Government schools and on the reservations, and eighty-eight associations with a membership well over two thousand bear testimony to the success of their endeavor.

Hampton has been especially interested in this work because Stephen Jones, a Sioux ex-student, has had the position of Indian secretary at large. His field has lain in the two Dakotas and Nebraska, south as far as Oklahoma and north into Manitoba and Saskatchewan. As fast as possible Associations have been established, so that the boys who had been members during their school days might find themselves welcomed by helpful friends on their return to the reservations. With such influences the temptations and hardships of the life opening before them may be met with far more strength and courage than is possible when one is single handed.

Only those who know something of reservation conditions can realize the immense importance of this work. As a means of spreading Christianity, and of binding together those who are trying to live right lives, its influence can scarcely be overestimated. To have the work dropped when strong foundations have been laid, and when its influence is so sorely needed, would be a step backward, and would leave open one more avenue for evil influence. It is most earnestly to be hoped that from some source this deficit may be met and the work continued.

Race Betterment Four hundred men and women of prominence, comprising the first representative group of scientific experts ever gathered in America for that purpose, met at Battle Creek, Michigan, January 8-12, to assemble evidence of race deterioration and to consider methods of checking the downward trend of mankind. The meeting was known as the First National Conference on Race Betterment.

Already the effect of the Conference is apparent in Battle Creek, where popular interest in mental and physical efficiency was awakened by a series of public school tests which showed an alarming percentage of defective children in all grades.

The Conference had its inception in the efforts of four men, particularly interested in race betterment: Rev. Newell Dwight Hillis, pastor of Plymouth Church, Brooklyn, N. Y., Dr. J. H Kellogg of the Battle Creek Sanitarium, Sir Horace Plunkett, former minister of agriculture for Ireland, and Prof. Irving Fisher of Yale University. At the invitation of a central committee, chosen largely by these men, fifty men and women of national prominence in the fields of science and education consented to share in the program. Their addresses, together with open discussions of many of the points considered, constitute a very widespread study of all phases of evident race degeneracy and the advocacy of many ideas of reform.

Some of the suggested methods of improvement are frequent medical examination of the well, outdoor life, temperance in diet, biologic habits of living, open-air schools and playgrounds, the encouragement of rural life, the segregation or sterilization of defectives, the encouragement of eugenic marriages by requiring medical certificates before granting licenses, and the establishing of a eugenics registry for the development of a race of human thoroughbreds.

Among those having a share in the program were Rev. Newell Dwight Hillis, Jacob Riis, Judge Ben B. Lindsey, Dr. Booker T. Washington, Dr. Victor C. Vaughan, Dr. S. Adolphus Knopf, Dr. C. B. Davenport, Dr. J. N. Hurty, the Very Reverend (Dean) Walter Taylor Sumner, and many others of equal prominence.

Some of the interesting statements of the Conference are summarized as follows :

"It will be no easy task to improve the race to the point where there will be no dependent children, but the elimination of the dependent child will be one of the best indices of the superiority of our national stock. "

GERTRUDE E. HALL, New York State Board of Charities

"Eugenics does not eliminate romance. We eugenists believe romance should be retained. Through the past it has proved a good thing. "
ROSWELL H. JOHNSON, University of Pittsburg

"In order that the race may survive it will apparently be necessary to make a eugenic selection of healthy mothers and to provide that the cost of bearing and rearing children shall be equally shared by all. "
J. McKEEN CATTELL, Editor *Popular Science Monthly*

"The boys are learning that they have a calling just as sacred as the call to motherhood and that is the call to fatherhood. "
WALTER TAYLOR SUMNER, Chicago.

"We must cultivate pure blood, instead of blue blood, if we would develop a race of human thoroughbreds. "
J. H. KELLOGG, Battle Creek, Michigan

"The Negro in the South, with all his weaknesses and handicaps, is not yet, in any large measure, in the ditch. "
BOOKER T. WASHINGTON, Principal of Tuskegee Institute

The Hampton Anniversary For many years Mr. Robert C. Ogden was accustomed to invite a company of friends to join him in a visit to Hampton at Anniversary time. When he became too ill to continue this custom, Mr. Alexander Trowbridge, a New York architect (62 West Forty-fifth Street), associated with him a committee of ladies and gentlemen to see to it that the annual pilgrimage to Hampton should not be given up.

Mr. Trowbridge has given much time and thought to organizing these parties and they have been most successful. The committee of arrangements for the present year announces that the party will leave New York on Wednesday morning, April 22, and, returning, will leave Old Point Comfort on the morning of the following Saturday. The cost of the trip will be thirty-seven dollars for each person, including railroad fare, Pullman seat, luncheons en route, and hotel accommodations for two days and three nights.

At Anniversary time an endeavor is made to give visitors a definite knowledge of the working of the Hampton School. President Eliot said that he found at Hampton the best combination of academic and industrial work that he had seen in the world. It is doubtful if there is any spot in this country where so much of historic interest centers as at Hampton. Last year's Anniversary program presented the work of the trade school and domestic science department by giving actual demonstrations on the stage of certain processes, such as bed-making and roof-construction. Similar demonstrations will be given this year, as well as stories of struggle for an education, by members of the graduating class. Accounts will be given also by supervising industrial teachers of the state, of how whole communities have been helped to an education, to better houses, better churches, better farms.

Anniversary time always brings to Hampton a distinguished company from North and South. While it is yet too early to say definitely who will be present, there is reason to believe that there will be a most interesting party. An endeavor will be made this year to give the visitors some knowledge of the very varied extension work which is being done by the school in Virginia and the other Southern states. If the weather is favorable there will be outdoor tableaux with plantation melodies and music by the school band.

A prominent citizen of Cambridge, Massachusetts, was asked not long since if he were going abroad. "Oh, no, " he said, "I am going to see something much more interesting than I could see abroad. I am going to Hampton." Almost every week brings to the school, visitors from different parts of the globe who have come to study Hampton's methods. The head of Trinity College in Kandy, Ceylon, spoke of his coming to Hampton as one of the great events of his life. Here, he said, he had seen worked out a system of education which he had dreamed about all his life.

SEE that red gleam—hear that whistle !
  That's the scarlet cardinal;
List that burst of joyous music —
  Mock-bird holds our hearts in thrall.

From our neighbor, Carolina,
  Comes the wren with notes of cheer;
Soon the cat-bird joins the chorus,
  "Spring is here ! Spring is here !"
                                    —F. F. Low

THE MAN WHO TURNED
GRAVEL TO DOLLARS

BY CLEMENT RICHARDSON

I found him in his bare feet and in extreme negligeé. Seated on the porch of his big farmhouse, to which he had come years before as a penniless hireling, he was trying to coax a breeze out of a hot night in Arkansas. As soon as I made myself known, he began to talk—talk full of shrewd observation and vivid rhetoric about the Negro farmer. Two hours later he remembered that I had not been to supper.

"You'll find me an ole, one-gallus farmer," said he, but I reckon I can find somethin' to eat."

As I passed along on his back porch I heard the soft bleating of sheep, the munching of cows on the cud, the stamping of horses in the stable. He brought me fresh fruit, fresh butter, fresh milk, and water from the ice-box. One-gallus farmer indeed! But that is the way of the old man.

Scott Bond, ex-slave and spare mulatto, came out of Mississippi in the early seventies and pitched his tent in Madison, Arkansas, now a bit of a lumber village forty-five miles from Memphis, Tennessee. He was illiterate and penniless. Like many a liberated slave, he carried all his personal belongings tied up in a red bandanna handkerchief, which he swung on the end of a stick and carried over his shoulder. At fourteen years of age he had worn his first pair of shoes, a pair which, after much instruction, he had put together for himself. At twenty-one he was the proud possessor of his first pair of store shoes.

Illiterate though he was, he came into Arkansas with a rare knowledge of soils. Now, Madison looks down into the luxuriant valley of the St. Francis River. Once a year when the Mississippi River is troubled she stretches forth her arm and washes all this forty-five miles of land between Memphis and Madison, leaving upon it heaps of loam and debris. Seeing this double source of enriching the soil, Scott Bond shook his head and exclaimed, "Lawd, dis is de place fur me—de open places are de places to live in."

However, he was poor. He labored as a plow hand for thirty cents a day. Evenings he went to the village and chopped wood for the grocery store and country club at twenty-five cents per two-horse load.   He recalled for me how in his courting days he and the woman who is now his wife used to pass by the big farmhouse in which he now lives, peep through the fence cracks at the luscious fruit in the orchard, and at intervals go in and beg a few windfalls.

"Lawd!" he used to say beneath his breath, "will I ever have anything that looks lak dis?"

When he had saved twenty-three dollars he married. This sum he invested in a bedstead, a dresser, and a chair or two. His bride made a mattress of crocus sacks, stuffed it with hay, and the couple moved into a cottage on leased land, ready to keep house.

A young mistress of the plantation, happening to be present when the furniture was moved in, asked,

"Unc Scott, is this all?"

"Yas'm. Ain't it ernough fur a pore nigger to start on?"

"But, Unc Scott, what are you going to cook in?"

"Why, dat so, I hadn' thought 'bout dat. But my money is all gone now."

The young mistress gave them an old teakettle and a skillet. The latter had a big hole in the side.

"Son, you oughter seen us tryin' to keep de corn dough from runnin' out of dat hole," said he.

With these items of furniture and utensils and with one dollar's worth of flour, twenty cents' worth of coffee, ten cents' worth of sugar, and a supply of corn meal and "middlin's," the couple launched forth into househeeping and farming. For six months there was no more sugar, coffee, or flour in that farm cottage.   At the end of that time some cotton had been sold.

"And what a eatin' we had," shouted the Arkansas farmer.

"But son, I began to work sho 'nough now," he went on. I worked from can't to can't—from ' can't see in the mornin' till ' can't see at night.' "

When other men were harnessing their mules, Bond had already turned half a dozen furrows, and when they were un-hitching to go home Scott Bond turned yet a furrow or two. When it rained or when he could not work his own fields, he cut and hauled wood for the white farmers round about, following always that "can't-to-can't" policy of his.

A mere accident led him into conceiving of farming on a business scale. Hitherto his highest ambition had been to pur-chase a small farm and from it to educate his children. He was already the father of two boys. His early and late hours had begun to yield profit, but he only rented a little more extensively. In those early days there were no banks in Arkansas. The country merchant was storekeeper, cotton merchant, and banker. The nearest bank was at New Orleans. To the country merchant

Scott Bond sold his cotton, receiving credit on the books. Whatever he needed he ordered. When his rent fell due he gave an order on the merchant, who paid the money over to the landlord. Scott Bond himself saw little cash in those days.

As chance would have it, however, the merchant and the landlord got at loggerheads, and ceased to speak to each other, the landlord vowing never to enter the merchant's store again. Whereupon the latter ordered Bond to get the money and pay it himself. Now the rent on the farm was $1500 a year. Down to the store the Negro farmer rode and gave his order for $1500.

"Son," said he, when telling me the experience, "I looked at all dem bills and looked at dem. I had never seen so much money in all my life. I jes couldn' take my eyes off it. After a while I took it up and put it down inside my overcoat pocket, and I hugged it and hugged it all along de road."

Out on the lonely highway he felt a desire to look at all this money again, to take it into his hand, He reached for it but feared the sudden appearance of a highwayman. Finally he rode into the forest. In a deep hollow he came upon a big log. Tying his mule, he took the money out of his pocket and spread it up and down the big log bill by bill. Then he stood back, folded his arms, and looked at the money, and looked at it. Unwilling to take his eyes off the bills, he began a circuit around the log, trudging round and round many times. Finally he spoke,

"Lawd, I made all dis money and hyer I am takin' it to somebody else. If I live I am goin' to have somebody doin' dis same thing for me. Son, let a man handle his money," he shouted. "Dere's a difference 'tween dat and paper orders. I don't kyer if it ain't but five cents, *let him handle it.*" Finishing his resolution, he collected his bills and went on his way.

A few days later, after a conference with his wife, such a conference as he always had before undertaking any business of importance, he invested his remaining three hundred-odd dollars in a small tract of land. Both his white and his colored friends called him a fool for paying so much for that particular spot. Part of it was in shrubbery, the rest a strip of sand on Crow Creek. This creek is a stream which riots over the lowlands in the wet seasons and simmers down to a contemptable rivulet in the dry season.

One day while he was plowing he saw a handsome carriage coming toward his fields.

"Who is dat fine white gentleman comin' dis way?" he asked himself.

"Is this Mr. Bond?" asked the fine gentleman, stopping by "Unc Scott."

"Tut, tut, none er dat now!"

The gentleman was taken aback.

"In de fus' place you know you don' mean it. And if you does you can't afford to call niggers "mister" in dis part of de country. You must be one of dem 'publicans fum de North."

Scott Bond has no very high esteem for the particular brand of Northerner that he knows.

"Well, what'll I call you then?" asked the stranger.

"Call me cross-eyed nigger," replied Bond, "dat's what dey says behind my back. And if you wants to do better'n dat—why, call me Unc Scott—dey calls me Unc Scott round hyer."

Thus instructed on the proprieties, the gentleman settled down to his purpose.

"They tell me you own this sand pit up here."

"Y-a-s, sir, I owns some little of it," replied Unc Scott, trying to be as ambiguous as possible. He hadn't the slightest suspicion of what the man wanted.

"Well, I am representing the Rock Island Railroad, and my firm has sent me here to buy sand and gravel off your pit. How will you sell it?"

There was a pause. Bond had never heard of selling sand.

"Well, I don' know, sir," he finally replied, "I allus consults my ole lady before I makes a trade. And if you can come back day after tomorrow I'll let you know."

"All right, Unc Scott," and the stranger was gone.

Scott Bond stood by his mule's head and waited until the carriage disappeared. Now the plantation which had the best of the sand and gravel on it was in charge of a colored man who had a two years' option on it. It comprised one hundred and sixty acres around Crow Creek, and the tillable land was very fertile. The farm was on sale for seventeen hundred dollars. Bond knew that the Negro who held the option planned to return the farm to the owners when the option ended. Leaping astride his mule as soon as the carriage was out of sight, Bond rode over to the field where the colored man was plowing.

"I had to be mighty calm," he said, "and kinder don't-care-like, for I didn' want to make him think anything."

He rode up, hailed the plowman, and talked with him.

Finally he asked casually, "Say, is you goin' to buy dis farm?" He knew the plans of the man already.

"Well, it is right next mine," said Bond, "and if you're not goin' to buy it I'll give you five dollars for your option, and you can stay right on here."

"When?" asked the other, anxious to get an easy five dollars.

"Right now, if you can go and sign the paper," and he showed the money.

Cash was scarce. "I'll go all right," said the other.

This was all the money Scott Bond ever paid out for the one hundred and sixty acres of land. The railroad bought more than seventeen hundred dollars' worth of sand and gravel out of this creek long before Bond's payments were due on the whole farm.

His resolution at the big log in the woods was beginning to be carried out. One by one he bought in the farms around him, and he peopled them with Negroes who paid him rent as he had paid the white landlord years before. One of the last estates to fall into his possession was that on which he had plowed for thirty cents a day, that through whose fence cracks he used to peep at the blushing peaches and luscious grapes. And he lives in the big farmhouse to which he used to go to beg a few windfalls from the master. He lives there with his sheep, cows, horses, and big Brahma chickens strutting proudly about, and the windfalls still dropping to the ground. His house is high up among the hills, and as he sits on the front porch, where he first went as an Arkansas hireling, he looks out northeast and southwest over forty-four hundred acres of his own farm land, some of the richest soil in the country.

The gravel-pit deal, the bringing of tenants whom he had to "carry," as the Southern term has it, until the crops were harvested, opened Scott Bond's eyes still wider to the business side of farming. And so he put up a big country store, selling groceries, dry goods of even the fanciest brands, hardware, and farm implements. The tenants of forty-four hundred acres of land are not a bad patronage in themselves, not to mention the floating purchasers who come to Bond's store in large numbers, for most of them have reason to know and esteem Unc Scott. Here the tenant may go and be "carried," getting any kind of merchandise he needs. Here he may secure cash money, and whenever "Scott Bond and Sons" buy from a tenant they invariably pay in cash—for Scott Bond applies his golden rule, "Let a man handle his money." The store is a successful business in itself, farming entirely apart.

Now the cotton on all these acres has to be ginned. Hence Bond's next step in the business of farming was to erect a cotton gin and cotton bailer, which is still another independent business.

On his farms along the banks of Crow Creek and the St. Francis River are gigantic oaks, pines, and sweet gums—indeed, lumber forests. He has built a sawmill back of the store and cotton gin, and near the river bank. The logs are floated down the river and lifted out of the water and sawed. He ships all the lumber he can turn out to the Chicago and Pittsburg markets.

But the gravel-pit business has again come to the front. Only last August a railroad contracted to take $21,000 worth of gravel from him each year for three years, a sum which in the aggregate would have paid for all his farms at the time he bought them. A gravel elevator is to be erected here, and Scott Bond and Sons will sell, not only to the railroads, but to contractors throughout the country.

"Son, it is all in the land. If you got dis land and treat it right it will give you what you ask for."

And then he propounded another scheme. He is already laying plans to establish a cement-brick factory. He has the clay on his farms and he has the water. For transportation he has the St. Francis River and the Rock Island Railroad cutting through his land. Moreover, the farmers all about are beginning to wall their ditches with cement bricks. They save the land from washing.

Scott Bond has three sons. Two of them are college graduates, the youngest is now in college. Waverly, one of the older boys, is storekeeper and cashier. He handles all the money of the firm. The other son, Theopholis, is superintendent of the forty-four hundred acres of farm land. And be it said to the credit of the latter that neither Euclid nor Greek syntax has been able to dislodge his appreciation of cotton growing or his knowledge of how to run a plow. Again and again I saw him take hold of a plow in the field and demonstrate to the tenant farmer how deep or how shallow the furrow should be made in laying by the cotton.

In the office of Scott Bond and Sons I sought still more accurate accounts of the Company's holdings. I found that the gin turns out 100 bales of cotton per day, and does from $4000 to $5000 worth of business a season; that 800 bales and upwards are shipped from the Bond plantation each year; that the sawmill turns out 25,000 feet of lumber per day, and that the Company owns about 500 mules with all the implements, wagons, etc. that go with such working stock. Footing it all up, estimating the values of the gin plant, town property, sawmill, gravel pit, bank securities, and a five-thousand-tree fruit orchard, which I have not mentioned before, Bond may be conservatively set down as being worth $280,000.00.

And then they took me to a back window of the store. From this back window we could see the spot on which, back there in the early seventies, Scott Bond chopped wood by the light of the stars for twenty-five cents per two-horse load !

A UNIQUE PEOPLE'S SCHOOL

BY J. E. DAVIS

A unique people and a unique school—both of these will be found by the determined traveler who penetrates to the heart of St. Helena Island off the coast of South Carolina. "Determined" is used advisedly, for one must have "a double 'termination in his heart" to succeed in reaching the Penn School on St. Helena. He may go by boat from Savannah or Charleston, or by train from north, south, or west to Beaufort, South Carolina. He will feel inclined to linger among the double-galleried white mansions, the orange trees, and the flower-filled gardens of this picturesque and aristocratic old town on the Beaufort River, "once the wealthiest and most cultivated of its size in America, which has produced statesmen, scholars, soldiers, sailors, and divines famous throughout the country." This inclination will be strengthened when the traveler reaches the primitive bateau serving as ferry over the mile or more of river which must be crossed en route to Penn School. Weather permitting, this goes semi-occasionally, and should live-stock, a carriage, or, rarely, an automobile, be part of the "freight," requiring the lashing of a "flat" to the little boat, then indeed must he "add to his faith, . . patience." Once across the river he starts on a pleasant, six-mile drive across Ladies' Island to St. Helena.

The little copses by the roadside are vocal with mocking birds and cardinals, the bare, brown cotton fields stretch on either side of the sandy road, almost to the horizon, with here and there a lonely cabin, a turbaned Negro woman, perhaps, in the doorway, a tall palmetto standing guard over the little homestead. On the uncleared land are groves of live oak and pine, draped with grey moss, in the distance golden marshes, the little streams winding through them shining like silver ribbons in the sunlight.   By the roadside, here and there, are smiling, brown-faced children.

The traveler enters at last an avenue of live oaks, their branches intertwined overhead and silvery moss hanging from them in long, waving fringes.   On one side of the road is a grove of live oaks, among them scattered buildings—a hall, a school-house, a small library, a barn, a grey, one-story Spanish-looking building with red-tiled roof, whence come sounds of hammer and saw—on the other side of the road, a gateway, a hedge of yucca, an attractive dwelling house, a large white building, several cottages.   The traveler has reached the Penn School—the heart of St. Helena—a community school for the six thousand black people of this island of the sea.

The history of this school is picturesque.   Begun in the stress of war, within sound of shot and shell, it continued through seed-sowing years full of struggle and privation.   Then, through easier, happier, harvesting years it reached, in 1912, its Year of Jubilee with the crowning joy of a beautiful trades building, the work of island men with island materials.   Not every school has for its very first Christmas a hymn written by a great poet, but Whittier in 1862 wrote for this school "The St. Helena Hymn."

 "Oh, none in all the world before
      Were ever glad as we!
 We're free on Carolina's shore
      We're all at home and free.

              .   .   .   .   .

 "The very oaks are greener clad,
      The waters brighter smile;
 Oh, never shone a day so glad
      On sweet St. Helen's Isle.

              .   .   .   .   .

 "Come once again, O blessed Lord!
      Come walking on the sea!
 And let the mainlands hear the word
      That sets the Island free. "

From the earliest days, when the patient black people were wont to say, "De big light am beginnin' to shine on St. Helena," through the years of patient effort, when the casual, "uncomprehending" children scuffled and fought in school, or, when the spirit moved them, curtsied to the teacher and went off to pick blackberries, down to that one when the picturesque old schoolhouse, sent down in sections from Philadelphia and used daily for thirty-eight years, gave out in spots and on rainy days obliged the teacher to raise an umbrella and the pupils to roost like hens on the tops of the benches—through all these amusing, pathetic, or inspiring experiences, even up to the present moment, the Penn School has struggled on, steadily holding

THE PENN SCHOOL ROAD

before itself the ideal of service to the people among whom it was established.

At first this service was given almost entirely to the physical needs of the people; the sick were cared for, the naked clothed, the hungry fed, the homeless sheltered. The island community was made up of slaves, mostly field hands, left on the plantations when their owners fled before the Federal army. From morning to night and the whole year long, all the Negroes had been accustomed to work in the fields tending the imperious crop of long-staple cotton. A peck of corn was the weekly ration and the slaves ground it themselves on Saturday night, taking turns until daylight. Their houses were of rough boards and had small windows without glass. The floors were of sand and lime. Long oyster shells served for spoons, and they did not know the use of a knife and fork.

To these people came, in 1862, Miss Laura M. Towne, of Philadelphia, and her friend, Miss Ellen Murray, of Canada—cultured, dainty women. To them these women devoted the remainder of their lives, cheerfully giving up home, friends, means, to help the least of God's creatures to self-respecting manhood and womanhood. For a year the Government ran the plantations and had the cotton crop gathered, paying the Negroes for their labor. Then the land, about seven hundred and fifty square miles, was sold to the Negroes in five- and ten-acre lots, thus helping them to self-respect by the ownership of land. The people remained on the plantations, forming little communities, each with its praise house, society hall, and burying ground. Penn School graduates began to teach in the county schools, married, and built good homes. The few whites on the island were always friendly, and the people, isolated and free from interference, worked their little plots of land, attended to their own affairs on the seventy or more plantations, developed into law-abiding citizens, and gave their love and devotion to the women who had come to live among them and who, they said, were "too [1] good to we."

Just before Miss Towne's death in 1901, the school was incorporated, at her request, to insure its permanence, and Dr. Frissell of Hampton Institute was made president of a strong board of trustees. Graduates of Hampton were sent to the island to inaugurate industries, for there were no good mechanics there. Two of the white teachers on the Hampton staff—Miss Rossa B. Cooley and Miss Frances Butler—undertook to help in the work. Unfortunately Miss Butler lived but one month. She was succeeded by Miss Grace B. House, also of the Hampton staff. These women, always with the help of a number of Hampton graduates, have continued in Penn School the spirit of service which has always characterized it.

Handicapped by small funds, the new workers have been able to move but slowly in carrying out their plans for serving the islanders. Preparing teachers for the county schools continued for some years to be the chief work of the school. This preparation has steadily improved in quality, and more and more effort has been made to bring the teachers in to the parent school for observation of an ungraded school maintained there, and for instruction. For the past two years, a skilled training teacher from Hampton has conducted institutes for them in the winter, and the schools are inspected regularly by the Principals of Penn School. A St. Helena Teachers' Association has been formed, and has an *esprit de corps* which promises well for the future of the county schools.

But this is only one of the community activities of the Penn School. Another is the instruction of the island farmers, not only by means of the school farm, but also by farmers' conferences, farm-demonstration work, and a co-operative society. In the farmers' conferences the men and women are encouraged to raise their food supplies and stop getting themselves deeper and deeper in debt at the store, to make a freer use of whitewash on houses and fences, to clean up the yards, to plant more trees and flowers, and to plough deeper. As a result of this work, the young men are more interested in the farm than in the city. An agricultural fair is held every fall, and last year there were as many as twelve hundred exhibits.

---

1 "Too," in the island vernacular, means "very."

ON THE PENN SCHOOL FARM

Although the school farm of one hundred and twenty acres is made up chiefly of poor land, by scientific methods it has been able to increase its yield each year. The superintendent in charge, a Hampton graduate, uses it, not only for the practical instruction of the pupils, but as an object lesson to show the farmers how to increase their crops, improve their stock and

IN THE SCHOOL COTTON FIELD

MISERY AFTER THE GREAT STORM
Inside the cabin a baby lies dead from exposure

HOME OF THIS FAMILY AFTER HELP FROM THE RELIEF FUND

poultry, introduce dairying and truck farming, and raise winter vegetables. In 1909 he was appointed a farm-demonstration agent by the United States Department of Agriculture, and since that time the number of demonstrators under his supervision on St. Helena and four adjacent islands has grown from 8 to 66 (with co-operators, 115), and they have increased the average corn yield per acre from 10 to 34 bushels.

A corn club has been formed for both boys and girls, and the white friends on the island have shown their interest by offering prizes for the best crops. Hundreds of trees have been planted by the school children as a result of the annual tree-planting contest by classes and individuals. Each pupil must plant at least three trees, one at home, one at school, and one by the road-

"MUDDERLESS" GOING TO THE PENN SCHOOL FOR HELP

side, a prize being given for the largest number living at the close of the year. As a result of this contest, there are about three hundred additional trees on St. Helena. The school is able to serve the community also by lending its mowing machine when needed by either white or colored neighbors, and by grinding sugar cane on shares for the colored farmers.

In 1911, after the great storm of that summer which destroyed many houses and crops, the St. Helena Co-operative Society was formed for the purpose of helping the farmers with loans at a fair interest. Its membership is one hundred and seven, with a Committee of Management numbering eight, which controls all its business. The rules of the Society have been adapted from those governing the co-operative societies in

Ireland, each member willingly accepting the "total liability clause" making the society liable for the debts of all the members. The men have thus, not only the opportunity of borrowing at a fair interest the cash which is so scarce in a cotton community, but are able to save money by buying seed and fertilizers cooperatively.

But it is not alone on the farming side that the Penn School serves the community. Formerly the islanders' broken wagons and plows had to be ferried to Beaufort to have the necessary work

THE FIRST SHOP AT PENN SCHOOL

done. Now they are taken to Penn School, where, in the new Cope Industrial Building [1], made of "tabby" (oyster shells, cement, and sand) by ninety-four island men under the direction of three Hampton graduates, there are well-equipped blacksmith, wheelwright, carpentry, and paint shops. Here horses are shod, and wagons, furniture, and tools made and repaired, while from these shops island boys will go out into the community to paint, or build, or repair churches and houses. The Cope Building also houses a cobbling shop where the island shoes are repaired, and a basketry room where the interesting native baskets, of marsh

1 Named for the Cope family of Philadelphia, for many years warm friends of the Penn School

"THIS IS WE BUILDING."

reeds stitched by hand with palmetto strips, are made for sale. The people say, "This is we building," and are inordinately proud of it.

The women of the island are served by Penn School in many

DR. FRISSELL AT THE DEDICATION OF THE COPE INDUSTRIAL BUILDING

ways, most directly, perhaps, by the "Community Class" of seventy mothers and grandmothers which meets weekly to hear talks on hygiene, to knit, sew, and make cornshuck mats or quilts. During the past year, at their own suggestion, they have been making quilts for their poorer neighbors. These women are very glad to buy the garments sent in barrels to the Sales House. Said one woman, after an earnest prayer of thanksgiving to "Massa Jesus," "Ooner [you] tell de frien's dat dese barr'ls has gold in dem for we."

"Community Maud," the school horse, has made many a visit to the homes, and after the great storm of 1911, the school nurse made 1404 visits, besides treating 265 patients at the school. From a relief fund, generously contributed by Northern friends, 234 houses were rebuilt or repaired, 277 people received rations, and 200 were given work for wages. The monthly temperance meeting started by Miss Towne in the early days is still continued on "Temperance Monday," when the island schools are dismissed and eight hundred children gather in Darrah Hall on the school grounds for a rally. The singing of the weird island spirituals by this body of colored children is an experience to be long remembered.

Between the school and the island churches there is close co-operation ; the teachers divide into squads on Sundays and attend the churches of various denominations, helping in the Sunday schools and speaking to the people on public questions. The call to church is given by the Penn School bell.

THE COMMUNITY CLASS QUILTING IN THE GROVE

THE NURSE'S VISIT

Through the training given the girls at Penn School the island homes are moving to a higher plane. The girls make their own dresses, weave rugs, cook the school lunches and teachers' meals, can fruit and vegetables, and make bread and "Penn School shingles[1]" for the island. Of the three hundred children in school, twenty-four are boarding pupils who are taking vocational training. The remainder are day scholars and walk from five to eighteen miles a day to and from school. The session does not begin until ten o'clock, to allow time for the long walks and for morning work in the fields at home.

1 A delicious cinnamon cooky

A ST. HELENA COUNTY SCHOOLHOUSE BEFORE BEING REPAIRED

A unique school institution is the "Public Service Committee," consisting of six boys and six girls from the two upper rooms. They are elected by the four upper grades, and a place on this Committee is considered a very high honor even after graduation, as the old members meet annually with the active members at Hampton House, the Principals' home. The badge,

THE SAME SCHOOLHOUSE REPAIRED BY THE PENN SCHOOL BOYS

WAITING FOR HELP AT HAMPTON HOUSE

a Penn School button, they lose only by misconduct. One of the duties of the Committee is to choose the school motto for the month—"Kindness," "Courtesy," for example—and to appoint a student to write a paper on it. It settles quarrels and all questions connected with tardiness and the children's behavior, on Sundays and holidays as well as on school days, on the roads, the playground, and the plantations. Its members serve as chairmen of the "Grounds Committee" appointed each week to keep

CO-OPERATIVE DITCHING

"BY THE ROADSIDE ARE SMILING, BROWN-FACED CHILDREN"

the grounds in order. The Public Service Committee gives repri-
mands, demands apologies, makes peace, and refers cases to the
Principals only when it thinks this necessary.

Thus, in this "unique experiment station," Negro boys and
girls are prepared for life and service—for life on their own Sea
Islands, in their home environment—as farmers or tradesmen,
housekeepers or teachers. Penn School has become a factor to
be reckoned with on the Island, an institution to be consulted
when new enterprises are on foot. The people, both white
and black, have confidence that its influence will be always on the
side of what it believes to be for the good of the island people;
and while there may sometimes be a difference of opinion in
regard to what this may be, it is still true that it is through Penn
School that "better days have done come to St. Helena."

*Note—Anyone desirous of obtaining more detailed information
in regard to the condition and needs of Penn School, should apply
to Penn School, Frogmore P. O., St. Helena Island, S. C.*

HOUSING CONDITIONS AMONG THE INDIANS

BY ELSIE E. NEWTON

IT has been the policy of the Government to invest a part of the Indian's individual capital in a good frame house of from two to five rooms. There are two reasons for this, one being the necessity of establishing him on his allotment and encouraging him in founding and conducting a homestead, and the other is the belief that he is better off in a house, especially a modern one. Among the Kiowas and Comanches and the Cheyennes and Arapahoes of Oklahoma, one finds these cottages pretty well kept, some exceedingly so. I recall one small village of whites and Indians where I was driven down an alley that divided the former from the latter. The contrast between the tidy back-yards of the Indians, and the unkempt ones of the whites would have made a good subject for a photograph.

Often, alongside the modern house, there will be one or more tepees, or more commonly tents, for which the family will frequently desert the house. There are some houses which are never occupied except for storage, especially during the warm months. There is no criticism to be made of this. Indeed, I should be loath to see the camping instinct disappear from Indian life, for I believe it is quite as necessary to the Indian's health as to that of the white man who seeks a yearly opportunity to return to the primitive life. I am convinced that camp life as such can be as readily attacked for sanitary reformation as the house, and that the Indian who has learned how to be clean in a tent or tepee will be the better prepared to live healthily in a house. But most of us do not think in terms of a tent, and we cannot associate sanitation with anything short of a house, and a frame and plastered house at that with bathtubs thrown in. It is difficult, therefore, to bring about a change in camp life, chiefly through our inability to teach, rather than through the inability of the Indian to improve it.

The bedstead is rapidly becoming a feature of all homes. Except in camp it will be found in every Indian home where there are sufficient means. The number of brass beds I have seen this year is astonishing. It may be that a part of the

family still sleep on the floor, but it is only a question of time
when there will be beds enough for all. Similarly, tables are
now in common use among such tribes as I have mentioned;
modern dishes are used, and especially on the Sioux reservations
there has been a movement towards cupboards. Most of them
are well kept; some are screened. These improvements may
appear insignificant, but when one stops to think that less than
thirty years ago the Sioux were nomads, warriors, and wholly
uncivilized, the changes will be appreciated.

The dirt floor is common in most log houses. The Navaho
housewife, if she is a good one, will periodically scrape the
surface of her floor, carry the dirt away, and sprinkle a layer of
fresh dirt in its place. Nearly all dirt floors are sprinkled with

CHIPPEWA HOUSES, SHOWING TENTS STILL IN USE

water to keep down the dust, and the adobe floor of the Pueblo
is hard and quite smooth. Such houses as have wood floors have
not always the best, and the wide cracks prove to be almost as
insanitary as the dirt floor. The modern houses which have been
built by the Government have matched flooring.

The custom of using utensils in common is a serious means of
contagion. Perhaps this and the family towel are responsible
for the spread of tuberculosis and trachoma more than any other
two things. The family towel is one step beyond having no
towel, so there is still a reason for thankfulness. At present the
style in towels is the Turkish, and it is a curious fact that all
the way from Wisconsin to Arizona it is the only style I have
seen. It is gratifying to notice that a crude lavatory arrangement

A SIOUX HOME WHERE A WOMAN WAS DYING OF TUBERCULOSIS

is becoming a part of Indian homes. Nearly always there will be a wash basin and soap, set on a stand, which, although not the latest thing in fixtures, represents a laudable attempt at cleanliness.

General uncleanliness brings the fly and, up to the present time, the Indian has little fear of a fly. It will alight on his jerked meat, or travel direct from carrion to the children's faces, with no one knows what results, though the baby is nearly always protected by a netting or some other cover when asleep. New

FIELD MATRON TAKING HOME PATIENTS AFTER AN OPERATION FOR TRACHOMA

houses are screened, but screens are not regarded, because the inhabitants have not been sufficiently educated. Either the doors are left open or the frames are broken and never replaced. Food is left uncovered and refuse thrown around the doorway.

Without segregation of contagious or infectious diseases, it cannot be expected that their spread will be limited, yet, except with such epidemics as the Indian has learned to fear, segregation has not been attempted. It is not difficult to vaccinate, or to separate the smallpox patient from his family; also when scarlet fever comes along, the family will probably submit to quarantine measures without trouble. But measles and whooping cough, although they have claimed their scores, have baffled quarantine. This is true also of trachoma and tuberculosis. These diseases are looked upon as part of the dispensation of fate, and that they can be prevented and cured is only beginning to be believed by the Indian. Many of the cases never reach the ears of the authorities, and their absolute control is one of the possibilities that has not yet been tested.

The conservatism of the Indian has been commented on at large ; his critics have even said that nothing can be done with him, and that it is of no use to try. But new ideas are taking root all the time. Within my own brief knowledge, the use of cans to collect sputum has become almost a custom among some tribes in the north. The airing of bedding has also become almost universal. The bedding may be ragged, or show the need of soap and water, but as long as it has a bath in that best of disinfectants, the sun, we should not complain. The introduction of beds and tables I have already mentioned. That many homes are commendably clean shows that a standard has been set, and this is a great stride. As the economic state improves, the home will improve *if* the right education has been imposed.

At this point it is well to sound a note of warning not to confuse the issue—not to confound the esthetic idea of cleanliness and sanitation with the things themselves. Those of us who are addicted to bathtubs must stop to think before we make any regulation affecting the Indian home. For the average Indian a bathroom is out of the question. His economic state forbids it or else there is no water supply. The Navaho uses the sweat bath and probably always will, as in most of his country water is scarce even for drinking purposes. He should be encouraged to retain the method best adapted to his needs. For the average rural family, a bath in a galvanized washtub is quite as effective as any other kind. It is idle to urge an Indian to build a larger house than he can afford, or one having more space and more rooms than he can care for, furnish, and heat. Congestion in a rural

AN AVERAGE CHIPPEWA HOUSE

home has few of the effects that overcrowding has in the cities, because of the ampler room for all the activities of the day. At night the porch, or even a tent, may be used to spread out the family and give better ventilation. Our particular efforts should be directed to reasonable order, not exact tidiness, and to closing the direct channels of the spread of disease germs—the use of individual towels, for instance, the sterilization of dishes, the killing of flies and other vermin, keeping down dust, preserving food and water from pollution, and care of sputum.

Compulsory sanitation of Indian homes has been advocated. The practical objection to it is the lack of adequate machinery to carry it out. On some of the large reservations it would be almost a physical impossibility ; among the citizen Indians it could not be undertaken at all, since they are under the health regulations of the state in which they live. I have no doubt that there are places where it could be applied with a reasonable degree of success, but it would have to be done with deliberation and judgment.

The only antidote to unsanitary housing is proper education, and I have persistently advocated a practical preparation of our Indian girls in those matters relating to the home and children. To every school should be attached a small, inexpensive, model house, built after the type which can be most readily imitated by the Indians of the locality, and in such a house, in small groups, the simple, elementary things of homemaking and child care should be taught. The equipment must be simple and inexpensive. The food stuffs of the reservation should be the starting point of all instruction in cooking ; and the making of a layette and clothes for small children should be included in the sewing course. Cost of materials, sanitation of a small home, personal hygiene, care and feeding of children, house management, the kitchen garden, home nursing, and the art of hospitality—these are the essential things to be taught. If they are taught on such a scale as approximates the average Indian home, the girl will be far more likely to begin at home where she left off at school than she will if she has become accustomed, during her school years, to all the complex machinery of a highly equipped

OUTDOOR HOUSEKEEPING ON THE PIMA RESERVATION

institution. This experiment has already been tried in some of the schools, and although it has been in existence but a few years, the results justify the experiment.

A general campaign of education has been inaugurated that includes a moving-picture machine illustrating the care of tuberculosis and trachoma and the dangers of insanitary living. This has visited every school and reservation in the southwest and this year it is in the north.

THE HAMPTON INSTITUTE TRADE SCHOOL*

III BRICKLAYING AND PLASTERING.

"Instruction must be considered as much as production. The shop is for the boy, not the boy for the shop."

SAMUEL CHAPMAN ARMSTRONG

"ABOUT the third day of my trade my instructor came to me and, commenting on my work, said, 'That is very good, Smith.' This was all I wanted to hear. That day I was so proud of bricklaying that I wore my work shoes to the dining hall. Everyone looked at them, but I did not care ; I wanted people to know that I was a young bricklayer."

These significant words were spoken at a recent Hampton Anniversary by a Negro bricklayer who had finished his trade and, as his final exercise, was giving, before a great audience of white and colored people, a practical demonstration of the stages through which the Hampton bricklayer must pass. Joy and pride in trade work characterize the Hampton student. Training and result go hand in hand in all of Hampton's classroom and workshop activity.

It was with radiant face and skill of hand that Hugh C. Smith told, with the aid of mortar, trowel, and bricks, the effective story of his first steps in bricklaying. Liberal quotations from this boy's Anniversary address will give, perhaps, a better idea of some of Hampton's aims and methods than any purely informational study.

"The first thing a student is taught when he enters the Hampton bricklaying department is how to take mortar up on his trowel. Our instructor told us not to push the trowel point into the mortar, but to take the trowel and cut the mortar angle shape.

* "Carpentry and Cabinetmaking," May 1913 ; "Blacksmithing and Wheelwrighting," January 1914

Being a very green fellow when I entered the department, I found this difficult to do, but I did not give it up. I worked away at this task for nearly a whole day, and late in the afternoon I found that practice was about to bring success. I could take the mortar up properly.

PLASTERERS AT WORK IN THE PRINCIPAL'S HOUSE

"Now I was ready to start spreading mortar. Spreading mortar properly is one of the hardest things a beginner has to learn to do. I have seen bricklayers who have worked at their trade for more than a generation and are still unable to spread mortar correctly. They take their trowels and simply shake off the mortar just as a man would shake seed from a board used in planting. We were first taught to spread mortar on a board. Every time I tried to get the mortar off my trowel, or tried to spread it as my instructor had shown me, every bit of it came off the trowel at once.

TECHNICAL WORK IN THE SHOP

"After five days' experience at mortar spreading I was actually ready to begin laying bricks. The first exercise in the laying of bricks is to place them end to end. The next exercise is to run a little wall, starting with four bricks and running up to one brick. A tedious thing that came into this exercise was pointing the joints; that is, smoothing the mortar in them. As soon as the wall is built it is torn down and rebuilt several times. Thus, at the beginning of the course, we get as much practice in tearing down as we do in building up.

PRELIMINARY WORK ON A LOGGIA

"The fourth exercise given to bricklayers is to form a corner. The square is used in squaring corners and jambs. After running the corner up three courses, it is time to stop and plumb it. The plumb rule is a very difficult tool to handle. One may see men standing in all kinds of positions when plumbing their work, but there is only one right way to stand in plumbing a corner. One should stand with the plumb rule in front of him.

"Last year's Senior bricklayers had a chance to demonstrate their skill in running English bond on Clarke Hall, our new Y. M. C. A. building, of which we are so proud.

"With the instruction I have received here at Hampton in the academic department, in mechanical drawing, and in bricklaying, I am about to go forth, ambitious to join the world's best mechanics."

The course in bricklaying and plastering consists of tasks of graduated difficulty. After having become proficient in laying a plain wall, students are given a little speed work. They are tested first, however, on their accuracy. Boys work from blueprints and complete an interesting series of practical shop exercises. They learn how to build a small corner, consisting of perhaps twelve courses ; how to lay a four-inch wall with the American bond ; how to raise a wall that must be built to a given line ; how to do foundation work ; how to construct piers, chimneys, and fireplaces ; how to lay off and construct segmental, circular, and

BUILDING THE SECOND STORY OF THE HAMPTON TRADE SCHOOL

STUDENTS CONSTRUCTING A GRANOLITHIC WALK

elliptical arches. The technical work which the bricklayers and plasterers do indoors is as nearly full size as possible. Indeed, the shop work, as far as it is carried, is full size and is made as practical as if it were to become permanent.

Negro and Indian tradesmen are taught how to use and care for the regular tools of their trade—the trowel, the hammer, the chisel, the plumbing rule and bob, and the steel square. They learn to make the practical calculations which are required in their everyday work. They are encouraged to read the standard trade journals and textbooks. The Hampton students have excellent equipment for all their trade work.

The bricklaying and plastering department was organized in 1896. The first construction work done by the department was the building of a wing of the school Laundry. The Armstrong-Slater Memorial Trade School was built in 1896 by non-student labor. Only one Hampton Institute bricklayer worked on it. Then, in 1898, the Domestic Science and Agricultural Building was constructed and four Hampton boys helped to build its walls. Next, Cleveland Hall, containing a large school chapel and a comfortable dormitory for girls, was erected, twelve Hampton tradesmen being employed. When the school's large barn was constructed in 1905 not a single outside man was hired to do any of the brick work. Other interesting building operations that have since been carried to completion without outside labor, except that furnished by Hampton ex-students, include the remodeling of the Huntington Industrial Works and the Pierce Machine Shop into boys' dormitories, and the construction of the substantial house now occupied by the school's assistant disciplinarian, as well as the erection of Clarke Hall, the new and attractive $30,000 Y. M. C. A. building, to which Smith referred in his Anniversary address.

The bricklaying, plastering, and granolithic work of the Institute is now done entirely by Hampton tradesmen. A few figures, giving the summary of one year's work, will be some indication of the unusual opportunity that the students have for practical training : Bricks laid, 237,816 ; granolithic walks constructed, 482 square yards, plastering done, 4049 square yards.

STUDENTS LAYING THE FOUNDATION OF THE Y. M. C. A. BUILDING

The students in the bricklaying and plastering department touch the life of the Hampton School at many points. They set boilers in the power house ; build the bake ovens which are used in the kitchens ; repair the plastering in the students' dormitories and other school buildings ; keep the granolithic walks in repair ; and do the necessary construction work in connection with the erection of new buildings. When one of the boys' dormitories was converted from an open dormitory into one with enclosed rooms, the students in the bricklaying and plastering department rendered excellent service. Then, too, when the school decided to add another story to the Hampton Trade School, bricklayers and plasterers did their part of the work most satisfactorily.

In building Clarke Hall, Hampton student bricklayers set all the stone and laid all the brick. The columns of the loggia, made of moulded brick and set on seven diameters, formed a very complicated piece of work.   In this structure the students had to construct flat arches and panels of various kinds.   This building, indeed, has been an excellent *demonstration* of the fruit of the practical training which Hampton tradesmen receive.

Builders and those who are in a position to pass expert judgment on Clarke Hall, as a specimen of good building activity, declare that it is first class in every way.

Instruction in plastering is also given to the Hampton bricklayers.   The boys begin with exercises in trowel handling and

CLARKE HALL, THE Y. M. C. A. BUILDING, COMPLETED IN 1912 BY
HAMPTON TRADESMEN

then pass on to work on plain walls and the different kinds of arches that are commonly used in modern building practice. They are taught how to use the common tools with which the average plasterer must earn his living.   Here, again, the Hampton students receive a wide range of practical training in the construction and repair work done on the numerous school buildings.

The agriculture boys at Hampton receive instruction in the bricklaying and plastering department one day each week for three months.   They are taught concrete work and the building of small piers, fence posts, and water troughs.   They also have some elementary work in plastering.   Boys who are taking the regular trade-school course in carpentry receive about twice as

A PRODUCT OF THE HAMPTON TRADE SCHOOL

much work in the bricklaying and plastering department as do
the agriculture boys. They are taught in the technical shop how
to do plastering and how to build piers, foundations, chimneys,
and fireplaces.

BARN AT HAMPTON INSTITUTE BUILT BY SCHOOL TRADESMEN

The Saturday morning shop talks cover a wide range of subjects. Sometimes a boy is assigned a subject and has to present his topic in the form of a practical demonstration before his classmates. Some of the subjects which are discussed by the instructor and the students during the Saturday morning sessions, are the methods and operations involved in brickmaking, the manufacture and use of cement, the principles of construction, and the meaning of important trade and technical terms used in bricklaying and plastering.

Laying bricks carefully and neatly to a given straight line, plumbing corners accurately, working with one another without friction, following blueprints exactly, tackling with enthusiasm difficult repair problems, getting ready to do things in the work-a-day world by doing practical work during school days, combining theory and good modern practice—these are some of the important lessons which Negroes and Indians learn in the bricklaying and plastering course in the Hampton Institute Trade School.

The test of all Hampton's work for individual and race uplift is found in the results which can be observed on the school grounds and in the records of the graduates and former students who are winning the respect and good will of the best white people throughout Virginia and the Southland. The bricklayers and plasterers who have gone out from the Hampton Trade School since 1900 are making their way successfully as journeys men, as teachers, and as contractors. They are carrying into their everyday living the lessons of thoroughness and reliability which they learned at Hampton Institute through constant drill, careful supervision, and wise counsel. They have gone forth, not only as builders of walls and chimneys, but also as builders of Christian character.

THE NEGROES
OF SAN ANTONIO

BY GEORGE S. DICKERMAN

IN looking over a report of the addresses on race problems
at the Southern Sociological Congress in Atlanta my eye fell
upon this statement by Professor Branson, "In only one city of
America, San Antonio, Texas, is the death rate of Negroes lower
than the death rate of whites." I at once recalled a day in the
winter of 1909 that I passed in this remarkable old city on the
Mexican border, when I felt the fascination of its ancient churches
with their atmosphere of historic association, and listened to wild
stories of frontier life among Indians and buffaloes from a gray-
haired veteran who had been on the ground from his childhood.
But of greater interest to me than all other things were certain
schools which I visited in San Antonio.

I was there on an educational errand, the same that has taken
me at one time and another to most of the cities in the Southern
states, and I was giving particular attention to educational efforts
for the colored people. On my way thither I had visited three
other cities of Texas—Marshall, Tyler, and Austin—each an educational center with two flourishing colleges for colored students
maintained by contributions from all parts of the country and
drawing their students largely from a distance. Here there was
no school of that kind, only the common public schools, but I
found these to be of such a character as to prove that they were
very uncommon. I have a number of photographs which were
taken at the time, and memoranda which I penciled in my note-
book ; as I bring these out and examine them in the light of Professor Branson's remark, the impression then received comes back
and is widened in the scope of its meaning.

Three of the photographs are here reproduced. They reveal
an air of respectability that is too seldom found in the public
schools provided for the children of this people. The buildings
are substantial and in good repair. They are surrounded with
appropriate fences on which not a picket is missing or broken.
Numerous trees have been set out, and are taken care of, so that
they are making a healthy growth and give promise of increasing
shade and beauty in the years to come. Space has been provided

FRONT VIEW OF THE NEGRO HIGH SCHOOL IN SAN ANTONIO

for a playground and here, too, good order is apparent.

As might be expected, the interior is quite as attractive as the exterior. In the high school one finds a carefully selected and well-arranged library on a suitable case of shelves, made accessible to the students and others who may wish to avail themselves of the books. In the rear of this building is a well-equipped shop for training in carpentry work and other industries. The Brackenridge school, named for a local friend and benefactor, is also provided with rooms for shop work, and, besides, has ground laid out in gardens where the children are taught to till the soil for vegetables and flowers. Another school building, which had been recently put up, contained rooms for dressmaking and millinery, and as this was not far from the

PLAYGROUND AND WORKSHOP OF THE NEGRO HIGH SCHOOL

THE BRACKENRIDGE SCHOOL

Brackenridge school the pupils passed from one to the other for industrial instruction.

Quite as significant as the buildings and equipment was the force of teachers that I found in charge of the work. How well prepared they were for their places may be inferred from the high character of the institutions in which they had been educated. The principal of the high school was a graduate of Virginia Union University and had taken post graduate work in Chicago University. One of his assistants was graduated from Lincoln University and the Yale Divinity School. Two others were from Fisk University, a third from Wiley University, and a fourth from Tillotson College, while two had taken a course at the State Normal School at Prairie View. The teachers at the Brackenridge school showed a similar record. The principal and one assistant were from Wilberforce University, while other assistants were from Fisk, Walden, and Roger Williams Universities.

With schools of such a character, conducted by men and women who have enjoyed these rare educational advantages, it would indeed be surprising if the Negroes of San Antonio did not show superiority in their mode of living to those in some other cities that one could name. Here are conditions that make for intelligence, for habits of industry, for wholesome recreation, for elevating employments in the home, and for worthy ambition in all the walks of life. Naturally, therefore, the death rate is conspicuously lower than in other cities which are not privileged in any such way.

THE NEGRO WORKING OUT HIS OWN SALVATION[*]

BY E. C. BRANSON

Professor of Rural Economics at the State Normal School, Athens, Ga.

AT present the drift of Negro population in the South is distinctly countryward. During the last census period our Negro population in general increased barely 10 per cent, but our Negro farm population increased more than 20 per cent. Just the reverse tendency is true among the whites of every Southern state except Kentucky.

In 1910 in the South the ratio of Negro farm workers ran far ahead of that of Negro population in general. For instance, in South Carolina the Negroes were 55 per cent of the population, but 68 per cent of the farm workers. In Georgia they were 45 per cent of the population, but 53 per cent of the farm workers ; in Alabama 42 per cent of the population, but 54 per cent of the farm workers ; in Louisiana 43 per cent of the population, but 64 per cent of the farm workers ; in Mississippi 66 per cent of the population, but 69 per cent of the farm workers. The Negroes were 30 per cent of our Southern population, but they were 40 per cent of all persons engaged in agricultural pursuits.

In Mississippi during the last census period Negro farmers increased at a rate nearly two and a half times greater than the rate of increase for Negro population in general, and in Georgia at a rate nearly three and a half times greater.

In every state of the South, except Arkansas and Oklahoma, the Negro is a dwindling ratio of population in general, but he is an increasing ratio of population in the farm regions, Louisiana alone excepted.

On the other hand, the Negro is a decreasing ratio of population in the cities of the South. In 1900 thirty-three Southern cities, each containing 25,000 or more inhabitants, had a Negro population amounting to 10 per cent or more. During the following census period, in all of these cities except Fort Worth, Negro population lagged behind the rates of white increase, in some of them far behind ; as, for instance, in Atlanta and Macon. In others there was an actual loss of Negro population.

[*] Excerpts from an address before the Southern Sociological Congress, reprinted from "The Human Way"

Between 1865 and 1880 the towns and cities of the South seemed in fair way of being overrun and overwhelmed by the Negroes. In 1910 it became evident that the Negro was resisting the lure of city life and sticking to the farm better than the Southern white man.

Some 50,000 Negroes are engaged in the various professions, mainly teaching, preaching, medicine, and law ; some 30,000 more are engaged in various business enterprises, some of them with conspicuous success and distinction. But here, all told, are fewer than 100,000 upward-moving Negroes.

On the other hand, 2,500,000 Negroes are engaged in agricultural pursuits as day laborers, tenants, and owners. With their families, they represent more than four-fifths of their race in the South, and they cultivate 100,000,000 acres of our farm land, or two-thirds of our total improved acreage.

The Negro, then, is wisely choosing or blindly moving, to work out his own salvation as a race, not in city but in country civilization.

In the farm regions he is achieving a new economic status. He is rapidly rising out of farm tenancy into farm ownership. In a large way he is coming to be a landed proprietor. During their first twenty years of freedom the Negroes made little headway in land ownership. They were absorbed either in politics or in religion, and this is particularly true of the leaders. The constructive achievements of the race were most marked in the direction of church building and church organizations. But during the last thirty years the Negroes of the South have come to feel that bank books and barns are more important than ballot boxes. At all events they appear in the 1910 census not as farm workers or tenants merely, but as owners in large numbers.

Nearly one-fourth of all the Negro farmers in the South own the farms they cultivate. In Florida they own nearly one-half of them, in Kentucky and Oklahoma more than one-half of them, in Maryland and Virginia more than three-fifths of them, and in West Virginia nearly four-fifths of them. In less than fifty years the Negro has acquired possession of twenty million acres of farm land. Altogether his farm properties are valued at nearly $500,000,000. Negro landholdings in the aggregate make an area a little larger than the State of South Carolina. The Russian serfs, after fifty years of freedom, have not made greater headway. They have not done so well, indeed, in their conquest of illiteracy.

True, cropping and share tenancy are increasing in the South faster than cash or standing-rent tenancy with its larger measure of independent self-direction—nearly seven times as fast during the last census period. But wherever land is abundant or labor scarce, or white farmers are moving out, the Negro rises out of share tenancy into cash tenancy and out of cash tenancy into ownership.

During the last census period the Negroes of the South increased less than 10 per cent in population, but they increased 17 per cent in the ownership of farms against a 12 per cent increase of white farm owners. In Mississippi, Alabama, and North Carolina the farms cultivated by white owners increased only 9 per cent, but the farms cultivated by Negro owners increased 19, 21, and 22 per cent in the order named. In Arkansas, while white farm owners increased 8 per cent, Negro farm owners increased nearly 23 per cent. In Georgia the white farm owners increased only 7 per cent, but Negro farm owners increased 38 per cent. Even in Louisiana, where there was an actual loss of Negro farm population, there was an increase of 14 per cent in the number of Negro farm owners.

In 283 counties, or nearly one-third of all the counties of ten Southern states, the Negroes are in a majority. In sixty-one of these counties Negro farm owners outnumber the white farm owners. This is true of 5 counties in Georgia, 6 in Oklahoma, 8 in Arkansas, 11 in Mississippi, and 17 in Virginia.

The Negro farmer now owns $37,000,000 worth of farm implements and tools, $177,000,000 worth of farm animals, $273,000,000 worth of farm lands and buildings. During the last ten years he has nearly doubled his wealth in farm implements, more than doubled his wealth in farm animals, and nearly trebled his wealth in farm lands and buildings.

In Georgia, in 1910, the farms cultivated by white owners numbered 82,930, an increase of 5776, or 7 per cent, during the ten years. The farms cultivated by Negro owners numbered 15,700, an increase of 4324, or 38 per cent, during this period. The rate of Negro increase in farm ownership in Georgia is more than five times the rate of white increase during the last census period.

In 1880 Georgia Negroes owned 580,664 acres of farm land, but in 1910 they owned 1,607,970 acres. It is nearly a threefold increase during the thirty years. Negro property upon the tax digests of Georgia now amounts to $34,000,000. Three-fourths of it is country property. Their gains in property ownership in the rural regions of Georgia are amazing, but they appear so uniformly on our tax digests that they have ceased to be surprising.

Here, for instance, is one of the sixty-six counties in the black horseshoe belt of the state. The Negroes outnumbered the whites more than four to one. In 1910 they owned nearly one-tenth of all the farm land, nearly one-third of the plantation and mechanical tools, more than one-third of all the household goods and utensils, nearly one-half of all the farm animals, and one-sixth of the total aggregate wealth of the county.

In another county there are 1148 Negro farm owners. They outnumber the white farm owners nearly three to one. In the census year only twelve mortgages were recorded against the Negro farms of this county. In an adjoining county four-fifths of all the farms cultivated by owners are cultivated by Negro owners. In the census year there were no mortgages whatsoever on Negro farms in this county.

In my own county in 1910 they owned 8283 acres of land; in one district more than one-fourth and in another nearly one-third of all the farm land. In all, 957 Negroes in the county, or more than one in every three males of voting age, are home or farm owners.

Where they are thinly scattered among white majorities, they make even more astonishing gains. For instance, here is a county in which the Negroes own 15,146 acres of land. Their gain in the ownership of farm animals in ten years was 291 per cent; in plantation and mechanical tools, 497 per cent; and in aggregate wealth, 310 per cent.

In the white belt is another county where the whites outnumber the Negroes nearly two to one. But the gain by Negroes in the ownership of plantation and mechanical tools during the census period was 376 per cent; in farm animals, 226 per cent; in total aggregate wealth, 230 per cent.

Here then, in brief, are the facts concerning Negro farm and home ownership in the South. They show that the Negro is a dwindling ratio of population in every Southern state except Arkansas and Oklahoma; that he is a decreasing ratio of population in the cities of the South; but that he is an increasing ratio of population in the farm regions of every Southern state except Louisiana. They show in every Southern state, without exception, that the Negroes are increasing in farm ownership at a greater rate than the whites; indeed, at rates varying all the way from two and a half to five and a half times the rates of white increase in farm ownership. Of course their farm holdings are small and their total acreage relatively little; but assuredly they are getting what Uncle Remus calls a "toe-holt" in the soil.

The Southern Negro, then, is working out his own salvation, not in terms of politics, not in terms of formal education, but in terms of property ownership; and mainly in terms of land in the rural regions. He is doing this without let or hindrance in the South, largely aside from the awareness of the whites, largely because of their indifference, but even more largely with the sympathy and help of his white friends and neighbors. He is lifting himself up by tugging at his own boot straps, a figure commonly used to indicate an impossible something; but in civilization, as in education, it is the only possible means of elevation.

The Negro is emerging from jungleism and winning civilization mainly and necessarily by his own efforts. He is coming out of darkness into light in accord with and in obedience to the laws of development. His progress every inch of the way is marked by struggle—struggle within himself for mastery over himself, and struggle with outward, untoward surrounding circumstances.

His real successes are achieved by himself. They cannot be thrust upon him by another. He cannot be coddled into civilization by an overplus of sympathy from friends far and near, North or South. We have tried to civilize the Indian with reservations and free rations, and we have failed.

The Negro as a race will never stand really possessed of anything that he does not win worthily by himself and for himself. His gains in property ownership, position, influence, and prominence in economic and civic freedom will keep steady pace with racial efficiency. His destiny will be wrought out in terms biologic, economic, and social; and, as usual, in dumb, blind struggle for self-defensive adjustment to surrounding conditions.

The laws of racial development have something like the steady, fateful pull and power of gravitation or any other natural law. These laws can be discovered and manipulated to accelerate or retard progress, just as all the laws of nature can be discovered and harnessed for constructive or destructive purposes. They can be recognized and applied as the laws of electricity have been recognized and applied. They cannot be invented and willed into operation by individual bumptiousness or legislative blindness.

The Negro problem will not be solved by editorials, creeds, or statutes; by conferences, congresses, or assemblies; by pride, prejudice, or passion.

The development of the Negro can be stimulated, safeguarded, and directed wisely and beneficently. The asperities of natural law can be softened. The stream of tendencies can be kept clear of injustice and cruelty, brutality, and inhumanity; and it will be so if we have any Christianity worth the name.

The way of salvation for the Negro is not along the paved highways of city civilization. In the cities he is waging a losing battle. The ravages of drink and drug evils, the vices and diseases of the slums, make swift and certain inroads upon the race as a whole in the congested centers of our population.

It would be beyond reason to expect a belated people to succeed in any large racial way upon the highest levels of competition. The chances of progress are upon the lower levels, where life is less intense, the struggle for existence less desperate, and surrounding circumstánces more propitious and helpful.

The Negro's chance is the countryside. Here he succeeds and achieves a new economic status for the race. The open country needs him as a farm worker. It holds out beckoning hands to him. The countryside has no slums. Fresh air, unmixed sunshine, and pure water are abundant. Fuel is everywhere plentiful. Nobody ever heard of a country Negro's freezing or starving to death or even suffering for the necessities of life in the rural South. In the country there are fewer temptations to irregularities of living. He sleeps more and works harder. He is less tempted into dissipation and vice. His home life is cleaner and wholesomer. His children are closer to him and under better oversight. Family life is less apt to be disrupted by immoralities or desertion. He easily saves money and gets ahead in the world somewhat. The Negro is waging a winning battle in the farm regions ; he is rising into a new economic level in the open country.

Negro farm ownership in 283 (or nearly one-third) of the cotton-belt counties in which the Negroes are densely massed is one problem. Farm ownership among Negroes thinly scattered in white counties among white majorities is another problem. In one case Negro property owners manifestly yield to the upward pull of the surrounding superior mass. Here they certainly acquire ownership with accelerated rapidity, and with advantage to themselves and the community at large. In the other case, Negro farm owners are thinly scattered in black counties among black majorities. Do they yield to the downward pull of the surrounding, inferior mass of shiftless, thriftless Negroes ? Is Negro life in these counties slipping back into savagery ?

The answer calls for complete acquaintance with the facts. There are now many Negro communities that are working out their salvation under conditions more or less sequestered. In Louisa County, Va., the Negroes own 53,000 acres of land ; in Liberty County, Ga., 55,000 acres ; in Macon County, Ala., 61,000. In Beaufort County, S. C., Negro farm owners outnumber white farm owners 17 to 1. Negro civilization in these counties is at hand for investigation. Mound Bayou, Miss., Boley, Okla., and Greenwood, Ala., are centers of Negro farm communities. There is abundant opportunitv for direct, first-hand study by non-partisan investigators. And there is need for race studies by scientific students, in scientific ways, and in a scientific spirit.

The Negro has suffered from the zeal of retained attorneys for preconceived opinions ; almost as much from indiscreet friends as from hostile critics. The skies ought to be cleared by impersonal, impartial acquaintance with the facts, whatever they are, concerning Negro problems and progress. Many good people in the South stand hesitatingly aloof because they are insufficiently informed and honestly in doubt about what is really best for the Negro and the community in which he lives.

Book Reviews

Afro-American Folksongs; A Study in Racial and National Music. By Henry Edward Krehbiel. Published by G. Schirmer, New York. Price, $2.00 *net*.

THIS attractive and interesting volume has been written with the avowed purpose of "bringing a species of folksong into the field of scientific observation and presenting it as fit material for artistic treatment." Toward this end the author has well done his part, writing with a keenness of appreciation and sympathy which will make his book a welcome addition to musical literature. He has gleaned in many fields and his deductions can hardly fail to convince both the scientific and the lay musician that there is in these wonderful songs a vast reward for careful study.

He speaks of Dvorak's symphony, "From the New World," which includes many characteristic elements of Negro songs, as a great step towards dignifying them in the eyes of the musical world, and perhaps of opening up a new school of composition.

He regrets, as do all who have ever known the genuine old-time melodies, that their finer qualities are so rapidly passing away, being pushed relentlessly into the past by the conventional music of church and school. Born of sorrow and oppression, they are passing with the condition that called them forth, and recognizing this, one hardly dares express the regret one must feel for their loss to science and to art.

Strangely enough the antithesis of the old spiritual, its "debased offspring," as Dr. Krehbiel calls ragtime and the African *tango*, is suffering a universal revival. Sloughed off almost entirely by the Negro himself, this remnant of his barbarisms, cultivated as a new feature in musical and terpsichorean art, is swinging round a curiously small circle to its early days in the African jungle.

Hampton recognizes the justice of Mr. Krehbiel's criticism of its book of plantation melodies—that the harmonization of its songs does not give any adequate idea of the Negro's own improvised rendering. The earlier writers, and perhaps the wisest, refused to give more than the air, frankly confessing their inability "to convey any notion of the effect of a number singing together."

Those who have attempted the rather thankless task have done so with many apologies, recognizing their limitations. Miss Hallowell, of the Calhoun School, who has made a more intimate study of the songs than any others appear to have done, confesses that it is "impossible to more than suggest their beauty and charm." Most attempts at harmonizing these songs have been made, not for scientific study, nor to guide the Negro singer, but to make them mean the most to the white amateur, just as Mr. Krehbiel has himself done in availing himself of the work of modern composers in harmonizing the songs given in his book.

The inspired pencil that can take down the best of these melodies with their many subtle peculiarities will find a vast field, not only in the American music of Negro and Indian, but in bird songs, with which they have many qualities in common. So far, no system of notation has been at all adequate to the task, and in the meantime rare things are passing away.

If Dr. Krehbiel, with his evident sympathy and understanding, might add to his scientific knowledge the invention of a new method of recording these elusive songs, he would find himself embarked on no mean enterprise. Going personally into the larger communities of the black folk, or even into the tobacco factories where singing is encouraged, he would find a world of new songs and be surprised to discover how much larger a proportion would be in a minor key than he has been led to suppose from the printed songs that have come to his notice. Instead of a " paucity of secular songs " he would find scores of them in the mines, on the railroads, in the cotton and peanut fields, and wherever a crowd of men or women need the encouragement of music to mark time for their work or to ring the changes on the more frequently used "spirituals." Many interesting game and dance songs are also extant. A collection of all these would make a- very interesting sequel to this new volume of Afro-American folksongs and cannot be begun too soon.   C. M. F.

In Freedom's Birthplace: A Study of the Boston Negroes. By John Daniels. Published by Houghton Mifflin Company, Boston. Price, $1.50 *net*.

THIS is an intensive and suggestive study of the Negro in a narrow field and with an environment, for a part of the time at least, exceptional. The earlier chapters of the book relate, briefly but interestingly, the story of the Negro in Boston from 1638 to the end of the Civil War. They set forth the treatment the Negro received, and make clear the not inconsiderable part he played in the struggle for American independence, and his vital part as "the decisive factor in the establishment of his freedom throughout he nation." An account follows of the Negro's consequent rise in public favor, his securing of equal rights, and his elevation to public office. It is shown that "all rendered at least ordinary, honest service," and that the "elevation of these members of the race to public office made the Negroes feel that they had a part of some consequence in the affairs of the community, and at the same time caused the community to form a higher opinion of them."

The influence of Southern opinion upon Northern sentiment, together with an influx of Negroes from the South, is shown to have brought a speedy reaction in Boston. Soon the Negroes were thrust upon their own resources. Out of this necessity, here and elsewhere, arose the general conviction that, "if the Negro people are to achieve real and lasting progress, they must be made to depend primarily, not upon the bestowal of favor from without, but upon their own independent effort from within." This marks the beginning of a new era with the Negro in Boston.

The author makes a careful, searching study of the physical, social, ethical, religious, political, and economic development of the Negro in Boston from this period, about 1895, to the present time. He finds that there has been a decided gain in the birth rate since ante-bellum days, and that it "is at present only slightly below that of the population as a whole, and is no doubt above that of the native-descended whites, so that, comparatively speaking at least, the Negro is not on this score very badly off." And since 1885 his death rate has undergone a continued and marked decline. This is due "chiefly to the steady betterment of both exterior residential environment and interior housing and living conditions among the Negroes."

Though pointing out the Negro's distrust of his own capacities, and his dependence upon others, his lack of genuine and substantial race pride, and other characteristics that retard social development, the author declares it to be clearly evident that the Negroes are making social progress in spite of all obstacles. Among other helpful agencies, the public free-school system is given as one of the chief permanent and fundamental factors in this progress. He believes that "Negroes themselves understand their own conditions far better, when all is said, than do the whites." He notes the small and decreasing extent to which Negroes fall into the hands of public or private charity. And what he regards as most promising and significant of all, are the "stronger race consciousness and the rudiments of a genuine race pride" which he sees springing up among the Negroes.

In regard to the Negro church Mr. Daniels is pretty severe. He feels that it has fallen far short of its opportunities in Boston.

But even here he notes a gain. He says that Negroes are now applying their religious resources in more practical ways and to better purpose.

On political grounds the Boston Negro has lost somewhat since 1895. This is due in the main, however, to causes over which he had no control, rather than to an improper or unwise use of the ballot, which the author does not hesitate to declare "the Negro's most direct means of safeguarding and promoting his well-being, so far as these ends can be accomplished through law and public action." In this connection he finds that Negro voters of today are better educated, more intelligent regarding political matters, and more interested in and disposed to uphold good government than was the case years ago.

As to the Boston Negro's economic situation the author finds him on an industrial level far below that of the white man. This is due to his industrial unfitness resulting from his early surrounding conditions and inherent shortcomings, and to discrimination. Nevertheless, he is forging ahead, and is, "in constantly increasing numbers and proportion, mounting into the ranks of those manual and clerical occupations which constitute the broad middle group of industry." The Negroes have acquired in greater Boston a surprising amount of property in homes, valued at over $3,000,000 ; and by means of practical industrial training are equipping themselves to take higher places in industry.

Altogether a long list of well-educated, capable, efficient Boston Negroes is cited, and the valuable services these men render their race and community are highly commended. Nevertheless, Mr. Daniels feels that, "so far as pertains to the past and the present, the *average* Negro—using this unscientific term for lack of a better—has always been, and still is, inferior to the *average* white man." Upon this inferiority is based the prejudice against the Negro. But he insists that, for the sake of justice and accuracy, the Negro should not be compared with the white man of today but with his own condition in the past. So measured, his advance is at least remarkable. Whether the Negro will ever reach a state of complete inherent equality with the white man the author is unable to predict, but he does not put it beyond the range of possibility. He says, "All we know is, that, though the Negro is still backward, he is steadily moving forward ; and that, though he is still below the other race in point of ability, he is gradually coming up." His inferiority is not only reducible but is actually being reduced. So his problem is "in process of measurable solution." For future advance the Negro must travel a double road : "On the one hand he must continue to make independent strides on his own account ; while, on the other, he must continue also to insist upon rights and privileges as a citizen, and thus more directly to combat the prejudice against him."

The book is critical of the Negro's shortcomings, but it shows what it is possible for him to do upon his own initiative and in accordance with his own best judgment under conditions that do not of themselves preclude progress. It is full of suggestion for the Negro and for those persons and communities that must deal with him.   W. T. B. W.

At Home and Afield

HAMPTON INCIDENTS

WASHINGTON'S BIRTHDAY

NOT until after the middle of February did the gleeful "snow whoop" of the Hampton students greet the winter's first tardy snowstorm, which made a sleigh ride in southern Virginia a possibility for a few hours. Washington's Birthday found snow on the ground and frost in the air. As the twenty-second of February fell on ·Sunday, the holiday was observed on Monday. An unadvertised event of the morning, which did not therefore come to the notice of many spectators, was the triumphal parade of thirty-seven students in overalls and work clothes marching blithely home from Hampton to their own "harmonizing" of "Dixie," appropriately armed with hatchets and axes, and led by a drum major twirling with dignified agility a stick that did duty for a baton. Not cherry trees, but the burned and useless portions of a Negro woman's house in Hampton, mutilated by a recent fire, justified the presence of the hatchets and axes; the volunteer wrecking crew had been at work getting the building ready for repair.

The event of the afternoon was the basket-ball game with Lincoln University, the last victory of the season for Hampton's team, resulting in a score of 27-12. A game between the 1914 and 1916 trade classes, won by the latter, preceded the inter-collegiate game and aroused much local enthusiasm. The usual holiday social, supplemented by a candy sale, was the final dissipation of the day.

ADDRESSES

THE work of Dr. W. D. Weatherford, of Nashville, Tennessee, student secretary of the International Y. M. C. A. Committee, in promoting sympathy and understanding between the black and white races of America is known and appreciated throughout the country, as are his books, "Negro Life in the South," and "Present Forces in Negro Progress," which have contributed considerably to the enlightenment of the white people and to the consequent solution of trying problems.

Dr. Weatherford spent Sunday, March 1, at Hampton, speaking to the students in church, at chapel exercises, and in Y. M. C. A. meetings. The subject of his morning sermon in Memorial Church was the need of leadership and the value of personality in leadership. In the afternoon he addressed the community service workers of the Y. M. C. A. and the Cabinet, and met with the committees, advising them in their various lines of activity. His stirring talk at the regular Y. M. C. A. meeting, on the temptations of young men, came from a life of broad experience in dealing with college men's problems.

At chapel exercises, Dr. Weatherford gave one of the most practical and convincing talks on foreign missions that has been heard at Hampton, showing the real advance, in the daily life conditions of Chinamen with the introduction of Christian sociology, and the consequent banishment of many harmful conventions, customs, and superstitions. The most moving appeal lay in his description of the eagerness with which even the coolies seize upon and absorb any scrap of Western civilization.

A further acquaintance with China and the Chinese was made through the visit on the following Sunday, March 8, of three members of the Chinese Educational Commission, on a tour of American institutions. Mr. P. W. Kuo spoke at the Y. M. C. A. meeting of the great opportunity for the establishment of Associations in China at this time when the students are reaching out for some religion that is more practical and soul-satisfying than Confucianism. The Y. M. C. A. is growing in popularity and strength through the main universities. It was practically the student class, the backbone of the republic, which brought about the revolution, and it is to them that the country looks for the installation of new educational systems and a new religion. At chapel exercises on the same day, Mr. Kuo talked about the relations existing between China and the United States and the growth of understanding between the two countries. He made the interesting statement that the life of Booker Washington, an account of which was given to him to read by an American lady while he was still a student, had ever since been an inspiration to him.

THE LIBRARY "BULLETIN"

THE Library issued on February 5 a mimeographed sheet, the "Library Bulletin," which lists the books recently added to the library, mentions the features of the current picture exhibition, and notes articles of especial interest to Hampton readers published in the trade and literary magazines. It is the plan of the Library to issue such a bulletin every two weeks. Copies are posted in public places that both teachers and students may see them, and are sent to heads of departments and others.

THE LINCOLN AND ARMSTRONG MEMORIAL

FACING the Library and on the other side of the road there has been erected a little white pavilion of Indiana limestone to house the bas-reliefs of Abraham Lincoln and General Armstrong done by Mr. A. B. Pegram, of London, the sculptor of the bronze equestrian statue of General Armstrong in the Library. The bas-reliefs were presented to the school some months ago by one of Hampton's devoted friends. The building, which is only sixteen by twenty feet, has very much the same architectural lines as the Library, and harmonizes attractively with the general arrangement of that section of the grounds.

RELIGIOUS WORK

ON March 1, at the King's Daughters' meeting, Miss Sherman showed some new and beautifully colored stereopticon slides of the Holy Land. Most of them were pictures of modern Jerusalem, including some particularly lovely views of the Lake of Galilee. The slides were purchased with money left by Miss Mary Briggs, in accordance with a memorandum found since her death stipulating that twenty-five dollars be sent to Miss Sherman for this purpose. The pictures are very much appreciated by the girls, whose Sunday-school study of the life of Christ they make so much more real.

At the communion service on March 8, twelve boys and ten girls joined the Church of Christ in Hampton Institute on confession of faith. Six of the boys and six of the girls are students who came to school last fall. Since January 11, Dr. Mix and Miss Johnston have been conducting communicants' classes for those who, during the Week of Prayer, showed a desire to become Christians, that they might have ample opportuuity to become firmly grounded in their convictions and Christian ideals before joining the church.

THE ARMSTRONG LEAGUE SUPPER

THE genial crowd which attended the supper given in the Gymnasium by the Armstrong League of Hampton Workers on Wednesday, March 4, between the hours of four and seven, was able, and apparently eager, to buy salads, cold ham, and oysters from trim French soubrettes; sandwiches from Sandwich Islanders decorated with flowery garlands; tea, coffee, and cocoa from Japanese brunettes in bewitching kimonas; cakes from fair Dutch *Mädchen*; candy from stately colonial belles; and ice-cream across a country-storekeeper's counter. The six booths, gay with the flags of the various countries represented, were arranged on either side of the big Gymnasium, the space between being filled with small round tables, at which the guests made merry over the delicious eatables. A victrola performed for the pleasure of those who "like music with their meals." One of the many pleasant aspects of the affair was the profit of eighty dollars realized for the Armstrong League.

VISITORS

HAMPTON has entertained many distinguished guests and a number of old friends during the past month. Fifty members of the National Education Association, Department of Superintendence, came down from the Richmond meeting on February 24 to spend the day inspecting the school plant. The party was made up of men and women who had had special training at Teachers' College, and was under the leadership of Professor George T. Strayer of that institution. After luncheon at the Mansion House, Dr. Frissell, Major Moton, and Dr. Abraham Flexner, explained Hampton's work to the visitors who assembled for a brief meeting in the Museum.

This smaller delegation was followed on the twenty-eighth by five hundred members of the National Education Association, who arrived about noon, lunched in Cleveland Hall Chapel with the teachers and workers, visited the Trade School, heard the chorus of Hampton students sing in Memorial Church, and listened to short talks from Dr. W. D. Weatherford, Dr. Frissell, and Major Moton. Dr. Weatherford's brief visit to Hampton and his help to the students during his stay are mentioned elsewhere in this issue.

Mr. Yong Chen, Mr. P. W. Kuo, and Mr. Tsuyi Yu, members of the Chinese Educational Commission to Europe and America, spent several days at Hampton early in March studying Hampton's methods of instruction. Mr. Kuo's Sunday evening address and his talk to the Y. M. C. A. are referred to on another page. Mr. Philip Van Ingen, of New York City, Dr. Wallace Buttrick, secretary of the General Education Board, Dr. Abraham Flexner, an assistant secretary of the General Education Board, and Mr. Elbridge L. Adams, the new chairman of the executive committee of the New York Armstrong Association, visited Hampton during the latter part of February. Mr. J. R. E. Lee, of the Tuskegee Academic Department, and Mr. W. A. Hunton, an international secretary of the Y. M. C. A. Colored Department, well known at Hampton, and always welcome, were on the grounds for a few days in the past month.

Former teachers and workers, who have been heartily welcomed by old friends at Hampton are Miss Orissa Baxter, teacher of home economics in the Hartford School of Religious Pedagogy, formerly in charge of the Teachers' Home boarding department; Miss Alice Boardman, teacher in the Ypsilanti Training School, Michigan, formerly teacher of manual training at the Whittier School; Mr. and Mrs. George D. Young, now located in Springfield, Mass., at one time in charge of Holly Tree Inn; Miss Rossa B. Cooley, of Penn School, Frogmore, S. C.; Miss Susan L. Cushman, who resigned from Hampton's academic department last year, and Miss Anna Vinton, formerly teacher of domestic science at the Holly Tree Inn.

Mrs. Alexander Purves and Miss Ruth Purves have returned to their home at "The Moorings." Dr. Frances Weidner, who was for several years superintendent of the Dixie Hospital and Training School for Nurses, has been visiting friends in Hampton and at the school. Dr. Weidner will in the future be connected with a new school for mountain children in Virginia which is now in the process of organization.

THE KING WILLIAM COLORED TEACHERS INSTITUTE

BY PERRY HARVEY *

ON January 23 and 24, there assembled at the Third Union Public School, King William County, a large number of teachers, patrons, and friends, who came to hear and help discuss the great problem of bettering school conditions. The meeting was held under the auspices of Mr. H. Ragland Eubank, the county superintendent. The first day was very beautiful and gave promise of a successful meeting. The presence of Mr. Jackson Davis, state supervisor of rural schools, added great interest.

Many subjects were discussed. Mr. Eubank introduced Mr. Alexander Dickerson, one of King William's most experienced teachers, who spoke on the subject of "School leagues and the teacher's place in the community." This talk was followed by a paper read by Mr. Jas. E. Dodson on the same subject. Superintendent Eubank introduced Mr. Jackson Davis, who urged the teachers and farmers to unite in order that they may bring about better conditions on the farm and in the schoolhouse.

The afternoon meeting was held in the church, which is about two hundred yards from the school building. Miss India Hamilton and the writer read papers on the subject, "Why manual training is so important in the rural schools." These were followed by a brief discussion. Mr. Jackson Davis gave an interesting talk on in-dustrial education, a subject which seemed to hold first place in the minds of the people. Mrs. A. S. Holmes read a paper on "The importance of a county colored teachers' association." After hearing this interesting and inspiring paper, the teachers organized an association.

The evening topics were "The necessity of a county colored school fair," and "How can the co-operation of the patrons best be obtained?" These were afterwards discussed.

The next day large attendance was made impossible by the rain, yet the meeting was fairly successful. The first speaker of the day was Mr. Beverly Allen [Hampton '81], who spoke on "The necessity of better moral training among the colored people." Mr. Allen was followed by Rev. Monroe E. Guerst [Hampton '88], who spoke on the same subject. The topics, "How to hold the attention of the rest of the pupils while a class is reciting," and "The importance of perfect, though kindly, discipline in schools" engaged the attention of many.

Mr. Eubank gave a brief estimate of the work of Mr. Jackson Davis, and emphasized his real worth to the state. King William thanks Mr. Davis for his visit and feels proud of her Division Superintendent, Mr. Eubank, who is doing a great work for the Negro schools of King William County.

* Hampton 1911

The Armstrong League

THE Armstrong League is an organization especially designed to interest the young men and women of the United States in the study of race questions, and particularly in the industrial education of the Negro and the Indian. The constitution is as follows:

CONSTITUTION

1 The name of this organization shall be the Armstrong League of——

2 The objects and purposes of the League are to disseminate information about the Negro and Indian races in America and to stimulate public interest in them; to further the movement for the industrial education of those races, and to extend the work and influence of the Hampton Normal and Agricultural Institute, founded by General Samuel Chapman Armstrong, and of other similar institutions.

3 Membership in the League may be extended to all in sympathy with the objects and purposes thereof.

4 There shall be a president, two vice-presidents, a secretary, and a treasurer, to be elected annually by the League, who shall perform the usual duties of such officers and who, with three associates, also to be elected annually, shall constitute the Executive Committee, which shall be charged with the direction of the affairs of the League and with the election of members. The Executive Committee shall meet three times a a year, in November, January, and April, and whenever called together by the president. A majority of its members shall constitute a quorum.

5 The annual meeting of the League, at which officers shall be elected and other proper business transacted, shall be held in April of each year.

6 Immediately after the annual meeting in each year, it shall be the duty of the Executive Committee to transmit a report for the previous year, including a list of members, names of officers, and the principal activities of the League, to the secretary of the Armstrong League of the United States in New York City.

7 This constitution may be amended by a vote of a majority of the Executive Committee, provided due notice of the proposed amendment is sent to all the members of the Committee.

THE first branch of the League to be formed was in New York City. This branch had its first meeting on February 16, at the house of Mr. and Mrs. William Jay Schieffelin. Miss Natalie Curtis, the compiler of "The Indians' Book," was to have talked of her experience among the Indians of the far West, but was prevented by illness from being present. In her absence the Rev. Charles W. Douglas gave an interesting talk about his trip through some of the Indian reservations last summer. Madikane Q. Cele gave one of his inimitable talks, in which he told the members of the League what Hampton had done for him and what ideals he was taking back with him to South Africa. This League has already about fifty members.

THE Andover League was formed on February 1. The whole school turned out, filling the chapel, and great enthusiasm was manifested. Principal Stearns presided and reminded the boys that Dr. Frissell was an old Andover boy, and that Mr. Sydney Frissell was also a graduate of Andover. The Hampton Quartet was present and sang several plantation songs, which aroused great enthusiasm. Mr. Jerome F. Kidder explained briefly the situation among the Negroes in the South and the work that Hampton is doing. The story of "John Henry" was then shown by moving pictures, and there were more songs, which were received with wild enthusiasm by the student body. Mr. Elbridge L. Adams, of New York, then outlined the purpose of the Armstrong League. He briefly recounted the chief events in the life of General Armstrong and urged the students to interest themselves in the great race problems of the country which General Armstrong had done so much to solve. The League was immediately formed, and since that time the students of Andover have raised money for Andover scholarships at Hampton.

IT was fitting that the first college league should be formed at Williams, which was General Armstrong's alma mater. The birthday of this League was February 4, 1914, on the occasion of the Hampton meeting at Williamstown. On account of the mid-year examinations, there was not as large an attendance of students as there would have been at some other time, but beautiful Grace Hall was nearly filled with an enthusiastic audience composed of people from Williamstown and North Adams. President Garfield presided and spoke of his father being one of the first trustees of Hampton. He then introduced ex-president Franklin Carter, a classmate of General Armstrong, who delivered a scholarly address on the life and purpose of his famous classmate. Major Moton also spoke. Mr. Adams, who is a graduate of Williams, then addressed the students and urged the formation of an Armstrong League at Williams. A committee of ten prominent Juniors was nominated and elected to perfect an organization. It is expected that the Williams League will have a general meeting in April.

A short Life of General Armstrong has been prepared and is now on the press. This, together with the constitution of the League, bibliographies on the Negro and Indian, and other information will form the League Manual.

Other college and school leagues are in process of formation.

———

Tbe Armstrong League

NEW YORK CITY

President, MISS KATHERINE G. CHAPIN
1st Vice Pres't, MISS MARY JAY SCHIEFFELIN
2nd Vice Pres't, MISS MARGARET CARNEGIE
Recording Secretary, MISS LOIS HALL
Corresponding Secretary, MISS EVA MCADOO
Treasurer, ALAN FOX

PHILLIPS ACADEMY (Andover, Mass.)

President, EDWARD J. WINTERS
1st Vice President, PARKER B. ALLEN
2nd Vice President, JOHN GRANT
Secretary and Treasurer, ALDEN DAVIDSON

WILLIAMS COLLEGE (Williamstown, Mass.)

President, CHARLES B. HALL
1st Vice President, T. A. LANGFORD
2nd Vice President, E. M. HEDDEN
Secretary, MASON TURNER
Treasurer, R. H. HODGE
Executive Committee, D. REMER, B M. SMITH, J. C. TYLER

THE
SOUTHERN
WORKMAN

MAY 1914

Press of
The Hampton Normal and Agricultural Institute
Hampton, Virginia

The Hampton Normal and Agricultural Institute

HAMPTON VIRGINIA

What it is An undenominational industrial school founded in 1868 by Samuel Chapman Armstrong for Negro youth. Indians admitted in 1878.

Object To train teachers and industrial leaders

Equipment Land, 1060 acres ; buildings, 140

Courses Academic, trade, agriculture, business, home economics

Enrollment Negroes, 1215 ; Indians, 37 ; total, 1252

Results Graduates, 1709 ; ex-students, over 6000
Outgrowths ; Tuskegee, Calhoun, Mt. Meigs, and many smaller schools for Negroes

Needs $125,000 annually above regular income
$4,000,000 Endowment Fund
Scholarships
A full scholarship for both academic and
industrial instruction   -   -   - $ 100
Academic scholarship   -   -   -   -   70
Industrial scholarship   -   -   -   -   -   30
Endowed full scholarship   -   -   -   -   2500
Any contribution, however small, will be gratefully received and may be sent to H. B. FRISSELL, Principal, or to F. K. ROGERS, Treasurer, Hampton, Virginia.

FORM OF BEQUEST

I give and devise to the trustees of The Hampton Normal and Agri-cultural Institute, Hampton, Virginia, the sum of   dollars, payable

The Southern Workman

Published monthly by

The Hampton Normal and Agricultural Institute

Contents for May 1914

THE SOUTHERN WORKMAN was founded by Samuel Chapman Armstrong in 1872, and is a monthly magazine devoted to the interests of undeveloped races.

It contains reports from Negro and Indian populations, with pictures of reservation and plantation life, as well as information concerning Hampton graduates and ex-students who since 1868 have taught more than 250,000 children in the South and West. It also provides a forum for the discussion of ethnological, sociological, and educational problems in all parts of the world.'

CONTRIBUTIONS: The editors do not hold themselves responsible for the opinions expressed in contributed articles. Their aim is simply to place before their readers articles by men and women of ability without regard to the opinions held.

EDITORIAL STAFF

H. B. FRISSELL   W. L. BROWN
HELEN W. LUDLOW   W. A. AERY, Business Manager
J. E. DAVIS   W. T. B. WILLIAMS

TERMS: One dollar a year in advance; ten cents a copy
CHANGE OF ADDRESS: Persons making a change of address should send the *old* as well as the *new* address to

THE SOUTHERN WORKMAN, Hampton, Virginia

Entered as second-class matter August 13, 1908, in the Post Office at Hampton, Virginia, under the Act of July 16, 1894

THE HAMPTON LEAFLETS

Any twelve of the following numbers of the "The Hampton Leaflets" may be obtained free of charge by any Southern teacher or superintendent. *A charge of fifty cents per dozen is made to other applicants.* Cloth-bound volumes for 1905, '06, '07 and '08 will be furnished at seventy-five cents each, postpaid.

VOL. I

1 Experiments in Physics (Heat)
2 Sheep : Breeds, Care, Management
3 Transplanting
4 Birds Useful to Southern Farmers
5 Selection and Care of Dairy Cattle
6 Care and Management of Horses
7 How to Know the Trees by Their Bark
8 Milk and Butter
9 Commercial Fertilizers
10 Swine : Breeds, Care, Management
11 Fruits of Trees
12 December Suggestions

VOL. II

1 Suggestions to Teachers Preparing Students for Hampton Institute
2 Experiments in Physics (Water)
3 Spring Blossoms : Shrubs and Trees
4 School Gardening
5 Drainage
6 Mosquitoes
7 Roots
8 Seed Planting
9 Housekeeping Rules
10 Prevention of Tuberculosis
11 Thanksgiving Suggestions
12 Some Injurious Insects

VOL. III

1 Proper Use of Certain Words
2 Winter Buds
3 Domestic Arts at Hampton Institute
4 Beautifying Schoolhouses and Yards
5 Responsibility of Teachers for the Health of Their Children
6 Manual Training in Rural Schools
7 Rotation of Crops
8 Life History of a Butterfly .
9 How Seeds Travel
10 Nature Study for Primary Grades
11 Arbor Day
12 Evergreen Trees

VOL. IV

1 Plants
2 How to Attract the Birds
3 The Story of Corn
4 The Story of Cotton
5 The Meaning of the Flower
6 A Child's Garden
7 The Winged Pollen-Carriers
8 Soils
9 Care of Poultry
10 Plowing and Harrowing
11 Transplanting of Shrubs and Vines
12 Transplanting and Pruning of Trees

VOL. V

1 Teaching Reading to Children
2 Culture and Marketing of Peanuts
3 The House Fly a Carrier of Disease
4 Culture and Marketing of Tobacco
5 Virginia's Fishing Industry
6 Farm Manures
7 Soil Moisture and After-cultivation
8 Patent Medicines
9 Hookworm Disease
10 Reading in the Grammar Schools
11 Oystering in Hampton Roads
12 Common Sense in Negro Public Schools

VOL. VI

1 Sewing Lessons for Rural Schools
2 Housekeeping and Sanitation in Rural Schools
3 Canning Fruits and Vegetables
4 Manual Training, Part II
5 Patrons' Meetings
6 Correlation of Industrial and Academic Subjects in Rural Schools
7 Southern Workman Special Index
8 Community Clubs for Women and Girls
9 Housekeeping and Cooking Lessons for Rural Communities
10 Fifty Years of Negro Progress
11 Approved Methods for Home Laundering
12 Number Steps for Beginners

Address: Publication Office, The Hampton Normal and Agricultural Institute, Hampton, Virginia

The

Southern Workman

VOL. XLIII   MAY 1914   NO. 5

Editorials

Conference for Education in the South
It is now seventeen years since a company of Northern and Southern men came together at Capon Springs, West Virginia, for the purpose of studying educational conditions in the South. Every year since that time important gatherings have been held annually in various cities of the South and have been attended by representatives of all parts of the country. During Mr. Ogden's lifetime, he was accustomed to take with him to these conferences a large party from Northern cities. Many of these Northern friends were thus given inspiration and help, for which they have expressed the greatest gratitude, and at the same time was brought together a body of Southern men who have become leaders of the educational movements in the South.

Education in its broadest sense has always been the subject of these conferences, and has been discussed, not only by those connected with academic work, but by farmers, business men, clergymen, physicians, and representatives of boys' and girls' agricultural clubs. The demonstration-farm work and rural-school supervision of the South has also had its representatives at these meetings.

The following program of a single day at the recent meeting in Louisville, Kentucky, April 7-10, may suggest the scope of the Conference:

12 noon—Country women's day : "The aspirations and needs of country women;" "What the household arts may mean in a country community"

2:30 P. M.—Business men's conference :   "Co-operative credit union for short-term credits"

2:30 P. M.—Farmers' conference :   "How can the co-operative associations make the community self-supporting ?"   "The tenancy problem"

2:30 P. M.—Southern Educational Association :   four separate sessions of the various departments

2:30 P. M.—Special conference of country women :   "How to make ready money;"   "Gardening, canning, and other home industries"

2:30 P. M.—Conference of country preachers: "The intellectual and moral life of the community;"   "Is the church developing character ?"   "How can profanity and immoral habits be rooted out?"   "How can standards be raised ?"

2:30 P. M.—Conference of country doctors :   "The rural fly problem;"   "The rural malarial problem;"   "The rural sewage problem;"   "The rural water supply"

3:00 P. M.—Recreation for country girls : games, etc.

8:00 P. M.—Country life: "Films for the farm;"   "Farmers' co-operative demonstration work;   "Boys' and girls' demonstration club work;"   "Co-operative cow-testing associations"

For a number of years the Southern Educational Association, which is made up largely of superintendents of public education and other schoolmen, has held annual meetings as a kind of Southern branch of the National Education Association. It was deemed wise this year to bring together the Conference for Education in the South and this Southern Educational Conference. The thought of the former has been from the first to associate with itself all existing educational organizations in the South ; hence, when the desire was expressed by the Southern Educational Association that the two societies be merged in one, the representatives of the Conference for Education in the South gladly agreed to the suggestion. At the meeting in Louisville, therefore, a formal merging was made of the two societies. The paragraphs of the resolutions adopted by the Conference which cover its merging with the Southern Educational Association, are as follows :

"That we favor the consolidation of the Southern Educational Association with the Conference for Education in the South, in the interest of economy of time and expense, and of the unity and correlation of all the related agencies heretofore included in both of these bodies, into one great annual co-operative conference.

"That we recommend the appointment of a committee of

three, consisting of the chairman of the executive committee of this Conference and two other members of that committee, to be named by him, to confer with a similar committee of the Southern Educational Association for the arrangement of the details of the consolidation of the two bodies; and that this committee be vested with full authority to act for this Conference in all matters pertaining to the consolidation of the two bodies and the fixing of the time, the place, and the program of the next meeting.''

The gathering at Louisville was of unusual interest. A very important feature was the presence of exhibits in different lines of educational work, especially those connected with rural life. A house was constructed, in the large Armory Hall in Louisville, which represented the best modern thought in connection with rural homes. All the most sanitary appliances for the kitchen, the dining-room, and the water supply were in evidence. While canning classes were being held, members of the Conference gathered in groups to discuss the best methods of improving home life. An interesting exhibit was made of the advantages to the farmer of the parcel post in the transportation of eggs, vegetables, and other farm produce. The representatives of rural schools had long and interesting sessions where most practical suggestions were made as to how rural schools can be improved, not only in the course of study, but in other details of school life. Business men gathered day after day and spent hours of study on the co-operative movement as related to rural life. The conditions in the rural church were discussed with great interest.

The Berea School of Kentucky had an interesting exhibit of the products of its hand work—weaving, basketry, and other industrial branches. Dr. Frost, its president, spoke to groups of men and women who wished to hear from him the story of his work among the mountain whites. Dr. Dillard, president of the Negro Rural School fund, presided at an interesting gathering, largely of Southern men, where the Negro problem was discussed. A representative of Mississippi made a most hopeful report on the condition of the blacks in that state, and of the movement of the white people there towards providing improved Negro schools.

Members of the Conference visited the schools of Louisville and were especially interested in the exhibit in the training school of a penny lunch for the children in attendance. Some of the members also visited the schools of the Presbyterian mission for Negro children, under the care of the Rev. Mr. Little. He is helped in this important work by some of the best white people of Louisville, a number; of whom are teaching in the various departments of the mission. Mr. Little shows wonderful devotion to this work, and the confidence which he has inspired in both the white and the colored people of Louisville is most hopeful.

The loss to the whole cause of education by the death of Mr. Ogden was felt by all present, and the first evening of the Conference was given up to a meeting in his memory, when Dr. S. C. Mitchell, president of Richmond Medical College, delivered an admirable memorial address. The Honorable J. Y. Joyner, superintendent of public education for North Carolina, who has served as president of the National Education Association, was chosen president of the Southern Education Conference, as the new organization is to be called, and there is reason to believe that the Conference next year will be one of the most important in its history.

⊠   .

Report of the Commissioner of Indian Affairs The annual report of the Commissioner of Indian Affairs for the fiscal year ending June 30, 1913 has just been made public. Honorable Cato Sells, the present Commissioner, who makes the report, took the office on June 4, 1913, so that the Bureau was under his direction for only a small portion of the fiscal year. Therefore the resumé which is given of the various activities of the Indian Office during the year is not so significant of the views and aims of the present administration as is the general statement of the needs of the Indian Service with which the report opens.

The new Commissioner finds the health conditions among the Indians deplorable. Approximately 25,000 Indians are suffering from tuberculosis, he says, while available hospital facilities for all will not exceed 300 beds. In the past year 1905 Indians were reported as having died from tuberculosis. Of the whole number of deaths reported from the various reservations, 32 per cent were due to this disease as against 11 per cent throughout the rest of the United States. The death rate among the Indians is 32.24 per thousand, while the Census Bureau gives 16 per thousand in the registration area of the United States. More than 60,000 cases of trachoma are estimated to exist among the Indians. Additional appropriations are needed to construct and equip hospitals to be located on Indian reservations, to check and control disease, and to improve the health of the Indians.

The housing conditions of the Indians throughout the country is a subject, the Commissioner thinks, which demands immediate consideration. Approximately 8000 Indian families are without other homes than mud lodges or tepees with dirt floors and revolting surroundings generally. These insanitary housing conditions continue to exist even where the Indians have been allotted from 80 to 320 acres each of valuable land. This state of things, the Report says, is a serious reflection upon Indian administration and should not be permitted to exist much longer.

Notwithstanding the fact that the Government has provided, since 1876, about $80,000,000 for schools, there are to-day some 10,000 Indian children without any school facilities whatever, principally in the Southwest and more particularly among the Navahos and Papagos. There are also about 7500 Indian children defective, either physically or mentally, for whose care and training no adequate facilities are available. Efforts will be made, the Commissioner promises, to procure increased appropriations for Indian school work, so that all Indian children may be provided with school facilities.

It is estimated that about 180,000 Indians have been allotted and that there are still about 120,000 unallotted. The earliest possible completion of the allotment work is desirable, as this is the main chance of perhaps 70 per cent of the Indians to become self-supporting.

One of the difficult problems which confront the Indian Service is the administration of the timber lands, which have a stumpage value of more than $80,000,000. To administer these lands so as to derive a sustained revenue for the Indians, and yet not to affect unfavorably the future needs in regard to the timber and water supply, will require, the Commissioner believes, the application of sound business foresight and scientific principles.

Other pressing needs are the determination of the heirs in thousands of cases of inherited lands, aggregating an enormous value ; the just settlement of the water rights on a number of reservations where the question of water rights has become involved ; and the probating and handling of the estates of many minors among the Five Civilized Tribes.

In this brief summary are presented pressing and perplexing problems enough to occupy the careful attention and enlist the highest abilities of all who have these matters in charge. It is a satisfaction to note, however, that the present head of the Indian Office has shown a zeal and a sincerity in behalf of the Indians which warrants expectation of genuine efforts for the protection and safeguarding of their interests. Meantime it is apparent that the policy of individualizing Indian property and the removing of restrictions from the Indian as fast as he demonstrates competency, together with the proper protection of incompetents and minors, will greatly increase the work of the Office for several years.

Clean-up Week in Virginia Last year over 130,000 heads of Negro families engaged in the Clean-up Day campaign which was organized by some of the thoughtful Negro leaders who have the confidence and respect of white and colored Virginians. The great possibilities for good to all the people of the Old Dominion, especially to the colored people, shown by the results of last year's Clean-up Day, convinced the Negro Organization Society that it would be well to devote at least a week this year to the work of cleaning up back yards, houses, barns, outhouses, schools, and churches for the promotion of better public health.

Before this issue of the Southern Workman reaches readers in distant states, thousands upon thousands of Virginia Negroes will have taken an active part in getting rid of accumulated rubbish and other disease-breeding elements.

Major Moton, of Hampton Institute, who is the president of the Negro Organization Society, has made clear to many thoughtful men and women throughout the country that the public cannot afford to have Negroes live amid insanitary surroundings. The principle of self-preservation demands that white men and black men must work together for the improvement of the living conditions of those who play a large part in the care of white children and white families.

That the Negro leaders in Virginia have succeeded in winning the co-operation of the State Board of Health, the white and colored papers of Virginia, and other agencies that help to create public opinion, shows clearly the reasonableness and usefulness of the public health work which has been undertaken by the Negro Organization Society of Virginia.

J. Hugo Johnston The state of Virginia loses one of its most efficient workers, and the Negro race one of its best representatives in the death of Dr. J. Hugo Johnston, the late president of the Virginia Normal and Industrial Institute at Petersburg.

He was graduated from the Armstrong High School in Richmond, and after ten years as a teacher in that city was asked by the Board of Visitors to take charge of the state normal school at Petersburg. President Johnston's faithful and efficient service as head of the only normal school maintained by the state for Negroes in Virginia was most genuinely appreciated, not only by the colored people, but also by the white people. He was a quiet, patient, tactful, and efficient administrator and educator who always had the respect and confidence of the state officials. The present standard of the institution is a testimonial to his character and ardent labors.

Dr. Johnston's passing away at this time is especially sad, because he was only fifty-five years old, and his influence in Virginia was tremendously helpful in the uplift of humanity in general. His life was one of service and devotion. The elevation of the morals of the people and improvement in their educational facilities were very close to his heart.' For over twenty years he was a deacon in the first Baptist Church in Richmond, to which he was always devoted.

Folk-Song Concert
Easter Day at the crowded and fashionable Hotel Chamberlin, at Old Point Comfort, came to a delightful close with a Negro folk-song concert, which was given in the large ballroom by the Hampton Institute choir, consisting of some sixty well-trained and well-blended voices.

That the Negro "spirituals, " or plantation songs, of the old South still possess soul-stirring power, was clearly shown by the enthusiastic applause with which the Hampton singers were greeted by the hundreds of hotel guests when they sang, "I'm a-rollin' through an unfriendly world, " "I want to be ready, " "O Freedom, " "Walk together, children, " "He is King of kings," "Couldn't hear nobody pray," "Roll, Jordan, roll," and the Easter plantation hymn, "Dust, dust, and ashes."

This concert of Negro folk-songs and the financial appeal which was made for the work of Hampton Institute became possible through the courtesy of Mr. George F. Adams, who for a number of years has thrown open the Chamberlin to the Hampton Singers on one Sunday evening during the height of the hotel season.

Dr. Frissell outlined the story of the growth of Hampton Institute since its organization in 1868 by General Armstrong on the old Camp Hamilton grounds, near the place where the white men first came in touch with the Indian and the Negro. He told how General Armstrong, who was the son of Hawaiian missionaries and neither a Northerner nor a Southerner, had seen the necessity of teaching the freedmen the dignity of labor and habits of industry. From two teachers and fifteen students, the Hampton School has steadily grown until now its enrollment includes nearly nine hundred boarding students and five hundred day pupils.

Dr. Frissell quoted the words of Dr. Charles W. Eliot, President Emeritus of Harvard, who said, "I know of no institution that so well combines these two elements—the academic and the industrial." Dr. Frissell told the Chamberlin guests about the everyday work of the Hampton students, which includes everything incident to life in an industrial village. He referred to the excellent record of the South in providing common schools for the colored people. He added that in Virginia last year about one hundred schools had no teachers, and that Hampton was unable to supply the increasing demand made upon it for tradesmen and teachers of industrial and academic subjects.

Arthur Harris, a Mohave-Apache Indian of San Carlos, Arizona, who is one of a group of thirty-six Indians who are now bravely working their way through Hampton Institute without any Government assistance, told the story of his struggle for an education and of his desire to remain at Hampton and finish the machinist's trade. Harris, who is a fine-looking specimen of American Indian, declared that Hampton affords the best possible kind of training for his people. He referred to the good influence that the returned students from Hampton are exerting throughout the West.

Major Moton, who has been connected with Hampton Institute for the past twenty-eight years, claimed that Hampton has taught the Negro to believe in work of the hand ; has established a platform on which people can meet for social service ; and has taught the Negro to respect himself and his white neighbors. He summed up the work of the Negro Organization Society which has been striving to secure the co-operation of white people and black people for the promotion of better health, better education, better farms, and better homes among the colored people of Virginia.

At the close of the meeting, the choir sang, "Hampton ! my home by the sea, " which was written by Mr. R. Nathaniel Dett, musical director at Hampton Institute.

STATUS AND NEEDS OF THE FIVE CIVILIZED TRIBES *

BY DANA H. KELSEY

THERE are two phases of the Indian situation in eastern Oklahoma which must be dealt with, one of which is the closing out of the tribal estate. My duties as superintendent having charge of the work of the eighteen districts into which this section has been divided, apply solely to the individual Indian, and this individual work must not be confused with the insistent demand for the winding up of the tribal affairs of the Five Tribes. This latter expression refers solely to the interests in land and money that all members of the tribes have in common. This tribal ownership, without doubt, should be soon done away with. The Cherokee and Seminole Nations have practically reached that condition. The Creeks have only one important unsettled question, which is the matter of the equalization of their allotments. The Choctaws and Chickasaws still have some large tracts of unallotted land, now advertised for sale, and their coal lands. The great complaint against Governmental supervision in the Five Tribes emanates from the educated part-blood who has an interest in the common property which he is unable to secure on demand Congress has been, and should be, urged to speedily provide the necessary legislation to close up and distribute this tribal estate.

From the standpoint of the individual of the restricted class, particularly the full-blood, it will necessarily be many years before he can safely be left without the protecting arm of the Government, and in speaking of the work among the individual Indians of the Five Tribes, I want to clearly distinguish between the highly educated professional or business part-blood—Indian only in name—and the uneducated, non-English-speaking, full-blood class. Too frequently we are pointed to such and such distinguished citizen of Indian blood as being typical of the kind of Indians over which the Government is attempting to exercise minute supervision. This is only true so far as withholding their share in the tribal estate is concerned, and I heartily agree with all who advocate a speedy distribution thereof, giving to this intelligent class their money or property, and thereafter utilizing

* Extracts from an address at the Lake Mohonk Conference, October 1913

the whole effort of the Government to protect the incompetent.

The real full-blood class reside in the remote localities. Too many of them live, or rather, meagerly exist, under the most undesirable and adverse conditions, as many as from six to ten living in a one- or two-room, unventilated log cabin, in many instances with one or more members of the family suffering from tuberculosis or trachoma, with almost a certainty that the disease will eventually afflict the entire family. These Five Tribes, having been for years considered civilized, have officially received no attention, from a medical standpoint. I have most earnestly urged specific appropriation for the employment of physicians, to be stationed in the full-blood settlements, who can seek out the many cases where Indians ought to be advised in regard to health and sanitary conditions. I have also urged appropriations for the construction of two or three sanataria, at which these Indians could be treated at the inception of these distressing diseases, their lives not only prolonged and saved, but many members of their families kept from similar affliction. The few sanataria already provided by the Government in the Western states are filled to overflowing with Indians from near-by reservations, and, besides, it is well-nigh impossible to get the proper results where it is necessary to take Indians too far from their home surroundings. They should be treated in a practical manner among their own people.

It is true that many of the part-bloods who have had sufficient education and whose environment has been such that they should have conserved the property placed in their hands, have squandered their allotments, or been defrauded in various ways. While we are unsympathetic with their lack of thrift this class has been anxious to accept self-responsibility, is amply able to cope with the adversities of life, and we cannot expect to exert continuous parental supervision over them, but this we must do with the older full-blood who has had no educational advantages, absorbing only what he could from his environment. Ample protection must also be given the helpless children. In addition to protecting the property rights of these minors, it must be our aim to see that they have every educational facility. I am frankly of the opinion that it is only through education that the difficulties of Indian administration will be met, and in the Five Tribes there are thousands of children, not officially recognized as members of the tribes, who are really Indians in every sense. The problem of this new unallotted generation, the eldest of whom are now seven years of age, is one seldom considered, but is to my mind the most serious from the Indian standpoint, that Oklahoma must face in the future. A visitor to the remote districts finds these children unable to speak English, scantily and slovenly clothed, presenting hopeless subjects from which we expect self-supporting American citizens within a few years. Unless the Government or the State realizes the vast importance of educating and training this younger element, it is not difficult to portray the conditions that will exist when the little they may inherit from their "allotted" ancestors is eaten up. If we are to have a self-sustaining Indian people, it can only be by a gradual process, and a vigorous educational policy. Every child of Indian parentage must be sought out, to see that it is regularly in school. If the ideal condition of education at home in district schools cannot be maintained, because of inaccessibility, or lack of interest of local officials or parents, then the Department should see that the children are sent to tribal or Government boarding schools. Every effort is made by the local officials to see that these children attend school, but the area to be covered is so wide that the machinery provided therefor is entirely unable to cope with the situation.

Speaking particularly of the more than 20,000 full-bloods, a large part of whom are non-English-speaking, it requires the utmost vigilance to protect these people in their property rights; and I must say that a great portion of the so-called grafting can, to a large extent, be charged to the activities of a small but unscrupulous element of part-blood Indians who are employed as interpreters or agents of landbuyers or lease-takers. These mixed-bloods gain an easy livelihood by overreaching their more ignorant brothers. This condition ought to be guarded against for the future by Indian schools especially impressing upon pupils their moral obligation toward the elder and uneducated Indians.

It should also be understood that the population of Oklahoma is not generally made up of a class that deals with Indians. The thousands of better citizens know very little, if anything, with reference to the Indian situation; and as a rule are indifferent at this time as to the effect that the actions of the elements that do overreach these people may ultimately have, when these ignorant Indians become public charges. With the unprecedented development in all lines, particularly the oil and gas fields, and marvelously rich properties, eastern Oklahoma has attracted a small element comparatively, who, like vultures, with nearly white interpreters and agents acting as their eyes and talons, reach out to take advantage of every opportunity to catch the ignorant full-blood and defraud him of his property, where it is not protected by Governmental supervision. This condition will continue to exist until the better citizens realize that the Indian question in eastern Oklahoma is going to be a serious one for many years, and elect courts and officials who will take a more active interest in the protection of the property rights of these Indians, particularly minors, and deal vigorously with crimes committed against them.

There is no question but that the officials are gradually growing more alive to this situation. The co-operation of state, tribal, and federal officials is bearing fruit, and there is a gradual molding of public opinion in favor of the protection of the Indian. I could enumerate a great many individual and specific instances where the officials of the Indian Service, in co-operation with the local officials, have saved the property of Indians. I recall one case of a full-blood Creek girl who lived in one county and who had a very valuable allotment adjacent to an oil field in another county some one hundred miles distant. About a week before this girl became of age, she was taken from her home with her young husband, put upon a train, carried to a city in western Oklahoma, and there entertained for several days and given only money enough for immediate wants. The night before she reached her majority she was brought back to her home, and at three o'clock on the morning of her birthday, upon a moving train, she executed a lease covering her oil land. When it was shown that this lessor had been taken away from competition that would have existed had she been accessible to other persons seeking the same lease, and the facts about its execution developed, this lease was disapproved, and one which she afterwards made for a larger bonus approved, and an additional $5000 secured for her, through the efforts of the Agency. This woman, although eighteen years of age, was as simple-minded as a child, and had never seen her allotment. The records are full of similar and much worse cases, many of which are entirely beyond the reach of the help of the Department, particularly where the land is inherited or the property is otherwise free from supervision.

In probate matters the great majority of the county judges are willing and anxious to do everything in their power to protect the rights of the minor Indians, but no parallel condition in this respect has ever existed in any state where approximately one-third of the realty in this vast area is owned by minors. It makes an unprecedented probate situation. The minors many times live in one county where the jurisdiction vests, while the estate is located in another county. Many complaints are received of probate sales being made for grossly inadequate considerations, where the heirs are full-blood Indians. The state courts have no machinery with which to investigate the condition of the properties, but must take the testimony of witnesses brought by the interested parties, and use interpreters hired by them. Many of the judges are now taking advantage of the opportunity of asking the Department to investigate these cases, but, with the great volume of them, it is a physical impossibility to give them all attention. In guardianship cases, there are instances where bonds are entirely inadequate, loans are made on insufficient security, guardians charge board for their wards while the children are in Government schools, etc.

I have just received a very interesting communication from one of our recently elected county judges, which portrays the situation in very vivid terms, and I cannot tell of the conditions better than by giving his letter :

"I have something like seven hundred guardianship and administrator cases on my docket, and the condition is something awful. It is not only in this county, but the same condition exists, I think, in every county on the east side, except Muskogee County. I have interviewed several county judges and find that in hundreds of guardianship cases the judges have taken straw bonds.

"A county judge is helpless to make a thorough investigation into the acts of each guardian without the assistance of your district agents, and even then the guardians will run in some of the most unreasonable expense accounts. In hundreds of cases the fathers of the Indian children are ignorant and many worthless and of no account, and they have squandered hundreds and thousands of dollars belonging to their wards. In many cases the fathers realizing their awful mistake in embezzling the money belonging to their wards, are only too anxious to resign and would like to turn over the estate to a Federal public guardian. They are unable to make any kind of a bond, and, Mr. Kelsey, I know I have at least two hundred such cases in my docket. It is not only in my county, but I am sure the same condition exists in most of the counties on the east side. Something must be done, and I ask you to pardon me for taking the liberty to write you and make these suggestions.

"Mr. Reynolds knows of the condition when I took this office, January 5, and I have gone over the matter with him and he can tell you the horrible condition that exists in my county."

Referring to the judge's suggestion that attorneys engaged in active practice should be prohibited from accepting guardianships, I mention the following case as emphasizing that suggestion. The day before I left Oklahoma, in the district court of Adair County, E. R. Horine was convicted of embezzlement and given a five years' sentence. Horine was an attorney. In 1908 he filed a petition asking for the appointment of himself as guardian for a full-blood Cherokee Indian minor. As such guardian he sold certain inherited land, representing that it was necessary to do this to support and educate his ward. The testimony developed that neither the minor nor his parents ever saw the guardian until brought into court to testify in the criminal proceedings; that Horine had embezzled all of the money derived from the sale of the land, and had never contributed one cent to the minor or his family for the maintenance or education of the ward. The facts in this case were developed by the representatives of the

Indian Agency, in co-operation with Tribal Attorney Hastings, who personally assisted the county attorney in the prosecution.

To summarize: The Five Tribes need, first, congressional action to close and distribute the tribal estate under proper Government supervision ; second, appropriations to improve the home life, and sanitary and physical conditions of the full-blood class; third, compulsory education; fourth, practical and careful administrative action to separate the competent from the non-competent; fifth, ample appropriations by Congress that temporary assistance may be provided the State to properly safeguard Indian probate matters—one of the most vital, present Indian problems; sixth, a change in the existing laws which permit the uneducated full-bloods to indiscriminately lease all their allotments without supervision, by which they many times improvidently dispossess themselves, for inadequate considerations, of land which they should cultivate and upon which they should reside—a condition which makes most difficult administrative action for their protection.

IN THE BOTTOMS

In the bottoms
Darkness falls like tones from heavy bells ;
And the quiet gloom is undisturbed
Save by mild music's sound.
Where candle-gleam betrays the hut of logs,
Whose outlines moult and melt into the gloom—
Hark, the tintinabulary tune
Of banjo serenade !

—*R. Nathaniel Dett*

FORTY-SIXTH ANNUAL REPORT
OF THE PRINCIPAL

To the Board of Trustees of

The Hampton Normal and Agricultural Institute

Gentlemen :

On the sixth of last August, Mr. Robert Curtis Ogden, for forty years a member, and for the last twenty years president of the board of trustees of the Hampton School, died at his summer home in Kennebunkport, Maine. It is very fitting, therefore, in the report for the present year, to dwell especially upon those parts of the school work which Mr. Ogden helped to make possible.

When General Armstrong, the founder of Hampton Institute, came to this country from the Hawaiian Islands in 1860 he brought with him a letter of introduction to Mr. Ogden. From the time of the presentation of that letter to the time of General Armstrong's death, Mr. Ogden remained his devoted friend, and when the General founded the Hampton School, Mr. Ogden placed his influence and money and time behind the enterprise. One of the first meetings held in Hampton's interest in the North was in Mr. Ogden's parlor in Brooklyn. From that time until his death he devoted much thought to the best ways of creating an interest in Hampton Institute and in the races which it represents.

Mr. Og
interest
Hampto

SPREADING HAMPTON IDEAS

The work which Mr. Ogden has helped Hampton to do in strengthening the faith of the American people in the Negro and the Indian, and in the Hampton method of dealing with race problems, has been of great value. Beginning with that little gathering in Mr. Ogden's house more than forty years ago, a series of campaigns has been held in nearly all the Northern cities. Armstrong Associations and Hampton Committees have been organized. In Carnegie Hall in New York City, in the Academy of Music in Brooklyn, in Boston, Philadelphia, Chicago, Cleveland, Detroit, and Pittsburgh, choruses of Hampton students have sung their songs ; Major Moton, Dr. Booker T. Washington, and prominent white citizens from both the North and the South,

have shown what Hampton, Tuskegee, and other schools are
doing towards the advancement of the races for which they are
working.

During the summer the shore and mountain resorts, where
are to be found representatives of every part of our great country, have been visited. The manly, self-respecting appearance and
the telling addresses of Dr. Washington, Major Moton, and other
Hampton graduates, both Negro and Indian, have done much to
strengthen a belief in the possibilities of their races, and they have
been important object lessons in the value of Hampton's training.

"THE STUDENTS CARRIED TENTS WITH THEM."

During the summer of 1912 the students carried tents with them in
which they ate and slept, cooked their food, mended their clothes,
and maintained regular military discipline. These camps were visited by many people of the community, and won words of praise
for their occupants. Next summer, thanks to the generosity of
one of the school's trustees, a yacht named the *Hampton*, manned
by Negro students and sailed by a Negro captain, will visit the
Northern coast summer resorts. The students will present the
story of the Negro and Indian races in song and tableau and moving pictures, as well as by addresses.

The campaign of the past winter, with songs, addresses,
and moving pictures, which extended through New York, New
England, and Pennsylvania, was one of the most successful in the
school's history. In addition to the large meetings, many schools
and colleges, both for young men and for young women, were
visited. Junior Armstrong Leagues have been formed in New
York City, Williamstown, Massachusetts, and at Phillips Academy, Andover, and others are in process of organization. A

Massachusetts Hampton Association, which includes such old friends as the Boston Hampton Committee and the Springfield Hampton Club, as well as other leagues in the state, has been recently organized.   A Hampton Committee has been formed in Philadelphia.   The school's thanks are due to the many devoted friends who, as patronesses and in other capacities, have supported the Hampton meetings and thus insured their success.

While these campaigns have much more than covered expenses and have secured for Hampton many lasting friends whose donations will extend through a series of years, the school would

Results Hampt Cam

READY FOR THE CAMPAIGN

not feel justified in spending so large a percentage of its funds for current expenses in the mere raising of money.   But when it is realized that Hampton is creating or strengthening, by its Northern campaigns, a belief in the possibilities of belated races, and at the same time presenting to thousands of discouraged men and women a solution for race problems, the expenditure seems more than justified.   It is also to be remembered that Hampton thus creates interest, not for itself alone, but for the whole Negro race, and that every other Negro school is helped by the pioneer work which Hampton performs.

MR. OGDEN AND EDUCATIONAL BOARDS

Major Moton, the school's Commandant, is accustomed to express in his addresses in Northern meetings his thankfulness to Hampton for affording a platform where the Northerner and the Southerner, the black man and the white man, can come together and discuss race problems.   Mr. Ogden did much to

Hampto affords platfo race ment

THE MARCH OF HAMPTON STUDENTS TO DINNER ON ANNIVERSARY DAY

bring this about. From the early days of the school he was
accustomed to bring parties of prominent Northern citizens to
Hampton for the Anniversary exercises. His business had brought
him into the South before the Civil War, and while he had
strong Northern sympathies, he also readily accepted the broad
views of General Armstrong, who, having been born in the
Hawaiian Islands, was neither a Northerner nor a Southerner, yet
keenly realized the heavy burdens that the freeing of the Negro
race threw upon the South.

When the Capon Springs Conference, made up of representative Northern and Southern men, met for the purpose of
considering how to forward the cause of education in the South,
Mr. Ogden saw in it great possibilities for bringing the different The
sections of the country together, and he threw himself into the Southe
movement with all the strength he possessed. He formed the Educati
Southern Education Board, made up for the most part of lead- Board
ing Southern men, many of them heads of Southern colleges.
While this Board devoted itself largely to a study of the white
public schools in the South, it gave to Hampton Institute and
other Negro schools the sympathy of a strong body of intelligent
Southern men whose influence can hardly be estimated.

The school's Principal and other officers have had the
advantage of intercourse and co-operation with these men. Edgar
Gardner Murphy, of Alabama, for a number of years secretary
of the Southern Education Board, was a devoted friend of the
Hampton School and a contributor to its current expenses. His
thought on the race problem, as expressed in his admirable book,
"The Basis of Ascendancy," was largely influenced by what
he saw at Hampton, and Hampton was much broadened by
Mr. Murphy and his writings. Dr. J. D. Eggleston, Jr., who, Help
as Superintendent of Public Instruction for Virginia, did so much Southe
to improve the public schools and especially the rural public Men
schools of the state, was for years associated in an official capacity
with Mr. Ogden and the Southern Board. The same is true of
the Hon. P. P. Claxton, the present United States Commissioner
of Education, and of Dr. Wickliffe Rose, whose remarkable work
in connection with the Rockefeller Sanitary Commission has given
an impetus to the improvement of sanitary conditions in the
South such as has come from no other single agency. These
and many other prominent Southern men have come, through
Mr. Ogden's influence, to know the Hampton School and to give
it the benefit of their thought and experience.

Following the example of the Co-operative Education Associ- Outgro
ation of Virginia, an outgrowth of the Southern Education Board, of the S
which has endeavored to bring together all the educational forces ern Ed
of the state, Major Moton, Hampton's Commandant, has been tion Bo

instrumental in forming an organization, known as the Negro Organization Society, which has successfully brought together all the various Negro schools, churches, and societies in the State of Virginia. No attempt is made to interfere with the business of these different societies, but all are asked to unite in securing better health, better schools, better homes, and better farms for the Negroes of the state. When a certain day was appointed, to be known as "Clean-up Day," and notice was given in the churches that the people were asked to devote the day to cleaning up their houses [and yards, 132,000 heads of Negro families responded. In a majority of cases the white people, feeling the importance of the occasion, released their servants from their duties. The whole movement has the cordial support of the white citizens of the state. At a recent meeting of the Organization Society in Richmond, the Governor of Virginia was the principal speaker; and the largest hall in the city, holding five thousand people, was filled, some eight hundred white people being in attendance.

General tion Mr. Ogden was a member of the General Education Board up to the time of his death, and for a time was its chairman. Hampton was thus brought into very close relations with all the important movements for education in the South which that Board initiated. Not only has the school received generous financial help from this source, but, what is of still more value, it has had the counsel and co-operation of its executive secretary, Dr. Wallace Buttrick. Hampton has had, too, the very great advantage of being associated with the movement for demonstration farms in the South, inaugurated by this Board in co-operation with the United States Department of Agriculture and that remarkable educator, Dr. Seaman A. Knapp.

It was the General Education Board also which made possible the work of Jackson Davis, supervisor of Negro rural schools in Virginia, and that of similar workers in other states. Mr. Davis has helped hundreds of Negro teachers in Virginia, not only by direct supervision, but by interesting the trustees and other white officials in the Negro schools, inducing them in many cases to appropriate increased funds for buildings and salaries. He has won the confidence of the Negroes of the state and has helped them, through the county supervisors under his charge, to form leagues for school improvement. Superintendent Daniel of Charlotte County writes as follows in regard to the results of the work of the industrial supervisor of his county under Mr. Davis:

" All over the county there is a manifest improvement—better schools, more interest, and a better grade of instruction. New school buildings are under way, the expenses being largely borne by the colored people; and definite organizations are effected in

AN EXHIBIT OF THE CUMBERLAND COUNTY COLORED SCHOOLS

every neighborhood. If we can keep this force at work it will result in great good for our colored people."

And Superintendent Dickinson of Cumberland County says:

"Some of our prominent white women have judged exhibits from Negro schools. There are many white people who are opposed to giving the Negroes any kind of education. I believe their number is decreasing in Cumberland County. As poor **Better** houses for white children are replaced by good buildings, the sen- **Negro** timent for better houses for Negroes is growing among the white **schools** people as well as among the Negroes."

Superintendent Washington of Caroline County summarizes Mr. Davis's work as follows:

"Mr. Davis has been our salvation in working up this senti- ment for higher ideals. His talks to the Negroes awakened them, not only to their responsibilities, but also to their abilities. I ver- ily believe the good Lord called Mr. Davis to do the work he is doing. I have often said that of all the men I know he is the only one who could do this mighty work. I suppose he has else- where, as he has in Caroline County, the perfect confidence and trust of the Negroes. They look upon him as their Moses to lead them out of darkness into a happy life. He is certainly doing it and doing well."

Many of the county supervisors and demonstration agents are graduates of Hampton, and thus the General Education Board increases the efficiency of the Hampton School by making it possible for its graduates to do this useful work for their people.

Negro
School
d

Mr. Ogden was also a member of the Negro Rural School Fund Board which controls the use of the interest of the million dollars given by Miss Anna T. Jeanes of Philadelphia for Negro rural schools. Dr. James H. Dillard, president of the Board (formerly dean of Tulane University, New Orleans), has used the interest of this fund in sending Negro supervising industrial teachers through one hundred nineteen counties, training the teachers in cooking and sewing and industrial work, cleaning the schoolrooms and yards, starting canning clubs in the homes, and interesting the Negro communities in better living.

MAKING HAMPTON'S WORK KNOWN

The publications of Hampton Institute, which are an important means of extending its principles of education, always appealed strongly to Mr. Ogden. He was a wonderful advertiser, having for years personally directed the advertising department of the great Wanamaker store, which he largely controlled. He had himself a remarkable power of clear statement, and was never entirely satisfied with the kind or amount of publicity which Hampton gave to its work.

It was partly in response to Mr. Ogden's suggestion that the school established a press service two years ago. The following statement will give some idea of the importance of its work :

" Hampton Institute is now in touch with a selected group of 672 white and Negro papers (white 437, Negro 235). The American Press Association, which supplies weekly syndicate service to over eighty Negro papers, has been most useful to Hampton in giving publicity to material of special interest and value to the colored people. Hampton has been able to secure, during the past year, several thousand columns of publicity. In the syndicate press stories it has been able to present the facts of everyday student life, the important happenings of the Hampton School year, and the school's extension work, which possessed news and human interest value. The *Survey* of New York has used several Hampton 'stories' in its weekly issues, and has sent out through its press service, which reaches 125 papers in 39 states with a combined circulation of 3,500,000 copies, some of the striking facts of Negro progress during fifty years of freedom. Hampton has also furnished the University of Wisconsin with material for its well-known traveling package literature dealing with 'The Awakening of the South.'

"The *American Schoolmaster*, published in Ypsilanti, Michigan ; a Maratha dialect journal, published in Belgaum, India ; the *African Times and Oriental Review*, published in London ; *East and West*, edited by Donald Fraser, Ontario, Canada ; and the

Bulletin of the Pan-American Union, published in Washington, are some of the agencies that have helped to spread Hampton ideas. "

The Publication Office helps to interpret Hampton to the outside world by sending out literature descriptive of the school's aims and methods. Prominent among the pamphets describing Hampton's purposes is one entitled "Education for Life," made

GENERAL ARMSTRONG

up of words of General Armstrong taken from his speeches, reports, and articles. The United States Bureau of Education has offered to circulate 15,000 copies of this pamphlet and has already sent out thousands of press notices calling attention to the fact that all the "familiar maxims of modern vocational training" have been preached daily at Hampton since its founding—"the training of the hand and eye, as well as of the mind, the moral effect of technical skill, the conception of labor as a moral force, the test of education in efficiency, and the vanity of education without discipline in thrift, self-help, love of work, and willing- ness to sacrifice. "

Officials of the United States Bureau of Education assert that "Hampton has taken on a new meaning for educators; that schoolmen everywhere are more and more attracted to its aston- ishing record of service; that the test of time has shown that General Armstrong's theory and practice were right, not merely for the races for whom they were immediately intended, but for boys and girls everywhere. "

The Publication Office issues many other circulars and bulletins descriptive of Hampton's work, including the annual catalogue, the Principal's and Treasurer's reports, conference reports, and various illustrated circulars, distributed in the Northern campaigns by the tens of thousands. Some of these have been written by Southern men or women.

tional
ets

The Hampton Leaflets serve an important purpose in extending the school's ideas on education among teachers and school officials. They are seventy-two in number and cover academic subjects, agriculture, animal industry, health, industrial work, nature study, schoolrooms and grounds, and Southern industries. They reach regularly over 1000 Southern teachers of both races and are in use from Oregon to Florida. About 20,000 copies of the Leaflets, either new or reprinted, have been issued during the past year. There is a constant demand by mail for material to be used by individuals, classes, and clubs in the study of Hampton methods and of conditions among the two races represented at the school.

onthly
trated
azine

The *Southern Workman*, the school's illustrated monthly magazine, which has a circulation of 5300 copies, contains numerous articles and editorials which express Hampton's ideas in regard to industrial education and methods of social work. Testimonies to its value have come from friends of the school in various parts of the country, from missionaries and social workers, and from Hampton graduates.

RACE NEEDS MET BY HAMPTON

Hampton does not prepare men and women for professions. While a number of its graduates have fitted themselves for professional life after leaving the school, the majority have devoted themselves to "helping the common people do common things in an uncommon way." Hampton is endeavoring to meet certain great needs of the masses of the Negro and Indian races. The first of these is for efficient teachers. More than a hundred

l-
ed
ers

Negro rural schools in Virginia alone have been without teachers the past year. Probably not one-tenth of the Negro teachers in the public schools are properly prepared, mentally or morally. One of Hampton's aims is to send out well-prepared teachers.

The second great need is for good homemakers. In slavery days the Negro hardly knew the meaning of the word "home." And even since emancipation, the masses of the race have regarded the houses where they have existed as merely places in which to pass the night. The church, instead of the home, has been the center of amusement and recreation. The stream cannot rise higher than its source. There is a tremendous need of

"THERE IS A TREMENDOUS NEED OF LEADERS IN HOMEMAKING."

leaders in homemaking, not only among the Negroes, but also among the Indians, who have only recently begun to make homes apart from the tribe. Every young woman who enters Hampton receives a thorough training in cooking, sewing, care of rooms and dining tables, and all else that belongs to home life. The school is endeavoring to provide well-trained homemakers.

Still another need of these races is for farmers with greater productive power and the ability to raise their own food supply.

Good h
makers

IN TRAINING FOR SCIENTIFIC FARMING

ntific
ers

Largely through the leadership of the men sent out from Hampton and other schools, Negroes have secured nearly 20,000,000 acres of land. Indians have large allotments. In order to hold this land they must be taught to cultivate it properly and to raise upon it much of their food supply.

LEARNING TO BE SKILLED MECHANICS

led
anics

Like other people, these races also need houses to live in and clothes to wear. The mechanics of the South before the war were Negroes. It is important that they hold the mechanical work of that section. The Indians need tradesmen of all kinds to aid them in their march toward civilization. Hampton's Trade School is sending out well-equipped carpenters, wheelwrights, blacksmiths, bricklayers, and other tradesmen, and the country welcomes them gladly.

PREPARATION OF TEACHERS

The report of the present year will show how Hampton tries to meet these common needs : (1) Teachers for the common schools. More than eighty per cent of the Negroes of the South live in the country, and practically all of the Indians. The needs of the rural school must therefore be especially considered. The country school needs teachers thoroughly trained in elementary branches and yet with sufficient knowledge of history, sociology, and economics to make them capable of leading in the communities to which they go.

Hampton's industrial system is of great value in helping **Words** its students to a knowledge of elementary subjects, especially **harness** English and mathematics. Favorable comments are often made **to things** by visitors at Anniversary time on the exact use of words by Hampton students. The reason for this is to be found in the fact

HARNESSING THINGS TO WORDS

that they associate words with things, according to the Squeers' method as explained by Dickens! Work in the laundry is connected with the laboratory and the classroooms. Classes in English deal largely with subjects with which the student has become familiar through his daily work. The Anniversary addresses have to do with the student's vocation or with his struggle for an education. Hence each word is full of meaning. The same is true of mathematics. Mathematical terms are connected at Hampton with the work of the shop, the farm, and the kitchen. Hence they have a content which is impossible where the student has to do only with abstract propositions. The work of the schoolroom is harnessed to actual life in a way which fits the teacher especially well for the many-sided work that is required in a rural community. Of the 844 boarding students enrolled this year, 374 boys are in the night school, which means that they are spending a large part of each day at the forge, the lathe, or the plow, where they are gaining an exact knowledge of things, and that their elementary academic studies are closely connected with their work. Of the remaining 470, 325 are girls, the majority of whom have definite duties in the kitchen, the laundry, or the dining- and sewing-rooms.

tional   Hampton has decided that it will not in the future give its diploma to any boy or girl who has not received definite vocational training. The result of this will be a better prepared body of rural teachers. In order to make their training more effective, much thought has been given to the selection of new students. The application department reports that 2328 letters have been written this year; 1536 application blanks have been sent out; 909 have been returned; 384 admission cards have been issued ; and 237 applicants have entered.

The Vice Principal's report shows a greater unification of the academic work, as a result of years of endeavor, by making the night and day schools follow the same course of study, so ved that a student may pass from one to the other with a minimum ization of loss. A plan has been successfully worked out by which pupils are no longer promoted by classes, but by subjects. They are made acquainted with their marks at the end of every two months. Much time is saved at the commencement of the term by bringing the new students to the school and assigning them to their duties a week before the return of the old ones. Tardiness has decreased. Better order is maintained. In many ways there is an improved organization which makes for greater care and exactness on the part of the prospective teacher.

The Hampton School is a normal school in all its departments, for the idea is continually impressed upon the students that what they receive is to be given to others. Each fall, at the opening of the school, hundreds of new students are being trained by older ones in the performance of their tasks. But in order that young tice men and women may be specially fitted for the work of teaching, aching the Whittier School, made up of five hundred Negro children from the immediate neighborhood, serves as a training school for the members of the Senior Class who are preparing to go out as teachers in public schools. Four months of their last year at the Institute are devoted to teaching, under careful direction, in the various grades at the Whittier. Perhaps in no other school in the country is a more thorough training given in the teaching of elementary subjects.

While the emphasis is thus laid at Hampton on elementary studies, attention is given also to such subjects as will especially fit the pupils to teach intelligently in that new type of rural g for school which includes the whole community. In addition to their unity study of agriculture and home economics, they are given sufficient instruction in history to enable them to give Negro and Indian communities a knowledge of their place in the world ; enough sociology to teach the meaning of the social organizations

"ENOUGH SOCIOLOGY TO TEACH THE MEANING OF SOCIAL ORGANIZATIONS"

of which they are a part—the church, the school, the home ; and enough economics to enforce lessons of thrift and the value of

A SENIOR PREPARING TO GO OUT AS A TEACHER

owning land. The study of the United States census, particularly that part relating to the Negro and Indian races, has been found especially helpful.

ral
ies
In connection with this special preparation for rural teaching, a careful outline of the Bible is given. Perhaps to no other people does the Bible mean so much as to the Negroes. Abraham and David and Joseph and Paul are very real in their lives. The events of the Exodus mean quite as much to them as do those of the Civil War. This year, Dr. Frank K. Sanders, president of Washburn College, Topeka, Kansas, and formerly dean of the Yale Theological School, has devoted much time to the preparation of a manual especially fitted to the needs of the races represented at Hampton, but which will be of value in all secondary schools. It has seemed wise to make all teaching of history in the school center in the Bible. Nowhere else is the rise of a nation from heathenism and idolatry to civilization so forcibly presented.

In the training of these prospective teachers much thought is given to instilling in them a love for the beautiful. They receive some instruction in art, especially as applied to taste in dress and home decoration. The head of the art department is in close relation with the school shops and with the department of home economics. He advises the boys as to the pictures for their rooms. He interests himself, and the students also, in the decoration of the school grounds ; everywhere he endeavors to create in these young people a love for the beautiful.

Hampton is fortunate in having secured as the head of its music department a graduate of Oberlin, a young colored man who has a thorough knowledge of his work and a real love for it. He contends that "the deplorable distaste of so many Negroes for their own music" comes from ignorance, and insists that we ought to have at Hampton a music trade school. "How much," he says, "it would mean to Hampton, to the graduates, and to the communities into which the graduates go if they were able to intelligently help the people with intelligent music." The Music School Settlement for Colored People in New York City has already demonstrated how much of a factor music is in the improvement of the Negro race. It may be that Hampton has not yet done all that it might do in developing the musical ability of this race, but it has always recognized the value of music as a factor in the training of the teacher.

ence
e
ry and
um
A valuable asset in the preparation of teachers is Hampton's beautiful Library, the gift of Mrs. Collis P. Huntington, with its well-selected collection of 38,943 volumes and its devoted librarian, who has given years of study to the task of developing a taste for reading in the young people of the school. Speaking of what the

THE HUNTINGTON MEMORIAL LIBRARY

Library is accomplishing, she says in her annual report: "There is no mathematical formula that will express the silent, sub-conscious influence of its beauty and order on a youth with no previous sense of such things. He himself can only vaguely suggest it when he says, 'I can learn a lot from this Library without ever opening a book in it.'"

Of great value also in the school's training of teachers is the Museum, where the students gain a knowlege of the homes, clothing, and customs of other peoples such as could not be given in any other way. While the collection is not large, it is carefully selected. Through the kindness of Miss Frances Curtis of Boston, a valuable addition of Philippine curios has recently been made. The room occupied by the collection is now crowded to overflowing, and additional space will soon have to be provided.

In their preparation for rural leadership Hampton students make a careful study of the needs of the community in the immediate vicinity of the school. Clubs of various sorts have been formed in which graduates and teachers co-operate for the improvement of the members. Mrs. Barrett's social settlement, the Weaver orphanage, the poorhouse, the jail, and the local Sunday schools are all used as training schools in social work for the young people who are soon to be the real leaders of their race. Inside the school, the Young Men's Christian Association, the King's Daughters, the boys' debating societies, the girls' literary society, the school battalion, and the girls' and boys' dormitories, afford opportunity for developing leadership; the football eleven and the baseball and basket-ball teams also do their part. "The school's success in athletics," as the Commandant reports, "has

Trainin rural le ship

tremendously increased the respect of the colored people for
Hampton and the ideas for which it stands. It has deepened the
loyalty and heightened the pride of the graduates and former
students in their Alma Mater as probably nothing else could have
done. But more significant still is the very important part the
school has had in making clean athletics and honorable sport possible in colored schools. For the first time Hampton won this
season the undisputed right to the championship, so far as Negro
colleges are concerned, in intercollegiate football in the middle
Atlantic states. ''

PREPARATION OF HOMEMAKERS

The second object which the Hampton School presents to
itself is the preparation of homemakers. For many years it

"WASHING AND RINSING"

seemed well-nigh impossible to connect the school's boarding
department with the domestic science department in such a way
that it should be a means of education, but this has now been done.
The Lady Principal says, in regard to the girls' training: "Systematic rotation is necessary. As soon as a girl is skilled in her
work she must move on to something else, just as she moves
from fractions to decimals or from the third to the fourth reader
in school. When one is conducting a large steam laundry and a
boarding house for nine hundred people, one must learn to resist

the temptation of holding on too long to a girl who shows a particular aptitude in some special line of the work.

"In order that the teachers may be sure that no one escapes **Rota·**
an important branch of training, each girl is given cards contain- **in work**
ing the following lists, and as soon as any part of the work is successfully accomplished, it is checked off."

LAUNDRY CARD	HOUSEWORK CARD
Sorting clothing	Bedmaking
Removing stains	Sweeping
Washing and rinsing	Dusting
Bluing	Washstand, wardrobe
Starching	Floors, rugs
Sprinkling and folding for	General appearance
ironing	Bathroom, sinkroom
Ironing unstarched clothing	Corridors, stairs
Ironing starched clothing	Table setting and clearing
Folding	Dishwashing, care of towels
Delivering	Scrubbing
Care of laundry	Silver cleaning, knife polishing
Mending	Waiting on table

In order to give the girls practical experience in real homes **Dom**
and at the same time enable them to earn money to help pay their **service**
way through school, they are encouraged to find places for domestic service during the summer vacations. The Lady Principal
reports; that of about fifty Hampton girls who were in service
last summer in places found by the school, six were reported dis-
appointing, but the majority were said to be most satisfactory.
A few extracts from employers' letters follow:

"———— was one of the best girls I have had. She had
not had much experience in a private family, but did her work
excellently, was always thoughtful and cheerful, careful in the
work assigned to her, and altogether to be recommended."

"———— was the best cook and I really think in all ways
the pleasantest and most efficient girl I ever had."

"We think we were exceedingly fortunate in having a girl
like ———— and we miss having her with us very, very
much. We enjoyed her quaintness and her personality, and if
we can again have the opportunity of doing anything for her we
shall feel it a pleasure."

PREPARATION OF FARMERS

The small farm where the boys help their father in the care
of his own land, live-stock, and buildings, and the girls, their
mother in the care of the home, is the best school that the Negro
or Indian can have. The youth who come to Hampton from such

homes, where independence, co-operation, thrift, and patience are taught, are by far the best material from which to produce leaders for these races. Hampton has done much and hopes to do more toward making such farms and homes possible.

In order to direct the minds of the students to agriculture, all of them, both boys and girls, are given some knowledge of plants, animals, and soils. But, in addition to this, two regular courses in agriculture are offered: (1) a four-year course designed to give thorough training in both the theory and practice of modern agriculture in order to fit the student for actual farming or for teaching agriculture; and (2) a short course (eight months) for strong country boys who are anxious to learn better methods of farming and who are unable to study agriculture in school for four years. Speaking of this course, the head of the department says: "The boy gets some experience in the different farm practices, and also has three hours daily of classroom work, where much of the regular course is covered but in a simpler and less thorough manner. However, as a farmer, he will know how to do things and why he does them, and, in the eyes of his neighbors, will be able to do many of the ordinary things about the farm in an extraordinary way."

The system of farm accounts which has been adopted at Hampton gives to the head of the agricultural department an exact knowledge of the income and outgo for every plot of ground on the farm, as well as a knowledge of the economic value of each cow and horse. The students also have practice in keeping accounts, which is of great value to them. The school's stock

ONE OF THE MODERN BARNS AT THE STOCK FARM

farm of six hundred acres, with its large herd of cattle, its
swine, poultry, and horses, and its modern barns, furnishes Hampto
a demonstration station in successful farming which means stock fa
much to the agricultural students.   The report for the last demons
year is most satisfactory.   Four hundred eight acres of crops,
exclusive of hay crops, were taken from 331 acres of cultivated
land.   Fifty-five acres were in hay, from which 155 tons were
harvested.   The average yield of corn was 24½ bushels per acre,
the best field yielding 52 bushels per acre.   There is every reason
to believe that the year's training given to the forty-five or more
first-year boys on the farm is of great value.   Some of the best
men the school has sent out are those who have had this experience.   An investigation recently made by the matron in charge
of the farm school in regard to the positions which these boys
have later held in the school, shows that ten of the twelve officers
of the Young Men's Christian Association are from the farm and
twenty-three of the ninety-five officers of the battalion.

THE TRAINING OF TRADESMEN

A fourth object of the Hampton School is the training of
Negro and Indian mechanics.   The Trade School reports a total
enrollment for the past year of 281, of whom 259 are Negroes
and 22, Indians.   Of these, 169 Negroes and 10 Indians are
taking full trade courses ; 1 Indian and 12 Negroes, special trade
training ; 40 academic students, manual training ; 7 agricultural
students, a special course of two weeks ; 10 agricultural students, a special course of three months ; and the remainder, one
or two work days each week.

Thirty-eight of the regular trade students have devoted
themselves to carpentry. Bricklayers, to the number of 33, come
next ; tailors numbering 24 follow, and blacksmiths, 21, come
fourth.   Seventy-three new students entered the Trade School
this year, which is an increase of about 24 per cent over the
number entering last year.   The total sales of the Trade School
amounted to $92,622.58, the sales to the Institute being $55,950.63.
Thirty firms have purchased 1431 trucks.

The carpenters and bricklayers have had exceptionally good Learning
practice in putting up a new dwelling house and the Shellbanks doing
barn, the contract price for the latter being $14,750.00.   In
all, 108 students worked on this building, including carpenters,
bricklayers, blacksmiths, tinsmiths, painters, and plumbers.

The director reports that there has been this year a better
class of work in the machine shop and a larger variety than ever
before.   There has been considerable increase in the automobile
and marine gasoline motor repair work.   The students are just

"THE STUDENTS ARE JUST COMPLETING A LATHE."

completing a twenty-two-inch, full-swing, side-carriage, turret lathe, which it would have cost the school about $1800.00 to purchase. This lathe was designed by the instructor, and all the work on the patterns and on the machine has been done in the shop.

The superintendent of the Trade School reports that last summer five industrial teachers from other schools came to Hampton for special instruction in drafting, painting, plumbing, machine work, upholstery, and wood-turning. During the year seven other teachers have at different times received instruction in special trade work. In addition to this, Hampton has filled orders for schools as follows: 42 for chair-caning supplies, 6 for shuck-mat material, 12 for basket material, and 8 for caning models and frames. The Trade School furnished eleven sets of blueprints of the trade courses to various schools, aided others by giving them information in regard to plumbing, general equipment, machine-shop equipment, and installation of water systems. The number of former students who are asking the school's help and advice in the way of purchasing material, fitting up shops, etc., is constantly on the increase, and this last year the Trade School has assisted tailors, wheelwrights, blacksmiths, steamfitters, carpenters, and bricklayers.

At the present time the trade students have from 4900 to 5400 hours' work in a three years' course in the Trade School. This is a longer period than is given in any other trade school in the country, but it has resulted in sending out thoroughly trained mechanics who have become leaders of their people in mechanical pursuits.

THE LARGER HAMPTON

A report of the Hampton School which confines itself to the work done on the school grounds is altogether incomplete. Dr. Wallace Buttrick in a public address commended Hampton on the ground that it lives, not for itself alone, but for the world outside. Some reference to the larger Hampton which its graduates have made seems necessary.

One of the rural counties most influenced by Hampton graduates is Gloucester in Virginia. Sixty former students, most of whom came to Hampton from Gloucester, are now living there. Among these are the principal of the Gloucester Agricultural and Industrial School at Cappahosic, four of his assistants, and eleven public-school teachers. In thirty homes the wife was a Hampton girl. A very successful Negro physician practicing in Gloucester is a Hampton graduate. Still another prominent resident is a teacher, lawyer, and farmer. Largely through the influence of these Hampton graduates more than ninety per cent of the Negro farmers of Gloucester County own the farms they cultivate.

In Northampton County, Virginia, are twelve graduates, six men and six women, besides a number of ex-students. One of the Northampton Negro families sent four of the five children to Hampton. A letter from one of the sisters gives some idea of what she and her brother have accomplished since graduation. She says :

"I have been teaching here at home for the last eight years. I began in a one-room schoolhouse which had been standing for thirty years. We kept the house in repair and did what we could toward beautifying the room and the grounds. We organized a school-improvement league and began raising money toward building a new, two-room schoolhouse. We have succeeded in getting this building and are now teaching in it. It cost $650, the school board giving $150 and the patrons the balance. My brother John built the schoolhouse. The superintendent says that it is the best arranged one for colored students in the county. John is kept very busy at his trade. This summer he contracted to repair two school buildings for white children which cost $2800; he has also built several houses. He has worked from four to eight men daily, some of whom were Hampton boys. Most of these jobs were for white people. They so often say that the one who can do the work is the one they will hire, regardless of color. Enclosed you will find a picture of our house. This he built his first year out of school, nearly six years ago. People then were unwilling to give him work, because he was a young .

Influen Hampt Virgi . countie

carpenter, so he built this to show what he could do. My brother
Nelson and I bought the land before he (Nelson) entered school.
There are two acres in the lot, the cost of which was $300. ''

l-round
pton
The story of a Hampton man in Mecklenburg County illustrates the all-round work which many of the school's graduates
are accomplishing. This man is a teacher, preacher, lawyer,
merchant, farmer, and home builder. As a teacher he has
reached about one thousand children, many of whom are now
heads of families or are teaching in various parts of the state.
As a preacher he has been instrumental in raising the standard
of morality, in correcting false ideas of religious worship, in
organizing a church, and in building a new house of worship.
He ministers to his people also in material matters, encouraging
them to buy land and build houses. He has more than once stood
security for homes for his people and has sometimes made their
first payments himself, writing their contracts and deeds, usually
free of charge, He himself sets an example by owning a well-
tilled farm of one hundred twenty-five acres and a store of general merchandise. His wife is post-mistress, to which position
she was appointed as the result of a petition signed largely by
the white residents of the town.

1
.C. A.
In Brunswick County an interesting rural work has been
organized by a Hampton graduate, who is the first county secretary of the Colored Young Men's Christian Association. The
general plan is to establish centers of influence through local
leadership, to interest the boys and men in better methods of
farming, and to endeavor to raise the religious and moral standard of the whole community. This work is most important and
might well be duplicated in every county in the South. Hampton
men are especially fitted for such an enterprise, which is akin to
the settlement work so successfully carried on by Hampton
women in various centers. These concrete examples are simply
illustrations of what has been accomplished by scattered Hampton graduates in rural communities throughout the South.

The school's graduates are active also in organized work for
rural betterment. Prominent among efforts of this kind is the
school-demonstration work. Last year there were industrial su-
·sing
strial
here
pervising teachers in one hundred thirty counties in the Southern
states, twenty-nine of these being in Virginia. Most of the supervisors are under the direction of Dr. Dillard, president of the Negro
Rural School Fund. The Hampton School pays the cost of maintenance of such supervision in ten Virginia counties and therefore
counts this as part of its extension work. A number of these
teachers are Hampton graduates, who are thus helping in a most
practical way to work out the problem of improving country life.

'' In the ten counties where supervising teachers paid by

Hampton Institute are at work, there are 240 schools; 149 of these are visited regularly by the supervisors ; 117 schools lengthened their term last year by a month ; 68 buildings were painted or whitewashed, and 41 sanitary outhouses were built.   To lengthen terms, to build new schoolhouses and repair old ones means an expenditure of money, and this money was raised, largely through

A RESULT OF SCHOOL-DEMONSTRATION WORK—THE OLD AND THE NEW

The old schoolhouse is on the right of the church in the upper picture.

the efforts of the supervisors, by private subscription, and by entertainments.   Last year the total amount of money so raised was $9278.14.   As the aggregate salaries paid these ten supervisors was $4200.00, it is evident that on an average each supervisor raised in cash a sum more than twice as large as her salary. Labor given and cash contributed are not included in this total. Had they been, the amount would have been much larger. ''

HOME OF THE GRADUATE WHO HAS DOUBLED THE NEGRO CORN CROP

Closely allied to this school supervision is the farm-demonstration work referred to in another part of this report. The Government agent for farm-demonstration work among Negroes in twelve Virginia counties is a Hampton graduate ; with the help of his nine sub-agents and one thousand demonstrators, he has doubled the corn crop of Negro farmers in certain counties of Virginia, and has improved their homes, churches and schools. Another graduate who has, under his direction on the Sea Islands, nearly one hundred farm demonstrators, is showing the people of the Islands how to double and in some
cases quadruple their crops. He has also formed a co-operative society for the purpose of helping the farmers with loans at a fair interest. The rules of this society, the first of its kind in the South, have been adapted from those governing the farmers' co-operative societies in Ireland.

In Southern cities, as well as in rural districts, Hampton graduates have been a tremendous power for good. In Richmond, Savannah, Roanoke, Augusta, and other Southern cities, as well as the towns of Norfolk, Portsmouth, and Hampton,
the school is represented by teachers, mechanics, and business and professional men who are loyal citizens and devoted to the spread of Hampton ideas. The Southern Industrial Classes, which introduced cooking, sewing, manual training, and gardening into the public schools of Norfolk, Portsmouth, Berkley, and the outlying communities, were largely under the direction of Hampton graduates. A Negro community near Portsmouth, built, inhabited, and governed by Negroes, where no liquor has ever been sold and no criminal arrest made, owes its

existence to one of the school's graduates.

In New York, Philadelphia, Boston, and other Northern cities Hampton graduates also stand for the ideas gained at the school. Some of them hold places of trust and are a strong influence for good in their communities. The same is true of Western cities. In Kansas City four of the Negro manual-training teachers are graduates, as is the principal of one of the graded schools. Three of the instructors at Western University, Quindaro, Kansas, were trained at Hampton.

Hampton graduates have also had an important part in spreading Hampton's ideas by starting other industrial schools, or by teaching in them. More than one hundred have served at Tuskegee, twenty-four being engaged there at present. The Calhoun School has fifteen Hamptonians in its teaching force, the Penn School, eleven, and the People's School at Mt. Meigs, *Outgro of Ham*

PRACTICAL FARM WORK AT CALHOUN SCHOOL UNDER A HAMPTON GRADUATE

six. The Cope Industrial Building on St. Helena Island was built under the direction of Hampton mechanics, instructors at Penn School. It would be impossible to mention all the institutions in the South and West where Hampton men and women are passing on to boys and girls of their own races the ideas of self-help and service to others which they gained at Hampton.

Hampton's returned Indian students have as good a record as the Negroes. The missionary spirit shown by many of them is well illustrated in the case of a Sioux man who, with his wife, is devoting himself to work among the Arapahoes. After writing of the opposition and discouragements he has had, he adds: *Return Indian dents*

"A good many people have asked me why I stay here as I do. I do not have to stay here. But if I can live my life for the good of others, why live for myself? Is my life so dear to me that I would be selfish enough to neglect my people? If

I could dare to get out among the Eastern people and make an appeal for these Indians I could bring tears from the hardest hearted palefaces that you ever saw. But I would rather do what I can and stay here with them."

Another Indian is doing most excellent work as secretary of the Indian Young Men's Christian Association. Of the 328 Indian girls now living who have had some Hampton training, 223 are homemakers, and of the 550 boys, 245 are farmers or stockraisers and 64, independent tradesmen. The others are following various occupations. The influence of Hampton's returned Indians on the reservations is excellent. They have done much to spread Hampton ideas among their people and it is to be hoped that they will always be represented at the school.

'nent
uates
Prominent among the Negro graduates who are making constant efforts for the general advancement of their race is Major Moton, Hampton's Commandant, whose work in connection with the Negro Organization Society of Virginia has already been mentioned. Major Moton has been asked to represent Hampton at the meeting of the Southern Sociological Congress in Memphis this spring. Dr. Washington's work is too well known to need description. He is an inspiration, not only to his own people, but, through the numerous translations of his book, "Up From Slavery," to many individuals of other races. Mr. W. T. B. Williams, a graduate of Hampton and of Harvard, as field agent for Hampton Institute and for the Slater and Jeanes Boards, carries Hampton ideas all over the South. Many of the schools he visits learn to look to Hampton Institute for direction, especially in their industrial and extension work. He is in demand as speaker at Negro teachers' institutes, conferences, and meetings of state and national education associations. As an executive officer of some of these organizations, he is frequently called upon for suggestions in forming new institutions or in reconstructing courses of study. Mr. Williams represented Hampton at the Southern Sociological Congress last spring.

ors who
d
pton
Another important way in which Hampton influences the outside world, is through its numerous visitors, more than 20,000 · of whom register at the school each year. The classes of visitors who are especially interested in Hampton's methods may be roughly divided into (1) students of social and race questions, who represent all parts of the world ; (2) educators—teachers, principals of schools, superintendents, supervisors, and representatives of educational boards. During the recent meeting of the National Education Association at Richmond, a party of fifty delegates, all of whom were, or had been, connected with the Teachers College of Columbia University, spent a day at Hampton. During the same week five hundred other members of the Association

THE HAMPTON CADETS, OF WHOM MAJOR MOTON IS COMMANDANT

also spent a day at the school inspecting its methods. Three interesting Chinamen, members of the Chinese Educational Commission, who came to America for the purpose of learning what kind of schools would accomplish the most good in their new republic, were told by the United States Commissioner of Education that Hampton was one of the important schools for them to see. The number of educators from India desirous of starting schools similar to Hampton, in the hope of solving the many perplexing problems of that country, has been rather remarkable. Representatives of Haiti, Thessalonica, South America, Sierra Leone, and Central and South Africa are among others desirous of introducing similar methods in their various countries.

GIFTS AND NEEDS

The year has been one of financial difficulty, for many of Hampton's friends have been unable to help because of pecuniary losses. Unusual efforts have therefore been made, through personal solicitation and campaign work, to supply the needs of the school. The General Board, the Slater Fund Board, Mr. Andrew Carnegie, and other generous donors have stood loyally by Hampton. The annual appropriations from the Land Grant and Morrill Act Funds for agricultural and mechanical work have been received, but the Government appropriation for the education of the Indians was withdrawn two years ago. The thirty-eight

SOME OF HAMPTON'S PLUCKY INDIANS

Indians at Hampton this year have worked for part of their expenses, as the colored students do, and have no doubt been made stronger by the experience.

A friend has promised $100,000 for a new dormitory which is greatly needed for the boys, who have been much crowded, some of them sleeping in the attics without sufficient air. We are indebted to another friend, who wishes to be anonymous, for two beautiful marble tablets in memory of General Armstrong and Abraham Lincoln, which have been placed in a small granite pavilion erected for the purpose opposite the Library. *The boy dormito*

Partly as a result of the memorial services for Mr. Ogden held in New York and Brooklyn, a suggestion was made that a building be erected at Hampton which should bear his name. For many years the school has needed an auditorium, neither Memorial Church nor Cleveland Hall Chapel being sufficiently large for the audiences which gather every Sunday evening. There is need also of increased dining-room space for the students, and it has been suggested that, if an auditorium is erected, Cleveland Hall Chapel be used as an addition to the present dining-rooms. Plans have been made for an auditorium to seat 1600 people, and $10,000 has already been subscribed towards the $100,000 which will be needed for the purpose. *The Og Audito*

During the past year over $68,000 has been added to the endowment fund, largely through legacies; $10,000 of this was the bequest of Mrs. Ann Maria Fisher, of Brooklyn, which is the first bequest and by far the largest amount ever received by the school from a Negro. It is gratifying also to report that the alumni have collected several hundred dollars for the school during the past year. *Additio to the endo*

The Schurz Memorial Committee has contributed to the endowment fund $15,000; as Mr. Schurz was Secretary of the Interior at the time when the Indians first came to Hampton, and had much to do with their coming, it seemed to the Committee very fitting that this money should be given to Hampton. It is proposed that Mr. Schurz's name be given to one of the Hampton buildings, or that in some other way his memory be perpetuated at the school.

Through the generosity of friends, a most delightful trip around the world was made possible for the Principal and Mrs. Frissell, which resulted in greatly improved health and a broader outlook. Everywhere they were received with the greatest courtesy. They had opportunities of getting glimpses of work in South Africa, especially among the mission stations of the American Board of Commissioners for Foreign Missions, and they were most delightfully entertained at Trinity College in Ceylon; but, owing to the disturbances in China, saw little of that country. Three *The Pri pal's tri* weeks were spent in Japan, where Saito, a former Hampton student, now associate professor at the Imperial Nautical College in Tokio, did all in his power to make the visit interesting and instructive.

It was gratifying to observe in how many places Hampton was known, and how grateful those who had seen its work were for the suggestions that they had received from the school for their own missionary work. One of the strong impressions made by the trip was the opportunity which Hampton has of being of service in all missionary work, and the tremendous chance it has for demonstrating how people of different races can work together in harmony and mutual helpfulness.

It was most gratifying also to the Principal to find on his return, that, owing to the loyalty of the workers at Hampton, the school had not suffered in any way during his absence.

IN MEMORY OF MR. OGDEN

The following resolution was offered by Dr. Francis G. Peabody at the meeting of the Board on January 31:

"The Trustees of Hampton Institute wish to enter on their records some slight expression of the affection and honor in which they cherish the memory of their late President, Robert Curtis Ogden. Mr. Ogden became a member of this Board in 1874 and for twenty years had the happiness of serving with General Armstrong and of reinforcing his creative work. In 1894, the year after General Armstrong's death, Mr. Ogden became President of the Board, and for twenty years has directed its affairs with self-effacing devotion, and with the discretion, foresight, and prudence of a man trained in the larger interests of business. We have leaned on his wisdom and shall sorely miss his counsel, but our deeper gratitude turns to his modest and generous character and to his deep and tried affection. He sanctified himself for others' sakes. He let his light shine, not that it should be known of men, but that it should illuminate the way we have to go.

"At this first session of the Board since his death, we offer to his family this inadequate testimony of our sympathy and commit ourselves anew to the task in which he has been our inspiration and guide."

Respectfully submitted,
H. B. FRISSELL, PRINCIPAL

SCHOOL SPIRIT *

BY JAMES HARDY DILLARD

President of the Negro Rural School Fund and Director of the Slater Fund

I am going to take for my subject the general thought of the right spirit for the schools to have. I was struck yesterday by a remark made by a speaker regarding the importance of having an ideal behind the work, because back of all good work there must be the vision, the spirit, the ideal. I wish, very briefly, to state something of what seems to me the right spirit for your institutions, and for all educational institutions.

First, I should like to emphasize what we might call the spirit of belief in the dignity of manual work. I think perhaps the colored people have the advantage of the white people in this. The white people have a longer line of tradition, wrong tradition, in the idea of what is honorable labor, what is dignified labor, and what is not. I do not know anything in which it seems to me the world needs a revolution more than in just this respect—the way in which it regards different kinds of labor. Will you tell me if you can see any reason why killing people, why settling the quarrels of people, why giving people drugs, should be more honorable in any way than laying brick or making a table or ploughing a furrow to produce wheat and corn and other good things? Yet we know that in some way we have the wrong idea that the sort of labor we call professional is more honorable than labor with the hands. We have the idea that labor with the hands lacks something intellectual, but it isn't true. Manual labor, when done rightly, needs brain. Why should not such work be as honorable as any? Why should we not begin in our schools to teach and get into the pupils' minds the idea of the real dignity and honor of any kind of true labor?

Secondly, I should like to call your attention to the fact that one of the best ways to raise our ideals about manual labor is to have manual labor done in the right way. The spirit of nice work would be the second spirit that I would try to infuse into educational institutions. I use the word "nice" in the true sense, as when we say "a nice use of words." This means that the words are used exactly right, that you get the right word to

* An address at the meeting of the State Agricultural and Mechanical Schools, held in Washington, D. C.

fit the meaning.   It means accuracy, and in addition to accuracy it means a certain beauty.   We have a good word that is used in a rather mystical way.   People talk about art as if it were something mysterious.   Now, what is art ?   Art is nothing in the world but doing in a nice and beautiful way the thing that you do. If you are going to make a table, you can make it rough and with the pieces so that they will not fit ; but if you make the table a thing of beauty, so that it gives one pleasure 'to look at it, then you are an artist.   If you make and cook a biscuit right you are an artist.   We should endeavor to instill into the pupils' minds this spirit of doing a thing just right.   This will give them an idea of the dignity of manual labor.   We people in the South need this second spirit that I speak of, this spirit of doing things "shipshape"; we need it perhaps worse than any other people in the United States.   We might just as well confess it ; we let things go.   Those of you who have charge of schools in the South need to stress this thought, that your pupils must not half do things.   Have them do thoroughly whatever they do.   Let us get it into the heads of the people that they must not only get things done, but that they must get them done in the right way. Every human being in the world ought to be an artist ; that is, we all ought to do our work in a nice and beautiful way.

The third spirit which I would try to put into the minds of the pupils in your institutions, and in all institutions, is the spirit of steadfast work.   We in the South need this too.   We need to learn that there are six days to work.   Especially I think our farmers need to learn this :   that not three days, but "six days shalt thou labor."   We might compromise on five and a half, with Saturday half-day off, but that much we must insist on.   I do not know of anything that needs preaching about more, that needs instilling into all of you young colored men and women more, than the spirit of steadfastness—sticking to the work.   You must learn, not to work three days in the week so as to make just enough to live or loaf on the other two days, but to work at least five and a half days in the week.

Now, then, if you can have these three spirits or thoughts in your students—first, the spirit of actually looking upon manual labor as just as honorable as any other kind of labor ;   second, the spirit of wanting to do the labor in a "nice" way ;   and third, the spirit of sticking to the labor—then you will send forth young men and women who will be capable and efficient workers.

The three kinds of spirit that I have just been talking about refer primarily to one's self.   Turn now for a moment to the spirit that looks out of itself.   We need very much, especially in institutions which may be called in a sense "higher institutions, "

institutions like these you represent, which have students coming from different parts of your state, institutions which are looked up to as the capstones of education, we need that these students should have infused into their minds what perhaps we might call the spirit of democracy in education. I think it is true in the colored schools of higher grade, as it is in the white schools, that there is too much of the spirit of exclusiveness, of the feeling that education is "for us." They are too apt to forget the great masses of their fellow-men out in the background who have not these advantages. The students should feel that they want everybody educated, not themselves alone. They should be taught that they must do their part in carrying advantages to others. They must have the spirit of inclusiveness, and not exclusiveness, as to the advantages of education.

Institutions like these ought to have, also, the spirit of co-operation with all other forces of education, and I should say especially with the public school forces of education. Your institutions should take special interest in all public school efforts, not only in the county that you are in, but throughout the state in which you are situated. As far as possible you ought to co-operate with every public school movement, in everything that tends to promote the betterment of the public schools. It would be well if the pupils in your institutions, at certain times of the year, could actually go out and see just what the educational conditions are around them, visit the little schools, get in touch with them, and where possible be helpful towards them.

This leads me to the last thought that I have in mind in connection with the democratic ideal. I refer to the spirit that is being preached in some churches, and is essentially the Christian spirit; namely, the spirit of social service. It is the spirit that makes us want improvement of conditions not for ourselves alone. It is the spirit of helpfulness towards all with whom you may come in contact and of wanting a better world for all God's people. We should value our advantages in order that we may go out and be helpful in our counties and states, trying to improve the homes of the people, favoring good schools, favoring good roads, favoring temperance.

If our schools can have these spirits that I have spoken of, how much good can be done by them in making the world a better place to live in. There is nothing new about these ideas, but they are the everlasting foundation of all true work. Let me enumerate these spirits again and ask you to think about them and develop the thought in your minds more fully than I have been able to do in this brief way: the spirit of the dignity of manual labor, the spirit of doing manual labor in a nice and beautiful way; the spirit of steadfastness in labor; and then, outwardly, the spirit of democracy in any of the advantages that we have—not wanting for ourselves what we do not want others to have. One of the finest things that has been said on this subject was spoken by Mr. Henry Watterson, talking to an audience of colored people. "I do not want," he said, "for me and mine that which I do not want for you and yours." That is the true spirit.

In conclusion, I would urge that in your special work you should not have the feeling that your school is all you have to think about in this great matter of educating all the people. Think rather of your school as a part of the whole educational movement going on in our country. If the pupils in your institutions can go out with this feeling of co-operation added to the spirit of honest and steadfast labor, you need have no fear of their failing to be, not only capable in themselves, but useful to their special communities and good citizens of the state and nation. These schools of yours, supported by nation and state, seem to have a very special call for dedication to the service, not of a select group, but of all your people.

Book Reviews

Progressive British India: By Saint Nihal Singh ; Published by Charles H. Kelly.   London.   Price, one shilling.

WHAT Englishmen think of India—commercially, educationally, and religiously—is not a state secret.   Traders, government officers, and missionaries, representing British interests that range from the most sordid to the most altruistic, have told the story of India's history, India's problems, and India's possibilities.   Now, Saint Nihal Singh, a native of British India, who is a journalist, a traveler, and a protagonist for the people of all India, outlines with clearness and fearlessness the struggle of the Indian millions for a chance to be more completely understood, and therefore better treated, by those who have gradually and effectively obtained the commercial and political mastery of a great land and an ancient people in spite of the open and secret opposition of the natives, who have regarded themselves as socially superior to the British.

Mr. Singh's book, written with the journalist's freedom of expression and power of summarizing, gives a clear idea of the world problem of race adjustment as it applies to British India. What this eloquent Indian writer says concerning the difficulty of people who differ so completely as to social ideas and ideals in understanding the thoughts and actions of so-called foreigners or alien races, may be applied, with the necessary changes of time and place, to the United States, South Africa, and other regions where the awakening of race consciousness stirs sleeping men and women into activity of body, mind, and spirit.

"Progressive British India" is issued as one of the Manuals for Christian Thinkers, edited by John Telford. Surely those who are Christians and who are also thinkers must soon realize that the man who forms part of any race problem has something to say, concerning his people and their innermost thoughts, that the men in authority would do well to read sympathetically and most attentively. What one man dares to say, thousands upon thousands are thinking and are governing their lives by. There is undoubtedly a serious aim in Mr. Singh's present work in the attempt to show what Great Britain was able to do through the agency of a powerful trading company, and later through govenment officers, to bring India from the battleground of "native jealousies and rivalries" to a land of possibility—for non-Indians.   W. A. A.

Furniture Designs for Schools and Shops: By Fred D. Crawshaw, Professor of Manual Arts, University of Wisconsin. Published by the Manual Arts Press, Peoria, Illinois. Price $1.00, postpaid.

TEACHERS of woodwork will get substantial help from Professor Crawshaw's new book on furniture design. His illustrations of typical designs, accompanied by suggestions for their re-arrangement and development, is a new feature in manual art publications, and one which cannot fail to appeal to teachers and students.

The discussions on the principles of design, as applied to furniture, are helpful even to those teachers who are well informed on the subject, and should be especially helpful to those who are entering the manual-training field, and to all pupils. These discussions, and the accompaning suggestive designs, are especially valuable to the pupil because they reveal to him a way in which to express himself in the re-arrangement and development of the suggested type of design.

Again, the practical nature of the numerous articles to be made, and the logical directions for constructing them, show that the author has a clear conception of the trend of thought regarding the kind of manual work of most value in the schools. He seems conscious of the fact, also, that the time is past when problems can be accepted which are weak in construction or design, and which are too difficult for the ordinary boy of grammar school age to make, without undue assistance from the teacher. This weakness in a course of study is sometimes met by allowing a boy to follow, unrestrained, a method of his own in designing and constructing an "original" project. We question the wisdom of this alternative unless the boy is fully competent to perform the work properly, and we welcome Professor Crawshaw's new book for the many valuable suggestions it gives for the development of the boy's power of initiative and originality.

Another interesting feature of this book is the practical treatment of design. Large surfaces are broken up whenever practicable, which not only gives relief and dignity to the design, but also introduces an economic feature into the furniture problem, which few authors seem to consider ; namely, that of presenting articles which are comparatively inexpensive to make, and are also good in design and logical in construction.

The cost of maintaining industrial work in a school, and especially in a country school, is a vital matter, yet one which is often overlooked. Most of the books on woodwork are written for highly organized schools, having boys from well-to-do homes, and racks full of lumber. While this excess of attention may be justifiable and readily explained, something more should be done than is now being done to encourage the teaching of industries in the ordinary school in the town or in the country.

Professor Crawshaw is a man of wide experience in the manual arts, and familiar with the needs of the ordinary boy, and he may have had their needs in mind when designing many of his projects. Whether he had or not, his book meets these needs to a considerable degree. So much so, indeed, that many of the smaller articles might be made from the wood obtained from selected dry-goods boxes, and with a very simple tool equipment. Work of this kind is being done in many country schools with marked success, and while this book is not intended especially for the much neglected country school, it gives many valuable suggestions which can be put into practice there.

We need more books of this kind. Makers of furniture, either in the school or in the shop, who are aiming to connect the work of the school with the boy's life, will find Professor Crawshaw's book on furniture design exceedingly helpful and instructive.   J. H. J.

Ezekiel Expands: By Lucy Pratt. Published by Houghton Mifflin Company, Boston. Price, $1.25 *net*.

TO many people Miss Lucy Pratt's "Ezekiel" is a real little colored boy, as strangers visiting the Whittier School

frequently testify by the eager question, "Can we see Ezekiel?"
Ezekiel's surroundings are real and very familiar to Hampton
readers, and Ezekiel himself is real in that he expresses the joys,
the longings, and the whimsicalities of many a little colored boy.

The author, who was for several years a teacher at Hampton,
has dedicated this new collection of ten stories about Ezekiel to
Miss Elizabeth Hyde, the Institute's lady principal, "a very
good friend of all the little Ezekiels." The book is illustrated
with six sketches of Negro children by E. W. Kemble, of which
the frontispiece portraying the hero is particularly good.

One or two of the stories are simply about Ezekiel, but most
of them include a sort of allegorical fairy story told by him in
characteristic dialect. With each of Ezekiel's absorbing fairy
stories, Miss Pratt registers a significant truth upon the minds
of her readers. If the innocence of the little Negro is sometimes
over astute, as in his generous declaration, "I'se gwine uplif' de
w'ite people," it is Ezekiel idealized who speaks, to emphasize
with gentle sarcasm some of the phases of the "race question"
which the author wishes more perfectly understood. The patronizing interest of a rapidly passing type of sentimental, impracti-
cal Northerner, the Negro's gift of originality in expression and
his often graceful turn of speech, his kindliness for the unfortunate, the occasional pathos of his social ostracism, and the unev-
enly sketched "color line" are the underlying texts of some of
the stories.

Some of Ezekiel's cleverest retorts may be too keen for a
careless little colored boy, but the author would have been un-
forgivable had she deprived us of their irresistible mischief and
humor. Friends of Ezekiel can heartily rejoice in his expansion.

M. I. H.

At Home and Afield

HAMPTON INCIDENTS

ON March 28, the evening of the third annual Adams Prize Debate, from the moment when the Douglass cheering section gave its first crisp message of enthusiasm and encouragement until the judges' decision in favor of the Dunbar speakers, the usual atmosphere of anxious tension pervaded the chapel. The well-organized cheering of the two clubs before the debate opened was the best that Hampton has heard. The promoter of the debate and donor of the prizes, Mr. Elbridge L. Adams of New York City, presided. The subject was, "*Resolved, That the United States should now grant the Philippine Islands independence.*" The affirmative argument was defended by the Dunbar Literary Society and the negative by the Douglass. The judges, Hon. Harry Houston, of Hampton, W. C. L. Taliaferro, Esq., also of Hampton, and Rev. Charles S. Morris, of Norfolk, gave a decision in favor of the affirmative, with one dissenting vote, and recommended for especial mention E. J. E. Lassiter of the negative team. One of the features which contributed to the success of the Dunbar speakers was their dignified, convincing delivery. Although some good points were made in the rebuttal, in which each of the six speakers took part, on the whole it was rather confused, proving the advantage of having in rebuttal only one representative from each team. The members of the winning team were presented with gold fob medals, and the banner held by the Douglass Society during the past year was given into the keeping of the Dunbar men.

Announcement was made, after the debate, of the winners in the Adams Essay Contest, who wrote on the subject, "Changes in the Philippines under American rule." The first prize was awarded to Blanche M. Briggs, of the Senior Class; the second to Frank B. White, a Junior who entered school last fall; and honorable mention was given Grace V. Stewart, also a Junior. The prizes in each case were books.

THE rural post office and general store with its mail delivery window, shelves containing dry goods and groceries all sold over one counter, lurid advertising posters, and airtight stove supporting something less than a mile of stovepipe and surrounded by dry-goods boxes and backless chairs for the convenience of the evening "social club," were all faithfully reproduced on the Cleveland Hall stage when the curtain rose at eight o'clock on Saturday evening, March 14. "The Village Post Office," presented by the Kings's Daughters and the Y. M. C. A. with thirty-five actors, was an entertaining cross-section of rural life, introducing village celebrities and eccentrics. The activity of the postmaster's son, an alert small boy whose interest in the cider barrel did not prevent him from giving his close attention to all that occurred, held the interest of the audience during much of the performance.

NEW GIFTS

A valuable acquisition to the equipment of Hampton is a large relief map of the Panama Canal which was lately presented by a friend of the school. The map is twelve feet, five inches long and four feet, five inches wide, made to a scale of 1 to 20,000. The vertical scale is 1 to 5000. It was made under the direction of the Isthmian Canal Commission by Edwin E. Howell, and shows the completed lock canal and also the Canal Zone. This map will be most helpful to the academic classes and is an interesting study for everyone. It is to be kept in the Library for the present.

A fascinating collection of curios from the Philippine Islands has been presented to the Hampton Institute Museum by Miss Frances Curtis of Boston. There are stiff pieces of fibre cloth and soft pieces of cotton material in bright color combinations, with a sample of the kind of loom on which they were woven. An interesting jacket is embroidered in an elaborate pattern in tiny pieces of shell, and there are other garments embroidered in bright-colored cotton and in beads. The Filipinos are evidently skilled in basket making, as the many baskets and large hats are beautifully woven, some in intricate patterns. Other curious things are bamboo mats, little baskets to be worn at the back of the head, a boat-shaped musical instrument, a queer wooden idol, and all sorts of knives, spears, head axes, and shields. Strangely enough the collection includes a bead belt made in exactly the same manner as those of the American Indians.

ADDRESSES

ON April 7, Mr. Andrew Carnegie, who, with his wife and daughter, were visiting Hampton, spoke to the students in Cleveland Hall Chapel. He expressed his appreciation of the courtesy shown him by all the students during his visit, commending their excellent deportment in speech and manner. He said that the more he looked into and examined Hampton, the higher he would place it as doing a great work for the whole country.

Mr. Carnegie earnestly advised the boys to abstain from smoking, drinking, and gambling, assuring them that he spoke, not from precept, but from example, in regard to all three. Drink, he said, has ruined more young men than any other sin, and gambling is dishonest, either taking what you have not earned, or throwing away what was given you for a good purpose. Mr. Carnegie reminded the students that in this country, "Every citizen's privilege is every citizen's right" and there is nothing to prevent them from making the most of their lives. His final words were an earnest plea to the students to live their lives so that they should leave the world a little better than they had found it.

THOSE who gathered in the Museum on the afternoon of March 30 to meet Mr. John Driscoll felt it a rare privilege to hear his simple but effective story of the famous battle between the *Monitor* and the *Merrimac*. Mr. Driscoll, who is living at the National Soldiers' Home, is one of the two known surviving members of the crew of the *Monitor*. The details became very realistic as one followed Mr. Driscoll's account, from the gloomy leave-taking of the *Monitor* from the Brooklyn Navy Yard without the customary cheering and salute, through the troubles caused by the gale that struck them the second night they were out, to their arrival at Hampton Roads on the night of March 8. On the following day the famous battle was fought, lasting for five hours. During this time the *Monitor* was withdrawn five different times, giving those on board the *Merrimac* the impression that they had won the battle, but they were always disappointed by seeing again the revolving turret of the *Monitor* and hearing the pounding of her guns. These withdrawals were made to allow the men to get some refreshment, to carry ammunition up the ladder leading to the turret, and to allow the *Monitor's* wounded commander to be removed to a tug. As soon as Lieutenant Green took command, the *Merrimac* turned and headed for Sewell's Point. The *Monitor* chased her and fired a parting shot, but she was out of range. The *Merrimac* was taken in tow by her two escorts and put in dry-dock for repairs, thus ending one of the most noted naval fights that the world has ever known.

The adverse criticism of the little *Monitor* is very interesting. She was condemned by shipbuilders and naval men, who declared she could never be launched and that, if she were, the first heavy sea that washed over her would swamp her; also that her crew must want to commit suicide. But after the gallant little "Cheesebox" received her baptism of fire and not only protected the *Minnesota*, but revolutionized naval warfare, and perhaps changed the destiny of a nation, a far different estimate was placed upon her value and ability.

TRADE SCHOOL

THE Senior Trade Class of 1914 held interesting exercises in connection with the unveiling of their motto on Saturday evening, April 4. After an address by the president, telling of the hopes and aims of the class, the motto was unveiled, and the words, "Virtue, Determination, Achievement," were made the subject of a stirring song by all the members of the class. Dr. Frissell was called upon and explained the derivation of the words of the motto, showing how much they might mean as an inspiration.

These exercises were followed by an exhibit of work in each department in the Trade School Building. A system of arrows allowed the many students and workers who visited the exhibit to inspect every room in the building in an orderly and logical way, and everywhere guides were stationed to explain the various exhibits.

ONE of the most interesting of these was that of the printing office, which, for the first time, was thrown open to the whole school. Here the interested visitor found the actual daily work of the department going on—printing on the various presses, folding, stitching, and cutting—while guides in the composing room explained the method of setting up type.

HAMPTON WORKERS

AT a very successful educational rally held by the Patrons' League of the Union Street School in Hampton on April 27, Major Moton advised the colored people to work together and to be persistent in their efforts for a better school. He assured them that they could get good schools if they only wanted them enough to work for them and would show their earnestness in the movement.

IN a musical prize competition given by the Music School Settlement for Colored People in the City of New York, Mr. R. Nathaniel Dett, the school's director of music, won the second prize of twenty-five dollars. Mr. Dett's composition was an anthem, based on the folk-song "Listen to the Lambs." The first two measures of the song were used as the theme, and the anthem was developed from this *motif*. It is written to be sung unaccompanied. Mr. Dett's purpose in this anthem was to show some of the possibilities of Negro folk-song themes for classical church music.

THE engagement of Mr. J. Blair Buck, assistant to the Director of Agriculture at Hampton Institute, and Miss Dorothea Dutcher of Milwaukee, Wisconsin, was recently announced.

THE position at Shellbanks resigned by Mr. J. W. Cline has been filled by Miss Ella L. Hoyt, of Penn Yan, N. Y., who has recently taken a special agricultural course at Cornell. Miss Hoyt will assist in the academic work and will have charge of the farm accounts.

THE following notice concerning an ex-Hampton worker appeared in a recent number of the *Survey:* "Miss Louise M. Goodrich, who for a year has been head resident of the Margaret Bottome Memorial, the King's Daughters' Settlement House in Harlem, New York City, became, on February 1, the first social secretary of the new club for girl students at Pratt Institute, Brooklyn. This club, which was opened early in the month, is designed to meet the social and recreational needs of the girl students, especially those boarding in the city. For thirteen years Miss Goodrich served in the general office and as instructor in the academic department at Hampton Institute."

THE WHITTIER SCHOOL

TENANTED birds' nests in the Whittier yard each year testify to the fact that small boys and birds can live happily in the same vicinity, if the small boys are properly educated. Regular bird lessons are given in the nature study classes, and Mr. Heath is correlating this work with drawing, giving the children a chance to color with the proper markings bluebirds and others. In one of the manual training classes they have made boxes, covered with chicken wire, in which suet may be put out in the trees for the smaller birds without fear of wholesale theft by the grackles and crows.

At this time of year the classes are studying seed germination, the kinds of soil, and the transplanting of vegetables from one flat to another until it is possible to set them out in the school garden.

ON the last Friday in March, Mrs. Frissell attended the meeting of the Parents' Association and told about her recent visit to Japan, showing the stereopticon pictures which she herself had taken and some additional slides on Japan presented by Dr. George L. Curtis of the First Presbyterian Church of Bloomfield, N. J. It will be remembered that Dr. Curtis a

few years ago gave the Whittier children their fine "magic lantern" in memory of his mother. There was an unusually good attendance at the meeting, and the parents were delighted with the afternoon's entertainment.

RELIGIOUS WORK

ON Sunday morning, March 29, Rev. Laurence Fenninger, assistant pastor in the First Presbyterian Church of Bloomfield, New Jersey, preached in Memorial Church, taking as his text Isaiah 40:31—"But they that wait upon the Lord shall renew their strength, they shall mount up with wings as eagles; they shall run, and not be weary; and they shall walk and not faint." At the chapel exercises in the evening, Mr. Fenninger spoke on the "art of listening," showing it to be really more difficult than the art of speaking, while those who can "listen" to the expressions of their companions while talking to them have learned the most helpful art of all.

Rev. Harris Ely Adriance, of Englewood, New Jersey, addressed the school at the chapel service Sunday evening, April 5. "Living life on the square" was his subject, the square being formed by the four words, sober, righteous, godly, and looking, which, followed out in their best and fullest meanings as explained by Mr. Adriance, would make a complete and perfect life.

AT the meeting of the King's Daughters on Sunday evening, March 29, the girls were addressed by Mrs. Firman, of the "Firman House," Chicago. This social settlement was named for Mrs. Firman's husband, a devoted settlement worker during his lifetime. She spoke on the word "Watch," showing how careful a watch should be kept on words, actions, thoughts, companions, and habits.

An interesting service was held by the King's Daughters in celebration of Palm Sunday. The room was decorated with palms. A chapter from the

Bible was read by Anne Scoville and a recitation was given by Elizabeth Jinks, after which forty little colored children marched around the room, singing a Palm Sunday hymn.

THE annual election of officers for the Y. M. C. A. for next year was held Sunday evening, April 5. The officers elected were George A. Scott, president; W. D. Dickey, first vice president; James Gayle, second vice president; P. L. Prattis, secretary; Mr. F. D. Wheelock, honorary secretary; and Captain Allen Washington, treasurer. It has been the custom for the past few years to elect the officers for the following year early in the spring, so that they may meet with the outgoing cabinet and get into harness, ready to take up the work when school opens in the fall.

A marked increase in attendance at the Thursday evening prayer meetings has been noticed during the past three weeks, due in large part to the appeal made by Dr. Turner one evening in chapel. For the last month, the regular Sunday Y. M. C. A. meetings have been given over to the discussion of an assigned topic. This type of meeting has proved to be the most helpful, encouraging, and inspiring form of service. The Y. M. C. A. is very grateful for the interest manifested in these meetings by members of the Faculty, and for the helpful words they have spoken from time to time.

VISITORS

THE first days of spring always bring many old friends to Hampton. Mr. Andrew Carnegie, who has done much for the education of the colored people, spent some days at the Chamberlin Hotel with Mrs. Carnegie and their daughter, Miss Margaret Carnegie. They visited the school several times, observing the work of the various departments. His words to the students appear else-where. Dr. W. J. Schieffelin of New York City, an ever welcome guest, visited Hampton about the middle of March with his youngest son. William J. Schieffelin, Jr. was a guest at the Mansion House for some days, and Alfred Olcott of New York, at the "Moorings." Ogden Purves and two school friends also spent their spring vacation at Hampton. Mr. Elbridge Adams, Chairman of the Executive Committee of the New York Hampton Association, came to the school for the Adams Prize Debate, accompanied by his two sons. Other old friends visiting Hampton were Mrs. Alexander Trowbridge (whose husband is chairman of the executive committee of the Brooklyn Armstrong Association) with her son; Mrs. T. J. Wattles of Norwich, Connecticut, whose father gave Pierce Hall to the school; and Rev. Harris Ely Adriance of New York with several members of his family.

Mrs. J. H. Gordon, in charge of the Howard Orphanage for colored children on Long Island, a description of which appeared in the March number of the Southern Workman, visited Hampton with her daughter on March 20. Other recent visitors were Mr. J. H. Binford of the Virginia Co-operative Education Association, Mr. Jackson Davis, and a number of students from William and Mary College, who, with Professor G. O. Ferguson, spent a day visiting the various departments of the school. Miss Margaret Armstrong and Miss Cushing, Seniors at Vassar College, spent their spring vacation at Hampton. A very welcome visitor was Mrs. E. E. Waters, of New York City, who was a schoolmate of General Armstrong.

Former workers whom Hampton has gladly welcomed this spring are Miss Elizabeth Metcalf of Buffalo, N. Y., Mrs. I. N. Tillinghast of Vassar College, Mr. George W. Andrews of Caldwell, N. J., Miss Martha Watt, Miss Charlotte Goodrich, and Miss Rose Alden, former academic teachers.

GRADUATES AND EX-STUDENTS

A recent visitor to Hampton was R. A. Jackson, an ex-student who left the printing department in 1892, and who has for five years been proprietor of a job-printing establishment, the Fraternal Press, in Chicago. His assistant is Charles H. Thornton, ex-student '93.

George W. Buckner, '04, has returned to Virginia Union University in Richmond to continue his studies there. William W. Wharton, '10, has this year entered the same institution.

William B. Scott, '90, last year resigned his work in the office of the New York and Long Branch Railroad in Long Branch, New Jersey, where he has been employed for many years, to devote himself to the ministry. He prepared for this work through private instruction, and is now pastor of the Pilgrim Church of Red Bank, N. J.

Cornelius C. Clark, '10, is, for the third term, principal of the Tar River Institute, Greenville, N. C., which has an enrollment of one hundred fifty pupils. This year he has entered the ministry and combines the work of preaching with teaching.

THE name of Aaron J. Starnes, '98, should be added to the list of four Hampton men mentioned last month as teachers of manual training in Kansas City.

Mary A. Spraggs, '10, has been teaching this winter at Irwin, Goochland Co., Virginia.

AFTER working several years as a successful contractor in Durham, N. C., Pinckney W. Dawkins, ex-student '08, accepted a position as teacher of manual training at St. Augustine's School in Raleigh. He is this year teacher of carpentry and manual training in Downingtown Industrial School, Downingtown, Pa., where he also has charge of the mechanical department. Thomas B. Patterson, '90, is director of the agricultural department at the same institution.

James L. Lawson, Trade Class '98, has been for nine years teacher of carpentry at the Kentucky Normal and Industrial Institute, Frankfort, Ky. This year he has been appointed director of the mechanical department in that school.

James D. Uzzell, '93, is now printer and linotype operator at the office of the *Star* in Newport News, Va.

Alma M. Stanton, '10, is teaching at Hamilton, Loudoun Co., Virginia.

Bertha A. Nelson, '09, who has been teaching for four years in the Virginia rural schools, is this year taking a special course in domestic science at Pratt Institute.

Martha L. Evans, ex-student '05, who was graduated in 1913 from Teachers College, Howard University, is teaching at Bridges, Gloucester Co., Virginia.

Wm. Hunter, ex-student '04, sends to Hampton a copy of the *World Progress*, a magazine published in Washington, devoted chiefly to descriptions of inventions, which contains a horizontal drawing and an explanation of a new valve construction for engines, on which he has recently been granted a patent.

THE Jamaica *Times* for November 8, 1913, gives a detailed account of the Government Farm School near Kingston, which has many of the features of Hampton. It speaks of Percival W. Murray, Hampton '03, the head master of the school, in very complimentary terms. The *Times* correspondent writes : "Mr. Murray took charge of the school at the beginning of this year, succeeding the former head master. He mixes his plans with ideas and common sense. In inspecting the school, I had the feeling of touching something that was living and developing, something instinct with that power of healthy life that keeps it on the lookout for the changes and adaptations made necessary by changing circumstances."

DEATHS

WORD has been received of the death of Seleah Hicks Harris, '90, at her home in Mecklenburg County on February 21, 1914. She had been teaching much of the time since her graduation, even after her marriage in '94. The testimony of those who knew her declares her "a faithful worker in home, school, and church."

John W. O'Kelly, ex-student, '01, after a long, painful illness died at his home in Raleigh, N. C. on February 7, 1914.

INDIAN NOTES

A recent number of the *Native American* contains the following item regarding a member of the Class of '08: "John Dodson, who has been assistant carpenter at this school for the past five years, has received transfer and promotion to Fort Apache School, Whiteriver, Arizona, and leaves shortly to take his new place. Phœnix loses a splendid employe and a capable workman, but is glad to have him go forward in his trade. John is a Shoshone, and a graduate of Phœnix and Hampton."

ONE of the graduates writes, "I often think of you all, and Hampton is as dear to me now as when I was there, more so now, as I realize the more I connect my school days with the business of to-day. The carpenter work I got there fitted me to build my own house, and the short time I was in the printing office helped me to form and write the heading of our business letter heads. I shall never forget the trips I made with dear Mr. Frissell in the North. He was always so kind to me, and made it a point to show me interesting places. The world is not so hard when one is true to himself and his neighbors, but of course one must not be afraid to work, even down to turning the washing machine for the wife and hanging out the clothes. I have done them all. I am not rich, a long way from it, but I have a comfortable home and am in business for myself. I am not bragging on myself, but I want to tell the boys and girls that the world is all right when one is not afraid to work; and by all means be honest."

AN article headed "What is wrong that Indian children starve to death in Wyoming?" was recently published in the *State Leader*, Cheyenne, Wyoming, by Charles Kealear of the Class of '89. It gives a vivid picture of hard conditions on the Wind River Reservation, where Mr. Kealear, a Yankton Sioux, has been working for many years. An editorial note preceding the article is of much interest to Mr. Kealear's Hampton friends. It reads, "Upon the request of several of the better class of Indians and some of the officials of the reservation, Charles Kealear, one of the most highly educated and respected Indians in Wyoming, has written of the true conditions of Indians in this state and leaves room for the reader to draw some of his own inferences as to causes and remedies. That Mr Kealear enjoys the confidence of his white associates and others is shown by the fact that he has just been named postmaster at Arapaho."

Mrs. Dorsie Ross Kearney, '09, writes of the Christmas celebration which the Hampton Indian students helped to make merry in a school in Montana: "I want to thank the dear Hampton boys and girls for the fine Christmas packages they sent me for the little Cheyenne children. I am at home now, but at Christmas time I was at Busby as temporary primary teacher. The packages arrived the evening we were going to have our entertainment and tree, and you don't know how glad we all were to receive so many presents for the children. There was about one present apiece, and you will never know how happy those little people were over the dolls, scrapbooks, etc. The larger girls were equally pleased over the sewing baskets and bags. Tell the boys and girls at Hampton that they will never know, until they get out in the field themselves, what joy and happiness one little present may bring to some little Indian child away out here in the West. I know when at Hampton I often thought to myself, 'What's the use, such trifling things !' I have found out that the things I thought small and trifling make the children as happy as more costly things would not. Tell the boys and girls to keep up the good work.''

THE NOTTOWAY COUNTY SCHOOL EXHIBIT

APRIL 3 was a red-letter day in Nottoway County. The day was fair and a large number of patrons and friends manifested by their presence their interest in the industrial work of the county schools exhibited at the Blackstone colored six-room schoolhouse. Members of the Patrons' League were busy selling lunches to those who had come to the meeting.

The exhibit showed marked improvement over that of last year, both in quality and variety. The garments were made of good cloth and the color scheme was excellent. Canned vegetables were on exhibition. Near a well-made bed stood a mattress made of corn husks and padded on one side with cotton, demonstrating that any school child can, with the use of home products, furnish a good mattress for his home. A most creditable bookcase had been made by the boys. The chair-caning was excellent. A three-course dinner was prepared and served to the visitors by the girls of the upper class of the Blackstone school. The county superintendent, a member of the school board, and the four white ladies acting as judges were unanimous in their commendation of the excellent work being done by the schools under the direction of Pauline Baskerville, Hampton '10, the industrial supervisor for Nottoway County.

Three of Hampton's graduates are teachers in the Blackstone school—Othelia Hoffman, '13, Louisa Reynolds, '13, and Janet Payton, '11. The rooms of these teachers were most attractively prepared for the reception of patrons and friends of the school. In one room a model farm was shown with an attractive two-story house, and with fenced vegetable and flower gardens. The well showed the care that had been taken in presenting facts connected with a sanitary water supply. The outhouses were made according to the directions sent out by the Virginia State Board of Health. A feature of this little model was the roadway showing several children with dinner baskets on their arms on their way to the schoolhouse in the distance.

An effective program was presented by the teachers of the county and members of the Blackstone High School. One girl read an excellent paper on bed-making. After the county teachers had completed their program, the county superintendent spoke most encouragingly to those present. He was followed by Mr. Connor of the Petersburg State Normal School who presented the work of the Negro Organization Society and spoke forcibly on the subject of health. Miss Virginia Randolph, of Henrico County, told of the work she is doing in connection with gardens. Mr. Jackson Davis was present and expressed his approval of the progressive work of Nottoway County.

Notes and Exchanges

A BOOK ON WOODWORK

"DESIGN and Construction in Wood," compiled by William Noyes, and recently published by the Manual Arts Press, Peoria, Ill., is a valuable book for the beginner in woodwork. Mr. Noyes has given much information in this work regarding tools, tool processes, and materials, and also full and lucid directions for making the articles presented in his suggestive course. With this book for reference, the worker cannot fail to have an intelligent grasp of the work in hand or to bring it to a satisfactory completion.

SCHOOL FOR WAYWARD GIRLS

THE following charter has been granted by the State Corporation Commission: Industrial Home School for Wayward Colored Girls (Inc.), Hampton, Va. No capital stock. Mrs. Henry Lane Schmelz, president ; Mrs. Harris Barrett, secretary—both of Hampton, Va.

Norfolk *Journal and Guide*

THE WOMAN ON THE FARM

SECRETARY Houston recommends a piece of long neglected social justice. He calls attention to the forgotten woman on the farm : "On many farms where there is always money enough to buy the latest agricultural appliances there is seldom a surplus to provide the woman in her productive work with power machinery that will lighten her physical labor, or running water that will relieve her of the burden of carrying from the pump all water that is used in the household."

The rural districts need a new standard of living. The neglect of the woman in the country is one of the most serious indictments that can be drawn against our civilization.

The *World's Work*

THREE NEW INDIAN TRIBES

THREE tribes of Indians hitherto unknown have been discovered by the University of Pennsylvania's Amazon expedition. They are in regions of Brazil never before penetrated by white men. The Indians call themselves Porocotos, Ajamaras, and Zapacas. Dr. Farabee, the head of the expedition, took vocabularies of their languages, took photographs, and collected many ethnological specimens. Archæological specimens of rare interest were also found.

KINDERGARTENS FOR COLORED CHILDREN

ANNOUNCEMENT is made by the Kindergarten Division of the United States Bureau of Education that a demonstration kindergarten has recently been opened for colored children at Chattanooga, Tenn., by the National Kindergarten Association, co-operating with the Bureau of Education. It will be supported temporarily by Miss Bessie Locke, of New York, in memory of her mother, Jane Schouler Locke. It is believed by those familiar with Chattanooga and its people that it will be necessary to support the demonstration kindergarten there but a short time when the local people will become sufficiently interested in this important work to assume the care and maintenance of the kindergarten, thus enabling the demonstrator to go to another city to repeat the demonstration. A second one will soon be opened in another Southern city, which will be maintained by Miss Elizabeth R. Wellington in memory of her mother, Mary D. Wellington.

HARVARD ORATOR A NEGRO

THE Harvard senior class elected A. L. Jackson, a Negro of Englewood, N. J., as class orator, and he will be the principal speaker at the commencement exercises in June. Although working his way through college, he has ranked well in his studies and has won his " H " on the 'varsity track team. He won his election from a field of six candidates by a large plurality.

New York *Sun*

JUNE 1914

THE SOUTHERN WORKMAN

Press of
The Hampton Normal and Agricultural Institute
Hampton, Virginia

The Hampton Normal and Agricultural Institute

HAMPTON VIRGINIA

What it is An undenominational industrial school founded in 1868 by Samuel Chapman Armstrong for Negro youth. Indians admitted in 1878.

Object To train teachers and industrial leaders

Equipment Land, 1060 acres ; buildings, 140

Courses Academic, trade, agriculture, business, home economics

Enrollment Negroes, 1215 ; Indians, 37 ; total, 1252

Results Graduates, 1709 ; ex-students, over 6000
Outgrowths ; Tuskegee, Calhoun, Mt. Meigs, and many smaller schools for Negroes

Needs $125,000 annually above regular income
$4,000,000 Endowment Fund
Scholarships
   A full scholarship for both academic and
      industrial instruction   -   -   - $ 100
   Academic scholarship   -   -   -   -   70
   Industrial scholarship   -   -   -   -   -   30
   Endowed full scholarship   -   -   -   -   2500
   Any contribution, however small, will be gratefully received and may be sent to H. B. FRISSELL, Principal, or to F. K. ROGERS, Treasurer, Hampton, Virginia.

FORM OF BEQUEST

I give and devise to the trustees of The Hampton Normal and Agricultural Institute, Hampton, Virginia, the sum of   *dollars, payable*

The Southern Workman

Published monthly by

The Hampton Normal and Agricultural Institute

Contents for June 1914

Statement of the ownership, management, circulation, etc., of the SOUTHERN WORKMAN, publish twelve times a year (monthly) at Hampton, Virginia, required by the Act of August 24, 1912.

    Editor, Hollis B. Frissell, Hampton Institute, Va.
    Managing Editor, J. E. Davis, Hampton Institute, Va.
    Business Manager, William Anthony Aery, Hampton Institute, Va.
    Publisher and Owner, The Hampton Normal and Agricultural Institute, Hampton, V
    non-stockholding corporation.

                WILLIAM ANTHONY AERY

                For The Hampton Normal and Agricultural Institu
Sworn and subscribed before me this 28th day of March, 1914

                HAMLIN NELSON, Notary Public
[SEAL]   My commission expires July 4, 1915

              EDITORIAL STAFF

H. B. FRISSELL   W. L. BROWN
HELEN W. LUDLOW   W. A. AERY, Business Manager
J. E. DAVIS   W. T. B. WILLIAMS

TERMS: One dollar a year in advance; ten cents a copy
CHANGE OF ADDRESS: Persons making a change of address should send the old as well as the address to

THE SOUTHERN WORKMAN, Hampton, Virginia

    Entered as second-class matter August 13, 1908, in the Post Office at Hampton, Virginia, u the Act of July 16, 1894

THE HAMPTON LEAFLETS

Any twelve of the following numbers of the "The Hampton Leaflets" may obtained free of charge by any Southern teacher or superintendent. *A charge of* fi *cents per dozen is made to other applicants.* Cloth-bound volumes for 1905, '06, ' and '08 will be furnished at seventy-five cents each, postpaid.

Address: Publication Office, The Hampton Normal and Agricultur Institute, Hampton, Virginia

The

Southern Workman

VOL. XLIII   JUNE 1914   NO. 6

Œditorials

The Southern Sociological Congress
: The third annual meeting of the Southern Sociological Congress was held in Memphis, Tennessee, from May 6 to 10. It brought together in sympathetic co-operation hundreds of white men and colored men, as well as devoted women, who are engaged in "a national crusade for social health and righteousness."

Hon. William Hodges Mann, a former governor of Virginia and a Southerner who served with gallantry in the Confederate Army, presided. He was re-elected by unanimous vote as the president of the Congress.

Dr. James Hardy Dillard, president of the Jeanes Board and director of the Slater Fund, presided over the special conferences which were devoted to a frank, sympathetic, and constructive consideration of race relations in the Southland.

Dr. W. D. Weatherford of Nashville, whose recent books on Negro life and Negro conditions have awakened in white Southern college men a new sense of personal responsibility for the welfare of their colored neighbors, pointed out clearly the need of treating Negroes as God's children, who are full of possibilities and are willing to receive kindly the best that the white man can give of himself, of his sympathy, and of his personality. Dr. Weatherford made a strong plea for the development of confidence and trust between white people and their colored neighbors.

The Southern Sociological Congress has achieved, through its generous founder, Mrs. Anna Russell Cole, and its devoted general secretary, Mr. James E. McCulloch, the sympathetic and real co-operation, for the promotion of social justice, of the strong Southern white leaders and the wisest and most respected colored men and women, who serve to interpret, the one group to the other, the life of a South which has an awakened social conscience and a sincere desire to give men, regardless of race, color, or creed, a square deal and an open field in the South's new and quickened life.

Dr. C. V. Roman, a colored physician of Nashville, outlined a sane policy of public health which emphasizes the value of modern methods of sanitation irrespective of race or social condition. He declared that in matters of health there is no real separation between "Quality Hill" and "Poverty Lane. " Disease respects no color line, and contact with contagion is always dangerous. He emphasized the importance of good morals as a factor in a campaign for better public health. "When all things are for barter, then ruin is imminent."

Major Moton of Hampton Institute pointed out the elements of the "Common Industrial Life. " After showing the relation of the Negro to the economic life of the South, Major Moton said: "It is fair to assume that, for the present at least, the South cannot depend on foreign immigrants for its farm operatives, its domestic and personal service, and its unskilled and semi-skilled labor. If the Negro is to constitute the mass of industrial operatives of the South, it is imperative that for the common good there should be sympathetic co-operation with white workers who are engaged in similar forms of industry. The laborer can be kept efficient and skillful only as his environment is wholesome and strengthening, and not weakening and demoralizing. It is the duty of every patriotic Southerner to use every possible means for practical, sympathetic training of these workers and their children through a thoroughly well-regulated school system. "

Major Moton made clear in his discussion of race segregation that the Negro does not want to be with white people because they are white. "The Negro has long since learned, " he said, "that property alongside of white people, in cities and towns, is more valuable ; that his wife and children have more protection ; that the streets are better and cleaner ; and that he gets better fire protection and greater police protection. "

Dr. George E. Haynes, who is director of the National

League on Urban Conditions among Negroes, showed that the increasing segregation is shutting off the Negro from helpful contact with the best white people. He declared that when benefits will not come to the Negro, then the Negro will go in search of the benefits, such as better police protection, better sanitary conditions, and better schools. The result of the present movement for segregation through legislation has been, in his opinion, the growth of suspicion on the part of the colored people and of apprehension on the part of white men. He declared that the so-called square deal is the foundation stone of community peace and progress.

The Southern Sociological Congress merits the hearty support of all those who believe in bringing together ''folks'' of all kinds to discuss in a straightforward, honest, and friendly fashion the variety of economic and social problems that the South is facing. The crusade of social service must be carried on by those who are brave and have the love of the Master in their hearts.

The Awakening of Caroline County   ''It's not so much education as the struggle for education that educates,'' was the sentiment expressed by Dr. Buttrick, secretary of the General Education Board. He was standing in a group, including the Governor of Virginia and state and county education officials, listening, in the burning sun, to a dignified colored patron of the Mt. Zion new, two-room schoolhouse, who described from the steps of the porch, whose roof was still unfinished, the building of this schoolhouse. The occasion was an ''educational tour'' to some of the white and colored schools of Caroline County, Virginia, and in the party which filled ten automobiles were, besides Governor Stuart and Dr. Buttrick, Mr. R. C. Stearnes, state superintendent, Mr. Jackson Davis, supervisor of Negro rural schools, Mr. John Washington, the Caroline County superintendent, Dr. Abraham Flexner of the General Education Board, Mrs. B. B. Munford and Mr. J. H. Binford of the Virginia Co-operative Education Association, and other Virginia educators. The route included two fine, new high schools for white children, which housed also the lower grades, and four colored schools, three of them shining with recently sawed lumber not yet painted. At each school some citizen told the story of ''How we built this schoolhouse,'' and it was easy to see that it was ''the struggle for education which had educated.''

No hard-luck appeal, but a very sturdy pride in achievement, shone in the eyes of the three colored men who spoke for their respective communities. Their simple statements that ''some folks just gave a lemon or a pound of sugar,'' ''the women helped put on the laths, " and "we're going to put the roof on this porch just as soon as we can and then we're going to paint the schoolhouse too, " were in no way artful ; they were merely facts for "white folks " who were showing a gratifying curiosity and interest.

The schoolhouses which the initiative of the people has produced and the teachers whom they have helped to hire will educate the minds of the children, and their hands along with their minds. In these days of "the rural school for the community, " this education of minds and hands will extend to the parents, who had fewer advantages. But it is the work these parents have done to get the shining schoolhouses, and the teachers who can teach communities, which has educated and will continue to educate their characters and their hearts—which has given them increased self-respect, judgment, ambition, and a larger social sympathy, and which has fired the spirit of progress among their people.

It was not only the demonstration of the fact that "the struggle for education educates " which was significant on that April afternoon. Successful struggle brings self-respect, which is valuable, and, in addition, the respect of others, which is powerful. When the highest official of the proudest Southern state travels many dusty miles to hear colored men tell how they built a two-room schoolhouse, it is a sign that encouragement and approbation, the most potent aids in any undertaking, will be measured out increasingly to the Negro race, as it continues to prove, by the spirit shining through its progress, that it is both worthy and appreciative of these gifts.

"High aims and Perseverance" An interesting ceremony took place in Hawaii on April 18 when fifty children, descendants of the first missionaries to that country, invaded Fort Armstrong and planted each a cocoanut tree. Fort Armstrong, which was named for General S. C. Armstrong, is a signal fort standing at the entrance to Honolulu harbor. The first tree was planted by a grandniece of the founder of Hampton Institute.

The General's favorite tree was the cocoanut, indigenous to his native island of Maui, Hawaii. "The cocoanut," he was wont to say, "stands for high aims and perseverance ; you work hard to get one and when' you get it, it tastes good. You feel that you have earned it. If I had a coat of arms, I'd have a cocoanut for a crest. " Its milk he called "distilled Pacific Ocean " and was never happier than when drinking it. A distinguished educator, hearing of General Armstrong's fondness for this fruit, said ; "Armstrong did not believe, however, in bestowing the cocoanut on a man who had not climbed the tree for it. He did not try to thrust an advanced civilization on a people that had not struggled to obtain it. "

▒

**Keeping Negro
Children in
the Country** Forty-odd social service "pilgrims "— Northerners and Southerners, black men and white men, all friends of Hampton Institute and the Hampton idea of education—recently visited three of the one-room Negro schools lying in Elizabeth City County in which the Hampton School is located.

What they saw was encouraging and may interest those who wish to keep on the land the country boys and girls, colored as well as white, by making the rural schools physically more attractive, educationally more interesting, and socially more useful.

The Negro school problem in Elizabeth City County may be briefly summarized as follows : There are 8 colored rural schools—one a seven-room school with 250 alert and promising children in daily attendance ; 2 two-room schools; and 5 one-room schools with an enrollment of from 25 to 70 pupils each and an average daily attendance of from 15 to 50. There are 17 teachers and all except 4 are Hampton graduates. The average school term is 7 months, from October to May.

The census of 1910 shows that the population of Elizabeth City County was 21,225 ; the population per square mile was 393 and the rural population per square mile 291 ; the number of whites 13,227 ; Negroes 7992, or 37.7 per cent.

These facts show that Elizabeth City County, like so many other counties of the South, has a distinct Negro rural-school problem to solve. What is being done to make the Negro schools in the region about Hampton Institute meet some of the community needs?

Mrs. Estelle M. Evans, a graduate of Hampton, has been making weekly visits for the past three years to the colored schools of Elizabeth City County to help the local teachers in the work of giving interesting lessons in sewing, cooking, basketry, chair-caning, corn-shuck mat making, weaving, and manual training. She has linked the schools to their communities.

Mrs. Evans, as a supervising teacher, has been carrying Hampton ideas of education to her own people. She has succeeded in winning the co-operation and good will of the rural teachers and the parents of the children. School-improvement leagues supported by the patrons have been doing excellent work. They have raised money to paint and whitewash school buildings and outhouses, have bought cooking utensils, and have co-operated with the teachers. Through sales and entertainments the parents have been brought into closer touch with the teachers and the problems of the classroom.

Those who recently visited Elizabeth City County colored schools saw evidences of school progress in the attractive exhibits consisting of well-made dresses, aprons, and underwear, attractive jars of canned vegetables and fruits, useful baskets of raffia and white-oak, fresh garden vegetables, and neat papers in arithmetic, spelling, and composition. Clean floors, well-made window curtains, soft green shades, ventilation boards, attractive pictures, and, above all, neat and happy children,—these are signs of progress in Negro education.

From the Hampton party's hearty words of endorsement it was clear that the so-called school-demonstration work, which is being carried on through the co-operation of the Virginia State Department of Education, the Jeanes Fund, Hampton Institute, and the local boards, appeals to the good judgment of men and women who wish to help people help themselves. What Elizabeth City County is doing to keep Negro children in the country, by making country schools more attractive and useful, is being carried on in at least one hundred nineteen other counties of the South. The movement is spreading rapidly. Men and women of vision see in it the solution of many of the perplexing problems which center in America's country-life development.

Hampton Afloat and Afield   For a hundred days in eleven states nineteen Negro and Indian students and graduates of Hampton, with officers of the school, will make a continuous campaign for funds.

Upon the little, eighty-five-foot schooner *Hampton* the chorus will set sail the last week in May upon the long voyage from Hampton Roads, Virginia, to Bar Harbor, Maine.

The camp of brown khaki tents which stood upon the lawns of Newport, Bar Harbor, and the North Shore and was carried to the resorts of seven states during the summer of 1912 will be taken ashore from the *Hampton* for campaigns into the White Mountains, the Adirondacks, and the Berkshire Hills.

The successful campaign of thirty students and officers of Hampton two summers ago was no junketing party. With a schedule of sixty meetings, and the necessity for speed of travel, with the need of continuous work for a hundred days upon sea and land, the little company on this summer's crusade has no light task.

To be crew, cast, and chorus ; to sing, to march, to sleep in the crowded forecastle ; to give the best of their peoples' songs and customs to strangers ; to try to gain new scholarships for new boys at Hampton—this is the gift of these fourteen colored boys and five Indians to their school.

The first landing of the crew will be made in Baltimore, where they will hold pageant on the grounds of the Gilman Country School the first Thursday in June. Sailing north through Maryland and Delaware, the chorus will sing in Wilmington at the first week-end of June. Philadelphia will welcome Hampton the following week with several church·meetings and an ideal site for the pageant upon the lawns of Haverford College. An overland journey to Orange while the crew round Cape May on the *Hampton*, and meetings at Orange, Elberon, and Asbury Park will end the second week in June.

At the home of Miss Grace Dodge at Riverdale, on the estate of Mrs. Wm. G. Wilcox on Staten Island, and at other handsome suburban estates near New York the chorus will sing and hold pageant until the last week of June, when it will travel to the Litchfield Hills.

July will find the *Hampton* sailing from New London to the far end of Long Island. Daily meetings from New Bedford to Norwich will carry the schooner "down Cape Cod" by July 20.

Meetings on the North Shore, at Bar Harbor, and on the Maine Coast are scheduled for the last days of July and the first week of August, after which a ten-day "hike" into the White Mountains will carry the camp and chorus inland as the schooner sails down the coast.

Newport, Narragansett, Long Island, and Mohonk at the height of the season through the last days of August, followed by a final dash into the Adirondacks and Berkshires, and pageants along the shores of the Hudson, will end the long summer crusade.

By sending out the best plantation chorus in America this summer, by giving the best of the Negro's music and folklore and the beautiful tribal dances and ceremonial chants of the Indian, the workers and students of Hampton hope to gain new friends and aid for their school and a better understanding of the two races for which it is carried on.

A National Hampton Association

On Friday morning, April 24, there was held in the Museum at Hampton Institute, a meeting of representatives of all existing Hampton organizations, for the purpose of forming a National Hampton Association, which should have the following objects :

"(1) To stimulate public interest throughout the country in the education and welfare of the Negro and Indian races, and especially in the work and influence of the Hampton Normal and Agricultural Institute at Hampton, Virginia, and to raise money for the same.

"(2) To open an office in New York at No. 1 Madison Avenue as a clearing house for all existing clubs or associations formed in the interest of Hampton, and to organize new clubs in sections of the country not now covered."

The idea of such an organization was launched in April 1913, during the special Hampton trip. A committee was then appointed to formulate plans and report at the meeting in 1914.

There were present at this year's meeting thirty-two persons, representing the Massachusetts, Brooklyn, New York, Philadelphia, Boston, and Springfield organizations. Reports from these societies showed encouraging work done during the past year. By-laws were adopted. A member of the Hampton staff will keep the New York Office in touch with the work at the Institute. The following officers were elected for the ensuing year : Mr. Alexander B. Trowbridge, Brooklyn, president ; Dr. H. B. Frissell, Hampton, first vice president; Dr. Charles J. Hatfield, Philadelphia, second vice president ; Mr. Harold Peabody, Boston, treasurer and recording secretary.

The above officers, *ex-officio*, and the following six persons were chosen members of the Executive Committee: Miss Gertrude Ely, Philadelphia; Mrs. W. B. Medlicott, Springfield; Mrs. Gilbert Colgate, New York; Miss A. P. Tapley, Boston; Dr. Wm. Jay Schieffelin, New York; Mrs. Charles J. Ide, Brooklyn.

Mr. Elbridge L. Adams, chairman of the executive committee of the Hampton Association of New York City, was unanimously elected executive secretary in charge of the New York Office and the organizing of new clubs throughout the country. All present were enthusiastic about the new Association and were confident that much will be accomplished by the executive secretary, who volunteers for this work out of his keen interest in and love for Hampton.

(Signed)   HAROLD PEABODY, Recording Secretary

The Hampton Alumni Triennial

Alumni of Hampton, attention ! On July 15 the twelfth triennial reunion will be held. Two or three hundred members are expected. The Association has been working very hard to raise money for a second endowed scholarship—$2500.

After the registration and the transaction of business, the alumni will have an outing—probably at Bay Shore Hotel, Buckroe Beach. Addresses from alumni members and Hampton officers will bring together in the spirit of good fellowship the men and women who are proud of their Hampton connection.

Write at once and tell Captain Washington that you plan to attend the triennial reunion. The treasurer, Mr. George J. Davis, will also be glad to receive your subscription or pledge to the scholarship fund.

THE MEXICAN SITUATION*

BY WILLIAM HOWARD TAFT

President of the Board of Trustees of Hampton Institute

WE are a great people. We admit it and therefore we don't have to prove it. The Lord has been very good to us. We have a great stretch of land, fertile and full of wealth. All the peoples of the world have contributed to the making of our people. We have had an enormous material expansion. We have worked vigorously on the problem of educating our people, and I believe them to be educated up to as high a standard as any in the world. We are a powerful people. When our energy is concentrated, with the resources we have at hand there isn't anything within our sight that we do not seem to be able to accomplish, if we unite together and make the effort we are capable of making. We are a young people, with all the energy and imagination of a young people.

The great resources and power we have, have thrust upon us responsibilities. The peoples of the world are growing closer together. There has been a great spread of the fraternal spirit. People today, and especially those who have made progress in civilization and education, are more interested than ever before in other peoples of the world. We become, therefore, more neighborly. We feel greater responsibility with reference to other nations, and while we have not constituted ourselves knights-errant to go about the world relieving political suffering and political anarchy, yet when Providence has thrust people and their woes upon us, we have not hesitated to take up the- burden and to help them. But we have always gone in for the purpose of helping. That is what we did in the Cuban war. We began that war to help the Cubans, but you never can tell where war will bring you out. We went into Santiago de Cuba, and we soon found ourselves ten thousand miles away in the Philippines, and we found there a people that needed our aid. But before we were able to render them any aid at all we had to restrain them by force. We learned to know, in doing such work, that if we are looking for the gratitude of a people as our chief reward, we had better go out of the business of philanthropic government.

Now, I have been hoping that we should not have thrust upon us the same burden with respect to the Mexican people. The

* An informal talk to Hampton students on April 23, 1914

Cuban war we went into because the conditions there had made Cuba an international nuisance at our door, and it was our duty, therefore, to go in and try to help that country to a better condition. We got the Philippine trouble in the same way.

Mexico for fifteen years under President Diaz seemed to be prosperous, and in a way it was. But in that fifteen years the government of that great country made an egregious error. It did not give any attention to the education of the people of Mexico or the improvement of social conditions. The condition of great ownership of land and concentration of wealth in a few people, peonage, and the absence of education continued until a younger generation arose and began to agitate against the tyranny of Diaz. They received promises from those who took up arms against Diaz that reforms were to be brought about, that lands would be divided, and that there would be a general millenium, if they were only given power. Such promises are not confined to Mexican politicians. It was as far from the truth in Mexico as it is in some other countries.

When Madero succeeded to the presidency, on the yielding of Diaz and the turning over of the government, he failed. His capacity for execution was not equal to his imagination and promises. He was overturned by Huerta and then he was killed, under circumstances that are not fully known. Then they had, as in the earlier history of Mexico, a regular succession of revolutions, and it has been going on ever since. The interests of the people have been injured. Foreign interests have been sacrificed. Lives of foreigners have been taken without due process of law, and a condition of anarchy has prevailed in the northern provinces, where Villa and Carranza have been asserting their purpose to establish a constitutional government with nothing to indicate that they know what that is, and a good deal of disturbance even in the south where the federals have been in control.

Now, in view of the disregard of international courtesy at Tampico and a salute of the flag as apology, we have finally come into hostile relations with the federal government carried on by General Huerta as provisional president.

If the flag incident were the only reason for our intervention, it might, in view of General Huerta's apology, seem very insufficient ground upon which to bring about war—if war is to follow. Some have hoped that this present movement may end with the seizure of the two ports, Tampico and Vera Cruz, and that it may not be necessary for us to proceed further. Those of us who know the kind of war that is to follow, if there is war, pray that this may be true.

We are in the face of a great crisis, and there is not any

reason why we should be blind as to the strong probability of war before us. It is on that subject I should like to give you a few of the inferences I draw from our previous experiences.

The technical reason for taking this course in seizing Vera Cruz and Tampico is the seizure of our men in Tampico and their subsequent release with an inadequate ceremonial expression of regret; but the real reason for the war, if it follows, as I hope it may not, must, in history and in justice to the American people, rest upon the seemingly hopeless condition that Mexico is in, and the obligation we have put upon ourselves to act in a neighborly way. I speak from an international standpoint.

Perhaps you will not think it neighborly when I tell you what is likely to happen. In an international way and in a historical sense, we have nearly reached the point where our position, in respect to this continent and also Europe, is that we assume the responsibility for peace in Mexico. For certainly Mexico has become a nuisance, from an international standpoint. If we engage in war, our only justification must be our neighborly obligation to go in and tranquilize the country.

I observe from this morning's dispatches that the moment we commit an act of hostility in Mexico, all parties there, however anxious they are to kill each other, will object to our coming. They do not wish to be interfered with in that killing by a neighbor. Therefore, it is not unreasonable to expect that ultimately we shall find a general feeling of active hostility to us on the part of our Mexican neighbors, when we go in and try to tranquilize them for their own good. That is what we found in the Philippines. We found a country in a state of anarchy, quite as it is in Mexico today. It was easy enough to subdue any organized forces of the so-called Philippine insurrectos. It took but a short campaign to disperse the armies of any size, and then the Filipinos conducted a warfare in which they are adepts, and which any people, partially civilized, can maintain for a long time and by which they present great difficulties to the tranquilizing of their country, especially where that country is tropical.

In a tropical country, the chief feature of the people is not energy in manual labor, but in Mexico, as in the Philippines, they take to guerilla warfare as we do to a picnic in this country. The country offers retreats in mountains, in forests, and on trackless deserts, from which they are able to visit the towns for food and to which they can retire again. To these places it is almost impossible for a military force to follow them. There were in the Island of Luzon perhaps three million and a half of people. In the whole of the Philippines there some eight million. In Mexico there are fifteen million. In order to bring about tranquillity in the Philippines it took an army of 75,000 at 600 different posts, so that the posts were generally in charge of officers of no higher rank than captain. Many were commanded by a first or second lieutenant and some even by a sergeant.

This was after the organized military forces had been dispersed. If we go to war with Mexico we shall see this same thing happen. Our army will be formidable enough to drive the Mexicans out of the large cities and the towns, and then will happen just what happened in the Philippines. There were little knots of insurrectos in the Philippines planted around every town. In Manila they waited on the tables of the large hotels in the day time and went out, got their rifles, and fired into the town at night. They were "amigos" in the daytime—"heroes" at night.

We shall probably have to have a garrison in every town in Mexico of any size at all. Then we shall have to teach our soldiers to hike. Do you know what hiking is ? You never tried it in any country like Mexico and the Philippines. You never hiked it in the Philippines through the rice paddies into the jungles, into the mountains with no trail. You never hiked it over a trackless desert like those in Mexico, where the sand is hot beyond expression and where the hot powdered sand blows and almost suffocates you. American soldiers will have to be trained to chase the Mexican over those plains and chase so him effectively that he can catch him, too.

It took us about three years in the Philippines to train our men for the work there. I am not attempting to discourage you from enlisting. On the contrary, if your country needs you, I am going to urge you to enlist. It is easy enough to enlist when you have great enthusiasm around you, when you don't see anything but the gold lace and hear good music. But what you must do, if your country requires it—and it has a right to exact it of you—is that you enlist with your jaws set fast ; with your eyes stern with the knowledge that you are going to encounter, not alone bullets, but, in great probability, loss of life or health from the diseases of a tropical country. You ought to go in with a knowledge of what you are undertaking. Do not go into it lightly like going to a ball. This is real soldier work, but without conspicuous glory and newspaper headline reward. It is the kind that tests character, the kind that brings out all there is in a man, that shows that he is a man.

It is possible, and I certainly hope that it is true, that my prognostications as to the extent of this campaign may not be well founded. But if we are going to enter upon this task, we ought to look at it from every side of it. If you feel called upon to respond to your country's call, you must realize what you are doing.

The young women to whom I am addressing my remarks may be equally tested, for the work of nursing is a most important work in the wake of the army. And the sacrifices women nurses have to make are very little less than those of the men who are expected to bear arms and fight the battles.

If, as I said, we go into this country and find a whole people hostile to us, it has been estimated to me by one who should be able to judge, that it would take four hundred thousand men and a million a day to carry us through the war. That means a great burden for this country to assume. But if we are called upon to do it and are in for it we can meet the test. We must assume the burden and show that our prosperity and success have come to men and women worthy to have them.

But our duty will not be ended when we have tranquilized the country. This country is not moved by a desire to acquire additional territory. We have enough responsibility with the territory we have, without seeking this additional burden. But when we have brought Mexico to a state of law and order through military compulsion, then we may have to train and organize them so they can govern themselves. And that is a more difficult thing than the military part of it will be. But we are equal to it.

The loss to be sustained in lives will seem certainly too great a sacrifice to those who are the immediate relatives of the dead and wounded—the mothers, fathers, brothers, and sisters. When nations act, however, this is essential and must be met. That is why war is so terrible.

We must be loyal first, be Americans all, and when duty is upon us we must be brave and meet it. No matter what the past may be, or how much we may criticise the policies that brought us to this point, no matter how much we risk, the people of the United States must do their duty. In the judgment of history, I believe we shall show ourselves to be, not only a patriotic people, but a people who are willing, when circumstances require it, to lend their aid to the promoting of law and order and to the progress of Christian civilization.

THE PLAINS CREE

BY ALANSON B. SKINNER

Assistant Curator in the American Museum of Natural History

OF all North American tribes the Cree Indians probably cover the greatest extent of territory. Their range runs, roughly, from the interior of Labrador to the foothills of the Rockies, and from two or three days' journey north of Lake Superior to a line drawn across the continent cutting the southern shore of Hudson Bay. Of course this is only an approximation of their domain, for they are found northward far up the Athabaska, southward in Montana and North Dakota, and their western range is cut into by the Assiniboine and Blackfeet.

Roughly speaking again, the Cree may be divided into two bodies, comprising the Forest or Wood Cree, and the Plains Cree. The former occupy the timbered portions of the country to the north and east; the latter dwell on the prairies of Manitoba, Saskatchewan, and Alberta.

The Wood Cree are people of rather simple life, who live in bark wigwams, manufacture birch canoes to travel on the water highways of the forest, and eke out a precarious existence by trapping and trading fur. The Plains Cree, on the other hand, were formerly a rather formidable body of mounted warriors, nomadic beyond all other tribes of the plains, subsisting upon the buffalo, and far more independent of the traders than their woodland brethren.

During last summer, the writer, who has already spent several summers among the Wood Cree on the shores of Hudson Bay, had an opportunity to visit several bands of Plains Cree in Saskatchewan in order to learn something of their ethnology.

Unable to subsist upon the buffalo, deprived of all their ancient means of livelihood, the Cree are now largely resident upon reservations, where they are supported by rations supplied by the Government, and the proceeds of such desultory work as it suits their wayward nature to perform.

To a certain extent they keep up the ancient religion and practices of their forefathers, but they are subservient to the white authorities ; and the Sun Dance, once the great Cree sacred ceremony, is a thing of the past. Most of them now reside in one-story log cabins, but every family has its huge painted teepee in which they live in summer, while wandering from

one place to another or digging Seneca root for the market.
The old-style blanket costume is frequently worn by the old men,
no matter how great the heat, but the younger set dress fully in
white man's garb, although most of them wear their hair long.

In many respects the Plains Cree have been strongly influenced by the Saulteaux and the Assiniboine, and many of their
customs and utensils seem to be connected with the Blackfeet.

PLAINS CREE YOUTH IN INDIAN COSTUME

Like the Plains Ojibway or Saulteaux, the Cree employ the
impounding method of taking buffalo, but their ceremonies concerning the erection of the medicine pole in the center of the
pound and the calling of the game are more elaborate. Like the
Ojibway, they have a series of war counts or coups by which
a warrior may become an *okitcita*, or brave, and the Sun Dance
is of great importance in their religious life.

Among all their neighbors the Cree have acquired a marvelous reputation as makers of charms. In fact "Cree medicine,"

for use in love, war, hunting, gambling, or any of the usual pursuits of Indian life, commands a high price throughout all the tribes with which they come in contact. The love medicines are generally considered the most potent and are eagerly sought after. One of the most famous of these consists of two tiny dolls, male and female, between which is placed some red medicine powder, with a hair, a finger-nail paring, or even a bit of the garment of the person desired. The dolls are then named after the persons involved and wrapped tightly together. Then the two people in question must perforce fall in love with each other. This is particularly the case when one has flouted or despised the other. The neighboring tribes make similar medicines themselves, but none are thought to be so efficacious.

The Cree have intermarried to a very great extent with the whites, particularly with the French, and this admixture has contributed to their culture. They possess a number of traits which can be traced to a European source, and this is particularly true of their folklore, where many Old-World stories have crept in. Thus the writer obtained the story of Cinderella, scarcely disguised at all. Due perhaps to this crossing of the races and to their long contact with the white traders, the Cree are among the most docile and amenable of Indians to paleface institutions. The Plains Ojibway are less easily converted to the white man's path, yet perhaps for this very reason the Ojibway seem to have more stamina.

One of the most important of Plains Cree ceremonies, yet one which ranks as decidedly inferior to the Sun Dance in their

FRAME OF THE LAST CREE SUN-DANCE LODGE

THE LODGE OF "GOD'S CHILD"

Note the Thunderbird in human form, his dream-guardian, painted on the tepee.

estimation, is "Smoking to the Great Spirit." We were told that such a ceremony was to be held on a certain night, and we were invited to be present. Accordingly, when the designated time arrived, we set out with a youth who served as interpreter, and drove many miles out over the prairies to the ceremonial ground.

Just as the sun was setting to the westward beyond the distant Qu'Appelle, we topped a little knoll, and saw pitched before us, in a huge circle, the painted tepees of the Cree. Women were cooking before the lodges or trudging back and forth with water from a little lakelet. Horses, with tinkling bells or bits of red flannel tied around their necks to ward off demons, were cropping the flower-spangled prairie, or straying to more alluring clusters of grass as fast as their hobbles would permit them. Groups of young men, in number from two or three to a score, lay idly on the grass, smoking or telling stories; the older men, full clad in blanket suits, were rambling about. In short, the sight was one which must have been common on those prairies from time immemorial, the only changes being that the tents were of cotton duck and not of buffalo hide, that the young men, though they wore their hair long and still clung to moccasins, were dressed in "store clothes," and that there were no armed braves watching for a Sioux or Blood attack.

We joined one of the groups of sluggards, and lying full length on the prairie, listened to their musical flow of Algonkin until the twilight began to dim. Just at dusk, a man, wrapped in a scarlet blanket and bearing a long, red-stone pipe in his arms, and followed by three youths whose arms were stretched

A PLAINS CREE'S OFFERING TO HIS DREAM-GUARDIAN

skyward, began to make the circuit of the camp. Four times he
went the rounds, and all the time he and his followers wailed
incessantly, "Aiiii-uh! Aiiii-uh! Aiiii-uh! Aiiii-uh!" Then they
disappeared under the cover of a great painted lodge that stood
in the center of the camp. Immediately afterwards, a naked
man, half-wrapped in a blanket, came out and began shouting in a
singsong voice an invitation to enter the lodge. So one by one
we got up, and went into the lodge, crawling under the back flap.

Inside, the lodge was festooned with offerings to be sacrificed
on the morrow. Blankets, rolls of scarlet broadcloth, food, garments, beadwork gifts, were suspended from the lodge poles and
piled on the floor. A circular altar, on which a fire burned, was
cut in the sod in the center of the floor and attended by four boys,
one at each point of the compass, who also kept incense of sweet-
grass constantly smouldering. The host, or master of ceremonies,
was naked; his body was covered with white-clay paint, and his
lank black hair dripped over his shoulders. He sat hunched up,
with his hand over his eyes, and only looked up to assign the
incoming guests to their places.

When all had gathered and the men had fully occupied one side of the lodge and the women the other, the host made a speech, telling us why he was giving the ceremony. When he had finished, food and tea were passed about to all of us.

When we had feasted, the host rose once more and made a circuit of the lodge, seizing a pole in each hand and praying, with many sobs and lamentations. Then he returned to his place, consecrated four stone pipes in the smoke of the incense, passed them, and then did the same with four rawhide rattles, which he likewise passed from left to right.

With the passing of the rattles the real ceremony commenced. One after another, in groups of four, the old men began to sing to the Great Spirit. They sang in strangling voices, choked with tears ; and the drops ran down their cheeks and spattered on their knees as they sat bent over. They sang of the long-ago, of the buffalo days "when everyone had enough to eat." They sang of the Sun Dance and the Medicine Lodge and their significance to the Indian. They sang of the passing of the years, the coming of the white man, of poverty, of hunger, and of despair. They sang begging mercy of the Great Spirit, praying for better days to come, and as they chanted to the monotonous swish of the rattles, the sun that had dipped down beyond the Qu'Appelle on the west, peeped up again far to the east, and the ceremony ended.

The last thing we saw, as we retired to a painted lodge to sleep, was the old men carrying out the offerings to be sacrificed to the Great Spirit by leaving them to rot on the prairie.

ROUND-HOUSE MISSION, QU'APPELLE RIVER, SASKATCHEWAN

THE NEGRO ALLEYS OF WASHINGTON*

BY EDITH ELMER WOOD

The Alley Bill was introduced about the middle of February in both Houses of Congress by the chairmen of the Committees on the District of Columbia. The Housing Loan Bill, which was introduced in the House of Representatives by Mr. Borland some months ago, was introduced in the Senate early in March by Senator Pomerene of Ohio. The press of Washington is united in hearty support of both bills. The Alley Bill has had two public hearings before the District Committee of the House of Representatives. Many distinguished citizens, including Commissioner Siddons, appeared in its behalf. The unanimity of public sentiment behind the bill is shown by the fact that only one person appeared in opposition to it, and he assured the committee that he was in full sympathy with its purpose and was only criticising the mechanism by which that purpose was to be obtained.

The Housing Loan Bill has also had two hearings, and the two bills had a joint hearing before the Senate Committee early in May, but neither bill has as yet been reported. The Housing Bill has been endorsed by a number of organizations, including several religious, civic, and philanthropic associations of Negroes. E. E. W.

IN 1909 there were over 15,000 people, of whom more than 13,500 were colored, living in the interior courts or alleys of Washington. This was approximately one-seventh of the total colored population. Since then the number has decreased both absolutely and relatively, partly through the condemnation of unsanitary houses and partly through the strong desire of the better class of alley residents to move onto the streets. This, in its turn, is due to the publicity that has been given the bad

---

* Three of the pictures illustrating this article have previously appeared in the *Survey*.

sanitary and moral conditions in the alleys. But the number of Negroes living in alleys is still more than 10,000, which is a little over one-tenth of the total for the city.

These inhabited alleys were not desired or foreseen by the founders of Washington. They came into use under the pressure of an emergency, and their danger was not realized until it was too late. Major L'Enfant, the French engineer who drew the plans of the projected city under the supervision of General Washington, made the lots deep so that every house might have an abundance of light and air, and tree and garden space. As the city grew, it became increasingly burdensome for people of moderate means to pay taxes on so much unproductive land. Finally, during the Civil War, simultaneously with the straightened resources of many families, came an influx of ex-slaves and refugees who had to be housed at once and could pay little or nothing for their shelter. Servants' quarters in back yards were pressed into service. Stables were converted into dwellings. Long wooden barracks intended merely for temporary relief were put up in those back-lot spaces, and some of them, patched and repatched, are doing duty as human habitations to this day. Gradually charity was replaced by business. The renting of these wretched makeshifts was found to be profitable. Rows of shoddy little brick or frame houses were put up facing on the alleys. More and more people were reaping disproportionate gains from this type of investment. And the evil was now fully entrenched.

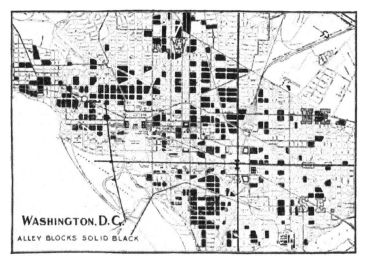

WASHINGTON, D. C.
ALLEY BLOCKS SOLID BLACK

THERE ARE IN WASHINGTON 258 BLOCKS WHICH HAVE INHABITED ALLEYS. THESE ALLEYS CONTAIN 3148 DWELLING HOUSES AND APPROXIMATELY 16,000 INHABITANTS.

In those days the alleys were unlighted, unpaved, and unconnected with water or sewer mains, so that the condition of the people living there was deplorable. This was soon recognized by physicians and others, and the fight against the alleys began (about 1872). Considerable progress was made for a few years, many of the worst shacks being condemned and torn down, but in 1878 the selfish interests got control and advance was checked. The eighties were a time of reaction and discouragement. Then matters took a turn for the better. Citizens awoke to their responsibilities. Careful investigations were made. A law was passed prohibiting any further erection of dwellings in alleys (1892). A law was passed (1906) providing for the condemnation of unsanitary buildings, under which 628 alley houses have so far been torn down and 376 repaired. A law was passed permitting the Commissioners to condemn unsanitary alleys and cut through minor streets, but the operation of this law has proved a great disappointment, owing to legal difficulties. President Roosevelt appointed the Homes Commission to investigate living conditions in the District of Columbia and make recommendations. Its report in 1908 found sanitary conditions in the alleys very bad and profits very high. It advised doing away with the inhabited alleys as soon as possible and loaning Government money under proper restrictions at a low rate of interest to such non-commercial building associations as would put up sanitary modern homes for working people at a moderate rental. Nothing,

WHERE SENATORS' CLOTHES ARE DRIED

A LIMITED NURSERY

These children are left alone all day in one room and this porch while their mother is at work.

however, was done at the time toward carrying out these recommendations.

The living conditions in the Washington alleys are, fortunately, not so bad as they used to be. The worst houses have been condemned, pavements and street lamps have been introduced, and each house has its hydrant in the back yard and a shed toilet connected with the sewers. Ashes and garbage are collected ; street cleaners come around once a week; inspectors from the health departments insist on a fair standard of repairs in roofs and drainage. City physicians and visiting nurses minister to the sick. District visitors from the Associated Charities relieve the worst cases of want. Most of the children go to school. The educated colored people of Washington have not been unmindful of their responsibilities. The Colored Social Settlement, which was founded in 1902 "for the improvement of social conditions in South Washington," is doing good work through a pure-milk station, medical clinic, boys', girls', and women's clubs, and classes in cooking, sewing, and gardening. The Alley Improvement Association conducts a day nursery and summer vacation school and has for years been holding nonsectarian religious services every Sunday in various alley homes.

Progress has, therefore, touched the alleys. But the conditions are still intolerable. The death rate on the streets of Washington in 1912 was 17.32 per thousand of population. In the alleys it was 28.52. Doesn't that tell the whole story in a nutshell ? In certain individual alleys it is higher. In four which the writer investigated last year, containing 540 inhabitants (Fenton, Madison, Essex, and Naylor), it was 51.85. In the worst of these (Madison) it was 78. Tuberculosis is a veritable scourge. Infant mortality is another. One baby of every three born in the alleys has been dying within the twelvemonth. Thanks to an energetic summer campaign, this proportion was reduced last year to one in four, but that is still a very bad showing. The tuberculosis death rate in the four alleys mentioned is three times as high as that for colored persons living on the streets of Washington (which is itself extremely high), and is about the same as the general death rate from all causes in Chicago or Kansas City. Some houses are so infected with tubercle bacilli that nothing short of total annihilation would render them safe.

What sort of people make up the alley population ? There are a few of the criminal and vicious class, of course, but they form a very small percentage, which attracts more than its share of attention. There is a much larger number of the shiftless and intemperate, who make themselves unpleasantly conspicuous and figure largely in the records of the police courts. But the largest number of all is simply unfortunate. There are widows and deserted wives by the hundreds struggling to keep their families together, old people who can no longer work as they used to do, people with all sorts of physical handicaps, the halt, lame, and blind. A few thrifty families who could afford to live elsewhere remain in the alleys to save money. A mother said to me, "We are saving money to buy a home. My husband can't think of anything else. But while we are doing it, our children are being ruined. "

It is obviously far harder for a mother to keep her children from bad associates in the forced intimacy of an alley community, hidden away in the interior of a block, than it would be on the street. The seclusion of the alley forms one of its greatest moral dangers. All sorts of disorderly conduct can go on unseen by the police or the general public which would not be tolerated a moment on the streets. And the respectable people in the alleys are too much afraid of their disreputable neighbors to complain of them. I know one good woman, a widow, who keeps herself and her house as neat as the traditional pin, who has worked hard to bring her boy up well and has succeeded. A very objectional group of people (not a family) has recently moved into the adjoining house, which has become a rendezvous for all the idle and vicious men and boys of the neighborhood. Liquor is drunk and probably sold on the premises, noisy quarrels and equally noisy merrymaking go on every night and all day Sunday, and the flimsy partitions transmit every sound. "He is a good boy, " she says of her son, "and he works hard and has been brought up to be straight and sober. But he is only seventeen. And how can he hear all that vile talk and profanity day after day and not be hurt by it?" Yet she will not complain to the police or be quoted to them, and if called as a witness, would probably say she knew nothing wrong about her neighbors.

Another fear besides that of physical vengeance from disreputable neighbors hampers the alley resident's efforts to better conditions. If he reports needed repairs to the health department

THE
BLIND ALLEY OF WASHINGTON,D.C.
SECLUSION BREEDING CRIME AND DISEASE
to kill the alley inmates and infect the street residents.

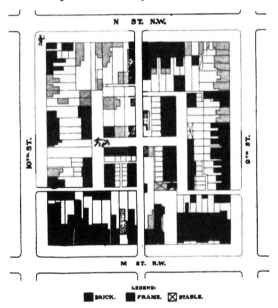

LEGEND:
■ BRICK.   ■ FRAME.   ⊠ STABLE.

or allows others to do it for him, he is liable to receive notice to move. The writer was the unwilling instrument in one such case, and it taught her a lesson. There was a row of five houses in very bad repair—roof and gutters leaky, plaster and woodwork atrocious. All were in approximately the same state, and the tenants, who seemed to be in abject terror of the agent, all agreed as to his disobligingness and the long time since any repairs had been made. But one family, who said they had lived in the house eight years and that nothing had been done in the way of repairs since or when they moved in, offered special

MADISON ALLEY

facilities to the visitor to see every part of the house, so
the report described that house in detail, including the others
only in a general way. The health department acted, the repairs
have been made, the neighbors express a sudden and suspicious
enthusiasm about that agent, but the house of the "informers"
stands vacant.

Most of the houses in the alleys contain four rooms and are
occupied ostensibly by one or, at most, two families. But the custom of taking lodgers is widespread and has a bad influence on

ALLEY LIFE IS NOT UNDULY STRENUOUS

family life.   There are very few tenements, but they are particularly bad ones.   Often a single room is occupied by a whole
family, and many of these families have five or six members,
or even more.   A cook stove, a bed, a table, a washtub, and a
couple of rickety chairs fill the room so full that one wonders, not
only how cooking and eating and laundry work go on, but how
they find even floor space to sleep on at night.   It seems superfluous
to say that children cannot be brought up to be good citizens
under such conditions—that health, morality, and self-respect
must suffer.   Yet some of these people are making gallant
fights.   I know one woman, handicapped by almost total deaf-

THE RISING GENERATION IN A WASHINGTON ALLEY

ness and the fact that her husband is serving a prison sentence,
who lives with her four children in one damp basement room and
keeps the children neat and clean and at school by washing and
ironing.   The neighbors speak well of her and of the children, and
she does it all herself, neither asking nor desiring assistance.

Last spring there was a sudden revival of interest in alley
conditions and of hope in the nearness of relief.   Many things
helped to bring this about; nothing more, perhaps, than the sympathy shown by the wife of the President.   Mrs. Wilson went
through the alleys and saw the conditions there for herself.
Then she loaned the White House automobiles to take Congress-
men and Senators on alley tours.   Finally, she attended the
various meetings which led to the formation of the Committee of

Fifty and then the meetings of that Committee.   Mr. Bryan said, on coming to one of those reunions on a hot June night, that he would not have been there except that he was ashamed to stay away when he knew Mrs. Wilson was going—and he was by no means the only one.

Out of the labors of this Committee (through a small sub-committee which worked devotedly all summer) grew the Alley Elimination Bill, which has received the endorsement of the Dis-trict Commissioners and the approval of President Wilson, and is being introduced simultaneously in House and Senate by the chairmen of the District Committees.   It provides that ten years after the passage of the act there shall be no more inhabited alleys in Washington.   In some cases streets are to be cut through to take the place of the narrow, tortuous alleys.   In oth-ers, the houses are simply to be closed for dwelling purposes. They can be used for warehouses or garages, but never again to shelter men and women.   Let us hope that no obstacle will be able to stay the passage of this long-awaited, sorely-needed law !

But some of us feel that the elimination of the alleys is only half the problem and that no solution is satisfactory which does not also provide modern sanitary homes for the inhabitants of the alleys who are to be turned out of the only homes they know. A bill to provide for this through a Government loan to non-com-mercial building associations (as was recommended by the Presi-dent's Homes Commission) has been introduced in the House of Representatives by Mr. Borland of Missouri.   It is a plan which has been successfully tried out on a large scale in England and Germany for the past quarter of a century, and more recently by a number of other countries, but it is new in the United States.

The Alley Bill will probably become law.   The Housing Loan Bill may.

Note :—The maps used in this article are loaned by the Housing Committee of the Monday Evening Club of Washington, which, under the direction of its chairman, Dr. Thomas Jesse Jones, has made an exhaustive study of alley conditions.

THE PALACE OF THE
GOVERNORS OF NEW MEXICO

BY PAUL A. F. WALTER

Secretary of the School of American Archæology

FOR more than three centuries the history of the Southwest centered in the long, low, massive adobe building at Santa Fé, New Mexico, known as the Palace of the Governors. It faces the plaza, the principal public park, which is also the center of the business district. Here reigned one hundred executives of New Mexico, some with high, autocratic hand, others weak and vacillating, under Spanish, Indian, Mexican, and American régimes. Stirring events which furnish abundant material for romance and history transpired within these walls. During the Pueblo revolution of 1680 one thousand men, women and children were crowded into this building and its *placita*, while hordes of Indians were hurling themselves against its two protecting towers, their arrows and their missiles falling in showers upon the cowering and frightened mass of Spaniards who replied feebly with cannon and firearms. The Spaniards finally made their escape and retreated in a memorable march to El Paso on the Rio Grande.

Under the Mexican régime, the old building began to fall into decay. From time to time, sporadic attempts were made at repairing the damage wrought by time and neglect. But it was not until a few years ago that the restoration was undertaken in a systematic and thorough manner. Dr. Edgar L. Hewett,

THE LOGGIA OF THE PALACE

director of the School of American Archæology, was the first to arouse enthusiasm for the proposition to restore to its pristine glory the Palace of Governors. Strange to say, he met with opposition and enmity in this undertaking, but he finally secured legislative assistance as well as powerful support elsewhere, and accomplished what many had told him would be a hopeless task. The restoration was completed a few months ago. The work of construction under the restoration plans was done under the supervision of Jesse Nusbaum, a member of the staff of the School of Archæology, and a master workman of rare skill.

THE MUSEUM OF NEW MEXICO

The building is one-twentieth of a mile long and is built in what is known as the Franciscan style, showing a mixture of the architecture of both Spain and New Mexico, as evolved by and adapted to the Southwestern environment. The simplicity of outline gives the structure a rugged beauty. A tower terminates each end and the picturesque portal recalls that the building was at one time a castle, a fortress, and a prison, in addition to being the Palace of the Governors. Today, it houses the Museum of New Mexico with priceless treasures of archæological interest taken from the numerous cliff dwellings in the immediate vicinity of Santa Fé. The installation of the Museum is recent and the specimens are scientifically arranged in glass cabinets or in cabinets built into the walls, some of which are eight feet thick and built upon the prehistoric walls of a village which may have existed a thousand or more years ago. Most striking and happy are the mural paintings which illustrate the environment that produced the specimens displayed in the same museum room. They are the gift of the Honorable Frank Springer, one of New Mexico's most famous scientists and ablest members of the bar.

The Palace also houses the School of American Archæology, one of the five archæological schools maintained by the American Institute of Archæolgy, the others being in Greece, Italy, Palestine, and China. The Historical Society of New Mexico, too, has its museum in the building. In addition, there are three fine libraries, one on linguistics, another gift of Mr. Springer, a library of New Mexicana, and a private archæological library.

New Mexico is proud of this Palace of the Governors and considers it the most famous landmark in the United States, as it certainly is the oldest government building north of Mexico. It is probable that a new wing will be added to it by the next legislature to serve as an art gallery. A notable collection of Southwestern paintings has already been made and three artists of note are connected with the school. Mr. Springer, above mentioned, recently gave a commission to Donald Beauregard, just returned from Paris, for seven mural panels of heroic size to depict the life of St. Francis d'Assisi. These paintings will be exhibited in the New Mexico building at the San Diego Exposition and upon their return will be placed in the proposed art gallery.

CENTRAL AFRICAN FOLK STORIES

COLLECTED BY AGNES E. MACKENZIE

Of the Livingstonia Mission, Nyasaland

HOW THE RABBIT SAVED THE HUNTER FROM AN OGRE

ONCE upon a time a hunter went out hunting with his dog for *sezi* — a small burrowing rodent. He had caught three when rain began to fall in torrents and he ran into a cave for shelter. But when he got inside he found an ogre there and he was very frightened.

He bowed low, saluted the ogre, and said, "O my father, please accept of these three sezi.

But the ogre answered roughly, "No, I do not want your sezi. Let your dog eat the sezi, then eat your dog, and then I will eat you."

At these words the hunter trembled and said, "Ah, no, my father, pray accept of the sezi."

The ogre refused the gift and again said, "Let your dog eat the sezi, then eat your dog, and I will eat you."

The hunter refused to do this, and the ogre and he began to dispute loudly. All at once they heard a voice outside say "Hodi?" (May I come in?)

The ogre answered, "Hodine" (Enter), and in came a rabbit drenched with rain.

"O dear me," he said, shaking his fur, "what a country this is for rain. I am glad to get shelter here. But I heard you quarreling, my friends, when I was outside. Pray tell me what is wrong."

Then the hunter said, "I came in here to take shelter, and when I found the ogre here I offered him my three sezi as a present. But he refuses to take them and says my dog must eat them, then I am to eat the dog, and then he will eat me."

"Ha-ha," said the rabbit cheerfully, "that is a good plan, but the ogre has left something out. Let your dog eat the sezi, then eat your dog, then the ogre will eat you up, and lastly I shall eat up the ogre."

"Not at all," cried the ogre angrily, "that won't do."

"Yes, yes," said the rabbit, "I am sure all you boys outside there agree with what I say," and with this he put his paw behind his back, and disturbed some white ants that were there. The white ants said "Waa-aa."

When the ogre heard this chorus of voices he feared greatly, and said, " I see there are too many of you against me."

With this the poor hunter saw his chance and escaped from the cave with his dog.

THE SELF-WILLED DEER

ONCE upon a time the beasts were gathered together to receive their horns, and to discuss how they should grow. Everyone said that the horns should grow at the back of the head, except one foolish deer, and he said, "I wish my horns to grow in front so that I can see them."

, The others laughed at him and said, "But all the rest of us think it is better that horns should grow out behind."

Then the deer said, "I don't care what you all say, I wish my horns to grow out in front." So he had his wish. All the others had horns branching out behind, but the self-willed deer had horns which stuck out in front.

All this took place in the beginning of winter, and the winter passed and now summer came, and all the streams began to dry up, and the water grew less and less. The other animals could easily stoop and drink at the stream even though the water was low, but the self-willed deer could hardly lap up any water because his horns were in the way when he stooped.

The water grew less and less till the streams were dry, and the only water to be had was in a little hollow among the rocks under a cave. The other animals could reach this pool with some difficulty, but when the self-willed deer tried to put in his mouth he could not reach the water because of his long, awkward horns. So he grew thinner and thinner and at last he died of thirst.

THE FISHERMAN AND THE GOAT'S HEAD

ONCE upon a time relish was very scarce in a certain village, and so several of the men said one day they would go to fish with hooks, and try to get some fish for relish. They went off to the lake to fish and they fished and fished, but could catch nothing till at last one of them fished up a goat's head. Then they returned to the village, opened their bag, and showed the goat's head.

Now one of the men in the village had lately lost a goat, and when he saw this head he declared that the fisherman had stolen his goat and killed it, and was now pretending he had found its head in the lake.

The fisherman protested that he was innocent, and that he had really fished the head up out the water. He called the other fishermen to witness that they had seen the head come up on his hook.

But the angry owner of the lost goat said that they were all liars and were deceiving him. So a great quarrel began, and at last the parties agreed to go to the nearest village to have their case settled.

When they drew near the village they heard a wailing, and they learned that a great head man had died. The chief asked what they wanted and they said, "O we cannot trouble you today, we did not know there was a death in your village, we came to ask you to settle our dispute."

The chief said, "Never mind about the death, it happened some days ago. Tell me about your quarrel."

The fisherman began and told how he had gone along with his friends to fish, as there was no relish to be had, and how he failed to get anything till he fished up a goat's head. Then the owner of the goats said that one of his goats had been stolen lately and that when he saw the goat's head in the fisherman's bag, he recognized it as that of his lost goat.

"Let us see the head," said the chief, and the owner of the goats, who had seized the fisherman's bag, now opened it to take out the head, but when he drew out the head it was no longer a goat's head, but the head of the head man who had lately died!

Then the case turned against the owner of the goats and not against the fisherman.

At Home and Afield

HAMPTON INCIDENTS

HAMPTON'S ANNIVERSARY

THE school's two-masted schooner, the *Hampton*, met the hundred or more Northern guests arriving at Old Point on Thursday, April 23, for Hampton's Anniversary exercises and sailed with them through the sunny, breezy spring morning to the school wharf. April had considerably decked the broad grounds for their festival days with the bewitching bronze and green of budding leaves on trees and shrubs, the lavender of the lilac, the flaunting purple-pink of the Judas tree, and the white of the dogwood, and had marked the green lawns with red and yellow tulip patterns and rainbow pansy beds.

Shortly after their arrival, these visitors, with other guests, were conducted through the Domestic Science Building, which houses also the Agricultural Department, where cooking and sewing classes and lessons preparing boys and girls for active farm life were going on. The work of the Agricultural Department was the emphasized feature of this year's demonstration, and the guests saw classes studying the selection of seed, the operation of stand-pipes and reservoirs, the use of gasoline engines on the farm, the dressing of poultry for the retail trade, dairy processes, home gardening, and the comparative advantages of different breeds of cows. The future woman on the farm or in the rural school, as well as the man, learns to make flower and vegetable gardens, to raise chickens for market, to make clean butter, to milk cows, and to be a good judge of dairy animals.

Before leaving the Domestic Science Building, the attention of the party was called to four exhibits in the upper hall. One, labeled "Health Conservation," consisted of a number of mounted photographs showing examination of the students' eyes, ears, throats, and teeth by specialists engaged by the school, physical tests and measurements being taken at the Gymnasium; gymnasium classes in action; boys' and girls' athletic sports; and some of the hospital equipment at Hampton. An academic exhibit displayed specimens of written work done by new students the first week in school last fall with contrasting papers below written by the same students seven months later. Two glass cases of dresses and table linen, fresh from the iron and with no faint suggestion of a wrinkle on their snowy surfaces, proved the efficiency of the school laundry. Plates of bread, cakes, and crisp cookies, and jars of clear preserves were shown behind glass doors.

AFTER a brief visit to the dairy and horse barns to see further and even more practical demonstrations of Hampton's training in agriculture, the guests were invited to witness a plowing match between representatives of the four agricultural classes—first year, second year, third year, and short course—the proud winner of which was a first-year boy. A "side show" at the match was a plow drawn by a single ox, driven by one of the older farmers of the community, and a modern, two-horse plow operated by a Hampton student, the two working side by side to show the evolution of the plow and of plowing, and of the efficient Negro farmer as well.

At noon the guests assembled] on the Mansion House piazzas to watch the midday drill which "gives a certain sparkle to the dull round of daily duty" six days of the week throughout the school year. On Anniversary days the sight of the girls, trim in their light gingham or percale dresses, brings added attractiveness to "the music of a band and the shining of an occasional epaulette." The impressive ceremony, when the lines of erect, bareheaded cadets form an avenue through which the girls, led by the band, march to the dining-room, is seen only at this time of the year. After luncheon at the Mansion House, Hampton's visitors were given a choice of three occupations for the afternoon—a visit to Shellbanks, the school farm six miles away on a beautiful salt-water "river;" an automobile trip to three of the rural schools in the county; or a sail on the *Hampton*, with an opportunity to examine its equipment as the home of forty campaigners on their trip next summer from Hampton to Bar Harbor.

THE TRUSTEES' MEETING

TWELVE of the fifteen trustees were present for the transaction of important business at the meeting on Thursday morning, April 23—Mr. Charles E. Bigelow, Mr. Arthur Curtiss James, Dr. William Jay Schieffelin, Rev. James W. Cooper, and Mr. Clarence H. Kelsey, of New York City; Rev. Francis G. Peabody, of Cambridge, Mass.; Hon. William Howard Taft, of New Haven, Conn.; Mr. Lunsford L. Lewis, of Richmond, Va.; Dr. William W. Frazier, of Philadelphia; Dr. Samuel C. Mitchell of Richmond, Va.; Mr. Frank W. Darling and Dr. Hollis B. Frissell, of Hampton, Va.

Mr. Taft was elected president of the board of trustees to succeed Mr. Robert C. Ogden, whose death in August left the office vacant for sev-

eral months. Dr. Francis G. Peabody, second vice president of the board, was made first vice president, and Mr. Clarence H. Kelsey was elected second vice president. The election of Mr. Taft was announced to the students and teachers and to a small part of the public at a meeting held in Memorial Church directly after supper to hear the ex-president of the United States discuss the present Mexican situation. The news was very heartily received, and it was several minutes before Mr. Taft was allowed to make himself heard. The full report of his talk, printed elsewhere in this issue, can give no true idea of the simplicity and genuine friendliness of his manner as he came forward and addressed the students as "Boys and girls," nor of his smile-provoking smile, nor of his inimitable chuckle. It was an unforgetable privilege to every member of the audience who heard his informal speech to glimpse Mr. Taft's lovable personality.

THE OUTDOOR TABLEAUX

THE entertainment in the evening, given on a stage on Holly Tree Inn lawn with a background of cedars and blooming dogwood and a canopy of China-berry trees, consisted of two parts—"The Indian's Gifts to the Nation" and "The Negro's Gifts to the Nation." An Indian medicine-man opened the scene with the story of the Indian's gifts of hospitality, land, food, and game. He then called together the representatives of different tribes, who came in tribal dress and smoked the peace-pipe in an impressive circle, while the Apache beat an Indian drum and chanted a song, strange with yodeling notes. A slow, dignified Apache dance with drum and song accompaniment followed the ceremony of the peace-pipe. The graceful ball-dance, which the Cherokees keep up the entire night before the tribal ball game, was performed by two lithe young Cherokee students to the accompanying chant of a third. Their yells, expressive of gleeful abandon, which occurred at intervals of the dance, particularly appealed to the audience. The scene closed with a war-dance in which all Indians joined, dancing and shouting. The second part of the entertainment graphically presented three of the Negro's gifts to the Nation— loyalty, song, and labor. Uncle Ben, dozing outside his cabin, is awakened by an impish young messenger from the Big House, to whom he tells the story of his Civil War experiences— how, after long, faithful search, he found his master's body and brought it home. He is interrupted by distant bugles and the song of Negro troops returning from the Spanish War, his son among them. The tramp of marching feet comes nearer and nearer and Sergeant Booker, with his right hand in a sling, at last rushes into his father's trembling arms. In the second scene the Rev. Ezekiel Brown arrives upon a scene of merry-making, rebukes a banjo player and stops a "buck and wing" dance, admonishing his brethren to praise the Lord with their true gift of song, rather than to serve the devil. The typical songs and responses of the Negro campmeeting follow. The first part of the last scene shows the singing field hands at work on the cotton harvest, illustrating the labor of the unskilled Negro which made possible the early economic development of the South. In the second part of this scene, the curtain rises, to the music of the "Anvil Chorus," on groups of busy Hampton tradesmen. On one side of the stage two carpenters are building a roof frame, on the other side a brick wall rises under bricklayers' skillful fingers, while in the background the blacksmiths' fire flashes, and tailors sit cross-legged on a cutting table. For the final tableau the workmen come forward with their tools and sing their trade song, " Men of Hampton !"

THE ANNIVERSARY EXERCISES

ON Friday morning the guests visited the Whittier Training School where Hampton boys and girls learn how to teach the children of their race. The Hampton Trade School was also inspected during the morning. At twelve o'clock came the battalion drill, and this time, following the line of girls, marched four hundred sturdy little Whittier soldiers. At two-thirty the line of parade formed again and escorted the guests to the Gymnasium, the usual scene of Anniversary exercises. The student body was accommodated on the raised platform at one end, with the graduating class in the front row, and visitors from far and near left hardly standing room on the floor of the building. On a smaller platform facing the audience were the trustees, the visiting speakers, and prominent citizens of the community.

On account of the long program, two of the Senior papers which had been selected for presentation were omitted, leaving the audience to wonder why the need was to tantalize them by the printed announcement of such promising subjects as "Hat renovating" and "The call to the farm," fulfillment being withheld. The first three speakers were members of the graduating class. "Why I wanted an industrial education" was the subject of Blanche M. Briggs's story of her coming to Hampton. Lula Owl, a Cherokee Indian of North Carolina, told the audience some interesting facts about "My mother's people—the Catawbas," including some of her own experiences as teacher of the children of that tribe during a summer vacation. A Georgia boy, B. Luther Colbert, then superintended the stage setting necessary for his demonstration on "The raising of a young calf." The properties required were a table, a small oil-stove for heating milk, a thermometer, a milk pail, skim milk, oil-meal, a brush and curry-comb, and a three-weeks-old Holstein calf. He explained the calf's digestive tract, also the proper food and its preparation, emphasizing especially cleanliness of pails and other utensils; and the thoroughbred baby animal enjoyed a hygienic dinner, unembarrassed by the close proximity of an ex-president of the United States and others of the nation's wise and famous men seated on the platform watching the operation with sympathetic interest.

THE next number on the program was an address by Miss Ella G. Agnew, state agent for girls' demonstration work in Virginia, on "The rural work in Virginia" which has given many a discouraged or indifferent little country girl an absorbing interest in her own home. She spoke especially of the tomato clubs and of their possibilities for putting life into the rural-school curriculum. Miss Agnew and her co-workers are doing for the white children, especially the girls, what Mr. Jackson Davis and his colored industrial supervisors are doing for the colored schools of the state. "The experience of a country physician," told by Dr. Charles H. Stokes, Hampton '91, of Gloucester County, Va., was enlightening to a large part of the audience, who, as Mr. Taft said afterwards, might find it difficult to realize that in this country at the present time there are communities where people die because they find it impossible to secure medical aid, and where other people, worse off, spend inefficient lives, beset by a series of communicable diseases, because they have no knowledge of sanitary precautions or of even ordinary cleanliness. The Negro race needs Negro doctors and there are not enough trained men to supply this need.

Mrs. Nannie L. Butler, of Bowling Green, Va., a graduate of Tuskegee in 1911, and now industrial supervising teacher in the Negro schools of Caroline County, told of "The awakening of Caroline County" in the past few years to an earnest, wonder-working enthusiasm for the best education possible for the colored children.

Dr. Samuel Chiles Mitchell, president of Virginia Medical College, Richmond, who for many years was associated with Dr. Robert C. Ogden in his educational work in the South,

delivered an address in memory of the late president of Hampton's board of trustees, expressing the mingled love, pride, gratitude, and sorrow that half of the members of the audience personally felt in the event of the recent death of this great and kindly man.

The last event of the afternoon was the presentation to the board of trustees of sixty-nine candidates for diplomas and sixty-six candidates for certificates by the Honorable William H. Taft, who, after congratulating the graduates on their share in the afternoon's exercises and upon the opportunities which were theirs through Hampton's training, gave them a small measure of advice with a large measure of encouragement and a blessing with which to start life. His address will be printed in the next number of the Southern Workman.

ADDRESSES

ON Monday evening, April 13, Miss Mary E. Frayser, who is in charge of the Home Economics and Extension work of Winthrop College, South Carolina, told the Hampton students of her work among white people in the rural districts. She spoke particularly of the woman's side of the country-life problem—the housing conditions. Women have progressed very little in their methods of housekeeping, while men have up-to-date machinery for their farms. If Mr. and Mrs. Julius Caesar were to return to earth, she said, Mr. Caesar would find himself in a strange world as regards farming implements and methods, but Mrs. Caesar would look around on Monday, see the big iron pot out in the yard with a little fire underneath, the woman running out from her hot kitchen to look after the washing, and would say, "I am perfectly familiar with my surroundings."

It is not entirely the men's fault, for women are much more conservative than men and do not take readily to new labor-saving devices. Miss Frayser went on to show how the house could be made convenient for housekeeping just as a man builds his office for the work to be done there. She emphasized the necessity for good health, plenty of water, and good food, and told of cases where water had been piped into the house very easily and cheaply. She also told how a fireless cooker could be made at small expense. These reforms are best accomplished through clubs for girls and boys, gradually drawing in the older people and getting them interested. The most important thing is to make the people feel that their co-operation is needed. The nineteenth century stood for equality, but the twentieth century strikes a far higher note—*mutuality*.

A former rector of St. John's Church in Hampton, Rev. John J. Gravatt, who used to work among the Indian students at Hampton Institute when General Armstrong was Principal of the school, and who made many trips to the Western reservations to bring back Indian boys and girls to Hampton, spoke at evening chapel on Sunday, April 19, on the life of the prophet Daniel and the value of determined purpose. Dr. Gravatt is now rector of Trinity Church in Richmond.

Rev. Henry Roe Cloud, a young Winnebago Indian who is an occasional visitor, always welcome, at Hampton, spoke to the students in chapel on Sunday evening, April 26, telling of his struggle for an education through the · Santee Mission School, Mt. Hermon, Yale University, and Auburn Theological Seminary, from which he was recently graduated. He is interested in starting a school for the training of Christian Indian leaders.

On the same evening Mr. Mornay Williams, a New York lawyer who is vice president of the Layman's Missionary Movement and a member of the advisory board of the New York Y. M. C. A., gave a short religious talk on the subject of "Building."

THE former Minister of Public Works in Liberia, Dr. J. Edmestone Barnes, now president and director of a society for establishing and maintaining the Liberian Industrial Training Institute and Schools, came to Hampton on May 11 with Dr. Weston E. Campbell, of Baltimore, Md., to study the methods of the school and the courses of instruction. Dr. Barnes spoke to the students at evening chapel of the colonization of Liberia in 1822 by American ex-slaves, outlining briefly its history, and dwelling upon the present need of the native tribes, a population of about two millions, for practical education. He hopes to establish eventually good elementary schools which shall reach the whole population, and a higher industrial training school similar to Hampton. His purpose in coming to this country is to acquire ideas, teachers, and capital. Dr. Barnes made an appeal to the Hampton students for teachers from among their ranks to take Hampton's training to the Liberian natives.

ENTERTAINMENTS

THE Sumner Literary Society, whose membership is made up chiefly of Hampton graduates at the school and in the vicinity, is able, with musical and dramatic talent summoned from its ranks, to offer excellent entertainments to the public every year. The Society gave a concert of much interest to music lovers at the Whittier School on April 17. An original piano composition—"Louisiana," described as a carnival waltz—by Mr. R. N. Dett was one of the numbers.

On Saturday evening, April 18, students and teachers enjoyed a too brief moving-picture show in Cleveland Hall Chapel, seeing a few views of the Coliseum at Rome and a two-reel "funny" picture of a runaway circus menagerie, members of which, released by a wrecked baggage car, investigated at will the homes and markets of a much excited community.

"Snakes" was the subject of a lecture given in the chapel on Saturday evening, May 2, by Mr. Raymond L. Ditmars, curator of reptiles at the New York Zoölogical Park. The talk was illustrated by living specimens and by moving pictures showing some of the snakes at home. Mr. Ditmars confined his lecture to facts about snakes whose habitat is the Southern states. Eight or ten more or less animated white bags were opened and yielded up snakes of different sizes and colors, all harmless, from the slender little green snake, known to both North and South, to the big, irridescent "indigo" snake and the powerful, brown-patterned pine snake. The lecturer has been curator of reptiles in the New York Zoölogical Park since 1889 and has written several books on the subject.

A little May queen reigned from a flowery throne on Holly Tree Inn lawn Monday, May 10. Her subjects were the children of the Whittier School and other Negro schools of the community. The May-day procession, with the queen and two tiny attendant maidens at the head in a low car covered with bridal wreath, drawn by six or eight pages, and followed by little ladies-in-waiting bearing flowery wands or hoops, marched around the grounds and up to the throne to the music of the Institute band. After this ceremony, the ladies-in-waiting made their obeisances to the queen, and then came the dance around the four blossom-topped maypoles, followed by folk dances, and, for a climax, ice-cream cones. From four until six o'clock the band was intermittently active and the lawn was gay with dancing children, proud parents, and admiring friends.

RELIGIOUS WORK

THE Rev. Laurence Fenninger, who preached in Memorial Church on Sunday, March 29, will, after the middle of June, be associated with Dr. Turner in the work of the chaplaincy. Mr. Fenninger, a graduate of Princeton and Union Theological Seminary, was formerly assistant pastor in the First Presbyterian Church of Bloomfield, N. J.

At the communion service on Sunday, May 3, six students—five boys

and one girl—joined the church upon confession of faith.

Dr Frank Knight Sanders, president of Washburn College, Topeka, Kansas, has recently delivered six lectures on the history of the Hebrew people, supplementing the study of the Old Testament, which is taken up in academic classes. It is hoped that it will be possible for Dr. Sanders to give a similar course of lectures each spring, and each fall another course to supplement the study of the New Testament, which is confined to the Sunday-school classes. Dr. Sanders has also prepared an outline to be used in the classroom study of the Old Testament.

On April 26 Mrs. Walter C. Roe, widow of Dr. Roe, missionary to the Indians since 1897, and herself now missionary-at-large for the Reformed Church of America, and Rev. Henry Roe Cloud, a Winnebago Indian who is her adopted son, spoke to the Indian students at their Christian Endeavor meeting in Winona.

THE King's Daughters Society sent three delegates, under the chaperonage of Mrs. Allen Washington, and the Young Men's Christian Association sent four delegates to the Negro Christian Student Convention held in Atlanta May 14–18.

At the Y. M. C. A. meeting on Sunday evening, May 10, George A. Scott, the president-elect for next year, announced the cabinet that he had chosen with the help and advice of the present cabinet.

TWO most helpful talks were heard in the Y. M. C. A. meetings of April 26 and May 10. On the former date, the Rev. Henry Roe Cloud told a few stories from his own life and experience which will be long remembered. He spoke of the Indian's conception of friendship as an indissoluble bond. When the two parties enter the compact, some sign is made by both, and thereafter nothing can part them in spirit, even though one be thousands of miles from the other. He then went on to tell of the time when he and another comrade entered into this bond of friendship with Christ. They each made a mark in the ground which should ever remain a witness to their pledge. Should one transgress this friendship, whenever his foot would touch the ground, the other would know it, and so long as their feet touched the ground, Mother Earth, the witness of their pledge, would keep reminding them of their promise to be true to Him.

ON May 10 Mr. Williams, the general secretary of the Colored Y. M. C. A. at Newport News, spoke on the topic of personal work. Mr. Williams is a man, who, by going down into the shipyards and mingling with the young men, has won them into the Y. M. C. A. The result of this personal work of a Christian man bringing others into a cleaner, stronger, purer life has been so noticeable in the general proficiency of the workmen, that the authorities of the shipyards have recognized its economic value by offering a cash bonus every week for those who have been prompt in reporting to work and for those who have shown marked faithfulness. This, Mr. Williams said, was the aim of the Y. M. C. A. —to make the men more efficient citizens. Through a banking club among the boys, many boys, who before hardly knew what it was to keep fifty cents from one week to another, now have a bank deposit of twenty-five or thirty dollars.

ATHLETICS

THIS year Hampton has had only two intercollegiate baseball matches. The school nine made the most of the opportunities given it, however, defeating Virginia Union University three to one in Richmond on April 13, and gaining an easier victory with a score of ten to two over the same opponent on the home diamond. It is hoped that a longer baseball schedule can be arranged for next year, as the successful team is naturally sighing for new worlds to conquer.

HAMPTON WORKERS

TWO representatives from Hampton, Mr. William Anthony Aery and Major R. R. Moton, attended the Southern Sociological Congress in Memphis, Tenn., May 6–10, Major Moton making an address before the Congress. Mr. Aery was present at the National Conference for Charities and Corrections held in Memphis May 8–15. Major Moton went from Memphis to Atlanta to the Negro Christian Students' Convention May 14–18, and from there to the Calhoun commencement and alumni meeting on May 19 and 20, being on the program for an address at each place.

A small prospectus announces the summer session from June 25 to August 4 of "the first teachers' college for the entire South"—the George Peabody College for Teachers in Nashville, Tennessee. In the list of the faculty, Miss Ethel Gowans, who resigned from Hampton's Agricultural Department in December, is mentioned as a teacher of agriculture. The prospectus states that "special emphasis is placed on courses in industrial education, home economics, rural education, rural life, sanitation and health, departments of education, history, English, and drawing."

EXTENSION WORK

A meeting was held in the Carey Chapel district school at Poquoson, Va., on Wednesday, April 15, to consider the building of a new schoolhouse, of which there is great need. Among the party which went from Hampton Institute and spoke to the colored patrons assembled in the school, urging them to unite with the Bethel District near by and build a three or four-room graded school in order to secure state appropriation for graded schools, were Rev. A. J. Renforth, division superintendent of schools in Warwick and York Counties; Mr. Frank K. Rogers, treasurer of Hampton Institute; Dr. George P. Phenix, Hampton's vice principal; Miss M. J. Sherman, in charge of the Record Office; Mr. William A. Aery, in charge of Press Service; Rev. A. A. Graham, pastor of Zion Church, and the following Hampton graduates: Mr. Thomas C. Walker, '83' of Gloucester, Va. ; Mr. William T. Anderson, '94' of Hampton, Va. ; and Mr. George J. Davis, '74' farm-demonstration agent in Elizabeth City County. The teacher of the school, Miss Mary Brandon, '92' has done excellent work with the equipment available.

ON Wednesday, April 22, a party from Hampton Institute and other parts of Virginia made a motor trip to the Buckroe, Northampton, Union Street, Bates, and Salter's Creek colored schools, at each of which they heard a report of the patrons' league with addresses by some of the visitors, and saw an exhibition of handwork done by the children and a demonstration of the industrial work recently introduced. Among those who spoke were Mr. J. H. Binford, executive secretary of the Virginia Co-operative Education Association; Mr. Jackson Davis, state supervisor of Negro rural schools; Dr. George P. Phenix, and Major Robert R. Moton, of Hampton Institute. A similar trip on the following afternoon in which about forty of Hampton's Anniversary guests joined, and another to the schools of Caroline County, Va., are mentioned editorially.

WHITTIER SCHOOL

AT the last meeting for the year of the Whittier School Parents' Association the election of officers was followed by a social given the parents by the teachers. The officers of the Association had served so acceptably the past year that they were re-elected, contrary to precedent. A very enjoyable musical and literary entertainment, including numbers by two favorites—a piano solo by Mr. R. N. Dett and a recitation by Mrs. R. R. Moton—was given after the business meeting.

DEATHS

THE death of Mrs. Harriet P. Hayward, mother of Miss Harriet S. Hayward, supervisor of the academic department of the school, occurred on Saturday morning, May 9, after an illness of several days. The funeral service was held in Memorial Church on Saturday afternoon at three o'clock. Mrs. Hayward has been living with her daughter at the school for the past five years.

Minnie B. M. Armstrong, of Fayetteville, N. C., a member of the Junior Class, died at the Dixie Hospital on April 9, 1914.

VISITORS

ANNIVERSARY festivities brought to Hampton about one hundred twenty-five guests from a distance, many of them members of the New York, Brooklyn, Philadelphia, Boston, and Springfield Hampton Associations. Among those who came down in the special party under the personal guidance of Mr. A. B. Trowbridge, who is chairman of the Executive Committee of the Brooklyn Association, were Mrs. Trowbridge, Mr. and Mrs. G. Colgate, Mr. Frissell and Miss Frissell, brother and sister of Hampton's Principal, Rev. Dr. Wilton Merle-Smith, of the Central Presbyterian Church, and Mrs. Merle-Smith, Col. Willis L. Ogden, his daughter, Miss Alice Ogden, and his sister, Mrs. Charles W. Ide, Mrs. St. Clair McKelway, Mr. and Mrs. Alfred T. White and Miss Katherine White, all of New York or Brooklyn; Mrs. Henry C. Davis and Mr. and Mrs. John T. Emlen, of Philadelphia; Dr. Alfred G. Rolfe, head of the Hill School, Pottstown, Pa.; Mrs. W. B. Medlicott, president of the Springfield Club; Mrs. W. B. Everett and Miss Rachel M. Stearns, of Waltham, Mass.; and Miss Corliss, of Providence. Trustees who came in the party are mentioned elsewhere. Mrs. Arthur Curtiss James and Mrs. William Jay Schieffelin, of New York, Mrs. Lunsford L. Lewis, of Richmond, and Mrs. Frank

Darling of Hampton, all wives of trustees, were present. Mrs. Darling was accompanied by guests, Mr. and Mrs. Lathers and Miss Julia Lathers, of New York.

Mr. John M. Oskison, an Indian journalist connected with *Collier's Weekly*, Mrs. Walter C. Roe, of Colony, Okla., missionary-at-large for the Reformed Church of America, and her adopted son, Rev. Henry Roe Cloud, a Winnebago Indian, attended the exercises.

Mrs. Alexander Purves entertained at her home, during Anniversary and the following week, her sister, Mrs. G. W. Crary, of New York; her aunt, Mrs. George Tilge, with her daughter, Miss Helen Tilge, of Philadelphia; and the Misses Annie and Eleanor Chalfant, Alleghany, Pa. Miss Brittingham, of Philadelphia, has been visiting Mrs. Purves for several weeks.

Mrs. B. B. Munford, Mr. Jackson Davis, and Mr. J. H. Binford, of Richmond, and Mr. W. S. Copeland, of Newport News, one of Hampton's state curators, came to Hampton for Anniversary days. Three Negro state curators, Mr. J. C. Carter, of Houston, Dr. W. T. Johnston, of Richmond, and Mr. J. S. Clark, of Danville, were present; also Dr. Charles S. Morris, of Norfolk, pastor of the Bank Street Baptist Church (Colored).

RECENT guests of the school, whose visit included Anniversary celebrations, were Mrs. F. C. Lowell and Miss Ethel Paine, of Boston, stopping at Hampton on their way home from the Penn School; Miss Alice P. Tapley, chairman of the Executive Committee of the Boston Hampton Committee and Miss Elizabeth Thornell, of Princeton, who were at the Mansion House for several days; Miss Henrietta Gardiner, of Gardiner, Me.; and Dr.

Francis G. Peabody, first vice president of the board of trustees, who gave the school the great pleasure of nearly a week's visit.

SOME of the distinguished visitors to Hampton during the past month have been Mrs. Lucian Newhall, of Lynn, Mass.; Mrs. James Bertram, whose husband is secretary of the Carnegie Corporation, and her little daughter; Miss B. B. Elder, head of the Eighth Ward Settlement in Philadelphia and her assistant, Miss Frances R. Bartholomew; Miss Frances Chickering, a former teacher; Rev. George McCune, secretary of the Presbyterian Mission in Korea; Dr. Lewis Francis, of New York; Mr. T. J. Woofter, Jr., of the United States Bureau of Education; Mrs. R. R. Reeder, whose husband is head of an orphan asylum at Hastings-on-Hudson; Secretary Wm. C. Redfield, with Mrs. and Miss Redfield; Professor Woodcock, of the University of Toronto; Dr. St. Clair McKelway, editor of the Brooklyn *Eagle*, who spoke to the students in chapel on Sunday, May 10; and Mr. A. J. Renforth, division superintendent of schools in Warwick and York Counties, with Mrs. Renforth and several white teachers. Five girls with a teacher from Miss Spence's school in New York City spent the week-end as school guests the middle of May. Miss Annie B. Scoville, who is doing campaign work among the girls' schools in the North, has been spending a week or two with her brother, Mr. Scoville.

Rev. Wm. H. Blaine, who is pastor of a Presbyterian church in Schieffelin, Liberia, recently arrived at Hampton with his son whom he wished to enter in school and who has gone to Shellbanks for the summer.

GRADUATES AND EX-STUDENTS

OVER a hundred graduates and ex-students registered at Marshall Hall on the Friday of Anniversary week. Ninety of these were from this vicinity—thirty-three from Hampton, twenty-four from Norfolk, sixteen from Portsmouth, eleven from Phoebus, and six from Newport News. Luncheon was served to the alumni on Friday in Cleveland Hall Chapel.

FOR the past four years, William R. Grigsby, ex-student of '97, has been engaged in the work of the ministry. During the past year Mr. Grigsby has been stationed at Sistersville, West Virginia.

Mrs. Millie Calloway Venable, '74, is, for the fourth year, the supervisor of the industrial work in the Holbrook Street School, Danville.

Robert H. Beverly, '02, who was graduated two years ago from the Bennett Medical College in Chicago, is now praticing medicine in Jacksonville, Illinois, with Dr. A. H. Kennibrew, formerly resident physician at Tuskegee Institute.

Philip F. King, '08, was graduated from the theological department of Lincoln University in Pennsylvania on April 21.

James T. Holly, ex-student '08, is now a druggist in Miami, Florida.

THE position of teacher of bricklaying at the new colored industrial school in Cincinnati, Ohio, is held by John F. Burrell, '09,

Burnett H. Gholston, ex-student of 1911, enlisted as a private in the United States Army in 1912, and has been in the Philippines since his enlistment. He has been promoted three times, first to the position of Company clerk, then to that of chief clerk at the regimental headquarters, and finally to his present position, topographic draftsman with the Military Survey Detachment, which is surveying the island of Zambales for maps.

MARRIAGES

THE marriage has been announced of Grace D. George, '11, to Mr. Solomon G. Slade, a graduate of St. Paul's School, Lawrenceville, Va.

Dr. Norwood A. Thorne, '04, a dentist of Chicago, Ill., was married on April 22 to Miss Helen Hunt Jackson, also of Chicago.

Word has been received of the marriage of James T. Morris, ex-student '13, and Miss Adell. Virginia Wells in Norfolk, Va., on April 27.

On April 29, Charles F. Stephens, ex-student '13, was married to Miss Ardenah L. Marcus, at the Fort Valley High and Industrial School, Georgia. Mr. Stephens is the teacher of manual training in the school.

DEATHS

ON April 14, Paulena W. Banks, ex-student of 1901, and daughter of Mr. Frank D. Banks, '76, died at her home in Anniston, Ala. She was married last June to Dr. Donald Wilborn. After leaving Hampton she was graduated from Spelman Seminary, and taught for several years before her marriage.

News has been received of the death in Boston, of William R. Kimball, '98, in March, 1914.

Ferdinand H. Calloway, '79, died in March at his home in Lynchburg. Since his graduation he had taught almost continuously within a radius of ten miles in Campbell and Bedford Counties. A Hampton graduate living in Lynchburg wrote of him a few years ago: "Mr. Calloway is a faithful, conscientious, Christian worker."

Robert Kelser, '76, died of tuberculosis at his home in Charlottesville, Va., in April. He did good work as a teacher until failing health obliged him to give up teaching about two years ago.

INDIAN NOTES

ONE of the first nine girls brought to Hampton in 1878 by Captain Pratt, Sarah Walker Pease, who left in 1887 to take charge of the sewing department in a mission school among the Crow Indians of Montana, where she afterwards married, writes from Lodge Grass of her family of nine children. She has eight sons, but the youngest child is a daughter, named for her old Hampton scholarship friend who has never forgotten them. There is a Baptist mission near by which she attends, being also a member of the women's society which holds its meetings at the different houses.

Alice Longfellow Chee, one of the Chiricahua Apaches, who came to Hampton from Mt. Vernon Barracks, Ala., and was returned to Fort Sill, Oklahoma, whither the band had been removed, is now at Mescalero, N. M., with that portion of the tribe which elected to go there rather than remain at Fort Sill when set at liberty by the War Department. She seems well content with the new location and already has a new house.

Bessie Peters, of the Stockbridge Tribe, Class '08, is enjoying her work as teacher in the Government School at Shawnee. She has the intermediate grades and finds her pupils showing a good knowledge of English.

Winifred Garrow, '11, is now a Senior in the Business Course at Haskell Institute. She writes, "I am chairman of the social committee of the Young Women's Christian Association, and we have to think up ways of raising money for the work. We gave an ice-cream social about a week ago, and last evening we gave an entertainment. We have sent sixty dollars for missionary work in Africa, thirty dollars for work in India, and now we are raising money to send to China. All this keeps me busy, but I enjoy the work very much.

"I have received a diploma from the Underwood Typewriter Company for writing forty words a minute correctly for ten minutes. They will give me a position as typist at any time, but I would rather work in the Indian Service."

Jacob Morgan, '00, has recently been appointed industrial teacher in the Pueblo Bonito School, Crownpoint, N. M.

Sallie Hood, who was a student in 1911-12, was married in March to Mr. Davis Tyner, of Shawnee, Oklahoma.

THE *Leader*, published at Haskell Institute, has the following to say in regard to John Block, who was a Hampton student from '89 to '91: "John is an industrious, thrifty farmer. Last year he had seven acres in alfalfa and cut it three times in the season; twenty-five acres in oats; thirty-five acres in wheat; twelve acres in millet. They also milk one cow, and his wife has many chickens and geese. They have been supplied with fresh eggs all winter."

Notes and Exchanges

SUMMER INDIAN INSTITUTES

DEFINITE arrangements have been made to hold institutes for employes of all departments of Indian schools as indicated in the following schedule :

Chilocco, Oklahoma, July 6–18

Flandreau, South Dakota, July 20–Aug. 1

Sherman Institute, California, July 20–Aug. 1

Tomah, Wisconsin, Aug. 3–Aug. 15

Chemawa, Oregon, Aug. 3–Aug. 15

Santa Fé, New Mexico, Aug. 17–Aug. 29

The charge for meals and lodging will not exceed $1.00 per day at any institute and at most places will not be more than $.75 per day. More complete information with reference to courses of instruction, lectures, conferences, etc., will be given in the final announcement.

A NEW NEGRO CORPORATION

THE African Union Company, incorporated under the laws of New York, March 20, is the name of an African trading company composed entirely of Negroes. The company controls the mahogany trees on 4900 square miles of Gold Coast territory, the value of which is several millions of dollars, and has a contract with one mahogany firm to take all the logs shipped for five years. It is incorporated for $500,000 with 20,000 shares at $25 each. Eleven thousand shares of the stock have been sold. Among the officers are Dr. W. R. Pettiford, of Birmingham, Ala. and Mr. E. J. Scott, of Tuskegee.

MOONLIGHT SCHOOLS

HOW illiteracy is about to be banished from a Kentucky county through the "moonlight schools" is interestingly told in a satement by Mrs. Cora Wilson Stewart, superintendent of Rowan County, addressed to the United States Commissioner of Education. The school workers have on record the name, location, and history of every illiterate in the mountain county, and are able to make a special study of each individual case. One by one the illiterates are interested in the work of such schools as the "Moonlight School on Old House Creek." In the past two years the thousand and more illiterates have been reduced to a few hundred ; and it is believed that the last vestiges of illiteracy will be wiped out by the close of the present year.

THE ARMSTRONG SCHOOL

THE school board, in naming the schools, honored the Cumberland Street School by naming it for one of the greatest men of this country, and one who has done so much for our race, Samuel C. Armstrong. The teachers placed an excellent portrait of him in the hall of the building, in the hope that the pupils will be inspired to go forward, accomplishing that for which he so bravely stood.

Norfolk *Journal and Guide*

THE INDIANS' ANCESTORS

RECENT investigation by many scientists indicate that the original Indian population of the United States was the overflow of the aboriginal population of southwestern Asia and Mongolia. Dr. A. Hrdlicka, who has recently visited that region, bases his belief in this theory, not only on the prehistoric remains found in this little-explored region, but on the striking resemblance of the existing race of natives to the American Indian. All the measurements, both facial and physical, tend to confirm the theory that they are the originals of the American Indian stock ; and some of the photographs of the living natives are so strikingly like the present-day Indians that it is impossible to tell them apart.

Billings [Montana] *Journal*

DE LIL' BRACK SHEEP

Po' lil brack sheep, done strayed away,
　　Done los' in de win' an' de rain ;
An' de Shepherd, he say, " O hirelin',
　　Go fin' my sheep again. "
But de hirelin' frown—" O Shepherd,
　　Dat sheep am brack an' bad. "
But de Shepherd he smile, like de lil'
　　brack sheep
　　Was de onlies' lamb he had.

Work at Home

JULY 1914

THE SOUTHERN WORKMAN

Press of
The Hampton Normal and Agricultural Institute
Hampton, Virginia

The Hampton Normal and Agricultural Institute

HAMPTON VIRGINIA

What it is   An undenominational industrial school founded in 1868 by Samuel Chapman Armstrong for Negro youth. Indians admitted in 1878.

Object   To train teachers and industrial leaders

Equipment   Land, 1060 acres ; buildings, 140

Courses   Academic, trade, agriculture, business, home economics

Enrollment   Negroes, 1215 ; Indians, 37 ; total, 1252

Results   Graduates, 1709 ; ex-students, over 6000
Outgrowths ; Tuskegee, Calhoun, Mt. Meigs, and many smaller schools for Negroes

Needs $125,000 annually above regular income
$4,000,000 Endowment Fund
Scholarships

A full scholarship for both academic and industrial instruction	$ 100
Academic scholarship	70
Industrial scholarship	30
Endowed full scholarship	2500

Any contribution, however small, will be gratefully received and may be sent to H. B. FRISSELL, Principal, or to F. K. ROGERS, Treasurer, Hampton, Virginia.

FORM OF BEQUEST

I give and devise to the trustees of The Hampton Normal and Agricultural Institute, Hampton, Virginia, the sum of   *dollars, payable*

The Southern Workman

Published monthly by

The Hampton Normal and Agricultural Institute

Contents for July 1914

THE SOUTHERN WORKMAN was founded by Samuel Chapman Armstrong in 1872, and is a monthly magazine devoted to the interests of undeveloped races.

It contains reports from Negro and Indian populations, with pictures of reservation and plantation life, as well as information concerning Hampton graduates and ex-students who since 1868 have taught more than 250,000 children in the South and West. It also provides a forum for the discussion of ethnological, sociological, and educational problems in all parts of the world

CONTRIBUTIONS: The editors do not hold themselves responsible for the opinions expressed in contributed articles. Their aim is simply to place before their readers articles by men and women of ability without regard to the opinions held.

EDITORIAL STAFF

H. B. FRISSELL	W. L. BROWN
HELEN W. LUDLOW	W. A. AERY, Business Manager
J. E. DAVIS	W. T. B. WILLIAMS

TERMS: One dollar a year in advance; ten cents a copy
CHANGE OF ADDRESS: Persons making a change of address should send the *old* as well as the *new* address to

THE SOUTHERN WORKMAN, Hampton, Virginia

Entered as second-class matter August 13, 1908, in the Post Office at Hampton, Virginia, under the Act of July 16, 1894

THE HAMPTON LEAFLETS

Any twelve of the following numbers of the "The Hampton Leaflets" obtained free of charge by any Southern teacher or superintendent. *A charge cents per dozen is made to other applicants.* Cloth-bound volumes for 1905, ' and '08 will be furnished at seventy-five cents each, postpaid.

Address: Publication Office, The Hampton Normal and Agric Institute, Hampton, Virginia

The

Southern Workman

VOL. XLIII   JULY 1914   NO. 7

Editorials

The South's Opportunity

The election of Mrs. John M. Glenn to the presidency of the National Conference of Charities and Correction, at the recent Memphis meeting, furnishes the South an excellent opportunity of showing the nation what it has done quietly and with little public demonstration to meet some of the social needs of the white and colored people and of learning, through closer contact with men and women in other sections, more about well-tried social relief measures.

Mrs. Glenn is herself a Southern woman of strong character. She has made a good reputation in social service work and should receive the co-operation of the devoted men and women who are giving the South the benefit of their training and their skill in social work. She should also command the loyalty of the vast army of members of the National Conference of Charities and Correction because she herself is an untiring worker and an able leader—a woman who knows from first-hand experience what constitutes a helpful program of social work. Mrs. Glenn will serve as an important contact maker between the North and the South. She will be able with the loyalty of the members of the Conference, and the co-operation of the social service workers in the South, and the enthusiasm of a large group of consecrated women, to spread widely and wisely the doctrine of a fair chance in social progress for everybody, regardless of color, creed, or present social status. How to prevent the spread of social dependence is a problem which should enlist the thought and activities of thousands.

The Memphis meeting was successful, not only in its rich program and its forceful speakers, many of whom were national and even international authorities in their special fields of social work, but also in the light which it turned on the city's segregated district in which commercialized vice was being carried on openly without very much popular opposition. The Conference members did more than criticize Memphis for its toleration of prostitution and offer some of the city officials that advice which the officials themselves were seeking. It actually took the Memphis police into its deliberations and joined forces with the representatives of the Trades' Council in discussing municipal problems. The Conference was constructive and only incidentally critical. Surely the social reaction on a city from contact with a large group of keen, warm-hearted social workers must be positive and good. The value of the National Conference of Charities and Correction to Memphis cannot be determined alone by the attendance, the addresses, and the discussions. It will find expression in the better organization of social uplift efforts and in the better understanding of civic problems.

When the National Conference of Charities and Correction meets in Baltimore next year, let us hope that the city officials will be as willing as the Memphis men and women were to receive frank, helpful criticisms and suggestions that represent the soundest opinion of fearless and discerning social workers.

The South's opportunity to demonstrate what it has done and is doing and the South's opportunity to profit by the costly experiments and mistakes of others comes in large measure at least by the election of Mrs. Glenn to the presidency of the National Conference of Charities and Correction.

⌗

Protecting the Indian from Liquor For the year ending June 30, 1912, the Government appropriated $75,000 for the suppression of the liquor traffic among the Indians. It has long been recognized that the use of intoxicating liquors is an insurmountable bar to Indian progress, and that education, campaigns for health, and efforts to encourage industry, all fail with the Indian so long as he uses intoxicants. The Indian Office has vigorously continued throughout the year the campaign against the illegal sale of liquor to the Indians, and even against its introduction into the Indian country. When it was found

that, in some instances, white employes of the Indian Service
introduced liquor upon the reservations under physicians' prescriptions, an order was issued to the employes strictly forbidding
their use of intoxicants, even when ordered by physicians.

To make this order more effective the present Commissioner
of Indian Affairs has recently addressed a personal letter to each
of the six thousand Government employes in the Indian Service
in a further effort to save the American Indian from the curse of
whiskey.

" I believe," says Commissioner Sells in his letter, "that the
greatest menace to the American Indian is whiskey. It does more
to destroy his constitution and invite the ravages of disease than
anything else. It does more to demoralize him as a man and
frequently as a woman. It does more to make him an easy prey
to the unscrupulous than everything else combined. Let us save
the American Indian from the curse of whiskey. There is nothing that could induce me, since I have taken the oath of office as
Commissioner of Indian Affairs, to touch a single drop of any
sort of intoxicating liquor, and this regardless of my attitude on
the prohibition question."

The Commissioner's viewpoint is that it should be the business of all the employes to do everything that might possibly be
helpful in saving the Indians, and that nothing could be more
helpful than to present an object lesson in banishing liquor.

While it might be argued academically that this order is an
invasion of one's personal privileges, yet all right thinking people in the Bureau and outside of it, cannot but recognize that the
Commissioner is setting a remarkable example of idealism in his
department and that it would be better to accept any such sacrifice of personal privilege than be guilty of an action which might
seem to justify the Indian in the use of whiskey.

⌗

**A Notable
Negro Concert**
An undertaking deserving of the highest praise is
the concert of the works of Negro composers as
given by four Negro artists, Mme. Anita Patti
Brown, soprano, Mr. W. Henry Hackney, tenor, Mr. Ernest R.
Amos, barytone, Mr. R. Nathaniel Dett, composer-pianist, assisted
by a local chorus of some thirty voices at Orchestra Hall, Chicago, on the evening of June 3. Possibly similar concerts have
been heard before ; notably, those of the Settlement School for
Colored People in New York. But these have invariably been
gotten up and arranged by white people ; the one in Chicago,
the very first of its kind in the northwest, was exceptional, in
that the conception of the idea and the execution of the necessary details, are to be credited to Mr. W. Henry Hackney, himself a Negro, who went to no end of trouble and expense in order
to exploit the creative talents of his people, and to show to the

world that the Negro is a significant and worthy contributor to musical art; a musical Moses, who would lead the geniuses of his race to the promised land of a wider appreciation.

The unusual event drew out an unusual audience; whatever may have been lacking from the standpoint of numbers being more than made up for in the significance of the personalities of those present; the fact that many of these were composers, critics, and professional musicians of national and international fame, not only gave tone to the occasion itself, but also attaches special significance to the subsequent criticisms.

The works of the following five Negro composers were presented: Samuel Coleridge-Taylor, Harry T. Burleigh, J. Rosamond Johnson, Will Marion Cook, and R. Nathaniel Dett. The next day all the Chicago dailies gave considerable space to reviews both of the works presented and the manner of presentation by the artists. One would be immediately struck by the almost universal note of surprise which characterizes these reviews. There was surprise at the "zeal" which lead a Negro to undertake such a thing as the concert; surprise at the "voices of great natural beauty," "astonishing volume," "excellent control," on the part of the artists who sang; surprise at the "striking signs of originality" and the "facility" as a performer, on the part of the composer-pianist who presented his own works; surprise at the "admirable" work of the chorus. The only disappointment expressed was that more of the compositions did not follow along what seemed to be a preconceived style of racial characteristics. It was plain that the Negro artists presenting the works of Negro composers scored a significant success, but what is none the less significant are the facts which their efforts brought to light.

It was evident that there is a general lack of understanding of what (outside of the so-called "ragtime") really constitutes the Negro element in American music, although a good deal was said about "cadences typical of his own racial chants," and a good deal more about the pieces being or not being "imitations of white man's music"; it was evident that an audience of cultured white American musicians did not know just what to expect of Negro artists, and were astonished that they should be able to intelligently compose, sing, and play as ones "having authority and not as the scribes"; it was evident that the audience was surprised and delighted both with the dignity of the thing presented and the manner of presentation; it was evident that the Negroes themselves, including both those who did and did not take part, were highly encouraged and enlightened as to their own possibilities; it was certain, that by the Negroes doing it themselves, Negro music was given an effective demonstration such as it could have had under no other circumstances, or only in years to come when present-day conditions have changed or have been forgotten.

Certainly there ought to be more of such concerts since apparently through no other medium does the Negro have the same opportunity of winning from the stronger race that real appreciation of his worth, which for some reason seems to be so long deferred; for after the concert the delightful feeling of mutual race appreciation was positively refreshing.

Colored Deaf and Blind Children "The measure of citizenship is not what a man heaps up for himself, but what he scatters abroad for the benefit of others ; not what he grabs, but what he gives to the commonwealth. The greatest citizen is he who does the greatest service. " These suggestive and prophetic words were recently spoken by Col. W. S. Copeland, one of Virginia's ablest editors, at the laying of the corner stone of the Elizabeth Houston Hospital, which will soon form a vital part in the organization and work of the Virginia State School for Colored Deaf and Blind Children, located near Newport News, Va.

About fifteen years ago, Mrs. William C. Ritter, wife of the superintendent, conceived the idea of building for Negroes a school similar to the one provided by Virginia for deaf and blind white children. Mr. Ritter, a Southern white man, who is himself deaf and mute, kept working on this idea. He interested some friends in this school project. The General Assembly of Virginia, however, moved slowly. The scheme for educating Negro deaf and blind children was at best experimental. The work of promotion in the Legislature fell on the shoulders of a few brave men.

Mr. Ritter and his second wife worked faithfully and wisely with a few other white people who understood their plans and sympathized heartily with Negro children who were growing up in ignorance and vice through no fault of their own. Deep faith and sound ideas won new friends for the handicapped Negro children. The governors of Virginia, beginning with Hon. A. J. Montague, saw the necessity of having a state school for colored deaf and blind children. The failure of Virginia in 1906 to find $5000 available for the appropriation that had been sanctioned by the Legislature, proved a blessing in disguise. In 1908, through the wide publicity that the school project had received, Virginia appropriated $25,000. Then the Newport News Chamber of Commerce became active and twenty-five acres were offered by the city and finally the school was located in a healthful, well-drained, and attractive spot.

Today there are seven modern and well-equipped buildings in which one hundred ten deaf and blind Negro children are being educated. Children who a little while ago knew not the name of God or their own name are now able to read, write, and communicate intelligently with signs. Children are taught to read by raised and punched letters, and also to write to their homes typewritten letters that are a rare comfort to parents and friends. Through the application of state funds and the co-operation of men and women .who appreciate from first-hand experience the trials of deafness and blindness, a most valuable work is being carried on. Hon. Harry R. Houston of Hampton and Dr. Clarence Porter Jones of Newport News have rendered most untiring service to Mr. and Mrs. Ritter in their heroic undertaking.

A brief review of the Virginia School for Colored Deaf and Blind Children shows clearly that whole-souled Christian men and women have won a battle for civic righteousness and community progress that should be given wide publicity. Some of the workers for the common good possessed unusual advantages of natural equipment and training for leadership; others were decidedly disadvantaged so far as the world could outwardly judge—all were loyally devoted to the idea of establishing a genuinely helpful school for the colored deaf and blind children of Virginia.

NOTICE OF ALUMNI REUNION

The twelfth alumni reunion of Hampton graduates will be held on Wednesday, July 15, 1914. Those who expect to attend are asked to write at once to the chairman of the committee on arrangements, Mr. F. D. Wheelock, Hampton, Va.

THE NEGRO CHRISTIAN STUDENT CONVENTION 1914

BY A. M. TRAWICK

" THE most significant gathering that was ever held in this country " was the statement of Dr. John R. Mott in calling to order the Negro Christian Student Convention which was held in Atlanta from May 14 to 18. These words were both prophecy and history. The prophecy grew out of a broad view of the hastening Kingdom of God on earth, and the historical facts growing out of the convention remain to be gathered up in years to come. If the purpose, message, and spirit of this convention can penetrate the heart of the church in the South, it will more than justify the memorable words of its chairman.

The purpose of the convention was fourfold : (1) To give to the present generation of Negro students in the United States a strong spiritual and moral impulse ; (2) To study with thoroughness their responsibility and leadership in Christian work at home and abroad, thus bringing them face to face with Christian life callings ; (3) to face responsibility resting upon Negro churches of America to help meet the claims and crisis of Africa; and (4) to consider what light Christian thought may throw on present and future co-operation between the races.

The committee calling this convention was one qualified to inspire confidence throughout the North American Christian world in its serenity of effort in attempting to attain this high objective. At the head of the committee was Dr. John R. Mott, Chairman of the Continuation Committee of the World Missionary Conference and General Secretary of the World's Student Christian Federation. Thus, in Dr. Mott's intimate relation to world movements, this convention was, at once, linked with two of the mightiest impulses which have stirred the Christian world within recent years. It is well to emphasize the fact that the Negro convention at Atlanta was not merely a Southern student gathering, but a movement which was vitally related to the world Christian enterprises of missionary and student leaders.

Co-operating with Dr. Mott in issuing the call and perfecting plans for the convention, were Bishop Walter R. Lambuth, founder of the African Mission of the Methodist Episcopal Church South, Bishop J. S. Flipper of the African Methodist Episcopal Church,

Dr. James H. Dillard, president of the Anna T. Jeanes Founda-
tion and director of the Slater Fund, Dr. Samuel C. Mitchell,
president of Richmond Medical College, President John Hope of
Morehouse College, Atlanta, Ga. Major Robert R. Moton, com-
mandant at Hampton Institute, Hampton, Va., Rev. R. E. Jones,
D. D., editor *Southwestern Christian Advocate*, New Orleans,
La., Miss Belle H. Bennett, of Richmond, Ky., president of the
Woman's Missionary Council of the Methodist Episcopal Church,
South, and Miss Lucy Laney, principal of Haines Institute, Au-
gusta, Ga.

NEED OF THE CONVENTION

It will not be difficult for those who have studied the movements of Negro life and thought in recent years to discern the
great need of just such a convention as was held in Atlanta. The
Negro is yearning for a better expression of his religious life. It
would be strange indeed if generations of Christian teaching and
exhortation had failed to produce in the Negro of the present day
an ambition to share his religious life in greater fullness with the
whole world. The Negro church has reached a point in its development where it is impossible for it to maintain its hold upon
vital principles unless there is a tremendous enlargement of its
vitality in relation to the world movements. It is as impossible
for the Negro church, as for the church of other people, to be
strong and vital without touching the needs of the entire human
family. Turned upon itself alone, the Negro church festers and
decays, but acknowledging its responsibility for its own interpretation of Christian life, it becomes vital with a new mission and
energetic with a new impulse.

The convention in Atlanta was one step forward in the racial
interpretation of Christianity which will be the Negro's chief
contribution to the progress of the world.

There was need of such a convention in order to provide an
expression of the religion which white men and women in the
South profess to practice. It is at variance with Christian integrity to confess the brotherhood of men and continue . to live in
complacent indifference to its claim at our own doors. It is no
insignificant thing for white men and women to be constantly
confronted with the fact that in the South they are not displaying an active brotherly life in harmony with their ideals. The
greatest of all evils growing out of the contact of the two races
on the Southern soil is the disregard of the claims of justice,
kindness, and brotherly love, and the absence of these essential
traits has too often masked the lives of even the best men and
women of the white church in their relations to their Negro
neighborhood. It has come to be unbearable in the minds of

many that there should be habitual injustice and unkindness in the treatment of the Negro, while Christian white people accept the circumstances as being outside the range of their lively interest. The existence of the Negro problem bears a menace to the white man's religion rather than to the Negro's ; for its effect is seen in the weakening and silencing of the corporate conscience, and this, in its ultimate consequences, is far more damaging than the injury suffered by any number of individuals. The Southern white church needed this convention in order to demonstrate to the world that its religion is henceforth as broad and complex as its life in contact with the Negro.

MUTUAL RESPECT AND CONFIDENCE

In reading over the list of the committee issuing the call to the convention, it is observed that white and Negro Christians co-operated in setting forth the objects and securing the speakers and the leaders.   Many of the speakers and leaders were South-ern Christians whose sanity and tact are unquestioned and whose ability to meet a delicate situation have been tested through repeated experiences.   Nothing was done at this convention, and nothing was said or purposed, which a spirit of cordial Christian co-operation can not reproduce in every local church throughout the entire South.   There was a free expression of opinion by both white and colored speakers, a sincere setting forth of ideals and problems resulting from deliberate purpose to understand one another, and the result was that each received the other's point of view.   In the spirit of this gathering the white Christian, addressing his fellow-Christians, can say : "Let us understand and trust the Negro. "   The Negro Christian, addressing a group of his fellow-Christians, can say, in turn, with equal sincerity : "Let us understand and trust the white Christians. "   This was the method pursued throughout the Atlanta convention.   Its spirit of mutual respect and confidence can mean nothing less for the South than a joint advance toward a brighter day when all men shall better understand one another and shall judge more kindly one another's motives and ambitions.

A convention is always significant as much for the things it fails to do as for those that it deliberately attempts.   So it was at Atlanta; the things omitted help to interpret its spirit and mes-sage.   Such questions as Negro criminality and lawlessness, defects of character which bulk so large in the public mind, were left out of the discussion, except only as their solutions were involved in the progress toward nobler and loftier aims.   There were no expressions of bitterness because of the past wrong doings or past evil history and no expressions of suspicion grow-ing out of mutual sufferings in days that are gone.   Throughout these days of preparation, as well as during the convention session, there was a total absence of motives sinister or judgments held in reserve. Everything was open and candid and uniformly brotherly. It would have been a distinct disappointment to every delegate and visitor if things unpleasant had been injected into the discussion, because in the thought of those who came to Atlanta there was only the expectation of helpful consultation.

Points of controversy between the races in the South were left out of consideration in the light of larger issues upon which all could agree. Race intermingling was not once mentioned except to declare that it was a dead issue, but on the other hand, racial pride and integrity were kept constantly in the foreground. This hated subject died a natural death in the light of the marvelous progress which the Negro race has made and the still more marvelous goal toward which it is hastening. Likewise, the question of the Negro's participation in state and local politics was not more than once or twice so much as hinted at. The failure to utter strong convictions on these issues was not because those at the convention held no opinion concerning their solution, but because it was tacitly assumed on all sides that political relations would adjust themselves in the event a larger citizenship was assured.

There was also nothing urged by the white delegates or controverted by the colored delegates on the point of segregation in matters of residence and business occupation. There was, however, much said on the subject of separation; but between segregation and separation there are broad and essential differences.

Segregation comes by force, separation by natural choice. Segregation is the voice of the stronger, saying to the less fortunate, "Thou shalt not;" separation is the voice of self-confidence saying, "I prefer to do this." All the good that any radical advocate of race exclusion desires to see accomplished through segregation is easily obtained through separation without attending evils of hatred, class prejudice, and other animosity, resulting from the exercise of force. No word was said at Atlanta to cause the Negro to feel that he was less of a man and less entitled to respect because of the fact that he was a Negro. On the other hand, much was said to cause him to be proud of his racial identity and to persuade him to accept his place in the divine ordering of things and to strive hopefully for the accomplishment of the evident purpose of his creation.

BASIS OF RACE CO-OPERATION

It would be strange indeed if, with all preparation in prayer and thought, the student convention at Atlanta had not resulted in a very definite movement toward a better reality in life adjustments. It may be said, without fear of contradiction, that the fourfold purpose with which the convention was called was left in the minds and hearts of all who came to Atlanta as seed-truths to bear fruit in future days. It is too early to attempt a portrayal of the purpose which was wrought into the lives of the delegates, but it is not a rash declaration to say that the religious life of students was tremendously advanced; that a definite missionary obligation was assumed by many; that a larger place was assigned to the church; and that religion was set forth as the only sufficient basis of race co-operation.

Many things were done that marked the creation of new friendships. Many of the delegates and visitors had known each other by reputation for years, but some of them were thrown together for the first time during the progress of this meeting. They learned by personal contact how to value each other's worth and how to estimate each other's purposes. Friendships were formed among students of various schools and among workers in various parts of the country which will endure when things less important have been forgotten. This friendship takes the comprehensive form of a determination henceforth to help each other, to believe in each other, and to bear each other's burdens in the spirit of Christian fidelity.

Among the things that were done, none will bear more important fruit than the emphasis upon home improvement. It was not an accident that put a discussion of home life at the very forefront of all the deliberations at the convention. It goes without the saying that there is no advance in race life or integrity without an improvement of family life, and a stimulation of family ideals. The honor of man, the protection of woman, and the safeguarding of little children were emphasized as the foundation stones of a permanent civilization.

Worthy of special mention among the things accomplished is the strong endorsement of the work of the Young Men's and the Young Women's Christian Associations. The activity of these student organizations in past years has been productive of an enlarged vitality in the spiritual, mental, and social life of many college groups; but the student field has been cultivated in only a small part. The traveling secretaries of both men and women student movements have accomplished results surprising in their richness and permanency, but the things done touch only a portion of the important field that remains to be exploited. A much larger number of young men and women is needed to enter the work of the secretaryship in colleges and universities and in this richly rewarding task heroic leadership and sacrificial devotion are qualities of the first consideration.

Students in all institutions of learning were urged by the

convention to study, through the Association's voluntary classes, the social problems confronting the North American church in order to enter sympathetically into their solution. Such study embraces the use of text-books issued by the Young Men's and Young Women's Christian Associations and extends to first-hand investigations of actual conditions in the college neighborhood. The acquisition of knowledge concerning these facts must, if the knowledge is to become vital, be attended at every step by definite service as often as the need is discovered.

Opportunities for service will be discovered through local churches, city and country mission stations and through organizations of allied agencies that are helping to promote the progress of God's kingdom upon the earth. Students can render invaluable service in evangelistic deputations, in visits to proclaim the social message of the church and in summer vacation activities, wherever the vacation months may be spent.

THE CHURCH'S CHALLENGE

Through a special commission, the convention issued a challenge to young men to enter the ministry. Many of the weaknesses which confront the present-day church were candidly confessed and it was resolved on all sides that the best means of correcting these weaknesses was to stimulate a strong ministry. The note was therefore sounded, which will be echoed throughout all the schools and colleges of the land, calling upon the best young men to accept the ministry as the call of God for their life work. The full report of this commission should be read and its message spoken from every pulpit and proclaimed through the church press, so that young men shall be without excuse if they refuse to confess their own obligation.

A special meeting of ministers and editors was held to devise plans to promote the publicity of the convention through the pulpit and the press. Ministers of all churches, both white and colored, are requested to preach upon the spirit and message of the Atlanta gathering and to do all in their power to help forward the good work that was here so wonderfully begun. It was also determined to ask editors of all church papers throughout the entire South to devote editorial space to the same worthy discussion. In this manner the result of the convention will continue to grow until all Christian people of all sects and creeds, both white and Negro, will have at least a part of the inspiration of this occasion. It was rightly judged that there are no agencies in the land better qualified to direct public opinion upon this all important question than the pastors in their pulpits and the editors in control of their periodicals.

Among the things that were done should be mentioned a richer and more comprehensive program of church activity. The spiritual message of the church was enlarged to embrace the obligation of the average church member, and it was also seen and duly recognized that the Negro church in America can never fulfill its destiny without the cordial co-operation of the white churches. It was boldly declared that one of the great needs of the times was for an interchange of visits between pastors of the white and colored churches involving preaching service in one another's pulpits. It was declared also that the churches have a place in the promotion of such fundamental matters as health, education, and the regeneration of social forces. The spirit of the convention was expressed in the sublime conception that whatever men need to have done for them, God expects His church to do, and the church in the South is composed of white Christains and Negro Christians. Therefore, it is only by working together that the churches can do the things the South needs to have done.

There are fields of labor in Southern territory which the Church has never occupied. There are neglected slums in the cities, groups of Negroes working upon plantations, in turpentine camps, in swamps, in railroad construction camps, and many other places where the voice of Christianity is seldom or never heard. This home field was held out to the awakening conscience of Negro students as a worthy place for a life investment.

CALL FOR MISSIONARIES

The convention also turned its heart towards Africa, the Negro's fatherland, and through the messages which were brought from that almost forgotten land, both the opportunity and the responsibility were laid upon the consecrated Negro students to respond to its call as the will of God for them in life service. But more important than all, was the exhortation to the Negro Church of the South to accept the whole world as its responsible field of Christian endeavor. The result of this world vision upon the Negro churches of the South, time itself can properly reveal.

It is not possible to tell, at this day, how many volunteers there were for definite religious service in the non-Christian fields, but there were many decisions during the convention days and there were others among the members of the convention who returned to their homes to deliberate concerning their personal duties in regard to the extension of the world-wide Kingdom. Many individuals solemnly arrived at conviction that their lives henceforth should be given to a declaration of the will of God to all human needs in whatever profession or life work they entered. Many were heard to declare that henceforth their religion should not find expression merely in the salvation of their own lives but in the transmission of their religious impressions into action which should deliberately seek to transform the whole corporate life into the likeness of the Kingdom of God.

The most important of all the consequences of the Atlanta convention was the dominant spirit of hope, giving character to all its utterances. There was no pessimism in any declaration, no despair in any address, no hate in any heart ; but there was an abounding, perfect confidence that the ever-living God is working His purposes in the lives of men. No one deliberately closed his eyes to the seriousness of the problem ; no one was unaware of the very difficult and delicate situation which confronts the two races in the South ; but the difficulties were not exaggerated and the dangers were not enlarged into imaginary fears. They were taken for their full worth, but over and above them all, there was the hope and assured confidence that what God has promised He will faithfully perform.

The convention closed, therefore, on the upward grade, and the delegates returned to their own fields of labor with a new confidence in the future augmented by the consciousness that there are many witnesses to the Christian enterprise upon which they have entered. The profound spiritual impact of this convention was comprehended by Dr. Mott who based his final exhortation upon the words of the writer to the Hebrews : "Let us fling aside every encumbrance and the sin that so readily entangles our feet, and let us run with patient endurance the race that lies before us, simply fixing our gaze upon Jesus, our Prince Leader in the Faith, who will also award the prize. "

A HAMPTON CRUSADE

BY SYDNEY DODD FRISSELL

A SLIM white schooner sailed out from Hampton Creek on a bright morning last May. Across Hampton Roads where the first English ships headed up the James, beyond Old Point where the Monitor steamed in fifty years ago, and seaward toward the Virginia Capes, through which a Dutch slave ship sailed with the first cargo of slaves, she kept her course.

On board was a white-clad crew with black faces and bronzed, a score of Negro and Indian youth picked from all the great family of Hampton for a voyage to eleven states.

With a hurrying of feet and a rattling of canvas and rigging, a swarming to mainsail, jib, and foresail one squad moved swiftly upon the deck, as the *Hampton* heeled to port or tacked to starboard under full canvas. Another squad below were folding the blankets, lowering the chain-hung sleeping-racks, and scrubbing the cabin floors. In the ship's galley another group moved quickly from stove to lazaretto as the odor of cooking bacon blew landward. The *Hampton* was off for her first voyage. Nineteen tradesmen, farmers, and teachers-in-the-making were at their first day of sea duty.

Upon the deck an Apache Indian sounded a sudden bugle call. From deck and forecastle the crew passed into the cabin, where pine tables were pulled down from the racks below decks and set with dishes by the "cook squads." A moment's hush and silence, with only the sound of waves from the open ports, then the melody of a score of voices filled the cabin, as crew and officers of three races joined in the Hampton grace. Hot coffee, oatmeal, and corn bread disappeared fast. Then, from bow to stern, below and above decks the eighty-five-foot schooner received a cleaning and scrubbing as she slid seaward past the dark pine woods and white sand beaches of the low Virginia shores.

IN PORT

A second bugle call from the deck and the crew gathered again in the cabin, washed clean now, with the tables hung from the ceiling, ditty-bags and blankets packed behind the lowered racks, and all hands ready for prayers. A plantation song, a chapter of Scripture, a word of prayer, a response in song, and the crew passed out to take their places, from the helmsman at the wheel to the bow watch at the anchor chains. A rigid inspection of decks, brass work, chains, and rigging, and the officers and skipper passed below decks to examine the lazaretto packed with trunks and tent rolls; the galley, with stove, pantry, and refrigerator; cabins and sixty-horse-power gas engine at the stern. Each member of the crew stood at attention to receive orders or to return the salute of approval. Thus began the first voyage of the *Hampton* with her working and singing crew.

Picked from all the men of Hampton to represent their school and their people, the nineteen black boys and Indians aboard were earnest with a strong purpose. For a hundred days these young students will hold a crusade for Hampton.

To be crew, cast, and chorus ; to act, to sing, to march; to sleep in the crowded forecastle afloat; to make camp ashore, to give the best of their people's songs and customs to strangers; to

UNLOADING PROPERTIES FOR THE FOLK FESTIVAL

try to gain new scholarships for new boys at Hampton—this is the task which these Hampton boys have undertaken for their school.

In this year of financial depression when some of the most loyal friends of Hampton have been forced to withdraw their support, the best chorus which the school has sent out for many years will give the scenes and songs of a pageant which will show the contribution of the Negro and Indian to American life.

Upon the lawns of Newport, Beverly, and Bar Harbor the curtain will rise as the chorus sings "My Old Kentucky Home." A white-haired Negro seated before his cabin door will tell how he was wounded in bringing his master's body home from the battle of Shiloh to his old mistress, who has never forgotten nor ceased to help him in time of need. His story is interrupted by the sound of distant bugles and the song of marching Negro troops returning from the Spanish War. The old man rises to listen to the bugle call and the old familiar marching song of the black troops. Suddenly his son David, who has been fighting with the Tenth Cavalry at Santiago, stands before the cabin home. The old man and his son grip hands in silence while the song of the marching troops grows faint in the distance.

In the next scene the chorus gives the typical responses of the Negro campmeeting, the true "spirituals" of their people, full of religious fervor and sad haunting harmony, beginning with the crudest and weirdest and ending with the most beautiful of the plantation melodies, proof of the Negro's true gift of song to America.

Again the curtain rises. The field hands are singing at their work in the cotton fields. After laying the cotton on the scales they dance with joy that the work is done. This scene depicts the labor of the unskilled field hand, whose service in the South made cotton king.

THE POWER BOAT OF THE "HAMPTON" TOWS THE BAGGAGE TO LAND

MAKING A LANDING

The work of Hampton tradesmen and the skilled Negro
artisans of today is shown as the curtain is again raised. Blacksmiths at their anvil, builders at their building, tailors at their
table, and cobblers at their bench—the tradesmen of Hampton
stand trained and ready to serve their country. The scene ends
with the singing of their trade song, ''Men of Hampton.''

Into the scenes of Negro life are woven not only the true
plantation songs, expressive of the longing and spirit life of a
people in bondage, but the buoyant gladness of the old-time
Negro dances and the dance music and labor songs of the black
field hands.

The Indians of Hampton have given generously of their store
of legend and ancient custom, adding a rare beauty to the
pageant, with the tribal songs and ceremonial dances of the
Cherokee, Apache, and Cheyenne tribes.

It is no light gift for these Indian youth to show to strangers
and to friends the customs of their people held sacred for many
centuries. In a spirit of reverence for their people's past they
give their rare and beautiful dances to win friends for the
school.

Below decks upon the little schooner *Hampton* are the khaki
tents which stood upon the lawns of Newport, Bar Harbor, and
Bretton Woods, and were carried through seven states two
summers ago. During the coming summer this moving camp
will be carried from ship to shore for expeditions into the White
Mountains, the Adirondacks, and the Litchfield Hills.

Baltimore, Wilmington, and Philadelphia heard the chorus the first week of June. While the schooner rounded Cape May the colored boys and Indians held festivals in Orange, N. J., and at Seabright. On June 11 the *Hampton* anchored off Riverdale-on-the-Hudson, and the pageant was given upon the beautiful estate of Miss Grace Dodge. The plantation songs were heard in the open air on Staten Island, at Greenwich, Conn., and upon the lawns of the handsome summer home of Mr. George Wickersham at Cedarhurst, Long Island.

After a journey into the Litchfield Hills with tents and camp, the chorus will sail about New London and upper Long Island, cruising later around Cape Cod through the first weeks of July, and holding festivals at the Cape resorts from New Bedford to Harwich. Upon the North Shore the crew will anchor off Beverly, to hold festival again where so many memorable meetings have been held for Hampton. Sailing to York Harbor, Portland, 'and Rockland, Maine, and touching at the islands the chorus will

THE REPRESENTIVE OF THE APACHES WHOSE FATHER
WAS A MEMBER OF GERONIMO'S BAND

"THE OLD MAN AND HIS SON GRIP HANDS IN SILENCE."

reach Bar Harbor the last week in July. A week of camping and festival in the White Mountains—at Bretton Woods, the Profile, Jefferson, Intervale, and Whitefield—and the company will stow their tents and baggage once more in the *Hampton's* hold and sail into Newport harbor late in August. Narragansett, Watch Hill, and Westerly will hear the singing before the schooner makes the long voyage under sail and power through Hell Gate and north again by the Hudson for inland marches to Mohonk and the resorts of the Adirondacks.

Thus for a hundred days in eleven states these colored boys and Indians will sing and hold pageant for their school. If they can win friends for their race and gain aid for their school they will return to the shops and fields of Hampton happy in the success of their crusade.

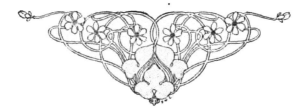

MEDALLIC PORTRAITURE OF
THE INDIAN

BY BRIGGS DAVENPORT

IN recent years, since it became evident that the savage red man of the United States of America was soon to disappear, leaving only his civilized and educated progeny to represent him, there has been much expressed regret that more care had not been taken long before the close of the last century to fix the features of the famous leaders of that race in some imperishable form of portraiture. Sculpture has given us many general and many idealistic representations of the North American Indian, but few that are of historic interest, and scarcely any that have the true documentary value. Yet no division of the human family could have afforded more picturesque subjects.

The most usual fault in the treatment of the red man in art has been the disposition to settle upon one type only and by narrow adherence to make it conventional ; while in truth the Indian tribes, large and small, afford among them a most strik-ing variety of facial conformation, as they do of customs and traditions. If the psychology of the red man had been search-ingly studied, perhaps as marked subjective differences would also have been found, both between tribes and between individ-uals as in the numerous civilized peoples of the globe. No sound ethnologist believes that the Indian tribes were of common racial origin. Everything that is known of them favors the theory that they represent many distinct strains of blood: that in atavic peculiarities some are as far separated each from the others as are the Chinamen and the Scotchmen of today.

After another generation or two, the full-blooded Indian, leading the life of savagery, or even merely wearing its costumes and respecting its traditions, will no longer exist in the domain of the United States of America. And probably, a half century later, his brother of the British North American dominion will also have lost, in the smelting-pot of what we define as civiliza-tion, nearly all the outward distinction of racial primitiveness.

It is therefore of great importance, both from the viewpoint of ethnology and that of history, that even at this late day all that is possible should be done to repair in this regard the negligence of the past. Of course, what may now be done is little in

comparison with what might and should have been done. Such
artists as Remington have finely illustrated some of the Indian
types; but they have done little to give posterity a vivid
individual idea of the great representative men of the Sioux,
Cheyenne, Shoshone, Ute, Nez-Percé and Apache peoples, for
instance, whose names sprinkle the pages of American military
annals, to say nothing of the tribes, with such leaders as Black
Hawk and Tecumseh, which flourished in the early years of
the republic. I have known personally a considerable number
of the leaders in war and statecraft of the Plains tribes,
among them Red Cloud, Spotted Tail, Old-Man-Afraid-of-his-

AN ARIZONA CHIEF

Horses, and Red Dog, of the Sioux; and Washakie, of the Shoshones. The true impression of their personality cannot be fully
gained through any description, joined even though it may be
to an eloquent account of their careers. The plastic art could
have done more than anything else to supplement their written
history. It ought, indeed, to be regarded as an essential aid
to all history. The Romans so considered it. The many por-
trait-busts of their great men with which their public buildings
and public places were adorned, as well as the multiplicity of
their medallic portraits, attest this fact; and from a study of the
higher types of their physiognomy we know more intimately
the race which ruled the world in the Latin era than we could

ever have known it by the mere recitals of historians and
biographers.

The bas-relief, as proved by the Greeks and Romans, and
some modern nations, is the form of sculpture best suited to
illustrate history. It is unfortunate that America has thus far
made such little use of this form. Not that numismatic portraiture of American origin is so rare; but that it has seldom been of
really important significance and merit. Of medals of historic
value made at the command of the United States Government
only eighty-six could be counted down to 1878: that is to say, in
more than a hundred years of political independence. The more
noted of these were designed by the French artists, Pierre
Simon Duvivier, Augustin Dupré, and Nicolas Marie Gatteaux.
The one important American medal of the last century bearing

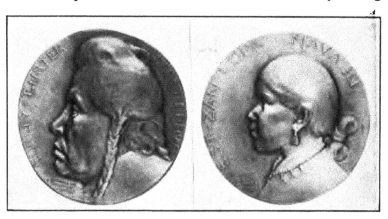

A SOLE SURVIVOR OF   A NAVAHO MAIDEN
CUSTER'S BAND

the effigy of a red man was designed by the celebrated astrono-
mer, David Rittenhouse, of Philadelphia. It is known as the
"Red-Jacket medal." But it is without value as original portraiture.

If the American people are to be tardily endowed with
numismatic memorials of the red Indians, it will be chiefly
because of the initiative of a young sculptor resident in Paris,
who has devoted several years to the procuring of clay studies
from life of representatives of that race. He has made periodic
visits to the reservations beyond the Missouri, and has spent
many months in wigwam villages and at Government agencies,
getting famous or typical Indians to pose for him and forming
the maquettes in their presence. Returning to Paris with these
first fruits of his labor, he prepares the moulds from his modeled

bas-reliefs and casts the medals himself in a furnace erected in a corner of his picturesque studio in the Rue Falguière. It seems strange at first thought that so many sculptors' ateliers suggest a mixture of chaos and art; really it is not strange at all. It is the mission of art to bring beauty out of chaos itself. In the studios of gifted painters, too, there is often a great deal of "clutter," distasteful as this commonplace word may be to romantic young women who enjoy only the outer unconventional view of art.

Disregarding by forced effort at first the great variety of objects more or less nondescript in Mr. Edward Warren Sawyer's studio, we at length discover the unpretentious sculptor himself, seated in a pensive attitude in an obscure corner. At his elbow

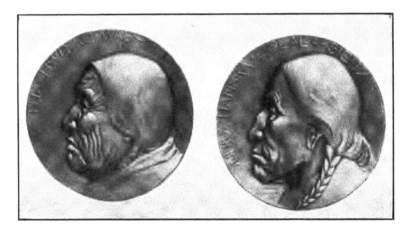

THE SIOUX CHIEF, LONG DOG   CRAZY HORSE'S CHIEF MEDICINE MAN

lies a medal freshly wrought in the preliminary clay, and on a big packing-case behind him is his slender statue of an Indian boy, remarkable for its simple and poetic realism. The artist himself is not tall, and is of rather boyish aspect; and it is almost a boy's smile, bright and optimistic, that illumines his face as he looks up expectantly at his visitor. His hand goes forth in greeting, but it passes the hand that is extended to meet it and offers the wrist instead. This the visitor clasps hesitatingly. Do you guess why there is no handclasp? It is because the hands of the sculptor are thickly knotted, almost solidified, by a rare and puzzling kind of rheumatism, defying the science of the doctors and their skill. For the last half dozen years this misfortune has had its grip upon him ; yet during all that period he has valiantly continued his work, has steadily advanced to better and better achievement. Heroism would be the best word to characterize such devotion to an artistic ambition—the tenacious refusal to rest, despite pain and the partial fettering of those noblest of all nature's instruments. What he has accomplished would be considered extraordinary, even without knowledge of his terrible difficulties ; with such knowledge, it appears marvelous.

It was ill health that first brought Mr. Sawyer in touch with the savage life. He had been one of the liveliest of all the joyous circle of art students in Paris and in Rome. He had exhibited notable sculptures in the Salons of 1902 and 1903. But the next year the doctors determined that he must go to a dry climate. He went to Yuma, Arizona, where Burbank, the eminent painter of red Indians, joined him. From Yuma he pushed up through the mountains into northern Arizona, to visit John L. Hubbel, the famous trader among Indians, whose knowledge of their peculiarities made his counsel in this instance invaluable. Another summer Mr. Sawyer spent in great part among the Agua Caliente Apaches. Subsequently he visited the Sioux, Cheyennes, Arapahoes, Utes, Shoshones, and Crows.

The idea of making a series of medallic portraits of typical Indians had been in Mr. Sawyer's mind for several years. The cost of its realization was, for him, a serious difficulty. Practical America looks askance at most art which does not serve as an emphasis to wealth or to material success. The young sculptor tried to get the men in charge of the great museums of his country to take a direct and helpful interest in his scheme, but could not. So at last he assumed all the initial pecuniary risk himself. It was a generous act, which only genius that is confident in itself can justify. He mortgaged a great part of his future to secure a large personal loan. After that he set out upon the longest of his tours among the Indians, again visiting Arizona, and later extending his leisurely travel through New Mexico, Oklahoma, Wyoming, Montana, and South Dakota.

" Americans will understand some day what they have lost in failing to obtain imperishable likenesses of Sitting Bull, Crazy Horse, Red Cloud, Spotted Tail, Chief Joseph, Washakie, Geronimo, and other remarkable Indians," said Mr. Sawyer, when I asked him about his latest modelings in bas-relief. "It is my greatest sorrow that I could not have commenced my work while most of the renowned chiefs of the later frontier wars were alive."

But Mr. Sawyer is happy over the fact that in a recent tour of the Indian reservations he got portraits in clay of several red men who had a noted part in the Custer battle in 1876. The search for them, the tactics used to win them to sittings, made his visits to Lame Deer, Pine Ridge, Standing Rock and the

Crow Agency intensely absorbing. It was near Manderson in South Dakota that he met what he calls "the old fighting type of the Oglala Sioux."

Everybody who can recall the day when the Custer massacre became known to the American nation still feels a tragic thrill at any realistic revival of its images of horror. For none, certainly, can this impression be more profound than for those who, like myself, rode over the track of Custer's ill-fated advance only a few weeks later, and who had previously been in battle with the very red men whom he encountered. Some of the old Crow scouts whom Mr. Sawyer found at the agency with their tribe

A BRAVE OF THE YUMA TRIBE

served with General George Crook's column when it moved northward in June, 1876, to its lively clash with the Sioux and Cheyennes under Sitting Bull and Crazy Horse on the Rosebud, just eight days before those same formidable warriors, on the Little Big Horn, annihilated Custer and the flower of his regiment. The two battle fields are less than forty miles apart. In one valley is now the post village of Lame Deer, and in the other the Crow Agency. My own last recollection of that region pictures it as enveloped, as far as the eye could reach, in a heavy pall of smoke from the dry August grass which the Sioux and Cheyennes had set on fire to embarrass our march, while at their leisure they cleverly dispersed towards the Yellowstone and the Little Missouri.

At the Crow Agency, which is only a mile and a half from the scene of the massacre, the young sculptor induced the scout Curley, the unique survivor of Custer's immediate command, to sit for him, and thus obtained one of his finest medals. Other Crow scouts who served the Government in that war and whom he has modeled are Other Medicine (Ech-spa-di-e-ash) and Big Ox (Besh-a-e-shi-e-di-nesh-a). Among the Cheyenne leaders are Two Moons (Esh-sha-e-nish-is), Old Bear (Ma-ki-na-ko), and White Bull (Ho-tua-hwo-ko-mas), chief medicine-man to Crazy Horse's band. All of these were conspicuous in the Custer fight. Among the Sioux of whom Mr. Sawyer has also made medallic portraits are John Red-Cloud, son of Red Cloud (Mok-pe-a-luta), head of the Oglalas, instigator of the Fort Phil Kearney massacre in 1866; Smoke (Sota), Long Dog (Sunka-Hanska), and Picket Pin (Hunkpa-Ka).

Mr. Sawyer hopes to get, on his next tour, many more studies at the Sioux and Cheyenne villages in the Dakotas and among the Blackfeet in northwestern Montana, near the Canadian border. He will also visit the Shoshones, one of the most interesting of all the copper-hued tribes, in the Wind River region of Wyoming.

There are many obstacles, some of them ridiculous, but none the less real, in the way of the artist who seeks to mould or to paint the yet untamed Indians of the elder generation. They must be treated in some respects as if they were children : they must be humored, flattered, cajoled, coaxed; but the dignity of their manhood must never be slighted in the least degree. Picture books have a sovereign fascination for them.

"Give a picture book to one of the old braves," said Mr. Sawyer, "and he will sit on the floor for hours with no other movement than that required for the turning of the leaves. Sometimes one of those old fellows would come to me and remain a long time without uttering a sound. Then suddenly, in a deep guttural tone, he would pronounce the word 'book,' and then I would know that I had him for a good sitting. I made many efforts to get my hand on White Bull, an ancient chief who stood greatly upon his dignity. At last I succeeded. But I doubted afterwards whether my success was not too great. Once an Indian is interested in you, he will bring his tepee, his dogs, his wife or wives, his papooses, all his belongings, in fact, and camp beside you, as long as your hospitality endures.

"No attempt to drive an Indian will do. Sometimes I capture my models through their curiosity. In Arizona I made a maquette of an old Apache who had a 'bad eye.' I took, of course, the better side of his face. He looked at my work after I had been at it an entire day. Then with an ominous grunt he

left me. By-and-by he came back, accompanied by a half-breed
Mexican, to whom he said:

" 'That fellow in there, he no good. He make me picture :
only one eye. Now I got two eye. I want other eye match one
eye.'

"The compliment which is implied in the wish to portray
their features does not greatly impress them. But they are fully
alive to the truthfulness or the non-truthfulness of the artistic

"REMARKABLE FOR ITS SIMPLE AND POETIC REALISM"

result. After I had finished the modeling of a medal a crony
of the original exclaimed, the moment he saw it: 'No need put
name on that old fellow!' and he laughed with the naive spon.
taneity of a child.

"Some of the most picturesque individuals have been spoiled
for the artist by their adoption in a certain degree of civilized
habits. Captain Coffee, an Apache warrior, was posing for me
one day when he was unceremoniously called away to have his

hair cut according to Government regulations and by the Government barber. When he came back one look at him was sufficient. I had to abandon my medal. Naiche, hereditary chief of Geronimo's famous band, has to submit at fixed intervals to the Government barber. With few exceptions I found that the Federal agents evinced but little interest in the making of the medals. They might have aided me in my negotiations with the Indians, if they had wished. But, instead of that, they allowed

CHEYENNE CHIEF, TWO MOONS, AND THE
SCULPTOR, EDWARD WARREN SAWYER

unessential routine to interfere with my work. I paid to nearly all the Indians who posed for me a day-wage of three dollars.''

Mr. Sawyer's excellence as a medallist is recognized by high authorities in art. Several of his bas-relief portraits are exhibited in the Luxembourg museum. He had twelve bronze profiles of Indians at the Ghent exposition. Private collectors have bespoken many of his medals; but it is most desirable that a complete series of his Indian effigies should be deposited in some great American museum, as the perpetual property of the nation.

Edward Warren Sawyer was born in Chicago in March, 1876. He first exercised his aptitude in sculpture as a boy in a wood carver's shop, in the intervals of schooling. Afterwards he entered the Chicago Art Institute. In 1899 he went to Europe in the steerage of a "crack" new steamship, and joined the life class at Calorossi's art school in Paris. He studied later under Fremiat, the immortal sculptor of animals, and did most of the modeling of the statue of an American bison bearing the latter's signature, which is one of the most striking ornaments of the Jardin des Plantes. He also studied under Gérome at the Ecole des Beaux-Arts, under Vernet at the Académie Julien, and under Auguste Rodin. He passed a year at the Academia delle Belli Arti and at the French school in the Villa Medici at Rome. In 1904 he received the bronze fine-arts medal at the Louisiana Purchase Exposition.

THE SPIRIT OF HAMPTON*

BY WILLIAM HOWARD TAFT

THOSE of us who come down to Hampton under the pretense that we are coming on a philanthropic errand may fool the rest of the world, but those of us who have enjoyed coming know that we come for one of the most real pleasures that men and women have in their lives. The inspiration of this anniversary ceremony we find in the improvement that is really being worked out through the spirit of Hampton, and the spirit of Armstrong, and the spirit of Ogden, and it comes to us with a lifting force.

What is it that you feel when you come to Hampton, when you walk about and see the cheery faces of those who are here receiving instruction and getting an inspiration of life ? It is an encouragement of our hope, and of our belief, that the problems which are before us, at least South of Mason and Dixon's line, are capable of solution, and that right here is the center from which shall radiate the influences that are to work out that solution. There is a great deal of talk from platforms by psuedo and sometimes real statesmen, and by politicians, about what is going to be done for people by legislation. It is a great rest to come to Hampton and hear what is being done by the people for them-

* Excerpts from an address to the graduating class at Hampton Institute Anniversary exercises, April 24, 1914

selves, through an encouraged community spirit, and the education that is being put into them by industrial and moral and uplifting institutions like Hampton.

Now young men and young women, I do not have to congratulate you on the great blessing that has come to you by having been educated at Hampton and having breathed in the spirit of Hampton. I know from what I have seen, I know from what I know of Hampton, that all your life long that which you have received here will furnish the basis for your action hereafter, and that when you fail, the thing that will humilate you most— if you do fail—and there are few of you who will—the thing that will humilate you most will be that you have fallen from the Hampton standard; and when those from whom you receive your inspiration, your principal and his associates, shall know you have failed, that will be the deepest punishment you can suffer. And the effect of that is going to lead you on to greater and greater effort to deserve the great benefaction which has been conferred on you by what Hampton has done for you. I do not wonder that Hampton, as you men and women go out from it, seems a kind of heaven and something from which you can derive inspiration for all the obstacles you need to overcome.

There is before you a great opportunity. You are coming into adult life just at a time in the course of the progress of your people in the South when the opportunity at your hand is greater than that of those who went before you. Definitely, what your people need is that they shall use the economic freedom they have. They are yielding to their thirst for education and to their land-hunger. These motives should lead them to work along honest, straightforward, industrious lines, improving the community life of which they are a part, and vindicating their value to society and the state. Let them be a felt part in progressive community spirit.

After this experience at Hampton today and after studying the North and the South, it seems to me that while the North has apparently been the more fortunate section for a number of decades, it is the South now that has a definite future before it which it can work out; and it is the North which is struggling amid changed and chaotic conditions, the future tendency of which is uncertain.

With the natural tendencies of the Negro, with his natural desire to be a farmer, with land easily within his reach, with the economic freedom that he has, with great opportunity for mechanical trades in country surroundings, with a definite goal before him, undisturbed by social theories, unaffected by political change or disturbance, taught that the labor of his hand is the most honorable thing that he can do, there is not anything that he cannot accomplish for his people by increasing their wealth and their economic importance, which are stepping stones to the other rights to which they aspire. Meantime, they will achieve real happiness, and under the influence of wisely ordered lives and the inspiration of religion, they will justify all the sacrifices and labor of men of their own and other races for their elevation.

Now, God bless you. May you go out with the spirit of Hampton, and as long as you continue to feel the gratitude that you ought to feel in your heart, as long as you have an earnest desire to live up to the standard of Hampton, as long as, whatever you do, you would be willing to tell the principal and officers of Hampton about it without embarrassment, so long will you be carrying the high standard of Hampton for the benefit of your race ; and whenever you end your lives, you may say, "I have contributed that which I owe to the help of my race, my country, and the world."

THE NEGRO AND THE SOUTH'S INDUSTRIAL LIFE*

BY ROBERT R. MOTON

Commandant of Cadets at Hampton Institute

THE Census of 1910 shows that two out of every five persons engaged in gainful occupations in the sixteen Southern states are Negroes. Of the entire Negro population in those sixteen Southern states, 63 per cent are in some form of industrial occupation, while only 47 per cent of the white people are thus engaged. Of all the Negroes who are engaged in industrial activities 60 per cent are agricultural workers. The large majority of industrial workers in the South are on the land ; and this is especially hopeful so far as the Negro is concerned. It is also significant that the number of Negroes engaged as agricultural laborers is about the same as it was fifty years ago, though the Negro population has increased nearly 150 per cent during that period. Something like a million Negroes have developed from agricultural laborers to farmers, there being, according to the Census of 1910, something like 890,000 in this class.

---

* Address delivered before the Southern Sociological Congress in Memphis, Tenn., May 9, 1914

After all of the efforts which have been made to induce foreign immigrants to settle in the South, less than 5 per cent have so far availed themselves of the opportunity offered, and a large portion of that 5 per cent has settled in the cities of the South. The Negro must be very largly depended upon to supply all the demands for labor in agricultural as well as domestic lines. According to reliable statistics, the Negro has not only hitherto done this more or less acceptably, but he has also gone rapidly into the fields of skilled and semi-skilled laborers. He is, therefore, an indisputable factor in the present and future development of our Southern states.

One reasonably familiar with the situation does not doubt that the South, within the next few decades, because of its splendid soil and climate, its abundant rainfall, its special adaptation to the raising of cotton, its new and growing spirit of enterprise which demands modern scientific methods of agriculture, will become one of the most important agricultural sections of the nation and the world. It is, therefore, important not only that labor and capital should work in harmony, but it is even more important that there should be inter-racial sympathy and co-operation along all lines of economic and civic endeavor.

NEED OF TRAINED WORKERS

Thoughtful Negroes as well as thoughtful white men are agreed that the South offers the largest opportunity for the Negro, economically, socially, and morally. It is also agreed by thoughtful people, black and white, that the rural districts in the South offer the greatest opportunity for the masses of colored people. It is fair to assume, then,

That, for the present at least, the South cannot depend on foreign immigrants for its farm operatives, its domestic and personal service, or its unskilled and semi-skilled labor ;

That it must depend on the Negro for the present and also the very distant future to recruit the ranks of this form of labor;

That, if the Negro is to constitute the mass of industrial operatives of the South, it is imperative for the common good that there should be sympathetic co-operation with the white workers engaged in similar forms of industry ;

That every effort should be exerted on the part of the South to make these laborers, black and white, more reliable, more skillful, and more efficient ;

That the laborer can be kept efficient and skillful only as his environment is wholesome and strengthening and not weakening and demoralizing ;

That it is the duty of every patriotic Southerner to use every possible means for the practical, sympathetic training of these workers and their children through a thorough, well-regulated school system.

It is frequently asserted by careless and thoughtless speakers and writers that all Negroes are lazy, shiftless, and inefficient; but the people who say this are not only out of accord with the facts of the case, but they often do not believe what they themselves are saying.

What they mean to say is that *some* Negroes in every community are lazy, shiftless, and inefficient; but in practically every district where Negroes are employed, whether as farm laborers or as mechanical laborers, the verdict is that the large majority of Negro workers are reliable, many of them are skillful and very efficient, and not a few are almost indispensable. There are very few places in the South where the employer would be willing to dispense with the services of his Negro employes.

The South has made marvelous strides in industries within the past forty years, but this would have been well-nigh impossible without its docile, cheerful, and willing Negro population. Notwithstanding the much discouraging talk and the more discouraging, not to say unfair and unjust legislation, there cannot be found, even where the ruling and the laboring classes are both of the same race, as much real, helpful sympathy and co-operation as exist at the present time between the Negro and the Southern white man. The relationship is one that is difficult to define, yet it is no less real. There are some individual white men who like individual Negroes, though they may think they hate the race. Individual white men will do any reasonable thing to help individual Negroes. Yet a single white man, here and there, may say any unreasonable thing against the Negro race. There are Negroes who are equally as inconsistent in their feelings and expressions regarding the white race.

The white South, for its own self-interest, if for no other reason, should strive to make the individual relationship which exists between the races a more general relationship, and make the large mass of Negro workers contented and happy. It should encourage Negroes to live on the farm and to buy up the waste and undeveloped lands of the South; it should offer every possible inducement for the Negroes to remain in the South and on the land where they can rear their children amid physical and moral surroundings conducive to their highest development and greater usefulness to themselves and to the state.

VALUE OF KNOWLEDGE AND CONFIDENCE

The two races in the South truly deserve to be congratulated—the Negro, because, notwithstanding all of the laws and all of the discussions regarding the various forms of circumscription and segregation, he has not become embittered and has not grown to hate the white race ; and the white people, because, in spite of all that has been said and done, they have not lost confidence in and respect for and desire to help the Negro.

Few white people know the Negro's real feeling on the question of segregation. The Negro rarely discusses this question frankly, for the reason that he does not think that because he is black he is cursed and that the Creator has limited his possibilities so that he is unfit for association with other human beings. But, as a matter of fact, 99 per cent, I should say, of the Negro race, if they should tell what they really feel, would say that they have no desire to be with white people *because they are white* ; that, so far as unforced segregation and separation are concerned, they are entirely in accord with it, not because of unfitness but because of racial incompatibility. One can observe this attitude in every Southern community and in most Northern communities where there is any considerable number of Negroes.

In Southern communities, long before segregation was ever spoken of, there were Negro sections in almost all towns where the Negroes lived happily, and there was practically no trouble or feeling of unpleasantness because of it. The only persons who presumed to disregard the unwritten law were certain white men who opened grocery stores, drygoods stores, and bar rooms which very frequently carried with them the lowest and most subtle sort of vices and degradation which would not be tolerated in white residential sections. What is true in urban communities is very much the same in rural communities. There were many counties in Virginia and in other states also where one could travel for miles on land owned by colored people and this happened without any law forcing white and colored people to separate.

The Negro enjoys the companionship of his race and never loses a chance to be with them, everything else being equal. Like every other human being, he enjoys being with his friends whether they are black or white. But because a few Negroes here and there in cities and in the country have bought property alongside of white people ; because the Negro traveling on the railroad wishes to ride in the Pullman car ; because at the railroad station he applies at the only restaurant for a meal ; because a few Negroes here and there go to Northern white universities ; and because the Negro protests against the " jim crow " car (which almost invariably means inferior accommodations) and the separation on street cars, the feeling in the minds of the average white person, is, perhaps, that the Negro wants to be white and that he wants to be with white people *because they are white*. There is absolutely no foundation in fact for this feeling.

NEED OF MORE PROTECTION

The Negro has long since learned that property alongside of white people in cities and towns is more valuable ; that his wife and children have more protection ; that the streets are better and cleaner, and that he gets better fire protection, greater police protection ; and that for such a section there are more adequate sanitary arrangements. The Negro farmer has discovered that if his land adjoins a white man's land the county roads are better cared for. The roads in the Negro sections, especially where the county roads are infrequently used by white people, as is often the case, are generally neglected, and it is often difficult to get the road master to pay any attention to that section of the public highway. In many cases it is never touched. The fence and stock laws are much more rigidly enforced by county officials and more carefully observed by both black and white wherever white people's property is concerned.

The truth is simply this. The white people are the ruling, controlling, dominating, directing element of this country and they have the best of everything—the best parts of the cities, the best hotels and restaurants, the best cars, and as a rule, the best schools, colleges, and universities. When a Negro shows an inclination to be with white people, it is not because he wants to be with white people as such, but because he wants to get the best as to land, position, education, comforts, conveniences, and protection.

It is self-evident that the Negro has practically no share in the making or the execution of the laws. He knows when he is segregated that underneath the segregation is the idea that he is inferior and unfit for association with decent people of every other race. He knows that in his section of the city the streets are not paved ; that criminals of his own race and often of other races are allowed to run at large and prey on the ignorant and innocent ; that in his section the health boards are not as particular as they should be regarding sanitary surroundings ; that street sweepers, who are often white, give little or no attention to sections where Negroes live ; and that Negro sections, because they are Negro sections, are almost invariably neglected by city as well as county officials.

WHAT SEPARATION HAS MEANT

Separation, as far as I have been able to observe, has never meant equal treatment or equal accommodations on railroads or steamboats, in restaurants or on street cars, or anywhere else.

Sometimes an effort has been made to make the public service equal, but those who have the supervision of it, because of lack of interest, or lack of sympathy, or perhaps lack of appreciation of the necessity of careful supervision, have allowed the accomodations to degenerate into places inferior and, in most cases, absolutely unfit for human beings of any race. In many cases, these places are as menacing to the health and lives of the white race as they are demoralizing and degrading, as well as menacing, to the health and lives of the colored people.

The Southern conscience ought to be aroused to the point of action where the white South will demand absolutely equal accommodations for both races in all places where there is local segregation. In many places, if there were Negro constables, Negro magistrates, and Negro policemen in Negro sections, there would be far less criminality on the part of Negroes, because these Negro officials would ferret it out and locate the vicious criminals of his race. He would, nine times out of ten, see that the offender was brought to justice. Negro street cleaners would be more zealous in their duties. The criminality of the South, as far as the Negro is concerned, would be reduced fifty per cent if the authorities would call into service colored men as constables and policemen. The white officers would get co-operation which they now little dream of.

No leader, either black or white, can give skillful, efficient, conscientious service when he is surrounded day and night by all that tends to lower his health, distort his mind, weaken his morals, embitter his spirit, and shake his faith in his fellow-men. The South's growth can come only when its laboring class is well housed, well fed, and surrounded by all that tends to make it strong mentally, morally, and physically. Under the system of segregation, which is at present being agitated and practiced in many quarters, it is impossible for the Negro to grow normally either in his physical, mental, or moral life. To that extent he is inefficient and unsatisfactory as a laborer. I much fear he will grow more so.

JUDGING A RACE BY ONE CLASS

The next largest group of Negro industrial workers, according to the Census of 1910, are the 1,324,150 of Negroes who are engaged in domestic and personal service. These come in little personal contact and have almost nothing in common, so far as actual occupation is concerned, with a similar though very much smaller group of white people. Nevertheless, because of the very intimate relationship which they sustain toward the dominant and law-making element, they are in many ways a most important factor in inter-racial problems. These domestic and personal-service workers have been for more than a generation very largely the ''ministers-extraordinary and plenipotentiaries of the Negro race at the court of Southern white public opinion.'' Their indifference, their laziness, their shiftlessness, their carelessness, their inefficiency, their immorality and criminality, have played no inconsiderable part in shaping the mental attitude of most Southern white people toward the Negro. Their interpretation of the sermons, lectures, lawyers' briefs, physicians' prescriptions, the conduct, character, feelings, sentiments, and longings of all the Negroes in the South, educated and otherwise, has been the infallible foundation upon which the reputation of the whole Negro race to a very large extent has been based.

Not all of this class are inefficient, shiftless, or criminal ; but the domestic- and personal-service element in any race, important as it is that they be efficient and satisfactory and able to hold their jobs, are not the best representatives of a race of people. They are apt to misinterpret and misrepresent the intelligent, well-meaning, property-owning, and progressive class. It is unfair to the white race that it should shape its opinion of the entire Negro race by the Negro cook or butler who may or may not be satisfactory. It is even more unfair to the Negro that the decision as to his morality, his intelligence, his ability, and his industrial efficiency should be determined merely by this element.

PROTECTION OF NEGRO WOMEN

A great difficulty that faces the Negro girls who are engaged in domestic service is the lack of attention and care on the part of their employers. This has had more to do with the moral degradation of Negro women than any other single phase of Southern life. Little or no interest is taken in these girls so long as they attend to their duties. Where they go, with whom they associate, the life they live, the environment in which they spend their off hours—these facts receive little or no consideration. This is perhaps natural, but it is certainly unfair, not only to the Negro domestic servant, but also to the white employer of the Negro servant. What is worse, it has made many a Negro woman ashamed of her job.

Many well-meaning white people take it for granted that the Negro wll be lazy, dishonest, and immoral. That very attitude, benevolent as it is, perhaps, is in itself most unfortunate and dangerous. It is most unfortunate for the Negro that the white man should set for him a lower standard either industrially, morally, or intellectually than for himself, and too easily offer a sort of half apology for Negro weaknesses, failures, and inefficiencies.

EDUCATION IS THE SOLUTION

This leads me to emphasize the very great necessity of education for the Negro. There has been much criticism and some fun and ridicule made at the expense of the educated Negroes, by perhaps well-meaning people. But, after all is said and done, the most successful and the most reliable and the most influential element in the Negro race, as in every race, is the educated class—the men and women who have done most to cement cordial and sympathetic relations between the races ; who have had the greatest influence for caution and conservatism upon the reckless, radical Negroes; who have been most patient and most persistent in their efforts to fit the whole Negro race for freedom and citizenship, in their broadest and most perfect sense, by practical Christian education and sane, wholesome advice.

It seems to me that the best means of cementing a more cordial, sympathetic, and helpful relationship between the two races is thorough, systematic training, and practical education for both races, which means loyalty and efficiency, and especially so for the more backward of the two races—the Negro. Our struggle, then, to bring all the laborers of the South to the point where they can make of this Southland, where cotton still remains the economic king, what it should eventually become, must be first to feed, clothe, and house them properly. For this they must be trained intellectually, morally, and spiritually ; and for this training the white people, the directing class, must see that all labor, black as well as white, has a full and complete opportunity to get the very best, broadest, deepest, and highest that the Creator has given to all mankind.

I plead for the continued co-operation and backing of the South in the efforts and achievements of such secondary and higher educational institutions as Hampton, Tuskegee, Howard, Atlanta, Fiske, and Virginia Union University, with a dozen other worthy institutions, not only for the training they give the Negro, but also for what this training has meant to the South and to the nation. It is only by broadening his horizon, enlarging his vision, increasing his ambition, deepening his pride in himself and in his race, and thereby increasing his respect for himself and otherselves, that the Negro will be made truly efficient—a permanent benefit to himself, to his race, and to his country. And this should be the Christian duty and patriotic obligation of every true citizen, black and white alike.

At Home and Afield

HAMPTON INCIDENTS

COMMENCEMENT DAYS

THE last week of May was fair and not uncomfortably warm for the ceremonies and merry-making of the Senior Class at Hampton. A succession of parties and socials, given the class by different instructors who had been closely associated with them during the past year, and the annual picnic, which was a very enjoyable day's trip on the schooner *Hampton*, to quaint old Yorktown kept the Seniors busy for a full week before the final commencement exercises.

ON Sunday morning, May 24, the sermon to the graduating class was delivered in Memorial Church by the school's chaplain, Dr. Herbert B. Turner, who took for his theme the class motto: "To co-operate and uplift." In the afternoon at three o'clock the battalion formed to march to the national and school cemeteries where memorial services were held. This beautiful ceremony, which occurs every year on the Sunday before Memorial Day, is attended by all the students and by the teachers and families on the grounds. A few words of prayer are offered and taps is sounded in the presence of a reverent group, and afterwards the flowers, which each man and woman, boy and girl, held as they followed the battalion to the cemetery, beautify some brave soldier's grave. It has been a custom among the students to find a headstone bearing their surname, or the grave of a soldier from their state, and there place a tribute.

After the soldiers' graves have been decorated, the battalion forms again and marches to the school cemetery where General Armstrong and a small number of teachers and students lie. Here again are prayer and taps and the decoration of graves with a more intimate feeling of mingled love, gratitude, and sorrow. General Armstrong's two sisters, Miss M. J. Armstrong and Mrs. Ellen A. Weaver, his daughter, Mrs. William H. Scoville, and four little Scoville grandchildren were among the number who helped to cover his unostentatious grave with garden blossoms.

THE annual band concert was given under the direction of Mr. William M. O. Tessmann in Cleveland Hall Chapel on Monday evening, May 25. The concert, which is yearly a demonstration of Mr. Tessmann's miraculous development, in a short time, of musical talent in raw material, was this year more than usually fine.

THE class-day exercises of the Agriculture, Business, and Trade Classes were held in the Chapel on Tuesday evening, May 26. Just before they began, the Senior Agriculture, Business, and Trade Classes of 1915 marched into the hall under a banner bearing the sententious motto, "Seeking higher things." The members of the three graduating classes took their seats on the platform and their representatives delivered brief addresses. Two boys received certificates in the business course, sixteen in the agricultural course, and thirty-nine tradesmen were graduated.

THE Seniors who had completed the Academic course, in addition to their se eral professional courses held their class-day exercises on the Mansion House porch at 10 o'clock Wednesday morning, May 27. Sixty-eight young men and women occupied the porch, the boys on one side of the entrance and the girls on the other; between them sat Dr. Frissell, presiding over the diplomas.

On the lawn, in front, an interested audience of teachers, parents, and friends listened to the brief exercises, which included the salutatory, class history, class will, valedictory, and the class and school songs. The historian gave many interesting facts and figures about the Senior Class, one significant statement being that there were among its members nine "Hampton grandchildren." The valedictorian delivered a manly address on "Present-day opportunities," and his final simple words of appreciation and affection to his classmates, teachers, and to Dr. Frissell were very moving.

The exercises closed with encouraging words from Dr. Frissell who called the class to a life of courage, co-operation, and devotion, and the sixty-eight graduates received their diplomas from the Principal and joined the ranks of Hampton's alumni.

The tree exercises followed, a little live oak near the entrance to the grounds being the center of attention during a short address and a song.

SUMMER SCHOOL

THE summer session for teachers opened on June 16 with an enrollment of over four hundred. Ninety per cent of the students, as is usually the case, are women. There are on the lists the names of a number of Hampton graduates and ex-students. Summer school teachers, who are not on Hampton's regular teaching staff are Miss Edna I. Avery, of the State Normal College, Albany, N. Y., whose subject is sewing; Mr. Benjamin Griffith Brawley, of Morehouse College, Georgia, literature; Miss Helen C. Clark, of Brooklyn, N. Y., cook-

ing; Miss Caroline W. Hotchkiss, of the Horace Mann School, New York, English composition; Miss Mabel I. Jenkins, of Dana Hall, Wellesley, English grammar; Miss Mary E. Kelton, of Ely Court, Greenwich, Conn., geography; Mr. John B. Pierce, farm demonstration agent of Wellville, Virginia, home gardening; Mr. John C. Stone, of the State Normal School, Montclair, N. J., arithmetic; and Mrs. Laura E. Turner, formerly teacher of sewing in Baltimore High School, sewing. All of the above-mentioned teachers with the exception of Miss Avery have taught in previous summer normal sessions at Hampton.

For the week beginning June 29 a clergymen's section of the summer school will be held for the ministers of Tidewater Virginia. The instructors are Dr. Frank K. Sanders, who has previously conducted excellent Bible courses at Hampton, and Rev. Laurence Fenninger, the school's newly appointed associate chaplain.

ENTERTAINMENTS

HAMPTON was favored on the night of May 20 by having Mr. Harry T. Burleigh, in a song recital assisted by the Hampton Choral Union, the Institute choir, and the school. The recital, which was held in the Gymnasium, under the auspices of the Hampton Choral Union, was, from all standpoints, one of the most successful in years. Mr. Burleigh presented a most varied program, ranging from grand opera selections to plantation melodies. Of the master songs, Massenet's "Legend of the Sage Bush," Coleridge-Taylor's "Corn Song," and Damrosch's "Danny Deever" deserve to be especially commended for their unusually effective interpretation; while in his rendition of his own arrangements of the Indian and Negro melodies, the artist carried his audience on the top wave of enthusiasm. The spontaneous outbursts of applause, the frequent encores, and the many flowers were some of the ways in which the audience showed its high appreciation of the artist.

Other numbers deserving more than passing mention were Mr. Tessman's violin solo, "Deep River," the singing of an Italian folk song, "The Gypsy Camp" and "Hampton! My Home by the Sea" by the entire student body, choir, and Choral Union accompanied by the band, and "Listen to the Lambs," a prize anthem for unaccompanied singing, composed by Mr. R. Nathaniel Dett, and sung by the Hampton Choral Union and the Institute choir.

When necessary, effective and musicianly accompaniments were played on the piano by Miss May Barrett, and Mr. Allen H. Gates, who, in this way, contributed not a little to the success of the evening.

ON the evening of May 16 the Shakespeare Dramatic Club presented scenes from Sheridan's play, "The Rivals," in Huntington Hall Auditorium. The acting of the whole cast was excellent, Sir Anthony Absolute, the imperious father, and Mrs. Malaprop of the oracular tongue, taking good advantage of the opportunities offered by their parts. The eighteenth century costuming—wigs, skirted coats, and knee breeches for the gentlemen and panniers and ruffles for the ladies—was very attractive, and in some cases truly magnificent.

A SCHOOL IMPROVEMENT

THE improvement of the school's grounds along the Jones Creek water front is now well under way. A line of reinforcing piles has been run the entire length from the previously improved front up to the Soldiers' Home bridge, and the new bulkhead and retaining wall are now being built. As soon as this is finished, the creek is to be dredged out and the dredgings used to fill in and make the necessary new land out to the tide line. This will give the school some new land and will make a very desirable improvement in the aesthetic and sanitary condition at that point.

ATHLETICS

THE fourth annual inter-class track meet was held on Monday afternoon, May 18, on the athletic field and was attended by a large and enthusiastic crowd. There were about a hundred entrants for twelve events—100-yard dash, 220-yard dash, mile run, half-mile, quarter-mile, shot put, discus, 120-yard high hurdle, pole vault, running high jump, and running broad jump. The Senior Middle Class won the meet with 43 points; the 1915 Trade Class was second with 29 points. Many of the athletes of the winning team helped to win the meet last year for their class as Junior Middlers, and the year before as Juniors. In the Junior meet held at the same time for the Newport News Y. M. C. A., the Whittier School, and the Excelsior Club, of Phoebus, there were three classes of entrants—80-pound, 90-pound, and unlimited. The Newport News Y. M. C. A. took first place with 98 points and the Whittier School second, with 72 points. There was a decided improvement over last year in the performance of each event.

THIS year the class crews rowed four races on the mile course from the red buoy in the Hampton Creek channel to the school wharf. On Tuesday, May 19, the Work Year Class won from the Juniors; on Wednesday, the 1916 Trade Class won from the 1915 Trade Class; on Thursday the Work Class, again victors, left the Senior crew behind at the finish; and on Friday, the final race between 1916 Trade Class and the Work Class was won by the Work Year boys in 6 minutes, 37 seconds.

The races were rowed in each case at five o'clock and the wharf was crowded with spectators who cheered excitedly for the gallant little Work Year crew as they left a steadily growing gap of sparkling blue water between their boat and that of their older, but in this respect, at any rate, less skillful opponents.

THE COMPETITIVE DRILL

ON Monday, May 25, the six companies of the school battalion competed in company drill for the Winston cup offered in 1911 by Major and Mrs. Thomas W. Winston, formerly of Fort Monroe. The drill was judged by Captain Richard I. McKinney, the adjutant at Fort Monroe, Lieut. R. M. Perkins, and Lieut. W. A. Copthorne, who selected the movements on which each company was graded. The cup was won by Company B, Bishop Brown, captain, score 79 per cent. Company A, under Captain Benjamin Davis, took second place, score 72 points.

In 1911, the first year of the competitive drill, the cup was won by Company B under Captain Roy L. Cordery. In 1912 Company C, under the leadership of Captain Karl E. Lay, a Seneca Indian, took first place. Last year, 1913, as this year, the cup was won by Company B, under Captain Bishop Brown. The winning company has the honor of being the color company during the following school year.

Following the drill the cup was presented with a short speech by Captain McKinney to the captain of the winning company and his lieutenants.

THE WHITTIER SCHOOL

THE Whittier Alumni Association was organized three years ago in a meeting called for that purpose, at which about seventy graduates of the Whittier School eighth grade were present. At the meeting last year it was suggested that money be raised to pay the scholarship of a Whittier boy or girl at Hampton Institute. As the dues are small and the Association has not yet been able to raise money in other ways, the growth of the scholarship is slow, but the effort is none the less earnest. At this year's meeting new officers were elected and papers were read by several members. Miss May Barrett is the present president of the Association.

HAMPTON WORKERS

ON June 13, Miss J. E. Davis, managing editor of the Southern Workman sailed from Montreal for several vacation weeks in Europe, it being her plan to spend the time principally in Norway and Tirol.

Major Robert R. Moton delivered the commencement address at the Alabama State Normal School, Montgomery, Ala., on Thursday evening, May 21.

At the commencement exercises of the Hampton Training School for Nurses held at the Dixie Hospital on Wednesday evening, June 17, Miss S. J. Walter, Major Robert R. Moton, and Dr. Harry D. Howe were among the speakers of the evening. Mr. Frank W. Darling, who is one of the directors of the Training School, presided and presented the diplomas.

On May 12, 1914, the *Hampton* took a chorus of twenty and Captain Allen Washington, the speaker of the evening, to Norfolk for a meeting in St. John's Church. "John Henry's" life at Hampton was shown in moving pictures, accompanied by plantation songs from the chorus, after which Captain Washington told the Negro audience some of the facts about Hampton and its work.

Captain Washington, who is traveling with the summer campaign crew on the schooner *Hampton* has a place on the program of the campaign entertainment.

The Samuel Coleridge-Taylor Music Club of Norfolk in May 1914, presented in recital Mr. R. Nathaniel Dett, director of music at Hampton Institute. Mr. Dett played among other things a number of his own compositions including the "Magnolia" and "In the Bottoms" suites, "Carnival Waltz," "Inspiration Waltzes," and "Go to sleep."

At a concert given in Chicago on June 3, the program of which represented Negro composers and Negro artists exclusively, Mr. R. Nathaniel

Dett was the pianist of the evening and played the suites mentioned above. Most complimentary press reports of the concert by the best music critics of the city appeared in Chicago's leading newspapers.

A LIBRARY EXHIBIT

IN connection with the annual meeting of the American Library Association held in Washington the last week in May there were some special meetings of high-school and normal-school librarians arranged by Commissioner Claxton, at which Hampton was represented by Miss Leonora Herron, Miss Mary Lane, and Miss Ethel Turner. A special school-library exhibit was shown at the Washington Public Library, including pictures of buildings, reading lists, charts, and statistics. Hampton sent to this exhibit a set of twelve cards, fourteen by eighteen inches, on which were mounted pictures of the library building and the different rooms with descriptions of the work done in these rooms. This exhibit will be kept as a permanent one for educational meetings and may eventually be sent to the Panama Exposition.

VISITORS

RECENT visitors to the school have been Rev. W. C. Johnston, a missionary to West Africa, who told in a general teachers' meeting on May 13 of the spread of the gospel in Liberia ; Mrs. Ella W. Brown, recently appointed superintendent of a new Indian industrial school in California ; Mr. Theodore R. W. Lunt, a secretary of the Committee on Education for the World Missionary Conference held in Edinburgh in 1912, and a brother-in-law of Mr. Alexander G. Fraser of Ceylon, whose visit to Hampton is remembered with pleasure ; Mr. Dennis Whittle, of London, who has been studying at Hartford Theological Seminary ; Mrs. Henrietta Fangel, of New York, daughter of General Armstrong's sister, Mrs. Ellen Weaver, who visited Mrs. Scoville for a week in May ; and Mrs. Alden Howe and Miss Emerson, workers at Atlanta University.

A delegation of about forty people from the Episcopal Sunday-school convention in session at Norfolk visited Hampton on June 18 under the guidance of Mrs. Frank Darling and Rev. Edwin R. Carter.

GRADUATES AND EX-STUDENTS

THE Hampton Alumni Association called, at the Bayshore Hotel, Buckroe Beach, May 25, a meeting of Hampton graduates and their husbands and wives, and the colored workers at Hampton Institute. The object of the meeting was to bring together for social purposes all persons in this section who have ever attended Hampton Institute. One hundred and fifty responded to the call and spent a pleasant evening renewing acquaintances, indulging in reminiscences, and enjoying the amusements of the popular resort. In response to the demand for more money for the scholarship fund now being raised, two hundred and twenty dollars were pledged at once.

Altogether the meeting was so successful, and the number that turned out so encouraging, that it was decided to form a permanent organization for furthering social life among old Hamptonians. Accordingly the Hampton Institute Association was created with the following officers : Mr. F. D. Wheelock, president, Mr. J. E. Smith, vice president, Mr. A. W. E. Bassette, treasurer, and Mrs. Harris Barrett, secretary. An executive committee composed of the following was also chosen : Mr. H. K. Jones, Mrs. R. R. Moton, Mr. N. B. Clark.

THE Hampton Choral Union is a body of about sixty people, nearly all of whom are graduates or ex-students of Hampton Institute. They are citizens of the community and invariably members of some church choir or music club. Their aim is the creation of a greater music atmosphere, and their efforts in this direction on the evening of May 20, with Mr. Harry Burleigh as star, was a signifiant success. But what was, and still is, more significant was the co-operating spirit which made this composite organization a strong unit working for the one desired end. It is not often that there is perfect agreement among different bodies of people, each enjoying the same especial talent; it is not often that the Hampton gymnasium is overtaxed as to capacity; nor is it often that the news of what is going on here at the school is so enticing as to lure hither our friends from the far-away counties. The success of the evening of May 20 is a demonstration of what can be accomplished when people work together, and proves that "co-operation" is still a worthy watchword for those who would uplift as they climb.

A number of Hampton graduates and ex-students have this year finished courses in other schools and colleges:

Elmer J. Cheeks, ex-student '05, graduated in June from Purdue University, La Fayette, Indiana.

William N. Colson, who was graduated from Hampton in 1908, after teaching a year at the Whittier School, entered Virginia Union University in Richmond, Virginia, from the College Department of which he recently graduated.

Andrew Foraker Evans and Henry P. Weeden, both of the class of 1908, were graduated in dentistry from Howard University, Washington, D. C., in June.

John H. Robinson, Jr., '08, graduated this year from the Medical Department of Howard University.

Philip F. King, '08, was graduated in April from the Theological Department of Lincoln University, Pa. His commencement address was on the "Problems of the country church."

Joseph Allison Marlowe, who finished the bricklaying course in 1907, and the academic course in 1909, graduated this year in dentistry from Temple College, Pa.

A girl who spent only one year at Hampton and that as a member of the Night School Class, Minnie Clayton Robinson, ex-student '01, is making herself very useful at Water View, Virginia. She writes:

"I am delighted with my work this year. This school has enrolled every year about 11 pupils; this year I have 35. We have raised money to lengthen our term one month and we are trying to raise enough for another month.

"I am very busy today with my pupils preparing some work for the school exhibit. Some are making aprons, collars, pillow cases, handkerchiefs, etc. Some of this work I have them hemstitch. They now want us to teach cooking. We have our teachers' meeting once a month. Things are now being brought up that I had in Hampton that year and it has been a great help to me in my work. This school works me very hard. I am not tired, only too glad that I can do it."

MARRIAGES

The marriage of Mrs. Nora Bell Satchell, '08, to Rev. G. C. Taylor of Roanoke, occurred at Bethel A. M. E. Church in Eastville, Va., on May 21, 1914. Mrs Satchell has for the past ten years been teaching the school at Birnsnest, Va., on the Eastern Shore.

Announcement has been received of the marriage of Horace B. Penney, who finished the carpentry course in 1905 and left Hampton in 1906, to Dolores Glaude, in Muskogee, Okla.

THE
SOUTHERN
WORKMAN

"De Mornin' Star"
J. E. DAVIS

Shall the Filipinos be Free?
HENRY FLURY

The Negro's Industrial Problem
MONROE N. WORK

Teaching Teachers at Hampton
WILLIAM ANTHONY AERY

Press of
The Hampton Normal and Agricultural Institute
Hampton, Virginia

The Hampton Normal and Agricultural Institute

HAMPTON VIRGINIA

What it is   An undenominational industrial school founded in 1868 by Samuel Chapman Armstrong for Negro youth. Indians admitted in 1878.

Object   To train teachers and industrial leaders

Equipment   Land, 1060 acres; buildings, 140

Courses   Academic, trade, agriculture, business, home economics

Enrollment   Negroes, 1215; Indians, 37; total, 1252

Results   Graduates, 1709; ex-students, over 6000
Outgrowths; Tuskegee, Calhoun, Mt. Meigs, and many smaller schools for Negroes

Needs $125,000 annually above regular income
$4,000,000 Endowment Fund
Scholarships

A full scholarship for both academic and industrial instruction	$ 100
Academic scholarship	70
Industrial scholarship	30
Endowed full scholarship	2500

Any contribution, however small, will be gratefully received and may be sent to H. B. FRISSELL, Principal, or to F. K. ROGERS, Treasurer, Hampton, Virginia.

FORM OF BEQUEST

I give and devise to the trustees of The Hampton Normal and Agricultural Institute, Hampton, Virginia, the sum of   *dollars, payable*

The Southern Workman

Published monthly by

The Hampton Normal and Agricultural Institute

Contents for August 1914

THE SOUTHERN WORKMAN was founded by Samuel Chapman Armstrong in 1872, and is a mon magazine devoted to the interests of undeveloped races.

It contains reports from Negro and Indian populations, with pictures of reservation and plantatio life, as well as information concerning Hampton graduates and ex-students who since 1868 have taugh more than 250,000 children in the South and West. It also provides a forum for the discussion of ethnologi cal, sociological, and educational problems in all parts of the world.

CONTRIBUTIONS: The editors do not hold themselves responsible for the opinions expressed in cor tributed articles. Their aim is simply to place before their readers articles by men and women of abili without regard to the opinions held.

[EDITORIAL STAFF

H. B. FRISSELL	W. L. BROWN
HELEN W. LUDLOW	W. A. AERY, Business Manager
J. E. DAVIS	W. T. B. WILLIAMS

TERMS: One dollar a year in advance: ten cents a copy
CHANGE OF ADDRESS: Persons making a change of address should send the old as well as the address to

THE SOUTHERN WORKMAN, Hampton, Virginia

Entered as second-class matter August 13, 1903, in the Post Office at Hampton, Virginia, und the Act of July 16, 1894

THE HAMPTON LEAFLETS

Any twelve of the following numbers of the "The Hampton Leaflets" may b obtained free of charge by any Southern teacher or superintendent. *A charge of fift cents per dozen is made to other applicants.* Cloth-bound volumes for 1905, '06, '0 and '08 will be furnished at seventy-five cents each, postpaid.

VOL. I

1 Experiments in Physics (Heat)
2 Sheep: Breeds, Care, Management
3 Transplanting
4 Birds Useful to Southern Farmers
5 Selection and Care of Dairy Cattle
6 Care and Management of Horses
7 How to Know the Trees by Their Bark
8 Milk and Butter
9 Commercial Fertilizers
10 Swine: Breeds, Care, Management
11 Fruits of Trees
12 December Suggestions

VOL. II

1 Suggestions to Teachers Preparing Students for Hampton Institute
2 Experiments in Physics (Water)
3 Spring Blossoms: Shrubs and Trees
4 School Gardening
5 Drainage
6 Mosquitoes
7 Roots
8 Seed Planting
9 Housekeeping Rules
10 Prevention of Tuberculosis
11 Thanksgiving Suggestions
12 Some Injurious Insects

VOL. III

1 Proper Use of Certain Words
2 Winter Buds
3 Domestic Arts at Hampton Institute
4 Beautifying Schoolhouses and Yards
5 Responsibility of Teachers for the Health of Their Children
6 Manual Training, Part I
7 Rotation of Crops
8 Life History of a Butterfly
9 How Seeds Travel
10 Nature Study for Primary Grades
11 Arbor Day
12 Evergreen Trees

VOL. IV

1 Plants
2 How to Attract the Birds
3 The Story of Corn
4 The Story of Cotton
5 The Meaning of the Flower
6 A Child's Garden
7 The Winged Pollen-Carriers
8 Soils
9 Care of Poultry
10 Plowing and Harrowing
11 Transplanting of Shrubs and Vines
12 Transplanting and Pruning of Trees

VOL. V

1 Teaching Reading to Children
2 Culture and Marketing of Peanuts
3 The House Fly a Carrier of Disease
4 Culture and Marketing of Tobacco
5 Virginia's Fishing Industry
6 Farm Manures
7 Soil Moisture and After-cultivation
8 Patent Medicines
9 Hookworm Disease
10 Reading in the Grammar Schools
11 Oystering in Hampton Roads
12 Common Sense in Negro Public Schoo

VOL. VI

1 Sewing Lessons for Rural Schools
2 Housekeeping and Sanitation in Rural Schools
3 Canning and Preserving
4 Manual Training, Part II
5 Patrons' Meetings
6 Relation of Industrial and Academ Subjects in Rural Schools
7 Southern Workman Special Index
8 Community Clubs for Women and Gir
9 Housekeeping and Cooking Lessons f Rural Communities
10 Fifty Years of Negro Progress
11 Approved Methods for Home Launderi
12 Number Steps for Beginners

VOL. VII

1 Manual Training, Part III

Address: Publication Office, The Hampton Normal and Agricultu Institute, Hampton, Virginia

The Southern Workman

VOL. XLIII   AUGUST 1914   NO. 8

Editorials

Hampton Trains Indians for Service

Two purposes present themselves in any general survey of Indian education. One of these contemplates only the benefit to the individual. The boy or girl in the school is to be trained intellectually and fitted industrially to go out into the world as an intelligent, independent citizen and a desirable member of the community. If, instead of returning to the Indian country, these boys and girls make for themselves places among the white people, the end and aim of their education is sufficiently fulfilled. And, indeed, no one would belittle the effort that brings to them success in this field.

The other purpose contemplates not only the good to the individual, but also the ultimate good of the race through the efforts of the school-trained youth among their own people. It is the aim of the educational institutions that work with this end in view to have the pupils return to their people after completing their education, and, by living example and altruistic effort, to work for the improvement of their own community morally and socially. This purpose involves a somewhat broader educational motive than the other and sets a standard in some ways more difficult of attainment.

It has always been the aim of Hampton to have its pupils go back to their people and carry the light of their education into the dark places of their own communities. This purpose is kept constantly before the students throughout their school course. It is taught not more by precept than by example. The missionary spirit is never absent from the school and is put in practice by the students among the poor and unfortunate of the neighborhood. The deeds of graduates who have accomplished anything of note in this direction are reported at the gatherings of the students. "Doing for others" becomes by constant association the familiar watchword.

One of the most distinguishing signs of the times in our present-day civilization is the spread and growth of all kinds of social activity and uplift work, and this movement is finding expression at graduation in our white schools and colleges. Thus far, however, the note has been pretty generally lacking on the graduation platform of our Indian schools. Perhaps the time is not yet ripe for much of it, although we recognize that the spirit of graduation in Indian schools is becoming more and more of a piece with that at the schools and colleges of our white boys and girls.

Surely there is no wider field for social service anywhere than is open to the Indian graduate—service that will make the lives of the less fortunate of their race brighter, happier, and more useful. Much may be accomplished, of course, by Indians in the various business and other pursuits, and education to that end is important. Inevitably the influence of success in this field will reach beyond the individual, too, because no man can win much that is worth while without setting an example that others might happily follow. But would it not be well to infuse more generally into Indian education the spirit of altruistic service also, so that an increasing number of Indians might be carrying the social gospel to their own people?

※

American Home Economics Association Very interesting programs were presented at the meetings of the American Home Economics Association, recently held on the beautiful campus of the College for Women, Western Reserve University, Cleveland, Ohio.

The keynote of the convention was struck by the president of the University in his scholarly address on the preservation of the family, in which he discussed the causes of family troubles and the means for their prevention. This subject was further developed by the Commissioner of Education of Massachusetts, when he attacked the system that educates people beyond their means, and pleaded for the most practical kind of teaching in homemaking, using the home itself as the laboratory.

Taking the family as a center, the addresses were, in the main, grouped around two divisions: First, the necessity of teaching every American woman her obligation in the matter of spending the family income, as 90 per cent of the money spent in the United States is said to be spent by women; second, community housekeeping, which was well introduced by Commissioner Claxton when he said, "The time has passed when the home is an isolated spot. In this day nothing affects the welfare of a city that does not touch the home."

Papers discussing the first division were presented on such subjects as "Buying for the household," "The visiting housekeeper in rural districts," "The consulting housekeeper," and "Teaching children to spend." In the second division the following community problems were discussed: water, waste, food, care of sick, education, recreation, and conditions of employment.

Miss Mildred Chadsey, chief inspector of the Department of Public Welfare, Division of Health, Cleveland, gave a most interesting talk on municipal housekeeping, as carried on in that city. This was followed by an outline of the work being done in municipal food control in New York by the Association for the Improvement of the Conditions of the Poor.

Part of one session was given to the discussion of art in the home and dress. Sectional meetings were held on such subjects as domestic art, domestic science, courses of study, and extension work. The great need for trained extension teachers was brought out, and a movement was started which it is hoped may end in the establishment of summer schools in different sections of the country to train teachers especially along this line.

On the last evening, Miss Sarah Louise Arnold, the president of the Association, gave a timely warning to the members that in the development of the efficiency of the household the *spirit* of the family must not be destroyed.

TEACHING TEACHERS AT HAMPTON[1]

BY WILLIAM ANTHONY AERY

The paragraphs that follow merely suggest the significance of reaching, through well-organized summer-school work, hundreds of earnest colored teachers who feel the need of Hampton's training. There is no attempt made to furnish a complete outline of the Hampton summer-school courses or methods of work. The marked success of the recent summer session for teachers was certainly due, in large measure, to careful planning and to thorough team work of teachers and students. — W. A. A.

OVER manual training workbenches, kitchen ranges, sewing machines, drawing tables, health charts and pamphlets, in the library and in the classroom, some 435 devoted colored men and women worked most faithfully and effectively during the recent four weeks' session of the Hampton Institute summer school for teachers (June 16 to July 14) and prepared themselves for more useful service to their communities. From Virginia and eighteen other states, [2] ranging from Florida to New York and as far west as Texas, there came to Hampton ambitious teachers, seeking fresh knowledge, higher standards, and the opportunity of obtaining vocational training which will help them to be of greater service to God and their fellow-men.

Neither statistics nor carefully worded paragraphs of description can possibly tell the whole story of Hampton's real service to those who attended its well-organized and skilfully conducted summer school. To estimate, on the other hand, the helpful reflex action on Hampton of the presence of so many consecrated servants of the people is correspondingly difficult. Hampton was able through its resources and excellent organization to give information, standards, and inspiration to those who came seeking aid, not for themselves alone but for the children and parents in their own communities. Hampton, however, gained new strength by contact with those who make the world better and happier through unselfish service.

---

1 The Summer-school talks, conferences, industrial exhibit, and experiences of Hampton graduates are outlined elsewhere in this issue.

2 Alabama, 10; District of Columbia, 6; Delaware, 1; Florida, 3; Georgia, 5; Indiana, 1; Kentucky, 4; Maryland, 16; Missouri, 2; North Carolina, 97; New Jersey, 4; New York, 1; Pennsylvania, 2; South Carolina, 13; Tennessee, 1; Texas, 1; Virginia, 260; West Virginia, 7.

NEW OUTLOOK ON LIFE

Dr. George P. Phenix, the vice principal of Hampton, who served as director of the summer school, emphasized in his short address at the opening session, the importance to men and women of studying subjects that give a broader outlook on life and a keener appreciation of music, art, and science.

That many teachers accepted this suggestion and pursued courses which would help them, not only in their class-room work and in their struggle for state certificates of higher grade, [3] but also in their every-day homelife, is clearly shown in the figures for enrollment by courses :

Agriculture, 46; arithmetic, 175; chair-caning, 191; civics, 66; cooking (advanced,) 36; cooking (elementary,) 34; community work, 36; drawing, 68; English composition, 55; geography, 106; English grammar, 64; hygiene, 52; literature, 61; manual training (advanced,) 87; manual training (primary,) 120; principles of teaching, 120; sewing (advanced), 62; sewing (elementary,) 67; singing, 85; poultry keeping, 30; elementary science, 22.

THE TEACHER'S OPPORTUNITY

The teacher is the school. A man or woman who has the requisite amount of initiative, tact, enthusiasm, and knowledge can go into the most unpromising community and induce the mothers and fathers of the children to band themselves together for the building or the improvement of the schoolhouse, the buying of desks, pictures, curtains, and the equipment that may be needed for putting in woodwork, cooking, and sewing, the beautifying of the schoolyard, and the spreading of sane ideas of education.

This sounds like dogma, but it is simply the recital of what has been done time and time again by colored teachers scattered throughout the Southland. This expresses Hampton's idea of the dignity of teaching and lays emphasis on personality, cooperation, and knowledge in building up schools for all classes and races.

BETTER RACE RELATIONS

What teachers have been doing to improve their schools and to establish more friendly relations between white and colored people was clearly shown at the two informal conferences that were held during the summer session. A typical story of educational progress among Negroes follows :

3 The following Virginia certificates were held by the summer-school students : 73 first grade; 1 special first grade; 69 second grade ; 7 third grade ; 34 professional ; 1 summer-school professional; 4 emergency; 10 high-school, first ; 2 high-school, second ; 21 high-school, unclassified ; 9 normal and industrial.

E. W. Wyatt, who lives in Emporia, Va., secured the co-operation of white and colored people so effectively that now his community has a school that is worth $8000. His first step was to talk over the educational situation with Henry Maclin, the white division superintendent of schools in Greenesville County, a man who has shown a hearty interest in the progress of Negroes. He went before the local school board and asked for the sale of the colored school which was then in an undesirable part of the town. He requested that the board should purchase property for a new colored school in a more desirable locality. The board agreed to help the colored people, if they would raise $500. Twenty Negroes banded themselves together and each one became responsible for raising $25. Within two weeks the colored people raised the money that they had pledged, but before they deposited their money, the white school board had deposited $500 to be used for the erection of a colored school.

  · The colored people then decided that it would be economy to build a brick school. After the superintendent and the members of the school board had been seen personally, on the question of a more expensive Negro school, Wyatt and his co-workers asked for an addition of four more rooms. The board agreed to this suggestion and simply laid down the conditions that the colored people themselves must raise another $1000.

One of the fine things about the Greenesville school project was the creation of a new school spirit among the colored people and the added enrollment of colored children. In one year the enrollment rose from 230 to 350 and the average daily attendance reached 80 per cent.

Other stories of corresponding interest and value might easily be recounted. The importance of presenting to teachers the possibilities for civic improvement that lie within their grasp is unquestioned. Through its summer school and conferences, as well as the regular courses for younger students, Hampton has been of untold benefit to thousands of Negroes in giving them new determination to go out into hard places and, as General Armstrong said, "do the impossible."

MAKING THE SCHOOL USEFUL AND ATTRACTIVE

Brief outlines, indicating the general and specific aims of some of the summer-school courses, will suggest what was offered to those who made the effort to reach Hampton Institute.

The course in community work, given by Miss Ida A. Tourtellot of Hampton Institute, included a study of the following topics : Average cost of living and average wages ; standards of living ; the home as a social agency ; co-operation ; statistics of the Negro race. It aimed "to give a larger knowledge of Negro life in the South, to take a survey of the Negro's progress, and to suggest lines of activity for the future. "

Mr. Leigh Richmond Miner, director of applied art at Hampton Institute, conducted a course in drawing which included "the study of color harmony in house-furnishing, school-room decoration, and the ornamental planting of school grounds. "

Anything that can be done to help teachers secure the co-operation of their pupils in having a clean and attractive schoolhouse—outside as well as inside—is well worth doing. "A little book, called 'Ornamental Planting,' was worked out in the drawing classes. One of the chief objects of the drawing course was to make of common things a work of art. "This little book," to quote Mr. Miner again, "introduces one to some of the native trees and shrubs and illustrates how with careful planting one may make a practical, picturesque entrance to a school building. Holiday work, blackboard drawing, how to know the trees, and simple color studies were shown as part of the course in drawing. "

BETTER FOOD AND BETTER PEOPLE

Good food, good health, and good morals—here is one of the common circles of life. The relation of one element to another in this circle of human happiness is real and, fortunately for those who attended the Hampton summer-school, was not forgotten.

In the cooking classes, both elementary and advanced, stress was laid on the *best methods* of doing the everyday work in the home—preparing food, planning and serving meals, setting the table, caring for the home, teaching subjects that fall to the lot of workers in rural schools, canning, preserving, and pickling.

While the fame of the colored cook has gone throughout the land, it is nevertheless true that thousands of Negroes are starving in the midst of plenty and are suffering from malnutrition because colored women have not had the advantages of learning how to cook properly for their families the most appropriate food. Hampton's task, then, of showing colored teachers, not only *what* to cook, but also *how* to cook, is important. The industrial exhibit, held at the close of the summer school, showed graphically the underlying aim of the cooking courses; namely, the correlation of good food, attractively cooked and served, and happier home life.

HEALTH FOR THE MASSES

Public-health safety is the crux of many problems that call for individual and group co-operation. The child that has a toothbrush and *uses* it regularly makes a contribution to his

community and helps to promote public-health safety. The child
that learns in school how to guard himself against disease
becomes a fine home missionary.

How to carry the common information concerning disease
and its prevention, which has been secured at great public
expense, to the average home is a problem that is claiming the
serious attention of wide-awake sanitarians and school officials.

Miss Sara Lane, of Hampton Institute, gave a course in
hygiene that included "topics relating to the health of children,
personal hygiene, the sanitation of the school and the home, and
public hygiene and sanitation." Her aim was "to make the
teacher a vital force in the community in which she works." The
avidity with which the Hampton students read health bulletins,
especially the *Hampton Leaflets* dealing with public health, and
the interest that they showed in a series of excellent charts
which presented graphically the influence of alcohol on health
and morals, indicated the eagerness of Negro teachers in their
search for reliable information and safe counsel regarding
personal and public hygiene.

MORAL TRAINING THROUGH WORK

Hampton has always emphasized the educative value of
industrial work that is done neatly, accurately, and honestly.
This tradition and practice were handed to the teachers
attending the summer school.

To saw thin wood to a knife line ; to cut from colored paper
figures that tell children a story or illustrate a school lesson ;
to weave an artistic rug ; to make a useful corn-shuck doormat or
picture frame ; to fashion a piece of furniture for the school or
home from a dry-goods box ; to take infinite pains in doing small
and large pieces of work in chair-caning and upholstery—this is
the Hampton idea of industrial work that trains and refines.

Were one looking for the opportunity of training people in
morals, surely the field of sewing, according to Hampton's
requirements of accuracy and neatness, would suggest itself.

In the elementary sewing course, Miss Edna I. Avery, of the
State Normal College, Albany, N. Y., had her students make the
common stitches, hems, and seams, for example, with special
reference to their uses and applications. The neat samples of
work and attractive note-books suggest the interest of the teachers in their work and give promise of good results that must
come wherever the Hampton trained teachers go to work.

Mrs. Thomas W. Turner, of Washington, D. C., a Hampton
graduate, gave in the advanced sewing course "instruction in
the selection, buying, and care of clothing; the drafting, cutting,
and fitting of a cotton dress ; clothing for infants and children ;

renovating and making over both dresses and hats ; and in simple house-furnishings. '' The dresses that were put on exhibition at the close of the summer school were tagged so as to show their specific uses and the cost of all the materials. The wonder was how such good-looking dresses could be produced so reasonably. Surely the school teacher who has herself made an attractive dress from her own drafted pattern and has worked out carefully the various items of cost, must be in a better position to help growing girls to have not only appropriate dresses but pretty dresses.

ALL-ROUND EDUCATION

Interesting and important work was done, of course, in the remaining courses. Hampton never neglects or considers lightly the academic subjects that are so fundamental for those who wish to become safe and efficient leaders in school teaching, homemaking, farming, and trade work.

To the regular class-room instruction there was added the benefit of a series of helpful addresses and demonstrations by men and women who were teachers in the summer school or were especially interested in the Negro's progress.

SPREADING HAMPTON IDEAS

Thousands upon thousands of worthy Negro children, living in the rural districts and cities of Virginia and other Southern states, will soon feel the influence of Hampton's idea of education for service, because nearly four hundred and fifty colored teachers attended the Hampton Institute summer school, and, after months and years, perhaps, of hard, self-sacrificing work, studied the best methods of presenting industrial and academic subjects to young people.

This assertion is made on the basis that each Hampton summer-school student represents the vital interests of at least forty pupils. Here again Hampton has employed the important principle of training individuals for civic responsibility and consecrated leadership in strategic positions.

Hampton is not simply satisfied to have young people go back to their home communities and do for a few what can be done through better organization for many more in that home community.

Hampton sends back into the needy rural districts and into difficult city positions those who can and must lead ; those who must carry heavy burdens ; those who must run with patience the race that is before them and faint not. Teaching teachers at Hampton means teaching ambitious ˏboys and girls, men and women, the art of living such pure, useful, Christian lives that they will work through silent example as well as through the conventional tools of the schoolroom.

THE NEGRO'S INDUSTRIAL PROBLEM

I LEARNING HOW TO WORK *

BY MONROE N. WORK

In Charge of Research and Records, Tuskegee Institute

WE are accustomed to think of the industrial problem among Negroes as arising where there is a lack of opportunity for work or where there is a threatened reduction of wages or where, because of prejudice or other reasons, they are prevented from getting or holding positions. The real labor problem for the Negro, however, is not getting opportunities to work but making the most of the opportunities that he has for working. A striking example of this recently took place in the Newport News, [Va.,] shipbuilding yards. There are employed at this shipyard some 4750 persons, about half of whom are Negroes. There are 29 different trades and occupations, in all of which except two, bell hangers and electricians, Negroes are working in greater or lesser numbers. Many of the colored workmen, mostly boys, spent so much of their time in idleness when their services were needed both by the shipyard managers and their fellow workers that for a time it appeared that foreigners would be brought in to take their places. Their pay was increased but this instead of making matters better made them worse and increased idleness and irregularity. The management of the shipyard stated that there was no desire to replace Negroes with other laborers except where they were unable to obtain Negroes to do the work of the company.

After a conference of a committee of colored workmen with the general manager it was decided to have Dr. Booker T. Washington come to Newport News and speak to the colored workmen in order that the problem might be brought squarely before them. He came and forcefully impressed upon them the importance of doing their full duty. He insisted that they should stick

---

* Part 2 will follow in the September issue.

to their jobs, keep their word, work regularly, save their money, buy homes, and in every way improve themselves. Their mothers and wives, the ministers of the town, doctors, lawyers, teachers, and business men were called upon to use their influence to see that the irregularity of work ceased.

MAKING THE MOST OF OPPORTUNITIES

In city and in country, wherever there are any large numbers of Negroes, they are confronted with the same sort of problem as confronted the colored workmen in the Newport News shipyard; that is, the problem of making the most of the opportunities for working. Nowhere in the country are the difficulties in securing work for colored persons as great as the opportunities for working. No Negro in the South has to be idle because there is no work he can get to do. On the contrary, jobs, especially in the trades, are continually hunting him. If the Negro loses his economic hold upon the South it will be because he has not made the most of his opportunities. There is everywhere, however, as at Newport News, always the likelihood of the Negro being displaced by foreigners unless he becomes a reliable, dependable workman.

At no time since his emancipation has the Negro lacked the opportunity to work, for beginning with his freedom the country entered upon its greatest era of prosperity and development. Since 1863 over three hundred million acres of land in this country have been brought under cultivation; two hundred thousand miles of railroad have been constructed and cities to the extent of over forty million in population have been built. All this development of economic resources has called for a great amount of rough, unskilled labor, just the sort that a poor, ignorant, and lately enfranchised people could do. From the standpoint of economic opportunity it is doubtful whether the Negro could have had his freedom at a more opportune time or in a country where his economic advancement would have been surer.

LEARNING TO WORK STEADILY

The Negro's industrial problem is learning how to work steadily and efficiently. That is, it is a matter of education. To the bondman there was but little distinction between slavery and labor. He observed that he was about the only one who had to work. Freedom he associated with being a "gentleman," that is, not working with the hands. What the freedmen had to learn was that emancipation meant more and constant work. The care of refugees by the Government and the spreading of the report that rations were being issued no doubt tended to confirm the idea that freedom meant not to work. The withdrawal of ra-

tions, the failure to receive the forty acres and the mule, and the
final abolishment of the Freedmen's Bureau, all tended to teach
the freedmen that emancipation meant work. This was their
first lesson in practical economics. It was, however, only prepar-
tion ; they had yet to learn to labor as free men.

THE NEGRO AND HAMPTON INSTITUTE

Samuel Chapman Armstrong, by means of his close association as a soldier with the freedmen and his previous experience
in Hawaii, saw what was their industrial need. He established
Hampton Institute in order that he might begin to teach them
what should be a free man's attitude toward work and how a
free man should work. Viewed superficially this may appear par-
adoxical. What need is there to teach those how to work who all
their lives have been laborers ? The labor of a slave is very different from that of a free man. The former is expected to bring
to his task the minimum of intelligence ; the latter, the maximum. The Armstrong idea was, through industrial education,
to equip the Negro so that he would bring to his task the maximum of efficiency.

As a slave, the Negro had not been in direct competition
with free labor. As a free man, he immediately came into competition with a body of free laborers who in the main worked
steadily and efficiently. As already indicated the great demand
for laborers, of just the sort that the freedmen were, had enabled them to gain a foothold. Whether they will be able to
keep their economic foothold depends, among other things, on
how well they will learn to labor as free men.

There are the problems of adequate wages, shorter working hours, etc., which concern all workingmen ; but today, 'as
fifty years ago, the Negro's most important industrial problem
is to stay on the job six days in the week and to do his work
as skilfully and rapidly as the white workingman.

A SCHOOL FOR ECONOMIC EFFICIENCY

The establishing of the Hampton Institute was an epoch in
the industrial history of the Negro. It was the beginning of a
systematic training through the school for economic efficiency.
It was a great task that Armstrong undertook. The ideas
and attitude of a people regarding labor had to be changed.
He could only begin the work. His great pupil, Dr. Booker T.
Washington, has further developed the idea of the dignity of
labor and the importance, in an industrially era, of a people
learning to work efficiently with their hands. Washington could
propagate the idea with an advantage that Armstrong did not

have. As a white man, the latter could advise the Negroes
that here was an opportunity of which they should take advantage
Washington, as a black man speaking to black men, could say
more forcefully and convincingly "these are the things which
we as a people must do."

There was also the further advantage that Tuskegee Institute was located in the very heart of the black belt of the South.
Here Negro labor, from the standpoint of constancy and efficiency, was at its worst. Here, in the one-room log cabin, in squal-
or and ignorance, lived the shiftless Negro farmer. Cornmeal
and fat bacon was his principal diet. He worked during the busy
season but from three to five days during the week. It is estimated that in the year he worked only about one hundred and
fifty days.

MUSIC

BY SARAH C. FERNANDIS *

UNDER the toil and the striving,
    Under the sorrow and stings,
Alway serene, aye persistent,
    Something in every heart sings.

And erst a grand oratorio
    Into life's harmony swells, —
Erst a song, plaintive and tender,
    Up from a slave's bosom wells.

Or in the high or the lowly,
    Still God's great, wonderful gift—
Music to bind all in kinship,
    Music to soothe and uplift.

* Hampton, '88

SHALL THE FILIPINOS BE FREE?*

BY HENRY FLURY

OWING to the recent change of administration in Washington, the subject of independence for the Philippine Islands has come again under discussion, and unless caution be used and legislative action be based upon actual knowledge of the conditions prevailing in the Islands, grave and serious blunders may be made. From my personal observations and study of local conditions while engaged in educational work there, it is my firm conviction that the only way the Filipinos can be made free is by a continuation and extension of the paternal guidance and self-sacrificing efforts of those engaged in their uplift. The granting of immediate independence to the Filipinos at this time would be equivalent to cutting adrift a helpless, untutored people and leaving them to the mercy of some nation more willing to exploit the natives than interested in their uplift.

It was suggested at the last Lake Mohonk Conference that the Islands be "neutralized" and governed by a Commission composed of members chosen from several of the great nations of the world. Of all the theoretical and impracticable schemes, this appears the most fantastic and undesirable. It would be a case of "Too many cooks spoil the broth," for what would be every nation's business would end in being nobody's.

As to the other plan, which has often been suggested by those ignorant of Philippine conditions—to give the Islands over to the Filipinos themselves—it is enough to say that this would leave the undeveloped people in the Islands to the mercy of the unprincipled few who would rule by playing upon the ignorance, superstition, and weakness of the many.

In discussing the Philippine problem it is well to examine the facts in the matter. The United States engaged in a war with Spain and at the end of it took over the Islands, beginning at once a program of sanitation, education, social betterment, and material uplift. Thinking that the United States was a duplicate of Spain, the natives rebelled, but after a bitter struggle were defeated. Instead of our Government following the

---

* Illustrated with photographs by the author

THE FILIPINO ANCESTRAL HOME

Spanish method of sending the Bible with the sword, the commander-in-chief of the army detailed soldiers as school teachers, distributed rice by the sack to relieve the distress caused by war, and sent the army surgeons to attend to the work of sanitation in Manila and the provinces. Then followed an era of twentieth-century methods to replace those of the sixteenth century—an era representing to the Filipinos a renaissance in all truth. To the uttermost ends of the Islands, to the tops of the mountains, to the innermost fastnesses of fever-laden jungles, the Government of the United States penetrated and held

CARABAOS AS NATIVE MOUNTS

DRESSING THE HEMP AT CATBALOGAN, SAMAR ISLAND

on with bull-dog tenacity. It was a conquering nation that defeated fever and ignorance as well as abject poverty.

Dr. Dean C. Worcester and Governor Wm. F. Pack, that "Grand Old Man of the Mountains," and others, stand as types of "conquerors" that justify, nay necessitate, American supervision. The work of sanitation, the development of irrigation, the opening of mountain trails, the building of roads, the institution of modern methods in agriculture, the suppression of murderous, plundering Moro pirates, the wholesale introduction of industrial, agricultural, and academic education, and the adoption of modern methods in the administration of justice, leave no doubt that the "conquest" of the Islands has been largely

BANCAS LOADED WITH HEMP GO DOWN THE RIVER TO MARKET.

THE TRADE SCHOOL ERECTED BY AMERICANS AT CATBALOGAN

economic as well as military. Nearly every undertaking in the Philippines is supported by the Filipinos themselves, and the American people are not taxed to support any of the projects.

Three things may enslave a people—economic conditions, the tyranny of a conquering nation, or the superstitions of their own minds. Certainly the United States is doing all it can to put the masses of the Filipinos in possession of the forces of nature by industrial and agricultural training and to free them from intellectual slavery by scholastic education. This nation has

IGOROT SCHOOL FOR GIRLS AT BAGUIO, THE SUMMER CAPITAL

granted a large measure of self-government and justice in the Philippine Assembly and has recently appointed a Filipino majority on the Commission which corresponds to the Upper House.

Comparisons are often useful (though sometimes odious) in an ethnological discussion, and from my limited experience as a teacher in the southwestern part of the United States and also in the Philippines, I beg leave to make a comparison between

LOOKING UP THE VALLEY ON THE WAY TO BAGUIO

the rural conditions in the two places that is more favorable to the Islands than to Arizona and New Mexico. The text-books in the Philippines were especially designed for the Islands and are unexcelled, and I believe the whole system there is more economically administered than in our Southwest. The rural Filipino gets a ten-months' school term and the teacher a living wage ($1200 to $1400 a year), while in the Southwest, the teacher is lucky to get a six months' term and he must have another source of income besides that of his profession. Right here I want to say that education is not forced on the Filipinos but each district in a province (county) must petition for and be able to support a school.

Another factor which is entirely ignored by many persons in discussing the Philippine problem is the matter of justice to the small army of men and women engaged in uplifting the Filipinos. Should they be given no consideration ? A body of men and women who have exiled themselves from their native country, who have detached themselves from the social life of their own race, and who bravely combat the subtle influences of climate and environment ? One who engages in the service must look to a life of isolation. If this country cuts loose from the Islands, this noble army will be banished, and think of their discouragement and the loss of skilled workers ! Left to their own devices, the Filipinos, like a lot of naughty boys out of school, would drive home their uplifters; then, after the mischief was done, they would try to call them back from over the thousands of miles of ocean waters. But never again would it be possible. A few would respond, but the rest, discouraged, would apply their efforts to work at home.

Let us hold tight to the Philippines; let us continue and extend the great work which already, in fourteen years, is transforming ten millions of people and offering the world an example of practical idealism. Freedom, like most other things, is an evolutionary process and it is only by giving the Filipinos the tools wherewith they can earn their freedom that they will get it.

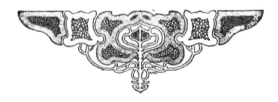

A GLIMPSE OF "DE MORNIN' STAR"

HAMPTON IN THE FIELD

I "DE MORNIN' STAR"

An account of the work of Hampton graduates now at the Calhoun Colored School, Alabama

BY J. E. DAVIS

A GROUP of white buildings, on a hilltop, shining in the sunlight, suggested the name, "De Mornin' Star," to the imaginative black people among whom the little settlement was established. The name took on new meaning when these neglected black people, living in the dark bypaths of ignorance and degradation in one of the most backward counties of Alabama's Black Belt, realized that the Calhoun School had indeed come to bring them light which would guide their footsteps into the highway of civilization.

During the years since the school was started in 1892 the light of "De Mornin' Star" has led the crop-mortgage farm tenant out of his serfdom into the freedom of the American small farmer; has shown many a mother the dangers to health and morals lurking in dark corners, in unclean cabins, in unkempt and neglected sons and daughters; and has drawn hundreds of boys and girls to study under its beams how to become useful men and women.

"Calhoun stands or falls," said its principal, Miss Charlotte R. Thorn, in an early report, "according as her boys and girls, when they go away to Hampton and other higher schools, come back to live in and do something for their home county, or remain away for good." During the eighteen years since the first class was graduated from Calhoun, many of its graduates have stood this test, 38 per cent coming back for a time to teach their neighbors' children, and 73 per cent returning to Calhoun to live. A number of these have bought land, built houses, and established homes that are object lessons to their less advantaged brothers and sisters. As a rule the Calhoun boys and girls develop at Calhoun, and strengthen at Hampton, a missionary spirit which sends them back to lend their help in making Lowndes County a model farming community.

Of the eleven Hampton men and women now teaching at Calhoun, five were once Calhoun pupils. The oldest of the latter group is Charles J. Edwards, who says of his life as a pupil at Calhoun: "It was my first experience in a well-regulated school

under well-trained teachers. A new day had come and everything seemed bright and hopeful." Graduating from Calhoun in
1897, he went to Hampton for further training, in 1901 receiving
his trade certificate in carpentry and the following year his
academic diploma. He then returned to Calhoun as teacher of
manual training and elementary carpentry, which department
has grown, under his guidance, more and more practical and
helpful each year. It furnishes the school with tables and bureaus, crayon and match boxes, nail and seed boxes, pencil-racks,
book shelves, settees, desks, and stepladders, and the community
with towel rollers, picture frames, washboards, ironing boards,
and tables. The boys have even made a pulpit for one of the
Montgomery churches.

MR. EDWARDS AND HIS BOYS COMPLETING THEIR SHOP

It is one of Mr. Edwards's rules that all training must result
in a finished article, with the result that many useful pieces of
furniture or devices for lessening work have found their way
into the homes. The carpentry classes have also helped to prepare very interesting exhibits for various fairs in the South and
for the Calhoun Club in Boston. It is significant that during the
past year white school principals and teachers of Lowndes County
have asked Mr. Edwards for models to use in the manual training classes which they were just starting.

Mr. Edwards married a Hampton girl, Celia Reade, '01, and
was the first Hampton graduate to have his home in the community. It is itself a small "mornin' star," being white and set
on a hilltop commanding a beautiful view. Five little Hampton
grandchildren are growing up there. This happy home life

among the people, together with Mr. Edwards's church and
Sunday-school work, has formed a strong bond between the
school and the community.   Mr. Edwards often conducts prayers
at the school and is the regular leader of the "spirituals," of
which Calhoun has its own interesting collection.

Another Hampton man, who was once a small boy in the
Calhoun School and is now one of its leading instructors, is
Robert W. Brown, farm manager and teacher of agriculture.
Coming from a little country school taught "in any outhouse on
any man's plantation where the people could agree to have it,"
he regarded his arrival at Calhoun as the beginning of his school
career.   He had been carefully taught, however, and his
religious nature developed by his mother and father.

CALHOUN'S SUGAR-CANE CROP

Looking back on his early Calhoun days he regards them as
the beginning of his Hampton life.   "The ringing of the bell,"
he says, "the military drill and discipline, the work in the classrooms and shops, the lessons from the life of General Armstrong,
the religious life, and in fact the whole influence of the place
might well be called 'Hampton adapted to the needs of the
people of Calhoun.'"   His decision to make agriculture his life
work was reached only by degrees.   At Hampton he first took
a course in carpentry and, after being graduated from the academic course in 1905, taught manual training in the practice
school there.   But, hearing the call of the land, he went North
to earn money for the agricultural course at Hampton, which he
completed in 1910, and was at once engaged to take charge of the
Calhoun farm.

STORING THE HAY

Under Mr. Brown's management this farm provides the school with fresh vegetables, milk, pork, veal, beef, corn, and hay. It serves the agricultural classes 'as an object lesson and practice field, and the community as a demonstration station. When two acres produced six hundred sixteen pounds of lint cotton, it furnished a significant lesson to the neighboring farmers, who raise, on an average, but five hundred pounds on *three* acres.

Through his knowledge of scientific agriculture Mr. Brown has redeemed land which was going to waste, terracing, ditching, and fencing it, thus adding twenty acres to the previous thirty-eight of cultivated land. He has made experiments with cotton, tending to give the boll weevil a cold reception on his expected arrival this year. Last winter the weevil reached the Calhoun railroad station but gave Mr. Brown no uneasiness. Each year more and more men ask him for advice and follow his methods with their crops. In order to keep the young men on the farm, it is necessary to increase their earning capacity, and Mr. Brown feels that there is great need in Lowndes County of an expert demonstration agent who can give his whole time to the work. By means of boys' corn clubs, farmers' conferences, and agricultural fairs, interest had been aroused, not only among the school children and their parents, but also among white land-lords, who have offered prizes to the Negroes for the best crops of cotton and corn.

Mr. Brown married Laura Witherspoon, also a graduate of Calhoun and Hampton ('09), and a former teacher in the settlement school. Their lives are most helpful in the community as well as in the school, and their home is a valuable object lesson.

The three women instructors who have been both Calhoun

and Hampton girls are Mary M. Bishop and Sallie A. Willis, ex-students, and Mittie B. Goldsmith, '07·

Miss Bishop went to Calhoun to assist the housekeeper while being trained to take charge of a department, if found capable. The following year she was put in charge of the students' dining room and kitchen, planning meals, ordering supplies, training cooks and pantry boys and waiters. The cooks and pantry boys are night-school students, often coming from one-room cabin homes, and are changed every two years. It was a hard position, but Miss Bishop has proved capable of carrying well all the work in her department. She has initiative and ingenuity, is systematic and orderly, and by much dignity has gained control, not only of the students working for her but of the whole student body under her care during meals. In the summer she not only has charge of the students' meals but also of canning and of the entire students' department. It was not easy for a young woman who had been the playmate of many of her charges to keep control of them, but Miss Bishop has "won out."

Another Calhoun girl who has "won out" is Miss Willis, as she has quietly gained, through her patience and conscientiousness, the respect and co-operation of her girls in the laundry. It was a happy day for the Calhoun School laundry when, last Fourth of July, after two years' hard work at drilling, the people of the settlement gathered to see water from a thousand feet below the surface gush fifty feet into the air when the engine was started. "Enough water for the first time" to wash, under otherwise primitive and hard conditions, thirty-two hundred pieces each week! The instructor's natural love of

MISS BISHOP'S COOKS

order and of cleanliness, added to her Hampton training, has made her mistress of the situation.

Miss Goldsmith has charge of the first-year primary work and of the playground at the noon hour. She has a strong influence, due to her quiet dignity and deeply religious life, and, readily gaining their love and confidence, easily controls the children. She has had but one year of previous experience, besides her experience at the Whittier Training School at Hampton.

This group, which has behind it both the Calhoun and Hampton training, with love and loyalty to both institutions, is most helpful to Calhoun's principal, and is her dependence when puzzling questions arise in the school or community. They are an excellent illustration of the wisdom of General Armstrong, who said, as long ago as 1872: ''The normal-school graduate of the South should be of the people, above them, yet of them, in order to make natural or probable a lifelong service in their behalf.''

Of the other Hampton workers at Calhoun, four are women and two are men. Annie E. Crawford is now completing her nineteenth year at Calhoun. Going there for one year of practice in teaching sewing and laundry work, she at once showed a habit of doing well whatever she undertook and an unusual ability in dealing with people. After five years Miss Crawford was put in charge of all the domestic-science classes and made housemother to the girls. Later she was released from the classes and, in addition to her work as housemother, made housekeeper of the teachers' home, which positions she still holds, having grown more and more useful year by year. ''Her sincerity and the depth of her loyalty and interest make her most valuable to Calhoun.'' Her careful, sympathetic, patient care and training of the forty-five boarding girls under her charge means much for the future of the community. On Friday evenings she meets them for friendly criticism of the week's life and for consultation and advice as to the best means of greater mutual helpfulness and advance.

Susie T. Townsley, now trained nurse for the school, was graduated from Hampton in 1904. While teaching for five years in rural Virginia, Miss Townsley, with the real Hampton spirit of serving the community, saw how much her people needed trained care when they were ill and decided that she could best serve them by becoming a trained nurse. Graduating from the Mercy Hospital and Training School in Philadelphia in 1912, she went to Calhoun first as a private nurse, the second year being regularly engaged by the school. For the first time in twenty years Calhoun has been, the past year, without a school physician, but Miss Townsley has done most satisfactorily all the work

"MISS CRAWFORD IS COMPLETING HER
NINETEENTH YEAR AT CALHOUN."

connected with the dispensary and the care of sick people on the grounds and in the community. She says regarding her work, "I am very happy here, happy in my lot—for at Calhoun the spirit of Hampton lives."

A CORNER OF THE GIRLS' DORMITORY

"One of the best teachers Calhoun has ever had " is Katie C. Hughes, Hampton, '04. Miss Hughes completed the high school course in a Northern city before coming to Hampton for special normal work. After her graduation she taught for three years before going to Calhoun where she has work with primary children in the day time, and with work students in the evening,

STUDENT BLACKSMITHS

doing equally well with both. At one of the community churches Miss Hughes seizes the opportunity to influence the parents as well as the children.

Still another academic teacher is Nettie E. Dolly, Hampton, '04, who has studied at Oberlin also for three years. This is Miss Dolly's first year at Calhoun, where she is considered a good worker.

The two remaining Hampton men are Shadrach E. Gray, Trade School '06, and James F. Ochard, '05. Mr. Gray is a

A CALHOUN COBBLING CLASS

trained blacksmith, and has had charge of the blacksmithing department at Calhoun for the past four years, as well as, for two years, of the work in leather, having taken a summer course in this branch at Hampton. He and his boys repair and care for the school harnesses and the leather on the carriages, and do the cobbling for the settlement, besides shoeing horses and doing other blacksmith's work. Mr. Gray is thoroughly interested and is a successful teacher, inspiring his boys to become careful and earnest workmen. Outside the school also his strong religious nature is deeply felt and he has been given much responsibility in the church to which he belongs.

Mr. Ochard, who left Hampton in 1905 with a diploma and a wheelwright's certificate, was put in charge, two years afterward, of the repair and construction work at Calhoun. He also acted for a time as disciplinarian for the boys. The repairs needed by eighteen buildings, and the care of the new engine house, with the pumps and piping, keep him and his boys very busy. With the other young men instructors, Mr. Ochard finds time, however, to help with the work of the White Cross League, an organization for the boys in which practical religious questions are discussed and much attention given to the subject of the respect due girls and women.

Mrs. Ochard was a Hampton girl as well as a trained nurse, and keeps a model home for her husband and child. Both Mr. and Mrs. Ochard are most helpful in the community life.

Thus these Hampton men and women, forming but one small group among a number to be afterwards described, make their school training tell, diffuse the Hampton spirit of service, and justify the expense of their education, as well as the confidence of the friends who made it possible.

·ARROW POINTS

BY HARLAN I. SMITH

POINTS chipped from stone for arrows, spears, and knives, are the most ancient, numerous, and wide spread of all known ancient objects of human handiwork. They are more common in most parts of the world than those ground out of stone. Those ground from bone and antlers are less numerous, except perhaps in a few regions, and those ground from shell are very rare. Arrows beaten from copper and whittled from horn are also very rare. Some arrows were used with wooden points, others merely with the shaft tip suitably shaped. Points cut from iron rapidly took the place of those of other materials among the Indians after the coming of white men, and the rifle bullet later took their place until now, when even it is falling into disuse.

Chipped points many thousands of years old are found in the earliest known deposits of human handiwork, and are still made in a few places. They are found in nearly all parts of the world— Japan, India, Egypt, France, Germany, Great Britain, Terra del Fuego, Peru, Mexico, Alaska, and Greenland. There is no part of Canada where they are absolutely known to be absent, though they are very rare on the coast of northern British Columbia and southern Alaska. Although they are numerous in southern Ontario, they are exceedingly rare on some sites where vast numbers of other specimens are found. On the coast of southern British Columbia, chipped points are perhaps as numerous as those ground out of stone, but not so common as those ground out of bone and antlers. In the interior they are numerous, while ground points are rare.

Most chipped points are made of stone that is brittle and chips easily. Flint, chert, chalcedony, jasper, quartzite, glassy basalt, obsidian or volcanic glass and stone of similar character are commonly used, although argillite, slate, limestone, and even sandstone, have been employed. The best material that was near seems to have been used in most cases. Glassy basalt was used for most points in the interior of southern British Columbia; black trap, much like it, and some other stones on the coast; grey chert or impure flint in Ontario ; and white quartzite in the maritime provinces. Some are made from pebbles, as on the coast of New Brunswick ; others from quarried rock, as the chert near Niagara and obsidian in Yellowstone National Park. A few points have also been chipped from glass in modern times. The stone was preferably chipped while containing the quarry water or before being weathered. Workshops where they were made have been found near Niagara Falls, Bathurst, New Brunswick, and elsewhere. The stone was no doubt chipped into form by blows from a pebble or stone hammer, but the final finishing work on some was done by flaking by means of a twisting pressure given with a grease-free bone or antler flaker.

The uses varied. The larger points would be unsuitable for arrows, but may have been used for spears or knives, although lances or javelins were not much used in North America. Lopsided points would not shoot or throw straight, but would serve as knives. Some points are broken, and usually they show no signs of use, except occasionally such as result from striking something hard, but a few are polished at the ends as if from use as knives. *Bunts* is the name given to those having the end blunt instead of sharply pointed, usually worked off about equally from each side. Generally these seem to be points redressed because the tips have been broken, although some were apparently originally made in this form. A few are polished on the end. Some believe that these were for stunning in order that pelt or plumage might be free from cuts or blood. There are relatively few, but these are widely distributed. Some very slender points were used as drill points, and some with an edge chipped only or mostly from one side, as scrapers, a few of each of these kinds being polished on the end from use.

The shapes vary, apparently largely due to accident in chipping, but the points are usually triangular or a pointed oval, called leaf-shaped. Some have slender blades and wide bases. Many have tangs or notches; some have two notches on each side, and many are more or less barbed. Some have serrated edges. A few have one edge chipped from one side, and the opposite edge chipped from the opposite side, giving them a rhomboidal section, possibly to make them whirl when shot, as a ball whirls from a rifled gun, but they are probably merely the result of a style of chipping. It has been suggested that, for war, points were loosely attached so as to come off in the wound, while for hunting they were firmly fastened so as to be easily withdrawn. For the former, triangular points would serve best; for the latter, notched points would be serviceable.

To shaft points they were inserted in the split end of the shaft, foreshaft, or handle, and lashed across the base or through the notches with cord, rawhide, or sinew, which later, on drying, would shrink and hold tightly; or glue, gum, or cement was used to hold them securely, and often both tying and sticking were employed. Some knives were probably simply grasped in **the** hand.

Caches or stores of points usually of unfinished or simple forms, are frequently found, as in Ontario and at Kamloops, British Columbia.

AN EXPERIMENT IN WRITING ENGLISH

BY JAMES HARDY DILLARD

President of the Negro Rural School Fund and Director of the Slater Fund

ALL agree that one of the things which schools should teach is the writing of fairly correct English. Whether a school teaches Latin or teaches agriculture, we believe that it should teach the pupils to write English with fair correctness as to spelling and capitals and punctuation. Of course there is considerable latitude, but there is at the same time a pretty well defined convention to which we expect ordinary writers to conform.

While I was recently visiting two well-known schools ranked among the higher institutions for colored youth, one for young women and one for young men, it occurred to me to give a simple test in correct writing.   I happened to have in my pocket a copy of ''Jane Eyre, '' and opening the volume at random, I dictated the following as rapidly as the pupils could write the words :

Long did the hours seem while I waited the departure of the company, and listened for the sound of Bessie's step on the stairs.   Sometimes she would come up in the interval to seek her thimble or her scissors, or perhaps to bring me something by way of supper—a bun or a cheese-cake—then she would sit on the bed while I was eating it, and when I had finished, she would tuck the clothes round me, and twice she kissed me, and said, '' Good-night, Miss Jane. ''

I was glad that I happened to select a comparatively easy passage in the way of spelling, as I wished mainly to test the pupil's spelling when writing simple words rapidly. I also wished to see whether they had a fairly good idea of punctuation. I was much pleased with the experiment, and was surprised at the general excellence of the papers, The handwriting was almost without exception distinct and neat, and most of the pupils showed good sense and good training in the use of punctuation. As would be expected, the most usual mistakes came in managing the quotation marks at the close.

The pupils in the two classes to which the test was given were in high-school work, and, as I have said, the test was an easy one, especially for pupils of that grade. One of the classes consisted of 28 girls in the first year of high school ; the other consisted of 32 boys in the second year of high school. The 28 girls made 275 mistakes, an average of about 10. The 32 boys made 241 mistakes, an average of about 7½. Eighteen of the girls were above the average, and ten below. Two of the girls, with 33 and 20 mistakes, were apparently in the wrong class, as were two of the boys with 17 and 16 mistakes. Of the boys, twelve were below the average and twenty above. The most correct paper was that of a boy whose only mistake was the omission of a comma after the word *said*, near the close. Five boys and seven girls missed the spelling of *scissors*, while twelve boys and seven girls missed *thimble*. In enumerating the mistakes I should say that I did not count the omission of the hyphen in the words *cheese-cake* and *good-night*, nor did I insist upon the two dashes, provided commas were used, or a semicolon or period for the second. I also disregarded the use or omission of the comma after the words *company, scissors, finished*, and the second *me*.

In conclusion I should like to say that in my opinion dictation is far the best method of teaching pupils to write correctly. The exercises should be taken from some suitable book published by any of the standard houses, all of which employ careful proof-readers. "Self-Help" by Samuel Smiles, published by Harper, is excellent for this purpose. Of course such exercises will be useless unless the papers are corrected with painstaking care, and are returned to the class with sufficient explanation of the corrections.

Book Reviews

In Black and White: An Interpretation of Southern Life. By Mrs. L. H. Hammond, with an introduction by James H. Dillard, LL. D. Fleming H. Revell Company. New York. Price, $1.25.

THIS brilliantly written book, "In Black and White" is an inspiring, sensible word on the Negro situation in the South. But for the unusual social development of recent years in the South, it would seem remarkable that this book should have come from that section, for the South has boasted of feeling rather than thinking about the Negro. With the broadening vision of the newer South, the author makes a significant "attempt to translate some fragments of Southern life into world-terms; to set sectional problems in their wide human relations, and so to see them as they really are." In this larger light, the South's great problem loses most of its wonted peculiarity. The community's debt to its poor, neglected, ignorant, and unprivileged classes, which happen in this instance to be black, in the main, is shown to be the same as that owed by other sections to similar classes of a more homogeneous population. The peculiar thing about the South is, as the author declares, that "we alone, of all the privileged of Christendom, have no widespread sense of obligation to achieve this task."

The book is a ringing challenge to Southern Christianity and civilization to acquaint themselves with well-tested Christian effort at social uplift the world over, and to apply this knowledge to trying local conditions—"to serve our neighbor, not according to the color of his skin, but according to his need."

This book could not have been written in the South ten years ago, although the service to which it calls so forcibly was as much needed then as now. It must needs wait for the awakening social consciousness of which it is, perhaps, the best single expression. Herein are recorded the efforts of those bodies doing the most significant social work in the South—the various organizations of the Southern Presbyterians, Methodists, and Baptists; the Carnegie libraries—"among the wisest investments in the South;" the Southern Young Men's Christian Association; the Negro Rural School Fund and the Phelps-Stokes Fund under Southern management; and the "once-so-hated 'Yankees'" who first made possible to Negro teachers a suitable preparation for their work. " Only time could bring the following hearty appreciation of the work of Northern teachers :

"But with all the mistakes and friction, the energy wasted or turned to loss, these people brought one thing with them which is never wholly lost. It may be hindered, partly negatived, robbed of its full fruition by many things : but always love bears fruit. They brought with them that principle of life. They kindled a light in dark hearts ; they sent out thousands of Negroes fired with ideals of service to their race. And they have saved the situation, so far as it has been saved, for our Negro public schools. "

The frankness and kindliness of spirit of the book are refreshing. The author writes out of a wealth of first-hand knowledge and experience, and there is no effort to blink at the facts. Over against the many acts of personal kindness to individual Negroes on the part of whites, she sets down the general indifference and neglect of the Negroes as a class and their exploitation at the hands of white people. The Negro's shortcomings are also given ample space. But she renders both the Negro and the white people a special service by repeatedly showing that the former's bad characteristics, instead of being racial, are due mainly to neglect and to conditions forced upon him. She says, "We criticize unsparingly the Negro's weakness and faults, yet fasten upon him living conditions which, the world over and among all races, breed just those things for which we blame him most. "

Mrs. Hammond writes not only with a full understanding of the Southern whites whom she represents, but with a rare appreciation of the thoughts and feelings of Negroes regarding many of the abuses to which they are subjected. She says, for instance, "If I were a Negro I should do just as Negroes do—resent with all my heart our stupid white assumption that when they attempt to buy property in our own desirable sections they are trying to force themselves upon us in impudence, and to assert their belief in and desire for 'social equality'." She understands that what these Negroes want is decency and sanitary conditions in which to live and rear their children. And she adds, "Their passionate desire for character in their children we do not begin to understand." If this book accomplishes no other end, it ought, at least, to open the hearts and minds of Southern whites to the iniquity of the Jim Crow cars, and wring from them a remedy. Mrs. Hammond understands that the fear of violence and lynching is ever present with the Negroes, and that "it hangs, a thick fog of distrust, between their race and ours." Again she says, "This sense of evil possibly impending, with the deep distrust engendered by it, colors all the Negro's relations with us." And she points out that the administration of the courts does not lessen this distrust. Accordingly, a strong appeal is made for justice for all, "for," she concludes, "if we fail to achieve justice for the poorest, our doom is written in the stars."

Mrs Hammond makes a stirring call to Southern whites for effective social service, although she realizes that there is considerable confusion still in the minds of many of them, when Negroes and social service are mentioned in the same breath. The paucity of effort on their part disturbs her, and will be a surprise to many others. As for the women, for instance, those "of the Southern Methodist Church are the only ones in the South as yet carrying on organized work for Negroes." But the most hopeful sign about whatever this and similar Southern organizations are doing is that their work "looks toward co-operation between the better classes of both races for the uplift of the Negro poor." "It is impossible," writes Mrs Hammond, "to serve the best interests of either race without this personal communication between the two." This is the most difficult part of her program. The spirit of this association will determine largely the effectiveness of these undertakings. The author's suggestion on this point is deserving of weighty consideration: "Our long indifference weighs heavily against us; and our assistance, where offered, is too often tinctured—or impregnated—with condescension. If Christ had come to us that way I think we would be savages still. However fine it may look on the outside, there is no lifting force in any condescending deed."

The book is not one of mere accusations. On the contrary it is filled with helpful, constructive, workable suggestions that require nothing more than ordinary thoughtfulness, commonplace sympathy and brotherliness—nothing that any human being need be afraid of. The ideals set up are not final or exhaustive. The author probably did not aim at any such achievement. They doubtless fall short of what some of the larger souls, black and white, desire, and they probably go beyond the point reached ·by many others. But they will serve as an excellent working basis for all who want to make of the South a finer place to live in.   w. t. b. w.

Out of the House of Bondage: By Kelly Miller. The Neale Publishing Company, New York. Price, $1.50 net.

IN his new book, for which he is to be congratulated on choosing such a superb title, Dean Miller pursues the general plan followed in "Race Adjustment," bringing together in one volume several of the papers that within the last few years have appeared in representative American magazines. There is about the book more unity of theme than such a method would normally imply, all of the essays dealing in one way or another with the general status in the United States of the people only fifty years "out of the house of bondage."

The book is of interest primarily in the field of sociology, and the method of the study is philosophical rather than technical. The general purpose is best stated in the author's own words: "Rather than describe the progress of the race in terms of definite data and tabular array of ascertained facts after the manner of the statistician, let us, if we may, clothe the dry bones of bare facts with the vital power of the living truth." In the pursuance of this method the author is sometimes led to review rather familiar ground, as in "Education for Manhood," "Fifty Years of Negro Education," "Negroes in Professional Pursuits," and "The Ministry." Much more original and interesting are "The Physical Destiny of the American Negro" and its companion essay, "The Ultimate Race Problem," "Crime among Negroes," "The American Negro as a Political Factor," and the essay reviewing Sir Harry H. Johnston's "The Negro in the New World" and Mr. B. R. Putnam Weale's "The Conflict of Color." One word is especially timely. Just at present, with the large amount of time given to the study of Reconstruction in representative American universities, there seems to be renewed emphasis on the incompetency of the Negro in political affairs as revealed by the events of the troublous decade after the Civil War. Major John R. Lynch, in his book, "The Facts of Reconstruction," also published by Neale, has recently shown that in Mississippi, where the Negro reached his highest degree of political power, he at no time had more than 34 out of 140 members of the legislature. Says Dean Miller along the same general line: "These much abused 'Negro governments,' as they are called, changed the oligarchy of the conquered states into true democracies, inaugurated a system of public instruction for all classes, and the general character of their constitutions was regarded as so excellent that many of them have not been altered up to the present time, except for the worse."

The style of the writing, a little ponderous at times, is at others exceedingly crisp and epigrammatic, as when the author says, "The world believes in a race that believes in itself." At the end of the book is the rhapsody, charming in its lyric quality, "I See and Am Satisfied," which originally appeared in the *Independent* a year ago. All told, the production is a highly creditable one and a work that no student of social conditions in America at the present time will want to fail to see on his shelves.

B. G. B.

Duplication of Schools for Negro Youth: By W. T. B. Williams. Published by The John F. Slater Fund.

Negro Universities in the South: By W. T. B. Williams. Published by The John F. Slater Fund.

A GRADUATE of Hampton and Harvard, W. T. B. Williams, who is the field agent of the John F. Slater Fund and a keen observer of Negro schools, has prepared an interesting and thought-provoking pamphlet on "Duplication of Schools for Negro Youth." Mr. Williams cites in some detail the facts of fifty cases of duplication and offers a map which presents graphically the serious problem of struggling Negro schools that seek public support and in many cases defeat the ends for which they were established.

Mr. Williams has come to this conclusion : "With the tendencies toward the consolidation of schools, even in the rural districts, with the resulting increased efficiency and economy, it is a great pity that the colored children in the elementary and secondary grades in the several schools in the same city must be taught in comparatively small groups at a high relative cost and lower deficiency.

"For example, in Birmingham, Ala., 986 elementary students are distributed among five private institutions. In Selma, 1162 pupils in the grades are divided among three private institutions. In Atlanta, 1256 such students are scattered around among five schools, and in New Orleans 1189 among three institutions. Certainly it does not seem possible that the great church boards will much longer delay some such adjustments as these for the good of the schools."

Dr. James Hardy Dillard declares in the preface to Mr Williams' discussion : "The bare sight of the facts contained in this publication should be sufficient to lead to some action. What stands in the way ? The main answer must be *denominationalism*. Denominations in religion will probably continue to exist so long as the thoughts and tastes of men differ; but when denominationalism leads to such waste of money and effort as is shown in the efforts to aid in providing education for the colored people of the Southern states, it is the part of wisdom and true religion to seek some basis of co-operation, rather than to continue in wasteful competition."

In an earlier study, "Negro Universities in the South," Mr. Williams showed clearly the relation of denominationalism to duplication in Negro educational effort and recommended a reduction in the number of schools offering college courses. Mr. Williams pointed out the need of colleges for Negro youth. He expressed, however, his firm belief in the value of giving added support to the better schools. The wonder has been that Negro schools having so little physical equipment and such small annual incomes have been able to turn out as good leaders as they have.

Today many of the helpful and safe leaders of the South have been trained in the schools concerning which Mr. Williams has made his reports. W. A. A.

Bookbinding for Beginners: By Florence O. Bean. Published by The Manual Arts Press, Peoria, Illinois. Price, $1.25.

THIS is a valuable book for teachers of hand work in the lower elementary grades and will be a direct help to those who may have to teach this subject. We welcome it because it gives one more form of useful hand work to our schools and one which will surely develop into a much wider field of usefulness in the near future.

The clearness with which the author has given the working directions, and the avoidance of unnecessary technicalities will do much to encourage its use in the public schools, especially in the fifth and sixth grades, where the hand work should take a definite form and should show evidence of considerable skill.

The concise and practical way in which the problems are presented convinces the reader at once that the author has worked them out to their completion, and removes any doubt about their being workable. Miss Bean leaves the subject at a very critical point—"the border line between educational hand work and technical bookbinding," which "cannot be crossed." Some writer will one day dare to break down this formidable barrier and stumbling block to progress in our schools and will link the "educational" and industrial work in a continuous chain of endeavor.

A fitting sequence to this valuable book on bookbinding would be a chapter on repairing school library books and text-books as a part of the pupil's training in book work. J. H. J.

At Home and Afield

HAMPTON INCIDENTS

SUMMER-SCHOOL TALKS

THE daily exercises held in Cleveland Hall Chapel between eleven and twelve o'clock for the summer-school students and teachers were not the least valuable of the month's activities. Addresses were made by members of the Hampton summer-school teaching force and by visiting educators as follows : two lectures, "Color in music" and descriptions of his piano suites, "Magnolias" and "In the Bottoms," by R. Nathaniel Dett; "The teacher as a social worker" by Rev. A. A. Graham of Phoebus, Va.; "Training deaf and blind colored children" by Hon. Harry R. Houston of Hampton, with exercises by the children themselves from the Virginia State School for Colored Deaf and Blind Children near Newport News ; two lectures on "The modernization of arithmetic" by John C. Stone of the State Normal School, Montclair, N. J.; "Thy word is a lamp unto my feet" by Rev. E. H. Hamilton of Hampton; The history of the Hebrews" by Dr. Frank K. Sanders, president of Washburn College, Topeka, Kan.; "Reckless waste of baby life" by John M. Gandy, president of the Petersburg Normal School; "Opening and closing exercises" by Miss Sarah J Walter, in charge of the Hampton Normal Training Department; "The care of the horse," with "Bonny Billy" from the Hampton stables on the stage as a demonstration, by Dr. R. R. Clark of Hampton Institute ; "Better country life" by W. T. B. Wiiliams, field agent of the Slater Fund, the Jeanes Board, and Hampton Institute ; "The

history of the Lower Virginia Peninsula" by Capt. Allen Washington, Hampton's assistant disciplinarian; and "The Negro genius" by Benjamin G. Brawley, dean of Morehouse College, Atlanta, Ga.

At the eleven o'clock chapel exercises on Monday, June 13, Dr. Frissell, who had recently returned from a Northern campaign trip, gave a most encouraging talk to the students, showing that their opportunities for making the world better, which may seem to them trifling in the narrow vision of the moment, are really tremendous and far-reaching.

On the final day, June 14, the audience enjoyed several selections from Mozart and Tschaikowsky played by a string quartet consisting of Dr. George P. Phenix, Mr. W. M. O. Tessmann, and Arthur and Emil Tessmann. Members of Mr. Dett's classes gave a demonstration of the chorus singing of children's songs, which they had learned for use in their schoolrooms.

TEACHERS' CONFERENCES

TWO conferences were held in July for the teachers taking the normal course, at which some of the more experienced Negro teachers spoke on subjects relating to community work, the co-operation of school and church, the schoolhouse and its relation to the community, the raising of money for school purposes, a campaign against tuberculosis, farming and teaching, and manual training and domestic science. The names of several Hampton graduates who spoke and summaries of their talks are given as graduate notes in this issue.

AN INDUSTRIAL EXHIBIT

ON Friday evening, July 12, from eight until nine o'clock, work of the cooking, sewing, chair-caning, manual training, and drawing classes was exhibited on the lower floor of Domestic Science Building. A demonstration of electric wiring, done by Benjamin Washington, a teacher in the Armstrong Manual Training School, Washington, D. C., who has been studying with Mr. C. S. Isham during the summer-school session, was also shown.

The motive of the exhibit was twofold : to show the normal students how to select and arrange effectively industrial exhibits in their own schools— a duty which falls to most of them at least once a year—and to let them see the classified results of the skill which they themselves, as a whole, had acquired during a month of study and practice.

The exhibit of the cooking class included tables correctly set for breakfast, luncheon, and dinner ; uniforms for cook and waitress on dressmaking forms ; jars of canned fruits and vegetables ; a tray arranged with proper diet foods for a diabetic patient ; and a number of dainty foods in a glass cabinet. The sewing exhibit displayed among other things samples showing the various stitches and very attractive dresses for house, street, and evening wear, the cost of material for one dress ranging from $.56 to $2.62.

Stools and chairs with woven seats of reeds, husks, raffia, and cane, and mattresses stuffed with hair, moss, or shucks, and finished with cotton tops were products shown by the class in chair-caning and upholstery. The manual training exhibit included silhouette pictures of schools and school surroundings mounted on cardboard, scrap books, boxes, trays, a furnished doll's house surrounded by pleasant grounds, and inhabited by contented-looking paper dolls, simple articles of home furniture made from dry-goods boxes, and a demonstration of rug-weaving on a small loom.

The drawing showed simple, artistic work with crayon, pencil, and brush, among which were cards with holiday designs and in particular representations of tastefully arranged school grounds planted with ornamental trees and shrubs and supplied with neat paths. The electrical exhibit included wiring in wood molding, metal molding and conduit, a design in miniature, lights, and an electric fan and a toaster in operation.

THE MINISTERS' CONFERENCE

THE conference for the Negro Ministers of Tidewater Virginia, held from June 29 to July 3, as a part of the regular summer school, was attended by forty ministers. The Baptist, Episcopal, Methodist and Presbyterian denominations were represented in this number. Four exercises were held each of the four days of the conference. Dr. Frank K. Sanders lectured on theology at the morning sessions and at the evening sessions on "The historical study of the Bible." Mr. Fenninger held a series of discussions on the general themes, "The minister and his message," and "The ministry of the church to the community."

Those who attended this conference on their own initiative formed a permanent organization, the purpose of which is to arrange for a regular annual conference such as was held this year. The future of this work was entrusted to the hands of an executive committee consisting of the following members : Rev. A. A. Graham of Phoebus, Rev. G. D. Jimmerson of Hampton, and Rev. Laurence Fenninger.

ENTERTAINMENTS

NINE members of the Douglass Literary Society on the evening of June 27 competed for prizes in an oratorical contest held in Cleveland

Hall Chapel. The orations were not original, but were, in most cases, eloquent speeches of famous statesmen or educators. The rules of the contest required that each speech should contain not more than 600 words. The delivery and bearing of the speakers were dignified and telling. The only criticism might be for occasional lack of force and of clear enunciation. The winner of the first prize, Lorenzo C. White, delivered "An appeal to the Georgia convention against secession" by Alexander Stephens. Felix Northern, to whom the second prize was awarded, gave "Claims of the Negro" by Booker T. Washington. The prizes were books.

ON the evening of July 3, several members of the summer school gave an entertainment in Cleveland Hall Chapel, consisting of vocal and instrumental music and recitations. All the numbers on the program were received by the audience with much appreciation, one of the most enjoyable being the reading of some of Paul Lawrence Dunbar's dialect pieces. An original poem on the Hampton Summer Normal called forth a burst of applause which seemed to indicate a concurrence, on the part of the entire summer school, with the sentiments expressed by the author.

On Monday evening, July 6, Mr. Edward Brigham, basso profundo and dramatic reader, gave a recital in Cleveland Hall Chapel. One of the most enjoyable numbers was the reading of Oscar Wilde's story, "The Selfish Giant," to the suggestive piano accompaniment written for the piece by Madame Liza Lehmann.

"The Feast of the Red Corn," an Indian operetta, was presented under the auspicies of the Treble Clef Club on the evening of July 9. A number of the actresses were summer-school students. The Indian costuming, which was under the direction of Mrs. W. T. B. Williams, the stage manager, was pleasantly striking, and the attractive dances, arranged with the help of Mr. C. H. Williams, were very gracefully performed.

ADDRESSES

IN the first week of the summer school, Mr. Jackson Davis, supervisor of Negro rural schools in Virginia, gave an illustrated talk on the improvement during the past few years in equipment and course of study of many Negro rural schools of the state.

On June 28 Rev. Wm. C. Bell, a missionary from Bailundo, Angola, W. Africa, who has had thirteen years of African life, told of the work which is being done there to correct insanitary conditions and to lessen superstition, polygamy, and the practices of witch doctors. He spoke also of the intention to build in that region a central agricultural and industrial school.

THE NEW DORMITORY

ON "Alumni Day," July 15, the cornerstone of James Hall, which is to be the new four-story brick dormitory for boys, was laid by Dr. H. B. Frissell in the presence of two hundred or more Hampton alumni. Dr. Frissell spoke of the building as a home where orderliness, cleanliness, and health will prevail. He told of the gift by Mrs. D. Willis James which made the building possible. Her husband was a devoted and helpful friend to Hampton during his life, and her son, Mr. Arthur Curtiss James, is one of the school's trustees. Mr. William M. Reid, '77, a lawyer of Portsmouth, Va., and president of the Alumni Association and Mrs. Sarah Collins Fernandis, '82, secretary of social work for colored people in Baltimore, spoke briefly for the alumni.

The new dormitory, which is situated at the left of Pierce Hall near Jones's Creek, which separates the school grounds from the Soldiers' Home, will cover an area 62 by 160 feet and will accommodate 175 boys.

The box in the cornerstone contains the Principal's Report for 1914, the

Treasurer's Report, a catalogue, issues of the Southern Workman from September 1913 to July 1914, the Newport News *Daily Press*, the *New York Times*, and the *New York Tribune* for July 14, the *Hampton Monitor* for July 10, the act of incorporation and by-laws of the school, a copy of "Education for Life," a copy of the Southern Workman for May 1898 containing the report of a speech delivered by Mr. D. Willis James at the dedication of Domestic Science Building, a copy of the Robert C. Ogden memorial pamphlet, "A Life Well Lived," "The Story of the Armstrong League," a memorandum signed by Dr. Frissell giving the names of the architects, builders, and donor, date of laying the cornerstone, and estimated cost of building, and coins of the following denominations : five dollars, one dollar, fifty cents, twenty-five cents, ten cents, five cents, and one cent.

CHARLES EDWARD ASHE

ON June 13, Mr. Charles Edward Ashe died, after several months of illness, at his home in Hampton.

Mr. Ashe was born in Portsmouth, Va., sixty years ago, and held his first position at Hampton Institute in 1875. Then for a number of years he was a building contractor. He returned to the Hampton School when the Domestic Science Building was being erected and became foreman of the carpenter shop in the Huntington Industrial Works. A few years ago he became the head of the carpentry department in the Armstrong-Slater Memorial Trade School of Hampton Institute.

The funeral service was held at four o'clock on the afternoon of June 15, in the Memorial Baptist Church of Hampton by Rev. James T. Haley. Mr. Ashe was buried in St. John's cemetery. The pallbearers included some of Mr. Ashe's associates at Hampton Institute and some of his friends in the city of Hampton. He is survived by three children and two married sisters.

In all of the Hampton Institute building operations during the recent years, Mr. Ashe played an important part and won the respect of his associates for his skill as a mechanic and for his devotion to duty.

GRADUATES AND EX-STUDENTS

SEVERAL hundred graduates assembled at Hampton Institute on Wednesday, July 15, for the twelfth triennial reunion of the Alumni Association. The program for Alumni Day was : Business session, 9 to 12 ; luncheon ; outing at Bay Shore, 2 to 5 ; laying of cornerstone for new dormitory, 4.30; reception at Mansion House at 5; banquet at 8 o'clock, Virginia Hall.

At the business meeting the following officers were elected: William M. Reid, '77, president; Ferdinand D. Lee, '79, vice president; William H. Harrison, '03, recording secretary; Don A. Davis, '09, corresponding secretary; Allen Washington, '91, financial secre-

tary; George J. Davis, '74, treasurer. The following executive committee was chosen: Fred D. Wheelock, '88, chairman; George J. Davis, '74; Frank D. Banks, '76; E. M. Canaday, '76; John H. Robinson, '76; Mrs. Laura Davis Titus, '76; Thomas C. Walker, '83; Mrs. Amaza Drummond Brown, '84; Harris Barrett, '85; Mrs. Phoebe Boner White, '88; Jesse Harris, '88; W. T. B. Williams, '88; R. R. Moton, '90; Mrs. Gertrude Peake Anderson, '92: Margaret H. Gordon, '06; Joanna Boyd, '09; Harvey A. Robinson, '10,

Wm. M. Reid, '77, and Mrs. Sarah C. Fernandis, '82, were called upon by Dr. Frissell to speak at the dedication of the new boys' dormitory, and expressed the interest and the pride of the alumni body in the constant growth of the school. Speakers at the banquet were W. T. B. Williams, toastmaster, William M. Reid, Augustus H. Hodges, '74, Joseph P. Weaver, '71, Mrs. Martha Brydson Armistead, '81, Ferdinand D. Lee, '79, Charles H. Williams, '09, Mrs. Sarah C. Fernandis, Mrs. Susan Edwards Palmer, '89, Louis Martin, '14, R. R. Moton, and Dr. France, of Portsmouth, Dr. Thomas Jesse Jones, Mrs. Ellen Weaver, Dr. George P. Phenix, and Dr. Hollis B. Frissell, who were guests of the Alumni Association.

AT a conference of summer school students held in Cleveland Hall Chapel on the evening of July 1, two of the speakers who told of their experiences in teaching were Hampton graduates. Lovie D. Galloway, '03, is teaching in a three-room school in Forsythe County near Winston-Salem, N. C. She has secured through co-operation good books, curtains, pictures, and a modern kitchen. She has taught boys and girls the value of keeping the schoolhouse clean and has herself scrubbed floors and cleaned windows with her school children as helpers. In her sewing work she has laid stress on neatness rather than mere decoration. She has tried to make her children see that tidy or untidy writing and drawing books tell the story of life in the children's homes.

Lucretia T. Kennard, '92, who is supervising industrial teacher in Caroline County, Md., read her annual report to the school board, extracts from which follow :

" The industrial work was taught in all the schools[21] with greater success than in previous years. Our teachers are graduates of normal and industrial schools and understand the work. One and a quarter hours are spent in industrial training each day.

"We are pleased with the way our school communities have responded to the needs of the schools. They are taking more pride and interest in the welfare of their children. This was demonstrated at our commencement, for we have never had our people present in such large numbers before.

" All the schools, except three, supported the industrial work. Those three schools partly supported theirs. In two communities a kitchen in one of the homes was rented and the girls, including all grades beginning with the third, were taught cooking and housekeeping. A number of *Hampton Leaflets* pertaining to the industrial work were bound in volumes enough for each school. The teachers were instructed to use them, making the work more satisfactory. They were given about two lessons a week to be taught from these leaflets. The work was to be done at the child's home or in school. A sample of that done at home was brought for the teachers to see.

"Our parent-teacher associations are in a flourishing condition. We have three mothers' clubs, three pupils' clubs, one Y. M. C. A., and a trustees' association. The parent-teachers associations and mothers' clubs meet monthly. The trustees' association meets twice a year. The ministers have helped us very much in all these organizations and in many other ways, enabling us to have better conditions in every community.

Mrs. Fannie Nicholson Ash, ex-student, '85, who is teaching in Portsmouth, Va., told of the fight against tuberculosis among Negroes which is being carried on there—a movement which was started by a few Negro women for the relief of a small boy who was suffering from the disease. For this case some of the Negro nurses and doctors gave their time and skill, but the work grew until it was decided to engage a regular nurse for the district. Half of her salary is paid by the Negroes and the other half by the city. Many patients have received treatment.

At a similar conference on Sunday evening, July 12, one of the speakers was Lucy F. Simms, Hampton, '77, who is now teaching in a seven-room school in Harrisonburg. She spoke of the effort Harrisonburg colored people have made to secure and maintain this fine school and of the generosity of the school board in recognizing their efforts.

ONE of the fifteen students to arrive on the day Hampton Institute opened in 1868 was Julia Gibbs

Stevens, '71· She has taught in South Carolina in public or private schools ever since leaving Hampton. She writes from Walterboro, S. C. :

"I am teaching four miles from Walterboro at Pringle's Crossroads where there has not been a school before. We have an enrollment of forty in such a short time. Some walk three miles every day—one little girl about six. It's nothing but hard work, but someone must go ahead. Hampton has done the sending out and we must do the work."

J. J. Tennessee, blacksmith 1911, visited the school in June. He is working at his trade in Wilson, N. C.

MARRIAGES

The marriage of Catharine W. Fields, '78· to John T. Gay occurred on July 6 in Williamsburg, Va. They will make their home in Hampton.

Announcement has been received of the marriage of Walter Douglas Jones who graduated from the Trade School, wheelwright's course, in 1899, to Mary L. Walker in Philadelphia on June 30.

The marriage of Ethel G. Dabney, '12· who has been teaching at Ivanhoe, Wythe Co., Va., and Joseph E. Herriford, '11· who for the past year has taught manual training at his home in Kansas City, Mo., occurred on June 30.

DEATHS

Dr. Bennett M. Starks, '00· of Baltimore, Md., died on July 12, 1914.

A death recently reported, which occurred some time this year, is that of Roscoe L. Lassiter, Trade School, '05· a journeyman shoemaker whose home was in Rocky Mount, N. C.

NOTICE of the death of the Rev. William D. Morris, ex-student '93· a preacher and farmer near Proffit, Va., has recently been received. For nineteen years he taught the public school at Eastham. At the time of his death, May 1914, he was pastor of two churches.

Word has been received of the death of Daniel Johnson, bricklayer '09· in Savannah, Ga.

INDIAN NOTES

IN a recent number of "Home and School," Michael Wolf, '13· disciplinarian of the Rainy Mountain School, Gotebo, Oklahoma, tells of his work among the Kiowas. He says, "Seven weeks ago an anti-tobacco campaign was begun for the Kiowa boys of this school. Previous to that time forty-three boys out of eighty-two, or more than fifty-two per cent, were on the threshold of the tobacco habit. Today there is not a single boy who uses tobacco in any form. The success of the anti-tobacco movement is due to the manly and courageous boys who resisted the appetite for tobacco. It is a noble fight for a clean, healthy body and for a strong character that these boys are engaged in, and one cannot praise them too highly."

On May 23, Flora Jamison, an ex-student from the Alleghany Reservation, New York, and Mr. Raymond Gordon were married by the Rev. M. F. Trippe. Mr. Gordon is a farmer, and the young couple will make their home in Red House, N. Y.

Robert McIntosh, an Apache who was a student at Hampton from 1881 until 1884, died at his home at San Carlos, Arizona, on Sunday, ·May 31.

A RECENT letter from Pierrepont Alford, Business Course '06· tells of his work with the engineers of the United States Indian Irrigation Survey. At the time of writing they were in the desert near the Stella Mountains, with plenty of poisonous lizards and rattlesnakes for company. William Emerson, an ex-student from the Pima Reservation, was acting as the guide during the trip through the deserts and mountains.

What Others Say

A NEGRO MOSES

A BRONZE tablet erected by the citizens of Auburn, N, Y., to the memory of Harriet Tubman was unveiled with appropriate exercises in that city on June 12. Harriet Tubman was born a slave in Maryland in 1821 and died in Auburn March 10, 1913. A part of the inscription on the tablet reads : "Called the 'Moses' of her people during the Civil War, with rare courage, she led over three hundred Negroes up from slavery to freedom and rendered invaluable service as nurse and spy." The principal address was delivered by Dr. Booker T. Washington, Hampton, '75, and speeches were made by Mayor Charles W. Brister of Auburn and by the former mayor, Hon. E. Clarence Aiken.

In reference to this occurrence, Mrs. Laura E. Titus, '76, writes : "While traveling with the Hampton singers General Armstrong in some way found out about Harriet Tubman and had the singers go to her little home and sing some of the old songs. She had very little prominence at that time and I think the General called definite attention to her in our travels. When I graduated in 1876 Harriet Tubman was the subject of my paper. The knowledge I had of her came mostly through this visit and the reading of a book of her life which was published through the efforts of one of her white friends."

INDIAN MILITARY SOCIETIES

U NDER the auspices of the American Museum of Natural History, Alanson Skinner, who has devoted four or five years to studying the customs of the Menominees and the Plains-Cree Indians in Northern Wisconsin, will visit Oklahoma this summer and will study the military societies and their ceremonials among the Kansas, Iowa, and Missouri tribes in that region. In August, Mr. Skinner will go to South Dakota and will live among the Sioux Indians for the rest of the summer. Mr. Skinner was adopted as a nephew by one of the Menominee chieftains, and among the Indians he is known as "Little Weasel."

New York Times

"GRANNY MAUMEE"

T HE Stage Society of New York City recently gave two performances of a Negro tragedy, "Granny Maumee," by Ridgeley Torrence.

Mr. Carl Van Vechten writes in the New York *Press* that Mr. Torrence has taken the Negro—just as Synge took the Irish peasant—to write about seriously and poetically and tragically, and he has written a great play. There is, as yet, no Negro theater. Several of the Negro writers are writing plays for the time when there will be one. This production is as important an event in our theater as the production of the first play of Synge was to the Irish movement.

Literary Digest

UNIVERSITY INDIANS

S TUDENTS of Indian descent in the University of Oklahoma have organized an Indian Students' Club, formed for the purpose of securing a larger and more representative attendance of Indian students from the various tribes. There are now about thirty students of Indian blood in the university, representing five tribes—Cherokees, Chickasaws, Choctaws, Delawares and Shawnees, and many of them are among the most prominent in student life.

Shawnee News-Herald

PHILADELPHIA NEGROES

T HROUGH the aid of the Philadelphia Hampton Committee, Negro workers of Philadelphia obtained jobs during the year which paid them a total of $35,000 in wages, according to reports of officers of the association made at the annual meeting at St. Stephen's Protestant Episcopal Church in May.

In addition to reports by the officers, addresses were made by the Rev. Dr. Carl E. Grammer, rector of the church, and Prof. J. P. Lichtenberger, of the University of Pennsylvania. These officers were elected : President, Dr. Grammer ; vice presidents, W. W. Frazier, Dr. Talcott Williams, the Rev. W. A. Creditt and the Rev. C. A. Tindley, and secretary-treasurer, John T. Emlen.

Philadelphia North American

THE ASIATIC EMIGRANT

THE
SOUTHERN
WORKMAN

SEPTEMBER 1914

The Hampton Normal and Agricultural Instit

HAMPTON VIRGINIA

What it is   An undenominational industrial school founded in 1868
Samuel Chapman Armstrong for Negro youth.   Indi
admitted in 1878.

Object   To train teachers and industrial leaders

Equipment   Land, 1060 acres ; buildings, 140

Courses   Academic, trade, agriculture, business, home economi

Enrollment   Negroes, 1215 ; Indians, 37 ; total, 1252

Results   Graduates, 1709 ; ex-students, over 6000
Outgrowths ; Tuskegee, Calhoun, Mt. Meigs, and m
smaller schools for Negroes

Needs $125,000 annually above regular income
$4,000,000 Endowment Fund
Scholarships
    A full scholarship for both academic and
        industrial instruction   -   -   -   **$**
    Academic scholarship   -   -   -   -
    Industrial scholarship   -   -   -   -   -
    Endowed full scholarship   -   -   -   -
    Any contribution, however small, will be gratefu
received and may be sent to H. B. FRISSELL, Principal,
to F. K. ROGERS, Treasurer, Hampton, Virginia.

FORM OF BEQUEST

I give and devise to the trustees of The Hampton Normal and A
cultural Institute, Hampton, Virginia, the sum of   *doll*
payable

The Southern Workman

Published monthly by

The Hampton Normal and Agricultural Institute

Contents for September 1914

THE SOUTHERN WORKMAN was founded by Samuel Chapman Armstrong in 1872, and is a mon magazine devoted to the interests of undeveloped races.

It contains reports from Negro and Indian populations, with pictures of reservation and plantati life, as well as information concerning Hampton graduates and ex-students who since 1868 have taug more than 250,000 children in the South and West. It also provides a forum for the discussion of ethnolog cal, sociological, and educational problems in all parts of the world.

CONTRIBUTIONS: The editors do not hold themselves responsible for the opinions expressed in co tributed articles. Their aim is simply to place before their readers articles by men and women of abili without regard to the opinions held.

EDITORIAL STAFF

H. B. FRISSELL	W. L. BROWN
HELEN W. LUDLOW	W. A. AERY, Business Manager
J. E. DAVIS	W. T. B. WILLIAMS

TERMS: One dollar a year in advance; ten cents a copy
CHANGE OF ADDRESS: Persons making a change of address should send the old as well as the address to

THE SOUTHERN WORKMAN, Hampton, Virginia

Entered as second-class matter August 13, 1908, in the Post Office at Hampton, Virginia, the Act of July 16, 1894

THE HAMPTON LEAFLETS

Any twelve of the following numbers of the "The Hampton Leaflets" may obtained free of charge by any Southern teacher or superintendent. *A charge of cents per dozen is made to other applicants.* Cloth-bound volumes for 1905, '06, ' and '08 will be furnished at seventy-five cents each, postpaid.

VOL. I

1 Experiments in Physics (Heat)
2 Sheep: Breeds, Care, Management ·
3 Transplanting
4 Birds Useful to Southern Farmers
5 Selection and Care of Dairy Cattle
6 Care and Management of Horses
7 How to Know the Trees by Their Bark
8 Milk and Butter
9 Commercial Fertilizers
10 Swine: Breeds, Care, Management
11 Fruits of Trees
12 December Suggestions

VOL. II

1 Suggestions to Teachers Preparing Students for Hampton Institute
2 Experiments in Physics (Water)
3 Spring Blossoms: Shrubs and Trees
4 School Gardening
5 Drainage
6 Mosquitoes
7 Roots
8 Seed Planting
9 Housekeeping Rules
10 Prevention of Tuberculosis
11 Thanksgiving Suggestions
12 Some Injurious Insects

VOL. III

1 Proper Use of Certain Words
2 Winter Buds
3 Domestic Arts at Hampton Institute
4 Beautifying Schoolhouses and Yards
5 Responsibility of Teachers for the Health of Their Children
6 Manual Training, Part I
7 Rotation of Crops
8 Life History of a Butterfly
9 How Seeds Travel
10 Nature Study for Primary Grades
11 Arbor Day
12 Evergreen Trees

VOL. IV

1 Plants
2 How to Attract the Birds
3 The Story of Corn
4 The Story of Cotton
5 The Meaning of the Flower
6 A Child's Garden
7 The Winged Pollen-Carriers
8 Soils
9 Care of Poultry
10 Plowing and Harrowing
11 Transplanting of Shrubs and Vines
12 Transplanting and Pruning of Trees

VOL. V

1 Teaching Reading to Children
2 Culture and Marketing of Peanuts
3 The House Fly a Carrier of Disease
4 Culture and Marketing of Tobacco
5 Virginia's Fishing Industry
6 Farm Manures
7 Soil Moisture and After-cultivation
8 Patent Medicines
9 Hookworm Disease
10 Reading in the Grammar Schools
11 Oystering in Hampton Roads
12 Common Sense in Negro Public Schoo

VOL. VI

1 Sewing Lessons for Rural Schools
2 Housekeeping and Sanitation in Rural Schools
3 Canning and Preserving
4 Manual Training, Part II
5 Patrons' Meetings
6 Relation of Industrial and Academ Subjects in Rural Schools
7 Southern Workman Special Index
8 Community Clubs for Women and Gir
9 Housekeeping and Cooking Lessons f Rural Communities
10 Fifty Years of Negro Progress
11 Approved Methods for Home Launderi
12 Number Steps for Beginners

VOL. VII

1 Manual Training, Part III

Address: Publication Office, The Hampton Normal and Agricultur Institute, Hampton, Virginia

The
Southern Workman

VOL. XLIII   SEPTEMBER 1914   NO. 9

Editorials

Alexander McKenzie   The Rev. Alexander McKenzie, for many years vice president of the board of trustees of the Hampton Institute, died at his home in Cambridge, Massachusetts, on August 6. He was pastor of the First Congregational Church of Cambridge from 1867 until 1910, when he was made pastor emeritus.

He was born in New Bedford, where he spent his boyhood and gained a love for the sea and a knowledge of the ways of sailors which stood him in good stead when he became a minister of the gospel. Later he went to Boston and acted as bookkeeper for a firm of lumbermen. Here he roomed with Cornelius N. Bliss, who afterward became a great woolen merchant in New York and a Secretary of the Interior under President McKinley. This practical training and environment gave him a knowledge of men that was of great value to him as a pastor and preacher.

At the age of twenty-one he entered Phillips Academy, Andover, where he enjoyed the instruction of that famous teacher, Samuel Taylor. He graduated from Harvard in 1859 and from Andover Theological Seminary in 1861. Soon after graduation he was called to the large and influential South Church in Augusta, Maine, where James G. Blaine and a

number of noted men worshiped. From here he went to Cambridge, where he spent more than forty years of his life as pastor of a single church.

He was always interested in educational affairs and was overseer of Harvard University, trustee of Bowdoin College, trustee of the Cambridge Hospital, member of the Cambridge school committee, president of the board of trustees of Wellesley College, of the Boston Congregational Club, of the Boston Seaman's Friend and Boston Port Societies, lecturer at Andover Theological Seminary and Harvard Divinity School, and vice president of the board of trustees of the Hampton Institute.

He was a powerful preacher and was in great demand among the students of the colleges and schools. He was accustomed to come to Hampton some days before the meetings of the trustees and his sermons in the school church were thoroughly enjoyed. Certain of his sermons were long remembered by the graduates of the Institution. One of them on the text, "He shall be like a tree," made a deep impression. He was an enthusiastic friend of the school and did much to make its work known throughout New England. After his health became infirm, he was unwilling to give up his yearly visit to Hampton. In Dr. McKenzie's death Hampton loses one of its most devoted friends.

The Passing of the Cherokee Nation

An event of more than usual interest in our relations with the Indian occurred in July when the Cherokee tribe was dissolved by a proclamation issued in due form under the arrangement of the Secretary of the Interior and the Commissioner of Indian Affairs. By this action the largest of the Five Civilized Tribes passes out of history as a tribe, its members, numbering over forty thousand (nearly one-eighth of our total Indian population), becoming citizens of the Commonwealth of Oklahoma with full rights of American citizenship.

This event is the direct outgrowth of the negotiations begun by the Dawes Commission more than twenty years ago. The chief interest which attaches to it lies, of course, in the fact that it is the first large achievement of the Government in its policy of bringing about the cessation of all tribal relations among the Indians. Incidentally it may be presumed to pave the way for a similar proceeding to be followed with other tribes as fast as their condition may warrant. The first step to this end is the allotment of the tribal lands and this has now been more or less generally accomplished with all the tribes. Aside from the question of education and training in self-support, the next great undertaking in each case must needs be the disposition of the tribal funds held in the United States Treasury for the benefit of the tribes. This has been provided for in the case of the Cherokees and the tribal funds amounting to some $600,000 will be divided among all the members of the tribe. Thus ends the direct supervision by the Federal Government over these people.

It is generally conceded that the Cherokees lead all the Indians in their progress in civilization. A peculiar distinction attaches to them because they were the first Indians to have a written alphabet—the invention of Sequoyah about a century ago. Undoubtedly this invention had much to do with their advancement, but, be that as it may, they have shown remarkable progress in material and intellectual development. Though very generally of mixed blood they have conspicuously demonstrated the inherent capacity for citizenship in the American Indian.

But the other civilized tribes have also developed in the same way and to almost the same degree, so that perhaps the most significant thing about the abrogation of the tribal relations among the Cherokees is the promise it implies of a similar step to be taken soon with the other four of these tribes, representing altogether (including the Cherokees) about one third of the Indians throughout the country. It is an experiment not without danger to many of the people involved and it will be watched with much interest. Upon its success will probably depend the course to be pursued in due time with all the Indians.

The National Association of Teachers in Colored Schools held its eleventh annual session in Savannah, Georgia, during the last two days of July and the first two days of August. In many ways this was the best meeting in the history of the organization. The leaders have held the idea all along that this body has a peculiar and important service to render, but the Association seems to have found itself more completely this year than ever before. Representatives were present from every state south of the Potomac and the Ohio, with the exception of Kentucky. Texas, as usual, sent a good delegation from beyond the Mississippi, and Ohio and the District of Columbia were represented.

From all quarters there was expressed the growing consciousness that for education to be of the greatest value to the Negro it must result more and more from the Negro's thought and initiative and his understanding of the needs of his race under present-day conditions. It was clear, too, that the Association was conscious of the weakness of colored schools of all grades, and that they understood that the ineffectiveness, especially of the public schools, was due not only to insufficient financial support and to the lack of proper supervision, but often also to incompetence and neglect on the part of colored teachers and indifference on the part of colored patrons. It was pointed out, however, that delinquencies on the part of the colored teachers were induced by the practically total exclusion of the colored patrons whom he serves from any participation in the management of their schools. To overcome all these unfortunate conditions in some appreciable degree is the task the Association sets for itself and for the public generally.

It was very evident that the younger and better trained members of this body—Harvard, Yale, Columbia, Pennsylvania, Brown, and Oberlin University men, for example—have very clear and positive ideas of the practical service efficient schools may render. These men and others are giving helpful consideration to the schools and other means of social uplift. The remarkable addresses by Dr. R. R. Wright, Jr., on "The Teacher as a Social Leader, " and by Dr. George E. Haynes on "City Conditions " would have been notable in any educational assembly. And the fact that nearly every speaker and most of the delegates are engaged in educational work of more than ordinary importance made this meeting of unusual value for consultation.

In addition to the colored members in attendance, the state supervisors of Virginia and Tennessee were present and delivered addresses. Superintendent Otis Ashmore of Savannah told of the splendid new school for colored youth in his city. He said it would offer manual training, but would not neglect the elementary academic training, the least a city should provide its colored children. The United States Commissioner of Education, Hon. P. P. Claxton, closed the meeting with a splendid address setting forth modern education. Savannah proved an admirable place for the session, and the meeting exceeded in value all expectations.

The First Church at Kecoughtan Four years ago, on July 19, 1910, exactly three hundred years after the founding, on July 19, 1610, of the Episcopal Church in Elizabeth City Parish, Virginia, the foundations of the first known church in the Indian village of Kecoughtan, now the town of Hampton, were re-dedicated. On July 26, 1914, a monument to mark the site of this church was presented to the parish by the Daughters of the American Revolution.

The foundations of the old Kecoughtan church, the first church in the parish so far as is known, are located in an old graveyard on the Tabb Farm, about one-half mile east of St. John's Church. They were discovered after a long search by Mr. Jacob Heffelfinger who had given a great deal of time to the study of Hampton's early history, and were presented to the parish by Mrs. Tabb and her children. The foundations are of cobble-stones with a few bricks, and mark out a rectangle, inside which are fragments of the church floor which was made of earthen tiles. The Association for the Preservation of Virginia Antiquities has placed a high iron fence around this property.

The monument which was unveiled on July 26 is a rough granite cross and pedestal cut from a single piece of stone. On one side are the dates 1611-1624 and underneath the names of the three ministers who served the parish during that time—William Mease, George Keith, and Thomas White. The other side bears this inscription: "Here stood first the known church at Kecoughtan, erected 1624—Jonas Stockton, Minister, William Gauntlett, Edward Waters, Church Wardens."

The stone was presented to the parish by Dr. C. Braxton Bryan, a former rector of St. John's Church, Hampton, now of Grace Church, Petersburg, who is an authority on Virginia church history. Dr. Bryan made a short historical address, telling the names of the twenty-three ministers who served in Virginia from 1607 to 1634, with some interesting facts about each. He also read a list of the different plantations along the James, showing how the quaint old names themselves are historical material, being in many cases the record of the family that lived there, or perhaps of some occupation carried on there. Dr. Bryan showed that Elizabeth City Parish formerly included territory in Nansemond, Norfolk, Princess Anne, and Elizabeth City Counties.

The monument was received on behalf of Mr. Heffelfinger and St. John's Church by the rector, Rev. Edwin Royall Carter, who said that while this was certainly not the first place in Kecoughtan where religious services were held, it probably was the first building the people felt to be worthy of the name of church.

It was, Mr. Carter said, their reverence for hallowed spots and sacred things which caused the Daughters of the American Revolution to erect this stone, and surely no spot could be more worthy of veneration than this, where the early settlers of Hampton first placed their church and met for religious services. It is one of the landmarks of our colonial history and cannot be too carefully preserved.

During the week, August 10-15, Major R. R.
Moton of Hampton Institute, accompanied by a
party of well-known colored men—principals of
various schools in Virginia, ministers, and business men—made an educational tour through the
Shenandoah Valley. The trip was made under the auspices of the
Negro Organization Society. It was the second annual trip of
the kind. It testifies to the vigorous and effective work this
organization is carrying on in the interest of better health, better
homes, better schools, and better farms and business among the
colored people of the state.

The Negro Organization Society Campaign

This interesting and unique society keeps an agent in the
field all the while. Once a year, Major Moton, its president,
heads a party on a special campaign into some section of the
state. This year an invasion was made into the Shenandoah Valley where the colored people are relatively few in number, and
where the work of the organization was hardly known. In this
beautiful section the colored people, though only small landowners, live under fairly favorable conditions. They are generally
above the average in intelligence, they have in most cases good
homes and churches, and in the main they live in friendly relations with their white neighbors.

Both races, however, appreciated the simple, direct, homely
lessons which the party taught on improving the health and homes
of the colored people, and on bettering their schools and farms,
and all accordingly joined in welcoming them to the various communities. The large numbers of colored people who came to
hear the addresses indicate somewhat their eagerness to improve
their conditions. And the presence of white people in all the
audiences shows something of their interest in the betterment of
their colored neighbors. At Roanoke, Staunton, Clifton Forge,
and Harrisonburg the mayors delivered addresses of welcome;
and white ministers, college professors, and superintendents of
schools testified to their appreciation and approval of the work
of the Negro Organization Society.

In leading colored people to secure better schoolhouses, to
put into effect better sanitary conditions in their homes, schools,
and churches, in distributing health bulletins, and by its
general campaigns in the many sections of the state, this
society has amply justified its existence. Its greatest achievement, however, is its remarkable success in uniting the colored
people in a single movement for their own uplift.

THE NATIONAL ASSOCIATION OF COLORED WOMEN

BY EMILY H. WILLIAMS

THE Ninth Biennial Convention of the National Association of Colored Women held at Wilberforce University August 4-7 was in many respects a notable gathering. It was the largest meeting ever held by the Association. There were present four hundred and four delegates and many visitors from twenty-eight states having state federations and from fourteen states having too few clubs each to form separate state organizations. The delegates represented fifty thousand colored club women interested in every phase of race development. Their work is done through twenty-one departments, including those devoted to the various phases of civic betterment, suffrage, temperance, literature, art, music, business, domestic science, religious work, and charities.

The president, Mrs. Margaret Murray Washington of Tuskegee, carried out her program accurately: every department, every state, every club having a representative present, reported; every speaker on the program for an address, who was present, read his paper at the time appointed, and all the distinguished guests present were introduced and spoke ; every session began and ended at the time appointed. Mrs. Washington's gracious presence, good humor, and charm were as unfailing as her stern insistence upon the time limit.

Individual club reports showed that the twelve hundred clubs are doing social uplift work of all kinds. Hamper basket clubs are helping the poor. Homemakers' clubs are learning to improve their own homes and teaching domestic science to others. Many clubs are actively engaged in church work and so noticeable was the number of ministers' and bishops' wives present, that a conference of these women was held after one of the sessions. The president called attention to the importance of this phase of the work of the Association, saying: "When you get the Negro minister's wife, you get the Negro minister; when you get the Negro minister, you get the Negro people. "

Though the clubs are each doing special work, they unite in their state organizations for state work. Alabama, having established a reformatory for boys, reported progress in establishing an institution for girls. Virginia reported the purchase of a farm for a school for wayward girls and the securing of state aid for its maintenance. Michigan reported the establishment of two homes for the aged, and persistent work in keeping open to colored people the doors of the various institutions where they are now received along with people of other races.

Heads of departments distributed literature along their special lines and made interesting reports. Mrs. J. C. Napier, of Nashville, Tennessee, reported that the Educational Department had raised money for a scholarship. The Art Department, under Mrs. C. W. Posey, of Homestead, Pa., had a large and valuable exhibition of work done by colored women during the last two years in china painting, millinery, and fancy work of every kind. A very timely address was made by the head of the Health Department, Dr. Mary F. Waring, of Chicago, Illinois. Her department distributed an instructive pamphlet. Music by colored composers was on exhibition in the music room. A committee of trained musicians demonstrated this music and entertained the convention. Among them were Mrs. Florence Cole Talbert, soprano, of Columbus, Ohio, Miss Sarah Mae Talbert, pianist, of Buffalo, Mr. R. Nathaniel Dett, pianist and composer (sent by the Treble Clef Club of Hampton), Miss L. Pearl Mitchell, Miss Inez Richardson, and Mrs. Winona Stewart, of Wilberforce. Mrs. W. T. B. Williams, the head of this department, read a paper on the progress the Negro has made in music during the past two years. She suggested that the most effective way to fight "ragtime" is to encourage our own composers and musicians and to popularize their more serious work. At the close of the session, the delegates voted to offer biennial prizes of twenty-five dollars each for the best compositions, vocal and instrumental, by colored women. Following inspiring addresses on the Negro woman in literature by Mrs. G. W. Clinton, of Charlotte, N. C., and Miss Anna Jones, of Kansas City, Mo., the convention voted to offer a prize of one hundred dollars to the colored woman who shall in the next two years produce a work of real literary merit. Interesting and profitable discussions on temperance and on suffrage were led by Mrs. Haynes of Nashville, Mrs. Logan of Tuskegee, and Mrs. Haley of St. Louis. Progress was reported in the work of persuading firms to discontinue, in their advertising, the ugly caricatures of colored people so often seen. The Northeastern Federation of ninety clubs affiliated with the Association has a boycott department and the National Association voted to establish one also to oppose such business houses as the National Biscuit Company which has suddenly discharged its thousands of colored employes. Thus all departments can boast of something accomplished at this convention.

The delegates received much inspiration from the many distinguished visitors, both white and colored. Mrs. Shears of the Douglass Center, Chicago, Miss Zona Gale, chairman of the civic department of the General Federation of one million white women, and Mrs. Harriet Taylor Upton, president of the Ohio Suffrage League, all urged the wiping out of prejudice between the races for their mutual benefit.

When the aged mother of Paul Laurence Dunbar told of her struggles to educate her sons, and of how they taught her to read; and when the beautiful pageant of the history of the Negro woman in America was enacted by the Ohio clubs, one could realize that:

> " Out of the wilderness, out of the night,
> Has the black woman crawled to dawn of light ;
> She has come through the valley of great despair,
> She has borne what no white woman ever can bear;
> She has come through sorrow and pain and woe,
> And the cry of her heart is to higher go. "

LIFE AMONG THE CATAWBA INDIANS OF SOUTH CAROLINA[*]

BY LULA OWL

LONG ago when Indians roamed over the South, as well as over the North and the West, the Cherokee and the Catawba were the two largest tribes of the Carolinas, the Cherokee being the larger and more powerful of the two.

My father was a Cherokee and my mother is a Catawba, so, you see, I have a right to be equally proud of both tribes, although I do rank as a Cherokee and not as a Catawba. The fact that I am called a Cherokee, instead of a Catawba, will perhaps seem strange to those who know anything at all about Indians and their customs, because it is customary for Indian children to go by their mother's tribe or nationality rather than by their father's. However, this custom is not always kept among the Cherokees ; for if a Cherokee man married an Indian woman of another tribe and continued to live on the Cherokee reservation, their children would be enrolled as Cherokees and would be entitled to all Cherokee rights. The children of an Indian mother and a white father are also Cherokees, but the children of white mothers and Indian fathers are not enrolled as Cherokees, and they are not entitled to Cherokee Indian rights—such as Indian money, land, and the privilege of attending Indian schools that are supported by the Government.

It is about my mother's tribe, the Catawbas, I am going to speak. Indian history tells us that during the year of 1760 the Catawbas were continually having petty warfare among themselves, as well as with the Iroquois and other Northern tribes. The colonial government tried to persuade them to stop killing each other and go to killing the French. The Indians were always friendly with the English, and during the Revolutionary War a number of them became valuable scouts for the English army.

During all these wars the tribe kept getting smaller and less powerful. At two different times smallpox broke out among them and more than one-half of the whole tribe died of it.

In 1763 the Catawbas were confined on a reservation fifteen miles square in the northwestern part of South Carolina. The

[*] A paper read at the Hampton Institute Anniversary exercises in 1914 by a Cherokee Indian student from Cherokee, N. C.

Indians soon rented their land to the whites for a few thousand dollars, and later sold all of it, except a single square mile on which they now reside. This small reservation is situated about eighty miles north of Columbia. The nearest large town is Rock Hill.

The tribe has grown so small that its number now averages about ninety-nine. A few Indians enlisted as soldiers in the Confederate Army and fought until the close of the Civil War. Since then the state government has had them in charge. Each year the legislature of South Carolina provides a sum of money that is equally divided and paid to every Catawba Indian residing in that state. The money is paid out to the Indians by a capable agent who is appointed by the legislature to act as a wise white father to the Indians.

MORMON MISSIONARIES

In 1884 Mormon missionaries from Utah came to the reservation and soon succeeded in converting a number of Indians. At the same time there were two Presbyterian missionaries at work on the reservation, and for a time their work was successful, but soon misunderstandings and other things came up that made the Indians dislike the Presbyterians and also distrust them. That is one reason why the Mormons succeeded in getting such ready converts.

As soon as it was known among the surrounding whites that Mormon elders were at work among the Indians they began to threaten and said that if the elders were not out of the country in the time given they would be put to death. The elders failed to move out, and in the meantime took pains to impress upon the minds of the Indians that the reason they were not afraid to die was because they believed that they were sent to be true prophets of God. The threats made by the whites were carried out and the two elders were put to death by a large mob.

Indians are great worshipers of brave men, so the death of their brave and beloved elders only caused them to become firmer believers in the Mormon faith. Two or three weeks after the mobbing, two more elders appeared on the reservation, and to this day two elders are always there to see that church laws are kept, and to make sure that ministers of other denominations do not have a chance to win away any of their members.

At present all the Indians excepting a few families are strict Mormons. My mother's family is one of the families that do not believe in the Mormon faith.

Perhaps some wonder whether or not the Indians practice polygamy. The majority do not. There are a few, however, who have more than one living wife or husband, but in every

case the husband has tired of the wife and has left her for some
one he loves better, or the wife has found some one whom she
thinks she likes better.   Their first marriage ceremony was perhaps performed by a minister of some other church and the second one by a Mormon elder.

The Mormon elders have really a wonderful influence over
the Indians and are now encouraging them to lead clean, moral
lives.   Tobacco, whiskey, tea, and coffee are some of the things
the church forbids the people to use.   The man or woman who is
found using them is liable to be turned out of the church.
Because the church laws are so strictly kept and lived up to, the
men hardly ever become intoxicated, and the home life seems to
be a happy one.

The families are all large.   The homes are nearly all poorly
built and furnished.   Men earn their living by raising cotton, and
cutting and selling wood to the town people.   Most of the land is
cleared and used for cotton and pasture land.   I think that the
people would work harder if they did not receive the yearly payment from the state, but as it is, they depend largely upon it for
paying their debts and for buying their food and clothing.

There is a small church and a schoolhouse on the reservation.
The church was erected by the Indians with the help of their
Mormon elders.   It is painted and boasts of a bell and an organ.
The schoolhouse was built with money furnished by the state.   It
is a one-room building, painted and well equipped with desks and
blackboards.   All books for the children are also furnished by the
state.

CURIOSITY AND LEARNING

Until this year the school terms have been about four months
long.   The children and parents did not seem to be interested in
the school, so longer terms were considered a waste of time and
money.

During my last summer's vacation the chief of the tribe came
to me and asked me if I would take the Catawba school for the
summer, or at least two months.   He said that it was to be an
experiment to see if it were possible to arouse the interest of the
people so that a longer school term would be possible for the next
year.   I consented to take the school and opened up the twenty-
first day of July with thirteen pupils.   The children came at first
just to see what the Indian teacher was like, but I noticed that they
soon became regular in attendance.   When school closed—the
latter part of September—I had thirty-two on roll.

In order to awaken the interest of the people I got up programs and had little social gatherings at my home and at the

schoolhouse. The first gatherings were not largely attended. I was not at all surprised, because I knew that the majority of the Indians did not want me to take the school. They said that I was too young to manage the children. This was because they did not know my real age.

One day in planning a writing lesson, I made a neat copy of an invitation to attend an entertainment given by the children. In the right-hand corner of the card I drew a black-eyed Susan and colored it with yellow crayon. I had the children make copies and then carry their cards home to their parents. To my surprise these special written invitations did what a spoken "All are cordially invited to attend" did not do; for almost every one who had received an invitation was present when we gave our entertainment. After this, all I had to do when I desired a large crowd, was to send out written invitations.

I was very glad to learn only a few days ago that the interest in the school is still kept up and that the school term is to be lengthened from four months to nine months next year. The schoolhouse is to be made larger and perhaps there will be two teachers instead of one.

Hampton makes it possible for every girl who goes out to be a helper in her home community. I am sure that I never should have been asked to take that school and certainly could not have been the helper that I tried to be if I had not had Hampton's training and its good reputation to back me up.

THE AWAKENING OF CAROLINE COUNTY

BY MARY HASKELL

"GOD votes for you an' de Deb'l votes agen' you, an' de way you votes you'se'f ·is de way you's gwine ter go." If this is true, the people of Caroline County, Virginia, have voted 'Yes," and have already gone several steps on their long, hard journey towards material, intellectual, and moral prosperity through the agency of good education.

Caroline County has almost as many black people as white people—about 8000 of the former and 9000 of the latter—and a big percentage of both races are doing their best to coax their living from a sandy soil and at the same time to increase its fertility.

In April, 1914, ten automobiles, carrying about thirty educators to see what the white and colored schools of Caroline County have been doing in the past few years, struggled through the heavy roads until it seemed to the unfortunate rear guard that, at worst, there could hardly be much sand in the road ahead, as most of it appeared to be in the air. A frequent cover crop of clover or alfalfa on either side of the road demonstrated, however, that some of the farmers had learned the secret of economic fertilization of unproductive land.

In the party were the Governor of Virginia, the state superintendent of schools, the state supervisor of Negro rural schools, members of the Virginia Co-operative Education Association, members of education boards, officers of normal schools, and county education officials. The route included two white high schools, one colored "academy," and three graded Negro schools.

TWO WHITE HIGH SCHOOLS

Both white high schools are two-story buildings, well ventilated and splendidly lighted, with rooms for the grades on the lower floor. The Bowling Green School, located in a settlement of about 700 people, was built last year. The Sparta School, which is six years old, but which was enlarged last year at an expense of $1500, is in a smaller and more scattered community

THE SPARTA HIGH SCHOOL
"At this high school the children of the county can fit for college."

and has an enrollment of 119 pupils. At these high schools the children of the county can fit for college without any intervening boarding-school courses. The patrons have not yet succeeded in introducing courses in agriculture, domestic science, or other industrial work, in the schools, but the bountiful and delicious luncheon served to the visitors at the Sparta High School by the mothers demonstrated that at least the girls need not suffer for want of training in cooking.

THE TRANSFORMATION OF A COLORED ACADEMY

The Bowling Green Industrial Academy has been a struggling private school—built, owned, and operated by a board of trustees representing the different colored churches of the county. Last winter the trustees decided to turn over the two buildings and ten acres of land to the county school board, if the county would maintain there a training school for Negro teachers. The county board with help from the state and from one or more independent education boards has agreed to do this. The agreement is a shining example of the good will and cooperation between the white and colored people in their efforts to improve the county. A white resident of Bowling Green who was a member of the touring party explained gratuitously and enthusiastically, "We have the best set of colored people in Caroline County that I ever knew. There is never any difficulty between the races," and received the astute answer, "That's because you have the best class of white people in Caroline County."

FOUR NEGRO GRADED SCHOOLS

Within the last two years the Negroes of the county have
built, unassisted, three two-room graded schools costing $1200
each and one three-room graded school costing $1800. The
impetus for this work was supplied by Mrs. Nannie Lee Butler,
Tuskegee, '11, the industrial supervising teacher of the county,
and was strengthened by the state's offer, which she conveyed
to the patrons, to pay the salary of a second teacher in every
community that would build a school of two or more rooms according to state plans.

The automobile party visited three of these schools on that
sunny, blossomy April day. At each place the children were
gathered on the porch, dressed for the most part in spick-and-
span clothes and showing rather dazed countenances—ten automobiles and the Governor and the superintendent of schools! At
each school the first procedure was a speech by a patron of the
school telling how the new schoolhouse was built. An account of
the File School from a paper, delivered by Mrs. Butler, the supervising teacher, at the Hampton Institute Anniversary exercises on April 24, is significant.

WOMEN AS CARPENTERS

"Some of the league members [Patrons' League], becoming discouraged, because funds were exhausted and the gathering of crops faced them, said the work must stop. But these
were men. A woman never becomes discouraged in well-doing.
This time the women vowed the work must not stop, that the

WELCOMING THE GOVERNOR OF VIRGINIA

The old one-room school building at the left of the picture is now used for cooking,
sewing, and manual-training classes.

THE MEETING AT MOUNT ZION GRADED SCHOOL

" A patron of the school telling how the schoolhouse was built "

building must be ready for their children at the opening of the school term. The Mothers' Club borrowed $100 on ninety days' time. To push the work more rapidly we gathered at the school, and while the men of the community put on the weather-boarding, we women nailed on the laths on all side walls, and finished without a mashed finger.''

DETERMINATION AND ENTHUSIASM

At the Mount Zion school, the representative of the community speaking from a porch said, "The roof of this porch is not yet finished—we went as far as we could. But we're going to finish it, and," with fire in his eye, "we're going to paint the schoolhouse too." The secretary of the General Education Board of New York City, standing in the group of listening visitors, murmured, "It's not the education that's educating these people—it's *getting* the education." At this school the little old one-room schoolhouse was used, as is generally the case as soon as equipment can be secured, for an industrial room. An exhibit of sewing, manual training, and cooking showed that the industrial teacher had been practical and thorough in her instruction.

. At the Bowling Green three-room school the speaker said, "Some gave a lemon and some gave a pound of sugar and there was lots of folks with us when we started to build this schoolhouse, but many fell by the way." It was this school, which, when finished, did not meet with the state requirements in the dimensions of one room, due to a fault of the contractor. If a schoolhouse does not follow the state plans the state will not give money for its support from the special Graded Rural School Fund. But the State Board of Education, being men instead of a machine, waived the technicality, and Bowling Green Negro children are reaping a well-deserved harvest.

One of the visitors held the following conversation with a patroness of the same school:

" Have you any children at this school ? "

"Oh, yas'm, I has three. But I had to take my boy out. I had to take him out an' let him go to work. He's fo'teen. But he's cert'n'y comin' back. He isn' through his schoolin' yet.'

It is in a great measure the industrial work which makes these mothers struggle to keep their fourteen-year-old children in the schools. They want them to know how to earn a *good* living when they start to earn. They know that if the children learn some practical facts and methods of cooking, sewing, farming, and making simple home furniture and tools, along with their academic studies, they will be so much more valuable to their future employers and so much more successful in any enterprises of their own. As Mrs. Butler said during her talk at Hampton Institute, in reference to the improvement of schoolhouses, " We know that our people have not done all they could, but this we also know—that much more has been done in these two years than would have been done in ten had not the industrial work been in operation." The summer canning and garden clubs do much to enlist the sympathy of the mothers and fathers.

The question was asked at the Bowling Green School, " Don't you have cooking lessons ? " and the mother of the fourteen-year-old responded, "Yas'm, they cooks 'roun' at the houses. We's fixin' to have cookin' here, but the room isn' done yet."

CAROLINE COUNTY'S ACHIEVEMENTS

In the past two years the four schools already mentioned have been built. At present there are three Negro schools under construction which will be ready for use in the fall of 1914. Two are two-room schools costing $1200 and the other is a four-room building at Dawn costing $2500, where, later, high-school subjects will be taught. These seven rural graded schools have been built entirely by colored people at a conservative total estimate of $10,300. All but one of them will receive the annual state aid of $200; that one receives $100, making the annual state aid to Negro rural schools in the county $1300. These figures do not include the gift of the Bowling Green Industrial Academy and 10 acres of land, the whole estimated as worth $2500, by the

colored people, nor the $175 annual state aid which that school as
a teachers' training school will receive.

The colored people of Caroline County have done well and
the white people have not been slow in acknowledging their
achievements.   The school term for colored children in the county
was formerly five months.   Next year in the seven new schools
the term will be eight months and only qualified teachers will be
employed.   This means a much-increased appropriation from the
county board.   It is proof that these Negroes are doing something worth while when the highest official of the proudest Southern state is willing to travel all day over sandy country roads and
stand in the hot spring sun to deliver ten-minute speeches to the
pathetically eager little groups of black people who are not his

" THE HIGHEST OFFICIAL OF THE PROUDEST SOUTHERN STATE "

constituents but who have gathered to do him honor.   "We want
the Negro to be able to enjoy among his own race every right that
the white man enjoys," elicited a shower of "Amens."

Each race is making an effort to understand the other and to
be generous. Concessions must be made on both sides. That is the
spirit in which the Negroes build schoolhouses entirely without
aid from the state or county government or from individual
white people, and view the results of their sacrifices with pride
rather than with resentment.   And that is the spirit in which
the county boards help to equip and maintain these schools, in
which the state board offers aid from the Graded Rural School
Fund, and in which the best Southern white people, after visiting
the schools, go forth to exert their influence for school improvement and for the further advancement of both races together
towards material, intellectual, and moral prosperity in the South.

THE LOT OF THE ASIATIC EMIGRANT

BY SAINT NIHAL SINGH

IN the list of inter-racial questions perplexing our age and crying out for solution, an important place must be assigned to
the problems arising from the persistence of Asiatic emigrants in
proceeding to countries where they are not wanted. The United
States of America being such a land, it may be of interest briefly
to state the main racial and economic issues bound up in them.

The Asiatics who emigrate hail mainly from Japan, China,
and India. Each of these lands has a large population which
more or less presses hard upon the agricultural and economic
resources of the respective countries.

Japan (not including its colonies and possessions) has a population of 52,000,000 and an area, roughly speaking, of 148,000
square miles. Fully five-sixths of the area is so mountainous
that it is unfit for growing crops. What land is available for
farming requires incessant labor to make it productive. The
Japanese peasant is industrious and patient. Compulsory primary
education has done much to whet his naturally sharp wits. His
government has gone to the length of placing within his reach
loans advanced at low interest to enable him to buy superior seed
and implements. But, withal, agriculture in Nippon requires
back-breaking drudgery, yields paltry profits, and is heavily
taxed.

The Sunrise Empire, in addition to Japan proper, has outlying possessions—Korea, with an area of 71,000 square miles and a
population of about 12,000,000; Formosa, 13,500 square miles in
extent and with about 3,080,000 inhabitants; Saghalien, or Kara-
futo, some 12,000 square miles in area and with a population of
25,000; and the Pescadores, nearly 53 square miles in area. It
also has the lease of the Liao-Tung Peninsula, and certain rights
in Manchuria. These possessions and spheres of influence provide
valuable opportunities to the Japanese and they have not been
slow to take advantage of them. Large numbers of Nipponese,
during recent years, have emigrated to these colonies and possessions, and many more are going to these parts to exploit the
resources and grow rich.

EAST INDIAN IMMIGRANTS LANDING AT VANCOUVER

There is a large body of Nipponese, however, upon whom the lure of these Asiatic lands is entirely lost. Indeed, even the Philippines and the Hawaiian Islands have no charms for them. If they want to leave their homeland, they are desirous of going to North America—and nowhere else. Frequent and serious attempts have been made to deflect the tide to Mexico and South America. Many shiploads of Nipponese have gone in those directions, many more are going there, and still more are likely to go there in the future. But even so, a considerable number of Japanese remain who want to make their way into California, Oregon, Washington, and British Columbia, and, if possible, to push eastwards, both in the United States and Canada.

China (proper) has a population estimated to be between 400,000,000 and 500,000,000 and an area of over 1,500,000 square miles. Much of the land is fertile, in a great or small degree, but the soil has been under cultivation for ages and needs careful manuring and hard labor. The Chinese peasant is patient, industrious, and intelligent. But he is illiterate and knows nothing of human progress. His implements and methods have not changed for centuries. His incessant labor gives him a poor living. In normal times he has little to spare. When scarcity through lack of rain, or floods, or pests such as locusts comes, he starves. Even in the most prosperous seasons he has practically no diversion to infuse joy into his monotonous existence.

Variations in population are great in China. Certain provinces are very densely, others are extremely thinly peopled. There is some movement from the congested to the sparsely settled areas; but a considerable stream of migration has a tendency to pour out of the country. Large bodies of Chinese have settled in the near-by Asiatic lands—the Philippines, Malaysia, Burma, and even India proper. These outlets, however, are inadequate. There is a strong inclination on the part of Chinese residing in the thickly populated districts to go to lands which are considered by the white people to be reserved for their exclusive use, by right divine.

India has a population of over 315,000,000 and an area of 1,773,000 square miles. Most of the land is more or less fertile, but large portions of it are deserts or semi-deserts. The fertile land, having been in use for ages, and being very primitively worked, requires extraordinary patience and industry to make it yield any kind of a harvest. Besides, agriculture in India largely depends upon the rain (monsoon); and that cannot be relied upon. Some years the rains are scanty and the tropical sun scorches the crops. Some years the rains are over-abundant, and floods ruin the harvests. In either case, there is scarcity and famine. The husbandman makes so little out of his hard and incessant toil that despite his most abstemious life he can save little or nothing. He more often is chronically in debt to the village money-lender (*bania*). In consequence, scarcity of food and fodder deals harshly with him.

During recent years much has been done to build irrigation canals and reservoirs in India. In one case several million acres of desert have been reclaimed by the wizardry of water. But when due credit is allowed for what these projects have done to shift population, this redistribution is so slight as to be almost imperceptible. The density of population in huge tracts continues to be very great, and the people residing in these congested areas show an irrepressible tendency to emigrate.

Burma, which, though for some decades politically a portion of India, is not, properly speaking, a part of Hindustan, has absorbed a number of Indians (or *Kallas*, blacks, as they are called by the Burmese). Others have gone to Malaysia, some to

China, and a few to the Philippines. British colonies being integral parts of the Empire in which India is included, the emigrants naturally proceed to the British dominions. Adventuresome East Indians have gone to the United States and other foreign parts.

STRENGTH OF THE OPPOSITION

How very strong is the impulse which drives people from all these lands—Japan, China, and India—to North America and the British Colonies, can be realized only when it is borne in mind that the emigrants proceed to these lands dominated by white men, knowing full well that Oriental settlers are often treated with open and unmitigated contempt by the latter, and that newcomers from Asia will be regarded with firm and uncompromising hostility.

The best way to illustrate the hostility of white people that Oriental settlers must face is to set down a list of their chief disabilities in one of the countries to which they go. In South Africa—a British Colony—the natives of India, who are fullfledged British subjects, have to put up with the following restrictions and indignities: All East-Indian immigrants are required to register themselves precisely as criminals are registered, that is to say, by finger prints, etc. They are compelled to live by themselves, in reservations outside the pale of civilization. The quarters assigned to them are unhealthy and insanitary. Educational facilities are grudgingly given their children. No matter how high their rank or deep their culture, no matter how much money they may be willing to pay for the ride, they are forced to travel in inferior railway and street cars. It is practically impossible for them to buy or even lease property. They are hampered in every conceivable way when they attempt to secure licenses to engage in trade or peddling. In some instances, East Indians who had built up commercial enterprises in South Africa have been financially ruined because the authorities refused to re-admit them after a temporary absence out of the Union, and would not allow them to import their countrymen to serve as employes.

A poll tax of $15 a year is imposed on each East Indian who elects to remain in South Africa after the term of his indenture expires, and he must pay a like amount each year for his wife and for each son above sixteen and each daughter above thirteen years of age. The authorities harrass the settlers by refusing to allow their wives and children (even though the latter may have been born in South Africa) to join them. The legality of marriages contracted according to Hindu and Moslem rites is denied, and children born in such wedlock are deemed illegitimate.

Religious observances are interfered with by barring out priests and preceptors.

In some cases the hostility towards Asiatic immigrants has led to their absolute exclusion or to the restriction of the number who are admitted. Chinese, for instance, are barred from the United States, and have to pay a poll-tax of $500 to gain entry to Canada. Japanese immigration to Canada is restricted. East Indians who proceed to Australia must successfully undergo the language test before they are admitted; and this provision is so ingeniously used as absolutely to prohibit such immigration, for the authorities always set for the test a tongue which the candidate has not the remotest chance of knowing.

In spite of all opposition and contemptuous treatment, Indians, Chinese, and Japanese remain in and continue to go to these countries. Some even do not hesitate to smuggle themselves in when they are excluded, or when restrictions making their entry almost impossible are placed upon them. The way the Chinese are smuggled in across the Mexican border is too well known to Americans to need to be referred to.

It may well be asked : Why does this immigration continue in the face of such open hostility?

The only answer that can be made is that it is to the economic advantage of Asiatics to settle in the United States and outlying British dominions. They find monetary opportunities in these lands such as they do not come across in Oriental countries. Many Asiatics prefer to live in Western countries because they like the environment. They appreciate American and European civilization. It is strange that this appreciation should continue to exist, considering the contemptuous treatment they receive. Some of the better educated Orientals stay on in these countries in order to carry on a relentless struggle for human rights, for democracy.

There are many East Indians, for instance, who feel that they must offer the stoutest resistance to efforts on the part of British dominions to deny to natives of India the right of domicile in any portion of the British Empire, to which they are entitled as British subjects. They believe that the British, who monopolize the best posts in the civil and military service of Hindustan, and who use their political advantages to secure for themselves a pre-eminent position in East-Indian industry and commerce, have no right to bar them out of their dominions. They contend that if the white man is not out of place in the brown man's land, the brown man is not out of place in the white man's country, especially in those lands where but a short time ago the colored man reigned supreme, and over which the white man only recently asserted his dominion.

TWO SIDES OF THE PROBLEM

The question rises: Why do the Oriental immigrants meet
with determined opposition?

A multiplicity of reasons are advanced, which may be briefly
summarized. These Easterners, it is said, belong to inferior
races. Their standards of life are lower than those of Caucasians and therefore they can underbid the white laborers.
Though many of them show a disposition to appropriate Western
enlightenment and urge that they are quite capable of acquiring
Occidental culture, yet they cannot be assimilated by those of
European stock. It is contended that some of the Asiatics are
unclean in their habits and lead insanitary lives. In the case
of the Japanese, it is asserted that their devotion to the Mikado
is so strong that it is chimerical to hope that they would be
faithful to the country of their adoption, especially if it went to
war with Nippon.

These contentions are hotly answered by Asiatics. Each

AN ADVENURESOME EAST INDIAN WHO IS
NOW AN AVIATOR IN THE UNITED STATES

and all of them say that they possess an enlightenment that stretches into the misty past, and that their forefathers were civilized when Europeans were savages. They aver that they can underlive Americans and Europeans chiefly because they do not indulge in expensive vices. They contend that life in the West is far too complex, far too costly, and point to the cry for the simple life as testimony to prove the strength of this argument. They assert that in any case the standards of life are constantly rising in the East. Many of them would remove the economic objections urged against them by a regulation being made by the authorities that Asiatics shall not cut the wages which the white men demand. They triumphantly point out that

A GROUP OF EAST INDIANS IN SOUTH AFRICA

more and more Asiatics are standing up for higher wages. The educated among Asiatic immigrants are of the opinion that they can live among Europeans without being a disturbing element, and make valuable intellectual, moral, and material contributions to the community in which they are settled, if the white people will only give them a fair chance. Finally, they affirm that discrimination is made against them only because they have yellow or brown, and not white, skins, and fling the retort at Caucasians that it is ungracious for professing Christians to boycott people just because of color prejudice.

Thus rages the controversy, each side urging its arguments in its own way, and neither relenting in the struggle. Indeed, at the time of writing, the polemic has reached a very critical

stage. Bills are pending in the House of Representatives at
Washington to exclude Japanese and East Indians. One ingenious scheme which is being urged to get rid of the Nipponese
without contravening the treaties that Japan has with America,
now being mooted, is to prescribe the military test for male
immigrants. That is to say, it is proposed that each man entering the United States must be from eighteen to thirty-five years
old, five feet four inches to six feet one inch tall, and 128 to 176
pounds in weight. This measure, if passed, would certainly be
effective in keeping out many Japanese, who, as is well known,
are very short in stature. The height of the average Japanese
man is just a little over five feet. The military regulations of
Japan prescribe five feet three inches as the height for A-grade

A GROUP OF EAST INDIAN WOMEN IN SOUTH AFRICA

soldiers, five feet two inches for the Auxiliary Transport Service,
and five feet one inch for the Medical Corps. Even with these
low standards of height, every year a large number of Japanese
youths who, under the law, are compelled to offer themselves
as conscripts, are rejected because they are not tall enough to
meet the military requirements. It therefore is apparent that
if the United States were to prescribe five feet four inches as
the minimum height for male immigrants, not many Nipponese
would be able to enter the country.

   If, for the sake of argument, it be conceded that these bills
to exclude Orientals were to be passed, would they solve the
problems of Asiatic immigration? Rather the reverse would be
the case. Measures of this sort are apt to hurt the susceptibili-
ties of the nations whose emigrants are thus excluded, and

the jingoes among them might precipitate armed intervention. Quite apart from that, such action might lead to commercial boycotts. Even if an open rupture may not take place, relations are bound to be strained. In any event, such steps could not but be against the interests of racial concord and amity.

THE REMEDY

No satisfactory prescription has been offered. It is not possible to reason with prejudice. Possibly the problem will have to drift as best it may until the general level of civilization rises.

Meantime, the restriction instead of the exclusion of Asiatic immigrants is suggested. It appears that progressive Orientals are quite ready to agree to limit the number of their people to be admitted yearly into the United States, Canada, etc., but as a necessary condition to this compromise, they demand that those Orientals who are admitted shall be treated on even terms with the other newcomers, in other words, that there shall be no discrimination against them after they enter.

This can be only a temporary measure, for it is inconceivable that Orientals, who are becoming more and more awakened and progressively more powerful, would accept such a destiny once for all. They are sure to insist upon being treated on the same terms that Occidentals exact from them. On account of their political and military weakness, at present they are not able to insist that the right thing shall be done by them. But it is to be remembered that they are fast leaving behind them the stage of helplessness and impotency. When Asia becomes really awakened it will not accept from America and Europe anything short of equal treatment.

However, until the time comes when Orientals can demand—and get—equal rights with Occidentals, the restrictive measures proposed may serve very well as a temporary solution. In the meanwhile, let us hope that racial discord will become minimized and men of different races and colors will live side by side without friction.

THE NEGRO'S INDUSTRIAL PROBLEM

II FARMING, TRADES, AND BUSINESS

BY MONROE N. WORK

In Charge of Research and Records, Tuskegee Institute

NEGRO FARMERS' CONFERENCES

THE second epoch in the Negro's industrial history was when, in 1891, seventy-five Negro farmers, ministers, and teachers met at the Tuskegee Institute in the first Negro farmers' conference. Here the farmers began to get at the fundamental things that needed to be done, if conditions were to be improved. They were told that they must work six days in the week and use improved methods of farming. This conference almost immediately became national in scope. The idea spread. Farmers' conferences and farmers' institutes for Negroes began to be held in every part of the South. To further aid in the work of improving Negro farming, Tuskegee Institute secured a trained agriculturist. Thus it came to pass that the black farmers of the South began to receive scientific instruction in agriculture about as soon as the white farmers of this section did.

THE SUCCESS OF NEGRO FARMERS

It was not an accident that Deal Jackson, a black farmer of Georgia, for over ten consecutive years enjoyed the distinction of putting the first bale of cotton on the market in that state, a distinction eagerly sought after by all farmers, white and black. It was not an accident that in 1912, Isaac Martin, a Negro farmer of Jefferson County, Alabama, in open competition with all the farmers of that state, raised two hundred bushels of corn on one acre of ground and thereby won the second state prize of one hundred and fifty dollars for the largest yield of corn on one acre of ground.

Neither was it accident that an ex-slave seventy-five years old, Samuel McCord, of Wilcox County, Alabama, by raising seven bales of cotton on two acres of ground, set a great example for the small farmers of the South. So impressed was the

United States Department of Agriculture with McCord's achievement that a special study was made of his methods and the result printed in a bulletin entitled "An Example of Intensive Farming in the Cotton Belt. " McCord was formerly a shiftless farmer working in a haphazard manner some fifty acres of ground and raising a quarter of a bale of cotton to the acre. He, however, grasped the essentials of modern agriculture, cut down his farm to two acres, and established a record in cotton-raising that is going to be hard to beat.

The figures of the last United States Census also appear to indicate that the Negro is successfully competing as an agriculturist in the South. From 1900 to 1910 the increase in the number of Negro farmers in the South, 20 per cent, was greater than the increase of white farmers, 17 per cent. The increase in the number of farms owned by Negroes was about 50 per cent greater than the increase in the number of farms owned by whites in the South. The amount of land in farms operated by the white farmers of the South in the last census decade decreased eleven million acres, while for the colored farmers there was an increase of four million acres. The value of land and buildings on farms operated by whites increased 122 per cent, the value of land and buildings on farms operated by Negroes increased 136 per cent. According to the census, three states in the South had a loss in their Negro population. On the other hand, all the Southern states showed an increase in the number of Negro farm owners. While Maryland, in 1910, had three thousand less Negroes than in 1900, it had six hundred and eighty more Negro farm owners. Kentucky had twenty-three thousand less Negroes, but five hundred more Negro farmers. Tennessee had seven thousand less Negroes, but twelve hundred more Negro farm owners.

Although Negro farmers have held their own and even made gains in agriculture, the majority of them are yet to be taught to work steadily and efficiently. From a pedagogical standpoint, however, the hardest part of a task has been accomplished. An interest has been created in agriculture and the occupation of farming has been dignified. Each year it is attracting a larger number of young and intelligent Negroes.

NEGROES IN TRADES AND TRADES UNIONS

The Negro is also making gains in the skilled trades. The number of Negroes in manufacturing and mechanical pursuits increased 32 per cent from 1890 to 1900. The occupation returns for the 1910 Census will no doubt show a larger per cent of increase in the number of Negroes in trades. In 1911, the English Government made an elaborate report on the cost of living in

American towns. This report gave important information concerning the occupation of Negroes in cities and indicated that the
number of Negroes in the trades was increasing. Another indication that the number of Negroes in the trades is increasing and
has become an important factor therein, is the efforts that are
being made to organize Negro labor. In 1910 and again in 1918,
the executive council of the American Federation of Labor
announced that special efforts were being made to organize
Negro workmen. At the meeting of the Southern Labor Congress in Nashville it was decided to admit Negroes as members.
This organization is representative of all the trades unions in the
South.

At the present time, only nine out of sixty of the most important unions bar Negroes from membership. It is significant that
the unions which bar Negroes from membership, such as the Locomotive Engineers, the Order of Railway Conductors, and the
Order of Railway Telegraphers, are generally those in occupations
where the Negro does not compete. On the other hand, in those
occupations where the Negro has come into the most direct competition with white labor, he has held his own and even increased.
In all of these occupations, the Negroes are admitted to the
unions. Although there is often discrimination on union jobs
against the Negro, it would appear that being admitted to labor
unions is not a problem.

THE NEGRO'S LACK OF BUSINESS ENTERPRISE

In contrast to the making of gains in those occupations where
he came into sharpest competition with white labor, the Negro
has almost completely lost out in the occupations where, a few
years ago, he had a monopoly. Why was it that he lost ground
in barbering, waiting, and shoe-shining which were formerly
almost entirely in his hands ? It was due not so much to competition as it was to the fact that in these occupations he did not
keep up with the times. He continued to conduct his barber shop
in the same old way, to have only a bootblack box or a bootblack
chair. The white man came and instead of a bootblack stand, he
opened a " shoe-polishing parlor." Instead of a barber shop, he
opened a "tonsorial parlor." This left the Negro hanging on
the outskirts of these occupations where he gathered in a few
stray nickles, dimes, and dollars, while the white proprietors of
the shoe-polishing and tonsorial parlors grew wealthy.

Just about how seriously the Negro is endeavoring to compete in these occupations for the trade of a great city, was well
illustrated recently in New York City. A Negro bootblack had
taken two old dilapidated chairs and placed them at the entrance
of a saloon. Hanging over the front of one of the chairs he had

placed an old broken sign "Shoe-shining parlor." He lounged lazily
in one of the chairs. A few feet away, just around the corner, an
Italian had a shoe-shining establishment with three alert attendants.   His place was always full.   The irony of the situation was
that this was in a Negro district.   Who would have supposed
twenty-five years ago that today Italians would be growing
wealthy shining Negroes' shoes?

THE INDUSTRIAL PROBLEM AN EDUCATIONAL ONE

The Negroes' industrial problem is an educational one.   It is
the problem of teaching them so that they will work six days in
the week and, if need be, at night.   They must also be taught to
do their work as efficiently as the white laborers with whom they
are in competition.   The problem of teaching the Negroes brings
up the meaning of making education common.

Making education common means not only that every person
has an opportunity to secure an education, but in a· more vital
way it means that education is to be adapted to the needs of the
people.   Since the majority of the Negroes will continue in the
occupations that they are now in, there should be facilities provided for educating them to do the best sort of work in these
occupations.   There is at present no place where a Negro can go
and learn the science of barbering.   Shoe-shining is becoming a
very profitable business and the indications are that the science
of the occupation is being developed.   There is, however, no
place where a Negro can go to learn this trade.   With possibly
one or two exceptions, it is likewise true of the science of waiting and servant work in which occupations there are more than
a quarter of a million Negroes.

WHAT NEGROES DO

In the South 2.5 per cent of the Negroes in gainful occupations are engaged in the professions ; in trade and transportation,
6.5 per cent ; in manufacturing and mechanical pursuits, 7 per
cent ; in domestic and personal service pursuits, 30 per cent ; in
agriculture, 53 per cent.

In the North the distribution of Negroes in gainful occupations is as follows : professions, 3 per cent ; agriculture, 5 per
cent ; the trades, 14 per cent ; business   and transportation
pursuits, 17 per cent ; and domestic and personal service pursuits,
60 per cent.

From the point of view of numbers it appears that in the
South the development of agriculture is first in importance.   In
the North the personal service occupations are first in importance.
It is necessary that the personal service occupations should be
taken up, dignified, and systematically taught in the same way

that agriculture and the trades are being dignified and taught. The domestic and personal service occupations are developing. They are demanding a much more intelligent and efficient service. In order that the Negro may gain ground and rise in these occupations it is necessary that facilities be afforded so that he may have opportunity to learn the barber trade, the shoe-polishing business, the science of waiting, valet and butler service, just as he has now throughout the South the opportunity to learn carpentry, blacksmithing, or agriculture.

DISTRIBUTION OF NEGROES IN GAINFUL OCCUPATIONS

SOUTH

Professions: 96,000; 2.5 per cent

Business: 270,000; 6.5 per cent

Trades: 300,000; 7 per cent

Domestic and personal service: 1,237,000; 30 per cent

Agriculture: 2,181,750; 53 per cent

NORTH

Professions: 17,000; 3 per cent

Agriculture: 25,000; 5 per cent

Trades: 70,000; 14 per cent

Business pursuits: 90,000; 17 per cent

Domestic and personal service: 310,000; 60 per cent

TUSKEGEE INSTITUTE COURSES

What should the industrial schools do in the matter of attempting to give instruction in the domestic and personal service pursuits? Already nurse training is one of the most important vocations taught at Tuskegee. As soon as the new laundry building is erected there, instruction in laundering will be give in a much larger way than it is now done.   This is important for there are over 200,000 Negroes in the South in this occupation. In a number of other schools nursing and laundering are taught. It is doubtful, however, whether the present industrial schools can do more than successfully teach the various trades and the several branches of agriculture.   Including agriculture, the industries for girls, and nursing, forty different trades and professions are now being taught at Tuskegee Institute.   They include general farming, truck gardening, fruit growing, care and management of horses and mules, dairy husbandry, dairying, swine raising, beef production and slaughtering, canning, veterinary science, architectural and mechanical drawing, blacksmithing, brickmasonry, plastering, tile-setting, carpentry, electrical engineering, founding, harness-making, carriage-trimming, machine shop practice, plumbing and steamfitting, painting, printing, woodturning, sawmilling, steam engineering, shoemaking, tinsmithing, tailoring, wheelwrighting, greenhouse work, road building and landscape gardening, bookkeeping and accounting, nurse training, dressmaking, millinery, ladies' tailoring, cooking, laundering, soapmaking, basketry, broommaking, mattress-making, and upholstering.

TRAINING SCHOOLS FOR DOMESTIC AND PERSONAL SERVICE

The instruction in public schools can be made the ground work for training in agriculture, the trades, and the personal service pursuits.   First of all, if there were throughout the South a good system of public schools, the average of intelligence would be greatly raised, and, as a result, labor of every sort would be more intelligent and efficient.   In the next place, in addition to literary work, industrial training could be given in a much more comprehensive way than it is now given.   In Southern cities the public school facilities for Negro children are generally inadequate.   If these facilities were increased and improved so that every Negro child could secure a good common-school education and, in addition, receive industrial training, it would probably be much easier than it now is to secure an intelligent, efficient Negro servant.

Another way to train individuals for efficient service in the domestic and personal service pursuits is to have local schools specially established for this purpose in Northern and Southern cities.   A particular school could teach one thing or a number of things, as the local situation might demand. Persons desiring the services of individuals trained for domestic service should be willing to contribute toward the expenses of a school established for training along this line.   Because of the competition for their services, good servants are at present scarce and often hard to keep. This competition has sometimes tended to discourage the idea of having efficient servants. If, however, competent servants were as common in the South as good blacksmiths or good carpenters there would not be the difficulty that there now is in keeping them. It is more than probable that the establishing of special schools for training in the domestic and personal service pursuits would tend to dignify these occupations and increase the number of competent persons therein.

CENTRAL AFRICAN FOLK STORIES*

COLLECTED BY AGNES E. MACKENZIE

Of the Livingstonia Mission, Nyasaland

THE RHINO AND THE HIPPO

ONE day the rabbit was out walking when he met a rhino. "Well my boy, where have you come from?" said the rhino.

"Why do you call me 'boy'?" said the rabbit. "I am as big as you are, and if you tug with me you will see that I shall beat you."

The rhino agreed to try, and so the rabbit ran away and fetched a long rope and gave one end to the rhino.

"Now I shall go far off," he said, "and when you feel me pull, then begin to tug."

The rabbit then ran down to the lake shore where he saw saw a hippo. The hippo said, "Well, my boy, where have you come from?"

"Why do you call me 'boy,'?" said the rabbit. "I am as big as you are, and if you tug with me you will see that I shall beat you."

The hippo agreed to try, and so the rabbit gave him the other end of the rope. "Now I shall go far away," said he, "and when you feel me pull, then begin to tug."

Then the rabbit ran quickly to the middle of the rope where neither animal could see him and pulled. When the rhino and the hippo felt the pull they began to tug with all their might, and each was very much astonished when he felt the powerful

*A number of "Central African Folk Stories," were published in the Southern Workman for June, 1914.

tug at the other end.   So they tugged and tugged, till they were quite tired out.

Then the rabbit ran to the rhino and said, "Do you agree now that 1 am as strong as you are ?" The rhino agreed.

Then the rabbit ran to the hippo and said, "Well, do you agree now that I am as strong as you are ?" and the hippo too agreed.

So the rabbit went on his way laughing to himself.

THE WIDOW AND THE LION

ONE upon a time there was a widow who was so poor that she had neither a cloth nor a skin with which to strap her baby son on her back.   One day when she was carrying the child in her arms she met a lion with a beautiful gazelle skin.   She begged the lion to give her the skin, and said that in return he could have her son when he grew up.   The lion agreed, and gave the skin to the widow.

Some years after, the lion came one day to the widow's house and claimed his prey.   "No," said the widow, "the boy is still too young, wait till he is grown up."

So the lion went away, waited some years, and then came again when the boy was a young man.   The widow told the lion to come at night.   In the middle of the night she woke her son up, and told him to go out on the veranda and set the mouse trap.   The son obeyed his mother, but on the way he changed himself into a mouse.   After a little he turned into a man again, and came in and lay down to sleep.

Next day the lion came, very angry indeed at having been deceived.   The widow told him to go and hide near the stream and she would send her son to draw water in a calabash.   The son again obeyed his mother, but on the way to the stream he changed himself into a large dragon-fly, and then he returned safely with the water.

Next day the lion came, very, very angry, and demanded his prey.   The widow told him to come again at night, and he would certainly not be cheated this time.   At night she fastened the door insecurely and told her son she wanted him to sleep across the doorway.   The son obeyed her, but he kept awake and only feigned sleep.   As soon as he heard that his mother was sound asleep, he rose, lifted her, and laid her across the doorway.   Soon the lion came and carried her off.   The woman cried out, " You have made a mistake, my son is in the house."

But the son called, " No, no, go off with your prey."

HOW THE RABBIT GOT THE LIONS' SKINS

THE rabbit wished to be betrothed to a young maiden, and he went to talk the matter over with her father. The father agreed to the betrothal, but said, "I do not wish cattle as the dowry, you must bring me a lion's skin."

So the rabbit got ready his bow and arrows, put some salt in a bag, and set off. He had not gone very far before he saw two lions feasting on the raw flesh of a deer. "Hello," said one of the lions gruffly, "where do you come from?"

"O, if you please, sir," said the rabbit meekly, "I am just taking a walk."

"Here then," said the lion, tossing him a bit of flesh.

The rabbit kindled a little fire, rubbed salt into the flesh, put it near the fire, and sat down to watch it roasting.

"Hello, what are you doing?" said the lion.

"It is our custom, sir," said the rabbit meekly. "We never eat raw flesh."

"Hum" said both lions, "it has a very good smell."

"Please taste my meat, sirs," said the rabbit, and he handed some roasted meat to the lions.

The lions tasted the meat and said it was much tastier than theirs, and they begged the rabbit to cook some for them. The rabbit agreed, and built up a big fire, laid bars of wood across, and put the lions' meat to roast near his own.

Presently the lions said, "We are very thirsty and wish to go to the stream to drink. Will you watch our meat till we come back?"

"Ah sirs," said the rabbit, "I may be tempted to eat your meat when you are away. Please tie me up before you go."

"O no," replied the lions, "just you watch the meat. We shall be back soon."

"Ah no, sirs," said the rabbit, "you had much better tie me up."

So the rabbit took a knife, and cut up thongs of leather from the skin of the dead animal, and gave them to the lions, and they bound his paws behind his back and laid him in the sun and went off.

When they came back they untied him, and all sat round the fire together. Presently the rabbit said, "O sirs, I am very thirsty. I must go to the stream and drink. Will you please watch my meat till I come back?"

"Well," said the lions, "we may be tempted to eat your meat, you had better tie us up before you go."

"Not at all," said the rabbit, but the lions said, "O yes, you must tie us up."

So the rabbit took long thongs of leather and tied up both
lions firmly, and then laid them on their backs in the sun. He
then went off to the stream, and he stayed a long time, and the
sun grew so hot that the thongs dried and grew tight, so tight
that the poor lions could not move. Then, late in the afternoon,
the cunning rabbit came back, took his bow and arrows, and shot
first one and then the other lion. Then he took off their skins
and went with them to the father of the girl he wished to marry.
And so the matter was ended.

THE FISH AND THE GRASSHOPPER

ONE day a widow went to the stream with her little boy to
    draw water. When they got there they saw a foolish fish in
the water. Instead of darting away as most fish do, it remained
quite still, and so the widow caught it in her hand quite easily
and carried it home, saying, "We shall have good relish along
with our porridge to-night."

After they got home she put the fish down, covered it with
a basket, and went out to get firewood· While she was out the
boy called some of his playmates and said, "Come and see the
strange fish my mother has caught, it does not run away." He
lifted the basket to let the children see the fish, but alas ! this
time the fish did not lie still, and when the boy tried to catch it, it
was so slippery that he could not hold it.

When his mother returned she was very angry, and said,
"O my fine fish, what shall I do ! you must go to the stream and
catch my fish."

So the little boy went, and after some time he caught a fish
and took it to his mother. She held it in her hand and looked at
it and said, "No, that is not my fish. I want the fish I caught
myself."

So the little boy went back, and tried again. He caught
many fish and brought them to his mother, but she always said
he must bring her the very fish he had lost. He tried all day
long, and at last at night he caught the fish she wanted, and she
was satisfied. She cooked the fish, and they ate it for supper.

Next day the boy went out to play in the bush, and he
caught a large grasshopper and took it home. He said to his
mother, "Look at my fine grasshopper." She took it in her
hand to admire it, but she did not hold it properly and it
escaped.

The boy cried out, "O my fine grasshopper, I must have it.
Go and search for it till you find it."

So the mother went and tried to catch the grasshopper,
but whenever she got near it, it hopped away from her, and

the poor woman went on trying to catch the grasshopper till she died.

THE TORTOISE AND THE ELEPHANT

ONE day an elephant was taking a walk when he met a tortoise. "Get out of my way," he called rudely.

The tortoise stepped meekly aside to let the elephant pass, but as he did so he said, "Why do you speak so rudely to me? Do you think I am a person of no importance? If you try a race with me you will soon see that I can beat you."

"The elephant laughed loudly and said, "You can never beat me; however, to please you, I shall race with you just now."

"No thank you, not today," said the tortoise, "but I shall meet you here early tomorrow morning and we shall run a race together."

Then the tortoise ran off and told all his friends, and they agreed to help him. So very early next morning he placed his friends at intervals along the road where the race was to take place, and then he himself went to the spot where he was to meet the elephant.

They started off together and the elephant ran till he was tired. Then he called out, "Where are you now?"

To his great surprise a voice answered, "Here I am," and he saw a tortoise in front of him.

So they set off once more, and again the elephant ran till he was tired. Then he stopped and called out, "Where are you now, friend?" and again to his great surprise a voice answered him, "Here I am in front of you."

The poor elephant ran on and on, but whenever he stopped to take breath he found a tortoise just in front of him. At last he felt he could run no further, and was just about to lie down when he saw a tortoise in front of him again. "Well," said the tortoise, "are you satisfied now?"

"Yes," said the elephant, "you were quite right, you can certainly run faster than I can." And so he shook hands with the tortoise, and they parted good friends.

At Home and Afield

HAMPTON INCIDENTS

HAMPTON WORKERS

THERE have been several changes in the staff of workers during the past month. Rev. E. L. Chichester, who for some years has been engaged in campaign work in the North, has resigned and is now managing a large stock farm in Stockton, N. J.

Miss Ella L. Hoyt, who was a teacher and bookkeeper at Shellbanks, is now secretary in the Agricultural Office. Her place at Shellbanks is filled by Mr. E. L. Faust of New York. Another new worker in the Agricultural Office is Miss Sadie Drummond of Hampton.

The position of matron, left vacant by Miss Bernice Paul, has been taken by Miss Lillian Clark, of Hampton Institute.

James Scott, who graduated from Hampton in 1911, has been appointed captain to fill the vacancy in the Commandant's Office left by Captain George W. Blount, who has taken a position in the Crown Savings Bank of Newport News.

In the Trade School, Mr. Bentzel has taken the position of instructor in carpentry, left vacant by the death of Mr. Ashe, and a new worker, Mr. L. K. Snyder of Elizabethtown, Pa., who was fitted at the Williamson Trade School in Pennsylvania, is filling Mr. Bentzel's place as instructor in drafting.

TRI-STATE DENTAL ASSOCIATION

THE Tri-State Negro Dental Association of the District of Columbia, Maryland, and Virginia, which met for its second annual convention at Buckroe Beach July 23 to 25, held a public meeting in Cleveland Hall Chapel on Friday night, July 24. The subject of the session was oral hygiene and several interesting papers were read. Dr. John Lattimore, of Hampton, gave a talk on oral hygiene in the home, using as a practical demonstration of his remarks twenty small boys from the Lincoln Street School in a vigorous toothbrush drill. Hampton graduates and ex-students who are members of the Association are Dr. J. T. Lattimore, '04, Dr. J. M. G. Ramsey, '02, Dr. A. O. Reid, '03, and Dr. A. J. Gwathney, who left Hampton in '88.

VISITORS

SINCE the close of the summer school, there have been quiet days at Hampton and few visitors. Dr. Thomas Jesse Jones, of the Bureau of Education, and his little daughter Gwendolen, spent a few days at the school. Another former Hampton worker who was gladly welcomed was Miss Jessie Coope of Washington, D. C., who was for several years instructor in physical training. Miss Mary Fletcher, a former worker at Hampton, visited Mr. and Mrs. Betts the first week in August.

Dr. John H. Reed, principal of the Caroline Donovon Industrial Institute in Liberia, visited the school in July for the purpose of studying the plan of the grounds and getting ideas and inspiration to carry back to his school. He was accompanied by Dr. Ernest Lyon, the consul-general from Liberia at Washington.

GRADUATES AND EX-STUDENTS

THERE is no town in the state of its size, that has a larger precinct of intelligence than has the town of Franklin, Va.

The educational facilities there are good and above the average. For these conditions Mrs. D. I. Hayden, [Hampton, '77] the founder and principal of Franklin Normal and Industrial School, is entitled to much commendation. The enlightened atmosphere of Franklin is responsible for the acknowledged church pride and the many beautiful homes in that little town.

Norfolk *Journal and Guide*

SEVERAL years ago two students at Hampton Institute pledged themselves to devote their lives to social service. They had been brought to this determination primarily by the instruction of General Armstrong and secondarily by reading Besant's "All Sorts and Conditions of Men." One of the girls was Sarah Collins, ['82] who became Mrs. John C. Fernandis, and who now has an international reputation as a successful social worker.

After teaching a while Mrs. Fernandis did effective work under the auspices of the charities organization of Baltimore. Coming to Washington she was offered the position of resident in the Colored Social Settlement. Her consecrated and efficient service here will always be remembered no less by her co-workers than by those for whom she labored. Her name is still a name to conjure with among the poor of South Washington. When the call came to her to place on a practical working basis the settlement at East Greenwich, R. I., the Washington settlement was being carried on in ten rooms instead of five and one thousand dollars had already been pledged for a new building.

Mrs. Fernandis is now employed by the Women's Organization (white) of Baltimore as a sort of consulting specialist on social work among colored people and she enjoys the confidence and respect which cultured people always give to intelligence and worth.

The other girl is now Mrs. Harris Barrett, ['84] of Hampton, Va.

Washington *Sun*

A homemaker who is also a community worker, Mary Bosley Truxon, '88, writes of her work. She was at Hampton only two years, but she has put to good use in her home and her community the lessons learned in those years.

"I have moved near Denton [Md.] on a farm of 57 acres which we are struggling hard to pay for and call it our home. I have seven children living; the eldest one is nineteen; how I wish I could send him to Hampton. I hope to send some of my children there soon.

"I am still teaching Sunday school whenever I can get to the church. I love to do the things that I think no one else cares to do and then I feel as if I am not crowding out anybody. I pity the girls of my race in this community and I am trying to do all that I can to help them.

"Last Sunday was Woman's Day at John Wesley Church and they invited me to make an address. The church was crowded; everyone seemed to be delighted with my talk but that did not satisfy me, because I was afraid that I did not say the right things in the right place. I want to help my people, not please them so much, but give them real help. There was also being held in Denton on the same day that I have mentioned a Sunday-school mass meeting. I was sent to represent the church to which I belong, and I read a paper on the possibilities of the Sunday school in the Negro church.

"I know that it is better children and purer homes that are needed by my people, not homes free from grease and dust only, but free from filthy habits and thoughtless, wicked speech."

SINCE her graduation in 1909, Joanna J. Boyd has been teaching at her home in Joyceville, Mecklenburg County, Virginia. She writes as follows :

"Last year was a good year for me in my school work. During the year I raised through quilts, concerts, and entertainments, the sum of $40.92. With a portion of this money my patrons extended the term six weeks and put in new window panes. A fifteen-dollar Christmas tree was given the children, all expenses taken from the remaining sum of money raised in the school the preceding term. The children were delighted with the useful presents of stockings, gloves, tooth-brushes, hairbrushes, gingham aprons, handkerchiefs, and combs.

"From one o'clock to four o'clock every Wednesday afternoon I teach the girls to cut and sew gingham aprons, shirt waists, undergarments, and dust caps. I also give them lessons in mending, darning, and button-hole-making. The boys are taught to put bottoms in chairs with shucks, make shuck brooms, shuck picture frames, and shuck whisk brooms.

"I am the only teacher, but I believe I am doing some good with such a large number of children, because all the leading white families, as well as colored, speak of such a striking improvement in the children that attend the school. No one could pay a boy that comes to my school any sum of money to pass a lady and not raise his cap, or even to keep his seat in a church, or any building, and allow a lady to remain standing. I am enjoying my work at home where I have taught every term since leaving Hampton. The Superintendent of Mecklenburg County has raised my salary."

AFTER teaching one year in Middlesex County, Alida P. Banks, '09, became industrial supervisor of the rural schools in Cumberland County, Virginia, a position which she held for two years—until she was called home by her mother's illness. She has during the past year been supervisor in Surry County where her home is situated. She is one of the three students from Surry County who have graduated from Hampton. The other two—Martha A. Tucker, '10, and Grace George Slade, '11—have been teaching in the county during the past year. Four ex-students—Lillie R. Clayton,

'09, Annie Williams Cypress, '93, Bertha J. Price, '06, and Lulu Price Tucker, '04—have also taught in the schools of Surry County this last winter. Alida Banks writes of the work of the county as follows :

"This being the first year for the industrial work in the schools of this county makes it difficult for me to say just what our success is. But I hope that we will accomplish some of what other counties are doing. There are 17 schools and 19 teachers in Surry. At my own home school, where I spent twelve years as a pupil, the people are doing much to help improve their conditions. Heretofore it has been a crowded one-room building, enrolling from 90 to 110 pupils. Last summer in June we organized a league to help in defraying the expense of an assistant teacher, providing the school officials would add another room. Consequently we now have a very nice two-room building according to the state health plans, and two teachers, one from Thyne Institute, and my sister of Virginia Normal and Industrial Institute. Our senior league has raised $130 , and our junior league $15 since the last of the past September [December 31, 1913].

"Miss Grace George is teaching in a very good school which has been made possible in a similar way through her efforts. If there is any one school that needs earnest workers and efficient teachers it is the country school."

THERE has recently been issued from the press of the National Baptist Publishing House a very neat and creditable directory of Nashville's colored citizens. Directories of colored business men and women have been got out in Chicago, Philadelphia, New Orleans, Atlanta, Savannah, and other cities, but this recent directory is perhaps the first of its kind ever published.

The book, which contains over 100 pages, with a list of the businesses, professions, societies, churches, etc., was compiled by Whittier H. Wright, [Hampton post-graduate, '09,] a son of President R. R. Wright of the Georgia State College, Savannah. Mr. Wright is attending the Meharry Medical College of this city and is a recognized expert and specialist in this particular line of work, having made studies and published directories of Negroes of Philadelphia, Savannah, Ga., Chester, Pa., and other cities.

The directory proper contains the name and address of every colored family in the city, and there is also a list of all those owning property. The book is illustrated with cuts and sketches of buildings and leading business and professional men and women.

Nashville *Globe*

A Hampton graduate of 1909, Patrick T. Beauford, after remaining at Hampton for one year to complete the advanced agricultural course, became farm manager at the Broadneck Farm, Hanover, Virginia, a reformatory for colored boys. He writes :

"Since leaving Hampton, August 1910, I have tried not to be idle during my spare moments. In September 1911 I began a course in poultry husbandry in the International Correspondence School, Scranton, Pa. By using my spare time, after my usual work hours here, I have been able to complete my course with credit, for which, on March 5, 1914, I was awarded a diploma.

"We who are engaged in this reform school work are able to do but little at a time among the community people since much of our time is required here, but in a small way we are trying to help. As the children in the public school have but five months' schooling, the teachers and several other officers here thought to prolong the term by raising money to pay the teacher for one or two months longer. We gave an entertainment, got the parents to bring things to sell, and formed two clubs, one for the women and one for the men, in which they competed. In various ways we collected the sum of forty-four dollars and some cents with which to pay the teacher.

"I go every other Sunday to the community church and teach Sunday school and take part in the church services."

A letter from Florence G. Anderson, who finished the Home Economics course in 1911, tells of her work of the past year in Kentucky :

"This year I am supervisor of Clark County, Kentucky. I enjoy my work very much. In the county there are ten one-room rural schools, but we have succeeded in teaching sewing and industrial work in each school, closing by having an exhibit. I began work the first of September and stopped the first of April to begin again in July.

"We have eight mothers' clubs and two agricultural clubs. We have added a room to one of our schools; fenced in another ; purchased a stove at one ; a stove and bookcase in the fourth. We are giving a series of entertainments to lengthen our school term, which is now six months. We have raised over one hundred fifty dollars and have in the treasury over fifty dollars. We have a Sunday school in eight communities, and debating societies in two.

"The spirit of friendly rivalry exists throughout the county, and the people are improving the conditions of homes, farms, and churches, and they are interested in beautifying the school. They do not place so much stress on sanitation and ventilation as they might.

"We have a farmers' conference that meets in Winchester; the mothers as well as the farmers are interested and take an active part. Next year we shall have the 'Housekeepers' and farmers' conference,' and give the mothers a chance to show just what they have done during those long months.

"Leaders are in demand in this state."

This letter shows how a Hampton girl gets along without much that she needs and in the midst of trying circumstances. She holds the position of matron in a large boarding school.

"We have one hundred forty-two boarders this year and are terribly crowded.

"The girls have done well in furnishing their sick room which was set apart one year ago. Through the Y. W. C. A. we have been able to get two beds all furnished, a washstand, new shades for the windows, a new rocker, and an invalid chair. We have had the wall kalsomined and the girls have painted the floor and all of the woodwork themselves.

"I have not been able to have any repairing done in my department as yet, but I hope to get something done next spring. Last spring my four girls painted the ceiling and all of the woodwork in the kitchen, borrowed brushes and would have kalsomined the walls, but could not get enough money to get the wash, so we had to leave it off until now.

"I was very fortunate last year in getting five dollars with which I bought several little utensils for the kitchen. This year I had four dollars and fifty cents given me and with it I was able to get a tin lunch box such as we used at Hampton. I shall use that for sending meals to the boys' dormitory and also to send meals out on the farm when the boys are there at work."

A Hampton graduate of 1911, Josephine Cole, who has been teaching in Caroline County, Maryland, since her graduation, writes as follows:

"Just a week before the holidays, the children and I planned to have the school and grounds in good order when Mr. Walker came to visit us. Before he arrived, we raised our new flag for the school. I had on exhibit several tables with work, such as shirt waists, dresses, dust caps, aprons, quilt squares, and neckties made by the children. On our table of cooked things done by the girls, we had biscuits, cakes, canned fruits, pickles, pies, jelly, potato salad, and a few other things. The boys brought some vegetables which they had grown. Mr. Walker gave a very interesting talk to the patrons and children and seemed well pleased with our school and work. The girls are continuing in their sewing and the boys are doing woodwork. At present I have a very full school—forty-six on roll and a very good attendance."

ONE graduate writes from a small place in Virginia of an inexpensive way to improve the school grounds:

"There has been no partition between the boys' and girls' yard. Saturday one of the boys and I went to the woods, got twenty-two cedar trees, and made one. It looks very nice already. The trees were all small, but will make a splendid partition as well as give shade in future years."

NEW YORK INDIAN NOTES

DURING the past year Caroline Hewitt, Julia Snow, and Alice Jamison have been employed as regular teachers in the Indian district schools on the New York reservations, and Helen George has been acting as substitute on the Cattaraugus Reservation.

Asa Patterson, Tuscarora, is employed as a pipefitter in Akron, Ohio. His sister Kate keeps house for their father in Niagara Falls, and has recently been taking the civil service examination for assistant chemist.

Wallace George, Carl Parker, and Leroy Jimerson are all employed in one of the large shops in Silver Creek, New York, where milling machinery is made.

Mrs. Fleeta Patterson Seneca is very successfully raising chickens on the Cattaraugus Reservation. She has about four hundred ard fifty, and does a good business selling broilers.

Winifred Garlow has recently finished the Business Course at Haskell Institute, and is at her home on the Tuscarora Reservation awaiting an appointment in the Indian service.

Gertrude Pierce is employed in the laundry of the Thomas Indian School, Iroquois, N. Y.

ON the evening of July 3 the Hampton returned students on the Cattaraugus Reservation held a most successful reunion in the Presbyterian Church. About sixty students from that reservation have attended Hampton, but so many are now living in other places that those who were present constituted the majority that could be reached in the short time given to preparing for the gathering. They were Mr. and Mrs. Wallace K. George, Mrs. Fleeta Patterson Seneca, Mrs. Elnora Seneca Lee, Mrs. Rose Poodre Parker, Irene Jemison, Caroline Hewitt, Clara Schingler, Gertrude Pierce, Rogene Pierce, Frances Halftown, Helen George, Leroy Jimerson, Carl Lay, Leroy Snow, Carl Parker, Nicholson Parker, Archie Tallchief, and Levern Jimerson. In addition to these there were a goodly company of husbands, wives, children, and parents, Mr. and Mrs. J. E. Fisher, the Presbyterian missionaries on the reservation, and Mrs. Lincoln and Mr. Brennan from the Thomas Indian School.

Carl Lay presided, and after a few remarks introduced Miss Andrus from Hampton. She was followed by Leroy Jimerson, who spoke on the Hampton idea of service and of how forcibly Dr. Frissell's talks come home to the students after they have left school and begun their lives in the world.

The evening was most delightful and it is to be hoped that it is the first of many such gatherings, for it is proposed to form a Cattaraugus Hampton Club. If this is done it will not only add a very pleasant social feature to the life of the reservation, but the club can be of very real service to the school, particularly in helping to interest new students. The idea is so good, and the beginning was so successful, that it is to be hoped the plan may mature, and the example be followed by Hampton's sons and daughters on other reservations.

What Others Say

NEGRO Y. M. C. A.

THE dedication of the $100,000 Negro Y. M. C. A. in Kansas City marks an important step in the advancement of the moral interests of the Negroes of the community. Of the total amount of money expended on the building half was subscribed by the white citizens of Kansas City and half of the remaider was subscribed by the Negroes themselves, one-fourth of the whole being the gift of Julius Rosenwald of Chicago. A significant feature of the new Y. M. C. A. is the self-sacrificing response made by the Negroes, to whom $35,000 is more, in proportion to their financial ability, than would ten or twenty times that amount be to the whites. The latter have shown themselves willing to help the Negroes to help themselves, and that is the most emphatic and effective assistance that can be rendered.

Kansas City, [Mo.] *Journal*

THE raising of $33,160.30 in ten days by the colored citizens of Nashville, Tenn., to meet the conditions of a gift of $25,000 from Mr. J. Rosenwald of Chicago and $45,000 donated by the Central Young Men's Christian Association for erecting a modern building for the work of the colored young men of Nashville was a most notable achievement. The campaign began March 20 and closed on March 30 with more than the required amount raised. Nashville *Globe*

THE colored boys of Rock Island have recently celebrated the opening of the Y. M. C. A. playgrounds for their special benefit. The grounds will be provided with tennis and volley ball courts, croquet, swings, turnpoles and a merry-go-round for the small boys.

Officers of the association announce that specific work along religious, educational, physical, and social lines is being successfully carried on. The majority of colored men and boys in Rock Island have enrolled and there continues to be a steady growth in membership.

McKinley Baptist Chapel has offered use of the church basement for winter quarters, making it possible to continue the work all the year round. Inside attractions will be a library, a shower bath, and gymnasium.

Moline [Illinois] *Dispatch*

CO-OPERATIVE BUYING

THE tenth annual session of the Negro Farmers' Conference of the St. Paul School in Lawrenceville, was held on July 30 and 31. The questions taken up related to crops, farms, homes, morals, land buying, crime, schools, churches, payment of capitation taxes, and county fair.

The organization of the Brunswick Farmers' Co-operative Company, Inc., with a capital stock of $15,000 to buy land, fertilizers, and other commodities, was perfected, and $2500 worth of stock was subscribed on the first day. This company is an organization of the Conference to save expenses by co-operative buying in Brunswick County. The shares are $10 and may be bought for cash or on installment plan.

CHEROKEE CITIZENS

THE Cherokee Indians have abolished their tribal form of government and have become citizens of the United States, thus ending the separate existence of the most numerous and prosperous tribe of red men in North America. In this connection it is interesting to note that so far as our knowledge goes there is no record of their savagery. When the white race came into contact with these Indians they lived in houses, had an organized government, and obtained their living through pastoral pursuits. They were farmers first, resorting to war only when it was impossible to escape fighting.

Utica *Globe*

TRACHOMA IN THE MOUNTAINS

TWO years ago a cry for help came from Kentucky. Miles from the railroad, up in the mountain counties, the people were suffering from trachoma. Dr. John McMullen, Passed Assistant Surgeon of the United States Public Health Service, in the summer of 1912 made an investigation in the wilderness on the Kentucky side of the Appalachian Mountains, where they form the great divide between Kentucky on the west and Virginia, West Virginia, and Tennessee on the east and south. He found that 60 or 75 per cent of families were infected in some neighborhoods.

Last September a hospital for these folk was opened at Hindman, Ky. In November, another was opened at Hyden, in Leslie County. A third hospital was opened in March at Jackson. Up to June 6 there were 6,726 treatments, 521 hospital cases, and 549 operations to the credit of the three hospitals.

World's Work

NEGRO KINDERGARTENS

KINDERGARTENS for colored children are being adopted in different parts of the South as one of the agencies for improving social conditions that have troubled two generations. Richmond, Va., has just opened an experimental kindergarten which has already created such interest among Negro parents and the school authorities that it is expected it will soon be made permanent. The Richmond kindergarten was opened by the National Kindergarten Association of New York at the request of Richmond people who knew of the success of the demonstration given among the colored children of Chattanooga, Tenn., where the local association assumed the care and support of the school on March 1.

CORRECTION—The editors of the Southern Workman wish to correct a misstatement which appeared in these columns in the August issue of the magazine. In a notice headed "Philadelphia Negroes," incorrectly copied from the Philadelphia *North American*, which reads "Through the aid of the Philadelphia Hampton Committee, Negro workers of Philadelphia obtained jobs during the year which paid them a total of $35,000," the words "Armstrong Association of Philadelphia" should be substituted for "Philadelphia Hampton Committee." The two organizations have no official connection with each other. The work of the Philadelphia Hampton Committee is for Hampton Institute. The work of the Armstrong Association of Philadelphia is chiefly for Philadelphia Negroes.

The Hampton Normal and Agricultural Institute

HAMPTON VIRGINIA

What it is   An undenominational industrial school founded in 1868 by Samuel Chapman Armstrong for Negro youth. Indians admitted in 1878.

Object   To train teachers and industrial leaders

Equipment   Land, 1060 acres ; buildings, 140

Courses   Academic, trade, agriculture, business, home economics

Enrollment   Negroes, 1215 ; Indians, 37 ; total, 1252

Results   Graduates, 1709 ; ex-students, over 6000
Outgrowths ; Tuskegee, Calhoun, Mt. Meigs, and many smaller schools for Negroes

Needs $125,000 annually above regular income
$4,000,000 Endowment Fund
Scholarships
A full scholarship for both academic and
industrial instruction - - - $ 100
Academic scholarship - - - - 70
Industrial scholarship - - - - - 30
Endowed full scholarship - - - - 2500
Any contribution, however small, will be gratefully received and may be sent to H. B. FRISSELL, Principal, or to F. K. ROGERS, Treasurer, Hampton, Virginia.

FORM OF BEQUEST

I give and devise to the trustees of The Hampton Normal and Agricultural Institute, Hampton, Virginia, the sum of   *dollars, payable*

The Southern Workman

Published monthly by

The Hampton Normal and Agricultural Institute

Contents for October 1914

THE SOUTHERN WORKMAN was founded by Samuel Chapman Armstrong in 1872, and is a m magazine devoted to the interests of undeveloped races. .

It contains reports from Negro and Indian populations, with pictures of reservation and pla: life, as well as information concerning Hampton graduates and ex-students who since 1868 have more than 250,000 children in the South and West. It also provides a forum for the discussion of ethn cal, sociological, and educational problems in all parts of the world.

CONTRIBUTIONS: The editors do not hold themselves responsible for the opinions expressed in tributed articles. Their aim is simply to place before their readers articles by men and women of a without regard to the opinions held.

EDITORIAL STAFF

H. B. FRISSELL   W. L. BROWN
HELEN W. LUDLOW   W. A. AERY, Business Manager
J. E. DAVIS   W. T. B. WILLIAMS

TERMS: One dollar a year in advance: ten cents a copy
CHANGE OF ADDRESS: Persons making a change of address should send the old as well as
address to

THE SOUTHERN WORKMAN, Hampton, Virginia

Entered as second-class matter August 13, 1908, in the Post Office at Hampton, Virginia the Act of July 16, 1894

THE HAMPTON LEAFLETS

Any twelve of the following numbers of the "The Hampton Leaflets" ma; obtained free of charge by any Southern teacher or superintendent. *A charge of cents per dozen is made to other applicants.* Cloth-bound volumes for 1905, '06· ' and '08 will be furnished at seventy-five cents each, postpaid.

Address: Publication Office, The Hampton Normal and Agricul Institute, Hampton, Virginia

The
Southern Workman

VOL. XLIII   OCTOBER 1914   NO. 10

𝕰𝖉𝖎𝖙𝖔𝖗𝖎𝖆𝖑𝖘

The Negro in Business More than ten thousand business enterprises in this country are owned, controlled, and operated by Negroes. This is one of the positive results of fifty years of freedom in a land of democratic institutions and wonderful possibilities for men and women who will hereafter think less about race friction and more about mutual helpfulness.

Dr. Washington helped to organize the National Negro Business League fourteen years ago in Boston. Today this association is an asset to the entire nation, for it acts as a clearing house of information concerning the Negro in business and as an inspirer of Negro men and women.

The recent meeting of the League in Muskogee was unique in that it emphasized the opportunity afforded *groups* of Negroes, especially in the rich and growing Southwest. It is well, indeed, that Negroes should have brought to their serious attention the value of co-operation in race enterprises and the importance of meeting more of the race's wants. The Negro farmer, stockraiser, merchant, builder, banker, undertaker, newspaper publisher, and mechanic have succeeded individually, of course; but a larger success awaits each class when co-operation in business, based on mutual good will and exchange of valuable service, becomes a matter of constant daily practice as well as an accepted theory in business. This lesson the Negro Business League has been effectively teaching, not only through its annual meetings but also through its inner workings through the entire year.

In Muskogee, white men and black men had presented to them in an agricultural and industrial exhibit, as well as in a most creditable industrial parade, the victories that earnest, hard-working Negroes had won in tilling the land, in buying and selling general merchandise, in operating real estate, in developing coal, oil, and gas lands, and in conducting various types of shops.

To compare notes on business methods, to exchange ideas on many topics of current interest, and to gain fresh inspiration several thousand Negroes assembled in Muskogee for the fifteenth annual session of the Negro Business League. To these fine representative Negro men and women, Dr. Washington brought a presidential message of rare force.

How the Negro business leagues throughout the country may be made more effective ; how energy commonly used in criticizing may be coined into improved methods of doing business ; how neglected opportunities may be converted into riches ; how foresight and initiative may give the Negro his fair chance in business; how white and black men may live together in peace and harmony—these were some of the topics covered in Dr. Washington's leading address.

That the Negro in Oklahoma and the neighboring states has been marching quietly forward to success in business, is shown by the large number of stores, farms, homes, and churches which he owns and the respect that he has won for thrift and industry among white people, who have been most helpful to individual Negroes in spite of any political program of segregation. In Muskogee alone the property of Negroes, together with their stock in merchandise and business equipment, amounts to several million dollars.

The annual declaration of the League called attention to the material wealth of the race—$700,000,000 worth of taxable property and 20,000,000 acres of land; ''the educational and civic progress which our material progress has accelerated;'' the development and extension of business among members of the race; the golden opportunities offered to 2,000,000 Negroes living in the Southwest; and the progress through peace ''under the inspiration of leaders who counsel patience, persistence, earnest efforts, provident ways, and upright, moral living.''

The Boley Idea   Boley, Oklahoma, is the largest Negro city in the United States. It is surrounded by some of the richest land in the world and has in its neighborhood most valuable mines of coal and wells of oil. Recently it was the scene of joyous activity when Dr. Booker T. Washington and some four hundred delegates to the National Negro Business League came to its citizens from Muskogee, through Okmulgee, Boynton, and Clearview, where Negroes are succeeding in farming, in cattle-raising, in mining, in the oil and gas fields, and in store-keeping.

Boley was founded in 1904 by Thomas M. Haynes of Texas, in the rolling prairie land on the Fort Smith and Western Railroad between Deep Fork and North Canadian Rivers, and is in the heart of a vast region capable of producing such diversified crops as corn, wheat, cotton, potatoes, alfalfa, apples, peaches, grapes, berries, and the common garden vegetables.

This Negro town is "making good." Today it has over eighty business concerns, an electric lighting plant, efficient water works, two banks, several attractive churches, a high school worth over $15,000, a normal and industrial school supported by the C. M. E. Church, flourishing fraternal orders, a Masonic temple of the Oklahoma jurisdiction worth $35,000, a telephone system, several cotton gins, a chamber of commerce, a city hall, a Negro station agent, and a Negro mayor.

From fifteen to twenty thousand people live in the region surrounding Boley—3000 are in the township of Boley and 1300 are in the city of Boley. Here, then, is the beginning—really an excellent beginning—of a demonstration in Negro city building which will be watched closely by those who are interested in the Negro as a factor in business.

The people of Boley, all of whom are Negroes, have shown rare pluck in going into a new country and doing *together* what most people said Negroes never could do—exercise initiative and judgment in building up business enterprises apart from white men. They have won their present success by making their lot one with the man on the farm.

Boley is in many ways a substantial evidence of the ambition, thrift, and capacity of the Negro who takes life more seriously than the average man of the race, and is not interfered with by unwise friends or out-and-out enemies. Boley reflects credit on Mr. Haynes and his co-workers. It gives promise of great things. It ought to be better known by young, doubting Negroes, especially city Negroes, who are dissatisfied with their lot and are ignorant of what the South and the Southwest offer in golden opportunities for the sober, hard-working, cheerful man, regardless of color.

What the future of Boley will be depends not only on the men and women who have planted a thriving city in a rough country, but also upon the Negroes who are trained (and will be trained within the next few years) for leadership in education, business, and public health, as well as in religion and law.

Whether the Boley idea should be carried to its logical conclusion and an effort should be made to induce great masses of Negroes to organize themselves into corporate groups, depends on whether white men and black men are willing to do away rather arbitrarily with the natural contact of the two races and run the risk of greater misunderstanding in race relations—the inevitable forerunner of racial friction.

Dr. Washington's visit to Boley, his words of encouragement and advice, together with his vital relation to problems of race adjustment, give this demonstration in "big business" for the Negro more than passing significance.

▓

Legislation for the Indians   Two items included in the Indian Appropriation Bill for the current year will be especially welcome to readers of the Southern Workman. The bill, which was passed by Congress in August, is for the most part an excellent piece of constructive legislation and carries provisions which will help the Indians in several new directions, but two of the items call for special mention here.

One is the considerable increase in the appropriation for educational purposes. Provision is now made for educating the deaf, mute, and blind children, who have hitherto been unprovided for. Some foundation for the education of the deaf mutes already exists, by the way, in the very general knowledge of the sign language possessed by all the Plains tribes. Special provision is made also for the education of the Navahos who have hitherto been but inadequately supplied with schools. Attention has frequently been called to the several thousand children of this tribe, who have entirely lacked school facilities. This tribe is one of the most promising although one of the most backward of them all, and it has long been urged that all the children should have some schooling.

The other item is the appropriation of $300,000 for improving health conditions among the Indians. Nothing like this sum has been appropriated for this purpose before. Of this amount $100,000 is to be used for constructing hospitals at a cost not to exceed $15,000 for each. This is in addition to the three hospitals which the Indian Office is now building for the Sioux on the Rosebud, Cheyenne, and Pine Ridge reservations, and does not include $50,000 appropriated out of the Chippewa Indian funds for a hospital for that tribe in Minnesota.

The investigations which have been made at different times into the health conditions among the various tribes, and the oft-repeated and widely published reports of the enormous death rate among the Indians and of the threatening spread of tuberculosis and trachoma among them, seems to be bearing fruit.

The campaign for health has been a long one. Most of the societies organized in behalf of the Indians have enlisted in it and the
Indian Office has urged it. Meantime that office has done what it
could with the means at its disposal to arrest the spread of the
two diseases which are the special scourge of the Indians, but
the means have been inadequate for effectively handling the situation. It is therefore gratifying to note that there is now a prospect for larger accomplishment. Surely there is no more important effort to be undertaken for the Indian than the conservation
of his health. All the money spent for his education and development and all other altruistic efforts for his welfare will be
wasted if his race cannot be saved from physical deterioration.

Distrust a Cause of the War When we look into the causes of the dreadful war
which has brought sorrow and death to thousands
of homes in Europe and her colonies, and poverty
and business depression to all parts of the world, we find
that perhaps chief among them was distrust of one country by
another. If the nations of Europe could have trusted each other
this bloody war could have been averted. If there is to be any
lasting settlement of their differences it must come through trust
and co-operation and recognition of the fact that the success and
growth of one nation are helpful to all others.

Major Moton, Hampton's Commandant, in his addresses to
Northern audiences, is accustomed to refer to the words of Mrs.
B. B. Munford of Virginia, a leading Southern woman, spoken
at a meeting of the Negro Organization Society held in Richmond
last winter and attended by an audience of five thousand whites
and blacks, when she declared that the best thing the white race
could do for the blacks in the South was to trust them. Major
Moton, speaking later at the same meeting, said that the best
thing the blacks could do for the whites was to trust them. Mrs.
Munford and Major Moton were right.

General Armstrong, Hampton's founder, was a great statesman as well as a great educator. One of the most important
lessons he taught his pupils and co-workers was the duty of
trusting and loving one another. In his memoranda he said,
"Cantankerousness is worse than heterodoxy." He advised his
successors to get rid of any workers who could not co-operate.
It was because of that teaching that Booker Washington was
able to say in his Atlanta speech, "No man, either white or
black, from North or South, shall drag me down so low as to
make me hate him." When the Tuskegee School was established
and grew to even larger proportions than the mother school, drawing its support largely from Hampton's constituency, the older
institution was able to realize, through General Armstrong's
teaching, that Tuskegee's success was Hampton's success. At

the twenty-fifth anniversary of Tuskegee the Principal of Hampton spoke of what Tuskegee had done for Hampton.

Governor Blease of South Carolina, whom the people of that state have rejected as their leader, was accustomed to think that the way to political distinction was through stirring up one race against the other. It is a cause for satisfaction that the people have spoken in emphatic tones against that method of self-aggrandizement. They are beginning to understand, as Dr. Washington said in the same Atlanta speech, that "you cannot fatten one finger of the hand without fattening the others;" that ignorance and poverty and superstition in one race in the South mean the same things for the other.

There is really no reason for the white man to distrust the black man, for the Teuton to distrust the Slav. The more advanced people should understand that ignorance and superstition in any race are to be dreaded, and everything possible should be done to abolish them—but that is quite a different thing from race hatred.

The President of the United States has done well to set apart a Sabbath, October 4, for the preaching of peace on earth, good will to men. Mr. Carnegie and his co-laborers deserve the thanks of the whole world for their valiant struggles to bring peace. But there can be no peace where there is distrust.

Hampton's Summer Work The past summer has been a very busy one for Hampton workers. An account was given in the August number of the Southern Workman of the summer school for teachers where four hundred and thirty-five colored men and women from Virginia and eighteen other states, ranging from Texas to New York, spent four weeks under an admirable corps of instructors, learning improved methods of teaching and how to introduce cooking, sewing, chair-caning, and other forms of manual training into their schools, studying hygiene and the care of the home, and obtaining a knowledge of how to carry on community work. The testimonies which these men and women gave at the close of the session as to what the school had done for them brought tears to the eyes of many of the listeners. One of the interesting classes of the summer school was that made up of a company of colored clergymen who spent a week under the direction of Dr. Frank K. Sanders and Mr. Fenninger in the study of the Scriptures.

An account was also given in the August number of the triennial gathering of the graduates, the largest in the school's history. After a morning spent in listening to the story of the school's progress and in the discussion of plans for increasing the helpfulness of the graduate body, the graduates assembled for the laying of the corner-stone of James Hall, the fine, new dormitory for boys, in whose construction the Trade School students have been occupied all summer. Mr. William S. Reid, once Gen. Armstrong's secretary, and for several years president of the Alumni Association, and Mrs. Sarah Fernandis, a pioneer in social settlement work in Washington and Baltimore, gave expression to their gratitude for the opportunities which the generous friends of the school have made possible at Hampton.

But perhaps the most important summer work that Hampton has conducted was the three months' crusade into the North of nineteen student representatives of the school. On a Chesapeake bug-eye, with a colored captain and crew, this company of students journeyed from Hampton to Mt. Desert, telling, on the lawns of Newport, Magnolia, Bar Harbor, and other popular resorts by songs, pageant, and addresses, the story of the struggle of the Indian and Negro out from barbarism to civilization, and showing the part which they have had in the progress of this country. Thousands of people from all parts of the country witnessed the pageant and listened to Major Moton and Captain Washington as they described the methods by which Hampton is endeavoring to help the white and black races to believe in one another and work together in harmony and mutual helpfulness.

It is hard to estimate the value of these, gatherings, where some of the most representative people of America assembled and were convinced of the possibilities, under proper education, of the black and red races. At Newport, Bishop Perry of Rhode Island said that Hampton had "changed what has been a race problem into a race program." Mrs. Beverly B. Munford, of Richmond, Virginia, paid an eloquent tribute to Hampton's work in her state and spoke strongly of what the school means to the white people of the South. Dr. Wallace Buttrick, at Bar Harbor, spoke of the *genuineness* of the school and described what he has seen of the work of its graduates in developing good Christian homes. He referred to Georgia Washington's work at Mt. Meigs, and to Celia Bradley's at Purves, Alabama. Dr. Francis Peabody, who presided at the meeting at Northeast Harbor, told of his pleasure in leading morning prayers with the students on the *Hampton*, and of how the religious life enters into all of Hampton's work. President Eliot dwelt upon the practical character of the school's religious training and explained how the students are fitted for the actual work of life.

Although the weather was by no means always propitious and the breaking out of the war interfered with the collections, the financial returns were satisfactory and many friends were won for Hampton. We are glad of an opportunity to express the school's thanks to the friends who so generously offered their

grounds for the pageant, and to the patronesses whose social
influence did so much to make the meetings a success.   ·

The appeals which Hampton is obliged to send
Hampton's out each month of the year in order to raise the
Appeal $150,000,over and above its assured income, which
is needed to carry on its work, have already been frequently met
with the answer that the war has reduced income and that a continuation of help is impossible.

Hampton has a most loyal body of friends. General Armstrong's appeal in his memoranda—"Hampton must not go down.
See to it, you who are true to the black and red children of the
land and to just ideas of education,"—has always met with a
loyal response. Poor women have given their mites; children in
mission schools have year after year kept up their scholarships;
and generous wealthy friends have made Hampton possible.

Devoted Hampton workers have lived on small salaries and
used every means of making the funds subscribed by the friends
of the school go as far as possible. Perhaps in no institution in
the country is there a more efficient treasurer's department than
at Hampton. The state auditor has again and again expressed
his pleasure with the admirable system of accounts and the
careful use made of money.

Hampton is a national institution. Just as war taxes have
to be levied so that the departments at Washington may not
suffer, so special efforts must be made for Hampton at this
critical time. The school is a demonstration station, one of the
most important in the world, illustrating how different races can
live together in peace and harmony. To quote again Bishop
Perry's words, "It has changed a race problem into a race
program."

Already expenses at Hampton have been cut down and the
greatest economy is being practiced. Certain of the school's
employes have voluntarily reduced their salaries.

Let us see to it that Hampton does not go down.

The Hampton School and its Alumni Association
Mary E. Melvin have sustained a serious loss in the death, on
September 5, after a long illness, of Mary E. Melvin, of the Class
of '74· With the exception of four years, the forty years since
her graduation have been spent in educational work—two years
as teacher in rural schools, sixteen in a Norfolk graded school,
four at Tuskegee Institute, two as assistant matron at Hampton,
after taking the school's course in matron's work, and twelve as
lady principal at the Agricultural and Mechanical College at

Tallahassee, Fla., from which position she resigned only a few weeks previous to her death. She was considered by the principal of this school an invaluable helper, having built up in the institution, from small beginnings, a strong woman's department. This principal, Mr. Young, writes of Miss Melvin as follows:

"During all these years she was my right-hand supporter and without her assistance I am sure that we could not have had the success that we have had."

Another of her co-workers writes, "Her consistent, beautiful life was an example and an inspiration to all who came into contact with it."

Most appropriate was the text of the rector's brief funeral sermon, "Not to be ministered unto, but to minister." Miss Melvin spent her life for others and has influenced for good thousands of young people of her race. Soon after beginning her work at Tallahassee she wrote: "I so often say that I am glad that I was born a Negro. Had I been born white and as poor as I am, I should have had the 'door of opportunity' closed in my face. As it now is no one can keep the *best things* from me. And I owe all this to Hampton and to the accident of being born a Negro. I tell my girls that all the good things have come to me that I may pass them to others. General Armstrong always made us feel that Hampton students 'gathered to scatter.'

At the funeral service in little St. Cyprian Chuch in Hampton the white garments of relatives and friends, the gray casket covered with beautiful flowers, the sunshine streaming over it through the open windows of the little church, and the singing of the choir as it preceded the body to the gateway were all in keeping with Miss Melvin's wishes.

"And may there be
No sadness of farewell
When I embark."

SCHOOL CREDIT FOR HOME INDUSTRIAL WORK *

BY L. R. ALDERMAN

State Superintendent of Public Instruction for Oregon

WHEN I arrived at the town of about two thousand people where I had been engaged to teach, the chairman of the school board accompanied me to the schoolhouse on the Friday before my new school was to open. Among the other bits of advice he gave me was that one particular boy should be expelled upon the first provocation. The boy had given trouble the year before and should not be allowed to contaminate the whole school. He had stolen things and had been in a street fight. For two years running he had been expelled at the beginning of school. The boy's father and mother were good people, but they had no control over the boy.

This was not very encouraging to me, as I had not had such an experience before, in fact had never taught in a town so large. I was looking for the boy the next Monday morning. He was pointed out to me as he came down the long walk to the schoolhouse. Instinctively I studied him as he came up the steps, measuring him with my eye as if to get an estimate of his physical strength, as well as of his mental make-up. He was large for his age, carried his head low, and looked up from under the brim of his hat. He looked at me as if to say, "I do not like you, nor any who are in your sissy business." He chose a seat in the back corner of the room, signed his name in a scrawly hand, and gave his age as seventeen. It seemed to be generally understood that he would make some trouble, so as to be expelled the first day.

During my vacation I had read "Jean Mitchell's School," and I remembered Jean Mitchell had scrubbed her schoolroom. I had noticed on the Friday before that the schoolroom had not been scrubbed, nor the windows cleaned, so I said after the morning recess, "How many of you would be willing to help scrub out the schoolroom this afternoon? As this is our home for the year, we want it clean." All seemed willing to help, and this boy threw up his head and took a good look at me as if he thought I had some little glimmer of intelligence. The pupils

* Extracts from an address delivered before the National Educational Association

were to bring brooms, mops, and pails from home. Harry brought a broom, mop, and a package of Gold Dust, almost full, which he had stolen from his mother. He scrubbed harder than any other boy in the school. He seemed to be a leader when it came to doing things with his hands. I was much delighted to see in him a willingness to help. I found out that he was totally lost when it came to studying grammar and fractions. These were not in his line, and unless the school took into account some active work it could not reach Harry. We had no manual training in the school, but we had football, baseball, and gardening. In all of these he excelled. I became convinced that in order to reach a boy like Harry the school would have to broaden out and give credit for home activities.

Next year in high school there was a girl who had a great deal of time to run the streets. I would see her going to the post-office and to the train every day. She hardly ever had her lessons. I clearly saw I was not reaching her. She was a large, healthy, good-looking, happy-go-lucky girl. Going home one night from school with one of the teachers, I was told that Mary's mother was coming down the street. As I felt she and I had a big job on our hands, I wanted to meet her. I saw in the face of the faded little woman signs of one of life's tragedies that we see so often in overworked, disappointed mothers. Her daughter had broken away from home influences. I realized that Mary was as cruel as the Spartan boy she and I had read about in history, who had been taught to slap his mother in the face that he might be hardened for battle. This was her first year in high school. I realized that the nebular hypothesis and quadratic equations could not reach the real Mary, nor the real Harry, who was also in this school.

That evening I thought it all over, planning how I could come to the aid of Mary's mother. The next morning before the algebra class I said, "How many of you girls swept a floor or made a bed before coming to school?" Some hands, not Mary's. "How many of you helped get breakfast this morning?" Some hands, not Mary's. "How many helped get supper last night?" Some hands, not Mary's. "None of you need to be told that the best friend you have or ever will have, perhaps, is your mother. Let us see what we can do to show our appreciation of our parents." I was struck with the real interest the class showed. "Tomorrow," I said, "I am going to give you ten problems. Five will be in the book, and the other five will be out of the book. The five out of the book will be: (1) help get supper to-night; (2) help do the supper dishes; (3) help get breakfast; (4) sweep a floor; (5) make a bed." I also gave certain duties to the boys. I said, "These tasks are going to count the same as algebra

problems." The next morning I was delighted to see the eagerness with which they responded; they had worked the five problems in the book and the five problems out of the book. Mary
continued holding up her hand after I had asked how many had
worked all the problems. I said, "Mary, what is the matter
with your hand?" She said she had worked five problems in
advance in the book. I had never associated the working of
problems in advance with Mary.

The tasks were changed during the year. We had at different times credit given for home work, the same as for school
work. During a discussion at an institute meeting, a very good
principal asked me, "If we give credit in algebra for home
duties, what will become of the algebra?" I never have been
able to answer his question. Once I was arguing with the residents of a small district that I wished would consolidate with
another district. A man rose and said that he believed in consolidation in general, but this particular district had the graveyard
deeded to it. If this district's identity was lost in consolidation,
what would become of the graveyard?

At the next county election I was elected county superintendent. My belief in encouraging home work had become a working conviction by this time, and I am sure I bored some very good
teachers nearly to the point of death talking about it. I was
asked, "Why should school credit be given for work not done
in school? Let school credit be given for school work, and home
credit for home work. It is dishonest to give credit at school
for work done at home. The more we can keep home out of
school the better it is." Some good, staid teachers looked at me
as if I had broken the Ten Commandments. I had some qualms
of conscience, and wondered if I could bring myself to a condition of being satisfied with seeing school credit given only for
work done in school, of being content if the subjects in the books
were taught, and of not caring if the children did spend their
time on the streets.

On my visits to the country schools, I at first made speeches
upon the importance of education, how it would pay the pupils to
be well prepared before taking up the duties of life. I prided
myself upon my ability to make this seem wonderfully ponderous
to them. But I noticed that nothing happened. They looked
dazed and glanced at the clock to see if it were nearly time for
school to close. But when I asked them to do something, to make
bird-houses for their back yards, or for the school yard, they
were alert, and I had over nine hundred bird-houses built by the
children of our county that year.

One day, as I was visiting a country school, I saw a boy taking up a collection in his hat. I was told they were taking this

up to buy popcorn, as one of the boys was going to town Saturday. I asked why they did not grow their own popcorn. I knew it would grow there, for I was born and raised in that part of the country. I told them I would give five dollars to the boy or girl who could raise the best popcorn that year. This seemed to interest them. I asked how many had raised watermelons. I was told nobody did, for the boys in the neighborhood were so bad about stealing them. I asked "If everyone were raising watermelons, who would there be to steal them?" All you have to do to get a grin the full width of a child's face is to mention watermelons. Going home that night in my buggy, some ten miles, I concluded we should have a school fair and give prizes for watermelons and muskmelons. When talking it over to my wife that night we added vegetables, jellies, bread, canned fruit, and sewing to the list for which prizes should be given at the fair.

A trip down one side of the business street and up another and I had all the prizes I needed to advertise the fair in the fall. It was not long before a father brought his boy to the office to learn more about the contest. The father patted the boy on his head and said : "John has a garden. He has pumpkins as big as a bushel basket. " How John's eyes sparkled at the praise of his father ! They went out and got into the wagon, and I could imagine the conversation John and his father had on the way home. It seemed worth while for us to go into some outside work and give credit for it. The fair was a great success, and it has grown with every year. This last year, its seventh, there were four thousand exhibits. The crowd at the fair is the largest that ever gathers at the county seat.

. The first year of the fair I heard high-school girls say, as they looked at the long rows of bread, "I am going to learn to make bread ;" as they looked at the ruby and amber jellies, "I am going to learn to make jelly. " I had mothers call me in, as I drove past their homes, to show me the sewing of their daughters. We had a large attendance at our parents' meetings after the fair was started. It became evident that we must co-operate along the line of activities of the child if we wished to secure the co-operation of the parents. They could not co-operate along the line of decimal fractions, infinitives, and principles. People I had not known were interested in education at all, would comment upon the interest the children in the neighborhood were taking in things. In order to raise better products they had to read bulletins. It created a real interest upon which the teachers could build in educational progress.

I was next elected superintendent in a city of about ten thousand people, and found the children were just as eager for

activity as they were in the smaller towns and in the country.
We had school gardens for the seventh and eighth grades, and
did the work during school time, on the condition that the children would keep up their school work. This they did for the sake
of working in the gardens. Certain teachers were willing to take
into account home activities in the school. We had sewing
taught. We had bread day. Hundreds of people came to see the
loaves of bread the children were able to make under the guidance
of their mothers. We had bird-house day. Nearly five hundred
bird-houses, some of them wonderfully made, were exhibited by
children who had learned from their fathers how to handle a
hammer and how to saw off the end of a board.

I have heard teachers say that it is too bad the schools do
not have accommodations for industrial work, but every girl lives
in a place where there is a stove and cooking utensils. Every
country or small-town boy lives where there is a saw, a hammer,
and an ax. If every school will furnish the child with a desire
to make something, he will surprise you with his ability to make
it. If you can create a desire in a girl to make an apron, or a
dress, or a skirt, she will find someone to show her how to make
it. I have noticed that the girls in some of our larger schools in
the domestic-science class were perfectly happy making loaves
of bread, tucking the little loaves into shining new pans, and
putting them into the gas oven. They would watch eagerly
when they were taken out, delighted with the beautiful, well-
shaped loaves of a perfect brown. I have seen the same girls
look with scorn at the big cook-stove oven at home, and the
large, unpolished tins. I have seen the mothers make the bread
and cook the meals, as the girls of the domestic-science class
were too busy with their school work, which was supposed
to mean so much to their future, to apply any of the results
learned. I knew a teacher in a manual-training class who spent
six months teaching the boys how to use a chisel, a plane, and
boring bits. The superintendent had to have the truant officer
compel these boys to attend the manual-training class. They
wanted to make something.

Children do not like to play a life—they want to live a life.
I have seen girls shrink from making little models in sewing,
and the boys look as if they were afraid to say out loud what
they were thinking while they were learning to use tools—just
to use them. I have seen the bored looks upon the faces of
pupils who were engaged in writing essays to be passed in to
the teacher, and sent to the waste basket. I have seen the
animated looks on the pupils' faces when they were learning
to write letters which were to go to some real place and would
bring back a reply.

GOOD READING FOR NEGROES

To give Negro boys and girls the opportunity of coming in contact with the heart stories of the noble men and women of bygone days; to fire their imagination; to bring them the privileges once reserved for the few; to help them form the habit of reading the best literature—this is the task that is outlined in the following sketches.

That Mr. Carnegie's investment in a library for the Negroes of Louisville is already bringing big returns in the lives of thousands of young people who are prospective citizens, there can be no question. That the work of supplying good reading for Negroes in Tennessee is well worth while, even a casual reader must discover. — THE EDITORS

I THE LOUISVILLE FREE LIBRARY

BY GEORGE T. SETTLE

Librarian

THE FIRST colored branch of the Louisville Free Public Library was opened in temporary quarters on September 23, 1905, and the new building was completed and opened on October 28, 1908. It was the first institution of its kind in existence.

The building occupied by the Western Colored Branch is seventy-seven by forty-five feet with a main floor and basement, built of brick, concrete, and stone with tile roof. The cost of the plant was $45,568.74. This included the following items: Site, $3180; improving grounds, $1048.68; building proper, $27,511.74; light fixtures, $433.55; furniture, $3395.34; and books, $10,000.

The library contains 10,046 volumes and receives ninety-one periodicals as issued monthly. The attendance in eight years has been 330,715, and since the opening 7132 persons have registered as borrowers of books for home use.

The library has the open shelf system which allows every one to go directly to the shelves and choose his own books, the librarian assisting in the selection, if it is desired. The children's section of the room is under close supervision of the children's librarian and children are assisted in making their selection of books. During the eight years that the library has been in operation it has issued in all 404,122 books.

The library serves as a reference library for the high schools, ward schools, and other educational institutions in the city. It is in close touch with the grade schools through the collections of books which are placed in the classrooms. These books are drawn by the children for home use under the supervision of the teachers. A large amount of reference work is done with the pupils of the schools. Information is looked up on all subjects and all kinds of topics, and all sorts of practical questions are answered. Since the opening of the library, information on 12,034 subjects has been found and 20,571 persons have been assisted in reference work by the library. This does not include the large number of persons who visit the library daily to read and consult the reference books for themselves.

Aside from furnishing facts in reference work and circulat-

THE WESTERN COLORED BRANCH OF THE LOUISVILLE FREE
PUBLIC LIBRARY
"The first institution of its kind in existence"

ing books, the library encourages and assists all efforts to an educational end and the advancement of the colored people in the city. The people feel that the library belongs to them and that it may be used for anything that makes for their welfare. During a single month thirty-two meetings have been held at the library. The following clubs and reading circles meet regularly in the building: Bannecker Reading Circle ; Dunbar Literary Club ; Fisk Club; Normal Alumni; Sunday School Training Class Story Hour ; Girls' Reading Club ; Douglass Debating Club ; Wilberforce Club ; and Young Women's Christian Association. Other meetings held at the library have been: State Medical Association,

Business League, Annual Conference of the Young Men's Christian
Association, State Federation of Colored Women's Clubs, Teachers' Institute, and illustrated lectures on social and educational
subjects.

The library conducts an apprentice class for those who desire
to enter library service. An examination is held in June and the
class puts in three months of actual work in the library in all
departments preparing for service. Nine persons have taken
this course.

The work at the Western Colored Branch has been so successful and is held in such high favor that the library trustees
have established a second colored branch in the eastern part of
the city. This is known as the Eastern Colored Branch Library

THE EASTERN COLORED BRANCH OPENED IN JANUARY, 1914.
Louisville is the only city having two colored branch libraries.

and was opened with appropriate exercises January 28. John H.
Buschemeyer, mayor of the city and president of the board of
trustees, presided. Addresses were delivered by Dr. Charles R.
Hemphill, president of the Southern Presbyterian Theological
Seminary, Prof. W. H. Bartholomew, ex-principal of the Girls'
High School, and others. Exercises were also held on the evening
of January 26 conducted by principals and teachers of the colored
schools of the city, and on Friday, January 30, conducted by the
colored ministers. The exercises on Saturday afternoon, January
31, were presented by the children of the colored public schools.
Louisville long enjoyed the distinction of having the only colored
branch library in the country ; it now has the distinction of being
the only city having two colored branches.

The Eastern Colored Branch building is one of the best in the country, adapted for library and social center uses. The size of the building is 60 by 80 feet on a splendid site 75 by 150 feet. The first floor contains the library room accommodating 10,000 volumes and an auditorium seating 350 persons. The basement has three classrooms for meetings and clubs and a playroom 37 by 40 feet. In addition, arrangements have been made for a playground 60 by 75 feet in the rear, and an experimental garden in the ell of the building.

The cost exclusive of the site was $22,574.20, paid for out of Carnegie funds. The site, which is a splendid location for a library, cost $5000, $4000 of which was paid for by the city and $1000 by colored citizens.

The number of books borrowed the first day the building was opened for circulation was 125 volumes. The average attendance the first week netted 234 persons daily. Judging from the interest taken, the success of the Western Colored Branch in Louisville will be repeated at the Eastern Colored Branch.

The two colored branch libraries are a part of the library system of the Louisville Free Public Library, of which George T. Settle is the librarian.

The staff of the colored branch is as follows: Thomas F. Blue, branch librarian; Western Colored Branch, Elizabeth I. Finney and Jane J. Simpson; Eastern Colored Branch, Rachel D. Harris and Lillie S. Edwards.

Since the acceptance of the above manuscript by the editors of the Southern Workman, the following press notice has appeared in Southern newspapers:

"Thomas Fountain Blue, librarian of the branch library for colored people of the Louisville Free Public Library, is a native of Farmville, Virginia. He was educated at the Hampton Normal and Agricultural Institute [class of 1888] and the Richmond Theological Seminary, graduating from the latter in the class of 1898 with the degree of bachelor of divinity. He served as Young Men's Christian Association army secretary of the Sixth Virginia Regiment Volunteers during the Spanish-American war. He went to Louisville in 1899 and was secretary of the Louisville Young Men's Christian Association for colored men from 1899 to 1905. For the past nine years he has been a member of the committee of management and treasurer of the Association.

"He has been librarian of the Western Colored Branch of the Louisville Free Public Library since its establishment in 1905. As a recognition of efficiency and faithful service, he was appointed librarian of the new Eastern Colored Branch Library in addition to his former duties, when it was opened in January, 1914. Mr. Blue is courteous, obliging, and untiring in his efforts to render every service for the profit, pleasure, and convenience of the many patrons of the libraries. He is held in the highest esteem by both white and colored citizens of Louisville. He has the distinction of being the first colored man in the United States to be appointed librarian of a public library exclusively for Negroes."—THE EDITORS

A STORY HOUR GROUP OF THE COLORED SCHOOL DEPARTMENT
OF COSSITT LIBRARY, MEMPHIS, TENNESSEE

II A MEMPHIS LIBRARY

BY CECILIA K. YERBY

Supervisor

IN September 1913 the Colored School Department of Cossitt
Library of Memphis, Tenn., was established, with the writer
as supervisor of the department. The purpose of this department of the library is to cultivate among the students of the
colored schools the habit of reading the best literature, to assist
the teachers in selecting good books and periodicals for themselves and pupils, and to cultivate and extend the scope of reading generally among the colored people of Memphis. Whether
the department is succeeeding or not depends upon how well it is
meeting the object it has in view.

The plan of work has been to visit the schools and find just
what class of literature, if any, a boy or girl is interested in,
and then select the best for them along the lines indicated. If
the student has no preference, an effort is made to select a
book, magazine, or periodical that will both interest and benefit
him—that will tend to create an interest in other books. If
the student likes history, we try to find something to please
his particular taste ; and the same if the inclination is to read
books on travel, fiction, science, or art, always selecting that
which tends most to elevate. The library furnishes this department some of the best books, magazines, and periodicals. The

students are encouraged to read these. Suggestions are made with reference to the contents of the books, and attention is called to any special articles in the magazines or other publications. By these efforts we have succeeded during the past school year in distributing 11,724 books, no account being kept of the use of magazines and other periodicals.

In order to instill in the students a desire for reading, we have had during the past year a weekly story hour at the Howe Institute Branch of the department. At these story hours the supervisors and others, usually some one or more of the public school teachers and members of the different professions of the city, tell the children gathered, usually of the primary grades, stories of general interest to children, informing them that they can find these stories and many others of great interest in the books of the library and in the publications furnished the department.

We have been fortunate in being furnished by the library with a stereopticon and illustrative views for a number of the stories. These have been very serviceable in helping to make the story hour a success. The average weekly attendance has been 120. The little ones were very interested from the beginning. As a result of the efforts made in the story hours, many of the children have asked for, and have received books, which they have read and returned. This branch of the work has been open not only to the school children, but to those so unfortunate as not to be in any school. One can judge something of the general interest manifested by the children by their large attendance.

Another activity of the department has been the book reviews held every two weeks. These have been on the whole very interesting to those attending, but unfortunately they have been poorly attended. At these reviews some one or two of the teachers or members of the different professions of the city, interested in keeping abreast with what the best authors have written and are writing, review the story of some book previously assigned to them. As a rule two books are reviewed at each gathering, after which questions are asked the reviewers, and different features, points, and topics are discussed. Of course, these reviews are of more interest to the "grown-ups." We regret that more interest has not been manifested on the part of teachers and the public generally.

The Howe Branch of the Colored School Department of the Cossitt Library is located in three well-lighted and well-ventilated rooms of the girl's dormitory of Howe Collegiate Institute, corner Wellington and Frazier Streets, Memphis, Tenn. This institution, owned and controlled by the Negro Baptists of Tennessee, was established in 1888 under very humble circumstances. The main building of the institution was given by Mr. and Mrs. Peter Howe of Illinois, and the institution took the name of its principal benefactors. The school has served mostly to benefit the people in the territory surrounding Memphis, the majority of the students coming from the country districts of West Tennessee, East Arkansas, and North Mississippi. The aim of the school has been ''to do thorough English and academic work, giving the students an easy command of the best in our language and literature, and a thorough preparation for teaching, and for entrance into college. '' The school has been fortunate during the past twelve years in having at its head a very progressive and capable leader in the person of Rev. T. O. Fuller, Ph.D., and has done excellent work under his administration, although it has no endowment, and depends solely upon its friends for support. The branch of the library located at Howe will serve a two-fold purpose ; to enlist the interest of the students coming from the country as well as that of those in the city. The location is central, and no better place for general service and convenience could have been selected.

Though our beginning has been small and modest, we hope in the near future to have every child and its parents interested and enjoying in some way the benefits of the Colored School Department of Cossitt Library. They are invited to make use of every facility offered.

AMONG THE ALIBAMU INDIANS

BY M. R. HARRINGTON

Assistant Curator in the Section of American Ethnology, University of Pennsylvania Museum

PROBABLY not one person in a thousand, unless especially interested in our native race, has ever heard of the Alibamu tribe of Indians, who are little known even to students of the subject. To me they were little more than a name, until I had actually visited them in their Texas home. Here they enjoy the distinction of being the only tribe left within the borders of the state, the others having all been massacred or driven out by the whites in retaliation for the raids made by the Kiowas and Comanches from the North. The Texan idea of justice, in those days, when they could not catch the Comanche raiders, was to take revenge on some entirely different tribe within their own borders, which was usually innocent of wrong-doing and practically defenceless. How the Alibamus ever escaped is a mystery, unless their location in a heavily wooded section caused them to be overlooked.

They are classed with the great Muskhogean group of tribes, for their language seems to lie somewhere between the pure Creek or Muskogi on the one hand, and the Choctaw on the other. In this respect it resembles the language of the Kwasadi tribe, their relatives, who live just across the Texas border in Louisiana.

Historical records tell us that the Alibamu tribe formed a part of the old Creek Confederacy, and lived, when first encountered by the whites, on Alabama River near the junction of the Coosa and Tallapoosa Rivers, in what is now the state of Alabama, which received its name from them. The earliest mention of them may be found in the records of De Soto's expedition, as far back as 1541 ; but little seems to have been known about them until 1702, when the French first came to Mobile Bay and found there several deserted Indian villages from which the inhabitants had been driven by the "Alibamons" who must have been on the warpath at the time.

The Alibamus lingered near the old homes, in spite of the encroachment of the whites, until about 1763, when they began to drift westward, stopping for a while near New Orleans, then crossing the Mississippi. Today there are a few in western

Louisiana among their kinsmen, the Kwasadis ; where, in 1908, I had the pleasure of meeting the first of their nation I had ever seen. There are also a few among the Creek nation in Oklahoma ; but the main body, about two hundred, lives in Polk County, Texas.

After conversing with the few Alibamus living in the Kwasadi settlement, I made up my mind to visit the Texas band; but the opportunity did not come until 1910, when I was working among the tribes of Oklahoma for the Heye Expedition of the University of Pennsylvania Museum at Philadelphia. When the chance came, I lost no time in taking a train to Houston, from which I made my way to Livingston, a little old "cote-house" town, buried in the "Big Woods" of Polk County.

THE HOUSE OF THE MISSIONARY, REV. C. W. CHAMBERS

Livingston is a sleepy little old-fashioned Southern town, where cows drowse peacefully on the sidewalks ; where cellars are practically unknown, most of the buildings being perched on stilts ; where pigs squeal and quarrel all night beneath the hotel floor ; and where they serve "hominy grits" with every meal.

Here I asked about the Indians, and was told that there were plenty of them a few miles east of town. Nobody seemed to know the name of the tribe, until I found one lanky individual who "reckoned they mote be called Alabams. "

After some search I succeeded in hiring a driver and team to take me out. It was said to be only seventeen miles to the

Indian settlement, but it seemed nearer seventy before we reached our destination. At last, thoroughly tired, we approached a log cabin where some children were playing, [and] a glance at their bright coppery faces told me that my goal was reached. A little further on was the house of the missionary, Rev. C. W. Chambers, where I soon made friends with the family and established very comfortable headquarters.

Mr. Chambers and his wife have been doing a fine work among these people for many years, Mrs. Chambers teaching

"THE ALIBAMUS HAVE RETAINED THEIR PURITY OF BLOOD."

school during the week and her husband preaching on Sunday, besides their very important service as friends and advisers at all times to the tribe. The scene of their labors is a little building which serves for both school and church. It stands in the same clearing where once the tribal dances were held. ·

The Indians are remarkably hospitable, polite, and friendly, and seem very industrious, some working their own or other people's farms, some in the sawmills, some cutting timber. In fact they were all so busy that it was hard to find an interpreter. The fact that during my entire stay, in all my travel from house to house, I did not see a single intoxicated Indian, speaks well for the condition of the tribe.

In this settlement the Alibamus have some twelve hundred acres of land; the deed of which is held by the chief, but which is made out to the tribe as a whole. However, they recognize individual ownership among themselves ; and many take considerable pride in their little farms which are scattered in every direction through the forest.

John Scott was chief in 1910, but he was so old at the time— said to be over one hundred—that it seems hardly possible that he can still be alive.

AN ALIBAMU FARMER AND HIS FAMILY

The Alibamus have retained their purity of blood to an unusual degree ; consequently many fine native American types may be seen among them. They still retain their ancient language in common use ; and while most of the men can speak enough English to transact their simple business affairs, but few adults have any real command of the white man's tongue. The young folks are better prepared, however, having enjoyed the advantages of Mrs. Chambers's teaching.

Mr. and Mrs. Chambers did not give me much encouragement when told of my wish to hunt for relics among the people. In all the years they had been in the settlement they had seen practically nothing in the way of Indian handiwork, except a few cane baskets and a silver brooch or two. A surprise was awaiting them,

for when I was ready to leave, the floor of the room they had assigned to me was fairly covered with specimens.

No one had ever asked the Indians about their beadwork and other things, laid carefully away as keepsakes; and they had not volunteered to show them to the missionaries, because they thought their teachers disliked everything connected with the old life.

No trace of the old costume can now be seen in use, except an occasional pair of moccasins which, like those of the Seminoles

" BEAUTIFUL BEADED SASHES AND ORNAMENTS
HAMMERED OUT FROM SILVER COINS"

of the Everglades, are made from one piece of buckskin, puckered to a single seam in front. But many pieces of the old-time finery had been preserved by the different families, including beautiful beaded sashes like those of the Choctaws; shoulder pouches, some woven in handsome patterns, with colored yarns, some beaded; gorgeous woven beadwork ornaments something like those of the Florida Seminoles in design; ruffled calico shirts and coats; leggings, some of cloth decorated with appliqué designs cut from colored fabrics, some of deerskin; and homemade brooches, earrings, arm bands, rings, bracelets, head bands, and breast ornaments, for the most part hammered out from silver coins.

Among the most curious of the old-time things were a number of earthenware pots and bowls made by hand from selected clay. When these were unpacked at the University Museum in Philadelphia no one could believe they were the work of modern Indians. They looked ancient enough to have come from the mounds, for in style and texture they are the same as pottery made before the coming of the whites. With these pots the

"MANY PIECES OF OLD-TIME FINERY HAVE BEEN PRESERVED."

Alibamus used long-handled wooden spoons very similar to those still made by the Seminoles and Creeks.

The gun has, of course, long been the favorite weapon for hunting the deer and other game that still linger, in diminished numbers, amid the forests and canebrakes. Yet some bows and arrows may be seen in the hands of the sturdy little bright-eyed lads; and the blowgun, typical weapon of the Southern tribes, still occasionally serves for hunting birds and squirrels. This is a long straight tube of cane, through which a tiny, sharply-pointed dart, winged with thistledown or cotton, may be blown with surprising force and accuracy.

EARTHENWARE BOWL MADE BY HAND
FROM SELECTED CLAY

But most of the native manual arts are practically extinct. With the loss of the old-time dances, held twice a year in the big clearing near the present schoolhouse, went the last need for the gay ornaments and picturesque garments of the past, long before superseded for workaday use by the cheaper jeans and calicoes of the whites. This was the end of the art of beadwork; silver work died for a similar reason, as did the art of weaving, seen in the pretty pouches, cunningly wrought of fiber threads and yarn.

And what is the use of spending days in gathering and preparing clay, building up the great pots coil on coil, smoothing, and burning them? They are easily broken at best, while a tin bucket or saucepan costs only a few cents, and will stand a lot of dropping and battering.

The only Indian art that really lives today among the Alibamus is that of basketry; for nothing the white man produces cheaply by machinery can take the place of the light, strong, durable baskets of split cane—the handiwork of the deft-fingered women of the tribe. There are large baskets shaped something like an hour-glass, for carrying burdens on the back with the aid of a pack-strap across the chest; baskets with handles and covers for carrying in the hand; large baskets for storage, made just about the right height to slip under the bed; flat shapes for use as dishes, and in larger sizes as trays for winnowing meal; while some with openwork bottoms serve as sieves and colanders. Besides these there are the heart-shaped baskets, "elbow" baskets, wall baskets made in two or three stories, and other fancy forms.

The weaves and patterns resemble those of the Mississippi Choctaws, and are quite attractive. But none can equal the exquisite fineness and beautiful coloring which characterizes the work of those wonderful basketmakers, the Chetimacha Indians of Louisiana, in other respects quite similar. Both Alibamu and Choctaw baskets would be far more attractive if the makers could be persuaded to use the lovely, fadeless native dyes of their ancestors, instead of the gaudy and short-lived chemical colors bought at the stores. This is not impossible by any means, for the Chetimachas still use their ancient colorings with great success ; and their products, besides being more artistic, bring a much higher price when offered to the better class of buyers.

But the Alibamus, so far as I know, have never tried to find a market for their baskets outside of the country folk about them, who might not appreciate the soft old dyes. The tribe might make considerable money if they could develop a market for basketry in places like Galveston, Houston, and San Antonio, where such attractive and useful articles should find a ready sale. Their distinctive style of beadwork might even be revived for the tourist trade—the handsome shoulder pouches and sashes, so different from the ordinary run of Indian goods, might take well if shown as the product of the only Indian tribe left in Texas.

A BUILDING WHICH SERVES FOR SCHOOL AND CHURCH
" It stands in the clearing where once the tribal dances were held."

SIGNS OF GROWING CO-OPERATION *

BY ROBERT R. MOTON

A T a meeting held recently in Virginia an old colored preacher in opening the service prayed thus : " O, God of all races, will you please, Sir, come in and take charge of de min's of all dese yere white people and fix dem so dat dey'll know and under-stan' dat all of us colored folks is not lazy, dirty, dishones', an' no 'count, an' help dem, Lord, to see dat most of us is prayin', workin', and strivin,' to get some land, some houses, and some ed'cation for ourselves an' our chillun, an' get true 'ligion, an' dat most every Negro in Northampton County is doin' his lebel bes' to make frien's an' get along wid de white folks. Help dese yere white folks, O Lord, to understan' dis thing. Lord, while you is takin' charge of de min's of dese white people, don' pass by de colored folks, for dey is not perfec'—dey needs you as much as de white folks does. Open de Negro's blin' eyes dat he may see dat all of de white folks is not mean an' dishones' an' prejudice' ag'inst de colored folks, dat dere is hones', hard-workin', jus', and God-fearin' white folks in dis yere com-munity who is tryin' de bes' dey know how, wid de cir'umstances ag'inst dem, to be fair in dere dealin's wid de colored folks, an' help dem to be 'spectable men an' women. Help us, Lord, black an' white, to understan' each other more eve'y day. "

The prayer of this old colored man expresses, in a crude but effective fashion, the feeling and desires of the best Negroes and the best white people of the South. The sentiment of this prayer is becoming more and more universal, and it is actuating as never before the best thought and the highest aspirations of our South-ern people. This, then, is the first fundamental sign of growing co-operation in our South. One who is reasonably familiar with Southern conditions cannot but see on every hand unmistakable evidences that the two races are growing more and more to understand and sympathize with each other in the common life which they now lead and must of necessity continue to lead.

It is comparatively easy for a person to become discouraged regarding the situation, especially if he is governed by the reports which he sees in the average daily paper. There seems[S]

* An address delivered before the Negro Christian Student's Convention held in Atlanta, May 6-10, 1914

to be a popular desire, on the part of press dispatches, to emphasize the unsavory side of Negro life.

How often one sees in a paper—front page, first column—in glaring head-lines a report of some crime alleged to have been committed by a black man ; whereas, in the very same paper, on the last page, and often in a most insignificant place on that page with very modest head-lines, one finds a report of a white man charged with the same sort of crime ! If there is a misunderstanding between black and white people in any community, often in cases where there are less than a half-dozen in the disturbance, the papers will report a *race riot* and give the impression that practically all the Negroes and white people in the community are up in arms against each other.

This sort of propaganda, which has been indulged in for several decades and with increasing exaggeration, cannot but prejudice many people of both races against the Negro, and cause the casual observer to wonder if it is possible after all for the black and white races, whom God in His infinite wisdom and goodness has seen fit in His own way to place side by side in large numbers on Southern soil, to live helpfully and harmoniously together. But there is no real reason for discouragement. The apparent hostility is more or less superficial and far from the actual facts of the situation, for, on sober second thought, there comes to mind the rank and file of the Negro race—the law-abiding citizens who keep out of courts and out of the papers; the earnest, thoughtful, growing numbers who are working side by side with the best white people for the solution of the race problem.

INDUSTRIAL RELATIONS

Immediately after the war there was naturally a certain sort of paternal relation that existed between the white man and the Negro, but this was of rather a patronizing sort. This relationship exists even now to some extent, but it cannot long continue. There must come a different and more lasting, and, in the long run, a more wholesome relationship. The younger generations of the white and black races have now come on the stage of action. Their dealings are less cordial and less patronizing, they are more cold and businesslike. The Negro stands on his manhood. Few favors are asked except such as may be reduced to a dollars-and-cents basis.

There was developed during the days of slavery a spirit of suspicion on the part of the Negro against white people which the reconstruction period did not by any means lessen and which has hampered the Negro, perhaps, more than it has the white man. This the Negro is rapidly outliving and that is encouraging. Notwithstanding all that has been said against.

the Negro from the press and platform, the real situation was never more hopeful and encouraging than it is at present. Even the casual observer must see that there is growing a spirit of real co-operation and sympathy between the races, and that never before has there been a more earnest and sincere effort on the part of both races for mutual help and co-operation. There is a growing and genuinely honest disposition on the part of the Negro everywhere to seek the advice as well as the assistance and co-operation of white people in every movement for the common good of the Negroes. There is an increasingly strong feeling on the part of Negro laborers and mechanics for unity and co-operation with similar groups of white artisans, and the white unions are seeing more and more the necessity for a closer union of the various classes of skilled workers, and this feeling will continue to grow as men become better trained, better educated, and better Christians.

EDUCATIONAL CO-OPERATION

In educational matters there is a growing sympathy and spirit of co-operation between whites and blacks as never before. The Negro is calling on school officials for a fair and equitable distribution of school funds. He is asking for better schools, longer terms, better pay for teachers, and better equipment; in many cases the Negroes, out of their own earnings, are buying land for the school and often putting up the schoolhouses, sometimes supplementing the pay of the teacher, this generally being done with the advice and approval of the local school officials, who are making appropriations for school purposes with a liberality such as was never before witnessed.

Hampton Institute, through its principal, Dr. Frissell, and its trustees, notably the late Robert C. Ogden, and through the institutions that have grown out of Hampton, has done more than perhaps any other single institution in making possible the sort of co-operation that counts for most in the development of the two races here in the South. Hampton Institute has established a platform upon which Northern men, Southern men, black men, and white men can work together for the good of humanity and the glory of God. More phases of life, more creeds and colors are constantly meeting at Hampton for the discussion of vital questions and inspiration for greater work than in any other place, perhaps, in America.

Dr. Booker T. Washington has done more than any other single man to bring the colored people to realize the wisdom and absolute necessity of calling on the white people for advice and aid, and I need not say that the response in most cases has been most helpful and gratifying; and this attitude on the part of colored people has encouraged the white people to take more interest in what is going on among colored people in almost every line of endeavor.

We all know of the work of the Jeanes Board through which Dr. James H. Dillard has accomplished such splendid service for God and humanity; and we all know also of the work of the state supervisors of rural schools, of whom Mr. Jackson Davis was the pioneer. These two agencies are linking, not only the common rural schools in the communities in which they are at work, but are doing what is to me more important—they are linking the two races together on the ground of common brotherhood, common needs, and common sympathy, in the cities as well as in the country. Here is a great forward movement toward the co-operation of the races. In Savannah, for example, organizations like the National Negro Business League are co-operating with the white people for a greater and better city. The same is true in Nashville, as well as here in Atlanta and in other Southern cities.

DR. WASHINGTON'S TRIPS IN THE SOUTH

Dr. Washington, usually under the auspices of the National Negro Business League with other prominent colored men, has gone on what he calls "educational tours" through almost all of the Southern states, where thousands of people, white and black, have gathered. These thousands have received from the distinguished Negro leader frank, yet sane, advice as to the best methods of real co-operation and a more helpful relationship. These addresses have had as cordial a response from white as from black people. It would be difficult to estimate the value of such trips in cementing more cordial, sympathetic feeling between the two races in these states.

UNIVERSITY COMMISSION ON RACE QUESTIONS

The unstinted thanks of the Negroes of the South are due Dr. James H. Dillard who brought into being, at the right time, the University Commission on Race Questions, a commission composed of representatives of all the Southern state universities—men who, without sentiment, are getting at the real facts regarding the Negro, with a view to helping, not merely the Negro, but the South and the nation as well. The Negro is perfectly willing to be judged on his merits by unbiased men, especially when they have before them the actual facts.

SOCIOLOGICAL CONGRESS AT MEMPHIS

In Memphis there was held from May 6 to 10 what was in some ways the most remarkable gathering I have ever witnessed.

This was the third annual meeting of the Southern Sociological Congress. There came together a large body of Southern men representing all phases of Southern life, and an equally interesting and representative body of Negroes. These men expressed frankly, dispassionately, and in a kindly way their views on the race situation, offering sane, helpful suggestions as to adequate remedies therefor. Is it not a hopeful sign when black men and white men can thus counsel together on common problems?

CO-OPERATION AMONG WOMEN

Our Negro women have shown consummate wisdom and tact in securing the co-operation and help of the leading white women in their civic movements. The Women's Civic League of Baltimore, led by Mrs. S. C. Fernandis, and all of our Virginia movements, have been and are now headed by the most prominent and aristocratic white women. And here in Atlanta, Mrs. John Hope could not have accomplished what she has so successfully achieved had she not asked the help and co-operation of the white women of the city.

The fact that the Negroes are themselves becoming better organized and are willing to accept the advice and leadership of their own race for racial betterment and civic improvement makes it all the easier for the leaders of these organizations to throw the weight of their influence on the side of sane co-operation with the best element of our Southern white people. Few private schools are started in any community but that the Negroes always ask certain of the leading white people to become members of the board of trustees. If they do not wish to make them real trustees, which means owners of the property, they will devise some kind of an advisory board, so as to link white people to the movement and thus secure their advice and counsel, and finally their assistance and often their influence with the county school officials.

BUSINESS CO-OPERATION

There are in the South today about seventy Negro banks owned, controlled, and operated by Negroes, also numerous building and loan associations. In many of these banks the presidents or cashiers of the white banks have not only given advice to their Negro competitors as to the best methods of banking, but have opened up their first set of books and started them off, and in many places overlooked their methods and work until the Negro banks could get on their feet. Only recently a Negro bank in Richmond came near having a " run " on it because of some erroneous report that was circulated in the community to the effect that the bank was in trouble, and several of the leading white banking institutions, through their presidents, told the Negro bank to pay all claims promptly, and that they would furnish the necessary money if it did not have the available cash. These banks knew that the Negro bank was absolutely safe and solid and they had absolute faith in the honesty and integrity of its black president. In almost every community the Negro and white business men are on terms of harmony and co-operation, loaning and borrowing and crediting as if both were white or both were black. This spirit of business co-operation must and certainly will continue to grow.

CO-OPERATION FOR BETTER HEALTH

It is perhaps along lines of health and sanitation that one finds the heartiest co-operation between the white and colored people. The Negroes have seen the possibility of a stronger and a more appealing plea to the white people for help and co-operation along lines of sanitation and hygiene than perhaps along any other line of racial activity. It is quite as important for white people that the Negroes should be clean and healthful, physically, mentally, and morally, as it is for colored people, and white people see and understand this and are willing and glad to lend assistance and co-operation as perhaps in no other movement. Disease is common to all, and though germinated in the Negro cabin, is very apt to find its way to the white mansion. Disease, like vice and crime, knows no color line. As a result of the very important meeting recently held in the city of New Orleans to start a health campaign throughout the South, the white people are urging the Negroes to enter into this movement and have met with a very general response.

NEGRO ORGANIZATION SOCIETY

There grew out of the Hampton Negro Conference a movement which we have called the Negro Organization Society of Virginia. This movement has for its object the federation of all existing organizations in the state of Virginia of whatever kind or character, whether religious, benevolent, or secret societies, social or business conventions, farmers' conferences, or what not, for the common purpose of general improvement of conditions among Negroes throughout the Old Dominion. Its motto is, "Better Schools, Better Health, Better Homes, Better Farms" among colored people. The Negro Organization Society seems to have federated about all of these organizations, for never in the history of the race has any movement taken hold of the various phases of Negro activity as this movement has done; and though the movement is only about three years old, it has inspired the erection of some twenty-five graded schools in the state, to say nothing about improving the equipment and surroundings of two score more.

We have just closed what we call in Virginia a "clean-up week." A year ago we had a "clean-up day," but we made it a clean-up week this year for the reason that it was not convenient in many localities in the state, because of storms, etc., to clean up on the day appointed. We asked the State Board of Health, as well as the county boards, for their co-operation and help. We prepared a special bulletin giving instructions, in simple language that could be easily understood by colored people, as to the best methods of preserving their health, which we called the "Negro Health Handbook." The State Board of Health published, almost as we gave it to them, at no expense to the Organization Society, about thirty thousand of these books which were put into the hands of the school teachers and preachers as well as other Negro leaders throughout the state ; and special sermons and health talks and lectures were delivered throughout the state of Virginia. We asked the white people who employ colored people to excuse their employes and encourage them as far as possible to clean up their premises ; and while we have not the facts for the present year, we know that last year 130,000 people devoted the day to a general cleaning up of their premises, disposing of rubbish, whitewashing their houses, outhouses, and fences, and destroying breeding places for flies and mosquitoes. The most significant thing accomplished in this health movement is that we got absolutely the co-operation and the backing of the leading papers and leading white people of Virginia. The new "Handbook" has just been published and forty thousand copies distributed, with results even more far-reaching than a year ago.

Last November in Richmond, six thousand people gathered to hear the reports of the year's work of this Society. Something like a thousand of these were white and they represented the leading people of the city of Richmond and the state of Virginia. There were present and on the platform, the Governor of the State, the President of the Richmond Medical College, the Principal of Hampton Institute, and many leading Negroes, among them Mrs. Maggie L. Walker, and such men as Dr. Charles S. Morris and Dr. Booker T. Washington. Mrs. B. B. Munford, one of the leading white ladies of Virginia and president of the Virginia Co-operative Education Association, was asked to speak on the subject "What white people can do to help colored people." Mrs. Munford opened her address with these words:

"The best way," she said, "for white people to help colored people is for white people to believe in colored people." In my opinion the best way for colored people to help white people is for colored people to believe in white people.

It seems to me, then, that if we live up to the spirit of the colored minister whom I quoted in the beginning of my talk, and accept the equally sincere and earnest advice from Mrs. Munford, we will have a clue to the maze of race prejudice and race misunderstanding, and a key to the door of Christian co-operation and brotherhood, which is the spirit and purpose of this Negro Students' Christian Federation.

A SEVENTEENTH CENTURY COUNCIL

BY JOHN CARL PARISH

AT two o'clock in the afternoon of a late October day in the year 1678, there gathered at the Chateau St. Louis in the town of Quebec a score or more of men. They were men of weight and influence in the colony of new France, and they came not only from Quebec but from the village of Montreal, lying out on the edge of civilization farther up the river, and from various outposts and wilderness settlements.

They had come in accordance with an order of the King of France, issued to Governor Frontenac, and his council, and requiring them to assemble the principal men of the colony and get their advice upon the question of selling brandy and other liquors to the Indians.

The intrepid La Salle, close friend of the Governor, was there from Fort Frontenac, his frontier post at the east end of Lake Ontario. His canoe had already, on many a long trip, cut the waters of the Great Lakes and the Ohio River, and his mind was now often turning toward the mysterious river that ran down the valley beyond the Lakes—the great Mississippi at whose mouth he was to set up the arms of France four years later.

Louis Joliet was there and many were the tales he could tell to La Salle of the voyage he had made with Father Marquette on that memorable river five years before.

From Montreal there was Jacques Le Ber, probably the most influential merchant of that energetic town. He could tell to La Salle no great tales of adventure, for he stayed close to his own

counter and drove a thriving trade with Indians and whites.
And the time was to come when, in all of Canada, La Salle should
have no more bitter and persistent enemy than this same merchant.

The others in the assembly were men of similar mold—
knights and squires, merchants, aldermen, and soldiers of the
New World. The clerk read the order of the King, signed by
Louis and by his minister, Colbert, and to these colonial men of
affairs the vexing question was put : Should the sale of liquor
to the Indians, in the towns and in the woods, be allowed, or
should it be regarded as an evil politically and morally—a mortal
sin as the fathers of the Sorbonne had declared it three years
before—and barred from the colony ?

Then the twenty men took pen and paper and each one wrote
his private views on the subject. They were vigorous men and
they expressed themselves in positive terms.

"The trade in brandy is absolutely necessary, " wrote
Du Gué, "in order to draw the Indians into the French colonies
and prevent them from taking their furs to other nations. "

For the sake of the country's commerce and the livelihood of
the inhabitants, chimed in a dozen others, the selling of liquor
must be permitted ; otherwise all the trade in furs would go to
the English and Dutch on the Hudson River.

And then, having given this—the real reason for their favoring the liquor trade—they began to cast about for further points
to support their position. It was the priests who had been protesting most vigorously against the sale of brandy, and to combat the argument of these Catholic missionaries they turned
their pens to the religious phases of the question. If the trade
were not permitted, wrote one, the Indians would go to the English and Dutch, who, instead of giving them a knowledge of the
Gospel, would oblige them to fall into heresy or else leave them
in their own superstitions, and they would never come back to
the French. This wail was echoed by the Sieurs de Repentigny
and de Bécancourt, who pictured the poor Indian remaining in his
own idolatry or taking up the evil religion of those two Protestant nations.

Others contended that not only was the trade not a hindrance
to religion, but that it was really a help, since only by allowing
the Indian the same liberties as the white man could they draw
him into Christianity ; and one man ingeniously bolstered up this
argument by referring to the Ottawas, among whom liquor was
not used and with whom, impliedly for that reason, the progress
of Christianity had been small.

The Ottawas proved a convenient example also for those who
minimized the effect of the liquor sale upon the increase of crime.

Look at the Ottawas, they said—they do not use brandy, yet they commit daily all manner of crimes. Other advocates of the trade contented themselves by saying that the sale should be permitted, but that the Indians should be chastised when they were guilty of disorders caused either by drunkenness or otherwise.

Several of the men, among them La Salle, predicted war as a result of the prohibition of the liquor trade. The Indians, turning to the English and Dutch for their liquor and fur trade, would ally themselves with those nations and make war upon the French. One patriotic Frenchman gave as one of his reasons for continuing the sale the fact that the brandy of the Canadians was far superior to that of the Protestant nations toward the south.

The prevention of bootlegging was an argument continually used. If the trade were prohibited by order of the King, *coureurs de bois* and vagabonds would carry on an illegal and highly harmful trade in the distant camps of the Indians, doling out poor liquor and demanding high prices.

The arguments of La Salle are reported at greater length than any of the others. He firmly believed in the trade as necessary to both the peace and commerce of the country. His experience at Fort Frontenac made him greatly apprehend war if they refused the Indians a commodity of which they were so fond without having other means of attracting them and dissipating the feelings of hate with which they were inclined to look upon the whites.

He did not regard it as a moral question and considered that since it was a matter which concerned the commerce of the country so vitally, it was a question to be settled by the laymen and not by the priests. La Salle's well known antipathy to the Jesuits no doubt prompted this remark, and since he was so deeply engaged in the fur trade himself, it is not surprising that he should oppose any move which was likely to divert that trade to the markets of the English and Dutch.

He indulged in a little mathematics in connection with the beaver trade. The Canadian trade amounted to from 60,000 to 80,000 beavers per year, he said, and the Indians who purchased liquor were about 20,000 in number. The ordinary price of a beaver skin was a pint of brandy. He therefore drew the conclusion that if each of these Indians drank 'but once a year the returns in beaver would amount to a third or a fourth of the entire commerce. Thus the country would draw from this source alone 20,000 beavers and would be giving in exchange to each Indian a quantity of liquor that was not sufficient to intoxicate him more than once at most.

The assembly was not, however, unanimous in advocating freedom of trade in liquor. Louis Joliet expressed himself as believing that it was necessary to prohibit, on pain of death, the transportation of liquor into the woods, but that the sale to Indians by the habitants in their own houses and stores at the settlements was permissible, providing the trade was carried on with moderation and with every effort to avoid making the Indians drunk.

Jacques Le Ber—himself a merchant of Montreal and no doubt enjoying a profit from the trade in his own place of business—expressed much the same opinion as Joliet. He favored the sale of liquor to Indians at the settlement with due moderation, but would prohibit its transportation into the woods and to the lodges of the red men.

There were three men out of the twenty who opposed the Indian liquor trade both in the towns and in the Indian's country. There should be no such trade with the Indians at all, wrote Duplessis Gastineau, since it was the ruin of religion. Those who had formerly been assiduous at prayers and in their attendance upon religious rites now lived as atheists and committed all kinds of evil deeds. The trade put both Frenchmen and Indians in a state of damnation—the former because of the contempt which they made of the orders of the church, and the latter because they drank only to intoxicate themselves. The trade, moreover, was the ruin of commerce as well, because of the tendency of the Indians to run in debt for drink.

The Sieur d'Ombourg was equally emphatic. If the trade were prohibited, he said, one would see no disorders. The Indians would live in peace and no one would loiter about to secure their peltries for a little liquor. The French would apply themselves to the cultivation of the soil, which would cause the land to flourish. On the contrary, if the trade were permitted, the country, far from improving, would decline and God would be badly served.

He reiterated the contention of Gastineau that the Indians drank only to intoxicate themselves, and he enumerated in great detail the murders and other foul crimes which the Indians were wont to commit when drunk. It was a great sin, he contended, to give twenty sous of brandy in exchange for six or seven pounds of beaver skins. When the Indians had drunk they sold everything they had for more liquor and sometimes gave a gun in exchange for a half pint of brandy. They drank in such quantities that they died of the effects.

Such were the opinions of the men of Canada who had been assembled by order of the King. When the written statements were all collected, they were paraphrased and combined in a report for the benefit of the Court of France. Of the twenty men, fifteen had declared themselves in favor of the sale of liquor to the Indians without let or hindrance. Two—Joliet and Le Ber—were willing to compromise by prohibiting transportation to the Indian country but allowing it in town, and three were totally opposed to the trade.

It is not surprising that three-fourths of such an assembly should declare for the liquor trade. They were men who were concerned most vitally with the success of the colony from a commercial standpoint. If anything diverted the commerce in furs to other markets they were in many cases ruined. The question to them was a matter of self-interest, and the history of the world has shown few cases where the mass of the people would consider the moral aspects of a public issue when the results were subversive of their personal interests.

It might be said that the liquor question did not appeal to them in the light of a moral issue, since the Frenchmen themselves used liquor freely and could probably see little reason for barring the Indians from a like privilege. The force of this defense, however, is dulled by the fact that for more than a third of a century the missionaries among the tribes had been emphasizing the fact that the Indian did not use liquor in the same way and for the same purpose as the white man; that the red man for the most part desired drinks not because of their pleasant taste, but solely that they might reach thereby a state of intoxication.

In the *Jesuit Relations* of 1637, Father Paul Le Jeune wrote of the Indians' desire for brandy and wine "which they love with an utterly unrestrained passion, not for the relish they experience in drinking them, but for the pleasure they find in becoming drunk. They imagine in their drunkenness that they are listened to with attention, that they are great orators, and that they are valiant and formidable, that they are looked up to as Chiefs, hence this folly suits them; there is scarcely a Savage, small or great, even among the girls or women, who does not enjoy this intoxication, and who does not take. these beverages when they can be had, purely and simply for the sake of being drunk. Now as they drink without eating, and in great excess, I can easily believe that the maladies which are daily tending to exterminate them, may in part arise from that."

Dozens of others had given expression to the same idea, and the Indians themselves had, in several cases, asked that liquor should be kept away from them. But the interests of those engaged in commercial pursuits—and this class did not exclude Governor Frontenac himself—discounted these protests of the priests and their red-skinned parishioners, and the sale of brandy continued.

The Canadians clung jealously to the liquor trade in order to preserve the commerce in furs, and the tilling of the ground went largely by the board. And in the course of time the prediction of d'Ombourg that the country would decline found its justification. For the people who had sought to build a commercial empire in the New World were forced to give it all up to a nation which, more prosaically but more wisely, had set itself to the cultivation of the soil.

COLORED WOMEN OF CHICAGO

BY FANNIE BARRIER WILLIAMS

WHAT is the status and general improvement of the colored women of Chicago? Anything like statistics is out of the question. Whatever the general improvement of the condition of women in the city, it is shared alike by all women who are susceptible to progress.

To see colored women on the streets, in public assemblies, and in the everyday walks of life, they seem altogether prosperous and sufficient. If they feel the sting of race prejudice, they seem to be confident of their own worth and hopeful for better conditions.

One important evidence of progress is the enlargement and improvement of the home life of the Negro people. Ten or fifteen years ago they lived in districts of the city bordering on what may be called the "slums." Vices of all kinds menaced the morals and health conditions of their families. But it is now easy to discern a great improvement in this respect. Better economic conditions have enabled them to purchase and occupy residences on some of the finest avenues and boulevards of the city.

It scarcely need be stated that in reference to employment in the trades, shops, and stores, colored women are the least favored of any class of women in the city, yet it is impossible for them to be idle and respected. While only a few colored women are fortunate enough to gain positions in what are considered the higher callings, they are nevertheless industrious and increasingly willing to do whatever their hands find in order to earn a respectable living.

About fifty colored women have won positions as teachers in

our mixed public schools. There is also a surprising number of young women holding good positions as clerks and stenographers. One young woman through civil service examination secured an important position with the Board of Education in Chicago, and is now private secretary to the assistant superintendent of schools.

Young colored women may also be found acting as assistants in dental offices, as court stenographers, as demonstrators of special goods in large department stores, as meat inspectors at the stockyards, a few in canning and hair factories, a few as clerks, and scores of them earn a comfortable living as manicurists, chiropodists, and hair culturists in private families.

In addition to these there are a number of colored women who have their own millinery establishments, beauty shops, and dressmaking and costuming parlors that are elegantly appointed and up-to-date in every detail. There is also an increasing number of professional nurses, several of them holding positions as nurses in the public schools and members of the Visiting Nurses' Association. There are several colored women connected with the Juvenile Court acting as probation officers, and one adult probation officer. There are half a dozen colored women physicians, three dentists, and one practicing attorney. Eight or ten young colored women are employed in the Public Library. There is a large number of music teachers, both vocal and instrumental. As a further evidence of progress, young colored women are eagerly crowding the night schools of the city in order to equip themselves for business positions.

A class of women that cannot be ignored, in this story of the life of the colored women of Chicago, is the women who work with their hands in the humbler walks of life, as cooks, housecleaners, laundresses, caretakers, and domestics. One of the most interesting sights in our public streets in the early morning hours is the large army of colored women going in all directions to their day's work. These women deserve great credit for their eager willingness to aid their husbands in helping to provide a living for themselves and their families.

Another phase of the life of these colored women is their passion for organization. There are clubs for the study of civics, social clubs to promote the refinements of life, clubs for the care and protection of dependent children, religious organizations in the interest of churches, and a number of social settlements and secret societies.

The most important undertaking among colored women is the establishment of the Phyllis Wheatley Home. It was organized and incorporated some years ago, for the purpose of giving shelter and protection to the young colored women who wander into Chicago unacquainted with the snares and pitfalls of a great city. The Home is a comfortable brick building, simply furnished, and offers a home for young women until they have secured employment, and one to which they can appeal and find a welcome at any time. Mrs. L. A. Davis is the founder and promoter of this enterprise, and is president of a progressive club of colored women who look after and support this noble work.

A new and important responsibility has come to Chicago women in the franchise. It is believed that this power granted to the women of the state of Illinois is going to lift colored women to new importance as citizens. They appreciate what it means and are eagerly preparing themselves to do their whole duty. They believe that they now have an effective weapon with which to combat prejudice and discrimination of all kinds. There need be no anxiety as to the conduct of these newly made colored citizens. They have had a large and varied experience in organizations and we expect to see in them an exhibition of the best there is in the colored race.

This splendid extension of the Fourteenth and Fifteenth Amendments will make many things possible and open many avenues of progress that have heretofore been closed to colored women. It is the hope of the leaders of the race that these new citizens will cultivate whatever is best in heart and mind that will enable them to meet the common tasks of life, as well as the higher responsibilities, with confidence and hope.

THE STORY OF KWAATTEE, GOD OF THE QUILLAYUTE INDIANS

BY ALBERT B. REAGAN

SAID the chief medicine man : "Kwaattee was the creator god ; but after the creation he set about changing things to make the world better. He also destroyed the evil monsters of the earth and water, and placed man on the footing on which he is now.

"Once, while he was walking up and down the earth, he learned that a certain tribe of Indians had captured the Sun and had it hid in a box, and that they only allowed so much of it to shine as just lighted their own territory and only as they needed it ; all the other peoples of the earth were in darkness. So Kwaattee went to secure the Sun for all peoples. He wandered into the village of the people who had the Sun, as though he were a lost slave of some other tribe. He was captured and set to work. At first they were very cautious with him lest he should run away. But finally they began to trust him with many things. Once they had a feast. So all went out, all the slaves, to get wood. But Kwaattee pulled up a great area of the forest by the roots and dragged it into the camp. In one move he had secured wood enough to last them for years. From that time on Kwaattee was practically a free man.

"Soon after the big feast, the people with whom Kwaattee was staying decided to go clam digging. Clams are dug out of the sand at low tide and a sharpened stick is usually used in this digging. Kwaattee went with them. He had been waiting for this. They took the Sun with them in the box. It was placed in the front end of the canoe. As they needed the light they opened up the lid a little ; then shut it up when they no longer needed it. They landed and went to digging the clams and carrying them to the canoe in baskets. Kwaattee caused a number of clams to be found at quite a distance from the canoe. A great rush was made for these clams, as the turn of the tide would soon cover them. Kwaattee was carrying clams. At the opportune moment, when all were going for clams but himself (he was returning with a basketful of them), he shoved the canoe out into the waves and before he was noticed he was out of swimming distance. He then hallooed back and asked them if they

wanted some Sun. They shot at him and ran to get other canoes
and follow him, but he paddled on and on and finally landed. He
then took the Sun out of the box and with a big toss hurled
it in the sky where you see it every day.

"In that far-off time there were giant wolves. Kwaattee
had a fight with them. Kwaattee had a basket of combs suspended at his back. He killed Chief Wolf. He was then
attacked by the whole wolf tribe. He had skinned Chief Wolf,
but before he could don the skin, the wolves, the whole pack,
were upon him. Out of his wigwam he went and down the ocean
beach from Cape Flattery along the west coast he ran. As the
wolves would overtake him, he would stick a toothed comb in the
ground between him and them, and on he would run. This
comb they would climb over and on they would come, and again
he would put down another comb. This was kept up till the
wolves, tiring, gave up the chase. Later Kwaattee came back
wearing Chief Wolf's skin for a cloak and the wolves dared not
attack him. The combs that Kwaattee placed are now the ridges
and promontories of the west coast of the Olympic Peninsula; the
larger combs extend far out into the breaking waves.

"Kwaattee once got married. While on his honeymoon,
he was attacked by a band of Indians. As Kwaattee had
departed his wife's home, his father-in-law had given him some
tallow and told him it would be of help to him on his journey.
Onward came the enemy to attack Kwaattee and his wife in
their canoe, to capture them and the white shining tallow. The
foremost canoe was within bow-shot; but no resistance was
offered. The man at the helm of the attacking canoe prepared
to leap into Kwaattee's canoe to take possession of it. Its
capture was sure; there was only a weaponless man and a
helpless woman in it, while in his canoe alone there were twenty
warriors. With a shout he leaped into the air to seize the prize.
Kwaattee simply raised his hand. Quicker than the flapping of
the thunderbird's wings the leaping man sank to the bottom of
the sea, a stone, and his companions instantly followed him.
Other canoes rushed to the attack, only to meet the same fate.
At last only two attacking canoes were left, and these, panic-
stricken, dashed for the shore and their inmates took refuge in
every possible hiding place they could find in the village. But
that did not save them. From every side and down every street
of the village Kwaattee hurled tallow over every house. At once
everything in the village turned to white stone. It is now the
rocky point on the coast six miles north of the Quillayute River.

"At this time the representative of evil was a giantess
named Duskia. She was the opposite of good. She even went
about the earth devouring little children. Kwaattee thought to

destroy her. He went to where she was digging wild onions on Quillayute Prairie. He had dressed himself up so that he appeared to be a stranger. He offered to help her carry her onions. He took two of her baskets, one of which he suspended in front of him and the other at his back by bands placed across the front and back parts of his head and over his shoulders. As soon as he got out of Duskia's reach he began to eat the onions, grabbing whole handfuls at a time and putting them into his now big mouth. Duskia ran after him but he just kept out of her way and ate till he had emptied the baskets. These he threw at her. She then recognized him and in anger ran after him to kill him. But he eluded her. Once she got so near that she reached for him, and he changed himself into a tiny bird and flew away. (You know Kwaattee was a god and could do anything.) As soon as he was at a safe distance, he changed himself back into his natural form and again the chase was on. Then he changed himself into a cricket and got away from her. Then after another chase he suddenly changed himself into a tiny fish in a little brook, and Duskia, coming to the brook and being thirsty from running, drank, and in doing so swallowed the little fish. Instantly Kwaattee changed his form into a monster whale and Duskia died of heart disease.

"In the Cape Flattery district there was a monstrous sea fish called Sumbus. This was the devourer of everything that came to the sea. Fishing in that part had to be abandoned. People who went out to fish never came back. So the people prayed Kwaattee to rid the sea of the monster. So Kwaattee went. He got a big whaling canoe, and having prepared many sacks of sharpened clamshell knives and some obsidian instruments, also lots of bait, he went out to the halibut banks and went to fishing. He had got his canoe almost filled with fish when Sumbus attacked him. The monster rushed at him with open mouth, and its mouth was so terribly, awfully big that Kwaattee and his canoe rushed down the monster's throat like a boat down the rapids in a stream. Once inside, Kwaattee stood his canoe on end in the great stomach, climbed up its rounds, and began cutting at the heart strings of the pounding heart. As it would beat and bring itself towards him he would strike it with his clamshell knives. One sack full of knives was used up with no effect; another, and another, till all were used. Then Kwaattee took his obsidian knife. With this he struck one terrible blow. One heart string was severed, then another. The beast was felt to plunge upward, then downward, in awful agony. Kwaattee gave another cut, a raking cut, and the big heart rolled down the great cavity. There was one terrible shaking and jerking of the beast, then all became quiet and the great hulk floated dead on the surface. On for days the beast floated. Kwaattee was inside and could not get out. At last the carcass floated ashore near Quillayute and the natives at once went out and began to cut it up for its blubber. As one man was removing the meat he cut into the inner cavity, and at once Kwaattee hallooed and asked them to cut a large hole so he could get out. This was done. Kwaattee at once crawled out, but he was bald, as the juices in the beast's stomach had taken all the hair off his head. But he went to a neighboring stream and washed his head and soon came back with hair reaching almost to the ground. As he was approaching, the people all shouted : 'That's Kwaattee, our god !'

"Kwaattee then journeyed on down the beach southward. Coming to Quinault Lake he saw one of his brothers swallowed by a monster that then occupied the lake. His brother had been out in a canoe and the beast swallowed him, canoe and all. So Kwaattee heated all the big rocks in the vicinity, and with a pair of tongs he hurled them into the lake, and when the water was heated boiling hot, the monster floated dead on the surface of the lake. So Kwaattee cut up the beast and saved his brother, but he wished a moment afterward he had not done so, for his brother changed his form into that of a hermit crab, the father of all the hermit crabs of our day. Disgusted, Kwaattee hurled the pair of tongs into the sea, open and up. You can see them today. They are the 'split rocks' near Tahola, Washington.

"After Kwaattee had traveled about the world much and had decided that he could make no more changes for its betterment, he climbed upon a rock overlooking the Pacific and there, as he looked at the gleaming, glittering rays of the setting sun shining back over the mirrored waters, he pulled his blanket up over his face, and as the sun went to his home in the west he turned to stone. You can see him sitting near Point Grenville, [Washington] at any time you go down the coast. His spirit has gone to the happy world in the direction he is facing."

GEORGE MOSES HORTON:
SLAVE POET

BY STEPHEN B. WEEKS

"Honor and shame from no condition rise ;
Act well your part, there all the honor lies. "

THUS wrote Alexander Pope, and his lines had a unique fulfillment in the life of George Moses Horton, a slave of
Chatham County, N. C., who has been recently characterized by
a modern North Carolina scholar as "a slave who owned his
master ; a poet ignorant of the rules of prosody ; a man of letters
before he had learned to read ; a writer of short stories who published in several papers simultaneously before the day of newspaper syndicates ; an author who supported himself and his family in an intellectual center before authorship had attained the
dignity of a profession in America. "

The documentary evidence on the life of George Moses
Horton is small and the traditional accounts are more or less
conflicting, but it is believed that the following is substantially
correct. According to the preface to "The Hope of Liberty"
George was born a slave in 1797. Professor George S. Wills, a
careful and enthusiastic scholar who has gone into the matter of
George's history at some length, says that George was born the
slave of Mr. William Horton on Roanoke River in Northampton
County, N. C.; that when he was about six years old his master
removed to Chatham County, N. C., where he died in 1815.
George then came into the possession of Mr. James Horton, son
of William, with whom he remained until his death in 1832. It
was necessary to sell Mr. Horton's property to settle his estate
and George was bought by Mr. Hall Horton, son of James. This
third owner is said to have been a hard master, but he allowed
George to go to Chapel Hill, the seat of the University in the
adjoining county of Orange, and later permitted him to hire his
time at twenty-five, or, as others say, at fifty cents per day.*

. George is described by the old people around Chapel Hill who
knew him as a full-blooded Negro who boasted of the purity of
his black blood. He was of the type known today as negroid ;
was more Aryan than Semitic in features, and more like the
natives of India and North America than those of the Sahara.

On the other hand Negroes who knew him in Philadelphia report that he was of mixed blood.

As a slave George was usually employed on the farm, but besides some personal service to his master it is said that his main occupations in winter were hunting and fishing, and in summer attending protracted meetings, or, as they were then called, camp meetings. Like all of his race George was fond of melody and these meetings gave him an opportunity to cultivate his budding poetic temperament. At these services, like Cædmon, the earliest of the English poets, he became familiar with the Bible story by hearing it read. He also made completely his own the melodies and the words of the Methodist hymnal then in use. The melodies were in his heart and the forms of the corresponding words became fixed in his brain. These furnished him the first elements of a literary education. He begged a blue-backed spelling book from somewhere and from this learned his letters. After learning the letters he learned to spell by matching the words in his hymnal which he already knew by sight and by heart with the words in the spelling book—a practical evolution of the word-method by a man who was innocent of pedagogy. In this way he learned to read the Bible. From that he learned grammar and prosody and above all acquired a simple, straightforward style and wrote good idiomatic English. It is said also that he became quite a voracious reader of books that were loaned him by Dr. Caldwell and other friends at the University. There is even a legend that James K. Polk, of the class of 1818, first started him in the art of writing, and that this was perfected by Professor Manuel Fetter ; that Mrs. Caroline Lee Hentz, novelist and poet and wife of Professor Nicholas M. Hentz, gave him instruction in versification and corrected his work. It seems to be certain that he was ambitious to learn, with a good memory and power of imitation, and that he was fond of the poetry of Byron and Moore.

He published his first poems in 1829. The volume was issued by Joseph Gales and Son and was entitled "The Hope of Liberty." The preface, dated at Raleigh, July 2, 1829, was probably written by Mr. Weston R. Gale, the junior member of the publishing firm, and may be taken as the final authority in the matters of his life so far as it goes. It says :

"George, who is the author of the following poetical effusions, is a slave, the property of Mr. James Horton, of Chatham County, North Carolina. He has been in the habit, for some years past, of producing poetical pieces, sometimes on suggested subjects, to such persons as would write them while he dictated. Several compositions of his have already appeared in the Raleigh *Register*. Some have made their way into the Boston newspapers and have evoked expressions of approbation and surprise. Many persons, some of whom are elevated in office and literary attainments, have now become interested in the promotion of his prospects. They are solicitious that efforts at length be made to obtain by subscription a sum sufficient for his emancipation, upon the condition of his going in the vessel which shall first afterwards sail for Liberia. ''

The author of the preface then continues : ''To put to trial the plan here urged in his behalf, the paper now exhibited is published. Several of his productions are contained in the succeeding pages. Many more might have been added, which would have swelled it to a larger size. They would doubtless be interesting to many, but it is hoped that the specimens here inserted will be sufficient to accomplish the object of the publication . . . . . It is proposed, that in every town or vicinity where contributions are made, they may be put into the hands of some person who will humanely consent to receive them. . . . . As soon as it is ascertained that the collections will accomplish their object, it is expected that they will be transmitted without delay to Mr. Weston R. Gales.

''None will imagine that pieces produced as these have been should be free from blemish in composition and taste. The author is thirty-two years old and has always labored in the field on his master's farm, promiscuously with the few others whom Mr. Horton owns, in circumstances of the greatest possible simplicity. His master says he knew nothing of his poetry, but as he heard of it from others. George knows how to read and is now learning to write. All his pieces are written down by others ; and his reading, which is done at night and at the usual intervals allowed to slaves, has been much employed on poetry, such as he could procure, this being the species of composition most interesting to him. It is thought best to print his productions without corrections, that the mind of the reader may be in no uncertainty as to the originality and genuineness of every part. We shall conclude this account of George with an assurance that he has been ever a faithful, honest, and industrious slave. That his heart has felt deeply and sensitively . . . . is impressively confirmed by one of his stanzas :

> Come, melting Pity, from afar,
> And break this vast, enormous bar
> Between a wretch and thee ;
> Purchase a few short days of time,
> And bid a vassal soar sublime,
> On wings of Liberty.

It is of interest to call attention to the title of this little pamphlet for the important light it throws upon the condition of slaves in North Carolina at the date of its publication. It is usually said that all higher aspiration in the slave was crushed and that those individuals who were intelligent enough to desire freedom were ruthlessly suppressed, but in North Carolina Horton was not only allowed to express his feelings privately on the subject, but even to print and openly publish his desires, and in doing this he was aided and abetted by some of the best men in the state. Not only was Horton allowed to do this in 1829, but he continued to enjoy the same liberty after the enactment of the harder laws that were passed as a result of the Nat Turner insurrection of 1831.

The persons who were interested along with Dr. Caldwell and Mr. Gales in the purchase and manumission of Horton are said to have been Governor Owen and a Dr. Henderson, probably Dr. Pleasant Henderson of Chapel Hill. The matter of manumission was laid before his master, but the valuation placed on the slave poet was so great that the project was necessarily abandoned. It is probable that these gentlemen were in his mind when George wrote his "Lines on hearing of the intention of a gentleman to purchase the poet's freedom : "

> Some philanthropic souls as from afar,
>   With pity strove to break the slavish bar ;
> To whom my floods of gratitude shall roll,
>   And yield with pleasure to their soft control.

Although the plan for manumission failed, it is more than probable that it was as a result of this discussion that George was allowed to leave the farm and go to Chapel Hill about 1834 for, notwithstanding the printed recommendation in the preface to "The Hope of Liberty," it was currently reported that, George was worthless as a farm hand, since his Pegasus resolutely refused to be harnessed to a plow. In and about Chapel Hill George spent most of his time for the next thirty years, waiting in the University itself, or on the students individually, or serving in the hotel kept by Miss Nancy Hilliard, and in this university town, the center of literary life and learning for the state, George's gift for versification secured him ready employment and produced for him considerable revenue.

During this University period of his literary career, George's work consisted mainly in writing, to supply orders from members of the student body, acrostics on ladies' names, and in the composition of love songs and amorous verses for ladies' albums. His scale of prices was modest enough : twenty-five cents for an ordinary effort and fifty cents when an extra amount of warmth and passion was demanded. The following specimen on "Love "is one of his earlier efforts and was dictated before he had learned

to write, but it is of the type of those poems by which he earned
his fame and money at the University:

> Whilst tracing thy visage, I sink in emotion,
>   For no other damsel so wond'rous I see;
> Thy looks are so pleasing, thy charms so amazing,
>   I think of no other, my true-love, but thee.
>
> With heart-burning rapture I gaze on thy beauty,
>   And fly like a bird to the boughs of a tree;
> Thy looks are so pleasing, thy charms so amazing,
>   I fancy no other, my true-love, but thee.
>
> Thus oft in the valley I think, and I wonder
>   Why cannot a maid with her lover agree?
> Thy looks are so pleasing, thy charms so amazing,
>   I pine for no other, my true-love, but thee.
>
> I'd fly from thy frowns with a heart full of sorrow—
>   Return, pretty damsel, and smile thou on me;
> By every endeavor, I'll try thee forever,
>   And languish until I am fancied by thee.

The fortunes of the poet seem to have declined after the
death of Dr. Caldwell, his patron, in 1838. The publication of
"The Hope of Liberty" had not been a financial success and the
idea of purchasing his freedom and going to Liberia was
abandoned. He remained in and about Chapel Hill, but all the
savings that he had accumulated for the Liberian voyage now
went for drink, as did all that he could earn or beg. A favorite
scheme to raise money was to write verses setting forth the sickness and distress of his family, and close with an appeal to the
students to "lend a helping hand to the old, unfortunate bard."
This he would take from room to room and read to the students,
and these patrons of literature usually responded liberally. Dr.
Battle tells us in his "History of the University of North Carolina," from which some of these facts are drawn, that George's
manner was courteous and his moral character good.

In the meantime the fame of George's poetry had reached
as far as Warrenton, N. C., where Miss Cheney, of Connecticut,
who afterwards married Horace Greeley, was teaching school.
Through her influence Greeley became interested in the poet, who
addressed to him the following, "Poet's Petition," which
appeared in the *Tribune*:

> Bewailing mid the ruthless wave
>   I lift my feeble hand to thee;
> Let me no longer be a slave,
>   But drop the fetters and be free.
>
> Why will regardless Fortune sleep
>   Deaf to my penitential prayer,
> Or leave the struggling bard to weep,
>   Alas, and languish in despair?

He is an eagle void of wings,
        Aspiring to the mountain height,
Yet in the vale aloud he sings
        For Pity's aid to give him flight.
Then listen, all who never felt
        For fettered genius heretofore,
Let hearts of petrifaction melt,
        And bid the gifted Negro soar.

George remained in and around Chapel Hill till the end of
the civil war. In 1865 he accompanied a U. S. cavalry officer,
presumably Captain Will H. S. Banks, to Philadelphia. He was
there in 1866, for the following extract from the published minutes of the Banneker Institute is furnished me by Mr. Daniel
Murray of the Library of Congress, along with much other material on the career of the poet, as follows: "A special meeting of
the institution was held on the evening of August 31, 1866, the
object being to receive Mr. George Horton of North Carolina, a
poet of considerable genius, it was claimed. The feasibility of
publishing his book was submitted to Mr. John H. Smythe, but
found too expensive."

Professor Collier Cobb, of the University of North Carolina,
is authority for the further statement that after going to Philadelphia Horton wrote a number of poems in imitation of the
"Passionate   Shepherd   to   his   Love"   of   Marlowe   and
"The Nymph's Reply" of Sir Walter Raleigh. He developed
also while living there some talent as a story teller. Like Cædmon
again his prose tales were based on the stories he had learned
from the Bible in earlier days. This was always the source of his
inspiration. It furnished him the themes and he decked them
out in modern garb in such a way as to suit the immediate
demands of the occasion. Professor Cobb also points out the
curious facts that little of Horton's poetic work was done before
he was forty ; that the most productive period of his life began
when he was sixty-seven and extended to his death, which is
believed in North Carolina to have occurred about 1883. Others
place it about 1880.

Horton was about five feet, eight inches in height, of medium
build, quick in his movements, of pleasing address, and popular
with the students whom he served. He married a slave of
Mr. Franklin Snipes and had two children, a son who was
known as Free Snipes, and a daughter Rhody who married
Van Buren Byrum. The son died in Durham, N. C., in 1896.
The daughter was still living in Raleigh, N. C., in 1897.

A second edition of "The Hope of Liberty" was published
by L. C. G. in Philadelphia in 1837 under the title "Poems by a
Slave." A third edition appeared in Boston in 1838 as a supplement to the "Memoir and Poems of Phillis Wheatley." Both of

these editions were issued as a part of the anti-slavery propaganda and add nothing to our knowledge of the poet.

In 1845 there was published a volume of his miscellaneous poems. It was issued at Hillsboro by Dennis Heartt, editor of the Hillsboro *Recorder*. No copy has been seen.

Other editions of his poems are said to have been issued in 1850 and 1854. It is possible that such was the case and that they were published through the interest of his student friends in the University of North Carolina, but no copies have been seen. It is also said that a small duodecimo volume of his Poems was published in Boston early in the fifties, with his autobiography, but this is possibly a mistaken reference to the edition of 1838. It is also said that short stories and essays were published by him about this time, but I have seen none of them.

There is an interesting reference to Horton in a letter dated at Chapel Hill, N. C., February 27, 1843, addressed to the *Southern Literary Messenger* and signed "G."—possibly Professor William Mercer Green. The letter says :

"Mr. Editor :

"A volume of manuscript poems was lately placed in my hands by their author, George Horton, a Negro belonging to a respectable farmer residing a few miles from Chapel Hill, from which I extract the following : [here a sample was inserted.] I have no doubt but that they will prove interesting to the readers of the *Messenger*. Should they meet with a suitable reception, I will continue them for several numbers, together with some sketches of the life, genius, and writings of their author." It does not appear that this offer was accepted.

The last known edition of his poems contains the following :

"Naked Genius by George Moses Horton. The Colored Bard of North Carolina. Author of 'The Black Poet,' a work being now compiled and revised by Captain Will. H. S. Banks, 9th Michigan Cavalry Volunteers, and which will be ready for publication about the 1st of October, 1865. This work will contain a concise history of the life of the author, written by the compiler, and will be offered to the public as one of the many proofs that God in his infinite wisdom and mercy created the black man for a higher purpose than to toil his life away under the galling yoke of slavery. Revised and compiled by Will. H. S. Banks, Captain 9th Mich. Cav., Wm. B. Smith & Co., Southern Field and Fireside Book Publishing House, Raleigh, N. C., 1865."

The accuracy of the above title is not vouched for, but the book was a duodecimo of 100 pages and there is said to be a copy in the library of the Boston Athenæum. It was the last contribution of the slave poet to the literature of his native state.

Book Reviews

In Red Man's Land: By Hon. Francis E. Leupp, former Commissioner of Indian Affairs. Issued under the direction of the Council of Women for Home Missions, by the Fleming H. Revell Company. Price, 50 cents *net*.

THE author's many years of service for and among the Indians fit him to speak with accuracy concerning them. Under such headings as The Aboriginal Red man, The Red Man and the Government, The Red Man and His White Neighbor, The Red Man and Our Social Order, Aborigines Who Are Not Red Men, and The Red Man as Teacher and Learner, Mr. Leupp tells much that is interesting, instructive, and valuable, not only to the worker among Indians but to the public at large.

The Red Man and Our Social Order will be found a particularly interesting chapter, dealing with various phases of the Indian's culture and the difficulties encountered in leading him to accept a standard so many times diametrically opposed to all he has been trained to consider as right and proper.

The closing paragraph sums up the author's purpose far better than any description of the book. He says, "My aim has been to show what difficulties confront us in our effort to lead, not the well-qualified few, but the great ignorant mass of the dwellers in Red Man's Land, from their ancient to our modern environment, from the age of stone into the age of steel, out of the shadows of a barbarism swarming with myths and mysteries into the sunlight of a culture rooted in eternal truth."

A supplementary chapter on Indian missions, by Dr. A. F. Beard, will make the book valuable to the Mission Study Classes now so popular. C. W. A.

The American Indian on the New Trail: By Dr. Thomas C. Moffett. Published by the Missionary Education Movement of the United States and Canada. Price, 60 cents.

FOR a number of years Dr. Moffett has been in charge of the mission work done among Indians by the Presbyterian church. He has spent much time on the reservations, and knows very thoroughly the conditions of the people about whom he writes. He deals first with his impressions of Indian characteristics and primitive religion, and then gives a resumé of some phases of their history and the Government's policies, thus bringing the reader to a consideration of many questions which have arisen during the progress from the old life to the new.

"The Red Man of the United States and the Christian Gospel" is the sub-title of the book. As this suggests, its main purpose is to acquaint the public with the Christian work that has been done for these people from the time of John Eliot to the present day, when over 31,000 Indians are known to be communicants of Protestant churches. The work among different tribes by the various denominations is reviewed with considerable detail, but results are summarized in the words: "When the Indians were without Christ it needed a standing army to control them. . . . The old restlessness is passing; they are settling down on allotted land and building homes. For years military force tried to subdue these people in vain. Nothing but the religion of Jesus Christ could have brought about the changes now evident."

As a contrast to this picture it is disheartening to learn that seventy-eight tribes and bands still need Christian missions, and that, according to figures gathered by Government officials, 177,000 Indians in the United States and Canada are non-Christian. "The anomaly exists today of one-half of the native American race unclaimed by any Christian church and thousands still in unrelieved paganism, without a missionary or the first instruction in the faith. What missionary appeal takes precedence of this? What duty and obligation rests more insistently upon the Church of Christ in America?"

Dr. Moffett has brought together a great deal of information which is presented in a most interesting way. The book is well indexed, and with its maps and statistical appendixes will be found most helpful as a reference work.   C. W. A.

Correction: "Bookbinding for Beginners" by Florence C. Bean, reviewed in the August number of the Southern Workman, is published by The School Arts Publishing Company, 120 Boylston Street, Boston, instead of by the Manual Arts Press, Peoria, Ill., as stated.

At Home and Afield

HAMPTON INCIDENTS

ENTERTAINMENTS

ON Saturday evening, August 1, the Douglass Literary Society held a recitation contest, in which two prizes, both books, were given for the two recitations most effectively delivered. The judges awarded the first prize to Augustus N. Brown, who spoke "Marco Bozzaris" by Halleck, and the second to Frank B. White for his delivery of Scott's "Lochinvar."

The present European war, its causes, the participating nations, and the possible results form the chief topic of discussion everywhere. The Hampton summer audience of students and workers were glad of the opportunity to hear a talk on these subjects by Major Moton in Cleveland Hall Chapel on the evening of August 21, and to see stereopticon pictures of European rulers and of cities and towns in the war zone.

On Saturday evening, August 22, the Dunbar Literary Society presented George W. McCorkle in recital in Clarke Hall auditorium. Ten of Dunbar's poems and one of the reader's own, with music by the Dunbar orchestra, made up the program. The poems were given with a very sympathetic interpretation and an irresistible humor which delighted the audience.

ATHLETICS

FROM June 8 to August 15, the three baseball teams which compose the Hampton Institute League—the Y. M. C. A. team, the Cubs, and the Giants—waged battle four days a week for the championship of the school diamond. The teams were well matched and the games, particularly toward the last, were very close, the scores being 2-0, 2-1, etc. The last game was played on August 15, leaving the Y. M. C. A. team the champions for the season with a score of 16 games won and 11 lost. The Cubs won 13 games and lost 16, while the Giants stood third with 11 games won and 16 lost. The victory of the Y. M. C. A. team entitles them to a pennant bearing the year and the name of the team.

THE "HAMPTON'S" RETURN

ON Saturday morning, September 5, the good ship "Hampton" sailed into the creek, bringing home from their three months' campaign in the North the boys who gave their time and energies this summer to the task of securing funds for the school. Hard work has agreed with them, to judge from their appearance, and has certainly not impaired their good spirits. On Sunday night at the chapel exercises, the chorus sang some of the songs they had used on the campaign, and Captain Washington gave a brief sketch of the trip as a whole. He spoke particularly of the good spirit shown by the boys, of the feeling of comradeship which had grown up between them, and of how they had learned to appreciate each other's good qualities.

Captain Washington said that the meetings had been well attended and by enthusiastic audiences. Everywhere they went they were most cordially received and, in his estimation, the campaign was the most successful one that has ever been made.

SHAKESPEARE PRIZE DEBATE

FOR several years the Douglass and Dunbar Literary Societies have held a debate in September. This has been variously known as the Blount Prize Debate and the Eureka Prize Debate, but is now to be permanently called the Shakespeare Prize Debate, being given under the auspices of the Shakespeare Dramatic Club, which also gives the prizes.

This year the subject for debate was: "*Resolved*, that the Federal Government should control public utilities." The decision rendered by the judges was in favor of the Dunbar Society, making the fourth year they have won the debate. In giving the decision, the judges praised both sides for their delivery and clearness of argument.

While the judges were consulting, Mr. B. Franklin Jones, a graduate, spoke to the students of the value of debating, especially as good training for public speaking. The prizes awarded were medals.

SENIOR TRADE CLASS PICNIC

ON Labor Day, September 7, fifty-ty-two members of the Senior Trade Class held their annual picnic. This year they went in the sail and power boat, *Wild Duck*, to Gloucester County, leaving the school early in the morning. The people of Gloucester gave them a royal welcome and entertained them with an outdoor picnic feast which was lacking in neither quantity nor quality. The class band played with enthusiasm, and the boys sang several plantation songs for their entertainers. They arrived home late that night after a most enjoyable day.

HAMPTON WORKERS

THE work of the school Y. M. C. A. for the coming year will be in charge of Solomon D. Spady, who was graduated from Hampton in June.

Mr. Barton White, for many years instructor in gardening at the school,

has taken a position at the A. and M. College in Greensboro, N. C. His work is being done at present by Fredrick A. Goings, who took the short course in agriculture last year.

THE fate of Americans in Europe during the past few weeks has been the subject of much anxious interest everywhere. It is a relief to know that the various Hampton workers who spent their summer abroad are now safe in this country. Hiss Harding arrived on August 30 after a trying passage on the *Espagne*. Mrs. Purves, Miss Ruth Purves, and Mr. Ogden Purves, and Miss J. E. Davis came on the *Rotterdam* arriving on September 6. Miss Ethel Shaw reached New York on the *Kroonland* on Sunday, September 13. They will probably have interesting tales to tell of their experiences in the war zone.

HAMPTON WEDDINGS

THE wedding of Miss Amelia Cooke and Mr. Alfred Gilbert took place on August 15 at Miss Cooke's home in Montville, Conn. They will live at Shellbanks, where Mr. Gilbert is the manager of the farm.

Mr. Elmo Christy was married on August 19 to Miss Millie Tierce at her home in Glenoia, Ontario.

At Magnolia, Mass., on September 19, occurred the marriage of Mr. J. L. Blair Buck to Miss Dorothea Dutcher of Milwaukee, Wis. They are expected at Hampton the first of October.

On Saturday, September 12, Mr. William V. Betts, the youngest son of Mr. and Mrs. C. W. Betts, was married to Miss Bessie Ashby Cannon of Charlottesville, Va.

A marriage of interest to Hamptonians was that of Miss Ellen Young, assistant librarian and a graduate of the class of '95, to Mr. Thomas C. Walker of Gloucester, Va., which took place on September 19 at Miss

Young's home in Hampton. They will live at Gloucester, Virginia, in the county which owes much of its progress to the untiring efforts of Mr. Walker.

Mr. Thomas Howard was married on Wednesday, September 16, to Miss Beulah S. Wilder of Baltimore, Md., a graduate of '99·

GRADUATES AND EX-STUDENTS

A minister who is also a farmer and is doing much to help his people get homes of their own, Rev. Geo. D. Wharton, '80· writes of a land company he has formed :

"Did I tell you that I had organized a company to be known as the 'Home Realty Company' which has a maximum capital of $25,000 and a paid-up capital of $1000? The company has a charter and has bought since January [April 1914] $12,000 worth of real estate. We are going to cut this up in small farms to sell to thrifty farmers of our race. We hope to help many of our people to get homes in this way. One man, who is a stockholder, has contracted for 50 acres and another one for 31 acres. They each made a cash payment, one of $100 and the other $125.

"I sold one man 75 acres of land, planned and had built for him a beautiful home, and allow him to pay for it on easy terms. He is doing well with his payments. He farms with me and received last year $1000 as his part of the crop. He will soon be free of debt. "

A GRADUATE of '09· Paul V. Smith, has had charge of the manual training in the colored public schools of Roanoke ever since his graduation, and in addition to that has been appointed principal of the Gregory graded school in that city. He wrote in March of his work :

"I have my hands full with an enrollment of over five hundred pupils and eleven teachers. I have from the introductory grade through the sixth grammar grade—seven grades—the eighth grade being in the other school. Three classes a day come to me from the seventh and eighth grades for manual training work. They receive an hour and a quarter's training. Last month my boys filled an order for four dozen chairs for introductory pupils. The chairs were 24 inches high at the back, 12 inches across seat, and 12 inches deep. They were caned on the bottoms with a herring-bone weave, and the backs were caned with a porch weave. Most of the chairs were put into the white schools. The furniture in my office was made in the manual training classes, and consists of a library bookcase with cupboard, two wall racks for books, and a library table.

"The entire school forms in line on the front playgrounds for devotional exercises when the weather permits. We have no assembly room and the children march in after the exercises. In my fire drill the building is cleared and the pupils are marched back to their rooms inside of five minutes. We have sanitary drinking fountains in our halls—a welcome improvement.

AFTER leaving Hampton, David J. B. McAlister, '11· spent two years at Virginia Union University in Richmond, going last fall to Howard University to study law. He wrote in February of his experiences since leaving Hampton:

"Since I have been away from Hampton I have served as mechanic, cook, missionary leader, janitor, and in some cases industrial adviser. At no time since I have been away from Hampton have I been without work and through this alone I am educating myself. "

ON August 24 the first quartet of the Hampton School and the Enterprise Quartet of the town of Hampton gave a concert under the supervision of Mr. William T. Anderson, Hampton, '94· at York County High School in the interest of the white and colored public schools. The audience, consisting of some five hundred white people of that section, manifested their appreciation by constant applause and encores. Through the efforts of Mr. Anderson the people of this county are awakening to the importance of educating their children and thus a collection of $52.10 was taken, one-half of which went to the white school for the continuation of its work, and the other half to the colored people that they may complete the building which is now in progress.

MARRIAGES

ON August 19, Elizabeth Driver, '13, was married in Troy, Ala., to Mr. Andrew H. Flake.

Leland S. Wharton, '12, was married on August 15 to Miss Julia E. West of New York City.

Harvey A. Robinson, '10, was married on August 24 to Miss Aline E. Campbell. They will make their home in Norfolk, Va.

In Athens, Ga., on September 2, Lurine M. Hawkins, '11, was married to Mr. William F. Holsey.

ON September 9, William C. Lewis, Trade Class '03, was married to Miss Letha M. Lightner of Chester, S. C. Mr. Lewis is teacher of harness making at the State College in Orangeburg, S. D., where he has been employed for the past nine years.

ON September 30, Susie E. Wharton, '09, daughter of Rev. George D. Wharton, '80, of Averett, Va., was married to Robert S. Saunders, '13. Mr. Saunders is principal of the public school at Averett.

DEATHS

Mary Allesia Watts, '07, died recently at her home in Indianapolis. After graduation she taught in Gloucester County, Va., for three years. She then accepted a position at Tuskegee, where she remained for one year. For the past three years she has been an assistant in one of the public graded schools of her own city.

ON September 11, after a very brief illness, there passed away Charles B. Randall, '99, one of Hampton's most useful and promising sons. His loss sadly cripples the Y. M. C. A.

work in Brunswick County, Va., where he had been doing for several years most successful work as the first county secretary of the Colored Men's Department.

Friends of Hampton will remember the striking addresses made by Mr. Randall at the Anniversary exercises in 1907 and on Founder's Day 1911— "The Evolution of a Hopeless Case" and "A Lazy Fellow's Awakening"— both indicative of the modesty and frankness of the speaker."

After graduation in '99, Mr. Randall took a graduate course in carpentry and spent a year at the Hart Farm School near Washington as teacher of carpentry, holding later similar positions in the Slater School at Winston-Salem, N. C., and the A. and M. College in Greensboro. Although he had become a contractor and builder and was doing an excellent business, he left it to go home to Powhatan County, Va., where he devoted himself to his mother, building her a new and substantial home, and becoming a successful farmer as well as a useful neighbor and citizen. After three years there he took up Y. M. C. A. work in Brunswick County, writing in reference to his decision :

"I am giving up my work here to become the first secretary of the Y. M. C. A. for county work among colored men. I look upon it as a movement with a great future for my people if we can make it go, and I see no reason why we cannot, because with the help of the Master ' to will is to can.'"

INDIAN NOTES

EARLY in September Hampton had the pleasure of a visit from Mrs. Elsie Fuller Bruce and her daughter, Miss Louise Bruce, of Pawhuska, Okla. Mrs. Bruce was a student from 1885 until 1888, and this is the first visit she has made since leaving here at that time. She found many changes, and was greatly interested in going about the school to see the progress made in twenty-six years. Mrs. and Miss Bruce were accompanied by Mrs. Laura Cornelius Kellogg, an Oneida who is now living in Washington, and whose name is well known as a writer on Indian matters.

Another Indian visitor during September was Esther Moose, a Sioux who was at Hampton from 1902 until 1905. She is at present living in Williamsburg, Va.

Rachel Sheridan, Omaha, has accepted a position at the Southern Ute School, near Ignacio, Col. She writes of the beautiful location of the school, with snow-covered mountains in the distant view.

TWO of the Indian girls who were graduated from Hampton last May are now taking nurse's training. Lula Owl, Cherokee, has entered the Chestnut Hill Hospital, Germantown,

Pa., and Susie St. Martin, Chippewa, the City and County Hospital, St. Paul, Minn.

Carl E. Lay has accepted the position of disciplinarian and athletic director at the Thomas Indian School, Iroquois, N. Y. During his last year at Hampton Mr. Lay was captain of the company which captured the silver loving-cup offered by Major Winston of the United States Army. He is well fitted for the duties of his new position.

Lena Ludwick, Graduate Course '10, has begun another year of teaching in the Government Boarding School at Oneida, Wis. Rachel Somers is filling a position as substitute teacher.

What Others Say

ART METAL WORK

TEACHERS of manual training will find helpful Arthur F. Payne's new book "Art Metal Work with Inexpensive Equipment," published by the Manual Arts Press, Peoria, Ill. The subject of metal working is treated in a masterly and exhaustive manner and all important tool processes are effectively illustrated. The book also contains much valuable information relating to the history of art metal work, to the composition and value of the metals used, and to the sources of materials and equipment.

NEGRO PRIZE WINNERS

Everybody's Magazine for September 1914, published in New York City, contains the announcement that its first prize of $500 for the best letter on the subject—"What we've learned about rum, or rum and remedies," has been awarded to Isaac Fisher, formerly of Vicksburg, Miss., but now of Tuskegee Institute, Ala.

A Negro, John Shepard, who was the winner of the bonus for the first bale of cotton to come to Dallas last year, has again received the bonus for

the first cotton bale. He was awarded $25 from the Chamber of Commerce, and $5 from the Dallas Cotton Mill.

The Dallas *News*

CANNING AT CARLISLE

" Up to August 29, the kitchen and dining-room force had put up for winter use the following : 257 gallons of corn, 792 gallons of tomatoes, 1273 of beans, and 200 gallons of cucumber pickles. Other vegetables keep coming in and the canning goes on. "

The Carlisle *Arrow*

INDIAN FAIRS

THE Commissioner of Indian Affairs has issued an urgent plea to superintendents of Indian reservations throughout the country to encourage Indian agricultural fairs and Indian agriculture in general, not only for the benefit of the Indians themselves, but because of the opportunity offered them by the European war to do a service to the nation by bringing their agricultural pursuits to the highest state of efficiency. Mr. Sells has pledged himself to attend as many of these fairs this fall as he can.

New York *Evening Post*

mpton Normal and Agricultural Institute

HAMPTON VIRGINIA

An undenominational industrial school founded in 1868 by Samuel Chapman Armstrong for Negro youth. Indians admitted in 1878.

To train teachers and industrial leaders

Land, 1060 acres ; buildings, 140

Academic, trade, agriculture, business, home economics

Negroes, 1282 ; Indians, 42 ; total, 1324

Graduates, 1779 ; ex-students, over 6000
Outgrowths ; Tuskegee, Calhoun, Mt. Meigs, and many smaller schools for Negroes

$125,000 annually above regular income
$4,000,000 Endowment Fund
Scholarships
    A full scholarship for both academic and

industrial instruction	$ 100
Academic scholarship	70
Industrial scholarship	30
Endowed full scholarship	2500

    Any contribution, however small, will be gratefully received and may be sent to H. B. FRISSELL, Principal, or to F. K. ROGERS, Treasurer, Hampton, Virginia.

FORM OF BEQUEST

e and devise to the trustees of The Hampton Normal and Agri-
nstitute, Hampton, Virginia, the sum of   *dollars*,

The Southern Workman

Published monthly

The Hampton Normal and Agricultural Institute

Contents for November 1914

THE SOUTHERN WORKMAN was founded by Samuel Chapman Armstrong in 1872, and is a monthly magazine devoted to the interests of undeveloped races.

It contains reports from Negro and Indian populations, with pictures of reservation and plantation life, as well as information concerning Hampton graduates and ex-students who since 1868 have taught more than 250,000 children in the South and West. It also provides a forum for the discussion of ethnological, sociological, and educational problems in all parts of the world.

CONTRIBUTIONS: The editors do not hold themselves responsible for the opinions expressed in contributed articles. Their aim is simply to place before their readers articles by men and women of ability without regard to the opinions held.

EDITORIAL STAFF

H. B. FRISSELL   W. L. BROWN
HELEN W. LUDLOW   W. A. AERY, Business Manager
J. E. DAVIS   W. T. B. WILLIAMS

TERMS: One dollar a year in advance; ten cents a copy
CHANGE OF ADDRESS: Persons making a change of address should send the old as well as the new address to

THE SOUTHERN WORKMAN, Hampton, Virginia

Entered as second-class matter August 13, 1908, in the Post Office at Hampton, Virginia, under the Act of July 16, 1894

THE HAMPTON LEAFLETS

Any twelve of the following numbers of the "The Hampton Leaflets" obtained free of charge by any Southern teacher or superintendent. *A charge cents per dozen is made to other applicants.* Cloth-bound volumes for 1905, ' and '08 will be furnished at thirty cents each, postpaid.

Address: Publication Office, The Hampton Normal and Agri Institute, Hampton, Virginia

The Southern Workman

VOL. XLIII   NOVEMBER 1914   NO. 11

𝕰ditorials

Henry Lane Schmelz

The Hampton School has been most fortunate in having devoted friends among its neighbors. Such a one was Mr. Henry Lane Schmelz, a prominent banker of Hampton and Newport News, who passed away on October 13 at his home in Hampton.

Hundreds of men, women, and children—rich and poor, learned and ignorant, colored and white—recently stood shoulder to shoulder in old St. John's Cemetery, before an open grave and paid in silent reverence their last token of respect and affection for this noble man. Members of several fraternal orders, co-workers in business, tradesmen, and townspeople, joined with Mrs. Schmelz and other relatives, in the simple and dignified rites over the body of the man whose "clean life, manliness, wholesome usefulness, and good name" are left a priceless heritage.

There is common agreement that Mr. Schmelz played an important part in the building up of Hampton and Newport News; that he had won an enviable reputation for his "large sympathy, generous heart, loyalty of spirit, integrity, and faithfulness to duty;" that he had a simple faith in Christ; and that he was to many, irrespective of business or social position or race, "a brother, comrade, and long-time friend."

Mr. Schmelz, in serving Hampton Institute for a number of years as one of its curators, not only attended regularly all routine meetings and rendered efficient service, but also took a deep and personal interest in the school. He did not hesitate to speak to the Hampton students whenever he was invited to do so. The earnest words of encouragement and good cheer that Mr. Schmelz brought to the Y. M. C. A. group, for example, were listened to gladly, for the Negro and Indian boys, with their keen insight into human character, realized that they were being taught by one who knew from rich experience how hard it was to win success in a busy world of competition. Mr. Schmelz showed in his words and in his life how completely satisfying it is to have and to hold the Christian religion.

Mr. Schmelz was a most loyal friend of Hampton. Scarcely a day passed when he was in health that he did not drive or ride on horseback through the grounds. On Saturdays he was accustomed to come to the school library to study his Sunday-school lesson. He and his devoted wife were interested in every plan for the betterment of the colored people of the State of Virginia and the South. He acted as treasurer for the Virginia Industrial Home School for Wayward Colored Girls, which secured, through Mr. Schmelz' activity, an appropriation from the last legislature. Mr. and Mrs. Schmelz accompanied Mr. Robert C. Ogden, the president of the Board of Trustees of the Hampton School and president of the Southern Education Board, on some of his trips through the South. Mr. Schmelz was a most kindly man and his death will be sincerely mourned by the community in which he passed his life.

Born in Hampton in 1853, Mr. Schmelz attended the local private schools and later went to Richmond College. Then followed busy days in business, with success won through untiring effort and attention to the details of his work. In 1888, together with his brother, Mr. Schmelz entered the banking business. Then, step by step, he began his more rapid progress that finally meant the establishment of a sound reputation in banking and a fortune of several hundred thousand dollars. That Mr. Schmelz was skillful in business, devoted to his co-workers, and, above all, ready to be cordial and friendly to all men, regardless of their business relations with him, there is now no doubt. Not only do men speak well of Mr. Schmelz in death, but many of them are willing to say frankly that they owe to him much of their own success in business. His counsel was wise and his financial assistance was timely.

Although Mr. Schmelz had been ill for many months, his death on the evening of October 13 was a shock to the people on the Lower Peninsula of Virginia. The measure of the man is what he wrought for good in the business life of his community and in the lives of his fellows. Though Mr. Schmelz taught a large Bible class for men, he was not a preaching Christian. He did most of his good deeds quietly. He shed sunshine along the common walks of life and loved his fellow-men.

The Indians' Conference The fourth annual Conference of the Society of American Indians was held in Madison, Wisconsin, October 6 to 11. Very unfortunately Mr. Arthur C. Parker, the secretary and treasurer, was unable to be present, and his absence was keenly felt. Because of the time consumed in deciding questions of organization, policy, and finance, there was less discussion of Indian affairs as a whole than in previous years. As in most infant organizations the annual dues and the few donations received, have not met the expenses. The deficit was made up by the members present, and pledges were given which insure the beginning of an inccme for the future. All of the officers were unanimously re-elected, and it is hoped that Mr. Parker will see his way clear to give his whole time to the Society. If this can be arranged it will be the beginning of its larger usefulness, and it is justly felt that he is the one man who can carry on the excellent work already begun, especially as editor of the *Quarterly Journal*. A determined effort is to be made to make the Society more widely known, and local secretaries were appointed on several reservations. It was suggested that this plan be followed also in the large Government schools. The constitution remains as heretofore, except for the change necessary to permit the president's re-election.

At the close of the Conference there was a general feeling that its affairs were on a firmer foundation than ever before, and that the good work already accomplished justified all the efforts that had been put forth. Mr. Coolidge spoke at one of the sessions of the active work done by the Society in helping to free the prisoner Apaches, in getting larger appropriations for the education of the Papahoes, and in other lines of work. He also outlined what the Society proposes to do in the near future. It is hoped that the Robinson Bill, which will codify the laws and determine the status of the Indian, may be pushed, and that the Court of Claims may soon be opened to the native American, the only race in the country to which it is now closed.

The resolutions adopted are of the same broad character as in former years—"for the good of the country and the honor of the race" their paramount idea. Commissioner Sells was thanked for his work in the Bureau, and recognized as a "man of lofty purposes, constructive ability, and sincere devotion to the work committed to his hands."

Between fifty and sixty active members (those of Indian blood) were present, as well as a number of associates representing various lines of work being done among Indians. With the great confidence felt in the officers of the Society, and its infant stage successfully passed, it is believed to be ready for even greater usefulness than has marked its course since the beginning.

The Mohonk Conference For more than a quarter of a century the Smiley family of Lake Mohonk have called together each year at their beautiful home in the mountains the friends of races which have been at a disadvantage in the life struggle, in order to discuss the best means of helping these races. Many a tired missionary out on the plains of the West has gained courage and hope from his visit to Mohonk. Many a Washington official has obtained a new conception of the meaning of race problems. The place, to those who have attended the Conference for years, is full of memories of the men who have labored and pleaded for better laws, better homes, and better schools, for Indians and other belated races.

The Conference just closed was in some ways the most interesting of the series. The day devoted to the Philippines, when General Wood, ex-Governor Forbes, Dr. Heiser, and other representatives of work among the Philippines told of improved sanitation in the Islands and of the model schools and prisons which have been established, was of extraordinary interest. The work which these men have accomplished is heroic. The discussion of the Jones Bill by the chairman of the meeting, who is also chairman of the Appropriation Committee of the House of Representatives, gave the Conference a clear conception of what seemed to most of those present an admirable bill.

One whole morning was given up to veteran missionaries among the Indians. The discussion by Dr. Thomas Riggs of Santee of what is meant by "a friend of the Indian"— an appeal for a sympathetic, intelligent interest in our brother in red—was most convincing.

The Indian race was ably represented by Mr. A. C. Parker, one of the leaders in the Society of American Indians, and by Henry Roe Cloud, a Yale graduate who is commanding the respect of the best men of the country. Mr. Parker pleaded for a codification of Indian laws which will give to the Indian some definite standing as a citizen. Mr. Roe Cloud advocated a school for the training of Christian Indian leaders. General Pratt told of some mistakes which the Government has made in its dealings with the Indians. The Young Men's and Young Women's

Christian Associations and the Indian Rights Association told through their representatives of the constructive work they are accomplishing in the West.

Again Mr. and Mrs. Daniel Smiley, who cared for every want of their guests, have placed in their debt all who are interested in race problems.

A New School Contest   A new method of extending the influence of the Negro school as a benefactor to both colored and white people in a community has been evolved by J. B. La Fargue, principal of the Peabody (Negro) Public School in Alexandria, Louisiana. Prof. La Fargue's idea is to get his boys, in competing for prizes, to take interest in work which will make for improvement in sanitation and neatness in the city.

The school contest idea is not a new one by any means, nor is the idea that the ideal school now makes its influence felt for twelve instead of nine months, but it remained for the Alexandria principal to combine the two and give us a new school contest to be listed along with the corn clubs, the canning clubs, and the home-garden contests.

The Peabody school enrolled 513 in 1913, about half of whom were boys. In addition to a school garden and some work in domestic science, a home-garden contest was organized in which some sixty were enrolled. This, however, was not enough. Principal La Fargue felt that his pupils should be influenced by school to stay out of the gutter during the demoralizing summer months. He proposed to do this by getting them to work.

He therefore interested some of the white merchants of the town to the extent of offering first, second, and third prizes to boys giving the best evidence of industry during the summer of 1914, the contest beginning in January and ending in September.

The boys were to solicit odd jobs from the white people of the town and to receive, upon the completion of each job, a certificate signed by their employers stating the date and the amount paid for the work. The boy who held the largest number of these certificates by the opening of the school year in September was to receive first prize for industriousness.

When the contest was but a month old, according to Prof. La Fargue, one boy whom he had considered rather lazy had amassed twenty-two certificates, stating that he had mowed lawns, cut weeds, and drained mud puddles, and had received from ten to twenty-five cents for each job.

This stimulus may mean a turning point in a boy's life. It may mean the inculcation of industrious habits in one who would have otherwise grown up to be a "no account" Negro. It may mean the cultivation of such habits in a score of the Negroes of

Alexandria. It may mean better sanitation on the premises of both white and colored people, for these boys are looking for work that needs to be done. In fact, the significance of such a movement is almost unlimited, for it touches the life of the Negro in three vital spots:

It keeps the children out of mischief for at least a part of the demoralizing vacation by substituting profitable employment.

It teaches them to grow up with the proper ideals of neatness and cleanliness of property ; and the lesson is impressed by the fact that they themselves are to look for the defects as well as to apply the remedies.

It centers in the school the interest of the Southern white people, who receive the benefit of the labor, and arouses the interest of the whole community in an institution which raises the standard of living.

La Fargue's contest, therefore, deserves good rank among the many children's activities outside of the classrooms in the modern school.

Tuskegee and Hampton "We must face the fact that both in the case of Hampton Institute and Tuskegee Institute, the cost of conducting the work is large ; especially is this true in regard to the extensive and constant activities which both schools carry on in extension work and through their publicity campaigns, " says Dr. Booker T. Washington in his annual report.

"While both the extension and publicity work are costly, nevertheless, from every point of view, it is believed that such work pays. Our justification for large expenditures in these two directions is found in the fact that but for the activity of Hampton and Tuskegee in keeping the cause of Negro education before the people in the North and South, interest in the subject would be waning instead of waxing as it is ; in a word, every dollar that these two institutions expend in extension work and publicity is helping all the institutions in the South and the whole subject of Negro education.

"Indeed, not a few of the most prominent white people in the South have expressed the opinion, both in private and in public, that both races in the South are constantly indebted to these institutions for newer and better methods of education. "

Here is a clear-cut statement of the larger work of Tuskegee and Hampton—the work of making these schools of real service, not only to all Negro schools and to the South, but also to the whole nation and especially to white schools that wish to harmonize their aims and methods with the real problems found in the everyday life of ordinary boys and girls.

That this patriotic work should be bravely and successfully carried forward, even in times of financial stress and uncertainty, there can be no doubt when the facts concerning these schools are fully understood. The report of Dr. Washington to the trustees of Tuskegee Institute is clear and forceful.

Tuskegee's enrollment for the school year ending in May 1914 was 1527—896 men and 631 women—representing 32 states and territories and 17 foreign countries and colonies of foreign nations. In addition, there were 201 in average attendance at the Children's House, which is the teacher-training school; 275 were enrolled in the agricultural short course; and 412 attended the summer school of 1913.

Like other schools which have a large student enrollment and a corresponding staff of workers, Tuskegee has practiced rigid economy. From within, its business committee has kept close track of the small as well as the large business transactions, striving constantly to secure the maximum return in efficiency for the money which has been spent—money that comes in small and large amounts from many classes and represents in many, many cases the sacrifices of whole-souled people for struggling black boys and girls.

Tuskegee has had to look far ahead and plan for permanent improvements which will keep the school up to a high physical as well as educational standard. Public health in a school community which is literally an industrial village must always be an important factor, not only in planning for future growth, but also in handling day by day groups of active boys and girls who are constantly learning many new things from their environment, outside of the classrooms and shops as well as under the direct supervision of teachers, matrons, and battalion officers.

The appeal of Tuskegee and Hampton to the public for complete support is based upon the usefulness of these schools in helping to point the way to a better understanding between races, classes, and sections of the country. Both schools aim to advance the best interests of all men through mutual good will.

THE MOHONK CONFERENCE

BY WILLIAM L. BROWN

THE Conference of Friends of the Indian and Other Dependent Peoples, which met at Mohonk Lake by invitation of Mr. Daniel Smiley in the middle week of October, with Honorable J. J. Fitzgerald, M. C., of New York, in the chair, confined its discussions this year to the Indians and the Filipinos. On the side of the Indian the affairs of the Five Civilized Tribes, in some ways the most advanced of the native Americans, received rather the major share of the attention of the Conference, while on the side of the Filipinos it was the Moros and the head-hunting tribes of northern Luzon, the most backward of the natives, which were chiefly considered.

As a whole the Conference was pervaded even more than usual, perhaps, by the spirit of helpful service and Christian uplift. In the men and women from the active field who told modestly but with enthusiasm of what they have tried to do in the Indian country or in the far-away islands one recognized a noble devotion to the high ideals of Christianity, and felt the spiritual influence of pure, unselfish motives. High officials and humble assistants alike seemed to be imbued with the desire for real service to the simple, backward people with whom their lives were for the time thrown. One realized that their work was done with a genuine feeling of the brotherhood of man and that they themselves were Americans of a type of which we may well feel proud.

One case in point was that of Dr. Victor G. Heiser of Manila, chief sanitation officer of the Philippines, who told of the establishment of the leper colony on the island of Culion and of the removal and isolation there of all the lepers of the Philippine Islands. Cottages and living quarters were erected, hospitals built and equipped, sanitary provisions completed—a whole village planned and constructed, and all provision made for the happy and contented life of a stricken community. It was only one of the many splendid achievement in sanitation, education, and administration which have marked the American occupation of the Islands. Then came the removal of the lepers, and this was the crowning glory of Dr. Heiser's achievement. With infinite tact, sympathy, and patience he induced these unfortunates to leave their homes and take up their residence in the leper settlement, so that the removal of one little shipload after another was effected without the use of force.

Another case in point of a different type but bearing the same marks of unselfish devotion in aid of the unfortunate, was that of Miss Kate Barnard, Commissioner of Charities and Corrections of Oklahoma, who has been engaged for years in a losing fight in behalf of the neglected and defrauded minors of the Five Civilized Tribes against a set of grafting guardians and a corrupt political ring and lobby.

Still another manifestation of the active spirit of the Christian religion in this Conference was the demonstration of missionary work both at home and in the Islands, to which the Conference listened with sympathetic interest and frequent applause. The session on Friday morning was devoted largely to a symposium of missionaries, in the course of which seven veterans of the field, led by Rev. Thomas L. Riggs of North Dakota, testified to the need of a firmer religious faith among the Indians as a basis of character, and told of the efforts being made by the churches to supply that need.

Turning to the more secular aspects of the Conference, perhaps no more important and pressing need of the Indians was presented for discussion than that voiced by Mr. Authur C. Parker, State Archæologist of New York and Secretary of the Society of American Indians, in an able address on "The Legal Status of the Indian." Mr. Parker is a capable and highly educated young Indian of the class rapidly coming to the front, largely through the activities of the Society of American Indians—a class that will presently supply the frequently expressed need for Indian leadership. He pointed out that in our efforts to civilize the Indian we have neglected to give him proper legal status, and he emphasized the belief that until there is provided a definition of the Indian's legal status, there will continue to be human waste, because the Indian inevitably loses spirit and hopefulness through not knowing what are his rights. Out of uncertainty comes despondency, and hope often dies. Mr. Parker quoted the platform of the Society of American Indians touching this subject and urged the passage of the Carter Code Bill now before Congress, which provides for the appointment of a commission to study and codify the laws affecting the Indian.

The discussion of the Five Civilized Tribes turned upon the wholesale cheating and robbery of the full-blood and backward Indians by the shrewder half-bloods and the unscrupulous whites. This robbery has gone on for years in several ways. Sometimes it is the minors and orphan children who suffer, through the misappropriation of their property by their guardians, and Miss Barnard and Mr. Hobart Huson of Oklahoma outlined the campaign that they have waged against this kind of graft and robbery of Indian wards. When the Department of Charities and Corrections, of which Miss Barnard was the head, entered the fight in aid of the orphans, the legislature cut the appropriation and crippled the department. All efforts to get state legislation in aid of these children were defeated. The grafters even tried to get rid of Miss Barnard by offering her a position, with a good salary, in Washington. In one instance her attorney was shot and she was threatened. It was a thrilling story.

Sometimes the Indians were victimized by being robbed of their lands, for which robbery the way was paved by the removal of the legal restrictions upon the alienation of certain Indian lands. By being plied with liquor or by other ingenious devices the more ignorant Indians were persuaded to execute deeds parting with their property for a song, and any attempt on the part of the Indians to interfere with this procedure and to recover the lost property was defeated by what seemed to be a nation-wide conspiracy.

Meantime the Federal Government has entered the field, and Mr. A. N. Frost, Special Assistant to the Attorney General of the United States, in an address on "Some Legal Aspects of the Situation," described the legal fight which has been waged against the Government in its efforts to recover several thousand deeds fraudulently taken from the Indian. The speaker thought that no greater wrong had been perpetrated upon the Indians than the removal of the restrictions upon certain classes of allotments.

That there are many good people in Oklahoma who are opposed to these proceedings and that a campaign has been started among them for arousing the public conscience was revealed in the course of the proceedings. How seriously the Mohonk Conference regards the situation is shown in its platform, which includes the recommendation that, if the Oklahoma legislature shall fail to give early and adequate protection to these Indians, "the Federal Government should resume full jurisdiction over all the "restricted" Indians of that state."

The application of the principles of the civil service both in the Indian Department and in the Philippines was urged by several speakers, and addresses on this subject were made by Charles F. Meserve, LL. D., and Hon. William S. Washburn. An interesting sidelight was added by Mr. Duncan C. Scott of Ottawa, who told of the civil service in the Indian Department of the Canadian Government, where the principles of tenure of office and promotion based upon merit are strictly followed and are productive of good results.

A subject, which has not come up before at Mohonk, to which this Conference gave careful attention is that of peyote or mescal, the use of which is spreading alarmingly among the Indians. This narcotic, the use and effects of which were described in the Southern Workman some time ago, has now become a serious menace to the Indians. Mescal societies have been organized upon the reservations, ostensibly with a religious foundation and motive, for indulgence in this drug, and the excess to which it is carried is seriously undermining the moral and physical stamina of the Indians. The subject was introduced, along with the liquor problem, by Mr. Henry A. Larson and was the theme of addresses by Mr. F. H. Daiker and Rev. G. A. Watermulder.

The Indian program included a number of other speakers, among them being Brigadier General R. H. Pratt, U. S. A., S. M. Brosius, M. K. Sniffen, Henry Roe Cloud, Rev. C. L. Thompson, D.D., and Rt. Rev. T. P. Thurston.

This year was no exception to the rule of extraordinary interest in the discussion of the Philippines at these conferences. The program included three speakers of nation-wide fame; Honorable W. Cameron Forbes, formerly Governor-General of the Philippine Islands; Hon. W. Morgan Shuster, formerly Secretary of Public Instruction in the Philippines and some time Treasurer-General of Persia; and Major General Leonard Wood, U. S. A.

Mr. Forbes, after reviewing the attitude of the two principal political parties towards Philippine independence, explained his own views as follows:

"I now want to say a few words explanatory of my own position and policies, because I have been generally criticised by those who have opposed me or my policies, as one opposed to Philippine independence, who does not believe in their ideals and aspirations, and who has worked to bring about a permanent control on the part of the United States against the wishes of the Filipino people. These representations are widely at variance with the facts. I have never advocated permanent retention of the Islands by the United States against the will of the Filipino people, although I am not at all sure that some permanent affiliation would not be the best thing for both countries; neither am I sure that it would. My position, outlined at the time that I took up the reins of government, and constantly adhered to in every public utterance that I have made from that time to this, has been a very simple one. I have said, and I say now, that I don't know what political relationship will prove to be wisest for both countries to assume at any given time in the future; that without entering into the political capacity of the Filipinos for self-government, they are not economically fit to maintain a separate government because they can't maintain an army and a navy and pay the expenses of their own development from their slender revenues. and need outside assistance in order to protect them from being swallowed up by other countries. Even before the utter worthlessness of international agreements of neutrality had been demonstrated by recent events in Europe, I have ridiculed the idea of substituting a silly scrap of flimsy paper for a strong administrative control backed up by the guns of Corregidor, recognizing as I did that without any outward gain we would have given up the strong argument of our administration, our flag, our soldiers, and our guns, for the weak one of some verbal promises which would last only as long as they remained in the interest of all parties concerned, and no longer.

While I was Governor-General of the Islands, I devoted myself to increasing the material resources of the country, without which increase any real independence, either of nations or of individuals, is impossible."

Considerable discussion of Philippine independence ensued, in the course of which Honorable J. J. Fitzgerald explained the provisions of the Jones Bill, providing for a more autonomous government for the Islands, which was passed by the House of Representatives during the week of the Conference. Mr. Martin Egan, formerly editor of the Manila *Times* pleaded for a non-partisan treatment of the subject and thought the Conference should deprecate the pernicious misuse of it in party politics. Professors William R. Shepherd and Paul Monroe, of Columbia University, presented certain arguments in favor of continued American control of the Islands, as a benefit to the Filipinos themselves for an indefinite period until they have demonstrated the ability to maintain a stable government. Mr. Shuster, on the other hand, thinks there is no justice in our refusing to give to the Filipino people the full measure of self-government. As to what would constitute a stable government by them no one can say. It must be worked out by the Filipinos themselves. "We have declared," he said, "our intention to grant them independence some day. If they are to have a fair trial it must be sometime within the limits of the present generation, else they will probably never have it at all. It is idle to talk of a policy that is to wait three or four generations for its inauguration." Mr. Shuster endorsed the acts and policies of the present Administration and approved of the Jones Bill as an excellent, just, and wise measure.

General Wood's topic was the Moros, and the manner in which this formerly savage, crude, and wild people had gradually been led step by step to adopt and abide by a systematic government partly in their own hands. These people and the wild tribes of northern Luzon were the subject of further addresses by Major I. L. Hunt, U.S.A., Lieutenant Colonel C. D. Willcox of West Point and Mrs. MacIlvaine. Mr. John D. de Huff, formerly superintendent of schools at Manila, discussed the educational aspects in the Islands, and Rev. J. C. Robbins, the religious aspects, while the business man's view was presented by Mr. G. H. Fairchild and Mr. C. M. Swift. Mr. Fairchild believes that the Philippine Islands are enjoying only a portion of the prosperity which should normally be theirs, the limitation being due to a lack of capital and to the restrictions of the American laws. Mr. Swift testified to the good qualities and natural abilities manifested by the Filipinos as railway employes.

The Philippine program ended with an address by Honorable Manuel L. Quezon, Resident Commissioner in Congress from the Philippine Islands.

EXTRACTS FROM THE MOHONK PLATFORM

IT is the chief concern of this Conference that our dependent peoples shall have so much, and only so much, of fostering care and protection as shall assure their continuous progress toward self-government. We repose the greatest confidence in those agencies of education and religion which are engaged in cultivating the elements of personal character and intelligence, upon which the hope of ultimate self-government must rest. We recognize also the educational value of experience in self-direction, and we desire that a dependent people should be left to their own resources and the ordinary course of civil government, and human co-operation whenever such procedure shall not obviously incur the danger of individual and racial disaster.

Indians

IT is evident that at certain points the dangers which threaten our Indian population are still so great as to call, not only for the maintenance of the governmental protection now afforded but for a considerable increase of such protection. This is particularly the case where the property interests of the Indians, in money and in lands, are so great as to arouse the intense cupidity of powerful and unscrupulous foes, some of whom are white men while others are themselves of Indian blood.

Conditions in the State of Oklahoma, affecting particularly the Five Civilized Tribes, call for the closest scrutiny. In the event that the Oklahoma legislature shall fail to give early and adequate protection to these Indians, we see no alternative but that the Federal Government should resume full jurisdiction over all the "restricted" Indians of that state.

The land suits begun by the Federal Government in the interest of the Indians of Oklahoma should be prosecuted, if necessary, to the courts of last resort, to the end that the lands of the restricted allottees shall be preserved from spoliation and that as much as possible of that which has been wrongfully taken from the unrestricted allottees may be recovered.

It is now well known that the increasing use among the Indians of the mescal bean, or peyote, is demoralizing in the extreme. We recommend accordingly that the Federal prohibition of intoxicating liquors be extended to include this dangerous drug.

The codification of our laws relating to the Indians is a matter of vital importance. The Conference accordingly recommends the immediate adoption of the necessary measures to accomplish this end.

The Philippines

THE American people, having accepted the privilege and responsibility of fitting the inhabitants of the Philippine Islands for self-government, their undertaking should be prosecuted with conviction and fidelity by Government officials, by teachers in the schools, and by teachers of religion, in order that a moral basis may be secured on which a stable government can rest. The desire for self-government on the part of the Filipino people is a legitimate and praiseworthy ambition. It should not only be encouraged but it should be coupled with the endeavor to cultivate the essential virtues of a self-governing people.

The object of our Government should be, not so much to hasten the time when it shall be freed from responsibilities, as to advance the time when the Philippine people shall be so fused in common purposes, a common language, common sentiments and ideas and character, that they shall be clearly competent to determine their future relations with the United States. It appears from the Jones Bill, now under discussion, that in the view of the present Congress, as thus far indicated, a definite time cannot yet be fixed when this momentous question of the status of the Philippines shall be finally decided. It is a view with which this Conference is in full accord.

With all the divergence of opinion in this country regarding our relations with the Philippines, there has been a manifest drift towards agreement on some of the main principles involved. The time seems opportune for urging that our national obligations towards the people of those islands be recognized as obligations of the whole body of the American people ; that they be no longer treated as a question of party politics ; and that proposed legislation relating to the Philippines be considered from a non-partisan viewpoint. Such unusual procedure seems warranted by the magnitude of the national interests and interests of humanity which are involved in the Philippine situation.

We urge that Congressional legislation on economic matters be guided by the welfare of the Filipino people and not by the economic interests of groups of American people or of foreigners, whether they be agriculturists, manufacturers, or consumers.

We recommend that under the present conditions of world-wide stagnation of commerce, which seriously affect the Philippine government, Congress extend all possible assistance to the work of the Philippine Bureaus of Science and Health.

This Conference records its gratification at the progress that has been made by the American Government in the Philippines in economic, scientific, agricultural, educational, and political development. We assure the great body of official, educational, and religious workers in the Philippines of our hearty recognition of their devoted and efficient labors, and our earnest desire that they may be given adequate facilities for their important tasks.

CIVILIZING A WILD TRIBE

BY MABEL COOK COLE

WHAT are we accomplishing in the Philippines ? Are our efforts bringing returns, or are we merely wasting money and energy in our Far Eastern experiment ? Politicians at home and in the Islands, the casual tourists, and the old residents are far from coming to an agreement on these questions when their answers refer to the Christianized natives ; but the few who have seen the district agree that a convincing answer is to be found in the non-Christian province of Bukidnon in north central Mindanao.

Five years ago this district was practically unknown. Its miserable, half-starved inhabitants were virtually slaves of the coast natives. The villages were deserted, and the rich lands were unused. Today the visitor enters the district over an excellent horse trail never exceeding a six-per-cent grade. At night he stops in a model village built about a plaza the grass of which is cut with a lawn mower. The carefully cleaned streets are bordered with stone drains, and, in some cases, even with sidewalks, while every yard is free from the customary animals and litter of a typical Filipino village. In this province we find, not one but a dozen "spotless towns" surrounded by fields of rice, corn, camotes, hemp, and coffee ; and the greater part of the work has been wrought in the last few years.

Why this district should have remained so long unknown is unexplainable unless it is that to American and Filipino alike the names Mindanao and Moro are synonymous, and it is little dreamed that in this same island there lies a great section of the finest country in the Philippines quite free from the lawless followers of Islam.

The entrance to the province is from Makabalan Bay which lies off the north central shore of the great southern island. Shortly after leaving the seacoast, a long ascent brings one to a high table land which stretches back for more than a hundred miles, broken only here and there by deep canyons at the bottom of which torrential rivers rush over great rocks.

In place of the herds of cattle which might be grazing on these broad, rolling plains of cogon grass, only the tracks of deer and wild hog appear. One may ride for hours through this land

A STREET IN A MODEL VILLAGE

of great possibilities and see no human life until one of the scattered villages is reached.

The development of these villages tells a story of evolution. Until a few years ago, the Bukidnon had practically no towns.

AN ABORIGINAL HOME

Each *dato*, or head man, had a large house in which a number of families lived, while near by were a few smaller houses where his retainers lived in times of festival or danger; but the people loved their scattered homes in the hills, and it was there that they spent most of their lives.

At times they gathered hemp or coffee, which they raised in small clearings on the mountain side or along the stream banks, and carried to the coast, where it was exchanged for bright cloth and ornaments. In their ignorance they were mercilessly robbed, or perhaps forced into debt to unscrupulous coast people who ever after kept them in subjection; and it is little wonder that the timid, wild people preferred to draw back into their hill homes, whose scattered and hidden positions made them practically free from intruders.

"A SPLENDID HORSE TRAIL" BUILT BY NATIVES

Their religious belief taught them to make a raid after a death and to bring back the hands of the slain as trophies, or, if a captive was taken, to make a celebration in which they and their friends danced and sang around the victim and finally speared him to death. But the Bukidnon were not a warlike people, and even today their greatest concern is for the good will of the numerous spirits who watch over their every act.

The greatest of these superior beings is Diwata Magbabaya, who is so awe inspiring that his name is never mentioned above a whisper. He lives in the sky in a house made of coins. There are no windows in this building, for if men should look upon him they would melt into water. There are many lesser spirits, some

who favor mortals, others who bring illness and bad fortune ;
and numerous ceremonies are made with offerings of rice, chicken,
and betel-nut to appease these immortals and to gain their
good will.   Their wishes are learned through omens, and never
does a man make a new clearing until he has besought the spirits
in the stones, the beliti trees, the vines, the cliffs, and the holes
not to be angry with him for disturbing their dwellings, but to
prosper him and to grant a good crop.   Every thought and act of
the Bukidnon are so filled with belief in the powers of the unseen
world that personal endeavor need play little part in their lives.

They meekly accepted the scourge of locusts which destroyed

A BUKIDNON WARRIOR

their scanty crops, the pest which killed their cattle, and the
exactions of the coast natives as the will of the spirits against
whom it was useless to strive, so that when the Government first
took an interest in them, they were leading a poor, half-starved
existence.

The almost hopeless task of freeing these people from the
coast people and inspiring in them a desire for more comforts was
assigned to Governor Frederick Lewis. His success has been that
of a wizard.   Indolent natives have been induced to build a splendid horse trail for a hundred miles across their country.   They
have learned that dynamite is more powerful than the spirits of
the cliffs.   They have seen the invisible rulers of the torrential

streams thwarted by the thirty-nine strong bridges which they themselves have constructed. To appreciate the enormous laʙor involved in building these bridges, one must realize that only the *bolo*, or long knife, was available for cutting out the heavy beams and planks in the forests, and that the heavy timbers had to be dragged by hand for miles to the places where they were needed.

To induce the people to leave their mountain homes and move into villages on the plains where they could be reached and governed was a still greater task, for the sturdy cogon grass had proved an almost unconquerable enemy to the primitive farmer with only his *bolo* and sharpened stick with which to fight it.

A PICTURESQUE GRASS-ROOFED BRIDGE

The Government introduced some inoculated carabao and Indo-Chinese oxen and put them at the disposal of worthy natives who were taught to use the disk plow and harrow, and in a few months considerable plots of food stuffs surrounded each village. The value of these plots was soon realized by the people, for a disastrous flood destroyed the plantings along the stream and river courses, and only the village crops kept them from starvation. This experience was an effectual aid to the energetic teacher, and more land came under cultivation. Today the native is self-supporting and independent of his former masters, who had taken advantage of his poverty and ignorance to rob him of the little he produced.

The public schools in this section are conducted along most practical lines, and the coming generation is being given an industrial education with the hope of bringing into the homes comforts which will induce the people to settle permanently. In the school gardens new fruits and vegetables have been introduced, and the boys are taught how to care for them. The girls are taught to weave and sew, while the boys construct beds, chairs, tables, and other useful articles.

The amount of skill, energy, and infinite patience necessary to make these care-free, ease-loving savages into members of law-abiding, industrious communities has been great. It was an experiment begun almost in the dark, for the resources of the country were untried and the Bukidnon themselves unknown ; but Governor Lewis has proved that with proper handling even the wild Filipino can make magical progress toward civilization.

With the introduction of more animals and machinery, more people will be called in from the hills, and this splendid land will be brought under cultivation. Surely Bukidnon gives an affirmative answer to the question, "Is it worth while ?"

THE "NESTOR OF NEGRO BANKERS"

BY CLEMENT RICHARDSON

In view of the recent death of Dr. Pettiford, readers of the Southern Workman should find of special interest the following appreciation of his work.

Editors.

"YOU SEE," said he, "we want to keep the money within the race, to conserve our financial strength. Every time a dollar gets back into the hands of a white merchant or a white banker no one of us can get it back except a laborer. We don't want to antagonize, of course, but we want the money to circulate within the race, so that in the future when immigrants come into the South, they will be a blessing to us instead of a hindrance; because our children will have land and business and the immigrant can trade with us too."

Thus spoke the "Nestor of Negro Bankers," Dr. W. R. Pettiford of Birmingham, Alabama; and this "conserve our money and give employment to our boys and girls" was the burden of his theme. Politics, religion, the story of the founding and development of his bank,—all came round to an abrupt lifting of the finger and the statement, "You see we want to conserve, so as to protect our folks."

Twenty-odd years ago, Dr. Pettiford was riding out from Birmingham to Ensley, a mining suburb. The street car chanced to be filled with Negro miners and their women folk, who were all laughing, jesting, carousing, quarreling. In the midst of the confusion a woman reached beneath her seat, pulled forth a half-gallon jug of rum, and held it to her lips. This set Dr. Pettiford to thinking and thinking hard. There were thousands of these people in and about Birmingham, earning wages of from a dollar and a half to two dollars per day. How to reach these men, since they didn't go to church, and teach them to "conserve" some of their money was the one question that took possession of him. Day after day he ruminated, until the subject began to inject itself into his sermons and midweek talks; he was then pastor of a large Baptist church. Three times a day he dinned the matter into the ears of his family at table. He buttonholed his friends in the streets; he lectured on the theme in the conventions, in the lodges, in the business meetings of his church, in general Negro business gatherings, referring again and again to the woman in the car with the jug of whiskey, and pounding away

at the principle of conserving money to protect and educate Negro
boys and girls.

Finally, either actually persuaded, or anxious to hear the end
of the matter, the Negro Progressive Association, a business club
of Birmingham, agreed to aid Dr. Pettiford in starting a Negro
savings bank. Plans were drawn and stock was sold. The savings
bank now seemed assured.   Dr. Pettiford began to go among the
laborers, preaching on his favorite theme, in order to have a rush
of depositors on the opening day. But obstacles began to rise and
multiply.   To enlist stock buyers and to persuade miners to
deposit their earnings were the merest child's play alongside the
vexing problems which bore in upon him.   At one of the early
meetings of the directors the question arose as to who would be
president.   Why, Dr. Pettiford of course, it was urged, since it
was Dr. Pettiford who had solicited the funds and established
confidence.   But he had no such ambition.   He had only undertaken the task as a bit of missionary work incident to his pastoral duties.   He therefore declined. Here the stockholders threw
down the ultimatum, "You'll be president or there'll be no bank.
Your name is necessary to maintain confidence."

His consent to serve as president for one year, while continuing his pastoral duties, cleared the horizon for further business.
At the end of the year agreed upon, the confidence argument and
the ultimatum again confronted him ; a third and a fourth year's
end brought the same result, until finally he resigned his pastorate—"Though I'll have you understand," he protested, "I'm
still a preacher"—and became the full-fledged president of the
Alabama Penny Savings Bank, an office he held for twenty-
three years.

But knotty problems of various kinds confronted the directors.   The president having been chosen, there came the question
of salaries and employes.   As to salaries, there were no funds
for the purpose.   As to employes, barring the janitor and the
scrub-woman, there were none worth a salary.   Where in all the
world could a trained Negro banker be found ?   Where would he
have obtained his training ?   In Africa business men had risen
only to the point of bartering in slaves, rum, and elephants'
teeth.   In America the highest positions the Negro had reached
in the banking business were those of janitor and elevator boy.
Those who were chosen to help consented to work for a time for
nothing.   To learn the business they set to work in the white
banks in Birmingham to learn bookkeeping and the like, employing city officers and white bankers to look after their work until
some degree of skill was attained.

Then, just as they thought they were making a good beginning, there came the panic of '93.   The laboring folk formed a

"bread line" to the bank, demanding their funds. They had
been none too sure of this new bank anyway, still less so, since
it was run by members of their own race. What infinitely surprised them, however, was that they all got their money back!
An investigation of banks in the city brought the fact to light
that the Penny Savings Bank was substantial. The clouds now
began to break. In 1895 the bank was incorporated by a special
act of the state legislature of Alabama, with a capital stock of
$25,000, and the privilege of increasing it to $100,000. A year

DR. W. R. PETTIFORD

later it bought a $6500 building. Another year and this building
was sold for $20,000, so rapidly does property appreciate in Bir-
mingham. The directors now bought an $18,000 house which
they sold a few years later for $35,000. Finally the bank built
its own house, the one which it now occupies. The building has
five stories and a basement, a store front, tile floors in the bank,
and a renting capacity of sixty-four rooms. Its rent amounts. to
$8000 per year, all the rooms save one being occupied by Negro
business men of Birmingham and surrounding towns.

The Penny Savings Bank now being established, Dr. Pettiford conceived of what is popularly known as a trust, but which
he thought of as a missionary scheme. With the Birmingham
bank as a center, he planned to establish branch banks in every
large town and in every city in the State of Alabama. He had
planted one in Selma and one in Montgomery, when the Alabama
state legislature passed a law prohibiting the further extension
of branch banks.

However, Dr. Pettiford was not wholly checked. The fame
of the Penny Savings Bank had gradually spread abroad among
the black folk throughout the country. Letters of inquiry as to

THE ALABAMA PENNY SAVINGS BANK

how to start a bank besieged him every day. Many cities with a
large colored population invited him to come and lecture on the
subject, offering him one hundred dollars per night and expenses.
Some of these invitations he accepted, remaining in the place he
visited until the bank was under way. Many other cities he
reached through the Negro weekly papers and through pamphlets. In this way the banking fever among Negroes raged until
there are in America sixty-three Negro banks in a sound, healthy
condition. They range from one in a state as far north as

Massachusetts and Pennsylvania to eleven in Mississippi and twelve in Virginia.

All these twenty-odd years the Alabama Penny Savings Bank has held to its old policy of saving the funds of the laborer. The money of Negro business men is handled by another flourishing Negro bank in Birmingham. But Dr. Pettiford, remembering the scene in the car, kept his bank open on Saturday and other "pay" nights to help "conserve" the money of the ten thousand Negro laborers who had become his depositors.

NEW YORK STATE INDIANS

BY CAROLINE W. ANDRUS

IN traveling across New York State, visiting such prosperous cities as Buffalo and Syracuse, one cannot but wonder if there really is an Indian problem waiting for solution within a few miles. The general ignorance of reservation conditions in the places that are geographically so near adds to this impression, and it is only when one sees for one's self that realization begins.

There are six reservations in New York State besides the tract of land on Long Island occupied by the Shinnecocks. The writer did not visit the St. Regis Reservation, which lies partly in New York and partly in Canada, on the trip she took last summer, but spent about three weeks traveling over the Cattaraugus, Alleghany, Tonawanda, Tuscarora, and Onondaga reservations.

The census of 1910 gives these reservations a population of six thousand, and because of their peculiar land conditions many of the people have retained their Indian customs to a surprising extent. The title for the land on which the reservations are located goes back to the grant from England to the Massachussetts Colony. A later grant to the New York Colony overlapped the former, and the two states compromised by giving New York jurisdiction over the disputed territory, while Massachusetts kept the pre-emption right to the land claimed by the Indians. Later, this became the property of the Ogden Land Company. The company now claims to own the fee to the land on which the Cattaraugus and Alleghany reservations are located, but not

Onondaga, Tuscarora, or Tonawanda.   Under this claim the Indians have the right of occupancy as long as they exist as a tribe. The Indians argue that they have the full ownership of the land, with the right of the Ogden Land Company to purchase when they choose to sell.   For years this claim has been contested in the courts.   Nothing has been decided, and on none of these reservations has there been any allotment of land in severalty.   The Indians may buy and sell among themselves, but not among the whites.

Another factor preventing progress is found in the fact that the Indian code of laws is entirely separate and distinct from that governing the white population.   As an example, divorce, among the pagans, consists in simple separation, while the marriage ceremony is equally primitive.   Other laws are as far removed from the white man's standard, and the first steps

THE "LONG HOUSE" AT ONONDAGA

toward progress will be their thorough revision and an adjustment of the land question.

On every reservation one finds a number of pagans.   Usually it is the older men and women who cling to these customs, but there are always some children of the uneducated and unprogressive who fill vacancies in the ranks.   Among the pagans the old-time dances are kept up with more or less regularity, and English is spoken but little.   As the years pass this element is bound to grow smaller and it would seem as though this problem would settle itself in a few years.   The tribal organization is kept up to some extent and chiefs are elected on some of the reservations.   At Onondaga one finds a modern edition of the ancient "Long House"—the council house of the Iroquois.

AN ONONDAGA HOME
Two students have come to Hampton from this home

In spite of all obstacles, conditions are changing, and changing for the better. The best element among the returned students is gaining more influence throughout the reservations; people are building better houses and are doing a higher grade of work on the farms and in the shops of the near-by towns.

Cattaraugus is the largest reservation, and is by many considered the most progressive. In addition to several district schools the state here maintains the Thomas Indian School, a fine institution accommodating nearly two hundred pupils, and with a far-reaching influence for good on all the reservations. Mrs. Lincoln, the superintendent, knows personally every child in the school and the conditions from which he comes. She

A GRADUATE'S HOME AT ONONDAGA

makes a point of visiting the homes during vacation, and the
knowledge that she is likely to come is an incentive to keep up
to the school standard.   The returned students on Cattaraugus
Reservation also have strong friends and helpers in Rev. Mr.
Fisher and his wife, missionaries who are working under the
Presbyterian Board.   This was the pioneer church among these
people, its work having been started about a hundred years
ago.   Many of the Indians are active in church work, as was
shown when a bazaar which brought them $122.00 was held this
summer for the purpose of raising funds to repair the church.
One ex-student of Hampton is superintendent of the Presbyterian
Sunday school and president of the Christian Endeavor Society,
while another holds an important position in the church.

On all the reservations work in the neighboring towns makes
a strong appeal to the men and boys.   At Cattaraugus one finds

THE ALLEGHANY RIVER AT WOLF RUN

many away from home, working in Silver Creek, Dunkirk, and
Buffalo; from Tonawanda they go to Rochester and the gypsum
mines, and from Onondaga to Syracuse.   This is but natural and
what white men would do under the same circumstances.   One
can but wish that more of the young men would study agriculture and cultivate the really fine land of the reservations, for
they could find an easy market for all they could raise, and
could wield a strong influence over their own people.

The Alleghany Reservation is beautifully located in the southwestern corner of the state, with the river from which it takes
its name flowing peacefully throughout its length.   This reservation is a standing reminder of the trickery by which the white
man has so invariably gotten the better of the Indian.   As the
story goes, the Indians were offered their choice of a tract
of land forty miles square or one of forty square miles.   The

result is that they have a reservation forty miles long and one mile wide. On this reservation is located the city of Salamanca, the ,land on which it stands being leased to the whites for ninety-nine years, dating from 1890 or 1891. For this the Indians receive an annual rental of $7000. At Tunesassa is a school which has been maintained by the Quakers for over a hundred years, the only mission school among the New York Indians except the Catholic mission at St. Regis. The people at Alleghany are mainly Presbyterians, and splendid work has been done among them by Rev. M. F. Trippe, who has been their missionary for about thirty years.

There are two temperance societies among the Iroquois. One, founded by Pleasant Lake, is still kept up among the pagans and the vow he made is still used by those taken into the society:

A GRADUATE'S HOME ON THE ALLEGHANY RESERVATION

"I will use it nevermore. As long as I live, as long as the number of my days is, I will never use it again. I now stop." In the early days of Christian work another association was formed. This is known as the "Six Nations' Temperance League ", and has been a great factor for good. Charles Doxon, a Hampton graduate of '89, was for some years its president. In spite of these organizations liquor is here, as everywhere, the Indians' greatest curse.

At Tuscarora and Tonawanda there are several district schools maintained by the state, and on both of these reservations Hampton girls have been teaching successfully. Churches under native preachers are doing good work. In addition to this the Rev. Mr. Trippe goes from Alleghany to Tonawanda once in three months to hold communion services.

A GRADUATE'S HOME AT TONAWANDA

At Onondaga there are perhaps as good homes as on any of the reservations. They are close together and conditions seem more those of a small town than of a farming community. Here the women have one great advantage, for, by virtue of a contract with the Solvay Process Company, all the houses on the main road of the reservation are supplied with running water.

Compared with conditions on Western reservations those in New York State seem very easy, but comparison with the conditions in neighboring towns brings a realization of the very great need of continued efforts in Christian education. Many of

CROSSING THE ALLEGHANY RIVER IN A "JOHN BOAT"

the people are very poor, and that in the midst of a most prosperous region. Poorly kept homes are too often the result of lack of proper training for the girls and perhaps are partly responsible for some of the intemperance among husbands and sons. As in all Indian communities, there is a lack of organized social effort. It would be interesting to see how much a social center, with a good library, would do towards keeping the young people contented at home after they leave school, and how it would affect the standards of the community.

During the time spent on the reservations the writer saw seventy-four Hampton graduates and ex-students. Some own good homes; some are working as skilled tradesmen in the shops of neighboring cities, holding their own side by side with white workmen; some are farming; some are teaching. The great majority of the girls are married, living in homes of their own, and ambitious to give their children a better start than they had themselves. Their loyalty to Hampton and the standing they have won in their respective communities, can perhaps be shown in no better way than by the fact that from these reservations seven new boys and girls have this fall come to work their way through Hampton.

A NEGRO MERCHANT IN THE MAKING *

A PERSONAL NARRATIVE

BY CHARLES W. GILLIAM

IN March 1886, my father died, leaving my mother with eight children, four boys and four girls, without a home and without money; and as I followed his remains to the cemetery, barefooted, together with my three little brothers, I saw my condition, and resolved that I would not see my mother and little sisters and brothers suffer. But it was at a time when work was scarce and the weather cold. We *had* to suffer. It is painful for me to tell you that the cold cracked our little feet open and my mother had to grease them at night with tallow that we might rest. And further, I remember that one morning we had nothing to eat but bread, and there had just come to town an old man buying scrap iron and bones, now called a junk dealer. I got me an old burlap sack and hunted bones, found some, and sold him ten cents' worth, with which I bought some molasses; I think I got about a quart, so we had breakfast, though a little late.

During the summer of 1886 I peddled fruit and ice cream on the streets of Okalona, Miss. The marshal of our little city at that time seemed to have much sympathy for me, and said to me one day: "Charley, do you think you can sell some grapes? I have lots of them and will pay you well if you can sell them." I told him that I thought I could. The next morning, by appointment, I went to his house for the grapes, put them in little paper sacks, and started out through the streets to the depot hallooing "Grapes! Grapes!" I failed to make a single, solitary sale on the trip. On my way back I still hallooed: "Grapes! Grapes!" The echo "Grapes" came back to me, and seemed to mock my little effort; the name seemed to sound a little harsh to the ear; there was nothing in it appealing or attractive, so I hallooed "Grapes" no more. I carried them back and told the marshal that I had had no luck that day but would be back and try again the next morning. So I began to think what name I might cry out or what I might say to attract the people's attention to the nice grapes I had for sale. I finally hit upon a name

* Address delivered before the National Negro Business League at Muskogee, Oklahoma

that I thought would fill the bill, and so I went back the next morning, got a basket of the same kind of grapes, and went down the street shouting at the top of my voice: "California Bells! California Bells! for sale." And don't you know, I began to sell them, and I sold them right along. They just went like hot cakes. Then it was that I learned the valuable business lesson that "There's something in a name," and I have followed that idea successfully even up until now.

I have taken a basket of bananas, as many as I could well carry, or a gallon freezer of cream, with saucers and a vessel of water in my hands, and walked down Main Street for three or four blocks and then two or three blocks up Meridian Street and three or four blocks down Washington Street, and sometimes I would not make more than one or two sales, and sometimes even none, though hallooing all the time that I had bananas and ice cream for sale. I came to the conclusion that there must be something wrong with my business method, so I remembered how, many a time after the fruit wagon had gone by, I had wished that I had bought; this memory whispered to me a new idea, and suggested that if I could first create the desire or want, and would then double-back over the same route shouting, "Bananas and ice cream," why, the women and children would meet me at their gates and doors and buy of me. So I learned, by actual experience, first to attract the people, create an appetite or desire for the goods I had to sell, and then push the sales with all my might; that's exactly what I do even unto this day and I have succeeded well by that method.

I went to Memphis the last of August, 1886, hunting work; got employment at the Gayoso Hotel as bell-boy at $15 a month. Bell-boys were allowed to shine shoes, so I made some days right nice little sums of money. I made it a rule to send my mother some money every week. I returned home in December of the same year with $65 and gave it all to my mother except $5, as she and the children were in need of clothing and shoes for winter. The next spring I went back to Memphis and again worked for the Gayoso Hotel awhile, and then for the Pullman Palace Car Company. After saving some money I decided to marry, took unto myself a bride, divided my money with her, and later moved home to Okalona.

On January 1, 1893, I succeeded Mr. T. W. Gregory, buying his little stock of groceries which amounted to a little over $81; this constituted my capital. With no previous experience in business other than selling fruit, peanuts, bananas, and ice cream on the street, I started a grocery. The building I began in was located on Main Street. It was a brick store, 20x45 feet, with a partition about half way back. I moved my family to the rear of the building so that I could save the money which I would have had to pay for rent in other quarters, and at the same time have my wife's assistance in looking after the business when I was out buying goods or drumming up customers. I need not tell you that we had a tough time. The panic of 1893 was on, but we worked and we sacrificed, and I studied the best way to invest my small receipts so as to get quick returns. On January 1, 1894, I found that I had made some little gains ; I might say the same thing of 1895 and 1896 ; the country was in a prosperous condition ; everybody was handling money and I profited by carrying out the old adage: " Make hay while the sun shines. "

In the spring of 1897 I decided to put in a small line of notions. I called on a white drygoods merchant, who was a neighbor, and asked him what he thought of the idea ; he said to me, "You are doing well, and you had better let well enough alone. " I next called on a white wholesale dealer, who gave me much encouragement and sold me my first bill of notions, amounting to $50. This step put new life into my business, and my friends and customers congratulated me. I studied the wants and needs of my people more and more, and my motto was to give them "value for value received, and to be courteous and kind to all," and at the same time I let them all know that I appreciated their support.

I soon put in a small line of drygoods, and that fall I went to Memphis, Tennessee, to market with Mr. P. McIntosh, who introduced me. I wish to say that Mr. McIntosh is supposed to be the oldest Negro merchant in the State of Mississippi and one of the most successful in this country. I bought $2000 worth of drygoods and notions, and $500 worth of shoes from a St. Louis shoe firm. My business continued to grow. In 1900, Mr. McIntosh and I formed a co-partnership ; the first year we did about $40,000 worth of business. Being a little ambitious, I thought I could do better by myself, so Mr. McIntosh and I dissolved partnership on perfectly friendly terms and remain strong friends to this day.

I bought a lot adjoining the house in which I began business. On this I built a brick store, 28x80 feet, with large plate-glass windows, the first on the street; ceiled the store with metal ceiling, lighted it with electricity ; put in modern fixtures, large floor cases, cash register, computing scales, typewriter, measuring tank, iron safe, and a soda fountain. I am carrying one of the best stocks of goods in our town and it is one of the best kept stocks. I go to market twice a year. My transportation is paid by the Commercial Association. Aside from my store and stock of goods, I have a handsome residence of twelve rooms, twelve tenement houses, eighty acres of farm land, several unimproved lots, and a little bank account, and should any of you visit me at Okalona, my home, I will give you a ride in my automobile.

Now, if you wish me to name some of the elements of success in conducting a mercantile store, I would say : (1) You must have some capital to do business with ; (2) you must have the support of your community and the backing of the farmers, and enterprises such as mills, gins, compress factories, etc., whose direct and indirect patronage and support will be helpful to you ; (3) the location of your store should be the best place obtainable ; (4) you should be very careful in buying and selecting your merchandise, for if you buy well your profit is already made; (5) you should study the wants and needs of your customers and keep the goods you know they must have or which they are accustomed to buy from your competitors ; (6) you must keep your store clean, and arrange your goods on your shelves or on your counters neatly and attractively ; (7) you must make your store as inviting as possible, a place where each and every one of your customers is cordially welcomed and courteously treated ; (8) if you have show windows, keep them looking attractive ; and it matters not what kind of a mercantile business you are conducting, make frequent changes in the manner of displaying and advertising your goods and wares ; (9) get the people to talk about you and your store, and when they come to your store, meet them at the door and greet them, have them feel that you are glad to see them, ask them about their families and neighbors, and above all, give them value received for their money.

It has been said, and well said, that a satisfied customer is the best advertisement one can have. I have also found it very helpful and beneficial to all parties concerned, to give frequent talks or lectures to my clerks. I tell them to cultivate the habit of being courteous and kind to all on the street as well as in the store, that they cannot afford to offend the humblest customer, as they are my best asset; my profits and my bank account depend on them, even their positions and wages depend on my customers. Occasionally there comes some misunderstanding between customers and my clerks, and sometimes between the customer and myself, but I make it a point to adjust the differences, and have the customer leave satisfied even if we have to make some concessions.

I have a regular time for opening and closing my store. I have my clerks understand that they must be on time ; I have certain duties for each and I see to it that he or she does his or her duty ; I am courteous and kind to them ; I make them feel that I am interested in their welfare as well as my own ; I make my store comfortable and pleasant for them ; I try to keep in touch with every detail ; I keep order ; I have no boisterous talking or debating within or in front of my store. I don't ask my people to trade with me because I am one of their race ; I ask them to trade with me if I can give quality and make prices equal to those of my white competitors.

I cultivate a friendly feeling toward the white people of my community and make it a point to be polite to them. Some of my best customers and friends are white people. I find that the better element of white people are always willing to help and patronize a polite, honest, honorable colored man or woman. I am interested in the building up of my town and community. I am interested in good streets, good roads, enterprises for labor, good schools and churches, the sick and the poor ; I am a taxpayer. I pay my bills promptly when convenient ; I discount my bills whenever possible, as this gives me good credit ; Dun and Bradstreet Mercantile Agencies say that my credit is good for from $10,000 to $20,000.

Now, I am told that our race numbers about ten millions, or one-ninth of the population of the United States. If this be true, we should sell at least one-ninth of all the groceries, one-ninth of all the drygoods ; one-ninth of all the clothing ; one-ninth of all the boots and shoes ; one-ninth of all the hats and millinery; in short, one-ninth of all the goods sold by American merchants to this nation. Don't be discouraged or afraid to enter business because there are so many white stores in this or that town. Go there and establish your business and fight your way through on your own merit. And last, but not least, if you ever expect to have or to own anything in this world, you must live within your means, for, in the words of our honored President : "We, like all other races, must deny ourselves today in order that we may enjoy ourselves tomorrow. "

INDIAN SCHOOL GARDENS IN EASTERN OKLAHOMA*

BY JOHN B. BROWN

Supervisor in the United States Indian Service

"Where's the second boy?"
"Please sir, he's weeding the garden," replied a small voice.
"To be sure," said Squeers, by no means disconcerted. "So
he is. B-o-t, bot; t-i-n, tin; bottin; n-e-y, ney; botinney.
Noun; substantive; a knowledge of plants. When he has learned
that botinney means a knowledge of plants he goes and knows
'em. That's our system, Nickleby; what do you think of it?"

SQUEERS is coming into his own as an educator. The generation of Charles Dickens forgot the cruelty of Squeers often
enough and long enough to laugh at the supposed absurdity of
the latter's pedagogy. The present generation is reversing itself
with sufficient promptness and decisiveness to demonstrate again
that the present majority thinks the former majority altogether
wrong. We do not believe that this is merely the ebb and
flow of an educational tide, but that we have made a permanent advance. We now with seriousness and earnestness spell
"P-l-a-n-t, plant," and while one section of the class punctuates
the other plants.

In the schools of the Five Civilized Tribes gardening is
begun soon after the Christmas Holidays by a study of the subject academically. As soon as the supply of seeds is received
they are tested in the schoolrooms, processes and results
being used in connection with language and number work. The
methods of seed testing may be found in any of the modern elementary texts on gardening or agriculture and will not be detailed here. As would be expected, the schools are not uniform
in their practices as to promptness, alertness, energy, and intelligence in carrying out this plan.

The testing of seed should closely precede planting time so
that the interest may not flag. Seed purchased from established,
reputable growers is rarely found defective, the greater danger
being from "home-grown seed." This is an important point,
one on which the general public is often wrong, and which the
young gardener needs first to know. There should be just time

---

*Reprinted, with permission, from *The Red Man*, Carlisle, Pa.

enough between the testing and the planting to enable the purchase of new seed when necessary.

Now comes the problem of individual gardens vs. school gardens. We have tried all plans and combinations of these. With some employees either system will work, and with others no system is worth the cost of the seed. All schools in the Five Tribes have had good gardens, and most schools have used the gardening educationally either by the individual or the class method, or both. My own plan has been never to insist on a system which the superintendent and teachers could not endorse hopefully and earnestly. Different plans from those in vogue have been suggested, explained, and even urged, but always with the closing injunction: "Do it this way if you can believe in it. It will work if *you* think so, but not merely because *I* think so, and if you think you are going to fail you have failed."

Individual gardens have been successfully grown at a few schools, notably at Armstrong Male Academy in the Choctaw Nation, near Bokchito, and the interest therein has been kept up from year to year. The difficulties ordinarily confronting teachers and superintendents in using this method are fully realized. In the first place, we meet the inertia and procrastination which so often spell failure before the work begins. These overcome, there is the tendency to grow tired of a new plaything or a new project, such tendency as is used by humorous writers in describing the efforts of older persons who essay gardening. Keeping up the enthusiasm which comes to most of us with the earthy smells of springtime, and making it last through the sultry summer days is only possible when the teacher is virile and wholly sympathetic.

In the Five Tribes, as on most reservations, pupils do not remain in school during the vacation, ordinarily the most important period of the garden's growth. We all have seen during July and August the weedy patch where the children's gardens had been planted and possibly for a time well cultivated. This problem we have solved in two ways. First, by planting only early vegetables which in Oklahoma mature before the close of school; and, second, by planting the gardens, whether "individual" or "class," in rows such as may be cultivated by horse power after the children are gone. This need not destroy the individuality of the space assigned to each pupil, and where we use this plan we are employing a few pupils during the summer, thus connecting in some slight degree the efforts of the springtime with the results of autumn.

In organizing for individual gardens the ground should be carefully measured by the pupils, and then before going further they should make a plat in the schoolroom, drawn to a scale, and make assignment of space to each pupil. Each pupil should have, not merely the same amount of space, but the same amount, kind, and quality of seed. The planting must be thoroughly discussed and the pupils taken to the garden in groups of proper size for handling. Children will "run wild" in a garden from sheer exuberance of spirits if this part of the work is not carefully planned and under good discipline. Keeping the pupil in his own territory and preventing waste of seed are the principal and the vital problems. After planting time, more individuality may be allowed.

The offering of prizes has been found very stimulating. Pupils compete not merely for the prize but for the joy of the game itself. They show energy, enthusiasm, and originality. Surface cultivation, the soil mulch, and the conservation of moisture mean something definite to the pupil who has seen one pupil win and another lose by their respective use or neglect of these well-established principles.

At Armstrong Academy competition in the individual garden contest has been voluntary, yet over 75 per cent of the boys have taken part. They were divided into two classes, the smaller boys having smaller space and having their gardens judged separately. At this school all individual garden work is done during the free time of the pupil. No better evidence of their interest possibly could be given, when it is known that it rarely is necessary to remind a boy when his garden needs attention.

It is very common for pupils to ask the teachers, the superintendent, or the farmer for advice as to what remedies should be applied to sick plants, how to destroy insects, or apply fertilizers. The competition at this school has become so keen that on one occasion, on the day the gardens were to be judged, one boy, in desperation that several plats looked about as well as the one which had cost him so much honest toil, got out before daylight and carried water to irrigate his tract, carefully concealing his somewhat questionable method by covering the water with dust. On that hot June afternoon his plants stood up in green, luxuriant contrast to the curled leaves of his rivals. He won, but there is now a new rule covering irrigation matters in connection with future contests.

One of our schools which has done excellent gardening by classes is Wheelock Academy, for Choctaw girls, at Millerton, Oklahoma. Here the girls, under the leadership of their teachers, are nature students and nature lovers. The two are not always synonymous. These teachers derive much personal benefit from the intimate association with their girls and with nature in the health-giving outdoor exercise. The girls at this school have an Agricultural Club and also voluntarily have assumed charge of the dairy, including the feeding and milking of the cows.

I have given some suggestions based on our experience, and referred to two schools where excellent results have been obtained. Recapitulating what now seem to me to be the most important elements entering into successful school gardening, the suggestions would be briefly as follows:

Preparation of ground by fertilization and deep fall plowing, and the collection of home-grown seeds.

Study of gardening, testing of seeds, and planning of gardens in schoolrooms during late winter.

Class gardens for primary pupils. Individual gardens for intermediate and grammar grades.

Similar tracts of ground, the same quantity and quality of seed, and careful organization at planting time.

Enthusiasm. Teachers and superintendents who love the smell of fresh earth and who faint not when the sun nears the zenith.   •

NEGRO ENFORCEMENT OF
THE LAW

BY A SOUTHERN UNIVERSITY STUDENT

EARNEST students of the race question in America are beginning now, when the evil days of Reconstruction are largely a memory and the progress of the Negro race has become a matter of pride to whites and blacks alike, to emphasize the part that the Negro himself can have in the solution of the problems arising from the position side by side of the two races.

One of the problems which both Negroes and whites in the South have to face is the prevalence in the rural districts and in certain parts of the towns of a widespread spirit of lawlessness. In many cases the indictment is brought in against the white man that he is guilty of innumerable lynchings and outrages in defiance of the law, and that he frequently exercises no discriminating justice even in the very courts of law themselves. Against the Negro the charge is brought of certain brutal assaults on virtue, an alarming number of murders, and a proneness to petty thievery exercised in all possible ways and forms. The people of both races are becoming gradually more sensitive to this sweeping arraignment of their so-called "lawlessness," and would gladly welcome any remedy which might place them in a more enviable light in the eyes of the world. It is the purpose of this brief paper to discuss in some degree the relief which many think would be the result of Negro participation in the enforcement of the law; that is, of Negro service under the executive department of the state.

Writing only ten years ago, Thomas Nelson Page, whose stories are not his only contribution to our knowledge of Negro characteristics, broached the subject in this way:

"It is the writer's belief that the arrest and prompt handing over to the law of Negroes by Negroes, for assaults on white women, would do more to break up ravishing and to restore amicable relations between the two races, than all the resolutions of all the conventions and all the harangues of all the politicians." * * * "The practical application of such a principle is difficult, perhaps, but not impossible. It is possible that in every community Negroes might be appointed officers of the law, to look exclusively after lawbreakers of their own race."

In 1908 Mr. Page's suggestion was commented upon by Professor Josiah Royce, of Harvard, as follows:

"Mr. Thomas Nelson Page in his recent book on the 'Southerner's Problem' speaks in one notable passage of the possibility, which he calls Utopian, that perhaps some day the Negro in the South may be made to co-operate in the keeping of order by the organization under state control of a police of his own race, which shall deal with blacks. * * * But this possibility is not Utopian. When I hear the complaint of the Southerner that the race problem is such as to endanger the safety of his home, I now feel disposed to say: 'The problem that endangers the sanctity of your homes and that is said sometimes to make lynching a necessity, is not a race problem. It is an administrative problem. You have never organized a country constabulary.'"

Again, in 1913, Sir H. H. Johnston, a distinguished Englishman in the South African service, who had toured the Southern states, made the following observations:

"The killing of Negroes by Negroes is a very common event and does not excite that horror throughout the Negro community that it should do. * * * But although this is an outrage on the Negro community, it does not directly affect the white man, and it should, in the first instance, be complained of and preached against by Negroes." * * * "What the United States wants is a good rural constabulary, white and colored; best of all a colored police, mounted or unmounted, under white officers, a police to be under the orders of the state governor."

It will be noticed that in these citations, the writers advocate only a Negro police force or constabulary. They do not advocate Negro courts. In fact, such courts would be open to the charge of "discrimination" under the Fourteenth Amendment; a conflict of jurisdictions would also be apt to occur in many cases. Many Negro courts have been conducted successfully, however, in such wholly Negro communities [1] as Mound Bayou, Mississippi, and Boley, Oklahoma.

In considering a Negro police to be used for the benefit of the members of the race, as outlined in the above quotations, four arguments marshall themselves in favor of the proposal and two against it. Those favoring it will be taken up first.

Eight millions of the colored people of the South still live in the country districts, sometimes in the ratio of six or seven to one white man. In a district or county beat covering twenty-five or thirty square miles of thick forest, dense canebrake, and deep swamp, there is usually one lone white "constable." He undertakes to enforce the law upon four or five hundred more or less disorderly Negroes, and attend to his private business at the same time. Many small offenders among the Negroes undoubtedly escape arrest altogether, or, with the aid of others, lie hid until "the trouble blows over." This, of course, is not calculated to produce an extremely great respect for the white man's law. A half-dozen Negro constables, hired at an equal expense, would probably bring every offender up for trial. They would be more familiar with the individual Negroes themselves, as well as with their haunts.

One scarcely ever sees a white policeman patroling constantly the segregated Negro portions of Southern cities. He dislikes such a "round." The colored corner saloon may bristle with crimes, but he never goes there unless he is called. Neither does this conduce to respect for the law. If the districts were patrolled by Negro policemen petty crimes could not flourish with the same ease and neglect.

The sense of order which comes to a people enforcing the law for itself is one of the boons of democratic government. This effect a system of colored police would probably have upon the Negro mind. These Negro officials would, little by little, by their embodiment of the principles of law and order, organize Negro public opinion against such atrocious crimes as rape and murder, and would make the shame of a small theft become much more sensible than is the prevailing case now.

In many of the small but oftentimes important cases which come before a mayor's or recorder's court, the officer of the law is the only witness to the crime. The decision of the judge depends in a large part upon his recital of the facts. In such

---

1 An interesting study is the relation of such "race towns" to a general movement toward segregation. See Booker T. Washington's "Story of the Negro, "Volume II.

cases when a white policeman makes the arrest the Negro may often rightly feel that he has been done an injustice. Such a feeling must naturally be modified in case the policeman is a member of his own race. Again, any visitor in a Southern police court, or, for that matter, any reader of the court news in a Southern newspaper, will notice with some vague sense of disapprobation a certain amount of levity on the part of officer and judge in cases of small crimes. The Negro defendant will often be heard with amused tolerance and then discharged with a smiling admonition "never to do it again." Such a system of condoning small crimes in him, offenses which would not be excused in the white man, has, as Edgar Gardner Murphy points out, its disadvantages as well as its more immediate advantages for the Negro. It does not inspire him, certainly, with any great respect for a code of law which may vary according to the mood of the judge or of the officer. Such mirthful or intolerant moods as may exist when both officer and judge desire to "teach these niggers a lesson," could not very well exist in common between a white judge and a Negro officer.

Two propositions rather stand in the way of the adoption of this proposal in the Southern states.

Would the Negro policeman enforce the law rigidly or would he be as susceptible to "graft" as his white colleague, or, as some might claim, even more susceptible? Would he rather shield his friends from the law than deliver them up to it, a course which he has so often followed in a private capacity? Evidently such a Negro police force would in all events have to be supervised and officered by white men, as Sir Harry Johnston has recommended.

Would the Negro be willing to serve in such a capacity? Or would his loyalty to his race really prevent the performance of such duties?

Perhaps the best way to satisfy one's doubts upon the queries brought forward is to receive testimony as to how similar systems of law-enforcement have worked out in practice.

Charleston, South Carolina, has a small "sprinkling" of Negro policemen; one or two Southern cities have a few such officials. Such forces have not assumed importance enough nor has the movement as a whole gone forward far enough, however, to justify any conclusions. The evidence must come from outside our own borders. Mr. Page says:

"The English manage such matters well, under equally complicated and delicate conditions. In Hong Kong there are several classes of police—the English, the Chinese, and the Indian police."

Professor Royce, who made a summer journey through Jamaica, speaks of the system there:

"The English ruler provided a good country constabulary in which native blacks also found service and in which they exercised authority over other blacks. Black men, in other words, were trained, under English management, of course, to police black men. Hence he (the Negro) is accustomed to the law; he sees its ministers often as men of his own race, and, in the main, he is fond of order and learns to be respectful toward the established standards."

Both citations mention the success of such a plan under conditions of even greater race complication than our own is ever likely to be. Neither mentions either "graft" or an unwillingness to serve on the part of these racial police. In Jamaica we seem to have full testimony of the influence of Negro policing in forming Negro public opinion. The Jamaica blacks seem to be governed rigidly and justly. On the basis of these English experiments, therefore, may not this question of Negro law enforcement be deeply interesting to all those who are devoted to the welfare of both races in its relation to a greater and a better governed South ?

"FLATWOODS"

A BLACK-BELT STUDY

BY MARY A. E. PENISTON [1]

IN the Black Belt of Alabama there are hundreds of communities where the black people outnumber the whites two to one. To tell of all these communities separately is an impossibility, as each community has its own differences of custom and peculiarities. During the past five years I have been teaching in Alabama and have had fine opportunities for observation. About twelve miles from where I am now teaching is a little community known as "Flatwoods," where I taught a three months' school for two successive summers.

I can never forget the Sunday morning when I first left Snow Hill to take up work at Flatwoods. But before speaking of my work there, I should mention the beauty of the place. Flatwoods (and no more appropriate name could be given it) is a beautiful stretch of lowland, dotted here and there with tall, massive oaks and bright-colored flowers. In summer, as far as the eye can penetrate, may be seen large acreages of corn, peas, and the staple product, cotton.

[1] A graduate of Hampton in the Class of 1903

In the old "Quarters" are the one-room cabins, built of logs and supplied with antiquated mud chimneys. One bad feature of the cabins is that each contains only one window, and that without glass. In winter the window has to be closed to keep out the chilly winds, and this often makes the room extremely dark. Beyond the cabins are the kitchens, cribs, and cotton houses; further still, the barns, all made of logs. Around these cabins and out-houses are fences made of split-pine poles, put together in a primitive, overlapping fashion. Around a few of them, however, where the inmates have more modern ideas, slabs are used for the fences.

In the center of a beautiful grove is the little mission church occupying the site where the "Big House" stood in slavery days, and where "Ole Missus" graciously fed the hungry mouths from her well-filled larder. On my arrival I found the church surrounded by weeds and bushes. In front was the dusty road, and at the rear a large watermelon patch filled with that luscious fruit, though it was not ripe at that time. Down in the meadows were the cows and goats lazily grazing, and on the banks of the fishing pond were those who patiently passed the hours watching the little fish as they swiftly glided by. Below was the creek, and at the upper end where the water was most shallow, several boys were in for an afternoon's "dip." Further on was a group of smaller children whose chief occupations were riding goats, throwing stones, and chasing pigs. The passers-by seemed to have an abundance of time, and although the day was hot, the church-goers looked cool and refreshed.

While I was musing on my new surroundings, and enjoying the beautiful scenery, a bright-eyed little boy crept up to my side and after gaining my attention, said bashfully, "Miss Teacher, my Mama says please ma'am come and take dinner with her today." Such was my invitation and how grateful I was, for my appetite had been sharpened by my long drive. Dinner had been prepared by "Mother Thompson," an elderly, pleasant looking woman whose husband is pastor of the community church, and, because of his long service in the cause of Christ, has been given the name of "Father Thompson." The dinner was cooked in typical Southern style, and everything was tastefully prepared by experienced hands. The menu consisted entirely of home-grown products—chicken, potatoes, peas, tomatoes, corn, and corn-bread. It was during this meal that I realized that there is nothing more genuine than Southern hospitality, and nobody more loyal than the true Southern mammy.

After dinner there was a gathering in the church and the plans for the school work were put before the patrons. Never have I seen a set of people more anxious for a school in their community ; never have I seen people who looked forward to the coming of the teacher as did these poor, untutored people who sat before me. As this was my second summer with them, they felt more at home with me. Once more they listened with eagerness, once more they pledged their support when suggestions were offered them: As in the previous summer, they promised to board the teacher by each patron contributing a portion of the foodstuffs ; chickens, eggs, potatoes, meats, rice, tea, milk, etc., were promised in abundance.

" Miss Mary, " said a white-haired patron as he arose from his seat in the amen corner, "us didn' know las' year jes how to do, but us is done learn' now, an' us is gwine let you see dat us means to educate dese chilluns. " And he proved to me that he meant it. From the day school opened until it closed his children were always present and punctual. Another patron said, "If chickens an' eggs, taters an' peas, means anything at all, dey means dat I is gwine educate my little ones." And throughout the meeting such expressions were heard ; though crude in presentation, they were sincere and were the expression of noble hearts.

I opened school the following Monday with an enrollment of twenty-three pupils, an increase of twelve over the previous summer. Ribbon of every color which the local drygoods store afforded was represented there that Monday morning, for every child was dressed in his Sunday best. They had not forgotten the lessons of the previous summer and they came with clean hands, fingernails polished, faces bright, and teeth brushed. One little boy, in order to please his teacher, had not only had his feet and hands washed, but had had them well greased !

It was remarkable to note the eagerness to learn which was displayed by the children. Their greatest desire, however, was to learn how to spell correctly, and every time they heard a new name their first question was, "How do you spell it ?" The same was true when I told them of various places, as New York, Boston, etc. For instance, I told them of a visit I had made in Baltimore. Hardly had I finished speaking when one of the little boys called out jubilantly, "Miss Mary, I can spell that !" "I don't think you can, Willie, " I told him. But he was sure he could. Then in Josh Billings fashion he arose from his seat and proudly spelt : "B-a-l-l Ball, t-y ty, m-o mo. Ball-ty-mo. " They were a persistent set of children and if they failed in the morning, they succeeded in the afternoon.

Their reasoning was very crude, and yet very interesting. One day in class I asked the children where they thought the colored people came from. One little boy said they came from Georgia ; another thought from out of the ground ; imagine the merriment when one little girl held up her hand and said: "Miss Mary, I know where they came from, Booker T. Washington made them."

Like their contemporaries in Africa they distinguished between "black" and "colored." One morning they told me of the drowning of Billy Mitchell, and when I asked if he was a white or colored man, one of the little boys replied, "He wan't neither, he was a black}man." I afterwards learned that Mitchell was an *exceedingly* black man.

My pupils varied in many respects, and the variations were very pronounced. Often in the same class were pupils whose ages ranged from six to fourteen years. Most of them lived near the schoolhouse, but a few of them walked two miles to school. They learned rapidly and well. Those who did not know a letter at the beginning of the first summer were able to read in the Second Reader by the end of the second summer. They had learned also to add columns of three figures, to do easy sums in subtraction, and could easily write their names and simple sentences.

I have never seen a more religious set of people than the parents of these children. Their preaching hours on Sundays were from eleven to two o'clock, and usually one had to listen to two sermons, sometimes three, during which time the "amen" sisters took turns in getting happy and the brothers in shouting. The sad part of this service was the fact that even though a number of older men and women knew the hymns by heart, they seldom sang a word, but usually hummed a monotonous tune.

"Big-meeting Day" was looked forward to for months, and at last, when the end of the week of prayer came, came also the usual festivities. Pigs, chickens, and even fatted goats were not spared, and many a flour barrel was scraped in order to make the much-longed-for cake. This was a time of great rejoicing, and those who cherished grudges against their neighbors forgot them, and those who were on unfriendly terms became reconciled.

Their home life was simple and sweet. Their chief competition lay, not in adorning the house with finery, but in keeping it clean. Not one home boasted of an organ or piano, and such a thing as a victrola was unknown. One family that could have easily purchased an organ, and where the good dame wanted one, was denied this pleasure because the husband, a deacon of the church, objected on account of his religious principles. Most of the houses were kept scrupulously clean, but void of any floor covering. Lace curtains were a rarity and belonged to those of the higher class only. When company was expected it meant that the walls would be re-papered, always with newspapers; the bed would be made up to a tremendous height, and the best quilt put on top. The good housewife usually prided herself on her quilts, and could show you the patterns of "bear claw," "grandmother's dream," "Jacob's ladder," etc.

These people were the most generous, whole-hearted people that I have ever met. When the cry came for help, if at dawn or midnight, there was always a ready response. I have seen home, work, and pleasure put aside in order to fulfill the solemn duty of digging a grave, or to go ten miles for the nearest doctor, or to sit up all night with a sick neighbor. Sympathy was always given, not in words only, but in deeds, and often manifested by the gift of a portion of their meager savings.

It was amusing to watch them go to the fields to work, especially the women, as they usually went barefooted, their dresses tied up above the ankles, and a red bandanna or a big sun-hat for head covering. Shoes were reserved for Sunday wear or special occasions. Though living in this primitive fashion, they were happy and care free. I have seen men and women who have worked all day on the farm, in the heat of the sun, come from the fields and, after eating supper, walk five miles to church for prayer meeting.

Before I left Flatwoods I could see improvements. The parents had begun to take more interest in the church and Sabbath school, and a greater interest in their children. The churchyard, which I found filled with weeds, had been converted into a beautiful court, and the church had been whitewashed inside and out. There was no more snuff-dipping or use of tobacco in the churches, and in many cases hair-wrapping had disappeared. Clean newspapers on the walls took the place of torn and faded ones, and every yard received a good sweeping on Saturday as preparation for the Sabbath. The men paid more attention to the broken-down fences; the harness was kept in better repair; the stock received more attention; clothes were brushed more often, shoes polished until they shone, and collars that had long been stored away were resurrected once more. The children realized that a crime had been committed when they robbed a bird's nest or killed a bird. There was no more fighting and no more stealing of watermelons, for they did not wish "Miss Mary," as I was called, to know about it. They learned to love the Sabbath school more. They came every Sunday, and there learned the lesson, repeating it to me during the week.

The desire to have the school continue has been planted in rich soil. The patrons are now raising money to build a two-room schoolhouse with modern improvements, and to secure the services of two teachers. Last summer the children began a small farm with this end in view. The meetings are held regularly, and the enthusiasm is just as great as in the beginning.

I cannot forget these people, for they were certainly good and loyal to me. My work was a pleasure and the hours spent with them in their homes were hours of real joy. Their attitude was all I wished it to be, and the beautiful part of it was that they never changed in their manner toward me. "May God bless Flatwoods," is my daily prayer.

Book Reviews

Indian Blankets and Their Makers: By George Wharton James. A. C. McClurg & Company, Chicago. Price, $4.00.

THE art development of the human race is, as the author says, a fascinating study, and the reader will not go very deeply into this volume without realizing something of that fascination. Merely to turn the pages and to examine and compare the numerous plates reproducing in colors the old and the modern Navaho blankets affords a rare pleasure. One is reminded of those charming books, with which we are all familiar, describing and depicting Oriental rugs. The art is the same in both fabrics and in both we find the fascination of hand-woven materials and colors wrought into things of beauty. Nor does the simple, virile design of the Navaho suffer by comparison with the more highly developed and elaborated pattern of the Oriental.

To the collector of Navaho blankets this book offers an added interest in a favorite hobby. To one who is fortunate enough to own even two or three blankets it brings the joy of the collector. To him who has none it will come as a revelation.

It is perhaps inevitable under such circumstances that the text should be subordinated to the illustrations and the plates. The illustrations are poetry; the text is uninspired prose. Yet it, too, is of interest and value. Mr. James has made a considerable study of the history of Indian looms and a careful analysis of the symbols that are found in Indian designs. He defines also the sources of the materials used, and in this connection he imparts a welcome item of information. It seems that the deterioration in blanket weaving which began about 1892, through the introduction of the cheaper Germantown yarns and the use of aniline dyes, was carried to such lengths as to effect its own cure,

for it flooded the market with an unsalable article. The author
tells us that "out of the mere instinct of self-preservation the
Indian trader sprang into the breach he himself had made, and
refused to buy the inferior specimens of the loom. The result is
that, today, as fine blankets are being woven as were ever produced in the palmiest days of the art."

Probably few people realize the extent of this industry. The
official reports of the United States Government give, as the
product of the Navaho looms in 1913, nearly a million dollars'
worth of blankets. In view of these statements of the [quality
and quantity produced the future of the industry seems assured,
and the importance of Mr. James's book as a timely treatise on a
very live subject is thereby much enhanced.   W. L. B.

Masterpieces of Negro Eloquence : Edited by Alice Moore
Dunbar.   Published by the Bookery Publishing Company, New
York.   Price, $2.50.

IN "Masterpieces of Negro Eloquence" Mrs. Dunbar has made
an interesting and valuable collection of addresses by many
of the foremost Negroes of the last hundred years. Certain
omissions suggest themselves at once.   But the editor declares
that "the present volume does not aim to be a complete collection of Negro eloquence ; it does not even aim to present the best
that the Negro has done on the platform; it merely aims to present to the public some few of the best speeches " which he has
made.   However, the whole or parts of fifty-one addresses by
forty-nine speakers are included. Naturally they bear mainly
upon the peculiar conditions surrounding the Negro in this country.   "Since the early nineteenth century until the present time,
he is found giving eloquent voice to the story of his wrongs and
his proscriptions. "

The addresses are arranged chronologically, beginning in the
early years of the nineteenth century and coming down to the
present time. Step by step they present the views of the
Negroes regarding their conditions and the men and measures of
their times.   They show the important parts played by the more
capable colored men and women, and set forth the aspirations
and achievements, the disillusionments and duties of the race.
Much of the history of the Negro is related in them.   And they
show especially the particular views of the colored people—a point
too often overlooked in the study of the Negro.   In making these
addresses readily accessible Mrs. Dunbar has rendered Negro
youth and the general student an important service.   The selections begin with addresses of such well-known colored men as
James McCune Smith, Frederick Douglass, Richard T. Greener,
Robert Brown Eliot, John M. Langston, and Dr. Alexander

Crummell, and close with those of such men of today as Dr. Francis H. Grimké, Major R. R. Moton, Hon. W. H. Lewis, Professor Kelly Miller, and Dr. W. E. B. DuBois.   W. T. B. W.

To a Summer Cloud and Other Poems: By Emily Tolman. Published by Sherman, French & Company, Boston, Mass. Price, $1.00 *net.*

THIS attractive little book of verse was written by a former Hampton worker who has always retained her interest in and love for the school. The range of the poems is a wide one, and many of them have appeared before in various New England journals. The verses on nature are particularly graceful and pleasing, though those on patriotism and religion show, naturally, greater depth of thought. Two memorial poems—one on Cora F. Butler who was a former Hampton worker and one on Hampton's founder—will be of special interest to readers of the Southern Workman. We quote Miss Tolman's appreciation of General Armstrong:

GENERAL S. C. ARMSTRONG

Died May 11, 1893

Alike from lowly hut and lofty hall,
From cabin of the black man or the red,
A common lamentation comes from all,
            Our General's dead.

The dusky host of those whom Lincoln freed,
By thy kind hand from darker bondage led,
Cry out, "The man who was our friend in need,
            Alas, is dead!"

The swarthy Indians on the Western plain,
Inspired by thee the white man's road to tread,
In many tongues repeat the sad refrain,
            "Our Chief is dead."

Those palm-fringed isles on far Pacific's breast,
That for our land this generous hero bred,
Lament, "Of noble sons, this one, the best,
            Too soon is dead."

Above earth's moan, across the shadowy sea,
From Heavenly shore, methinks I hear reply;
"Who cares for least of mine doth care for me,
            He cannot die."

Indian Scout Talks: By Dr. Charles A. Eastman. Published by Little, Brown and Company. Price, 80 cents.

THE author's childhood on the Western prairies and in the woods gives him a thorough insight into the lore so coveted by all children, and especially by the Boy Scouts and the Camp-Fire Girls to whom the book is dedicated. They will find in it a charming guide book, its first lessons helping to put them in sympathy with nature that they may be mentally ready to adapt themselves to the physical training necessary for the woodsman.

Here they may learn how to read footprints in the snow or in the green forest, how to hunt with bow and arrow and how to trap wild game, how to make and follow blazed trails, and a great many other things which they will realize are just the things they have wanted to know.

There are interesting chapters on Indian games and dress, and it is to be hoped that some of the illustrators of Indian life may take to heart the fact that "no Indian girl may wear the feathers of the eagle." Perhaps as useful as anything in the book are the lists of Indian names with their meanings.

Dr. Eastman's work will not only be a valuable guide to the Boy Scouts and Camp-Fire Girls, but it will give them many lessons on the high ideals of courage and service the young Indians learned in the old days, and cannot but add to the espect in which they hold their red brother.   C. W. A.

Japan's Modernization: By Saint Nihal Singh. Published by Charles H. Kelly, London. Price, one shilling.

A BRILLIANT journalist of British India and an ardent protagonist of colored peoples, Saint Nihal Singh, has told within one hundred-fifty readable, small pages the dramatic story of Japan's modernization.

The chapter headings suggest Mr. Singh's method of treating his material : "The Nation Transformed ;" "Material Progress ;" "Intellectual Quickening ;" "Reformation of Society ;" "Towards Democracy ;" "Problems Ahead."

This book is one of the "Manuals for Christian Thinkers," and lays special stress on the relation of Christianity, education, industries, and the status of women to the development of Japan's economic and social life during the past two generations. Mr. Singh furnishes in this excellent handbook a good list of classified books and an index which is complete enough to be really useful. He refrains from the use of footnotes and tells his straightforward story in short paragraphs that are full of vivid pictures of everyday life in old and new Japan.

Again and again Mr. Singh points out the difficulties that Japan has had, in her struggle toward democracy, through the lack of sympathy on the part of Government officials and the race prejudice of Europeans. While Mr. Singh presents the striking facts of Japanese life with vividness and apparently does not aim to be controversial, nevertheless he leaves in the mind of his readers the impression that the people of the Occident, through

sheer race prejudice, have been decidedly unfair to the Japanese
and other colored peoples. While students of race problems recognize the fact that prejudice is a vital factor in such problems,
it is also true that wherever different races have come to understand each other and to see the *best* in each other, they have been
able to find a platform upon which they could stand and work
together for the best in life—religion, education, and economic
progress.

Mr. Singh has explained, with clearness and a good deal of
force, how Japan has met some of the important tests of modern
civilization—civilization as it was understood before the days of
the great war in Europe. His book should prove interesting
reading to those who wish to know what the Japanese people are
like in their common life. That "Japan's Modernization" should
be included in a series that is intended to appeal to Christian
thinkers is significant of the growing desire on the part of men
to understand, as far as possible, the facts of race progress and
race feeling. W. A. A.

At Home and Afield

HAMPTON INCIDENTS

SCHOOL ENROLLMENT

THE forty-seventh term of Hampton Institute began on October 1
with an enrollment of 899 boarding
pupils, and 425 day pupils in the Whittier Training School, making a total
enrollment of 1324. Of the 899 boarding pupils, 603 are old students and
296 are new. There is an unusually
large number of girls, 367 in all. An
addition of 16 new Indian students, 8
girls and 8 boys, an increase of 11 over
last year, encourages the hope that
the number will continue to increase
every year, in spite of the fact that
they now come without help from the
Government. There are now 42
Indians at Hampton.

Most of the new students go into the
night school, and work during the
day—the boys on the farm, in the
kitchens and offices, and in the schoo

buildings ; the girls in the domestic-
science work class. Thirty-three boys
are working this year on the Shellbanks Farm.

A new student who comes to Hampton from Portuguese East Africa,
is Columbus Kamba Simango of the
Ndau tribe. He received most of his
preparation at the Mt. Silinda School
at Melsetter, East Africa, being
taught for a time by Mrs. Julia Winter Hatch, a former Hampton worker.
Simango has entered the day school.
His purpose is to get the all-round
training which Hampton gives, in
order to fit himself to go back as a
missionary to his people.

COURSES OF STUDY

THIS year the classes have been
arranged on a new basis, making

an important change in the course. The work done in the Junior year is now to be considered of an elementary grade and forms a separate Junior or preparatory department. All the regular courses begin with what was formerly the Junior Middle year and continue through four years, now called the First, Second, Third, and Senior years. No certificate will be given without a diploma, and to earn a diploma the student must complete one of the four-year courses. These courses are, for the boys, the academic-normal, agricultural, and business courses, and a trade course in any one of thirteen trades; for the girls, the academic-normal, home economics, library, and matron's courses.

NEW WORKERS

THERE have been several changes in the teaching force at Hampton this year. Mr. Hugh W. Alger, of West Chester, Pa., who has been state supervisor of schools in the district of Norwalk, Conn., has taken the position of supervisor of the academic department formerly held by Miss Harriet Hayward. New academic teachers are Miss Dorothy Jones of New Hartford, Conn., a graduate of Smith College; Mrs. Elizabeth Brady of New York City; Miss Ruth Goodwin of Saco, Me., who was graduated from Colby College; and Mr. Fred E. Fossett of Brunswick, Me. Miss W. O. Nash and Miss Grace L. Morrison have returned to teach in the academic department.

Miss Ellen Cope, a graduate of Wellesley College, who took a post-graduate course in hygiene last year, is the new physical director for the girls. Miss Bertina A. Leete, of Claremont, N. H., formerly a teacher in the schools of Richmond, Va., is in charge of the domestic science department, and Miss May D. Stone of Lowell, Mass., is secretary to Dr. Phenix.

In the Trade School, besides those mentioned in a previous issue, are Mr. C. C. Jagger, of Westerly, R. I., assistant in the machine shop, and Mr. Lloyd M. Westcott of Syracuse,

N. Y., assistant in the paint shop. Other new workers are Mr. Benjamin L. Davis, '14, foreman in the dairy barn, and Mr. Louis Martin, '14, foreman in the horticultural department.

SUMMER TRADE WORK

BESIDES the general repair work which goes on most of every vacation, several pieces of work have been done this summer by the Trade School. A new kitchen wing has been attached to Marquand Cottage for the restaurant, the old kitchen being added to the dining-room. Two new dwelling houses at the north end of the grounds have been partially completed. A new feature in their construction is the use of stucco instead of weatherboarding, which makes a very attractive appearance. The boys' new dormitory, James Hall, is well under way. It is to be a four-story, fireproof building, with concrete floors, brick corridor walls, and partition walls of gypsum block, and will accommodate one hundred seventy-five boys. Concrete "benches" for rose beds have been made in the greenhouse.

ADDRESSES

ON Sunday afternoon, October 10, Miss E. F. Clarke, who came to this country from Natal, South Africa, gave a most interesting talk to the Hampton workers. She told of the life and characteristics of the Zulus, showing pictures of the country, the people, and their houses, which are huts made of saplings, thatched with grass, without doors or chimneys. The natives are ignorant and superstitious, but love their homes and their own people, and are glad to help support Zulu students who are ambitious for a good education.

Two important schools in Natal are Amanzimtoti Institute, with its industrial, preparatory, and normal departments, and the Inanda Seminary for girls. Miss Clarke spoke especially of the bad moral conditions in the town, making it unsafe for girls to live there. In Durban the people are obliged to employ boys to do the house work, as careful parents will not allow their daughters to go to the city.

ON Monday evening, September 21, Miss Davis gave a stereopticon talk in Clarke Hall, primarily for the students, but many of the workers and families on the school grounds were glad to take advantage of the opportunity to hear about her interesting experiences in Europe last summer. The pictures shown represented the principal buildings in several European cities, the troops of the different nations, and conditions under which Americans escaped from the war zone.

Miss Davis was in Munich when Germany declared war against Russia. She went from Munich to Lucerne, where she remained two weeks, during mobilization. She took the first opportunity to go to England by way of France, finally being obliged to recross the Channel to sail from Rotterdam. Miss Davis spoke of the difficulty all travelers had in securing even small amounts of cash on their checks; while she had a very strenuous journey without the usual accommodations, she met with uniform courtesy in all the countries through which she passed. Miss Davis said she was compelled to leave her baggage in Europe, adding that the only travelers who seemed certain of having their trunks with them were four e e - phants that she saw at Boulogne, apparently en route for Paris.

ENTERTAINMENTS

THE Work Year Boys gave their annual program on Tuesday evening, September 22, in Cleveland Hall Chapel. The program consisted of music, several papers on the value and dignity of labor, and a cleverly written class history, during the reading of which the trophies won during the year were displayed. They gave the incoming Work Year Boys a hearty welcome.

"A Merry Company" is the title of a bright and unusually well-acted little operetta which was given by the students in Huntington Hall Auditorium on September 26. A very pretty picnic scene was rudely interrupted by a tramp, whose many mishaps, and the efforts by three gallant policemen to restore order, caused much amusement. Music was furnished by the band under the direction of Mr. Tessmann.

The King's Daughters enjoyed a social evening among themselves on Saturday, October 3, when the old members renewed friendships and the new students were welcomed among them.

On Saturday, October 17, occurred the annual "getting-acquainted" social, the boys going the rounds to Winona, Cleveland Hall, and the Museum, where different teachers and girls, acting as hostesses, received them.

RELIGIOUS WORK

THE regular missionary rally of the students was held on Sunday morning, October 4. Dr. Turner and Miss Nettleton, who is to have charge of this work during the coming year, spoke to the students of the ways in which they can assist in this work for the neighborhood. Dr. Frissell also spoke of the rare opportunity which missionary work affords for practical Christian service. At the close of the rally, about two hundred of the boys volunteered as helpers.

The Y. M. C. A. has entered upon a year of activity under the leadership of Mr. S. D. Spady, the general secretary. Each year the Association sends a letter to every boy who expects to enter Hampton, and on his arrival he is given a handbook of information about the life of the school. This year a new feature was added to this phase of the work. The new students, on their arrival at Hampton, were met by members of a reception committee who cared for their comfort and sought to befriend and assist the newcomers in every possible way. On Saturday evening, October 10, a social was held for the new boys, which gave them an opportunity of making many friends among the old students.

At present a campaign for new members is being conducted, and it is hoped that at least two hundred will be enrolled. An invitation is being extended this year to the instructors to enroll as honorary members.

EXTENSION WORK

AT a teachers' institute for the colored teachers of Middlesex and Mathews Counties held at Mathews Court House on October 2 and 3, two of Hampton's workers were among the speakers. Mr. W. T. B. Williams made an address and took part in the discussions. Mr. L. R. Miner, Hampton's director of applied art, spoke on "Art in Common Things," making a point of the beautifying of school grounds. His drawings showed how wild shrubs and trees might be used effectively in school grounds. Mr. E. C. Percifull, the superintendent of schools for the two counties, was much interested in Mr. Miner's plans, and hopes to introduce them in the white as well as in the colored schools.

A GRADUATE HONO

FOR the colored people of Car County, Maryland, October 10 was a proud day. The weather was fine and a large number of parents and children, patrons, ministers, and teachers met in the new building at Denton, Md., for the purpose of dedicating it. Quite a number of white friends were present, among them the state and county superintendents, the lady who has charge of the girls' canning clubs of Maryland, the industrial supervisor of Baltimore County, and others.

The exercises were interesting and appropriate for such an occasion. After the opening, which was directed by Miss Lucretia Kennard, Class of

'92 the supervisor of the industrial work of Caroline County, the county superintendent took charge and introduced the state superintendent, Dr. Stephens, who gave an admirable address, near its close making the suggestion that on account of the fine service rendered by Miss Kennard to the children of the county, the name of the new school building should be the Kennard High and Industrial Training School. A motion was made to that effect and unanimously carried. Miss Kennard made a graceful speech in which she said that the school should have a motto, and that she hoped it might be the one she had learned at Hampton: "Not to be ministered unto, but to minister;" she added that she sincerely hoped the school might stand for service.

The patrons of Denton and Caroline County are to be congratulated upon this additional opportunity to carry on in a more advanced way the academic and industrial work of their county.

WHITTIER SCHOOL

THE Whittier School opened on Thurs , October 1, with a large attendance o. pupils from Newport News, Hampton, and Phoebus. There are many more chi dren from Hampton this year than e er before. Miss Ida A. Tourtellot, ho formerly taught in the academ department of Hampton Institute, i now principal of the Whittier Schoo Two new teac s are Miss Fredoni D. Banks and M Lucy C. Barrow both of Phoebus. ey were gradua from Hampton in e, and this , therefore, their firs ear of teacl ing. The manual training ot be in charge of a regu but the classes will be tau students from the Institute.

On Monday morning, tober 12, Miss Julia C. Lathrop vi ited the school and spoke to the chi n at morning exercises. She explain d to them the pledge they had just m de as they saluted the flag. They ha promised to support the Government and therefore to support their fathers and mothers, for all the homes together make the community and all the communities make the nation. Obedience to fathers and mothers is the first step toward supporting the Government. Miss Lathrop also referred to the work of the Children's Bureau, of which she is Chief.

VISITORS

A recent visitor at Hampton Institute was Miss E. F. Clarke, of Natal, South Africa, who spent some time studying Hampton's methods of training. Miss Clarke has worked under the American Board of Missions in Nata for fourteen years, the last five being spent in the normal department of the Amanzimtoti Institute. When she returns she will be connected with the Inanda Seminary for girls. Her sister, who is at the Mt. Silinda School in Melsetter, East Africa, visited Hampton last year. Miss Clarke hopes to put into practice some of the ideas

she has gained while in this country.

Miss Julia C. Lathrop, Chief of the Children's Bureau, Washington, D. C., visited the school for a few days. She was accompanied by Miss Margaret Armstrong, who is at present connected with her department. Mr. Jackson Davis, state supervisor of rural schools in Virginia, was a recent visitor. Mr. Channing H. Tobias, student secretary in the Colored Men's Department of the International Committee of the Y. M. C. A., spent a few days at Hampton. Friends of Hampton workers who have visited the school during the past month are : Mr. and Mrs. Van Antwerp of Washington, D. C., sister and brother of Miss Mabel Hodge ; Miss M. Gertrude Berry of Worcester, Mass., a friend of Miss Turner; and Mrs. F. A. Whitaker of Bellows Falls, Vt., visiting her daughter, Miss Ethel Buckman. Other visitors were Miss Lillie M. Edminster of Brooklyn, N. Y., and Miss E. Grace Browne of Waltham, Mass.

THE ARMSTRONG LEAGUE OF HAMPTON WORKERS

NOTICE is hereby given of the regular annual meeting of the Armstrong League of Hampton Workers to be held in the Museum at Hampton Institute on Wednesday, November 4, 1914, at 4:30 p. m. A full attendance is desired and all new Hampton workers are cordially invited to be present.

EMILY K. HERRON,
Recording Secretary

GRADUATES AND EX-STUDENTS

THE industrial supervisor of Albemarle Co., Va., Maggie L. Payne, is a Hampton graduate who completed the post-graduate course in 1910. She was recently married to Jackson P. Burley, '96, of Charlottesville, Va. She wrote last winter of her work in the rural schools:

"Four days every week I visit the schools in the county, and every Friday I have a class of boys from seven or eight schools at a time meet me in a conveniently located house rented for the purpose. I teach them to make shuck mats and white-oak baskets, and to bottom chairs. These lessons they teach the other pupils in these schools, and you would be surprised to see how fast the ideas are taken from pupil to pupil over the country.

"I copied that manner of getting my work around by seeing the work handed from the old to the new students at Hampton. From this class three stores in Charlottesville are being supplied with shuck mats, and the pupils are enjoying their work very much."

ONE of the most earnest and faithful graduates of Hampton, who has taught almost continuously since leaving the school, wrote in January in reference to the annual Christmas letter sent out to former students:

"It is with much pleasure that I read all those dear and helpful letters I get from Hampton, so full of thought and anxiety for my race. When I stop and think what God has done, what He will do for all those who fear Him and keep His commandments, discrimination and segregation do not worry me."

THIS letter will give some idea of the work of an industrial supervisor in rural schools. It was written in March by John W. L. Young, '12, who took a special course in manual training after graduation, and became an industrial supervisor in Georgia. He says:

"I have succeeded to a great extent in getting the patrons of the county to see and understand the aim of this industrial work. I have under my supervision fifty-one schools. The Board of Education gives five-month school terms, beginning November first, but not many opened school until after Christmas, after the cotton picking season. I spent nearly all of November going around holding meetings in the different communities to encourage the people to send their children to school as soon as possible, and a good many times I got them to consent to open school at once. All the schools were open in January and I then began taking up the industrial work. Most of the schools before I began my work were very badly kept, so practical lessons in housecleaning and talks on cleanliness and health usually preceded the other industrial work. I have taken up such work as cornshuck mat making, white-oak basketry, chair-caning, cardboard construction work, picture framing, a little upholstery, and simple furniture making.

"I have organized in the schools what are known as Jeanes' Fund Leagues. Their purpose is to raise money by giving entertainments or by self-taxation, with which to purchase materials for the work. I have taken up some form of work in thirty-nine schools and hope to take up work in the remaining eleven by the middle of March."

A GRADUATE of 1912, who has returned to his home to follow his trade, wrote in March of some of the difficulties which he has to meet. He refers gratefully to the Christmas letters sent out from Hampton to graduates and ex-students:

"The Hampton letters were of untold help to me. They came at a time when our church was in very low spirits and gave me encouragement to press onward, though I was tempted to give up. I am glad to say that our church is now on the upward march. Our preacher was turned out of Conference on account of his immoral life. The man we have now seems to be a good man, ready and willing to do all he can to uplift the church. I have greater hope for our Sunday school than I have ever had.

"In my trade work I have more than I can do. The last of last August I began my own and my brother's house. We have an eight-room house, twenty-six by twenty-seven feet. We are living in it now [March]. We have sixteen acres of land. My work on this house has been the means of my having more work offered me than I can do. I have had four houses offered me, costing from eight hundred to twelve hundred dollars each. I shall take two of them at twelve hundred and the others if I can get help enough.

"I have been doing a great deal of brick work. There is not a bricklayer in the town, but three near here. There are three white carpenters in town and a number near here. Nearly all my work so far has been for white people. Two of the houses that I spoke of are for Negroes, one at twelve hundred dollars."

Remus G. Torrence, Trade Class, '09, remained for two years' work in academic (day school). He then returned to his home, Huntersville, N. C., where for the past three years he has taught the school from which he came to Hampton. He and his assistant have now about a hundred children on roll. During the vacations he follows his trade—carpentry. Through his influence fifteen families have bought their own homes since he returned to his own community.

A GIRL who is trying to carry out the teaching received at Hampton, Effie C. Pointer, '13, wrote last January of her first attempt at teaching:

"This winter finds me teaching here in Henderson at the graded school. There are over four hundred pupils enrolled in our school and nine teachers. I am teaching the second grade and have on roll thirty-eight. I am very happy in my work. Our principal's wife, Mrs. Mary Eaton, who is a Hampton graduate, is one of our teachers. I am trying to become better acquainted with my pupils by visiting their parents and seeing the conditions of their homes. I have a Sunday-school class in one of the churches here and have carried in several new scholars."

A GRADUATE of last year, Irene E. Polk, has written enthusiastically of her work in Denton, Md. Her letter, received in March, said: "We have a well-organized Patrons' Association and a Mothers' Club; both are doing very good work in improving the school and home.

"I have all the classes from the third through the seventh in sewing and weaving. These girls have organized themselves into a little 'Busy Bee Club' for the purpose of buying games for the school. We have bought a croquet set and are expecting to get a basket ball with the next month's dues.

"Every Friday I have the larger girls of the school in my room for a talk. We have fine times together, talking over the things girls should know. I get a great deal of pleasure from these talks because I learn to know the girls better. Many of the girls are becoming more refined and I feel that they are helped by these little meetings."

AN ex-student of '86 who was at Hampton nearly four years, is now in a hotel in Pennsylvania. His letter of January, 1914, shows how fully he has followed General Armstrong's advice about getting property:

"I am still working in the hotel because there is no other avenue open to me where I can make an honest living. I have saved my money and bought a home. I paid $2700 for the land and a five-room house on it, and built a double house at the cost of $4475, borrowing $1300 from the bank at six per cent to meet my payments. I have succeeded in paying every cent that I owe; with the improvements that I have made on my property I value it at $12,000. I was told that I would have trouble in renting my houses because the colored people could not pay the rent and the white people would not rent from me. I found it quite the opposite. The white people are reluctant to give the colored people a chance to get them. A colored family rents my five-room house at $13 and a white family the nine-room house at $25."

LAST winter an ex-student of '92 wrote as follows of his various activities:

"I have been secretary of the Indian Woods Baptist Church for eighteen years; secretary to the board of trustees for eighteen years; either superintendent or principal Sunday-school teacher in the same church for over twenty-one years; and am secretary of a real-estate company which owns and controls over $4000 worth of land. I own two lots in the town worth about $700 each, and four shares in the real-estate company worth $1600, making my real estate value about $3000. I am in company with my brother in the merchant business. We carry between $1000 to $1800 worth of stock all the time."

A LETTER received in June 1913 from Robert E. Malone, Agriculture '09, formerly head of the Orchard Division at Tuskegee Institute, tells of some of his activities in the State of Kansas, where he has been for three years instructor in agriculture at Western University, Kansas City:

"I have recently received an appointment from Governor Hodges as the Kansas representative at the National Negro Farmers' Conference to be held at Birmingham in July. I am chairman of the executive committee of the Kansas State Farmers' Association."

A GRADUATE of 1912, Thomas H. McNeil, was during the past year principal of a rural school in Cumberland County, Virginia. He wrote in the spring as follows :

"I am teaching in a new building with large windows and plenty of light, good heaters and desks, which make it very comfortable. While the girls are sewing the boys are making mats. The old school building stands in the yard, so it is very convenient for the boys who are making mats and trying to do woodwork. I want to have them make a kitchen cabinet and a kitchen table for our cooking teacher. The night school, which I am teaching free of charge, is taking very well. We have only been open two weeks and we have seventeen pupils on roll, the oldest being seventy-one years old. I am expecting to have a full school in the course of two weeks.

" We have two leagues— the Senior and Junior Industrial Improvement Leagues. The former is composed mostly of the patrons, the latter of the school children. We have raised about sixty dollars since school began, the greater part of which has been invested in window shades, water cooler, lamps, chairs, tables, and other necessities for the school. We are now trying to raise money for an extra month."

THE industrial supervisor of the rural schools of Rockbridge County, Va., is Othelia Hoffman, '13.

Sarah C. Campbell, '11, for two years a teacher at Penn School, Frogmore, S. C., is now industrial supervisor of the schools in Middlesex County, Va.

Lucy Lee Jones, '01, has accepted a position at Kittrell College, Kittrell, N. C.

Zella F. Turner, '13, is now a teacher at the Penn School, Frogmore, S. C.

Lillian B. Weeden, '12, is a teacher in one of the public schools of Portsmouth, Va.

Gladys C. Austin, '13, died at her sister's home, Bluefield, W. Va., on October 8, 1914.

TWO of Hampton's women graduates have recently been honored by having buildings named for them in appreciation of their devoted service to their people—Miss Melvin, '74, whose recent death was chronicled in the last number of the Southern Workman, has been thus honored in the naming of a new girls' building at the Agricultural and Mechanical College at Tallahassee, Fla. An account of the dedication of the *Kennard* High and Industrial Training School at Denton, Md., will be found in another column.

ONE of the workers at the People's Village School, Mt. Meigs, Ala., who has served there for the past two years, Napoleon L. Byrd, '12, is now studying at the University of Wisconsin.

Arthur C. Shearer, '13, is teacher of blacksmithing at the State College for Colored Students in Dover, Del.

Chester A. A. Coles, graduate carpenter '04, has recently been appointed instructor in carpentry at the State Normal School in Montgomery, Ala. Mr. Coles for several years held a similar position at the State Agricultural and Mechanical College at Tallahassee, Fla.

Elijah A. Chisholm, '07, is now in charge of the agricultural department at the Robert Hungerford School, Eatonville, Fla.

Benjamin F. Jones, '13, who was last year teacher of carpentry at the Manassas, Va., Industrial School, has been appointed teacher of manual training at the new Cuyler Street School of Industries, Savannah, Ga.

Harrison A. Magill, '08, who has for the past six years been teacher of manual training at the Whittier Training School, Hampton Institute, has been appointed teacher of manual training in the public schools of Tulsa, Okla.

Thomas H. McNeil, '12, has accepted the principalship of the public school at Millwood, Clarke County, Va.

FOR the past eleven years, George W. Blount, '02, has been employed at Hampton Institute, first as bookkeeper in the Treasurer's Office and later as Commandant's assistant and teacher of bookkeeping. He has recently been elected director and general business manager of the Crown Savings Bank of Newport News, Va.

G. Hays Buchanan, '08, and Lincoln University, '14, has been appointed principal of the new county training school at Bowling Green, Caroline County, Va.

Thomas J. Edwards, '05, for the past two years supervisor of rural schools in Tallapoosa County, Ala., has been elected superintendent of the Negro Reformatory at Hanover, Virginia. Mr. Edwards has written a series of articles on rural life in Alabama which have appeared from time to time in the Southern Workman.

Robert L. Page, '07, is now bandmaster and teacher at the Agricultural and Mechanical College in Greensboro, N. C., where he was formerly instructor in bricklaying.

INDIAN NOTES

THERE were present at the recent Conference of the Society of American Indians in Madison, Wis., nine Hampton graduates and ex-students, a fine body of men and women of whom the school feels justly proud. They were Frank Gauthier, Menominee, who was at Hampton for a short time only, in '86 and '87, and who has since held various positions in the Government Service; Charles Kealear, '89, a Sioux, who is doing active Christian work among the Arapaho Indians, and who is postmaster at Arapaho, Wyoming; Mrs. Angel De Cora Dietz, Winnebago, '91, the well-known illustrator and teacher of drawing and native Indian art at the Carlisle Indian School; Lavinia Cornelius, an Oneida, who was at Hampton from '88 until '93, afterwards graduating from the New Haven Training School for Nurses, and now acting as nurse at the Government School, Hayward, Wis.; Louis Armell, and John Hunter, Winnebagoes, the former a farmer, the latter a carpenter at Winnebago, Nebraska; Elizabeth G. Bender, Chippewa, who left from the graduate course in '08, and has ever since been a teacher in the Government Service, being now at the Fort Belknap School in Montana; Stella O'Donnell, Chippewa, Graduate Class of '10, who taught for one year after leaving Hampton and is now stenographer at Pawnee, Okla.; and George Brown, Chippewa, '12, general mechanic at Yankton Agency, Greenwood, S. D.

Andrew Bellcour, Chippewa, is employed at White Earth, Minnesota, as a printer on the Tomahawk.

Joseph DuBray, a Yankton Sioux who was at Hampton from 1890 until 1895, and who has for years been farming in South Dakota, is now a student in the Theological Seminary at Alexandria, Va.

James Mannington, Pawnee, was married during September to Miss Bertie Allen, an ex-student of Chilocco.

What Others Say

INDIAN FRUIT GROWERS

THROUGH aid of the Government, under the reimbursing regulations and agreements to reimburse therefor, the Indians of the Morongo or Malki Reservation in Banning, Cal., have planted over 500 acres to oat hay and nearly 11,000 fruit trees, consisting of almond, apricot, peach, apple, prune, and pear trees. The largest single Indian ranch or orchard at Morongo, all fruit-bearing trees of the apricot, peach, and almond variety, is a little over twenty acres, and from this acreage the Indian owner realizes from $1500 to $2000 per year.

Native American

NEGRO BUSINESS

THE Industrial Savings, Loan, and Investment Company, with a paid-up capital of $25,000 is a Negro organization at Danville, Va., that is proving a great success. The company, in addition to helping Negroes secure homes in the city, owns considerable real estate, much of which is business property. A large auditorium of pressed brick is one of its holdings.

The *Tuskegee Student*

THE HAMPTON SCHOOL

THERE was recently published in the *Survey* an excellent account of Hampton Institute in the fiftieth year since Emancipation, with a cut of the school's shield and one of Major Robert Moton on its cover. Hampton is the pioneer industrial school for colored youth, being the torch from which Tuskegee, Calhoun, and Mt. Meigs, and smaller school centers receive their light. Hampton ought, in fact, to be called "Armstrong," after that great-hearted man to whose restless soul it owes its one hundred and fifty buildings, its thousand acres of land, its courses in thirteen trades, embracing teaching, homemaking, business and farming, for the 800 or more students in enrollment there. From among her 8000 former students you will find a representative in every part of the country. It is one of the most consoling thoughts that, in spite of the recrudescence of race feeling now uppermost, the colored man has had, and still has, true friends like Armstrong and the late Robert Ogden.

A. M. E. Church Review.

INDUSTRIAL SCHOOL IN LIBERIA

AN industrial school, modeled upon the Negro educational institutions at Hampton, Va., and Tuskegee, Ala., is to be established in Liberia with part of the $65,000 just turned over to the Liberian Government as a gift from the American Colonization Society.

ABORIGINAL FARMERS

THE Indians were the first to use fertilizers in Virginia, says the Norfolk, Va., *Pilot*. The finny tribe was much more abundant then than now, or at least more numerous in the smaller streams and thousands of coves that indent the shores. At high tide, when the fish were feeding up at the end of the coves, the Indians would draw across the stream a sort of hedge or fence made of reeds woven together, so that the fish would be left high and dry on the mud when the tide went out. This same plan the white people followed. Such fish would be, say six to twelve inches in length. Generally two would be put in a hole in the ground, and four kernels of corn planted on top of them.

A NEGRO FIREMAN

THE first Negro to become a member of the Fire Department of New York has been appointed by Commissioner Adamson. He is John Woodson and has been assigned for duty with Truck 106, at 124 Greenpoint Avenue, Brooklyn. He was third on the civil service list and successfully passed through the school of instruction.

New York Sun

A GERMAN-INDIAN

THE New York *Times* says that the first full-blooded American Indian ever born in Germany has appeared near Dortmund, Westphalia. The child's father is a Sioux, William Bear Shield, and the mother is Mary Bear Shield, who was a member of an Indian troupe touring Germany with a circus.

The birth took place in a typical American prairie wagon en route from Dortmund to Recklinghausen. The mother was anxious that her baby should be registered in the German records as an American citizen and a Christian. To that end she sought the nearest American Consul, G. E. Eager, at Barmen. The baby was christened Maria Consula.

DECEMBER 1914

THE SOUTHE WORKM

What Co-operation Can Accomplish

BOOKER T. WASHINGTON

Mescal and the Indians

G. A. WATERMULDER

A Social Work Worth While

W. D. WEATHERFORD

Hampton Principles at Work in China

H. B. GRAYBILL

Press of
The Hampton Normal and Agricultural Institute
Hampton, Virginia

The Hampton Normal and Agricultural Instit

HAMPTON, VIRGINIA

What it is   An undenominational industrial school founded in 1868 Samuel Chapman Armstrong for Negro youth. Indi admitted in 1878.

Object   To train teachers and industrial leaders

Equipment   Land, 1060 acres ; buildings, 140

Courses   Academic, trade, agriculture, business, home economi

Enrollment   Negroes, 1282 ; Indians, 45 ; total, 1327

Results   Graduates, 1779 ; ex-students, over 6000
Outgrowths : Tuskegee, Calhoun, Mt. Meigs, and m
smaller schools for Negroes

Needs $125,000 annually above regular income
$4,000,000 Endowment Fund
Scholarships
     A full scholarship for both academic and
         industrial instruction   -   -   - $
     Academic scholarship   -   -   -   -
     Industrial scholarship   -   -   -   -   -
     Endowed full scholarship   -   -   -   -
     Any contribution, however small, will be grate
received and may be sent to H. B. FRISSELL, Principa
to F. K. ROGERS, Treasurer, Hampton, Virginia.

FORM OF BEQUEST

I give and devise to the trustees of The Hampton Normal and
cultural Institute, Hampton, Virginia, the sum of   *dol*
payable

The Southern Workman

Published monthly by

The Hampton Normal and Agricultural Institute

Contents for December 1914

THE SOUTHERN WORKMAN was founded by Samuel Chapman Armstrong in 1872, and is a mon magazine devoted to the interests of undeveloped races.

It contains reports from Negro and Indian populations, with pictures of reservation and planta life, as well as information concerning Hampton graduates and ex-students who since 1868 have tau more than 250,000 children in the South and West. It also provides a forum for the discussion of ethno cal, sociological, and educational problems in all parts of the world.

CONTRIBUTIONS: The editors do not hold themselves responsible for the opinions expressed in co tributed articles. Their aim is simply to place before their readers articles by men and women of abili without regard to the opinions held.

EDITORIAL STAFF

H. B. FRISSELL   W. L. BROWN
HELEN W. LUDLOW   W. A. AERY, Business Manager
J. E. DAVIS   W. T. B. WILLIAMS

TERMS: One dollar a year in advance; ten cents a copy
CHANGE OF ADDRESS: Persons making a change of address should send the old as well as the address to

THE SOUTHERN WORKMAN, Hampton, Virginia

Entered as second-class matter August 13, 1908, in the Post Office at Hampton, Virginia, the Act of July 16, 1894

THE HAMPTON LEAFLETS

Any twelve of the following numbers of the "The Hampton Leaflets" obtained free of charge by any Southern teacher or superintendent. *A charge cents per dozen is made to other applicants.* Cloth-bound volumes for 1905, ' and '08 will be furnished at thirty cents each, postpaid.

Address: Publication Office, The Hampton Normal and Agric Institute, Hampton, Virginia

The
Southern Workman

VOL. XLIII　　　　　DECEMBER 1914　　　　　NO. 12

𝕰𝖉𝖎𝖙𝖔𝖗𝖎𝖆𝖑𝖘

The Negro Organization Society What is the Negro doing to work out some of his own problems and secure the fundamental things of life—"better schools, better health, better homes, better farms?" The answer is found in the story of the Negro Organization Society of Virginia which recently held its second annual meeting in the City of Norfolk.

To stimulate a desire for better education and better health; to help the people raise money for community improvements; to commit the leaders and the masses to the policy of self-help; to impress upon the people the value of fresh air; and to co-operate with the best white people in matters of public welfare—these have been some of the wise aims of the Negro Organization Society under the able leadership of Major Moton, its president, and his devoted co-workers, including members of church, school, business, and fraternal organizations—literally thousands of the best colored people in Virginia.

That these worthy aims have been carried into successful execution during two years, is clearly shown in the summary of achievement offered by the executive secretary, President J. M. Gandy of the Petersburg Normal School. The Negro Organization Society has stimulated, as he reports, the erection of 14 new school buildings; inspired the building of sanitary privies at schools, churches, and homes; distributed nearly 100,000 health bulletins; issued a "health creed and pledge card" and secured over 2000 signers; organized "clean-up" campaigns, and secured the active co-operation at one time of at least 150,000 colored people in getting rid of dirt and waste material about their homes, schools, and churches; organized farmers' conferences; conducted educational campaigns in five and health campaigns in four counties; and, best of all, secured the enthusiastic support and co-operation throughout Virginia of white public officials, newspapers, and prominent citizens.

President Wilson's attitude towards the constructive work of the Negro Organization Society is admirably shown in his recent letter to Major Moton. The full text follows:

"I have been very much interested in the accounts I have heard of the work you are attempting to do through the instrumentality of the Negro Organization Society, and feel that you are to be especially congratulated on the deep interest which has been manifested by the white people of Virginia and the South in the plans now maturing for the betterment of conditions among the Negro people. I think one of the happiest circumstances of recent times is this co-operation between the white people and the Negroes in the South in intelligent efforts to advance the economic success and comfort of the Negroes, and put them in a position where they can work out their own fortunes with success and self-respect. I wish I might attend the meeting at Norfolk in person, in order to express my interest and sympathy, but I cannot, and I hope that you will feel at liberty to read this letter to the meeting."

Governor Henry C. Stuart of Virginia has also given his cordial endorsement to the aims and methods of the Negro Organization Society. A letter from him was read at the closing meeting.

The kindly attitude of the white people of Norfolk towards this movement was strikingly shown by the fact that nearly a thousand of the best white citizens of the city came to the final meeting, which was held in the Norfolk Armory, and listened most attentively to Dr. Frissell, Mr. Barton Myers of Norfolk, Major Moton, Rev. A. A. Graham, President Gandy, Dr. Charles S. Morris, and Dr. Booker T. Washington. Then, too, the Norfolk Chamber of Commerce, under the leadership of its president, Mr. Barton Myers, co-operated most generously in securing for the Negro Organization Society the largest meeting place in the city. A young white lawyer, Mr. A. T. Stroud, and the secretary of the Chamber of Commerce, Mr. William A. Cox, spent a great deal of time and energy in perfecting the final arrangements for this excellent meeting. The white press of the city opened its columns freely to announcements and reports concerning the Negroes' progress towards better health and better education.

Reports from delegates showed that hundreds of communities are taking seriously the question of better public health and

better public schools. The annual meetings of the Negro Organization Society act as a clearing house of ideas. Men and women
return to their homes and put into practice suggestions which are
discussed with frankness and vigor in the Society's public meetings. Major Moton has well said that men and women hold office
in the Society, not merely as an honor, but as an opportunity for
larger and more effective service to their fellow-men.

Excerpts from Dr. Washington's [fine address appear elsewhere in this issue. To read them is to believe in the Negro's
usefulness to the Southland.

The Hampton Farmers' Conference   Through self-help and the co-operation of the best
white people, the Negro of the South, especially
the farmer, is coming into his own. Were one at
all skeptical of this proposition, he could not help
being favorably impressed with the excellent display of farm,
home, and school products which commanded the attention and
respect of hundreds upon hundreds of white and colored people
during the recent two days' session of the Hampton Institute
Farmers' Conference.

Those who are in a position to pass sound judgment on the
strong and weak points of exhibits, say frankly and enthusiastically that at this Conference they saw many encouraging evidences of Negro thrift, teachableness, and progress in homemaking and community building.

There came to Hampton hundreds of colored farmers, white
Southern men who are serving as state supervisors of Negro
rural schools, experts in school administration, and industrial
supervising teachers. These men and women, who are actively
engaged in improving rural life, were able to meet at Hampton
on a broad educational platform and there, during two busy,
interesting days, work in harmony for the better things of life.

Special stress is laid on the fine exhibits because they, after
all, indicate the trend in Negro education which meets the genuine needs of the masses and at the same time tends to make the
country, where the Negro lives in great numbers, more and more
attractive to boys and girls and to their parents as well.

To appreciate the progress that has been made, for example,
in the growing of corn, the canning of fruits and vegetables, in
the making of simple garments, and in the growing of the common farm crops, one must compare the actual products of today
with those of five or ten years ago. Before systematic attempt
was made to reach the small farmer through the helpful farm-
demonstration agent and the well-trained teacher who seeks to
co-operate with the commonly neglected workers in the one-room

country schools, relatively little could be expected of the farmer and his family living in an isolated and unprogressive community. New life and new hope have come through bringing sound ideas of education to the farmstead and by bringing the farmer and his family in touch with the best work of his distant neighbors.

In this educational process, Hampton and other schools which have conducted farmers' conferences have rendered important service to white and colored people alike. The real test of a farmers' conference does not lie in the number or even the excellence of the addresses, but rather in the visual evidences that it can furnish of success won through the application of good methods to the raising of farm crops, the improving of live stock, and the introduction of conveniences and comforts in the home, in the church, and in the school.

What the colored farm woman has done for the improvement of rural life throughout Virginia was graphically described by one of Hampton's graduates. She emphasized the importance of the work that colored women are doing in organizing and conducting school leagues and clubs for girls and mothers, and in raising money for the improvement of schoolhouses within and without. Indeed, colored women are playing an important part in everything that has to do with the work of rural uplift.

At an "experience meeting" men who had won success in the face of ignorance and poverty were listened to most attentively by several hundred delegates to the Farmers' Conference. "Making farming pay," not only in dollars and cents, but in fuller, richer living, was the recurring theme.

The Conference addresses covered topics which had a direct and valuable appeal to men and women interested in rural welfare. They contained ideas of co-operation, higher standards, and racial good-will that are well worth keeping before men and women who have to work out their salvation in the country districts more or less apart from direct contact with professional teachers.

That the recent Farmers' Conference was the best of its kind ever held at Hampton, there is no question. It was a striking testimony to the efficiency of the school's agricultural department and to the willingness of the colored people to come to Hampton to learn how to promote rural welfare.

Detailed information concerning the fine exhibits, the helpful addresses, and the prominent visitors appears in this issue under Hampton Incidents.

⊠

Dr. Washington in Williamsburg   That Dr. Booker T. Washington should have been so cordially invited to speak before the teaching and student body of William and Mary, an old and distinguished college which has trained many of America's best statesmen, and that he should have received such a generous welcome on the part of hundreds of young white Southerners who are preparing for service in strategic positions, indicate clearly the racial sympathy and co-operation which are spreading throughout the Southland.

President Tyler expressed his hearty appreciation of all that Dr. Washington has done during the past thirty-odd years to bring about peace throughout the South. He frankly declared that Dr. Washington has made for himself a conspicuous name and has influenced the entire country to a remarkable degree.

Dr. Washington outlined the story of his uphill climb from the little cabin and the coal mine to the founding and development of Tuskegee Institute. He referred to the remarkable progress that Negroes have been quietly making during fifty years of freedom. "Where the Negro has touched the life of the best white people," he said, "there have come progress and good will." He added that while the worst things concerning the Negroes in the South are commonly sent over the world, comparatively little is known of the friendly feeling which exists between the races in hundreds of communities throughout the South.

The close attention and hearty applause that the young men of William and Mary College gave Dr. Washington showed their kindly feeling toward one who has always stood for generous service, not only to his own people, but to the white race as well.

Before speaking in the college chapel, Dr. Washington addressed a mixed audience that overflowed the Williamsburg courthouse.

The real meaning of Dr. Washington's recent addresses in Williamsburg will not be known for a very long time. The good seeds of racial good will which he sowed will bear good fruit as the years roll by and as young men, who are now students, take their rightful places as leaders in the state and in the professions. Untold good for the South and the nation will come in proportion as men of different races and classes are willing to emphasize and discuss the things which they can agree on rather than spend their time and energy debating matters on which they naturally disagree.

Peyote and the Indians   In this issue of the Southern Workman appears one of the addresses delivered at the Mohonk Conference on the physiological and psychical effects of peyote or "mescal," and the alarming rapidity with which the use of this drug is spreading among the Indians.

Other articles have appeared in various periodicals calling
the attention of the Indians and their friends to the deleterious
effects of this drug. Dr. Murphey, supervisor of the medical
department of the Indian Bureau, has published an illuminating
article based upon his own knowledge and observation. The
Journal of the Society of American Indians in the June number
of this year gave the subject most practical comment. The
Journal of Religious Psychology also contained a valuable contribution on the peyote cult in Winnebago, Nebraska. The Indian
Bureau, too, has collected much valuable data.

The time has come for the Federal Government to deal with
peyote as it does with other deleterious drugs, and to authorize
the Indian Department to prohibit its use as it does the use of
liquor. Hampton Institute, always deeply interested in the welfare of the Indian, and especially in Indian youth, deplores the
fact that so many young men and women, so promising and with
such high ideals when they leave school, allow themselves to be
deluded, weakened, and in some cases debauched by the use of the
drug. It is with keen satisfaction that we endorse the resolution
of the Mohonk Conference concerning peyote and note that the
Board of Indian Commissioners, the Indian Rights Association,
and friends at large are using their influence to secure its prohibition. It is a deplorable fact that there should have been a vacillating policy in the past. It is responsible for the delusion, the
ruination, and even the death of many an Indian. We plead that
the Federal Government deal with this problem promptly and
effectively.

⊠

**The Philadelphia
Armstrong
Association**
The sixth annual report of the Armstrong Association of Philadelphia is a modest statement of the
valuable and far-reaching work done during the
past year by this organization in behalf of the
colored people of that city. Its work of finding opportunities for
colored men in the building trades—employment practically
closed to Negroes in Northern cities—and of making openings for
them in new kinds of mechanical pursuits, and its helpful investigations into housing and other conditions affecting the Negro
are suggestive illustrations of possible constructive work with
the Negro in cities. The Association not only does effective work
itself but makes a point of co-operating with every other agency
that may be induced to assist in the work of Negro uplift. The
public schools, churches, civic organizations, and business leagues
are called into the work. The Armstrong Association itself is
one of the representatives in Philadelphia of the National League
on Urban Conditions among Negroes. The success of the organization is due in no small measure to its hearty co-operation with

capable colored men and women, not only in its management, but also in direct work among the colored people.

As an indication of the nature and amount of the work done by the Association during the past year, it may be mentioned that four hundred fifty-five jobs were found for colored workers. These jobs called for bricklayers, carpenters, electricians, furnace men, painters, paperhangers, plasterers, plumbers, porters, printers, roofers, seamstresses, and stenographers, among many others. The report shows that the Association secured, within eight months, contracts for colored mechanics for an amount in excess of $35,000.

The home and school visitor employed by the Association made eight hundred visits during the year. Some of these visits were for the purpose of getting in school, children above and below the ages when they are required by law to be there. Homes of boys with working certificates were also visited. If the boy was idle he was reported to the school; if he was employed he was urged to attend night school. Other visits were made in cases of discipline, and to find out the home conditions of pupils. Further activities of this visitor are indicated by the directions she gave in the work of "clean-up" week, and by her supervision of the baths of fifteen hundred pupils of the "fresh-air" class.

Another significant phase of this work is that dealing with unsanitary conditions about the home. In this the Association has the co-operation of the City Housing Commission and the Bureau of Health. The reporting of bad surroundings usually brings improvement, and has the following effects besides: "The person entering the complaint, realizing that an inspector will call at her home, begins to tidy up the place; she speaks to her neighbor about it; the neighbor begins to clear out her rubbish. Not knowing just when the health officer will call, they continue to clean and thus the habit is quickly formed."

But of greater importance than all these direct activities among the colored people is the work of the Association in creating a better general feeling toward the Negro, and in educating the public to an appreciation of the value of his work. Successful public meetings have been held in white and colored churches and in important clubs. Such a meeting as the one held in the New Century Drawing Rooms, with "Business and employment among Negroes in Philadelphia" as the subject, when trades unions, vocational education, standards of living, and opportunities were discussed, must result in great good for the cause of the colored people.

The Oklahoma Indians' Friend

Whenever the Indians have been in special need of a friend to plead their cause before the public and to arouse the conscience of the nation against some particular injustice or dishonorable dealing, it has more than once been a woman who, has publicly championed their cause. The case of Bright Eyes, herself an educated Indian, who toured the country from the Missouri River to the Atlantic Ocean thirty years ago in company with the old chief, Standing Bear, for the purpose of telling of the wrongs which had been inflicted upon the Poncas, will be recalled by many readers. The addresses of Bright Eyes presented a clear, dispassionate elucidation of the wrongs her people had suffered and made an appeal for simple justice. In consequence of the public sentiment which she aroused an investigation was undertaken and an effort made to restore justice as far as possible.

The fight which Miss Kate Barnard, State Commissioner of Charities for Oklahoma, has been waging in behalf of the Indians of that state has made her a figure of almost national reputation. Her purpose is to secure passage by the state legislature of laws protecting the Indians against those who are seeking to gain possession of the Indians' great wealth in oil and mineral lands. The size of her undertaking may be realized when we are told that $200,000,000 is a low estimate of the money prize at stake. This wealth is now in the hands of some 33,000 "restricted" Indians, most of whom are ignorant and helpless, and the success of the plot which she is trying to frustrate would mean misery and poverty for thousands of these wards of the Government. It is a big man's fight.

Miss Barnard has been called a modern Jeanne d'Arc. She is a slight, frail-looking young woman with a large heart and great courage, who appears to combine in her nature a rather unusual religious fervor and an idealistic reliance upon divine inspiration, with a shrewd, practical knowledge and common sense, and an insight into the devious machinations of scheming men. If she has the dreaminess of her French prototype she has also the wakefulness of the weasel. No fair-minded person who has heard her speak as she spoke at the recent Mohonk Conference can fail to be impressed by her earnestness and sincerity, or by the unselfishness of her devotion to the cause of the weak and defrauded children of the red race. Nor will he fail to recognize her remarkable capacity and power of accomplishment.

It is to be hoped that the plea which she is now making very generally for funds with which to carry on her campaign will not be made in vain, and that her hands will be upheld in her efforts to right grievous wrongs. Indeed, there would seem to be but one answer to her appeal: "Shall we, in the

evening of the life of this people, rob the last survivor before
we pass with him down into the common silence of eternity?
Shall we send the last orphan of this dying race a penniless
pauper back to our common God?''

🗒

**The New
Petersburg
President**   The new president of the Virginia Normal and
Industrial Institute, which is generally known as
the Petersburg Normal School, is John M. Gandy,
who has had an interesting educational career.
Born in Mississippi in 1870, Mr. Gandy has spent all his life in
school work. After being graduated from Fisk University in
1898, he taught Latin and Greek for three years in the Virginia
Normal and Collegiate Institute. When Governor Montague of
Virginia came into office he ordered that Latin and Greek should
be taken out of the school curriculum. Mr. Gandy was then
selected to teach pedagogy. He continued at this work for about
twelve years, making an excellent record as a teacher and as a
student of psychology, ethics, the history of education, and
methods of teaching.

When the sad news came of the death of President J. Hugo
Johnston, who had served his race so faithfully and efficiently
as the head of the Virginia Normal and Industrial Institute, those
who knew Mr. Gandy and appreciated his fine qualities as a
schoolman and as a public leader, hoped that he would be chosen
as President Johnston's successor. It is fitting that one who has
served so continuously in the field of education should be selected
as the administrative head of the normal school which is doing
such fine work, and gives promise of growing influence in the
training of young colored teachers for more efficient service, not
only in the schools of Virginia but throughout the Southland.

To thousands of white and colored Virginians, Mr. Gandy is
already well known on account of his efficient work during the
past two years as the executive secretary of the Negro Organization Society. In his work of promoting better health and better education among the colored people of Virginia, he has
won the cordial support and hearty sympathy of the officers
of the State Board of Health, of leaders in school, church, and
fraternal organizations, and of the masses, through his straightforward and vigorous appeal for co-operation in saving the lives,
not only of colored people but of their white neighbors. Mr.
Gandy is in truth a public servant. His long and hard years
of struggle and preparation have well fitted him for the excellent work which he is now doing for the safety of the public
health and for the training of colored teachers.

WHAT CO-OPERATION CAN ACCOMPLISH*

BY BOOKER T. WASHINGTON

THE Negro Organization Society is so unique and at the same time so practical in its objects and results that it commands the respect, confidence, and support of all the best people of both races throughout Virginia. Not the least important part of the work of this society consists in teaching colored people to work together; and in showing them that they can accomplish more through union than through dissension. It is not only teaching our race to co-operate, but it is furnishing an object lesson in showing how white people can help black people; how we can be and are separate in strictly social matters, but one in all that concerns the fundamental things of life in the South.

The Negro Organization Society of Virginia is showing us that in the great big fundamental things of life, there is no one who can help us except ourselves, that no law of Congress or of the state legislature can help us as much, in the last analysis, as we can help ourselves. There are things that we can do, and the things that we can do are being emphasized through this practical and far-reaching organization, which is bringing religious denominations, educational movements, secret and fraternal organizations, business leagues, and civic organizations together for the purpose of seeing that throughout the State of Virginia better educational facilities are provided, better sanitary and moral conditions brought about, crime reduced, and friendly relations between the two races maintained.

Another thing that the Negro Organization Society is teaching is that we have advantages right here in the South in the way of soil and climate and white people who understand us and whom we understand, which are not accorded to any similar group of our people anywhere in the world. True, we sometimes have evidence of racial friction, but when we consider the large number of black people and the large number of white people scattered over an immense territory, such as we have in the South, the wonder is that there is not more racial friction instead of less. We must remember, too, that when a large territory is

* Excerpts from an address before the Negro Organization Society in Norfolk, Virginia November 12, 1914

occupied by people who are white, that they sometimes have trouble. This is manifest in what is now going on in Europe.

The mere fact that the Negro race is in the South in large numbers does not mean that we can always remain here in our present state of prosperity unless we prove to the people in every community where we live that we can get as much out of the soil, and as much out of the natural resources of the community, as any other race can. This places upon us a tremendous obligation.

The great bulk of our people are going to live, in my opinion, here in the South, where they are better off in proportion to their numbers than anywhere else in the world. We are going to live here because we do not want to leave and because the white man does not want us to leave.

I am glad that this organization is emphasizing the matter of health, the matter of cleanliness, the matter of better sanitary conditions throughout Virginia. In this work for better health both races can co-operate. When food is being prepared, the Negro touches the white man's life; when food is being served, the Negro woman touches the the white man's life; when children are being nursed, the Negro woman touches the white man's life; when clothes are being laundered, the Negro woman touches the white man's life. It is mighty important, in the interest of our race as well as in the interest of the white race, that the Negro woman be taught cleanliness and the laws of health. Disease draws no color line.

If by reason of filth and unsanitary conditions in Norfolk, growing out of ignorance, there comes to the black community, consumption, smallpox, or any other contagious disease, it is likely to reach, through the Negro community, the mansion of the richest white person in the city. In Alabama, a few years ago, an ignorant Negro woman was employed as cook in an aristocratic white college for girls. Little attention was given to the health or cleanliness of this colored woman. Little attention was given to the place where she slept or the way she lived. In the end a deadly contagious disease took hold of her body and from her spread among the white girls in the college. The result was that four of the most promising of these white girls were taken away by death and the college was disbanded for the year.

The entire South is dependent upon the Negro, in a large measure, for certain kinds of work. A weak body, a sickly body, is costly to the whole community and to the whole state, from an economic point of view. The average length of a Negro's life in the South is at present thirty-five years. It should be fifty years, and the Negro Organization Society of Virginia can prolong the life of the average Negro working man to fifty years. In

India, the average length of life is twenty-five years; in Massachusetts, where they have good public schools, it is forty-five years; in Denmark and Sweden, fifty years.

In the City of Norfolk there are practically 35,000 black people. Statistics show that 1800 of these people are sick all the time; $65,000 are spent every year in Norfolk for Negro funerals alone. All this, in the way of sickness and death, means a net loss to the City of Norfolk of at least $1,370,000. In the State of Virginia, statistics show that there are 41,000 black people who are sick all the time. This means a net loss to the white and black people of Virginia in the way of earning power of at least $23,000,000.

There are 450,000 Negroes sick in the South every day in the year. The average black man loses 18 working days in the year because of sickness. The sickness and death of so large a proportion of its population means an annual loss to the South of over $300,000,000. At least $150,000,000 of this amount could be saved by taking measures to prevent disease by the simple precautions which the Negro Organization Society in every way emphasizes. This $150,000,000, saved, would furnish six months of schooling for every white and black child in the South and, besides, would build good schoolhouses for every child in the South.

Through this organization, the Negro can do his part in ridding the state of the idle and loafing class. We must let our people everywhere understand that we will not hide crime, that the black loafer is a great burden, and that he gives our race a reputation which hinders its progress. Our white people, too, can help us in this matter of better moral conditions by encouraging the colored people who live upright, industrious, economical, and frugal lives by not advertising Negro crime quite so much in the newspapers, and by advertising, instead, more evidences of Negro thrift and Negro morality. While we are trying to do our part in bringing about a higher moral condition, the white people can help us by seeing that the Negro everywhere gets absolute justice in the courts, that throughout the South we get rid of the crime of lynching human beings, and that every man charged with a crime has an opportunity to come before a court of justice where his guilt or innocence can be proved.

The two races in Virginia can co-operate in encouraging the Negro wherever he lives to have a clean, sanitary, healthy community. I do not believe that this can be brought about by any laws meant to segregate the Negro in any certain part of a community or city. Wherever the Negro is segregated it usually means that he will have poor streets, poor lighting, poor sidewalks, poor sewerage, and poor sanitary conditions generally. These conditions are reflected in many ways in the life of the race to its disadvantage and to the disadvantage of the white race. Happily the Negro here in the South has pretty good common sense and he is not likely to thrust himself on any community where conditions are not congenial, where he is not happy, and where he is not wanted. Segregation is not only unnecessary, but, in most cases, it is unjust.

I am glad to note that in Virginia, as in most of the states of the South, there is a spirit of co-operation between the two races, which has never existed before in like degree, in helping our race to get education. For a good many years after the civil war white people were afraid to educate the Negro because they did not know what it was going to lead to, but just in proportion as the white people throughout the South see that education is used by our people in a way to make them simple, modest, earnest, never afraid to work on the farm, or in the shop, or in the house; in proportion as they see that education makes a better citizen, millions of dollars are going to be poured out throughout the South for the education of our race.

We must not deceive ourselves, however. The problem of educating the Negro, as well as the white child in the South, is just beginning to be solved. We have scarcely begun to educate. In the State of Louisiana, at the present time, each black child receives $1.59 a year for his education; in Georgia, only $1.42. Fifty-two per cent of all the Negro children in the South of school age entered no school last year. By reason of the poor salaries paid teachers and the short length of the school term, it would require 20 years for a Negro child, under present conditions, to complete a public-school education. In several of our Southern states, first-class Negro convicts earn $40 per month for 12 months in the year, while Negro school-teachers receive about $25 per month for teaching 4 or 5 months in the year. All of these conditions must be faced frankly in the interest of both races, in the interest of a higher and better civilization in the South. In proportion as we face them, both races are going to be happier and more prosperous. Ignorance cures nothing. We must all unite to blot out ignorance from the South by placing good, first-class schoolhouses for both races in every community in our beloved and beautiful Southland.

We must not become discouraged. Tremendous progress, in all the directions to which I have referred, has been made and is being made. When we consider all the struggles, all the difficulties through which both races have passed during the last fifty years, the wonder is, not that we have accomplished so little, but that we have accomplished so much. Both races are going to

live here in the South together. Year by year we are going to
understand each other better. There is going to be more racial
co-operation, more friendship, more peace, more harmony, more
prosperity. Despite evidences of racial friction which crop out
here and there, when you get to the bottom of conditions in any
Southern community it is found that each individual Negro has
his or her white friend; and each white man has his individual
Negro friend. The relations which exist between the individual
Negro and the individual white man are often closer and better
understood and more sympathetic than those obtaining in any
community outside of the South. In the matter of facing the
trying conditions in the cotton-growing states brought about
by the European War, there is a racial co-operation and sympathy
which I have never seen before in the South.

Our race is improving in the matter of health. Some ten or
fifteen years ago the death rate was about thirty per thousand;
at the present time, through such organizations as the Negro
Organization Society and others, the death rate has been decreased. It is now from twenty-four to twenty per thousand.

The Negro began life fifty years ago with practically no
property. He owns now in the South 20,000,000 acres of land.
Fifty years ago only 5 per cent of the Negroes could read or
write. At present 70 per cent can read and write. Twenty
years ago, there were in one year 250 cases of lynching; during
the past ten months, there have been only 33 cases of lynching.
This reduction has been brought about through racial co-operation and a better understanding. For these evidences of progress our race deserves great credit; and the white man by whose
side we live in the South deserves equal credit for the encouragement and the practical help which he has given us in all these
fundamental matters.

We of the black race and the white race here in the South
are going to present to the world a great object lesson, showing
how two races, different in history, different in color, can live side
by si deon the same soil in peaceand in harmony, neither hindering
the other but each helping the other towards a higher and
more useful civilization:

A SOCIAL WORK WORTH WHILE

BY W. D. WEATHERFORD

Student Secretary of the International Committee of the Young Men's Christian Associations

ONE of the most remarkable pieces of social service and Christian mission work being carried on anywhere in this country can be found if one will take the trouble to spend a day in Louisville under the guidance of Rev. John Little. Mr. Little is a Southern man, the son of slave owners, a graduate of the University of Alabama, a graduate of the Southern Presbyterian Theological Seminary, and yet for fourteen years Mr. Little has been giving his entire life to as interesting a piece of Negro work as can be found anywhere in this country.

Fourteen years ago a little company of six theological students of the Presbyterian Theological Seminary in Louisville fell into conversation one day about the needs of the Negro in their city, and what the men in the Seminary could do to be of some service. This little conversation led to forming a band for a Negro Sunday school. This was opened in an old, abandoned grog shop on one of the streets which is given up entirely to Negro tenement dwellers. The six theological students gathered together on the first Sunday afternoon twenty-six ragged little Negro children in order to try to give them the simple message of the gospel. One of these teachers found that in his class of six boys there was not a single child who even knew the name of Jesus Christ, although they had been living under the very shadow of the steeples of white churches, and had been within the sound of twenty church bells for all the years of their lives.

In order to increase the crowd of boys and girls who were coming to them in their little grog-shop meeting, the theological students made a canvass of the neighboring houses and invited both parents and children to be present each Sunday afternoon. The number rapidly grew until the room, which would not hold any more than a hundred, was filled to overflowing.

One day there appeared in this company a young boy who at the close of the meeting got up and invited the theological students to come over to Smoketown to start a similar meeting for the people of his section. The students refused to go because they had no money to rent buildings and they had no further time to give, so the boy from Smoketown was sent back empty-handed and disappointed. However, he was not discouraged, for the next Sunday afternoon he appeared with the same request, and then the next Sunday, and so on for a number of weeks, each Sunday insisting that they must have a similar work carried on in Smoketown. At last the students agreed that they would send over other theological students and open this new work. The result of these two little missions started fourteen years ago is that at the present time there are two large and fairly well-equipped buildings for carrying on all types of religious, social, industrial, and service work. In these two buildings, which now belong to the Mission of which Mr. Little is the superintendent, there are more than a thousand boys and girls

A SEWING CLASS IN THE PRESBYTERIAN COLORED MISSION, LOUISVILLE

who are regularly getting instruction, not only in the Bible, but in all forms of industrial work, including basketry, cooking, sewing, and light carpentry.

It is a delight to go into one of these buildings during a week day and find, as I found recently, a group of Negro girls of about twelve years of age all grouped around a white teacher (who, by the way, is one of the finest white women in Louisville) learning to use needle and thread in the making of garments for themselves. Some of them had on garments which they themselves had made in the sewing school. In another room I found another group of girls under the supervision of a well-trained Negro teacher, taking a lesson in cooking. In still another part of the building I visited a large carpenter shop in which a number of boys

"A SOCIAL WORK WORTH WHILE"

were gathered for study of the elements of carpentry. If one could have gone the same day to the other mission station he might have found a group of mothers in a mothers' meeting, and in another section of the building he might have found a group of young boys making baskets. Mr. Little and his associates believe that religion is living and that life ought to be religious; consequently anything that will help to make the homes of the Negroes of Louisville better and make the children more industrious is believed to be genuinely religious. This mainly accounts for the phenomenal success of the work which he is doing.

Some time ago Mr. Little decided to put a number of public

A MISSION CARPENTRY CLASS

baths into one of these mission stations for the use of the Negroes of that community. On making a careful investigation he found that in that entire community there was only one bathtub with running water. As soon as the shower and tub-baths were introduced in the Mission building whole families began to patronize them, the little children coming on Saturday afternoons, and bringing their clean clothes with them, to have their weekly bath. It was pathetic to note that many of them did not know anything about a bathtub or a bathroom. An amusing thing happened when the afternoon for the young boys arrived. After having their hot showers they refused to dress, for they said they had to have a plunge in those tubs since they never in their lives had been in a white bathtub. If cleanliness is next to godliness, there is not a particle of doubt that Mr. Little and his Mission are doing a wonderful piece of moral uplift work for the Negroes of the community in which this particular mission is situated.

Another interesting piece of service which this Mission has been able to bring about is the establishment of public libraries in the communities where these missions are located. Louisville has the distinction of having two public libraries for the Negroes, which, I believe, is more than any other Southern city has. The first library was built out of Carnegie funds, but it can serve only one section of the Negro population. There was great need of another library in the very center of Smoketown, the section where Mr. Little's work is being carried on; consequently the Negroes set to work, with Mr. Little's help, to raise the money to purchase a splendid corner lot for the erection of a library. This they carried through in a quick financial campaign with wonderful success and enthusiasm. The city then aided them in securing sufficient funds to build a public library. In the two Negro libraries in Louisville there are at present about ten thousand volumes and the average list of books drawn is close to six thousand per month. When I visited one of these libraries I found a whole company of boys standing around the door waiting for an opportunity to get in. I also found a group of boys inside preparing, through the reading of magazines, for their weekly debate, and I found some mothers there trying to get information about better housekeeping. There cannot be a particle of doubt that this library, which is so largely an outgrowth of the work of Mr. Little, is one of the best things which Louisville has provided for the Negro citizenship of that city.

Another remarkable thing about the work of Mr. Little and his Mission is the fact that he has drawn into sympathetic co-operation a number of the leading surgeons and physicians of the City of Louisville. A little girl was found by Mr. Little in a most deformed condition. She was taken to the hospital of one of the leading surgeons of the city, her limbs were broken and re-set, and after two months' time she stood erect and was able to return home. A large number of cases of this kind have been operated on free of charge by the best white surgeons in Louisville. Some of the best oculists have been freely giving their services in helping to remedy the large amount of defective sight among the Negroes in this settlement. Mr. Little says he has asked many people for money and been refused, he has asked not a few people for service of time in the teaching and work in his Mission and has sometimes been refused, but never has a surgeon, an oculist, or a physician refused to give attention to a needy Negro child. When one goes into these missions and sees children whose eyes were once very defective now seeing clearly, others whose limbs were deformed now walking

A MOTHERS' MEETING

straight, and still others with various maladies healed, he is reminded of the days of Christ when it was said to the followers of John as a testimonial of Christ's work that " the blind receive their sight, the lame walk, and the lepers are cleansed, the deaf hear, and the dead are raised up, and the poor have good tidings preached to them.''

Perhaps the most important thing about the work which Mr. Little is carrying on in this Negro section is the large number of splendid white people in Louisville who have given so liberally of their time in co-operation with this work. Recently, at a banquet served to the workers in these missions, there sat down seventy-five Southern white men and women from the City of Louisville, in the midst of whom were a number of leading surgeons, physicians, and oculists, some of the leading society

SOUTHERN WHITE TEACHERS IN THE LOUISVILLE MISSION

women of the city, and a number of public-school teachers, both
men and women. All of these persons were giving from one to
three hours per week in ministering to the needs of these lowly
people. Certainly the time has come when a new interest on the
part of the Southern white people is springing up, and the
number of those who are participating in social service among
Negroes is rapidly growing.

Mr. Little has, in the work which he is doing here, set
a standard for such work in any city in the South. His sane combination of religious, social, and industrial training commends
itself, not only to the best colored people, but to the best white
people of our section. To make Negro boys and girls more
healthy physically, to teach them to use their hands and their
brains, and to transform their hearts, is a thorough and fundamental work. The South can well be proud of two such people
as Mr. and Mrs. Little, who have brought to bear all their splendid
training, their culture, and their religion on the uplift of the
Negro boy and girl. If such an experiment could be multiplied
in every city, and if Mr. Little and those who, like him, are
attempting to help the Negro boy and girl, could have more
money at their disposal, the future years would see fewer
criminal Negroes, less shiftlessness, more of home building, and
the whole South would reap the splendid benefits in a larger and
truer life.

HAMPTON PRINCIPLES AT WORK IN CHINA

BY H. B. GRAYBILL

Principal of the High School of the Canton Christian College

I HAVE just seen Chung Wing Kwong reading with great interest the life of a Hampton graduate. The Honorable Chung Wing Kwong, called one of the five great scholars of south China, has for some years been the Chinese Dean of the Canton Christian College, and was, while the modern party was in power, the Commissioner of Education for the Canton Province. To be commissioner there means to have complete control of all public education ; so the ideas and ideals which the commissioner gets hold of exert an influence over a population of at least twenty-five millions.

At the college in Canton I have seen both students and teachers studying the work of Hampton Institute as shown in books and catalogues. It is not only because the work is an interesting novelty to them. It is because they are earnestly striving for the uplift of China, and they see that Hampton's principles are the ones needed in the making of a new China. Hampton has broken away from some of the traditions of education which have hindered progress, and has sought to discover and practice the principles of real education. So also China is just beginning

RAW MATERIAL

the modern chapter of her history, and education is the foundation of it. She wants the plain fundamental principles.

Imagine the Chinese adopting the European and American custom of wearing cap and gown in academic processions. It would be funny instead of dignifying. But the idea of the dignity of learning is a good one, and they express it equally well by a real seriousness of countenance and a respectful bearing. The Chinese people are remarkable for their common sense. They are very good at selecting the best of what they discover and refusing to imitate the useless or absurd.

GOING OUT TO BUY LAND FROM A VILLAGE "ELDER"

HIGH SCHOOL STUDENTS

When American college boys feel in the mood for fun and frivolity, they too frequently resort to intoxicants, or go out to break lamps, steal gates, or perform some other highly original feat. But Chinese boys will get up an entertainment. Witl in a very few minutes they will have a rousing program of songs, acts, humorous speeches, and various very original "stlnts." Once, I remember, they got up a most amusing act, which was evidently inspired throughout, though no mention was made of them, by three young women in the school. It was called, "The old king of the sea and his three daughters," who wanted to know what the young men of the world are like.

Like Hampton, the Canton Christian College teaches that labor of the hands is both ennobling and educational. The old-

PRIMARY SCHOOL OF THE CANTON CHRISTIAN COLLEGE

style Chinese scholar always had long fingernails and wore a
long, light-blue coat, so that anyone could easily see that he never
did any work except with his brain and pen. Also, when
the Chinese boy was first taken to school he was dressed in a
long blue coat and from that day he gave up all outdoor games.
Consequently it was at first very difficult to introduce baseball
or any other form of athletics. But the boys soon caught the
idea, saw the value of exercise in increasing health, and understood that athletics and manual labor do not interfere with dignified and earnest study. Now every one of the four hundred
and fifty boys and girls in the dormitories of the several schools

TAI-NGAN-KAI, OR "BIG-EYED CHICKEN"
A junk of the salt monopoly

is out for athletics or outdoor work every afternoon. Not long
ago I saw two teams play right through a hard rain as if they
had always been accustomed to dashing through the mud. Certain classes are required to do gardening or other manual work,
but they are so enthusiastic and industrious that more land is
assigned to voluntary gardeners than to the classes.

General Armstrong's aim "to build up character and fit
leaders and teachers" is being again realized in this work
around on the opposite side of the world. China's greatest needs
are for tens of thousands of teachers for the millions of children
who will be the men and women of the next generation when

China may be taking her place among the great nations of the world, and leaders to direct and control this great human force. America is training so many of these teachers and leaders for China that some newspapers have recently had the headline "America is running China."

Recently the first graduate of the Canton College high school was given control of all the magistracies of the province, and in a short time he succeeded in establishing real local self-government in a large part of the whole province. When I left China another one of my old students was giving to Canton for the first time in her thousand-year history a street broad enough for an ordinary wagon.

Hampton has helped to show that a modern young man's religion should include a large measure of the spirit of unselfish service. Our Chinese boys, like those at Hampton, catch this spirit quickly and go right to work helping to improve the condition of their people. The farmers in China all live in villages, and there are six of these villiages within a mile of the college. So the boys go out in every direction on Sunday afternoons to preach and teach in these villages and help with their schools. They conduct night schools, assist the faculty in summer normal-school work, and are now publishing a small magazine in Chinese, not to exhibit their learning but to uplift their people.

This college and its schools are growing up only by the support of those who believe in helping a people to help themselves, and in giving them the powerful impulse of the spirit of Christ.

OVER THE ROOFS OF THE INNER CITY OF CANTON

IN MICMAC SUMMER CAMPS

BY FRANK G. SPECK

MY travels among the Indians this past summer took me in the direction of the Micmacs of Nova Scotia, Cape Breton, and Newfoundland. This tribe, the easternmost of the Algonkian stock, is characterized by its numbers and its national conservatism. There are probably about five thousand Micmacs, and no one would suppose from an acquaintance with some of the bands near to the large towns of eastern Canada, that such a strong feeling of national unity pervades the whole group. It is largely among the Cape Breton bands that the best spirit is found, although I do not wish to undervalue the patriotism of some of the New Brunswick bands which I have not visited. The latter are under the excellent influence of Father Pacific at Ristigouche, who has done wonders in developing the economic independence of the tribe and in stimulating pride in language, literature, and customs. Outside of the New Brunswick bands, those of Cape Breton have had no particular encouragement. They have practically taken care of their own culture, and from the point of view of the ethnologist have done it quite well. It was here that I spent most of my time, attracted to the region by the favorable reports of the interesting life of the Indians and the fame of the beautiful Bras d' Or Lakes.

The Micmacs of Cape Breton occupy five native settlements—Eskasoni (the capital of the whole Micmac nation) on Middle River near Baddeck, Wycegamagh, Malagawatch, Chapel
Island, and Sidney. These villages are located amid the most
beautiful natural surroundings. Inland salt-water lakes, in some
directions fifty miles in extent, with rocky shores and dark spruce
and fir forests, characterize the geography of the island. The
nature lover and conservationist find a deep gratification in the
country because, in the first place, the population is not so dense
as to have disturbed nature too much and the temperament of the
inhabitants is mostly of the pastoral, conservative type. Indeed,
many of the interior settlements are composed of Scotch Gælic
folk whose everyday speech is Gælic. Aside from the interesting
possibilities for the study of old European economy and culture
transplanted from the heaths of Scotland to the evergreen forests of Canada, let us confine our attention to the native Micmacs, whose lot is cast in with the tranquil life of the Scotch
settlers.

We learn that, after the close of the conquest of Canada by
the English, many of the Micmacs who had been aiding the
French at Quebec returned to their homes in New Brunswick to
find English sentiment strong against them for having espoused
the enemy's cause. Accordingly, under their Great Chief,
Tomah Denys (1749), a number emigrated to Cape Breton where
the country was wilder, game more plentiful, and the English
fewer. Here they established the tribal capital. It is a satisfaction to state that the old Micmac régime is still in force here.
At the annual gathering on St. Anne's Day in the latter part of
July the present Great Chief, John Denys, the great grandson of
the leader just mentioned, sits at the head of the tribal council
composed of representatives from all the Micmac, bands even from

those of Newfoundland. Native costumes are worn, the people, to
the number of possibly a thousand, camp in birch-bark wigwams,
and the Christian religious ceremonials are followed by native
exhibitions of dancing and games, all of which foster the pride of
ancestry in the tribe and tend to develop its self-respect. Above
all, the memorials of the alliance between the Micmacs and the
Iroquois are kept alive by the preservation of the wampum records, which were sent in the early days from Caughnawaga, the
capital of the confederacy of the eastern tribes. No other tribe
in the East has kept this interesting and, to the Indians, serious
ceremony active up to the present day, although all of them had
it fifty years ago. The whole meeting consumes not less than
a week and forms the Micmac religious and political national holiday. To their credit it should be said that nowhere among the
Eastern Indians have I found such a general knowledge among
the people of their native institutions. Nor is this conservatism
maintained at the expense of English education. The Micmacs
seem to understand their own culture, at the same time showing
the same amount of other education as other Indians who may
have lost much of their tribal lore. I have often been surprised
at the skill with which even some of the young men have been
able to expound a point of Indian word analysis or grammar.

Perhaps most interesting of all the features of native literature is the system of hieroglyphics which was invented many

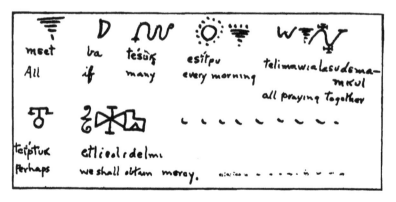

years ago for the transcription of church matter, partly by the
early missionaries, and evidently based upon the picture-writing
methods common to all the Algonkians. These hieroglyphics are
not related to any other system, being composed of rather complex figures which represent words and ideas. There is, indeed,
nothing phonetic in the system, it is purely mnemonic, picto-
graphic, and ideographic. Grammatical modifications are,
however, possible by employing marks denoting tense, person,

and some adjectival changes. These latter points are unquestionably the product of priestly ingenuity, but the foundation idea itself and many of the pictorial concepts are strictly native in origin. I give an example on the opposite page of a short text in the Micmac system to show its general appearance and character. Nearly all the Micmacs can read this writing, although it requires a great amount of memorizing. These people are very fond of discussing the features of their language and literature, in which many of them show much natural scholarship.

As a comparison with their mental life let us devote a few words to considering the material side of native existence. Originally the Micmacs were strictly a hunting people. Nowadays, however, the game will no longer support them. The complete change of mode of life has not been well bridged over by the Micmacs. They have not adapted themselves very much to farming. In consequence, the tribe is outwardly not to be considered a very prosperous one. I am inclined to attribute the agricultural backwardness of these people to the country itself as much as to the peculiar lack of physical concentrativeness of the Indians. This northern country, originally completely covered with evergreen forests, is not exceptionally fertile all over. Much of it is rocky and the soil sour. The European settlers inherit an inborn taste for clearing the land in spite of physical obstacles, which the Indians, who were primarily hunters, cannot equal. Land clearing is not only against the northern Indian's physical inclinations, especially where he sees the white man having a hard time with it, but he always has to subdue his feelings, which tell him that forests mean game, game means hunting and the elements of life and activity that he craves. How, then, with such feelings can the Indian develop into an aggressive land cultivator?

I am sure that, with favorable opportunities, the average nomadic Indian, of the northern tribes at least, is better fitted for a mode of life depending upon the exercise of his wits than for a physically hard-working life. Since his social environment among the white people is not conducive to entrance into mental occupations, the average Micmac has to choose between trying to farm under really difficult conditions and picking up a living by hunting and trapping and selling small wares. The latter course is commonly the one chosen. This whole question is of course a very perplexing one. Small farming to supplement steady hunting and fishing is the economic ideal to which the Micmacs and tribes in like situations are fitted by nature. While this may be quite impossible to attain in most parts of the country it is not so difficult a prospect in the less densely settled parts of Canada, with proper game laws for the white people. As for the Indians, they can take care of game protection as they did when their existence depended upon keeping up the supply.

In another respect the Micmacs have preserved an old feature of their life with the full realization of what it means. I am now referring to those of Cape Breton. Wigwams of birch bark are much used by these people in the summer, and only a few years ago were common as permanent dwellings. The birchbark wigwam is a most comfortable affair when properly kept, and nothing in the north country is more picturesque than a camp of them. Even discounting the esthetic influence on the Indians themselves of what is beautiful the wigwam is very important in Indian hygiene. Since abandoning the universal use of wigwams, many families who can well afford good houses spend part of the year in wigwams, claiming that they remain healthier than in houses. No one who has ever lived in north-country camps can well deny this. The camp, with its fresh air, cleanliness, and portability, is the fit environment of a strong, outdoor type of manhood. To see how thoroughly the Micmacs believe this one should visit their camps at their national festival. Recently the head chief has requested the people not to use tar paper at this time as a substitute for birch bark, as the ugly, cheaper material mars the appearance of the celebration. I might add that to be converted to admiration for the wisdom of a people who preach adherence to the bark camp, one only has to become an occupant of a wigwam a little while. The Micmacs are experts in camp construction.

Having survived the submerging wave of European intrusion, the Micmacs are still a national entity, with much of their inward culture intact and some of their exterior life. To the student of local folk life a visit to the home of the Cape Breton Micmacs yields much satisfaction.

MESCAL : A MENACE TO THE INDIANS *

BY G. A. WATERMULDER

ALTHOUGH much has been said and written in recent years concerning the use of peyote among the Indians in the United States, so that it is quite generally known and deplored, yet it is very evident that we greatly need to know the real facts.

Turning to the *Congressional Record* of last year, when the Indian Appropriation Bill was under consideration, and the words "and peyote" had been added to the section appropriating $100,000 for the suppression of the liquor traffic, we find that our lawmakers treated the subject as a joke, as a whimsical suggestion of some fanatical Indian enthusiast. This last year witnessed a repetition of the same indifferent consideration. It is very evident that we need to know thoroughly the chemical constituents, the therapeutic value, the psychological and physical effects of the drug, if we hope effectually to help our Indian brother who, today, groping under the sad illusion of having found a panacea for all the ills of body and soul, is drawn headlong into incompetency and final despair. He will not take kindly to the proffered help; he will reject the extended hand; he will spurn any superior knowledge on the subject—the habit has "got him "—but it becomes the duty of every Government official, of every Christian worker, of every sincere friend of the Indian, to deal with it most intelligently, most effectively, and most persistently.

Fortunately we are not left in the dark. The drug has for many years been most carefully and scientifically analyzed. Experiments have been made on both animals and human subjects. For years scientific articles have been published in medical journals. The United States *Dispensatory*, which is the legal and final authority on the chemical analyses of all drugs, contains a full and most illuminating article. The facts are, therefore, well known to the scientific man. They must be made known to the public.

Anhalonium Lewinii is the botanical name. The word "peyote" appears to be of Mexican origin, while the term

---

* An address delivered at the Mohonk Conference, October 14—16, 1914

"mescal buttons" is the commercial designation given to it. The United States *Dispensatory* says, "Under the name peyote are used in Mexico for narcotic purposes certain cacti whose tops have entered commerce under the name of mescal buttons." Every scientific description that I have read speaks of mescal and peyote as the same drug.

Peyote is a species of cactus grown in northern Mexico. It is pear-shaped. The top, about one and one-half inches in diameter, is cut off. It is very soft when moist. When dry it becomes brittle and hard. It has a disagreeable taste and odor. It is sold by dealers who gather the buttons for commercial purposes and sell them in the border towns of Texas for from three to eight dollars per thousand. It is generally eaten in its dry, brittle state, from five to fifty or more buttons being taken in one night. It is also frequently made into a tea. It is sometimes powdered and put in capsule form. From time immemorial it has been used by certain tribes in Mexico for the purpose of producing intoxication. From there it spread among the Kiowas of the Rio Grande, the Zunis in Arizona, and others. It is worthy of note that in the early days it was always used for the purpose of producing intoxication at religious ceremonies. It is said that the Zuni Indians selected a few to submit themselves annually to intoxication, but never habitually subjected themselves to frequent intoxication. As early as 1720 Spanish authorities prohibited its use, and in the old Spanish archives appears a record of prosecution against an Indian for having drunk the herb called peyote. In late years it has gradually spread to an increasing and alarming extent among the tribes of the United States, beginning in the south among the Comanches, Kiowas, Otos, Cheyennes, Arapahos, and their neighbors, and spreading to the northern tribes—the Omahas, Winnebagoes, Sioux, and others. Thousands of our Indians are now peyote drug fiends.

A chemical analysis has been made by the Pharmaceutical Institute of Leipzig, Germany, by Doctors Prentiss and Morgan of Washington, and by Dr. S. Weir Mitchell of Philadelphia, and other prominent names are given in the U. S. *Dispensatory*. The analysis shows that it contains a number of alkaloids (*anahalonine, mescaline, anahalonidine*, and a fourth, together with a residue). These alkaloids are described by the highest legal chemical authority "as powerful agents ranking in strength with some of our most potent drugs." The chemists also state that the physiological and psychical effects resemble those of such powerful and restricted drugs as *cannibis indica*, strychnine, and morphine, which, together with their derivatives, have been long restricted by law.

Not only has a careful chemical analysis been made, but

experimentation has been performed on animals and human subjects. These authorities found that four or five mescal buttons (our Indians use from five to fifty or more) "produce a peculiar cerebral excitement attended with an extraordinary visual disturbance." There was found a gradually increased dilation of the pupil, slowing of the pulse, and weakening of heart action from nine to thirty beats per minute, uncertainty of gait like that produced by alcohol, tremors, wakefulness, and in some cases nausea. There was an overestimation of time, minutes became hours, and hours became long periods of time. Distances were accentuated. There was nothing near. Objects close at hand appeared to be moving farther and farther away. There was a sense of dual existence. In some cases it produces delirium, often followed by seeing monsters, grotesque faces, and gruesome shapes like a cat with huge claws, crawling up the body to clutch the throat. But the things that fascinate and grip the imagination, producing unusual enjoyment, are the visual hallucinations and the extraordinary effect upon the hearing. The habitué enjoys "a regular kaleidoscopic play of most wonderful colors, an incessant flow of vision of infinite beauty, grandeur, and variety." The effect produced upon the hearing makes "each note produced on the piano the center of a melody of other notes which appear to be surrounded by a halo of color, pulsating to the music." Herein it largely resembles *cannibis indica* and opium.

About twenty years ago some of the leading drug manufacturing firms of our country, as the Parke Davis Company and the Merk Company, thinking that such a powerful drug might have some value as a remedial agent, began to prepare it in certain compounds. These preparations have been used to a slight extent in various forms of neurasthenia and hysteria, and also have been alleged to be useful in neuralgic and rheumatic affections. It should, however, be carefully noted that it is no longer prepared. Dr. Francis, the chief chemist of the Parke Davis Company, says "it is absolutely a dead issue so far as doctors and pharmacists are concerned. We no longer carry it in stock." Its remedial value has been pronounced very doubtful. The scientific aspect of the subject is thus well summed up by Dr. Wiley, formerly chief chemist of the United States Agricultural Department, when he says: "It is an evil and nothing but an evil." The injurious results which follow the habitual use of such a powerful and peculiar drug are well expressed in a warning given by Dr. S. Weir Mitchell, of Philadelphia. After careful experimentation he says, "I predict a perilous reign of the mescal habit when this agent becomes obtainable. The temptation to call again the enchanting magic will be too much for

some men to resist after they have set foot in this land of fairy
colors, where there seems so much to charm and so little to
excite horror or disgust."

Dealing as we are, then, with a most potent drug, producing
such extraordinary psychical pleasures, need we wonder that it
is eagerly sought, that its use is defended, and that it is playing
havoc within the ranks of our Indian population, already so
weakened by disease? Thousands of our most typical, virile,
and promising Indian youth, young men who have come from
our Government schools, are the chief promoters.   The old
medicine superstitions no longer appeal.   Here is something
new and wonderful.   It retains enough of the old to make it
Indian, and it adds what he has superficially learned and observed in our civilization and religion.   It appeals to his craving
for leadership and to the lusts of the flesh.   And today we have
a new, semi-religious movement among our Indian people, with
peyote as a fetish that is worshiped as something extraordinarily supernatural.

In many tribes meetings are now held every night with
all-night sessions.   The drug is passed in dry form or as a tea.
Everyone takes as much as he or she may desire.   Gradually the
majority present become intoxicated, enjoying the incessant and
wonderful flow of vision from the inevitable reaction, but with
no desire for a hard day's work.

The drug is also constantly used by many during the week.
It has become a daily necessity. Although it has no remedial
value and is most dangerous, it is used in all forms of sickness
and disease for old and young, for the strong and for the
new-born babe.   And we need not wonder.   The sick man
wants something to rid him of the sense of pain.   He wants his
nerves benumbed.   The white man administers his hyperdermic
doses; the Indian too enjoys alleviation from pain and stimulation of the nervous system.   Thousands and hundreds of thousands of people have no doubt gone out of the world in a very
happy frame of mind through the use of opium, morphine, or
cannibis indica.   The Indian ignorantly takes his supernatural
remedy by the pound instead of by the grain, by the cupful instead of by the drop or spoonful.   Need we wonder that frequently an emaciated, anemic, helpless, dying patient will, under
this powerful stimulation, rise from his bed, walk about, gather
his relatives and friends together, make a most wonderful speech
concerning the things he has seen, shake hands, bid farewell, and
then lie down and in a few minutes die?   To the untutored it
does seem supernatural and marvelous.   Or need we wonder that
infants troubled with the common ailments of children, when
given dose after dose of this drug, die of paralysis, or of digestive and nervous disturbances?   And need we wonder that the

plump, sunny faces of young men as they come from school soon
become sallow, inky, and sunken, or that their strong bodies,
debauched by the lusts of the flesh, hasten to an untimely
grave? What can we expect of any people whose bodies have
been enervated and ruined by any kind of a powerful drug?"
The American Indian, in his present physical condition, needs
every ounce of physical strength to resist the ravages of disease.

We are now face to face with the question, Is it a menace to
progress? Is it merely a pleasurable indulgence? Shall we
treat it with indifference—a joke of politicians? Or shall we
treat it intelligently as men and women of high patriotic and
moral purposes? The Indian thinks it is his salvation. Never
before has he seen such wonderful things. It is the herb that
God gave for the weak. It is the magic wand that dispels the
darkness and brings the light. But, ah, what delusion! What
fancied pictures! What castles in the air! Finally and certainly, what a debauched, ruined life!

The Indian has also been taught that it is a cure for the
liquor habit. And true it is that many drunkards have eaten
mescal and have stopped drinking liquor, but mescal is merely a
more dangerous and potent substitute. Many use both. Many
mescal leaders are also our greatest drunkards. Says Dr. Richardson of Denver concerning the relative effect of alcohol and
mescal: "So far as its results upon the human economy are concerned, from a pathological standpoint alcohol is altogether the
safer and less harmful. The alcoholic subject may, by a careful
system of dietetics, escape physical and mental weakness, but the
mescal fiend travels to absolute incompetency. It is a vicious
thing."

The Mohonk Conference, the Indian Department at Washington, and the nation at large have never taken a doubtful stand
as to the influence of liquor on the Indian race, but here is an
agent pronounced by the highest authorities as still more dangerous than liquor. The Indian drunkard has been taught and knows
his danger and penalty. The mescal eater, ignorant of the fatal
consequences of drug habits, gradually but certainly is going to
his destruction.

Friends, I feel confident that no intelligent person sincerely
and seriously devoted to the cause of the American Indian would
care to argue the question. We know that as a habit-forming
drug, stealing upon the victim like a thief in the night, this mescal will clutch him in its deadly grip. Not only this generation,
but the rising and future generation which will be the product
of the physically, mentally, and morally weakened present one,
must be considered. Immediate effects may in many cases be
apparently slight. Some of the Indians have strong bodies, and,

as in the case of the alcohol drinker, the effects may seem slight at first. But the normal functions of the body cannot be interfered with, day after day, week after week, year after year, without the most serious results. If the resistance to disease of the present generation is already alarmingly low, what shall we look for in the future ?

About sixteen years ago Dr. and Mrs. Roe met a powerful and intellectual Indian of the Comanche tribe of the Southwest. They discussed with him the philosophy of the ancient Indian ideas until the question of mescal was introduced. This man had four sons and a daughter. The father and four sons had contracted the mescal habit, using it throughout the following sixteen years in constantly increasing amounts. The four sons had married early in life and had many children. There remains but one child of the offspring of those four men. All their infant children were treated with mescal. The daughter, on the other hand, became a Christian, induced her husband to become a Christian, and now has a beautiful little family growing up around her. This is but one instance.

And then, industrially, mescal is bound to become one of the greatest hindrances to progress. Many Indians are now working their farms, but who will question the ultimate outcome of our industrial hopes for the race if this habit continues and increases ? Beautiful buildings, houses, barns, farms, implements, will be of no avail unless we get at some of the problems that lie entrenched in the lives of so many of our promising Indians.

And what will be the effect mentally when it destroys the power of concentration, logical thinking, strength of will, balanced judgment ? Let some of our Government schools—superintendents, teachers, and matrons—courageously tell the story of the mental depression and stupidity, the physical languor and destroyed aspirations, frequently found in their pupils who secretly use it.

And then, when I think of the moral effects, when I know that it needs a clear mind, a strong will, a pure imagination, to build character, when I know how hard it is to resist temptation and aim high under the best of circumstances, and then when I think of the likelihood of becoming morally strong with the use of a habit-forming, body-weakening, will-relaxing, imagination-exciting drug, I stand appalled and cry: "O God, we will fail in all our work unless Thou dost set these men free—and then they shall be free indeed. Help us to set them free."

Friends, we need definite Federal legislation to stop this drug at the border. We need definite Federal legislation to stop it in interstate commerce. We need state legislation to stop it within the states. We need power given to the Indian Department to deal with it as it does with liquor. We need this Conference and all the organizations it represents, and all the influence it can exert to get back of it.

I close with an appeal from the oldest daughter of Quanah Parker. Quanah Parker was the great chief of the Comanches, who also became the great mescal chief of Oklahoma, and who has so long and so astutely handled Washington legislation. Mrs. Cox, his oldest daughter, recently testified before a large audience as follows : "My father was the great chief of the Comanches. He ate mescal. He asked me to eat mescal. I did eat for a few years but I gave it up. I followed a better road. I told my father to give it up. He would not. He became very sick. I got six doctors to examine him. They all said it was because he ate mescal. I again asked him to stop, but no, he would not. Two years he was sick. He became paralyzed. One day he said he would again go to a mescal meeting, far away. He took a train. He attended the meeting. The next day, while coming home on the train, he died. O friends, I ask you to stop the use of mescal. "

Shall we answer the heart cry of the daughter of Quanah Parker ?

HENRY EVANS AND NEGRO METHODISM

BY STEPHEN B. WEEKS

WITH its strong appeal to the emotions and its emphasis on experience, Methodism has always been popular among Negroes. Indeed, among Southern Negroes the Methodists and the Baptists, who represent an essentially similar type of religious life, are in a very large majority, and to one of this race the whole Methodist organization in Fayetteville, N. C., traces its orgin.

The first preacher and teacher of Methodism in that town was Henry Evans, a Negro. We know very little of the life of this early preacher, and almost all that we do know with certainty comes from the autobiography of Rev. William Capers, bishop of the Methodist Episcopal Church, South, who was the preacher in charge of the Methodist congregation in Fayetteville at the time of the death of Evans. Another source of some information is the autobiography of Rev. James Jenkins, a traveling Methodist preacher of the Carolinas who visited him in 1802.

Bishop Capers introduces his story of Henry Evans in an unusual way:

"But the most remarkable man in Fayetteville when I went there, and who died during my stay, was a Negro by the name of Henry Evans. I say the most remarkable in view of his class; and I call him Negro with unfeigned respect. He was of that race without any admixture of another. The name simply designates the race and it is vulgar to regard it with opprobrium. I have known and loved and honored not a few Negroes in my life, who were probably as pure of heart as Evans, or anybody else. Such were my old friends, Castile Selby and John Boquet of Charleston, Will Campbell and Harry Myrick of Wilmington, York Cohen of Savannah, and others I might name. These I might call remarkable for their goodness. But I use the word in a broader sense for Henry Evans, who was confessedly the father of the Methodist church, white and black, in Fayetteville, and the best preacher of his time in that quarter; and who was so remarkable as to have become the greatest curiosity of the town, insomuch that distinguished visitors hardly felt that they might pass a Sunday in Fayetteville without hearing him preach."

It is said that Evans was born in Virginia of free parents, and as he was "almost too feeble to stand" at the time of his death in 1810 we may perhaps safely carry back the date of his birth to 1730 or 1735. He became a Christian and a Methodist when quite young and was licensed to preach in Virginia. There is a report also that he removed from Virginia to the neighborhood of Doub's Chapel in what was then Stokes, now Forsyth County, North Carolina, and while there was also licensed to preach. He stayed there about a year, but being a shoemaker by trade and thinking to improve his financial condition, he determined to remove to Charleston, South Carolina. It was while on his way southward from Stokes that he was detained for a few days in Fayetteville. Here, like St. Paul, his spirit was stirred within him "at perceiving that the people of his race in that town were wholly given to profanity and lewdness, never hearing preaching of any denomination, and living emphatically without hope and without God in the world."

Bishop Capers then continues his narrative as follows:

"This determined him to stop in Fayetteville; and he began to preach to the Negroes, with great effect. The town council interfered, and nothing in his power could prevail with them to permit him to preach. He then withdrew to the sandhills outside of the town, and held meetings in the woods, changing his appointments from place to place. No law was violated, while the council was effectually eluded; and so the opposition passed into the hands of the mob. These he worried out by changing his appointments, so that when they went to work their will upon him he was preaching somewhere else. Meanwhile, whatever the most honest purpose of a simple heart could do to reconcile his enemies was employed by him for that end. He eluded no one in private but sought opportunities to explain himself; avowed the purity of his intentions, and even begged to be subjected to the scrutiny of any surveillance that might be thought proper to prove his inoffensiveness.

"Happily for him and the cause of religion, his honest countenance and earnest pleadings were soon powerfully seconded by the fruits of his labors. One after another began to suspect their servants of attending his preaching, not because they were made worse, but wonderfully better. The effect on the public morals of the Negroes, too, began to be seen, particularly as regarded drunkenness and their habits on Sunday. It was not long before the mob was called off by a change in the current of opinion, and Evans was allowed to preach in town. At that time there was not a single church edifice in the city, and but one congregation (Presbyterian) which worshiped in what was called the statehouse, under which was the market; and it was plainly

Evans or nobody to preach to the Negroes.   Now, too, not a few
mistresses and some masters were brought to think that the
preaching which had proved so beneficial to their servants might
be good for them also; and the famous Negro preacher had some
whites as well as blacks to hear him.   Among these were my old
friends, Mr. and Mrs. Lumsden, Mrs. Bowen (for many years
preceptress of the Female Academy), Mrs. Malsby, and, I think,
Mr. and Mrs. Blake.   From these the gracious influence spread
to others, and a meeting-house was built.   It was a frame of
wood, weather-boarded only on the outside, without plastering,
and about fifty feet long by thirty feet wide.''

Unfortunately Bishop Capers gives no dates for these interesting occurrences, but we are able to fix them as antedating
1802, for in that year Rev. James Jenkins visited Fayetteville and
writes in his autobiography:

"We had no white society there at that time; I found, however, a small society of colored people, under the care of a colored man by the name of Evans, who preached to them regularly, and no ordinary preacher was he.   I visited him every
round and encouraged him all I could, and furnished him with a
steward's book in which to register whatever might appertain to
his office.   About this time he leased a lot for seven years and
commenced building a church, twenty by thirty feet, out of
rough-edged materials.   They met the expenses themselves, except $5, which was given them by a white man.   This was the
first Methodist church in the place; it was called 'the Negro
church.'   In a short time it became crowded, and an addition of
ten feet was made to it.''

In 1803 Mr. Jenkins writes: ''Old Sister Malsby, who was
then a member of the Presbyterian church, and who, as I was
told, had been led out of the public congregation for shouting,
asked me if she might come in among the Negroes ?   This was
the first white member we had in the place.''

If we turn again to Bishop Capers we will find the result of
the step taken by ''old Sister Malsby.''   He says: ''Seats, distinctly separated, were at first appropriated to the whites, near
the pulpit.   But Evans had already become famous, and these
seats were insufficient.   Indeed, the Negroes seemed likely to
lose their preacher, Negro though he was, while the whites,
crowded out of their appropriate seats, took possession of those
in the rear.   Meanwhile Evans had represented to the preacher
of Bladen circuit how things were going, and induced him to take
his meeting-house into the circuit and constitute a church there.
And now there was no longer room for the Negroes in the house
when Evans preached; and for the accommodation of both classes,
the weather-boards were knocked off and sheds added to the

house on either side, the whites occupying the whole of the original building, and the Negroes those sheds as a part of the same house. Evans's dwelling was a shed at the pulpit end of the church."

Of Evans himself Bishop Capers says: "I have not known many preachers who appeared more conversant with the Scriptures than Evans, or whose conversation was more instructive as to the things of God. He seemed always deeply impressed with the responsibility of his position; and not even our old friend Castile was more remarkable for his humble and deferential deportment towards the whites than Evans was. Nor would he allow any partiality of his friends to induce him to vary in the least degree the line of conduct or the bearing which he had prescribed for himself in this respect. And yet Henry Evans was a Boanerges, and in his duty feared not the face of man."

Of Evans's death, which occurred between June 13 and December 22, 1810, the inclusive dates of Bishop Capers' pastorate in Fayetteville, he has this to say:

"It was my practice to hold a meeting with the blacks in the church directly after morning preaching every Sunday. And on the Sunday before the death of Evans, during this meeting, the little door between his humble shed and the chancel where I stood was opened, and the dying man entered for a last farewell to his people. He was almost too feeble to stand at all, but, supporting himself by the railing of the chancel, he said: 'I have come to say my last word to you. It is this : None but Christ. Three times I have had my life in jeopardy for preaching the gospel to you. Three times I have broken the ice on the edge of the water and swum across the Cape Fear to preach the gospel to you. And now, if in my last hour I could trust to that, or to anything else but Christ crucified, for my salvation, all would be lost and my soul perish forever.' A noble testimony! Worthy not of Evans only, but of St. Paul. His funeral at the church was attended by a greater concourse of persons than had been seen on any funeral occasion before. The whole community appeared to mourn his death, and the universal feeling seemed to be that in honoring the memory of Henry Evans we were paying a tribute to virtue and religion. He was buried under the chancel of the church of which he had been in so remarkable a manner the founder."

Bishop Asbury also bears testimony to the thoroughness of Evans's work. He was at Fayetteville in 1811 and writes in his Journal: "Preached; our house is too small; preached in the afternoon; we must enlarge our house." By January 1814, this desire had probably been attained, for the congregation was then strong enough and the house of worship large enough to entertain the South Carolina Conference and thus, in the case of Henry Evans, were the Scriptures fulfilled, "for his works did follow him."

A NEGLECTED PHASE OF THE NEGRO QUESTION

BY D. HIDEN RAMSEY

Supply Instructor in Economics, University of Virginia

THE most serviceable leadership that the Southern white man can adopt in his role as one of the elements of the Negro question must after all be moral. Economic considerations may complicate the problem, legal aspects may introduce irritating situations, but the moral order of things must be trusted as the final solvent. Amid the conflict of varying opinions on other phases we are perforce impressed with the unanimity with which all leaders stake the issue upon a moral readjustment. When the two races pool their ethical forces, we see the light.

The Negro is imitative; the progress that is to be his must come through a response to the wholesome conditions which environ him. This is axiomatic in the field of race adjustment; the lower race rises by imitating the best life of the higher. Conversely, the lower race stagnates morally, or even hardens its immoral tendencies, by adopting the moral relapses of the higher as the pattern of virtue. James Bryce in his thoughtful lectures on "The relations between the advanced and backward races of mankind" has developed this idea, showing its importance in all questions which grow out of race relationships.

And the Southern white man who wishes to bring sanity and sympathy to bear on the Negro question must accept this negative responsibility no less than the more obvious affirmative responsibility which is pressed upon him. The Negro has the right to demand from his white brother something more than justice in the courts and industrial opportunity. The dominant race, by virtue of the privilege which it claims, should furnish in its life and teachings moral guidance for the submerged people. The "White Man's Burden" of which Kipling sang in verse, is largely a burden of moral responsibility—a responsibility which impels the man higher up to cultivate moral elegance that he may the better serve as a model for the man lower down.

In no other respect probably is the modern Southerner failing more disastrously in his relations to the Negro than in neglecting to provide this sensitive moral guidance, both in leaders put forward and in environment created. The white man too often feels that he does his duty when he gives the black man the full protection of the courts, public education for his children, and economic reward for his honesty and thrift. It is not necessary to defend the institution of slavery in lamenting the passing of that personal relation between the whites and the blacks which obtained under the old régime. The Southerner of today deals with the Negro as a race but not as an individual. The whites and the Negroes considered in large groups are in closer and more effective sympathy today than at any previous time in the history of their relations. But Elisha Smith, the Negro carpenter, seldom goes for advice to Marmaduke Smith, the white banker, who is the son of his father's master. And Marmaduke Smith, while he contributes generously to several Negro charitable foundations, rarely inquires after the health of Elisha. It is well for the Negro race to be sufficient unto itself; it is indeed a commendable effort that would develop in the Negro a deep pride in the achievements of his race. But the Negro question of the South will never be solved through institutional activities. There must be between the two races an abounding sympathy—a sympathy which stresses individuals no less than groups. The king of old who thought that he could convert his soldiers to Christianity by baptizing them in companies at the point of the sword was no farther wrong than the modern philanthropist who, in trying to solve the race question, ignores the personal element.

This occasional failure of the Southern white man to make himself responsible for the moral welfare of the Negro is illustrated in the conventional attitude toward the segregation of houses of prostitution. Every Southern town practically has its red-light district. Public opinion forces the houses of ill-fame to the outskirts of the community. At the same time, another law—a law of real estate—is working just as relentlessly to crowd the Negro into the same area. Apparently neither of the two parties has any choice. The keepers of the brothels must go where public opinion will be indifferent to their business ; the Negro must live where rent is cheapest. And, as a result, in most Southern towns and cities, "niggertown" and the red-light district are synonymous terms. Yet strange to say very few white people have been impressed with the tragic incongruity of the situation. We expect chastity from the Negro, yet we surround him in his childhood, in his home, with the spectacle of organized vice. We repose our faith in the ennobling influence of the church and the school, yet we often find the Negro church and the Negro school cheek by jowl with the white brothel. Human nature at best is frail, and especially so in a child race. The Negro cannot live in proximity to houses of prostitution and fail

to be contaminated; he cannot in his daily life be confronted
with the depravity of certain white men and then be expected to
imitate those finer white spirits whom he knows only by hearsay.

But white men have often protested—and successfully—
against these conditions, as is illustrated in the case of Asheville,
North Carolina. Two years ago Asheville, like most other Southern towns, had a red-light district situated in the Negro residential section of the town. But one good man in the community, Dr. R. F. Campbell, had been impressed with the unfair
strain that these conditions placed upon the virtue of the
Negro. The local newspapers at this time were carrying editorials of an anti-vice crusade nature, and Dr. Campbell took
advantage of this sentiment to protest in public print against a
species of segregation which unloaded the brothels upon the
Negro residential sections. The late William Garrott Brown, who
was then a visitor in Asheville, added the weight of his own
influence to the protest of Dr. Campbell. Investigation found
three houses of ill-repute adjoining a Negro public school with
an enrollment of twelve hundred children. The Negro ministers
joined forces with the white ministers in sending a protest to the
city police court justice. The judge exercised his full preroga-
tive, with the result that within a week the brothels were driven
out of the Negro district.

Abraham Flexner's study of "Prostitution in Europe,"
recently published under the Bureau of Social Hygiene by the
Century Company of New York, raises many interesting questions in this most repulsive field of social study. Dr. Flexner
demonstrates how completely regulation and segregation, the
two specifics employed for the evil on the Continent, have broken
down in practice. The future may point out a new path of correction along which the United States can travel. But segregation which segregates only for the higher classes is a social
experiment which discriminates against the man at the bottom
of the ladder. In the North the poorer immigrant classes suffer; in the South it is the Negro who must obey the laws of real
estate.

The next few years should furnish striking developments in
Southern race conditions. The complex educational machinery
which is now being built up will then be functioning; a new generation will have become set in the new modes of thought. But
after all has been said and done, we must look to the moral guidance of the Southern white man for the justification of our high
hopes. And it must be a moral guidance that speaks in the daily
routine of life across the social chasm that yawns between the
two races.

THE CALL FOR NEGRO FARMERS

BY SOLOMON D. SPADY *

EVERY man at some period of his life has a call to do some particular thing or kind of work. Moses was called by God to lead the children of Israel from the slave land of Egypt to the free land of Canaan. Alexander the Great and Napoleon were called to establish the kingdoms they represented in the world. General Armstrong and Booker T. Washington heard the call to help educate the black man and to teach him to love and appreciate the things that are highest and best. Today the call for strong young men to go to the country and teach our people modern methods of farming is ringing out loud and strong in every country district.

At my home in Northampton County, Virginia, the land is level and very suitable for truck raising, especially for white potatoes. There are a number of large farms under cultivation, the majority being cultivated by Negroes. Some of these farms are also owned by Negroes. But the Negroes, and the white farmers as well, have not as yet awakened to the fact that in order to be successful they must vary their work from year to year. They try to follow the old method of planting practiced by our fathers before the war ; that is, they plant potatoes in the spring and after the potatoes have been harvested they follow them with corn, and so on year after year. They do this until the land becomes, as they say, ''unproductive,'' when it is only worn out from lack of proper attention. No rotation of crops is used, no cover crop is sown to hold the land together and give it vitality. For these potato crops farmers spend thousands of dollars for commercial fertilizers, in their effort to make a larger crop and thereby more money, instead of adding fertility to the soil by manure and the use of cover crops. The lack of knowledge of modern methods of farming has led the Negro farmer to believe that farming is not a paying occupation, and has driven many a boy to the city, in some cases to his ruin.

Such are the conditions which led me to believe that there was no money in farming, and that the farm could not be worked

* A paper by a member of the graduating class, delivered at the Hampton Anniversary, April 1914

profitably even if it was conducted with the same skill and energy and backed up by as ample capital as other industries, and most of the farmers at my home believed the same thing. This erroneous belief must be changed and that very soon or the agriculture of Northampton County must go down.

In the year 1909 I decided that I could not stand the farm any longer, that it was not a paying business, and that I must change my vocation. I had a desire to be a lawyer or some other kind of professional man. So, naturally, I planned to go to college. I met Mr. T. C. Walker, who advised me not to go to college but to come to Hampton. After much persuasion on his part I took his advice and came to Hampton. My first year here was spent at Shellbanks, a large, six-hundred-acre farm about six miles from the school proper. Here I cooked for the students during the day and went to school at night.

About the middle of the term I was asked what trade I wanted to take, and with the idea of taking one that would help me through school, I decided to take carpentry. Very fortunate I thought myself to have my request granted. During this time I was studying some of the fundamental principles of agriculture every Friday night under the superintendent of Shellbanks Farm. These principles took root in my heart and commenced to grow, until I began to understand the real beauty in working with Nature and to see as never before the needs of my people—the need of someone to teach them that farming can be made a paying business, and that they themselves possess the very essentials to assure progress on the farm, such as capital and potential energy; that if these qualities are put into full use, then the vast land possessions will provide large quantities of food stuffs, and afford employment for a great number of people.

With this conviction I changed my mind and chose the course in agriculture. With the three years' training in the agriculture department, and two years' work in the academic department, I feel I shall go back to my people a professional man, not in the terms of a lawyer or doctor, but as a trained agriculturist, not to minister unto them through pleading at the bar for justice, or through medical treatment, but to minister unto them as one who has heard the great call from Mother Earth and from the farmer as well, to show to them by precept and example the blessings that may be obtained through scientific farming. I hope to give to my people what Hampton has given me, the knowledge that if farming is put on a firm basis, backed up by a sufficient amount of skill, energy, capital, and efficiency, it will pay, and that if the farmer starves and neglects his land and the soil remains poor and thin he has no right to expect good profits and abundant crops. As a man sows so must he reap.

PHILIPPINE INDEPENDENCE[*]

BY W. MORGAN SHUSTER

Formerly Secretary of Public Instruction in the Philippines

I BELIEVE that certain events which have occurred in the world during the last three months, when properly studied and realized, may throw a somewhat new light upon our attitude as a nation and a people towards the future of the Philippine Islands and the Filipino people. I think there has been a great deal of hypocrisy about our treatment of the question. We have laid the flattering unction to our souls that we are being truly altruistic toward the Philippines, that if we do not stay there they will fall into the hands of Germany, or into the hands of Japan, or some other nation.

I do not think any of these assumptions are correct. I think the fact that treaties have been violated somewhat rudely of late should not be taken as a sign that they will not be solemnly enforced between nations in the future. It behooves the United States, then, to consider how strong they can make themselves in the court of nations. It will not do to assume simply that we are right in whatever we do. We may think we are right, but we have something further to do. We must convince the world at large that we are right. It is a very easy thing to convince the world at large of the fact that we have a right to keep the Philippine Islands merely as a trade appendage. I think that any other nation which might have taken them by right of conquest, in the benighted phraseology of the times, would have retained them for exploitation, and America is entitled to the fullest credit for not having done wholly that. But the arguments which you have heard so often in favor of an indefinite retention of the Philippines under the United States flag are not based on altruism ; they are based upon a sentiment created by commercial and business interests in this country.

The question of when a stable government can be established in the Philippine Islands is one about which we will know just as much one hundred years from now, in my humble opinion, as we do today. I have been in the Islands for a number of years ; others have been there longer; and I do not think any man can say that the Filipino people could not start a stable and inde-

---

[*] Extracts from an address delivered at the Mohonk Conference, October, 1914

pendent government tomorrow, if given the opportunity, or that they might not maintain it without serious difficulty for the rest of time. It is entirely possible. I do not think any man could say that, even if they were drilled in the goose-step of government for one hundred years by the most successful tutors we could furnish and then given that independence, they would immediately enter upon an era of prosperity and idealistic self-government. I do not think that it is a matter of time or purely a matter of technical training.

We have, ourselves, in the United States the most incompetent set of municipal governments that can be found anywhere. That is generally admitted, I believe, as to our municipal go vrnments. I do not wish to make it appear that this statement is original on my part, for it is not; but we have some municipal governments which would get a mayor of a fifth-rate town in Germany sent to jail. And yet we speak of "efficiency in government." Efficiency in government is not technique; there is no means of knowing that what is technique for one town will be the same for another; there is no way of knowing that what is good legislation for one state will be good legislation for another state at the other end of the country; and there is no way of knowing just what will be a good government for the Philippine Islands. They will have to work that out for themselves, if they are ever given a fair opportunity.

That any nation which has been under foreign domination can suddenly develop great self-governing ability, I do not believe. You are all familiar with the struggles of our own country when we had two and a half millions of inhabitants; we came through gallantly and nobly and solved our problems, but if any European nation then in power had thought it advisable to shed the necessary blood and spend the necessary money to come over and retake the American colonies, it could have been done, because they were thoroughly exhausted, financially and otherwise, and there were a dozen pretexts for it any time. If we are going to expect the Filipinos some day suddenly to execute and put in force such a model government that no nation could find a pretext for objecting to something that happened there, I fear their hopes of independence are very slim.

The great fear urged against giving the Islands independence has been that the Japanese would probably come and take them. If the Japanese want the Philippines, they can take them whether we have our flag flying there or not. They can take them in four and a half days by putting so many troops there that for us to send an army across the Pacific and get them out would be almost beyond military possibility. We would probably try it; we would feel that we would have to. So, if Japan wants the Philippines, she can take them, whether they happen to be American territory with our flag flying over them, or whether they happen to be neutral territory with our guarantee and the guarantee of other nations back them, or whether they are wholly independent without any guarantee of neutrality. Japan's ability to take them is because of their physical proximity. Why don't we have any fear of this? I was talking with a well-known Japanese gentleman a few weeks ago and asked the question point blank. He said, "If my government could get out of Formosa and Korea and get back where we belong, without getting into financial ruin in those two countries, we should be very happy, and we are not looking for any further trouble; you could not possibly *give* us the Philippines." I really believe he expressed the attitude of the Japanese people. I believe they are just as anxious to observe their present high place in the family of nations as any other nation in the world. I think that their conduct has been admirable, both in peace and in war. They have scrupulously observed their treaty obligations, and any difference of opinion between this nation and the Japanese nation that I have been able to discover is due to some doubt as to whether we are exactly in a position to observe our obligations toward them. No charge at all has ever been made, that they have not scrupulously observed theirs towards every other nation, and if the Japanese made—as they undoubtedly would make—a treaty with the United States regarding the neutrality of the Philippine Islands, they would observe it and observe it to the letter; so that we may dismiss from our minds, when considering the question of Philippine independence, any doubts as to the efficacy of neutral treaties or anything of that kind.

We have declared through one branch of government that it has always been our intention to grant the Filipinos their independence some day. If forty or fifty years pass without this people being granted complete independence they will never get it, barring some unforeseen contingencies. That is why any policy looking toward the indefinite retention of the Islands, with the assertion that some day they will get independence, is bound to be more or less hypocrisy. It cannot be sincere. If they are to have their independence and be given a trial, a fair trial, at being an independent nation under whatever guarantees are deemed necessary or convenient, they must have it sometime within the memory of the present generation. It is perfectly useless to speak about letting generations pass, two, three, or four, and then giving them independence. It would be very much better for the American people, as well as for the Filipinos, if that is the policy, to say now that they shall never have it. But I take that what the American people really want, if they can find the way, is to be perfectly sincere and fair towards this situation. I believe that, irrespective of party ties, that is what they wish to be, and I believe that a very long step in this direction has been taken by the passage of the Jones Bill in the House of Representatives; and when it is passed by the Senate I shall feel like saying that a longer step has been taken. I hope yet to see, before my memory and eyesight grow too dim, a bill passed which shall grant to the Philippine people free and full independence, with such assistance and co-operation granted by this government as we may feel it to our interest to give them.

A NEGRO YOUNG WOMEN'S CHRISTIAN ASSOCIATION

BY LAURA E. TITUS [1]

President of the Norfolk Negro Young Women's Christian Association

IN July 1908 a meeting was called at Hampton, Virginia, by Mrs. Addie Hunton, national organizer of women's clubs, at which Mrs. Harris Barrett presided. The object was to organize a State Federation of Colored Women's Clubs. There were scarcely enough Virginia clubs to claim recognition, but being made state organizer I at once set to work to form new clubs, among them one at Norfolk, called the Norfolk Association of Colored Women, of which I was elected president.

We set to work to build up this newly formed club. A number of good Christian women took hold in earnest to establish a reading room for local girls and young women. This movement met with hearty approval. The club grew and we decided to change the name to the Young Women's Christian Association, and further to advance our work by trying to help girls coming into our city.

After two years we found ourselves handicapped for room. We had, through the kindness of the Y. M. C. A., been holding our meetings in their rooms. A permanent home was badly needed so that more substantial work could be done for the working girl. Captain John L. Roper, a white gentleman of Norfolk, offered us the lease of a suitable house for one year (and has still kept it up). The members hastened to furnish the house, which contained nine rooms and a bath. On the lower floor were the kitchen, dining-room, and living-rooms, in which met five or six clubs and the sewing and reading classes. We had also classes in cooking and gardening, Sunday meetings, and social gatherings of Sunday schools and clubs.

---

[1] Hampton, '76

In 1910 we secured a charter for the Association. The Golden Sheaf Circle, Colored King's Daughters, under Miss Sarah Brinkley, furnished a bedroom. Later, through the trustees of the Mary L. Mead Fund we were enabled to furnish another. This fund was donated by the Sunshine Library of Hampton founded by Mrs. George Davis, a Hampton ex-student. Captain Roper gave fifty dollars towards furnishings, and we found ourselves with five bedrooms holding twelve beds and cots.

In 1913 we had to change houses on account of a sale. The girls were increasing in numbers through the agents and other mediums. In April we had a membership rally which gave to the Association over two hundred new members. Application was then made for membership into the National Young Women's Christian Association, three Y. W. C. A. secretaries having previously visited our Association and found it in harmony with the requirements of the National Association. In June we had a financial campaign for $1500 and were successful in getting the pledges which are now being collected. In spite of all these things we could not show the results of the real hard work that was being done at the Association rooms because we had no permanent secretary to overlook the work properly and give the necessary reports. The National Association came forward with its splendid offer to assist us by recommending a general secretary, Miss Gertrude James, of the New York Association, who now has full charge of the work.

Numbers of girls apply for work through the Association and there are many calls for workers. We place between twelve and fifteen girls each month. If we were sure that our girls were well equipped for the service demanded more could be placed. We are hoping through our domestic science classes to fit the girls for that service which can demand a higher wage.

Many a stranded girl or woman has been kept at the Association rooms while waiting for work or money to return home. It is our rule to turn no girl away if we can accommodate her. Last winter girls sat up in chairs rather than leave the Association, and our housekeeper has slept on the floor to give a girl a bed.

The Association activities in regard to basket ball, physical culture, Camp Fire girls, and "Blue Birds" are growing. In summer the little ones are carried to the playground and to picnics in the park. They have been helped also through the fresh air fund of the white United Charities, which has given much encouragement to the Association, the Association in turn investigating and reporting helpless cases among the poor colored families of the city. Sunday afternoon service has always a good

speaker and good attendance. We also hold mothers' meetings.
We have the sympathy and hearty approval of the excellent ministers in our city. The churches are all open to our work and we
are always accorded a hearty welcome. The doctors are always
willing to give lectures and other assistance.

We are anxious to draw in more of the working girls from
laundries, factories, etc. We very much need books and papers
for the library, a larger cooking department, and a small loom
for weaving rugs. Among the fourteen associations of the
county we are ranked as one of the best. In all our work we
feel much encouraged and thank the Master for the gift of kind
friends, who have helped so largely in making this work possible.

At Home and Afield

HAMPTON INCIDENTS

THE ARMSTRONG LEAGUE

ON the afternoon of October 26 the
Armstrong League of Hampton
Workers gave a cake and candy sale
and flower show in the Assembly Room
of the Mansion House. The room was
beautifully decorated with roses,
dahlias, and even a few chrysanthe-
mums, which had appeared earlier
than usual to do honor to the occasion.
The delicious cakes and candy sold all
too fast for late comers. An added
attraction was the opportunity of
making trips about the harbor, two
motor boats leaving the school wharf
every hour. The sale cleared $70.67.

The annual reception of the Armstrong League to its members and
the new workers was held in the Museum on Saturday, October 31. A
pleasant evening was spent in making
new acquaintances, looking over pictures of the buildings and grounds as
they were in the old days, and finding
familiar faces in pictures of early
workers. A guessing contest with
portraits of famous men brought out
the fact that three at least of the
members of the League have a good

memory for faces. The prize, a bunch
of yellow chysanthemums, was divided among them.

ON November 4 the annual meeting
of the Armstrong League was
held in the Museum. The treasurer
reported that the Armstrong Memorial Fund has increased from $427.51
to $737.57, the social committee hav-
ing raised $227.22 during the year.
The executive committee reported
that copies of " Education for Life "
and the "Story of the Armstrong
League " had been sent to members
and that eighty-seven new names had
been added to the membership. Miss
Hyde, Mrs. Scoville, Mr. F. D. Banks,
and Mr. Howe gave very interesting
personal reminiscences of the early life
of the school, thus contributing
greatly to the enjoyment of all who
were present.

THE FARMERS' CONFERENCE

THE Farmers' Conference was held
this year on November 9 and 10.
Supervisors and farm-demonstration

agents began to arrive on the sixth, and from that time a steadily increasing army invaded the school grounds. Farmers and their wives from Tidewater Virginia, and from neighboring states; the farm-demonstration agents of Virginia, who are teaching the farmers better methods of raising crops; industrial supervising teachers of rural colored schools; and the white state supervisors of rural schools; representatives of the General Education Board : these were the different groups of people who came to the Conference to give and receive advice and inspiration.

A FINE EXHIBIT

THE farmers, demonstration agents, and supervising teachers, were all represented in the various exhibits which filled the school Gymnasium and overflowed into a large tent outside. Patchwork quilts, knit and woven rugs in all varieties of color and design, beautiful embroidery, and long rows of canned vegetables and fruits testified to the industry and efficiency of the farmers' wives. Each industrial supervisor had an exhibit from her county schools, consisting of sewing, canning, basket work, and furniture. The exhibit from Gloucester County took the first prize. Fruit and vegetables of all kinds were displayed by the farmers and farm-demonstration agents. The sweet-potato exhibit was declared by the judge, who has been judge of exhibits in three states, to be the finest he had ever seen, The girls' canning clubs had an especially fine exhibit.

A new feature which aroused great interest was an illustration of the use a farmer can make of the parcel post. A plow, which ordinarily would be shipped by freight and would be a long time on the road, was shipped in four packages by parcel post. A number of plow points, a harness, eggs, and various other things were also sent in this way.

The Whittier School sent an exhibit which made suggestions for work suited to the different grades in rural schools. There were drawings, map work, a loom, a homemade fireless cooker, and a "Virginia home"—a cardboard house, surrounded by a well-kept yard with a garden. The children from the Whittier demonstrated their industrial work one afternoon in the Gymnasium, weaving rugs, making cornshuck mats, bottoming chairs with shucks.

Besides competing in their exhibits, the farmers had an opportunity of comparing their skill in judging horses, mules, and cattle. There was also a plowing match in which rapidity and efficiency were the winning factors.

CONFERENCE MEETINGS

NOT only through the exhibits and the contests did the members of the Farmers' Conference learn the right and the wrong ways of doing things. Helpful talks on the different subjects of interest to farmers were given on Monday and Tuesday afternoons by men and women who are specialists in the subjects on which they spoke. Dr. Jarvis, director of the extension work of the Connecticut Agricultural College, told what Connecticut is doing for her farmers. Mr. A. B. Graham of Long Island showed the helpful relations which may exist between an industrial school and the farmers in its neighborhood. Miss Agnew, Virginia supervisor of girls' canning clubs, and one of the judges of the canning exhibit, showed the good and bad points of several cans of fruit and vegetables. She said that the exhibit this year was seventy-five per cent better than it was two years ago. Mr. John B. Pierce, graduate of Hampton and director of Negro farm-demonstration agents for Virginia and North and South Carolina, told of the work these agents are doing and of the help they are giving to the farmers. At a poultry meeting on Tuesday morning, Mr. Graham of the Institute gave an interesting lecture on eggs and the proper way of dressing chickens. Among the speakers at the afternoon meeting were Miss Lucy H. Tapley, principal of Spelman Seminary, Atlanta, Ga.; Mrs. Booker T. Washington, who told what the women are doing in one county in Alabama; Mr. Thomas C. Walker of Gloucester, Virginia; and Mr. F. H. Cardoza of the Agricultural and Mechanical College for Negroes at Tallahassee, Florida.

AN interesting and helpful "experience" meeting was held on Monday evening. One farmer after another told of what he had accomplished, of his failures and successes, and of the methods he had found best for increasing his crops. The help given by the farm-demonstration agents was emphasized again and again. Miss Elizabeth A. Jenkins, (Hampton, 1902) general supervisor of industrial work for Virginia, told what the colored women of this state are doing. She said that the better homes and higher standards of these women are due in great part to the industrial supervisors, who have roused them to take an interest in these things.

THE closing meeting of the Conference was held in Cleveland Hall Chapel on Tuesday evening. Addresses were made by Mr. W. T. B. Williams, field agent for the Jeanes and Slater Funds, Dr. Charles S. Morris of Norfolk, Dr. Booker T. Washington, Hampton's most famous graduate, and Dr. Frissell. Mr. Williams told the farmers that there was no finer crop than their boys and girls and that the schools ought to equal the farms of which they are justly proud. The children must be given a sufficiently thorough training to enable them to hold this land, and therefore there must be longer terms and better teachers.

Dr. Morris urged the people to remain in the rural districts of the South and to buy land. The city, he said, is ruinous to colored men. Slavery was necessary—a rough school, but the pupil was rough—and slavery had changed the Negro from "the African sitting under a banana tree, clothed by sunlight and fed by gravitation," to the hard-working, landowning Negro of the South today. It is for the colored race of today to give a new meaning to the word Negro; to make it mean character and service; and to achieve this, the race should continue to live in the rural districts of the South.

Dr. Washington, who was greeted with applause when he entered the Chapel, first addressed the students, telling them of the life at Hampton when he was a student, of crowded rooms in which six or seven had to sleep, and of the tent where he slept one winter, waking more than once to find his tent blown across the campus. He told them that they have a great responsibility, for it is their duty to educate the masses of their people who are still ignorant. The average Southern white man must also be brought to believe in Negro education, and it is for Hampton students to do this by showing themselves earnest, modest, and willing to serve.

To the farmers Dr. Washington gave the advice to go back to their homes and remove the "Negro earmarks" from houses and grounds—the broken fence, sagging gate, unpainted house, and broken windowpane. He said that farmers are just coming into their own and that they hold the key to the situation. He urged them to go on farming and make more than a mere living on their farms—enough to build better homes, churches, schools. Above all, he said, they should not get discouraged, for racial friendship is increasing every day and they should be proud of the race to which they belong and of the progress they have made.

In a brief speech Dr. Frissell expressed his pleasure at seeing the members of the Conference and his delight in the progress made during the past year as shown in the exhibit.

At this meeting it was announced that the farmers and their wives had presented to the school, in token of their appreciation of the assistance given them by Hampton, full scholarships for two boys in the agricultural department.

BESIDES the regular sessions of the Conference, several other important meetings were held simultaneously. One was the winter meeting of the school's trustees, on Tuesday morning, November 10. There were present Mr. Clarence H. Kelsey, second vice-president of the Board, and Mr. Charles E. Bigelow of New York; Judge Lewis of Richmond; Dr. S. C. Mitchell of Delaware College; Mr. Frank W. Darling and Dr. H. B. Frissell of Hampton. The white state supervisors of rural schools also had an informal meeting and discussion of their various problems with Dr. Wallace Buttrick, Dr. Abraham Flexner, and Mr. Sage of the General Education Board. Messrs. F. C. Button of Kentucky, Jackson Davis of Virginia, L. M. Favrot of Arkansas, George D. Godard of Georgia, N. C. Newbold of North Carolina, J. L. Sibley of Alabama, and S. L. Smith of Tennessee were present at this meeting.

SPECIAL COURSES

AFTER the Conference a two-weeks' special course was held at the school for the benefit of the supervising teachers of industrial work in Negro rural schools. The courses in chair-caning, cooking, sewing, manual training, poultry, games, school organization, rooms and grounds, and work in homes, were well attended by men and women eager to learn more efficient ways to serve their people. The enrollment numbered forty-nine supervisors from three states.

At the same time a short course in agriculture was held for farm-demonstration agents. Lectures were given by the agricultural instructors of the school, and by Mr. Jesse M. Jones, field agent in the Farm Demonstration Department of the United States Bureau of Agriculture. Nine men took this course.

On Monday evening, November 16, the supervisors met with Mr. Jackson Davis, Virginia state supervisor of rural schools, to discuss such problems as poor attendance, poor sanitation, indifference of parents and consequent difficulties in lengthening terms, raising teachers' salaries, and introducing industrial work. Supervisors who had successfully solved some of these problems exchanged experiences with those who had been able to deal with others. The reports of the supervisors showed that the parents, on the whole, are so enthusiastic in the improvement of schools as to be willing to make heavy sacrifices to put up a new building or hire another teacher, and that, in cases where indifference and opposition are shown, diplomacy will accomplish much towards conversion in a short time. Dr. Frissell, in speaking to the teachers at the close of the meeting, said that he considered these rural workers as valuable missionaries as any that he had seen in his travels in Africa, China, Japan, and other countries of the world.

THE CHORAL UNION CONCERT

ON Saturday evening, October 24, in the Gymnasium, the Hampton Choral Union scored a brilliant success before a large audience, in the presentation of Madame Anita Patti Brown, coloratura-soprano, of Chicago, in recital, assisted by Mr. Joseph Douglass, the well-known violinist of Washington, and Miss Eliza Coppage of Norfolk, dramatic reader.

The artistic merit of the whole program is beyond criticism. The singing of Madame Brown was a revelation to many; she possesses a voice of great natural beauty, perfected evidently by considerable study. It is high, clear, and sweet, with an unusual quality that is almost startling in its effect. The ease with which she projected her tones so that every syllable of even the most *pianissimo* numbers was caught by those in the farthest part of the Gymnasium was truly wonderful, and probably is very largely responsible for the enthusiasm with which her every number was received. Whether it was the "mad scene" from "Lucia," the scena and aria from "Traviata," or just the old familiar "Suwanee River," Madame Brown was equally at home. Miss Belasco, who accompanied her on the piano, showed rare taste and skill.

Miss Belasco gave an interesting talk on life in the British West Indies at the informal social held in the Museum after the recital. Mme. Brown also sang Sunday morning in church, in the afternoon at the Greenbrier School dedication, and in the evening at the King's Daughters meeting.

Both Miss Coppage and Mr. Douglass have been heard at Hampton before. Miss Coppage gave very effectively "Nydia, the blind girl of Pompeii" to incidental music on the piano by Mr. Dett, who also played the accompaniments for Mr. Douglass. Mr. Douglass presented, among his numbers, a new Coleridge-Taylor composition—"Gypsy Song"—for which all were grateful. His fame has been well earned and his playing shows no diminution of power through many years of public performance.

Other numbers on the program were the opening chorus, "Hymn to the Trinity" by Tschaikowski, sung by the Institute choir, and the "Laughing Song," by Van der Stucken, sung by the Hampton Choral Union. At the conclusion of the program "Hampton, my home by the sea" was sung by both choirs, the audience standing. All of the chorus singing was without instrumental accompaniment.

This is the second recital to be given at Hampton under the auspices of the Hampton Choral Union, which is directed by Mr. Dett, the school's musical director, one of whose aims is to create in all of his pupils a greater love for the best in music.

HAMPTON'S RELIEF WORK

THE Hampton School is not behind the rest of the world in extending a helping hand to the needy. "Help-

ing the Belgians" has become as general among both workers and students as elsewhere in America. Knitting by the teachers is in evidence at lectures, at all small gatherings, and even at table. Lessons are given free of charge, and tyros in the art unintentionally afford much amusement to the onlooker. But all prove to be persistent and the number of mufflers and wristlets is multiplying rapidly.

The King's Daughters Society, nearly four hundred strong, is busily engaged in fashioning warm petticoats and dresses for Belgian children. A group of Senior girls has called itself the "Red Cross Club" and is making hospital garments for the Red Cross Society. While some of the money for materials has been given by friends, the King's Daughters themselves generously contributed $50 of money raised by entertainments to a collection for the Belgian sufferers amounting to $216, which was taken at prayers on Sunday evening, November 8.

THE PRINTING OFFICE

FROM small beginnings the printing office has grown to be one of the most important departments of Hampton Institute. It has recently been moved to new quarters in the southwest wing of the Trade School building which have several advantages over the old ones in Stone Building. The press room is on the first floor. Each piece of machinery has its own individual motor to which it is attached and there is no overhead belting. The floor is made of cement. Over the press room is the composing room, a large, airy, and quiet room, in one corner of which is the instructor's office. A freight elevator runs from one room to the other.

ATHLETICS

THE first three football games of the season were played on the home field. On October 30 Hampton defeated the Livingstone College team from Salisbury, North Carolina, by a score of 39-0. Union University met Hampton November 6 and the game began with promise, but the Union team soon weakened and Hampton was able to score 42 points. In the third quarter Union made a goal from the field by a drop kick, making the final score 42–3.

Last year Hampton won the football championship of the Interscholastic Athletic Association by the defeat of Howard's long-time champion team with a score of 8–6. This year Lincoln University won from Howard by a score of 12–0 a week preceding the Hampton-Lincoln game, thereby causing itself to be regarded as Hampton's strongest opponent. Accordingly, the game on November 16 was well attended and excitement was high. The teams were well-matched, both maintaining strong lines very difficult to break through, and both being on the alert every minute. The only forward pass completed during the afternoon was executed by Lincoln. The Hampton secondary defense was very good, every forward pass made by the Lincoln team, except one, being caught by Hampton. In the last quarter Hampton made a determined fight and finally put the ball on Lincoln's three-yard line. On the next play the ball was carried across Lincoln's goal line by Flynt, but the Lincoln captain contended that the touchdown was not complete as the Hampton man was not "downed" before he was pushed back across the goal line in the field of play by the Lincoln team. The referee had been ruling all through the game in accordance with the football rules that the play ended where the forward progress of the player was stopped. Lincoln, however, left the field, forfeiting the game, and making the score 1–0 instead of 6–0, which it would have been had the play continued. The decision giving Hampton the touchdown was unanimous on the part of the officials.

HAMPTON WORKERS

THE Bureau of Education has started a new work, that of investigating and promoting home and school gardens. This work is to be under the direction of a specialist and an assistant, both experts in school gardening. Miss Ethel Gowans, formerly instructor in agriculture at Hampton, is now in temporary charge of the work.

At an educational rally held in York County recently, Major Moton addressed the School Improvement League. Mr. George Davis, farm-demonstration agent for York and Elizabeth City Counties, was also present and spoke.

A new worker in the Trade School is Mr. Walter F. Quast of Baltimore, Md., who is filling the position of instructor in drafting left vacant by the resignation of Mr. Staebner.

Several photographs taken by Mr. Miner, the school's director of applied art, have been used on the covers of the *Crisis*.

Dr. R. R. Clark, veterinarian at the Institute, has obtained leave of absence to sail as chief veterinary surgeon on the *Rembrandt*, which left Newport News November 18 with a load of 800 horses for France.

RELIGIOUS WORK

GREAT interest is being manifested in the Sunday evening meetings of the Y. M. C. A. During the last month the average attendance has been considerably over two hundred. The same interest is being shown in the group prayer meetings which are held on Thursday evenings after night school. The Membership Committee of the Association has been conducting a campaign for new members. More than two hundred have already been secured, and it is expected that the membership will be larger this year than ever before. The Bible-study groups began their work on November 15, at which time one hundred and sixty men had joined the classes. The Seniors, under the leadership of Mr. Aery, are to make a study of "Christianity as applied to life's problems." Under the leadership of Mr. Coughlin, the Senior and Junior Middle group will use the book written by Harry E. Fosdick on "The manhood of the Master." The Juniors will meet in several groups conducted by Hampton graduates, and follow the course outlined in Robert Speer's book on "The Man Christ Jesus."

The first communion service of the school year was held on Sunday morning, November 1. At this service two of the young men united with the church on confession of faith.

VISITORS

SOME friends of the Indians have lately visited the school. Mrs. Walter C. Roe of Colony, Okla., spent a few days at Hampton with her adopted son, Mr. Henry Roe Cloud, and Miss Anna J. Ritter, matron in the government school at Colony. Another visitor was Miss Lucy C. Bloxton of Amherst, Virginia, who is a missionary among the Indians of that county. Dr. Harley Stamp, an anthropologist who is making a comparative study of the blood pressures of different races, recently visited Hampton.

AMONG the visitors at the Conference who have not been mentioned elsewhere were Mr. and Mrs. E. C. Sage and Mrs. Clarence H. Kelsey of New York ; Miss Hughes, assistant to the Virginia supervisor of girls' canning clubs, and Mrs. Jackson Davis of Richmond; Dr. T. J. Jones and Mr. Walter B. Hill of the Bureau of Education ; and several Virginia county superintendents.

Miss Dorothy Kieland of Buffalo, N. Y., a graduate of Cornell University, spent a week at Hampton studying its methods of work. She expects to go to South Africa to assist Miss E. F. Clarke, who recently visited Hampton, in her work at the Inanda Seminary. Another visitor who came to study the school's methods was Miss Whitlow of New York City. She works with feeble-minded girls in New York, teaching them sewing, weaving, cooking, and housekeeping, and feels that her observation of the industrial work at Hampton will be of great help to her in her work.

Mr. Leo Bock, a professional moving-picture photographer from Linwood, Long Island, is spending some time at the school, helping the director of applied art to work out his scheme for a new series of moving pictures illustrating Hampton's work.

THE WHITTIER SCHOOL

A LARGE number of enthusiastic patrons were present at the Whittier School on the afternoon of Friday, October 30, for the first meeting of the patrons' association. The address of welcome was made by Rev. Mr. Nottingham, Hampton, '91. Miss Walter outlined the policy of the work for the coming year. An earnest appeal was made by Miss Tourtellot, Miss Walter's assistant, for the cooperation of the parents in caring for the girls and boys on the way to and from school. Major Moton told of the work of the Negro Organization Society of Virginia, and spoke so convincingly that the patrons' association unanimously voted to join the organization, then and there raising the membership dues.

On Monday morning, November 16, the industrial supervisors taking the special course at the Institute, visited the Whittier School to observe the work in the various rooms.

A battalion of Whittier boys has been formed by Captain Scott from the Institute. The boys drilled for the first time on Friday, November 13, and enjoyed it very much. They will drill every Friday afternoon during the year. The enrollment of the Whittier School has now reached 457.

GRADUATES AND EX-STUDENTS

AN ex-student of 1893 expresses her appreciation of two years of training at Hampton. For a number of years she was in domestic service, commanding excellent wages and doing very satisfactory work. In 1900 she married and in 1907 she and her husband moved to a small farm which he owned in Maryland. She writes:

"The old house on the farm, much dilapidated, consisted of two rooms, one above and one below, but I made the best of it until we could do better, for there were horses to be bought, land to be worked, farm utensils to get, and all buildings to be erected.

"First we built a barn and stable combined, next a corn house and a henhouse, and then a meat house. When these outbuildings were placed we had spent three years on the farm, working late and early. We then began to plan a house for our own comfort and completed it four years ago last November. The old house now serves as our carriage house and we have a very comfortable home. Our land is 104 acres; the house consists of seven rooms and a large hall.

"We have now four horses, two colts, two cows, thirteen hogs, and I raise and sell more than a hundred dollars' worth of poultry every year. I make country butter. We read the best farm papers.

"We grow principally wheat, rye, corn, and tomatoes besides a good bit of trucking. We now pay insurance on $2300 worth of property since we have come here."

AN ex-student of '98, Mary S. Booth, who graduated from the nurse-training department of the Freedmen's Hospital, Washington, D. C., in 1902, wrote last winter that she was head operating nurse in that institution, appointed to that position in 1913. She said:

"Since leaving Hampton in '98 I have completed a course in nurse-training at the Freedmen's Hospital, Washington, a Government hospital. I was graduated from that school in 1902. In May 1913, I took the Civil Service examination for the position of head operating nurse in the hospital. The examination was held in every state and the nurse passing with the highest per cent got the appointment. Very much to my surprise, I was the lucky nurse and received my appointment in June. I have absolute control of all operations and give the pupil-nurses the surgical part of their training."

A GRADUATE of the Trade Class of '08, Southey G. Johnson, last year completed the industrial course for teachers at the School of Applied Industries, Carnegie Institute, Pittsburg, Pa., and became teacher of manual training in the Dunbar High School of Okmulgee, Okla. In a letter to Hampton he describes his school as follows:

"The Dunbar School here is a frame building combining the grade and high-school work. The school board worked all last summer to equip the school for manual training and domestic science.

"The manual-training department is equipped for eighteen boys in woodworking with a set of general tools, grindstone, trimmer, and a set of wood finishes. Five hundred feet each of southern pine and white oak were given and the work was begun. The preliminary course was planned to develop habits of observation, accurate thinking, and skill in the use of tools. Shelves for the domestic-science and manual-training laboratories were constructed, a lumber rack, and a ten-foot service table for the sewing room; new Yale locks were put on the doors, and windowpanes were put in.

"We have now on exhibition some attractive magazine, newspaper, postcard, towel, necktie, book, and wall-china racks; a number of taborets artistically finished in Flemish, fumed, and mission oak; and footstools of plain and fancy design, some with cane bottoms.

"The boys are taught to repair and refinish furniture and also to repair tinware. They are encouraged to take orders for the construction of such things as are within range of their skill and ability. The training has enabled them to improve their homes and has given them a broader knowledge of their economic condition.''

A SUCCESSFUL contractor in Montgomery, Alabama, is James A. G. Johnson, Trade Class, '06· He said in a letter received last April:

"I am getting along nicely here. I am always busy. I have worked as many as eight men at once here and have done some very creditable jobs for some of the best white people of this city. The last job I completed cost about $4000. One white lady said that it was the finest house in the city."

A LETTER received last January from Anna Richardson, ex-student, '07· and a graduate of the Petersburg Normal School in 1911, expresses gratitude for a Christmas box sent to her through funds given by the Boston Hampton Committee:

"Words are inadequate to express the joy and happiness that came to the children and myself when we viewed the contents of the Christmas box sent to us. The American flag, which was one of the presents in the box, was hoisted in our schoolroom, it being the first one, I think, the school has ever owned. You can imagine the patriotic feeling it brought to our dear old fathers and mothers who were present.

"The presents for the children were placed upon the tree, the little Christmas bells were hung alternately around them, and gilt was intertwined through the branches. The little boys were very happy indeed over their balls and music-boxes, neckties, and other useful articles. The girls were all very much pleased with their dolls, bags, books, calendars, cards, and aprons. The stockings filled with candy brought gladness to all. The children's parents highly appreciated the givers' thought for their little ones."

Sarah F. Evans, '96· has begun work as housekeeper at the Young Women's Christian Association in Philadelphia.

Fanny Mabuda, '10· of Natal, South Africa, is now primary teacher at the Lovedale Mission in the Cape Province, a school which she attended before coming to Hampton.

TWO recent graduates, Ethel L. Pratt, '12· and Susie F. Bassette, '14· are teaching in the new Greenbrier School on the outskirts of Hampton. On Sunday afternoon, October 25, the school patrons, over a hundred strong, together with Mr. John M. Willis, superintendent of schools in Elizabeth City County, members of the Wythe District School Board, Major Moton, and friends from Hampton Institute, assembled in the well-built, attractive, two-room schoolhouse, and held a simple service of dedication.

Mr. C. H. Jones, the president of the patrons' league, told the story of Negro education in the Greenbrier community and outlined the struggle the committee has had in raising funds with which to build a schoolhouse in keeping with the good houses of colored people whose children were going to a crowded, one-room school.

Superintendent Willis referred to the new life that Miss Pratt had put, during two years, into the Greenbrier School. He commended her for the co-operation and assistance she has won from the school board, the county superintendent, the white people, the colored patrons, and the children through her "unselfish service, tact, energy, and courage." So well had this young Hampton graduate done her work that the school board, after considering a number of make-shift plans for improving the old, inadequate, one-room school, finally decided that she ought to have the very best it could give her.

Today there stands the new Greenbrier School, which (with the heating outfit) represents an outlay of $2500. Mr. C. F. Bailey, the chief of the engineering department in the great shipbuilding company at Newport News, looked very carefully after the construction work; a white architect drew special plans for the building; the superintendent of schools spent a great deal of time and thought over the plans; and, best of all, white people and colored people worked together with Miss Pratt and the industrial supervising teacher, Mrs. Estelle M. Evans, another Hampton graduate.

CLASS OF 1914

AMONG last year's graduates who went from Hampton to higher schools are Bishop Brown, who is studying at Ferris Institute, Big Rapids, Mich., B. Luther Colbert, who is fitting himself at Ohio State University to be a veterinary surgeon ; and H. Perkins Spivey, who is a student at Howard University.

There are each year a number of graduates who fulfill one of Hampton's ideals by teaching in country communities. This fall two graduate men are teaching the country schools at their own homes: Ira H. Godwin in Smithfield, Va., and Stevan R. Young In Upper Zion, Caroline County, Va. Hawthorne Smith is teaching a country school at Wattsville, Accomac County, Va., and James H. Williams is doing the same work at New Upton, in Gloucester County. Joseph E. Oliver is assistant to the principal in the high school at Blackstone, Va.

Teachers of trades are Lorenzo D. Debroe, who has blacksmithing and academic classes at Christiansburg Institute, Cambria, Va., and Linnaeus T. Pinn., instructor in carpentry at Mannassas Industrial School, where he studied before entering Hampton. Benjamin Barnwell is assistant in the agricultural department at Penn School, where he prepared for Hampton.

Graduates working at their trades are Hugh Jackson, tailor at Cape Charles, Va.; Robert B. Jones and Edward C. Rhodes, carpenters at Norfolk; J. D. White, printer in Harrisburg, Pa.; Clarence H. Slaughter, bricklayer in Sutherlin, Va.; Virgil L. Haskins, Nathaniel P. Miller, and Arthur J. Wells, bricklayers employed in the construction of buildings at Hampton Institute; and Frederick C. Scott, assistant in the electrical department at Hampton. Howard D. Massey is at work in the paint shop at Hampton Institute. James E. Johnson is assistant in community work at Thornton, Arkansas, where he is associated with Elsie J. Catlett, '96·

TEACHING becomes the occupation of a large percentage of the girls graduating from Hampton. Graduates of last spring who are teaching schools in their home communities in Virginia are Emma Cason, Princess Anne; Helen Chavis, Runnymede; Isabel Cosby, Charlottesville; Kate Kerr, Eastville; Harriet E. Laws, Avalon; Carrie B. Oliver, Crewe; and Blanche M. Briggs, who is teaching domestic science in Suffolk. Fannie L. Mack is teaching at her home in Athens, Ga.

Other teachers are Nannie G. Miles in Carloover, Bath County, Va.; A. La Perle Howard, assistant in the graded school at Blackstone; Lizzie L. Brooks, assistant in the public school at Averett, Mecklenburg County, Va.; Susie F. Bassette, who is assisting Ethel T. Pratt, '12· at the Greenbrier School near Newport News; Mary L. Biggs and Pauline C. Dungee in the graded public schools of Norfolk; and Lucille Hackley in Hollins, Va.

Mrs. Martha S. Boyd is in charge of the colored Young Women's Christian Association in Lakewood, N. J.

MARRIAGES

ANNOUNCEMENT has been received of the marriage of Ulysses S. Wharton, '04· to Cordella Hughes Murdock in Washington, D. C., on November 21. Dr. Wharton will practice medicine in Altoona, Pa.

On September 9, the marriage of Roy L. Cordery, '10· to Myria M. Furniss occurred in Philadelphia. The groom holds the positions of disciplinarian and teacher of carpentry at Princess Anne Academy, Princess Anne, Md.

On October 14, J. J. Scott, '97· was married to Mrs. Georgette Atkins of Smithfield, Va. Mr. Scott is an employe at Hampton Institute.

John W. Tull, an ex-student and former Hampton worker, was married on November 25 to Miss Phoencie L. Armstead, of Phoebus, Va.

INDIAN NOTES

A program and premium list of the third annual fair at Crow Creek, S. D., has recently been sent to Hampton. It contains many interesting announcements, but none of Indian dances, and on this the association is certainly to be congratulated, although the gate receipts will doubtess be lessened thereby. The premium list is one that can hardly fail to arouse the right kind of competition among the Indians. There are prizes offered for all the agricultural and domestic entries generally found at any county fair—for displays of corn, squash, hens, horses, cows, and pigs; for bread, cake, pie, doughnuts, aprons, quilts, and many other articles. In addition, there is a list of prizes for Indian handiwork, such as the best set of bows and arrows, or the best moccasins and beaded gloves. The most interesting features are the parade of all Indians who have four cows or heifers, or four mares or more; and the prizes for the best kept and cleanest tent on the grounds, the best set table for dinner, all food to have been prepared by the exhibitor as far as possible, the cleanest Indian baby on the grounds, and the neatest Indian girl under fourteen years of age. To cap the climax, the laziest Indian on the reservation is to receive thirty cents. One wonders how many

contestants there will be for this prize !

Among the officers of the association we find several returned Hampton students. Louis Fire is president of the association, and Henry Little Eagle, chief of police, while on the executive committee we find the names of Henry Jacobs and Medicine Crow. A fair of this kind seems to be a step in the right direction, and Hampton friends will look for its continued usefulness.

Harry Kingman, who was at Hampton from '87 to '93, has recently been elected treasurer of the Sioux Indian Council. In commenting upon this organization a Western paper says: "One of the most unique executive bodies of its kind anywhere in the United States is what is known as the Sioux Indian Council, a body composed of Sioux Indians, which has exclusive charge of the voluminous business affairs of the Indians belonging on the Cheyenne River Reservation. As there are several thousand of these Indians, and as they have large financial dealings with the United States Government, in the way of payments of interest and principal on funds belonging to the Indians which were derived from the sale to the Government of several hundred thousand acres of their surplus land, the Council is frequently called upon to transact business on a large scale."

Robert P. Higheagle, '95, is this year teaching the little Government day school at Bull Head, S. D., one of the sub-stations on the Standing Rock Reservation.

SOME PUBLICATIONS OF

The Hampton Normal and Agricultural Institute

Annual Catalogue (Illustrated)

Principal's Report (Illustrated)

Founder's Day Programs

Education for Life, Samuel Chapman Armstrong

"Hampton"

Hampton's Message (Illustrated) Sydney D. Frissell

The Regeneration of Sam Jackson, (Illustrated) J. W. Church

What Some Men Have Said of Hampton Institute

Hampton Sketches II, Johnson of Hampton, E. L. Chichester

Hampton Sketches III, The Woodman, E. L. Chichester

Hampton Sketches IV, A Change of Base, E. L. Chichester

General Armstrong's Life and Work, (Illustrated) Franklin Carter

Practical Training in Negro Rural Schools (Illustrated) Jackson Davis

The Servant Question, Virginia Church

General Samuel Chapman Armstrong, Henry Pitt Warren

Armstrong a "Statesman-Educator," Stephen S. Wise

Single copies distributed free. Prices per dozen and hundred on application to Publication Office, The Hampton Normal and Agricultural Institute, Hampton, Virginia. In applying for publications please state reason for request.